Five Column™

Verse-By-Verse Edition

The Synoptic Gospel™

FIVE COLUMN™

Verse-By-Verse Edition

The SYNOPTIC GOSPEL™

Using the **New American Standard Bible (NASB)** Edition of The Four Gospels

Compiled by: Daniel John

Smart Publishing Ltd.
Surrey, British Columbia   Canada

FIVE COLUMN:
The Synoptic Gospel

Verse-By-Verse Edition - *Paperback*   1.1 - *2025*
using the text of *FIVE COLUMN: Word-For-Word Edition*   3.7 - *2025*

ISBN 978-1-988271-79-8

Copyright © 2009, 2014, 2017, 2023

Smart Publishing Ltd.
Surrey, British Columbia Canada

fivecolumn.com synopticgospel.com

Compiled by: Daniel John
Cover design: Daniel John and Leon Nguyen
Cover image: *La Última Cena*, by Juan de Juanes (*c. 1562*)
The *Jesus Logo* trademark is owned by Smart Publishing Ltd. ® 2012.

All Rights Reserved Worldwide. No part of this publication may be copied, printed, reproduced or transmitted
in any form, for any purpose, with the exception of the specific *Permissions of Use and To Quote*
as defined on the following two pages, and at: *fivecolumn.com/copyright*

All Scripture used in the Four Gospel Harmony is from the NEW AMERICAN STANDARD BIBLE ®
Copyright © 1960, 1962, 1963, 1968, 1971, 1972, 1973, 1975, 1977, 1995
by the Lockman Foundation, La Habra, California.
All rights reserved. *www.lockman.org*

Printed by Amazon.

*   *   *   *   *   *   *

Other formats of this publication, **FIVE COLUMN: Verse-By-Verse** Edition
PDF: ISBN 978-1-998271-92-7   Hard Cover: ISBN 978-1-998271-93-4

Editions of **FIVE COLUMN: Word-For-Word** Edition
PDF: ISBN 978-0-993914-06-5   Paperback: ISBN 978-0-993914-01-9   Hard Cover: ISBN 978-0-993914-07-2

The unified *Fifth Column* text of this book is reprinted as **The Synoptic Gospel**: *The Story of The Life of Jesus*
ePub: ISBN 978-1-988271-49-1   Kindle: ISBN 978-0-993914-03-4
Standard Edition - PDF: ISBN 978-1-988271-27-9   Paperback: ISBN 978-1-988271-30-9   Hard Cover: ISBN 978-1-988271-28-6
Complete Edition - PDF: ISBN 978-1-988271-41-5   Paperback: ISBN 978-1-988271-44-6   Hard Cover: ISBN 978-1-988271-83-5
Audiobook - Download (.m4b): ISBN 978-1-988271-00-2   DVD (.m4b): ISBN 978-0-9939140-9-6

Editions of **The Red Letter Gospel**: *All the Words of Jesus Christ in Red*
ePub: ISBN 978-1-988271-10-1   PDF: ISBN 978-1-988271-06-4   Kindle: ISBN 978-1-988271-07-1
Standard Edition - Paperback: ISBN 978-1-988271-37-8   Hard Cover: ISBN 978-1-988271-33-0
Complete Edition - Paperback: ISBN 978-1-988271-47-7   Hard Cover: ISBN 978-1-988271-84-3

are available at: synopticgospel.com/purchase

FIVE COLUMN:
The Synoptic Gospel

Copyright Statement With Permissions of Use and To Quote

fivecolumn.com/copyright   *synopticgospel.com/copyright*

All Rights Reserved Worldwide. No part of this publication may be copied, printed, reproduced or transmitted in any form, for any purpose, with the exception of the following specific *Permissions of Use and To Quote*:

1. Use of The Fifth Column Synoptic Gospel Verses

A) **Use of Up To Nine Verses** - In exception to the above Reservation of Rights, and Fair Dealing (see Part 4. on the following page), short quotations of up to nine Verses from the *fifth column* text (*The Synoptic Gospel*) of this book may be used without the written permission of Smart Publishing Ltd. for **non-commercial use** in worship or for educational purposes, as when read aloud during a service, sermon or study, or when printed in a lesson, missive or newsletter, etc.

   Acknowledgement: All Verses that are read aloud or quoted verbally should be acknowledged as: "*The Synoptic Gospel, verse xxx.y*", where *xxx* is the *scene reference number* and *y* is the *Verse(s)*. When quoted in print the acknowledgement (as on the Copyright Page) should read "*The Synoptic Gospel* © 2009 by Smart Publishing Ltd. synopticgospel.com" and the individual Verse references can be shortened to *TSG xxx.y*.

   Commercial Use or Reproduction: For permission or license to reproduce TSG Verses for any commercial reproduction or use please request permission at: *fivecolumn.com/copyright/permission-request-form/*

B) **Use of Ten Or More Verses** - Up to and including one hundred (100) Verses may be quoted, reproduced or distributed from the *fifth column* text (*The Synoptic Gospel*) of this book for **non-commercial use** provided that the quoted Verses amount to less than 30% of the total work in which they are used, and that the reference to each Synoptic Gospel Verse or set of Verses is notated as *The Synoptic Gospel xxx.y*, or *TSG xxx.y*, or simply as *xxx.y* for acknowledgement types i) and ii) below - where *xxx* is the *scene reference number* and *y* is the *Verse(s)*.

   Acknowledgement: All Verses that are read aloud or quoted verbally should be acknowledged as: "*The Synoptic Gospel, verse xxx.y*", where *xxx* is the *scene reference number* and *y* is the *Verse(s)*. The written reproduction of ten or more Synoptic Gospel Verses requires that acknowledgement is included on the Copyright Page of the completed work, or where it is appropriate, of the most applicable of the following statements:

     i) All Scriptures are from *The Synoptic Gospel* © 2009. Used by permission of Smart Publishing Ltd. All rights reserved. synopticgospel.com

     ii) Unless otherwise noted all Scriptures are from *The Synoptic Gospel* © 2009. Used by permission of Smart Publishing Ltd. All rights reserved. synopticgospel.com

     iii) Scripture quotations marked *The Synoptic Gospel* (or *TSG*) are from *The Synoptic Gospel* © 2009. Used by permission of Smart Publishing Ltd. All rights reserved. synopticgospel.com

   Commercial Use or Reproduction: For permission or license to reproduce TSG Verses for any commercial reproduction or use please request permission at: *fivecolumn.com/copyright/permission-request-form/*

C) **Use of More Than One Hundred Verses** - For permission to quote or reproduce more than one hundred (100) Verses from the *fifth column* text (*The Synoptic Gospel*) of this book in a single commercial or non-commercial work, or fewer Verses if they exceed 30% of the total length of a short work, please obtain permission from the publisher and copyright owner Smart Publishing Ltd., using the form at:

fivecolumn.com/copyright/permission-request-form/

2. Reproduction of The Four Gospel Harmony

A) **Use of One Full Scene** - Up to one full Scene of up to two pages that includes the columns of the Four Gospel Harmony and *fifth column* word-for-word Merger of this publication may be reproduced for use in a **non-commercial** work if the acknowledgement reads:

FIVE COLUMN © 2009 by Smart Publishing Ltd. All rights reserved. fivecolumn.com

   Commercial Use or Reproduction: For permission or license to reproduce any part of the *FIVE COLUMN* Four Gospel Harmony for any commercial use or purpose please request permission from the publisher and copyright owner Smart Publishing Ltd. at: *fivecolumn.com/copyright/permission-request-form/*

B) **Use of More Than One Scene** - For permission to use or reproduce more than one full Scene from the *FIVE COLUMN* Four Gospel Harmony of this publication, please request permission from the publisher and copyright owner, Smart Publishing Ltd. at:

fivecolumn.com/copyright/permission-request-form/

FIVE COLUMN: *The Synoptic Gospel*

Copyright Statement With Permissions of Use and To Quote - *continued*

fivecolumn.com/copyright

3. Use of Other Content

The following specific permissions for **non-commercial use** apply to the other materials that are included in this edition of *FIVE COLUMN: The Synoptic Gospel*. To obtain permission for any **commercial use** or reproduction of the following materials please visit: *fivecolumn.com/copyright/permissions/* and then submit a request using the form at: *fivecolumn.com/copyright/permission-request-form/*

A) **Cover**: With the exception of the painting "*La Ultima Cena*" by Juan De Juanes (*c. 1562*), no element of the cover design, including the artwork, graphics or logos, may be used in any way without the permission of Smart Publishing Ltd., which can be requested at: *fivecolumn.com/copyright/permission-request-form/*
The *Jesus Logo* trademark is owned by Smart Publishing Ltd. © 2007. ® 2012.

B) **Articles**: The seven *Articles* included in this publication may be copied or reproduced in whole or in part for **non-commercial use** if the acknowledgement reads: *Written by Daniel John.* © 2014 by Smart Publishing Ltd. For any commercial reproduction or use please request permission at: *fivecolumn.com/copyright/permission-request-form/*

C) **Notes**: i) Note 1-4 - Beyond the uses defined in Part 4. below (*Fair Dealing*) no part of Notes 1-4 inclusive may be copied, printed, or reproduced for any type of use without the permission of the publisher and copyright owner Smart Publishing Ltd., which can be requested at: *fivecolumn.com/copyright/permission-request-form/*

ii) Note 5 - *An Overview of The Four Gospels* may be copied or reproduced in whole or in part for **non-commercial use** if the acknowledgement reads: *Written by Daniel John.* © 2014 by Smart Publishing Ltd. For any commercial reproduction or use please request permission at: *fivecolumn.com/copyright/permission-request-form/*

D) **Maps**: The Chapter Maps of Israel and of Jerusalem may be reproduced in whole or in part for **non-commercial use** and display if the acknowledgement reads: *The Synoptic Gospel* © 2009 by Smart Publishing Ltd. For any commercial reproduction or use please request permission at: *fivecolumn.com/copyright/permission-request-form/*

E) **Appendix 1**: Up to 7% of the contents (approximately one page) of *Appendix 1 - The Synoptic Gospel Scene Contents* may be reproduced for **non-commercial use** if the acknowledgement reads: *FIVE COLUMN* © 2009 by Smart Publishing Ltd. (or *The Synoptic Gospel* © 2009 by Smart Publishing Ltd. may be used). For permission to reproduce more than 7% of Appendix 1 in a single work, or for any commercial use, please request permission at: *fivecolumn.com/copyright/permission-request-form/*

F) **Appendix 2**: Up to 10% of the contents (approximately one page) of *Appendix 2 - Gospel Verse Cross-Reference* may be reproduced for **non-commercial use** if the acknowledgement reads: *FIVE COLUMN* © 2017 by Smart Publishing Ltd. (or *The Synoptic Gospel* © 2017 by Smart Publishing Ltd. may be used). For permission to reproduce more than 10% of the *Gospel Verse Cross-Reference* in a single work, or for any commercial use, please request permission at: *fivecolumn.com/copyright/permission-request-form/*

4. Fair Dealing

Fair Dealing is an exception (*Section 29*) to the Canadian Copyright Act (*R.S.C., 1985, c. C-42*) that allows for the use of small sections of a work (in the case of this work, fewer than five Verses of *The Synoptic Gospel fifth column* text, or one full Scene of the *FIVE COLUMN* Four Gospel Harmony) to be reproduced for non-commercial purposes without the prior written approval of the copyright holder. Common Fair Dealing uses include private study, education, research, review, news reporting, criticism, parody and satire. Detailed information is available at: *fivecolumn.com/copyright* and *laws-lois.justice.gc.ca/eng/acts/c-42/page-3.html*

All Verses and material used according to Fair Dealing best practices must be reproduced accurately, and acknowledged as: "*FIVE COLUMN* © 2009 by Smart Publishing Ltd." or for the following:

- *The Synoptic Gospel* © 2009 by Smart Publishing Ltd. may be used when quoting the *fifth column (Synoptic Gospel)* text, reproducing the Chapter Maps, and/or reproducing any part of *Appendix 1 - The Synoptic Gospel Scene Contents*.
- *Written by Daniel John.* © 2009 by Smart Publishing Ltd. may be used when quoting or reproducing any part of *Notes 1-5*.
- *Written by Daniel John.* © 2014 by Smart Publishing Ltd. may be used when quoting or reproducing the seven *Articles*.
- *FIVE COLUMN* © 2017 by Smart Publishing Ltd. may be used when reproducing any part of *Appendix 2 - The Gospel Verse Cross-Reference* (*The Synoptic Gospel* © 2017 by Smart Publishing Ltd. may also be used).

* * * * * * *

Updated Copyright Statement With Permissions of Use

In all situations and circumstances, the most current *Copyright Statement With Permissions of Use and To Quote* for this Smart Publishing Ltd. publication as found at *fivecolumn.com/copyright* (and mirrored at *synopticgospel.com/copyright*) are in force, and if different from what is stated in this printed publication then the current online version shall supersede these printed permissions.

fivecolumn.com/copyright/permissions/

"The Words That I Have Spoken To You Are Spirit, and They Are Life."

~ Jesus Christ

TSG 519.4 / John 6:63

This Gospel is Dedicated To Humanity's Savior,

Our Lord, Jesus Christ.

Thank You!

For best viewing results **Rotate the Book 90°** (1/4 turn) clockwise (to the right).

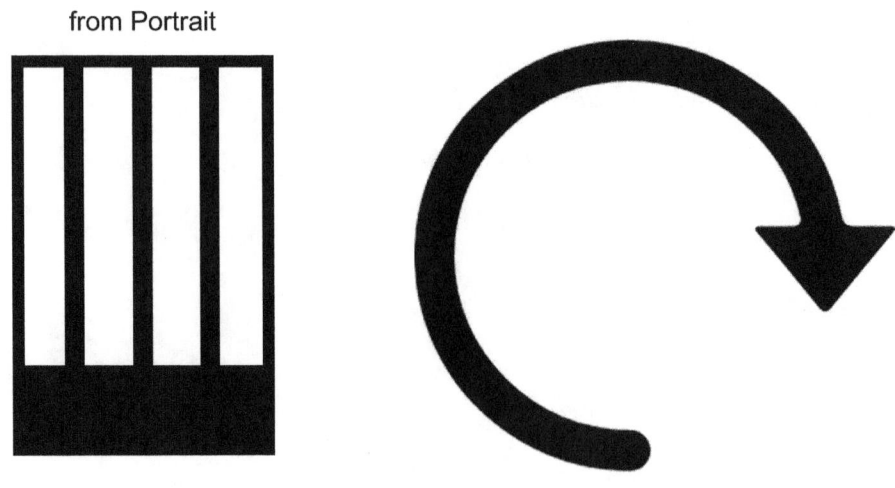

from Portrait

to Landscape

TABLE OF BOOK CONTENTS

	Page
Foreword	i
Introduction	ii

NOTES On Reading This Book
1. **How This Book Was Compiled**
   - Part 1. Order The Gospel Storyline . . . iii
   - 2. Harmonize The Parallel Verses . . iv
   - 3. Edit The Fifth Column v
2. **Dividing The Gospel Storyline**
   - Part 1. Storyline Divisions vi
   - 2. Split Verses vii
   - 3. FIVE COLUMN Verse Reference System viii
   - 4. FIVE COLUMN Verse Notations . . viii
3. **Dates Listed In This Book**
   - Part 1. Date Notations Used In This Book . . ix
   - 2. Assigning A Date To Each Scene . . ix
   - 3. The Synoptic Gospel Timeline . . ix
4. **Other Notes**
   - Part 1. Locations x
   - 2. Maps x
   - 3. Quotations & References . . . x
   - 4. Verse Indication Lines . . . x
   - 5. NASB Retentions x
   - Samples - *Compare VBV & W4W Editions* xi
5. **An Overview of The Four Gospels**
   - Part 1. Why Are There Four Gospels? . . . xx
   - 2. Overlap Among The Four Gospels . . xxi
   - 3. A Brief Overview of The Four Gospels . xxi
   - 4. Comparison Chart of The Four Gospels xxii

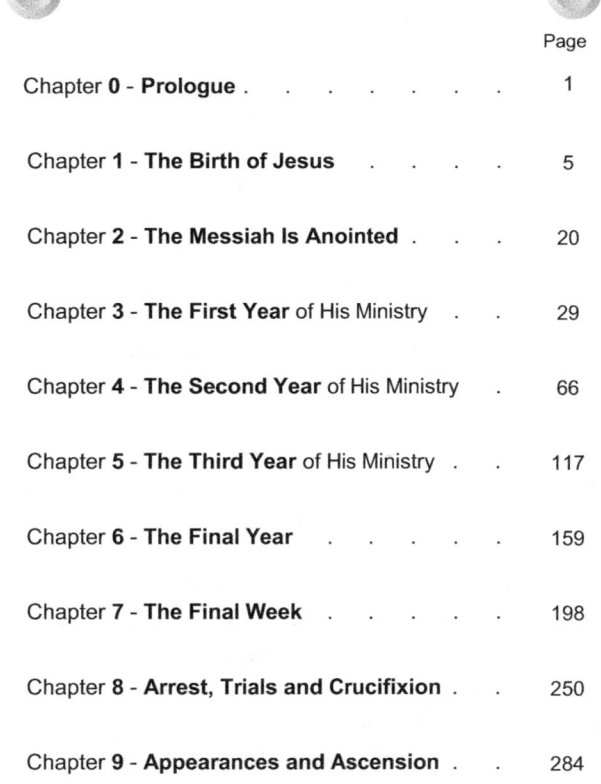

	Page
Chapter **0** - **Prologue**	1
Chapter **1** - **The Birth of Jesus**	5
Chapter **2** - **The Messiah Is Anointed**	20
Chapter **3** - **The First Year** of His Ministry	29
Chapter **4** - **The Second Year** of His Ministry	66
Chapter **5** - **The Third Year** of His Ministry	117
Chapter **6** - **The Final Year**	159
Chapter **7** - **The Final Week**	198
Chapter **8** - **Arrest, Trials and Crucifixion**	250
Chapter **9** - **Appearances and Ascension**	284

The **Acts** and **Scenes** of each **Chapter** are listed at the beginning of the Chapter, and in the **Table of Gospel Contents** on the following five pages, and in *Appendix 1 - The Synoptic Gospel Scene Contents*.

ARTICLES
1. Why Merge The Gospels? A-1
2. Have The Gospels Been Merged Before? . . A-1
3. Why Include The Gospel of John? A-2
4. Parallel Wording Differences A-4
5. Ordering The Gospel Storyline . . . A-4
6. Re-Versing The Gospel A-5
7. The Future of The Four Gospels A-6

APPENDIX 1 - The Synoptic Gospel Scene Contents A-8
- *includes Gospel Verses, Dates and Locations*

APPENDIX 2 - Gospel Verse Cross-Reference . . A-24
- *locate any Verse from the Four Gospels*

Improving **FIVE COLUMN:** *The Synoptic Gospel* . . A-36

TABLE OF GOSPEL CONTENTS

FIVE COLUMN

CHAPTER 0 - PROLOGUE — 1
Act 1 - Foreword
- Scene 1 Prologue — 1
- 2 The Word of God — 1

Act 2 - The Genealogy of Jesus
- Scene 1 The Genealogy of The Messiah — 2
- 2 The Genealogy of The Son of God — 3

CHAPTER 1 - THE BIRTH OF JESUS — 5
Act 1 - The Prophecy About John
- Scene 1 The Birth of John Is Foretold To Zacharias — 6
- 2 Elizabeth Becomes Pregnant With John — 7

Act 2 - The Annunciation To Mary
- Scene 1 Gabriel Tells Mary That She Will Birth A Son — 8
- 2 Mary Visits Elizabeth — 9

Act 3 - The Birth of John
- Scene 1 The Birth and Naming of John — 10
- 2 The Prophecy of Zacharias About John — 11

Act 4 - The Birth of Jesus
- Scene 1 An Angel Solves Joseph's Dilemma — 12
- 2 Joseph and Mary Journey To Bethlehem — 12
- 3 The Birth of Jesus — 13
- 4 Angelic Announcement To The Shepherds — 13
- 5 The Naming of Jesus — 14

Act 5 - Jesus Is Presented In The Temple
- Scene 1 Righteous Simeon Prophesies About Jesus — 14
- 2 Anna The Prophetess — 15
- 3 Return To Nazareth — 15

Act 6 - To Egypt and Back
- Scene 1 King Herod and The Magi From The East — 16
- 2 Joseph Is Warned To Flee to Egypt — 17
- 3 Herod Orders The Death of The Male Babies — 17
- 4 Joseph, Mary and Jesus Return From Egypt — 18

Act 7 - Young Jesus In The Temple
- Scene 1 I Had To Be In My Father's House — 19

CHAPTER 2 - THE MESSIAH IS ANOINTED — 20
Act 1 - John Becomes The Baptist
- Scene 1 John Begins His Ministry of Baptism — 21
- 2 John Warns The Pharisees — 22
- 3 The Teachings of John The Baptist — 23
- 4 John Preaches About The Coming Messiah — 23
- 5 John Denies That He Is The Christ or Elijah — 24

Act 2 - The Baptism of Jesus
- Scene 1 John Is At First Unwilling To Baptize Jesus — 25
- 2 Jesus Is Baptized By John In The Jordan River — 26
- 3 John Testifies That Jesus Is The Son of God — 26

Act 3 - The Messiah Is Tempted
- Scene 1 Jesus Fasts In The Wilderness For Forty Days — 27
- 2 Satan Tries To Tempt Jesus — 28

CHAPTER 3 - THE FIRST YEAR of His Ministry — 29
Act 1 - Jesus Begins His Ministry
- Scene 1 Jesus Meets Andrew and Simon — 30
- 2 Jesus Meets Philip and Nathanael — 31
- 3 Jesus Turns Water Into Wine At A Wedding — 32

Act 2 - The First Passover
- Scene 1 Jesus Expels The Merchants From The Temple — 33
- 2 A Pharisee Named Nicodemus — 34
- 3 The Disciples of Jesus Begin Baptizing — 35
- 4 Believe In The Son and Have Eternal Life — 35

Act 3 - A Journey Through Samaria
- Scene 1 King Herod Imprisons John The Baptist — 36
- 2 The Woman At Jacob's Well — 37
- 3 I Am The Living Water — 38
- 4 Many Samaritans Believe In Jesus — 39

Act 4 - Jesus Settles In Capernaum
- Scene 1 Through Nazareth and Cana — 40
- 2 Healing The Son of A Royal Official — 40
- 3 Jesus Resides In Capernaum — 41
- 4 Jesus Calls Peter and Andrew, and Others — 42
- 5 Jesus Calls James and John — 43

CHAPTER 3 - THE FIRST YEAR continued
Act 5 - Jesus Heals Many
- Scene 1 Healing A Demoniac on The Sabbath — 44
- 2 Jesus Heals Simon Peter's Mother-in-Law — 45
- 3 Many Come To Be Healed — 45
- 4 Preaching and Healing Throughout Galilee — 46
- 5 Cleansing A Leper — 47
- 6 Resurrecting The Son of A Widow — 48

Act 6 - John Enquires About Jesus
- Scene 1 John Asks Jesus, "Are You The Expected One?" — 49
- 2 John Is Elijah, Who Was To Come — 50
- 3 To What Shall I Compare This Generation? — 51

Act 7 - Jesus Attends A Feast
- Scene 1 Jesus Heals A Man at The Bethesda Pool — 52
- 2 The Father and The Son — 53
- 3 Those Who Believe My Words Will Live — 54
- 4 My Testimony About Myself — 55
- 5 The Parable of The Good Samaritan — 56
- 6 Jesus Visits Martha and Mary — 57

Act 8 - Events In Capernaum
- Scene 1 The Man Paralyzed In A Bed — 58
- 2 Jesus Is Accused of Blasphemy — 59
- 3 Jesus Calls Matthew Levi — 60
- 4 Matthew Gives A Reception For Jesus — 60
- 5 Why Do You Not Fast? — 61
- 6 New Cloth and Wineskins — 61
- 7 Picking Grain On The Sabbath — 62
- 8 Healing A Withered Hand On The Sabbath — 63
- 9 Lord, Teach Us to Pray — 64

Act 9 - The Death of John The Baptist
- Scene 1 The Demand of Herodias — 65
- 2 King Herod Has John Beheaded — 65

CHAPTER 4 - THE SECOND YEAR of His Ministry — 66

Act 1 - Jesus Chooses Twelve Apostles
- Scene 1 Miracles of Healing — 68
- 2 Jesus Appoints Twelve Apostles — 69

Act 2 - The Sermon On The Mount
- Scene 1 The Beatitudes — 70
- 2 You Are The Salt of The Earth — 71
- 3 You Are The Light of The World — 72
- 4 The Eye Is The Lamp of The Body — 72
- 5 I Have Come To Fulfill The Law — 73
- 6 Forgive Your Brother — 73
- 7 Settle With Your Opponent — 74
- 8 On Adultery and Divorce — 74
- 9 Make No Oath By Heaven or Earth — 75

Act 3 - The Sermon on True Wealth
- Scene 1 Give To Everyone Who Asks of You — 75
- 2 Love Your Enemy — 76
- 3 When You Give To The Poor — 76
- 4 When You Pray — 77
- 5 The Lord's Prayer — 77
- 6 When You Fast — 78
- 7 Life Is Not About Possessions — 78
- 8 Store Up Treasure In Heaven — 79
- 9 Do Not Worry About Food or Clothing — 80

Act 4 - The Sermon on Spiritual Fruit
- Scene 1 On Judging Another Person — 81
- 2 Ask, and It Will Be Given To You — 82
- 3 The Fruit of False Prophets — 83
- 4 Build On The Solid Foundation of The Word — 84
- 5 Jesus Finishes His Sermon — 84

Act 5 - Events In Galilee
- Scene 1 Healing A Centurion's Servant — 85
- 2 Perfumed Feet In The Home of A Pharisee — 86
- 3 Preaching The Kingdom of God — 87
- 4 Jesus Denounces The Unrepentant Cities — 87
- 5 Come To Me - My Burden Is Light — 88

CHAPTER 4 - THE SECOND YEAR continued

Act 6 - On Good and Evil Spirits
- Scene 1 You Heal By Beelzebul — 89
- 2 How Can Satan Cast Out Satan? — 90
- 3 The Unforgivable Sin — 91
- 4 On Good and Evil — 91
- 5 A Wicked Generation Seeks A Sign — 98
- 6 On Unclean Spirits — 98
- 7 Woe To You Pharisees! — 93
- 8 Woe To You Lawyers as Well! — 93
- 9 Who Are My Mother and My Brothers? — 94

Act 7 - Parables About The Kingdom
- Scene 1 The Parable of The Sower a) — 95
- 2 Why Do You Speak To Them In Parables? — 96
- 3 The Parable of The Sower b) Explained — 97
- 4 The Parable of The Tares a) — 98
- 5 The Kingdom of Heaven Is Like A Mustard Seed — 99
- 6 More Parables About The Kingdom of Heaven — 100
- 7 The Parable of The Tares b) Explained — 101

Act 8 - Mighty Miracles
- Scene 1 Jesus Calms The Stormy Sea — 102
- 2 A Demon-Possessed Man Named Legion — 103
- 3 Jesus Sends The Demons Into The Swine — 104
- 4 Jairus Implores Jesus To Heal His Daughter a) — 105
- 5 A Woman Is Healed of Her Hemorrhage — 106
- 6 Jesus Heals The Daughter of Jairus b) — 107
- 7 Two Blind Men and A Mute Demon — 108
- 8 Reading In His Hometown On The Sabbath — 109
- 9 The Nazarenes Take Offense At Jesus — 110

Act 9 - Jesus Sends The Apostles
- Scene 1 Jesus Sends His Twelve Apostles To Preach — 111
- 2 Jesus Instructs The Apostles — 112
- 3 Peace, To Those Who Receive You — 112
- 4 I Send You Out As Sheep Among Wolves — 113
- 5 You Will Be Persecuted, But Do Not Fear — 114
- 6 Whoever Confesses The Son of Man — 115
- 7 I Have Not Come To Bring Peace — 115
- 8 He Who Is Worthy of Me — 116
- 9 The Apostles Go Out and Preach The Gospel — 116

CHAPTER 5 - THE THIRD YEAR of His Ministry — 117

Act 1 - The Bread of Life
- Scene 1 The Apostles Return — 118
- 2 Jesus Feeds A Crowd of Five Thousand — 119
- 3 Jesus Walks On The Sea of Galilee — 121
- 4 Peter Joins Jesus On The Sea — 122
- 5 Healing In Gennesaret — 122
- 6 I Am The Bread of Life — 123
- 7 The Will of The Father — 124
- 8 Eat My Flesh, and Drink My Blood — 125
- 9 Some Disciples Stumble At This — 126

Act 2 - In Galilee, and Beyond
- Scene 1 Eating With Unwashed Hands — 127
- 2 The Things From The Heart Defile The Man — 128
- 3 The Wisdom of A Canaanite Woman — 129
- 4 Jesus Restores The Hearing of A Deaf Man — 130
- 5 Jesus Feeds Four Thousand People — 131
- 6 The Pharisees and Sadducees Seek A Sign — 132
- 7 Beware of The Leaven of The Pharisees — 133
- 8 Healing A Blind Man at Bethsaida — 134
- 9 Healing A Crippled Woman on The Sabbath — 134

Act 3 - A Trip To Trachonitis
- Scene 1 Who Do The People Say That I Am? — 135
- 2 Jesus Rebukes Peter — 136
- 3 If Anyone Wishes To Follow Me — 137
- 4 Jesus Is Transfigured With Moses and Elijah — 138
- 5 Why Must Elijah Come First? — 139
- 6 Jesus Cures A Demon-Possessed Boy — 140
- 7 Why Could We Not Drive Out The Demon? — 141
- 8 Follow Me — 142

Act 4 - Return To Capernaum
- Scene 1 Jesus Foreshadows His Death and Resurrection — 143
- 2 Paying The Poll-Tax — 143
- 3 The Greatest In The Kingdom of Heaven — 144
- 4 Do Not Cause The Children To Stumble — 145
- 5 On Stumbling Blocks and Hell Fire — 145
- 6 If Your Brother Sins — 146
- 7 On Forgiveness and The Unforgiving Slave — 147
- 8 He Who Is Not Against Us Is For Us — 148

TABLE OF GOSPEL CONTENTS

CHAPTER 5 - THE THIRD YEAR continued

Act 5 - Jesus Sends Seventy Disciples
- Scene 1 The Trials of Discipleship 149
- 2 Jesus Sends Seventy Disciples To Preach . . 149
- 3 King Herod Is Perplexed About Jesus . . . 150

Act 6 - On Dining Etiquette
- Scene 1 A Sabbath Meal With Pharisees . . . 150
- 2 Do Not Take The Place of Honor . . . 151
- 3 Invite The Poor, and Be Blessed . . . 151
- 4 The Seventy Disciples Return 151

Act 7 - A Collection of Parables
- Scene 1 The Joy Over One Sinner Who Repents . . 152
- 2 The Prodigal Son 153
- 3 Rejoice! Your Lost Brother Has Been Found . 154
- 4 The Shrewd Manager 155
- 5 He Who Is Faithful With Little Things . . 156
- 6 Lazarus and The Rich Man 157
- 7 Pray, and Don't Lose Heart 158
- 8 The Pharisee and The Tax Collector . . 158

CHAPTER 6 - THE FINAL YEAR of His Ministry 159

Act 1 - The Feast of Tabernacles (Booths)
- Scene 1 His Brothers Did Not Believe In Him . . 161
- 2 Why Do You Seek To Kill Me? 162
- 3 Where I Am Going You Cannot Come . . 163
- 4 Come To Me, and Drink 164
- 5 The Pharisees Are Divided 164

Act 2 - Discussions In The Temple
- Scene 1 Jesus Forgives An Adulteress . . . 165
- 2 My Testimony and Judgment Is True . . 166
- 3 You Are From Below, I Am From Above . . 167
- 4 Abraham Is Our Father 168
- 5 Your Father Is The Devil 169
- 6 You Have A Demon! 170

CHAPTER 6 - THE FINAL YEAR continued

Act 3 - Healing A Man Born Blind
- Scene 1 Jesus Cures A Man Who Was Born Blind . 171
- 2 The Pharisees Question The Man and His Parents 172
- 3 They Question The Man A Second Time . 173
- 4 Do You Believe In The Son of Man? . . 173

Act 4 - The Good Shepherd
- Scene 1 I Am The Door Of The Sheep . . . 174
- 2 I Am The Good Shepherd 174
- 3 I Lay Down My Life To Take It Again . . 175
- 4 Repent And Bear Fruit, or Perish . . 175

Act 5 - The Feast of Dedication
- Scene 1 Depart From Me, All You Evildoers! . . 176
- 2 I And The Father Are One 177
- 3 The Jews Try To Stone Jesus For Blasphemy . 177

Act 6 - The Resurrection of Lazarus
- Scene 1 Jesus Hears That Lazarus Has Died . . 178
- 2 I Am The Resurrection and The Life . . 179
- 3 Mary Goes To Meet Jesus 179
- 4 Jesus Calls Lazarus Forth From The Tomb . 180
- 5 The Pharisees Plot To Kill Jesus . . 181

Act 7 - Further Teachings
- Scene 1 Teachings On Divorce 182
- 2 Teachings On Adultery 183
- 3 A Word About Eunuchs 183
- 4 Let The Children Come to Me . . . 184
- 5 What Must I Do To Obtain Eternal Life? . 185
- 6 It Is Hard For The Wealthy to Enter The Kingdom 186
- 7 What Will There Be For Us? 187
- 8 The Generous Landowner 188
- 9 The Unworthy Slaves 188

CHAPTER 6 - THE FINAL YEAR continued

Act 8 - The Road To Jerusalem
- Scene 1 Shall We Command Fire From Heaven? . 189
- 2 The Ten Lepers of Samaria 189
- 3 What Will Happen To The Son of Man . . 190
- 4 To Sit On My Right and On My Left . . 191
- 5 The Greatest Is The One Who Serves . . 191
- 6 Jesus Restores The Sight of Bartimaeus . 192
- 7 The Salvation of Zaccheus 193
- 8 The Parable of The Good and Faithful Servants . 194

Act 9 - Anointed For Burial
- Scene 1 Mary Anoints Jesus With Perfume . . 196
- 2 The Disciples Question The Waste . . 197

CHAPTER 7 - THE FINAL WEEK 198

Act 1 - Sunday - Arrival In Jerusalem
- Scene 1 The Lord Has Need of Your Donkey . . 200
- 2 Jesus Rides on The Colt 201
- 3 The Approach To Jerusalem 201
- 4 Hosanna, To The Son of David! . . . 202
- 5 Jesus Weeps For Jerusalem 203
- 6 Jesus Enters Jerusalem 203
- 7 Jesus Cleanses The Temple, The Final Time . 204
- 8 Healing In The Temple 204

Act 2 - Monday
- Scene 1 Jesus Curses A Fig Tree 205
- 2 Who Gave You This Authority? . . . 206
- 3 Who Did The Will of His Father? . . . 207
- 4 The Parable of The Evil Vine-Growers . . 208
- 5 To Serve Me, You Must Follow Me . . 209
- 6 A Voice From Heaven 210
- 7 Believe In The Light 210
- 8 Believe In Me, and The One Who Sent Me . 211

CHAPTER 7 - THE FINAL WEEK continued

Act 3 - Tuesday

Scene		Page
1	Be Prepared For The Wedding Feast	212
2	The Pharisees Plot To Trap Jesus	213
3	Is It Lawful To Pay Taxes To Caesar?	213
4	In The Next Life, Whose Wife Will She Be?	214
5	The Greatest Commandment	215

Act 4 - Wednesday - Woe To The Pharisees

Scene		Page
1	How Is The Christ The Son of David?	216
2	Beware Of The Scribes and The Pharisees	217
3	The Hypocrisy Of The Scribes and The Pharisees	218
4	First, Clean The Inside of The Cup	219
5	You Shed The Blood of The Prophets	219
6	A Second Lament For Jerusalem	220
7	The Greatest Contributor To The Treasury	220

Act 5 - Wednesday - The End of The Age

Scene		Page
1	The Temple Will Be Destroyed	221
2	The Signs of the End of The Age	222
3	Your Testimony When They Persecute You	223
4	You Will Hated Because of My Name	223
5	Do Not Turn Back!	224
6	False Christs Will Arise	225
7	Signs In The Sun, Moon and Stars	226

Act 6 - Wednesday - The Return

Scene		Page
1	The Parable of The Fig Tree	227
2	One Will Be Taken, The Other Will Be Left	228
3	Be On The Alert!	229
4	Be Dressed In Readiness	230
5	The Lamps of The Ten Virgins	231
6	Separating The Sheep From The Goats	232
7	Judas Plots With The Jews To Betray Jesus	233

CHAPTER 7 - THE FINAL WEEK continued

Act 7 - Thursday - The Last Supper

Scene		Page
1	Preparing The Venue	234
2	The Last Supper Begins	235
3	Jesus Washes His Apostles' Feet	236
4	One Of You Will Betray Me	237
5	Judas Is Revealed	238
6	The Blood of The New Covenant	239
7	My New Commandment: Love One Another	239
8	Peter, You Will Deny Me Three Times	240
9	Two Swords Are Enough	241

Act 8 - The Holy Spirit and The Father

Scene		Page
1	I Am The Way, and The Truth, and The Life	242
2	The Holy Spirit Helper	243
3	I Go Away, and I Will Come To You	244
4	Abide In My Love, and Bear Fruit	244
5	My Commandment Again: Love One Another	245
6	The World Hates Me and My Father	245
7	More About The Holy Spirit of Truth	246
8	I Am Going To The Father	247
9	Jesus Prays To The Father	248

CHAPTER 8 - ARREST, TRIALS & CRUCIFIXION 250

Act 1 - Jesus Is Arrested at Gethsemane

Scene		Page
1	The First Agonized Prayer of Jesus	252
2	Jesus Prays A Second Time	253
3	The Third Prayer of Jesus In The Garden	253
4	Judas Leads The Authorities To Jesus	254
5	Peter Defends Jesus With A Sword	255
6	Jesus Is Arrested	256

CHAPTER 8 - TRIALS & CRUCIFIXION continued

Act 2 - Jesus Is Accused by The High Priest

Scene		Page
1	First, To The House of Annas	257
2	Then To The High Priest, Caiaphas	258
3	Peter's First Denial of Jesus	259
4	Peter's Second Denial	259
5	Jesus Is Charged With Blasphemy	260
6	Jesus Is Beaten	260
7	Peter Denies Jesus The Third Time	261

Act 3 - Jesus Is Questioned by The Sanhedrin

Scene		Page
1	The Sanhedrin Council Condemns Jesus	262
2	The Jews Take Jesus To The Roman Governor	262

Act 4 - Jesus Is Questioned by The Romans

Scene		Page
1	Pilate Hears The Accusation Against Jesus	263
2	Are You The King of The Jews?	264
3	Pilate Finds No Guilt In Jesus	265
4	Herod, Tetrarch of Galilee, Questions Jesus	266
5	We Romans Find No Guilt In This Man	266

Act 5 - Jesus Is Sentenced To Die

Scene		Page
1	Shall I Release for you Jesus, or Barabbas?	267
2	The Jews Cry Out To Crucify Jesus	268
3	Pilate Sentences Jesus To Die	268
4	The Soldiers Mock and Scourge Jesus	269
5	Pilate Tries Again To Release Jesus	270
6	Jesus Is Handed Over To Be Crucified	271
7	Judas The Betrayer Hangs Himself	271

Act 6 - The Crucifixion of Jesus Christ

Scene		Page
1	Simon of Cyrene Carries The Cross of Jesus	272
2	The Walk To Golgotha	272
3	Jesus Is Crucified	273
4	The Soldiers Divide His Clothing	274
5	Jesus Is Crucified Between Two Criminals	274
6	Pilate's Inscription of The Charge Against Jesus	275
7	Jesus Entrusts His Mother To John	275
8	Let This Christ Save Himself!	276
9	The Last Words of The Two Criminals	276

TABLE OF GOSPEL CONTENTS

	Page
CHAPTER 8 - TRIALS & CRUCIFIXION *continued*	
Act 7 - The Death of Jesus Christ	
Scene 1 Darkness Falls Over The Land	277
2 Jesus Dies On The Cross	277
3 An Earthquake At The Death of Jesus	278
4 The Body of Jesus Is Taken Down	279
Act 8 - Jesus Is Laid In Joseph's Tomb	
Scene 1 Joseph Asks Pilate For The Body of Jesus	280
2 The Body of Jesus Is Placed In Joseph's Tomb	281
3 Roman Soldiers Guard The Tomb	282
Act 9 - The Resurrection of Jesus Christ	
Scene 1 An Earthquake at The Resurrection of Jesus	283
2 The Soldiers Are Paid To Lie	283

	Page
CHAPTER 9 - APPEARANCES & ASCENSION	284
Act 1 - Sunday Morning	
Scene 1 The Women Arrive At The Tomb	285
2 Two Angels Greet The Women At The Tomb	286
3 The Women Tell The Apostles	287
4 Peter and John Run To The Tomb	287
5 Jesus Appears To Mary Magdalene	288
Act 2 - Appearances To The Apostles	
Scene 1 Jesus Walks To Emmaus With Two Disciples	289
2 They Finally Recognize Jesus	290
3 Jesus Appears To The Ten Apostles	291
4 Jesus Proves That His Body Is Real	292
5 Jesus Bestows The Holy Spirit On The Apostles	292
6 Jesus Manifests Himself To Thomas	293
Act 3 - Reunion In Galilee	
Scene 1 Jesus Meets His Apostles At The Mountain	294
2 Appearance at The Sea of Galilee	294
3 A Catch of One Hundred and Fifth-Three Fish	295
4 Peter, Tend My Sheep	296
5 The Promise of The Father	297

	Page
CHAPTER 9 - ASCENSION *continued*	
Act 4 - The Great Commission	
Scene 1 Jesus Sends The Eleven To Preach The Gospel	298
2 These Signs Will Accompany You	298
Act 5 - The Ascension of Jesus Christ	
Scene 1 Jesus Christ Ascends To Heaven	299
2 They Went Out and Preached Everywhere	299
Act 6 - Epilogue	
Scene 1 Final Words	300

FOREWORD

It is important that every person hear about the life and teachings of Jesus Christ. Few disagree that this story is found within the four Gospel accounts that open the New Testament of the Christian *Bible*, namely *Matthew, Mark, Luke* and *John*.

Within these four Gospel narratives there are many places where two, three, and even all four of them, mention the same saying, or describe the same event. In these many sets of parallel and overlapping verses there are almost always also differences within the specific details that each account records.

Over the centuries, many types of *harmonies* (which align the verses of the Gospels in parallel columns) and *mergers* (which combine or unify the individual words of the Gospels) have been created in an attempt to reconcile the differing chronologies of the four accounts, and to include or unify all of their words. This book goes beyond all previous works by unifying the details of the parallel verses of the four Gospels on a word-for-word basis, to produce one single and complete Gospel story of the teaching life and healing ministry of Jesus Christ.

As for the name, FIVE COLUMN is the title of this book which contains the database of the Four Gospel Harmony and the *fifth column* word-for-word Merger. The unified *fifth column* text is named *The Synoptic Gospel* and is the subtitle of this book, and as a separate work that reproduces just the *fifth column* text. Use this book to see how the words of the four Gospels were aligned and harmonized to produce the *fifth column* text, and read *The Synoptic Gospel: The Story of The Life of Jesus* if you just want to read the full Gospel story.

About The Verse-By-Verse Edition

This book is a condensed version of the *FIVE COLUMN*: *The Synoptic Gospel* database which only displays the full Verses as they appear in the *fifth column* text of *The Synoptic Gospel*. Notations in the four Gospel columns indicate the original verse divisions as they were split and arranged to create the *fifth column* Merger of the **Word-For-Word Edition** (ISBN 978-1-988271-79-8).

For some Verses in this book it may be difficult to see how the *fifth column* unified text was produced from the words that are shown in the four original Gospel columns, and this is usually due to the steps of the sixteen step harmonization and merging process that cannot be displayed using the format of this book which does not always show the full word-by-word division of every Verse. To see the full detail of how every word from each of the four original Gospel columns was harmonized and merged consult the *FIVE COLUMN*: **Word-For-Word Edition** (552 pages) available at *fivecolumn.com/purchase*.

As this Edition cannot currently be printed-on-demand in the intended landscape format this book was printed with a portrait layout, the contents of which are best viewed when the book is turned $90°$ (one quarter turn) clock-wise (to the right).

INTRODUCTION

The New Testament Greek word *euangelion* (evangel) means *good message*, which became *gospel* in Old English, meaning *god term* or *god-spell*, and is most commonly referred to today as *good news*.

Since at least the Latin *Vulgate Bible* of 405 CE the canon of the Christian New Testament has opened with the four Gospel accounts of *Matthew, Mark, Luke* and *John*, each of which records a version of the good news of the life and teachings of Jesus Christ. Each Gospel account was written by a different man, and told to a different audience, from a different point of view; and each narrative has a slightly different emphasis, focus and reason why it was written.

While the four Gospel accounts are generally united in their overall theme and storyline, they each also contain unique sayings and stories, which when taken together provide a more complete, composite picture of the teachings and the personality of Jesus Christ.

Within the four Gospels there are many instances where the same saying, teaching or story is recorded in two or more of the accounts, while some sayings and events from the life of Jesus are mentioned within all four. In the many places where more than one Gospel account is describing the same event, those verses are thought of as "parallel", in that their content is the same or similar, occasionally even using identical wording.

Because there is so much material shared between the four Gospels accounts, particularly *Mark, Matthew* and *Luke*, they are often referred to as "synoptic" which is a Greek compound word that means "seeing together" or "seeing as one". In this case, *synoptic* means seeing the four Gospel narratives of the New Testament as one single record of the things that Jesus Christ said and did and taught.

In the many places where the Gospel stories closely parallel each other, there are almost always also differences in the wording and specific details that each account records. While these differences are usually minor and inconsequential, they sometimes produce contradictions, and occasionally even apparent conflicts.

Despite their differences, because there is so much similarity and overlap shared between the four New Testament Gospels, they have long been used together, both as a **harmony** which displays the Gospels in columns side-by-side, and as a **merger** (also known as a *synopsis*) which eliminates the duplication between the sections of parallel verses, and combines the remaining words to produce one single, complete version of each saying and event.

In this book, with all of the events arranged in chronological order, the parallel and overlapping sections of verses were reconciled as they were being merged into the *fifth column* on a word-for-word basis using a precise system of notation, which was part of a harmonization and unification process that involved sixteen steps. The unified text that is produced in the *fifth column* of FIVE COLUMN is known as *The Synoptic Gospel*, and is the subtitle of this work.

The main consideration of this work ensures that every detail from each of the four Gospel texts is included or accounted for, and that not one single word is unnecessarily omitted. The process of removing the duplication between the parallel sections of words and verses reduced the word count from the 83,680 words of *New American Standard Bible* (NASB) version of the four Gospel accounts, to the 65,776 words of *The Synoptic Gospel* unified text, which is almost 22% shorter compared to reading each of the four individual Gospel accounts back-to-back.

While eliminating both the confusion caused by the differing chronologies of the four Gospels, and resolving the wording differences within their many sections of overlapping and parallel verses, this work produces an easy to follow narrative that preserves the full detail of every word, teaching, and miracle of Jesus Christ, as found within the four Gospel accounts of the New Testament.

The complete, unified *fifth column* text of this book is reproduced in a separate work titled, *The Synoptic Gospel: The Story of The Life of Jesus*.

May God continue to Bless and Inspire all who seek to know and understand the teaching Life and healing Ministry of Jesus Christ, The Son of God.

Daniel John

December, 2014

fivecolumn.com   *synopticgospel.com*

NOTES ON READING THIS BOOK

The following section of Notes explains how the verses of the four individual Gospel accounts of the New Testament were aligned and combined to create the unified text of the *fifth column* of the *FIVE COLUMN: The Synoptic Gospel* Four Gospel Harmony and Merger, and details some of the features of this book.

If the steps that involve the manipulation of individual words cannot be clearly seen in this *Verse-By-Verse* Edition use the 552 page *Word-For-Word* Edition, which shows the individual word splits that divide the text of the Gospel Verses into as many as 18 pieces.

NOTE 1

HOW THIS BOOK WAS COMPILED

The 83,680 words that are contained within the four Gospel accounts of the New Testament (*NASB Edition*) were ordered, aligned, harmonized and merged into a single, complete and flowing narrative, according to the following series of sixteen steps.

1.1 - Order The Gospel Storyline

Step 1 - Line Up The Four Gospel Accounts Side-by-Side

The texts of the four Gospel accounts of the New Testament were placed in four parallel columns side-by-side, next to which a "fifth" column was added on the left side of each page.

Each verse from each Gospel is placed on its own consecutive horizontal line within its column, except when the content of the verse is repeated or paralleled in one or more of the other Gospel columns, in which case those parallel verses will likely share the same line across the Gospel columns - see *Step 3 - Align The Parallel Verses*.

Step 2 - Arrange The Verses Chronologically

In order to create one contiguous storyline, the verses from each of the four Gospel columns were moved up or down as necessary within their respective Gospel columns to sequence all of the sayings and events chronologically, according to a timeline which was established for the life and ministry of Jesus Christ, which begins before His birth, and ends after His ascension. For more information see *Note 3 - Dates Listed in This Book* on page *xviii*. The detailed timeline used in this book will be published in the future as, *The Timeline of The Life of Jesus Christ*, by Daniel John.

In general, this work used *The Gospel of John* as a backbone to which the verses from *The Gospel of Mark* were added. To this, the verses of *Matthew* were ordered, and then the content of *Luke's* account.

Verses were moved up or down within their respective Gospel columns so that the combined chronological storyline of the four columns flowed as logically and smoothly as possible, from the *Prologue* and earliest events to the conclusion of the story. For more information see *Article 5 - Ordering The Gospel Storyline* on page A-4.

Step 3 - Align The Parallel Verses

Where two or more of the Gospel accounts contain verses that mention the same saying, or are describing the same event, those parallel verses and groups of verses were moved up or down within their respective Gospel columns to be aligned side-by-side on the same line with each other across the four columns. Verses were moved to be aligned with the chronological backbone established for the overall storyline (*Step 2*). For more information on aligning parallel verses, see the first two steps of *Note 1.2 - Harmonize The Parallel Verses* on the following page.

Step 4 - Arrange Groups of Verses Into Scenes of Action

When chronologically ordered, the 3,779 verses (*NASB Edition*) of the sayings and deeds of Jesus from the four Gospels were sorted into groups of consecutive words and verses called a *Scene*. In general, each Scene of action describes either a single event, or a group of related actions if they all happened in roughly the same place and at the same time. For more information about Scenes, see *Note 2.1 - Storyline Divisions* on page *vi*.

Step 5 - Assign A Date To Each Scene

Each Scene of Verses is assigned a chronological date for when the action occurred within the timeline that was established for the life and ministry of Jesus Christ. For more information about the dates assigned to the Scenes of this book, see *Note 3 - Dates Listed In This Book* on page *ix*.

Step 6 - Copy Unique (Unparallel) Verses Into The Fifth Column

The text of each line of a Verse that is unique, and does not have a matching set of parallel words from one or more of the other Gospel columns, was copied into the *fifth column* of that line. For the steps of the process used to unify the words of the parallel sections of words and Verses, see *Note 1.2 - Harmonize The Parallel Verses* on the following page.

1.2 - Harmonize the Parallel Verses

Step 1 - **Split Parallel Verses Into Pieces**

In order to reconcile wording differences between the parallel and overlapping sections of verses within the four Gospel columns it is almost always necessary to split and divide each synoptically shared verse into two or more pieces, where each piece is a word, or a group of consecutive words. For more information see *Note 2.2 - Split Verses*, on page *vii*.

Generally, each piece of each split verse is assigned its own new line across the five columns except where the words of a piece of a split verse exactly or closely matches or parallels the wording of a piece of a split verse from one of the other Gospel columns, in which case that repeated word or group of words (from each of the Gospel columns) is usually be placed on the same line across the other Gospel columns - see the next step.

Each piece (groups of consecutive words) of each split verse is numbered within its Gospel column using the *Verse Reference* notation system found on page *viii*.

Step 2 - **Align The Parallel Pieces of Verses**

Within each Scene, the parallel pieces of each split verse were moved up or down as necessary within their respective Gospel columns so that identical and similar words or groups of words - which contained the same basic meaning of thought or action - were aligned to be on the same line across the four columns.

The lines of parallel split verses were then moved up and down as necessary within their respective Gospel columns so that the overall narrative produced by reading them consecutively flowed smoothly and logically from one line of text to the next in the *fifth column*, from the beginning of the Scene to the end.

Differences in the individual words or the sequence of those words within the sets of parallel verses were reconciled according to *Step 4*.

Step 3 - **Copy Parallel Words Into The Fifth Column**

Where a line across two or more Gospel columns contained an identical word or set of words, a single copy of that word(s) was copied into the *fifth column* of that line.

Where in a line of text across the four Gospel columns there is a difference between the parallel verses of even a single word, a choice was made as to which word or words would be copied into the *fifth column* from which Gospel column(s), and which word(s) or word-form(s) would not be retained - see the next step.

Step 4 - **Reconcile Wording Differences**

Where in a line across two or more Gospel columns of parallel verses there is a difference of even a single letter within a single word, a choice was made as to which word, words or word-form(s) from which Gospel column(s) would be copied into the *fifth column* of that line, and which word or words from the parallel Gospel column(s) would not be retained.

There are several types of word differences that necessitated making a choice, including the use of synonyms (different words with the same meaning), differing action tenses (past/present/future), and the use of singular/plural. For more information on the types of wording differences that necessitated making a choice, see *1.3 Step 2 - Word Substitutions* on the following page, and *Article 4 - Parallel Wording Differences* on page A-4.

Word choices between the Gospel accounts were made to be inclusive of the differences between each individual word so that each line of the story created in the *fifth column* flowed smoothly to the next line, and logically from the beginning of the Scene until the end. For more information about *Word Substitutions* see *Step 2* on the following page.

After the chosen word or words from each line of parallel text were copied into the *fifth column* of that line, then the word(s), word-forms, and suffixes that were not retained to be copied into the *fifth column* were struck ~~through~~ within their respective Gospel column(s) (see *Step 4* on the following page).

1.3 - Edit the Fifth Column

Step 1 - Rearrange The Sequence of Words

In order to maintain a smooth and logical flow of thought and action from one line of text in the *fifth column* to the next line, it is occasionally necessary to rearrange the sequence of the individual words as they are being copied from one or more of the four Gospel columns. This rearrangement is possible because the sequence of those words as they appear in any English translation is usually different from the order of those same words in the original Greek manuscript. It is noted that whenever a language is translated the grammatical structure of the words usually necessitates the rearrangement of those words in order to fit the form and syntax of the language into which they are being transcribed.

As with any translation, the importance of the words lies in their full and accurate conveyance of meaning, and the particular order of their sequence is usually a secondary consideration. With this in mind, the sequence of the words was rearranged where necessary, as they were being transcribed into the *fifth column* from the four columns of that line, in order to maintain a smooth and logical flow of thought and action.

Step 2 - Words Substitutions

In order to maintain a logical flow of thought and action within the lines of the *fifth column*, especially where parallel sets of verses exist within two or more of the four Gospel columns, it is often necessary to substitute or replace a word from at least one of the parallel Gospel columns of that line with a word in the *fifth column* that has an equivalent meaning. An example is the substitution of the word *and* in replacement of *for* or *but*. To help identify individuals, especially if they are speaking (as at the beginning of a Scene), the name of a person was occasionally substituted in the *fifth column* in place of their pronoun from one or more of the four Gospel columns, such as *Jesus* for *He*, and visa-versa.

Every word that was substituted in the *fifth column* appears within square brackets [ ] as does its counterpart(s) within the four Gospel columns, where the words or letters that are not replaced (not used/unretained) are shown as struck [~~through~~] within its set of brackets.

Words from the four Gospel columns were also changed or added when being copied into the *fifth column* to correct for discrepancies between the English text of *The Nestle-Aland Novum Testamentium Graece, 21st Edition* (*Marshall's Interlinear © 1958*) upon which the translated text of the *New American Standard Bible* (NASB) version of the four Gospels is based. The *Westcott and Hort* manuscript *(© 1969)* was also a consulted resource.

In places of difference, word substitutions and/or additions (see next step) were made to more closely align the English text of the *fifth column* with the original Greek wording of those original verses from the four Gospel columns. Words that were changed for this reason have an asterisk * beside them within their Gospel column(s).

Step 3 - Added Words

In order to bridge all of the details while maintaining the flowing readability of each line, Verse, and Scene of the *fifth column*, especially within the many sets of parallel verses that are shared by two or more of the four Gospel accounts, a full word is occasionally added to a line of the *fifth column* that does not appear within any of the four Gospel columns of that line. Common added words include *and*, *the*, *of*, *he*, *He*, *Jesus*, and *they*. For clarity angle brackets < > appear around every word that was added to the *fifth column*.

Step 4 - Adjusted Suffixes

In order to maintain a logical and grammatically consistent flow of thought and action within each line of the *fifth column*, and from one line of text to the next, it is occasionally necessary to change or modify the suffix of a word from one or more of the four Gospel columns as it is being copied into the *fifth column*. The most common reason to modify a suffix is to unify the differing action tenses of the Gospel columns. To enhance clarity, suffixes were also sometimes added to words in the *fifth column* that did not have a suffix in the original Gospel column(s) of that line. All added and modified suffixes are shown within the *fifth column* inside [square] brackets, or in the case of very short words, where the modified suffix may replace all but the first letter or two of that word, the entire word may appear within the brackets. The original, unretained suffix is shown inside its respective Gospel column(s) as struck ~~though~~ and within [square brackets].

Step 5 - Punctuation

In the *Koine (Hellenistic/common)* Greek language, in which the New Testament and the four Gospel manuscripts were originally written, there is no punctuation; punctuation was added later as the Greek was being translated into other languages, including English. As such, punctuation is added or changed within the *fifth column* of this book as necessary in order to maintain a smooth and logical flowing readability of thought and action within the words and sentences that formed each Verse, and from one Verse or Scene to the next.

Step 6 - Assign Verses

The final step of the process used to produce the text of the *fifth column* text of this book was to order the groupings of consecutive words and sentences into numbered *Verses*. Verses assigned in this book generally consist of a single full sentence, but may contain two or three sentences if they are short, and the details that they contain are closely related in thought, action or meaning.

For more information on the assignment of Verses in the *fifth column* of this book, see *Note 2 - Split Verses* beginning on the following page, and also *Article 6 - Re-Versing The Gospel* on page A-5. For more information on the *Verse Reference System* that is used in this book, see *Note 2.3* on page *viii*.

NOTE 2
DIVIDING THE GOSPEL STORYLINE

For ease of reading and referencing, the entire *fifth column* text and four Gospel Harmony of this book is divided into three major types of divisions, based on the locations of the events, and the duration of time that they cover.

2.1 - STORYLINE DIVISIONS

1. **Chapter** - This largest division segments the entire Gospel storyline into ten pieces. The length of time covered by a *Chapter* can range from a single day, to a week, or a year, or even cover indefinite periods of time, such as the *Prologue* and *Genealogies* of *Chapter 0 - Before The Beginning*.

2. **Act** - Each *Chapter* is divided into as many as nine A*cts* of related events that all happened during the same shorter, period of time, and usually also in the same approximate geographical location. Generally, the period of time covered by an *Act* may take place during an afternoon, or over a few days, weeks, or months.

3. **Scene** - Each *Act* is divided into as many as nine Scenes of action, each of which describe a single parable or event, or a few related events if they all occurred in the same geographical location, and during the same short period of time. A *Scene* may relate the conversation of a few minutes, as a single teaching or parable, or cover a longer span of time, such as the two days that Jesus spent in Samaria. The *Prologue* and *Epilogue* Scenes of this book cover long, indefinite intervals of time. In terms of length, a Scene may consist of just on sentence, to more than thirty *Verses*. The entire unified *fifth column* text of this book is divided into 360 Scenes of action.

These three major storyline divisions are specified in:

1. the *Table of Gospel Contents* found at the beginning of this book
2. the *Table of Chapter Contents* that begins each Chapter
3. the *title block* that begins each Scene, as this example for *Scene 121*:

> Chapter **1** - The Birth of Jesus
>
> Act **2** - The Annunciation To Mary
>
> Scene **1** - Gabriel Tells Mary That She Will Birth A Son

4. *Appendix 1 - The Synoptic Gospel Scene Contents* - at the back of this book.

Scenes were further subdivided into the following smaller units of text:

4. **Verse** - For ease of reference, the groups of words that comprise each *Scene* are numbered as *Verses*, which generally consist of a single important detail, or a few closely-related pieces of information. A *Verse* can range in length from a few words to a full sentence, or three.

   For more information on the Verses and the reference system used to arrange the text of the *fifth column* of this book see the following two pages and *Article 6 - Re-Versing The Gospel* on page A-5.

5. **Line** - A *line* is a horizontal demarcation across the *five columns* of the *Word-For-Word* Edition of *FIVE COLUMN*. The lines that comprise the verses of the four Gospel columns of the *Word-For-Word* Edition are not shown in this *Verse-By-Verse* Edition.

2.2 - SPLIT VERSES

In reference to *The Bible*, a "verse" is a group of consecutive words and/or sentences that subdivides the chapters of each book of *The Bible*, including the four Gospels of the New Testament. In the many places where the Gospel accounts closely parallel each other, and are mentioning the same saying or are describing the same event, the parallel and synoptic verses almost always also contain differences within the specific wording and details that they each record. So that each line across the four Gospel columns of this database would contain the same word, words, or meaning of thought, it is necessary to split most verses that are part of a parallel set into multiple pieces, where each piece of the split verse consists of either a single word, or several consecutive words, or a complete sentence, or two.

Using a tilde ~ any verse from the four Gospels can be divided into two pieces, and the sequence of each piece shown. A **tilde to the right** of the original Gospel *verse reference number* indicates the **first piece** (*beginning*) of a split verse, and the second or **last piece** (*end*) of the split verse is shown with a **tilde to the left** of the *verse reference number*. (See *Split Verse* below)

While the second or end (last) piece of a split verse will usually be found within its Gospel column on the very next line below, the end piece will occasionally be found many lines below within that same Scene, or it may even appear in a different Scene, Act, or even in another Chapter. And while the second or end piece of a split verse is usually found after (below) the first or beginning piece of the verse, sometimes the end piece is placed before (above) the line of the first piece, usually within that same Scene, but occasionally in a proceeding Scene, Act or even Chapter.

Split Verse	Piece	Notation	Text
2 Pieces	beginning	John 12:36~	"While you have the Light, believe in the Light, so that you may become sons of Light!" ~
	end	John 12:~36	~ After Jesus spoke these things, He went away, and hid Himself from them.

A verse can be split into three pieces, and the middle piece designated by placing a tilde on either side of the *verse reference number* for the middle piece of the verse.

Double-Split	beginning	John 8:44~	"You are of your father the devil, and you want to do the desires of your father. ~
3 Pieces	middle	John 8:~44~	~ He was a murderer from the beginning, and does not stand in the truth, because there is no truth in him. ~
	end	John 8:~44	~ Whenever he speaks a lie, he speaks from his own nature, for he is a liar, and the father of lies.

As the purpose of splitting verses is to allow for the precise alignment of the differing wording used among the parallel verses of the four Gospel columns, it is often necessary to divide parallel verses into more than three pieces. This is accomplished by adding a number after the *right directional tilde* of the middle split pieces, and the *left directional tilde* of the middle split piece is no longer needed to represent the first or proceeding piece(s) of the verse, and is dropped and not shown.

By numbering the pieces of split verses in this way any verse can be divided into an unlimited number of pieces, and in the *Word-For-Word* Edition of *FIVE COLUMN* a Verse was split 18 times to form 19 separate pieces. In this *Verse-By-Verse* Edition the largest split verse consists of eight pieces (seven split) in *Scene 412*.

Triple Split	**Quad Split**	**Five Split**	**Six Split**
4 Pieces	5 Pieces	6 Pieces	7 Pieces
1st beginning 1:1~	1st beginning 1:1~	1st beginning 1:1~	1st beginning 1:1~
2nd piece 1:1$^{~1}$	2nd piece 1:1$^{~1}$	2nd piece 1:1$^{~1}$	2nd piece 1:1$^{~1}$
3rd piece 1:1$^{~2}$	3rd 1:1$^{~2}$	3rd 1:1$^{~2}$	3rd 1:1$^{~2}$
end / last (4th) 1:~1	4th 1:1$^{~3}$	4th 1:1$^{~3}$	4th 1:1$^{~3}$
	end (5th) 1:~1	5th 1:1$^{~4}$	5th 1:1$^{~4}$
		end (6th) 1:~1	6th 1:1$^{~5}$
			end (7th) 1:~1

Using this notation system each piece of every *separated split verse* can always be located, no matter how distantly separated those pieces may be within the 360 Scenes of *FIVE COLUMN: The Synoptic Gospel*. To locate all of the pieces of a *separated split verse*, use *Appendix 2 - Gospel Verse Cross-Reference*, located at the back of this book.

2.3 - FIVE COLUMN VERSE REFERENCE SYSTEM

For ease of reading and referencing, as with any long book or play, the text of the *fifth column* of *FIVE COLUMN (The Synoptic Gospel)* is divided into *Chapters*, *Acts*, and *Scenes*, based on the chronological time of the occurrence in relation to all of the other events in the combined Gospel story, along with the location and the duration of the event.

Scene Reference Number

The entire *fifth column* text of *FIVE COLUMN: The Synoptic Gospel* is divided into ten *Chapters* (0 - 9) each of which may consist of up to nine *Acts* (1 - 9) which are further subdivided into as many as nine *Scenes of action* (1 - 9). Using this system, each of the 360 Scenes within this book is designated by a three digit *scene reference number* (123).

From the *scene reference number* it can be roughly determined when in time the action of the *Scene* took place, in relation to all of the other events of the combined Gospel storyline. For example, a *scene reference number* of "111" indicates, beginning with the first digit on the left - the first *Chapter* (although there is a *Chapter 0 - Prologue*), while the second (or middle) digit indicates the first *Act*, and the final digit is the *Scene* number. Knowing that the title of *Chapter 1* is *The Birth of Jesus* gives an indication of when in time this Scene may have occurred, in relation to the sequence of the other events that are mentioned within the combined Gospel story.

To avoid confusion when quoting *fifth column (Synoptic Gospel)* Scene references, each number in the sequence should be read or said so that the number for the *Chapter*, *Act* and *Scene* is distinct, as in, "Scene one, one, one", and not "Scene one hundred and eleven".

Verse Reference Number

The text of each *Scene* of *FIVE COLUMN: The Synoptic Gospel* is subdivided into *Verses* which consist of from one to three full sentences. A Verse may represent a single line of text from the *fifth column* of this book, or be composed from more than a dozen consecutive lines. For more information on the assignment of Verses in this book see *Note 2.2* on the previous page, and *Article 6 - Re-Versing The Gospel*, on page A-5.

The Verses of each Scene are consecutively numbered, and the assigned *verse reference number* is listed after the *scene reference number*, and following a period. Verses are designated by either a single digit *verse reference number*, as 111.1 (Verse 1), or by two digits, as 111.23 (Verse 23).

To avoid confusion when quoting *Synoptic Gospel* Verse references, each number in the sequence should be read or said so that the number for the *Chapter*, *Act*, *Scene*, and *Verse*, is distinct; as in, "Scene one, one, one, Verse one".

2.4 - FIVE COLUMN VERSE NOTATIONS

As each Scene in *FIVE COLUMN: The Synoptic Gospel* is referenced by a three digit *scene reference number*, each complete *Verse reference* is a four or five digit number.

Following are examples of the notation system that references the *Verses* of *The Synoptic Gospel*.

Single Verse Reference

	Notation	Chapter	Act	Scene	Verse	digits
single-digit verse	111.1	1	1	1	1	4
double-digit verse	111.12	1	1	1	12	5

Multiple Verse Reference

Multiple Verses can be consecutively referenced using the following system of notation:

	Notation	Chapter	Act	Scene	Verses
verses 1 to 3	111.1-3	1	1	1	1-3
verses 1 and 4	111.1, 4	1	1	1	1 & 4
verses 3 to 12	111.3-12	1	1	1	3-12
verses 1 to 3, and 5	111.1-3, 5	1	1	1	1-3 & 5

Multiple Verse References From Multiple Scenes

Verses from multiple Scenes can be noted by separating each reference with a semicolon ";" as:

232.1; 234.6-8; 443.5; 845.1-3, 5, 8-12; 932.6, 9

NOTE 3
DATES LISTED IN THIS BOOK

3.1 - DATE NOTATIONS USED IN THIS BOOK

The Gregorian calendar, as used today throughout much of the world, is divided into two distinct eras of time that are derived from the year which was calculated as the one in which Jesus Christ had been born. This division produces a date in time that occurred either before the birth of Jesus, or one that happened after He was born.

In this book, these two eras of time are noted as:

BCE — denotes a date that occurred before the traditional year assigned as the one in which Jesus had been born, where **BCE** in English is an acronym for "**Before the Common Era**", or *Current Era*, or *Christian Era*.

BCE corresponds to the older dating notation that used "B.C." or "BC", which in English stands for "*Before Christ*."

CE — denotes a date that occurred after the traditional year assigned as the date of the birth of Jesus, where **CE** is the acronym for the "**Common Era**", or *Current Era*, or *Christian Era*.

CE corresponds to the older dating notation of "A.D." or "AD", which stands for the Latin *Anno Domini*, and is translated, "In the year of *the* (or *our*) Lord."

3.2 - ASSIGN A DATE TO EACH SCENE

So that the four differing timelines of the events that are mentioned within the texts of the four Gospels could be unified, each Scene of *FIVE COLUMN: The Synoptic Gospel* was assigned a date in time for when the recorded action in the Scene may have taken place. Dates are assigned to each Scene according to a chronological timeline which was constructed around the significant dates of the birth of Jesus, His baptism (as the *Messiah* - the *Christ*) and the beginning of His public ministry, as well as His arrest, death, resurrection, and ascension into Heaven. Other dates that help focus the timeline include the three Passovers and the other Feasts that Jesus attended in Jerusalem, which are mentioned only within *The Gospel of John*.

Details provided within the text of some Scenes allow the season, the month, and occasionally even the day of the week to be determined; and for those Scenes that narrate the arrest, trials and crucifixion of Jesus, sometimes even the hour of the day is mentioned, or can be determined, or estimated. As it was a major source of conflict with the Pharisees, another timing detail that is noted are those events that took place on a Sabbath.

Where no date or timing information is provided within the text of the Scene itself, only the year and the season or month is assigned, usually based on the date of the Scene that precedes it.

As it is not always possible to know with precision or certainty when in time the hundreds of individual sayings and events from the life of Jesus Christ may have occurred, it is unlikely that the dates assigned to each and every Scene in this book are always accurate, but they are reasonable, given available Scriptural and historical sources of information, and our current understanding of them.

While every effort has been made to be accurate in the dating of each Scene, beyond the important dates which establish the timeline, and the Feasts and Festivals that Jesus observed in Jerusalem, along with the Sabbaths, it generally does not matter very much if He healed someone in the year 31 or 32 CE, or whether it was during the spring or the summer, because in the end the Gospel story is about the things that Jesus Christ said and did, and not usually about when He may have said or did them, some 2,000 years ago.

The date and other timing details associated with each Scene of action in this book are listed in:

1. the *title block* that begins each *Scene*
2. *Appendix 1 - The Synoptic Gospel Scene Contents*

3.3 - THE SYNOPTIC GOSPEL TIMELINE

In order to chronologically sequence all of the many sayings of Jesus Christ, and to arrange all of the events that make up the full Gospel account of His life and ministry, it is necessary to establish a timeline, based in part on the dates of a few important events: the **Birth** of Jesus, His **Baptism** (as the *Messiah/Christ*) and the beginning of His Ministry, the **Death** of Jesus, and His **Ascension** into Heaven.

Against this basic timeline each *Scene of action* in this book is assigned a date, based on how those verses fit within the overall combined timeline that was established for the four Gospels. The assignment of dates to the Scenes of this book is done to be as accurate as possible, given the limited information provided within each of the Gospel accounts themselves, and the scarcity of supporting historical information about the life of Jesus. It should be kept in mind that the importance of the Gospel story of the life and teachings of Jesus Christ is found in what the Son and Word of God said and did, and excepting the major events of His life, it does not usually matter when during His life and ministry any specific event may have occurred.

The full details behind the selection of the dates used in *FIVE COLUMN* and *The Synoptic Gospel* will be made available in *The Timeline of The Life of Jesus Christ*, which will be published as a future work.

NOTE 4 - OTHER NOTES

4.1 - Locations

Excepting the *Prologue* and the *Epilogue*, each Scene of *FIVE COLUMN: The Synoptic Gospel* is assigned a geographical location for where the action likely occurred. When it can be determined from the Gospel account, the name of the town or location where the action took place is mentioned, along with the territory name which is *italicized*, as in, "Jerusalem, *Judea*". When it is possible, other location and geographical features are also included, as in, "Sea of Galilee, *Galilee*" or "Garden of Gethsemane, Mount of Olives, Jerusalem, *Judea*".

In those many places where a geographical location cannot be determined from the text of the Gospels or other related sources of information, the assigned location is usually the same location as that of the previous Scene. In those places where an outright guess had to be made, the listed location is usually only of the regional territory, as in *Judea* or *Galilee*.

The location of each Scene is listed before the date in each Scene's title block, and also in *Appendix 1 - Synoptic Gospel Scene Contents*.

4.2 - Maps

Excepting the *Prologue*, each Chapter of this book features a geographical map of either the country of Israel or the city of Jerusalem, as they would likely have appeared during the lifetime of Jesus, in the beginning of the first century CE. The border of "Israel" is that of the ancient kingdom as unified under Kings David and Solomon, but with the territory divisions that existed during the lifetime of Jesus. The legend in the bottom right corner of each map details its symbols and scale.

So that some of the places where Jesus traveled to at various points during His life and ministry can be more easily seen, each map of Israel in this edition of *FIVE COLUMN* highlights the locations of the Scenes of action which occurred during the timespan covered in that chapter by displaying those locations with a white center in the black circle that represents the location.

All Chapter Maps are © 2009 by Smart Publishing Ltd.

4.3 - Quotations and References

Included in this book are references to the complete and partial quotations from the Scriptures of the Old Testament, as they are found within the texts of the four Gospels. All quotations and references appear throughout the *fifth column* of this book in *italicized* font. To the right of the end of each quotation is a number in superscript which corresponds to the *reference footnote* at the bottom of the page.

Indirect and weaker secondary references appear within round brackets ( ). References to multiple sources within the same book of *The Bible* are separated by a semicolon ";" and references to multiple books are separated by a slash "/" (see *Note 2.3* on *page viii*). Additional references help clarify times and locations, and provide additional biographical information.

4.4 - Verse Indication Lines

Horizontal lines of varying thickness and darkness are shown in the *Word-For-Word* Edition of *FIVE COLUMN* to indicate the original structure of the Gospel Verses as they appear within the four Gospel columns. This *Verse-By-Verse* Edition only shows a single black line to indicate each of the four Gospel's last verse. The other types of lines used in the Word-For-Word Edition include the *Gospel Verse Division* Line, *Broken Scene* line, *Split Verse Continued*, and the *End of Scene*.

4.5 - NASB Retentions

Braces { } around verses and text within the four Gospel columns indicate that the surrounded words do not appear within all Greek manuscripts, but that they are included in the *New American Standard Bible* (NASB) translation of The Gospels.

FIVE COLUMN

Note 4 - Samples

xi

WORD-FOR-WORD SAMPLES

The following six examples show the **Verse-By-Verse** text of this book beside the full word-for-word divisions of the *parallel split verses* from the **Word-For-Word** Edition of *FIVE COLUMN: The Synoptic Gospel*.

P The first (top) part of each Sample shows the text of the Verse(s) as it appears here in the **Verse-By-Verse** Edition.
P The second (bottom) part shows the full word-for-word harmonization from the **Word-For-Word** Edition.

For some Verses in this book it may be difficult to see how the *fifth column* unified text was produced from the words that are shown in the four original Gospel columns, and this is usually due to the steps of the sixteen step harmonization and merging process that cannot be displayed using the format of this book which does not always show the full word-by-word division of every Verse. To see the full detail of how every word from each of the four original Gospel columns was harmonized and merged, consult the *FIVE COLUMN: Word-For-Word* Edition (552 pages) available at *fivecolumn.com/purchase*.

Sample 1 - from this book

7 - THE FINAL WEEK Act 7: **Thursday - The Last Supper**	Scene 2: **The Last Supper Begins** A house in Jerusalem, *Judea* Thursday evening, April 2nd / 33 CE	Page 235 *The United Gospel of Jesus Christ*
	Matthew / **Mark** / **Luke**	
1 When it was evening, <and> the hour had come, Jesus came <and> reclined at the table with [His] twelve apostles.	26:20 ~~Now~~ when evening ~~came~~, Jesus ~~was~~ reclining at the table with [the] twelve ~~disciples~~. 14:17 When it was evening ~~He~~ came with [the] twelve. 22:14 When the hour had come, ~~He~~ reclined at the table, ~~and the~~ apostles ~~with Him~~.	

Sample 1 - *Word-For-Word* Edition

Scene 2: **The Last Supper Begins**

Page 383

	Matthew	Mark	Luke
1 When	26:20~ ~~Now~~ when	14:17~ When	22:14~ When
it was evening	26:20⁻¹ evening ~~came~~,	14:17⁻¹ it was evening	
<and> the hour had come,			22:14⁻¹ the hour had come,
Jesus	26:20⁻² Jesus	14:17⁻² ~~He~~	22:14⁻² ~~He~~
came		14:17⁻³ came	
<and> reclined at the table	26:20⁻³ ~~was~~ reclining at the table		22:14⁻³ reclined at the table,
with	26:20⁻⁴ with	14:17⁻⁴ with	22:14⁻⁴ ~~and~~
[His] twelve	26:20⁻⁵ [the] twelve	14:~17 [the] twelve.	
apostles.	26:~20 ~~disciples~~.		22:~14 the apostles ~~with Him~~.

Five Column

Note 4 - Samples

Sample 2 - from this book

3 - FIRST YEAR OF MINISTRY	Scene 5: **Jesus Calls James and John**	Page 43
Act 4: **Jesus Settles In Capernaum**	Sea of Galilee, near Capernaum, *Galilee* late spring / 30 CE	*The Story of The Life of Jesus*

	Matthew	Mark	Luke
1 Going on a little farther from there, [Jesus] saw two other brothers; James, the son of Zebedee, and John his brother, who were partners with Simon.	4:21~ Going on from there [He] saw two other brothers, James the son of Zebedee, and John his brother,	1:19~ Going a little farther, [He] saw James the son of Zebedee, and John his brother,	5:10~ ~~and so also were~~ James and John, sons of Zebedee, who were partners with Simon.
2 [They] were in the boat with their father Zebedee, mending the nets.	4:~21~ in the boat with Zebedee their father, mending ~~their~~ nets;	1:~19 [~~who~~] were ~~also~~ in the boat mending the nets.	
3 [Jesus] called them, and when they had brought their boats to land, immediately they left everything, and their father in the boat with the hired servants, and <they> went away and followed Him.	4:21 ~~and~~ [He] called them. 4:22~ Immediately they left the boat and their father, and followed Him.	1:20 ~~Immediately~~ [He] called them; and they left their father ~~Zebedee~~ in the boat with the hired servants, and went away ~~to~~ follow Him.	5:11 When they had brought their boats to land, they left everything and flowed Him.

The Synoptic Gospel — *The Story of The Life of Jesus*

Sample 2 - *Word-For-Word* Edition

3 - FIRST YEAR OF MINISTRY

Act 4: Jesus Settles n Capernaum

Scene 5: **Jesus Calls James and John**

Sea of Galilee, near Capernaum, *Galilee*   late spring / 30 CE

Page 59

One Complete Gospel United from Four

	Matthew	Mark	Luke
1 Going	4:21~ Going	1:19~ Going	
on	4:21^{-1} on		
a little farther		1:19^{-1} a little farther,	
from there,	4:21^{-2} from there		
[Jesus] saw	4:21^{-3} [He] saw	1:19^{-2} [He] saw	
two other brothers;	4:21^{-4} two other brothers,		
James,	4:21^{-5} James	1:19^{-3} James	5:10~ ~~and so also were~~ James
the	4:21^{-6} the	1:19^{-4} the	
son of Zebedee, and John	4:21^{-7} son of Zebedee, and John	1:19^{-5} son of Zebedee, and John	5:10^{-1} and John, sons of Zebedee,
his brother,	4:21^{-8} his brother,	1:19^{-6} his brother,	
who were partners with Simon.			5:10^{-2} who were partners with Simon.
2 [They] were		1:19^{-7} [~~who~~] were	
in the boat	4:21^{-9} in the boat	1:19^{-8} ~~also~~ in the boat	
with their father Zebedee,	4:21^{-10} with Zebedee their father,		
mending the nets.	4:21^{-11} mending ~~their~~ nets;	1:~19 mending the nets.	
3 [Jesus] called them,	4:~21 ~~and~~ [He] called them.	1:20~ ~~Immediately~~ [He] called them;	
and		1:20^{-1} and	
when they had brought their boats to land,			5:11~ When they had brought their boats to land,
immediately	4:22~ Immediately		
they left	4:22^{-1} they left	1:20^{-2} they left	5:11^{-1} they left
everything,			5:11^{-2} everything
and	4:22^{-3} and		
their father	4:22^{-4} their father,	1:20^{-3} their father ~~Zebedee~~	
in		1:20^{-4} in	
the boat	4:22^{-2} the boat	1:20^{-5} the boat	
with the hired servants, and <they> went away		1:20^{-6} with the hired servants, and went away	
and followed Him.	4:~22 and followed Him.	1:~20 ~~to~~ follow Him.	5:~11 and followed Him.

Five Column

Note 4 - Samples

Sample 3 - from this book

4 - SECOND YEAR OF MINISTRY				Page 71
Act 2: **The Sermon On The Mount**	Scene 2: **You Are The Salt of The Earth** Mount Eremos, near Capernaum, *Galilee* spring / 31 CE			*A Complete Four Gospel Harmony*
	Matthew	**Mark**	**Luke**	
1 "You are the salt of the earth, [and] salt is good;	5:13~ "You are the salt of the earth;	9:50~ "Salt is good;	14:34~ "[Therefore], salt is good;	
2 "but if the salt has become unsalty <and> tasteless, with what will it be seasoned? How can it be made salty again?	5:~13~ but if the salt has become tasteless, how can it be made salty again?	9:~50~ but if the salt becomes unsalty, with what will you make it salty again?	14:~34 but if even salt has become tasteless, with what will it be seasoned?	
3 "It is useless for either the soil or the manure pile, [and] is no longer good for anything except to be thrown out, and trampled under foot by men.	5:~13 [It] is no longer good for anything, except to be thrown out and trampled under foot by men.		14:35~ "It is useless either for the soil or for the manure pile; it is thrown out.	
4 "Have salt in yourselves, and be at peace with one another.		9:~50 Have salt in yourselves, and be at peace with one another."		
5 "If anyone has ears to hear, let [them] hear."		4:23 "If anyone has ears to hear, let [him] hear."	14:~35 He who has ears to hear, let [him] hear."	

THE GREATEST GOSPEL

A Unified Four Gospel Harmony

Sample 3 - *Word-For-Word* Edition

4 - SECOND YEAR OF MINISTRY

Act 2: The Sermon On The Mount

Scene 2: You Are The Salt of The Earth

Mount Eremos, near Capernaum, *Galilee*   spring / 31 CE

Page 104

A Unified Four Gospel Merger

	Matthew	Mark	Luke
1 "You are the salt of the earth,	5:13~ "You are the salt of the earth;		
[and]			14:34~ "[~~Therefore~~],
salt is good;		9:50~ "Salt is good;	14:34⁻¹ salt is good;
2 " but if the salt	5:13⁻¹ but if the salt	9:50⁻¹ but if the salt	14:34⁻² but if ~~even~~ salt
has	5:13⁻² has		14:34⁻³ has
become	5:13⁻³ become	9:50⁻² become~~s~~	14:34⁻⁴ become
unsalty		9:50⁻³ unsalty,	
<and> tasteless,	5:13⁻⁴ tasteless,		14:34⁻⁵ tasteless,
with what will it be seasoned?			14:~34 with what will it be seasoned?
How can it be made salty again?	5:13⁻⁵ how can it be made salty again?	9:50⁻⁴ ~~with what will you~~ make it salty again?	
3 " It is useless for either the soil or the manure pile,			14:35~ "It is useless either for the soil or ~~for~~ the manure pile;
[and] is no longer good for anything except	5:13⁻⁶ [~~It~~] is no longer good for anything, except		
to be thrown out,	5:13⁻⁷ to be thrown out		14:~35~ ~~it is~~ thrown out.
and trampled under foot by men.	5:~13 and trampled under foot by men.		
4 " Have salt in yourselves, and be at peace with one another.		9:~50 Have salt in yourselves, and be at peace with one another."	
5 " If anyone has ears to hear, let [them] hear."		4:23 "If anyone has ears to hear, let [him] hear."	14:~35 ~~He who~~ has ears to hear, let [him] hear."

Five Column

Sample 4 - from this book

8 - TRIALS & CRUCIFIXION Act 1: **Jesus Is Arrested at Gethsemane**	Scene 2: **Jesus Prays A Second Time** Garden of Gethsemane, Mount of Olives, Jerusalem, *Judea* late Thursday evening, April 2nd / 33 CE	Page 253 *The Four Gospels United as One*

#		Matthew	Mark	Luke
1	When [Jesus] rose from prayer, He came to the [apostles], and found them sleeping from sorrow.	26:40~ And He came to the [disciples] and found them sleeping,	14:37~ And He came and found them sleeping,	22:45 When [He] rose from prayer, He came to the [disciples] and found them sleeping from sorrow,
2	<He> said to Peter, "Simon, are you asleep? Why are you sleeping? Could you men not keep watch with Me for one hour?	26:~40 and said to Peter, "So, you men could not keep watch with Me for one hour?	14:~37 and said to Peter, "Simon, are you asleep? Could you not keep watch for one hour?	22:46~ and said to them, "Why are you sleeping?
3	"Get up! Keep watching, and praying that you may not enter into temptation;	26:41~ "Keep watching and praying that you may not enter into temptation;	14:38~ "Keep watching and praying that you may not come into temptation;	22:~46 Get up and pray that you may not enter into temptation."
4	"the spirit is willing, but the flesh is weak."	26:~41 the spirit is willing, but the flesh is weak."	14:~38 the spirit is willing, but the flesh is weak."	
5	<Then> [Jesus] went away a second time, and <He> prayed again saying the same words; "My Father, if this cannot pass unless I drink it, Your will be done."	26:42 [He] went away a second time and prayed, again saying, "My Father, if this cannot pass away unless I drink it, Your will be done."	14:39 Again [He] went away and prayed saying the same words.	

THE UNIFIED FOUR GOSPEL HARRMONY

All The Words of Jesus Christ in Chronological Order

xvii

Sample 4 - Word-For-Word Edition

8 - TRIALS & CRUCIFIXION

Act 1: **Jesus Is Arrested at Gethsemane**

Scene 2: **Jesus Prays A Second Time**

Garden of Gethsemane, Mount of Olives, Jerusalem, *Judea*   late Thursday evening, April 2nd / 33 CE

Page 411

The Complete Gospel

#		Matthew	Mark	Luke
1	When [Jesus] rose from prayer,			22:45~ When [He] rose from prayer,
	He came	26:40~ And He came	14:37~ And He came	22:45⁻¹ He came
	to the [apostles],	26:40⁻¹ to the [disciples]		22:45⁻² to the [disciples]
	and found them sleeping	26:40⁻² and found them sleeping,	14:37⁻¹ and found them sleeping,	22:45⁻³ and found them sleeping
	from sorrow.			22:~45 from sorrow,
2	<He> said to Peter,	26:40⁻³ and said to Peter,	14:37⁻² and said to Peter,	22:46~ and said to them,
	"Simon, are you asleep?		14:37⁻³ "Simon, are you asleep?	
	Why are you sleeping?			22:46⁻¹ "Why are you sleeping?
	Could	26:40⁻⁶ could	14:37⁻⁴ Could	
	you	26:40⁻⁴ "So, you	14:37⁻⁵ you	
	men	26:40⁻⁵ men		
	not keep watch	26:40⁻⁷ not keep watch	14:37⁻⁶ not keep watch	
	with Me	26:40⁻⁸ with Me		
	for one hour?	26:~40 for one hour?	14:~37 for one hour?	
3	"+Get up!			22:46⁻² Get up
	Keep watching,	26:41~ "Keep watching	14:38~ "Keep watching	
	and praying that you may not enter into temptation;	26:~41 and praying that you may not enter into temptation;	14:~38~ and praying that you may not come into temptation;	22:~46 and pray that you may not enter into temptation."
4	" the spirit is willing, but the flesh is weak."	26:~41 the spirit is willing, but the flesh is weak."	14:~38 the spirit is willing, but the flesh is weak."	
5	<Then> [Jesus] went away	26:42~ [He] went away	14:39⁻¹ [He] went away	
	a second time,	26:42⁻¹ a second time		
	and <He> prayed	26:42⁻³ and prayed,	14:39⁻² and prayed,	
	again,	26:42⁻² again	14:39~ Again	
	saying	26:42⁻⁴ saying,	14:39⁻³ saying	
	the same words;		14:~39 the same words.	
	"My Father, if this cannot pass unless I drink it, Your will be done."	26:~42 "My Father, if this cannot pass away unless I drink it, Your will be done."		

Sample 5 - from this book

7 - THE FINAL WEEK Act 1: **Sunday -** **Arrival In Jerusalem**	Scene 3: **The Approach To Jerusalem** Bethphage, *Judea* Sunday, March 29th / 33 CE			*The Story of The Life of Jesus*
	Matthew	**Mark**	**Luke**	**John**
1 When the large crowd who had come to the feast heard that Jesus was coming to Jerusalem, <they> went out to meet Him.				12:~12 the large crowd who had come to the feast, when ~~they~~ heard that Jesus was coming to Jerusalem, 12:13⁻¹ ~~and~~ went out to meet Him,
2 As He was going, many [in] the crowd were spreading their coats on the road, and *others took leafy branches which they had cut from the palm trees,*[1.] and <they> spread them [on] the road.	21:8 ~~Most~~ [of] the crowd spread their coats ~~in~~ the road, and others ~~were cutting~~ branches from the trees and sprea~~ding~~ them [in] the road.	11:8 ~~And~~ many spread their coats ~~in~~ the road, and others spread leafy branches which they had cut from the ~~fields~~.	19:36 As He was going, ~~they~~ were spreading their coats on the road.	12:13~ took ~~the~~ branches ~~of~~ the palm trees

1. Leviticus 23:40

Sample 5 - *Word-For-Word* Edition   *(Page 319)*

	Matthew	**Mark**	**Luke**	**John**
1 When the large crowd who had come to the feast heard that Jesus was coming to Jerusalem,				12:~12 the large crowd who had come to the feast, when ~~they~~ heard that Jesus was coming to Jerusalem,
<they> went out to meet Him.				12:13⁻⁵ ~~and~~ went out to meet Him,
2 As He was going,			19:36~ As He was going,	
many	21:8~ ~~Most~~	11:8~ ~~And~~ many	19:36⁻¹ ~~they~~	
[in] the crowd	21:8⁻¹ [of] the crowd			
were			19:36⁻² were	
spreading their coats on the road,	21:8⁻² spread their coats ~~in~~ the road,	11:8⁻¹ spread their coats ~~in~~ the road,	19:~36 spreading their coats on the road.	
and *others*	21:8⁻³ and others	11:8⁻² and others		
took				12:13~ took
leafy		11:8⁻⁴ leafy		
branches	21:8⁻⁵ branches	11:8⁻⁵ branches		12:13⁻¹ ~~the~~ branches
which they		11:8⁻⁶ which they		
had cut	21:8⁻⁴ ~~were~~ cutting	11:8⁻⁷ had cut		
from the	21:8⁻⁶ from the	11:8⁻⁸ from the		12:13⁻² ~~of~~ the
palm				12:13⁻³ palm
trees,[1.]	21:8⁻⁷ trees	11:~8 ~~fields~~.		12:13⁻⁴ trees
and	21:8⁻⁸ and			
<they> spread	21:8⁻⁹ sprea~~ding~~	11:8⁻³ spread		
them [on] the road.	21:~8 them [in] the road.			

Five Column

Note 4 - Samples

Sample 6 - from this book

8 - TRIALS & CRUCIFIXION
Act 6: **The Crucifixion of Jesus Christ**

Scene 5: **Jesus Is Crucified Between Two Criminals**
Golgotha, Jerusalem, *Judea*   Friday morning, April 3rd / 33 CE

Page 274

The Gospel of Good News

	Matthew	Mark	Luke	John
1 There at that time, they crucified two criminals with Him; one on His right, and the other on His left, [with] Jesus in between.	27:38 At that time two ~~robbers were~~ crucified with Him, one on ~~the~~ right and ~~one~~ on ~~the~~ left.	15:27 They crucified two ~~robbers~~ with Him, one on His right and ~~one~~ on His left.	23:~33 there they crucified Him ~~and the~~ criminals, one on ~~the~~ right and the other on ~~the~~ left.	19:18 There they crucified ~~Him~~, and with Him two ~~other men~~, one on ~~either side~~ [and] Jesus in between.
2 And the Scripture was fulfilled which says, *"He was numbered with transgressors."* [1.]		15:28 {And the Scripture was fulfilled which says, "~~And~~ He was numbered with transgressors."}		

1. Isaiah 53:12

Sample 6 - *Word-For-Word* Edition

8 - TRIALS & CRUCIFIXION
Act 6: **The Crucifixion of Jesus Christ**

Scene 5: **Jesus Is Crucified Between Two Criminals**
Golgotha, Jerusalem, *Judea*   Friday morning, April 3rd / 33 CE

Page 448

The Synoptic Gospel

	Matthew	Mark	Luke	John
1 There			23:33⁻⁴ there	19:18~ There
at that time,	27:38~ At that time			
they crucified	27:38⁻³ ~~were~~ crucified	15:27~ They crucified	23:33⁻⁵ they crucified	19:18⁻¹ they crucified ~~Him~~, ~~and~~
two	27:38⁻¹ two	15:27⁻¹ two		19:18⁻³ two
criminals	27:38⁻² ~~robbers~~	15:27⁻² ~~robbers~~	23:33⁻⁷ the criminals,	19:18⁻⁴ ~~other men~~,
with Him;	27:38⁻⁴ with Him,	15:27⁻³ with Him,	23:33⁻⁶ Him ~~and~~	19:18⁻² with Him
one on His right,	27:38⁻⁵ one on ~~the~~ right	15:27⁻⁴ one on His right	23:33⁻⁸ one on ~~the~~ right	19:18⁻⁵ one on ~~either side~~
and	27:38⁻⁶ and	15:27⁻⁵ and	23:33⁻⁹ and	
the other			23:33⁻¹⁰ the other	
on His left,	27:~38 ~~one~~ on ~~the~~ left.	15:~27 ~~one~~ on His left.	23:~33 on ~~the~~ left.	
[with] Jesus in between.				19:~18 [and] Jesus in between.
2 And the Scripture was fulfilled which says, *"He was numbered with transgressors."* [1.]		15:28 {And the Scripture was fulfilled which says, "~~And~~ He was numbered with transgressors."}		

1. Isaiah 53:12

NOTE 5

AN OVERVIEW OF THE FOUR GOSPELS

5.1 - Why Are There Four Gospels?

So significant was the impact of the life and teachings of Jesus Christ on Judaism and the Roman, now western world, that within one hundred years after His death more than thirty accounts had been written about His life, His sayings, teachings, and miracles. Many of these collections of the sayings of Jesus, and stories about His life, were reportedly written by, or ascribed to, men who had been with Jesus during His ministry. Then as now, in addition to the four familiar Gospels of the New Testament, *Matthew*, *Mark*, *Luke* and *John*, there exists a *Gospel of Peter*, *of Philip*, *of Thomas*, *of Mary*, and yes, even a *Gospel of Judas*; as well as a *Gospel of The Apostles*, *of The Twelve*, and *of The Hebrews*, along with many others.

Some 120 years after the life of Jesus, a Syrian student of Justin Martyr named Tatian created a type of unified account of the four familiar Gospels known from the Greek as *Diatessaron*, meaning "of / from / out of" "four". In his work Tatian used 96% of *The Gospel of John*, and added to it from 50% to 85% of the content from each of the Gospels of *Matthew*, *Mark* and *Luke*. To eliminate the repetition and duplication between their stories, where two or more of the three accounts parallel each other but do not parallel *John*, Tatian generally selected the wording of the verse(s) from one of the Gospels over the other(s). When given a choice, it appears that Tatian generally chose to include the text of the longest, or most detailed version, of the saying or event. To this he often included additional details that were found within the other Gospels.

Tatian likely chose to combine the texts of these four particular Gospel accounts because they had all been accepted and read by the Church(es) for more than sixty years by that point in time, in about 160 CE. And while these four Gospels were sometimes read together, most Churches preferred one Gospel's version of events over all of the others.

Perhaps Tatian chose to include *Matthew*, *Mark* and *Luke* because they were so similar, and he sought to be inclusive, and to not offend any Church or group if he were to exclude their favorite Gospel.

That Tatian used *The Gospel of John* as the backbone for his work shows that he not only thought that it was authentic, but possibly *John* was his favorite Gospel, or he recognized that only *John* mentions the teachings and events from the ministry of Jesus that occurred in Judea and Jerusalem during the Feasts and the festivals, where Jesus came into conflict with the Pharisees and the scribes of the Law, as He taught in The Temple.

As to why Tatian chose to combine four of these Gospel accounts of the life of Jesus, and not three or five, from among all of the many "gospel" records of the life and sayings of Jesus that existed by his time, is likely because the other three accounts were so similar in wording and content that to leave one of them out - even *Mark* which only contributes about 7% unique, unparalleled content - would have produced a very incomplete record of the teaching life and healing ministry of Jesus.

Another reason as to why Tatian chose to combine four of these Gospel accounts, and not fewer or more, is perhaps because at that time, as anciently before, the number four represented a form of completeness; as in four corners, or the four directions, the four seasons of a year, and of course, the four elements from which everything was at that time, believed by some, to have been be composed (earth, water, air and fire).

Perhaps Tatian saw the complete Gospel of what Jesus Christ said and did and taught as a structure that required four legs upon which to stand firmly, even as the testimony of four witnesses is better than that of one person, or three.

Despite its editorial shortcomings, Tatian's more complete Gospel account of the life and teachings of Jesus Christ was used throughout the early Church, and exclusively by the Syrian, Eastern and Coptic Churches for more than two hundred years, until the Latin *Vulgate Bible* was completed by Jerome on appointment from the Catholic Church in 405 CE. Significantly, the *Vulgate* version of the New Testament opened with the same four Gospels that had been chosen by Tatian, but with *John* now being the fourth Gospel, as all Catholic and most Protestant *Bibles* still present them today. In the east, toward the end of the fifth century, the use of the unified Gospel *Diatessaron* was eventually replaced by the four Gospels of the Syriac *Peshitta*.

Despite the early use of these particular four Gospel accounts in favor or lieu of any and all others, the matter continued to be discussed and debated within the Church until being "officially" settled more than one thousand years later, at a session of the *Ecumenical Council of Trent* held in 1546, at which the Catholic Church finally sanctioned the four books of *Matthew*, *Mark*, *Luke* and *John* as inspired, faithful and true records of the life and teachings of Jesus Christ.

As each of these four Gospels have long been considered authentic and inspired accounts of the life and teachings of Jesus Christ, the words of their texts were combined to produce the Four Gospel Harmony of *FIVE COLUMN*, and the word-for-word Merger of their texts as *The Synoptic Gospel*.

For more information about the history and the formation of the four Gospels of the New Testament, watch the nine part *Overview of The Gospels* series at:

synopticgospel.com/overview-of-the-gospels-series

5.2 - Overlap Among The Four Gospels

Due to the large amount of parallel stories and overlapping material that is shared between *Matthew*, *Mark* and *Luke*, it is generally accepted that *Matthew* and *Luke* borrowed or copied material from *Mark's* Gospel, in addition to other sources, such as a yet unfound *Q* document (German: *Quelle*, meaning "source").

There are also theories that additional documents must have existed to account for the unique material that is found in the Gospels of *Matthew* and *Luke*, referred to simply as the *M* and *L* sources, which, along with other source documents, may have served as *pre* or *proto* versions of these Gospels. Many of these early source documents were likely transcribed from an oral telling of the sayings and events.

There are many theories about the original source documents that contributed to the "modern" Gospels of *Matthew* and *Luke*, and these origin hypotheses are noted in simplest terms by the number of source documents that may have been involved.

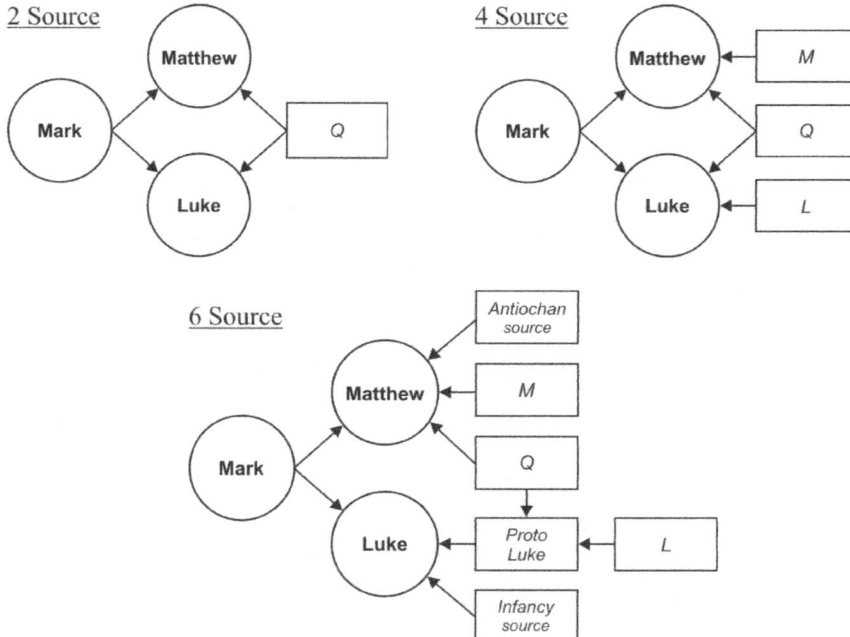

While it is interesting and useful to know which of the four accounts was written first, and which author borrowed or copied what material from whom, and to speculate about what their original source documents may have been some two thousand years ago, the purpose of *FIVE COLUMN: The Synoptic Gospel* is merely to align and harmonize the words of the texts of the four Gospels of the New Testament as they currently exist, in order to produce a single, complete, chronological Gospel account of the life and teachings of Jesus Christ.

5.3 - A Brief Overview of The Four Gospels

Of the four Gospel accounts that open the New Testament only two have traditionally been claimed to have been written by men that Jesus Christ Himself had called to be His apostles; *Matthew* Levi, a tax collector from Capernaum in Galilee, and *John* Zebeddee, the fisherman and younger brother of James ("*The Elder*"), also from Capernaum. For more information about the authorship of *The Gospel of John*, see *Article 3 - Why Include The Gospel of John* on page A-2.

Whoever the authors of any of these four Gospel accounts of the sayings and events of the life and ministry of Jesus Christ were, each writer was a unique person, who had his own individual personality, ancestral lineage, cultural heritage, education, occupation, beliefs and point of view on God, the world, Judaism, and the mission of The Messiah. Therefore, each author had a different reason as to why he chose to add his version of the events from the life of Jesus Christ to the other accounts that already existed. Each Gospel account was written to satisfy the needs and interest of a different group of people, and each Gospel narrative has a slightly different focus and emphasis; whether to prove to the Jewish peoples that Jesus is their long promised Messiah, or to show the Gentiles of the Greek and Roman worlds that He is also the Savior sent by God for the salvation of all of humanity.

As the unity between the four Gospels is seen when they are read together, as they have been since before the *Diatessaron* of 160 CE, and ever since at least 405 CE as the opening books of the New Testament of the *Vulgate Bible* of the Catholic Church, it is of interest to note some of the ways in which the four Gospel accounts differ from each other, as detailed in the Comparison Chart that begins on the following page.

It is likely that all four of the Gospel accounts were originally written in Greek, the language of trade and commerce in that region of the world at that time, although some believe that there may have been a *proto-Matthew* source document that was originally written in Hebrew or Aramaic, although no such manuscript has yet been found.

While all four of the New Testament Gospels show the humanity and the Divinity of Jesus as The Messiah - The Christ - The Anointed One - the *Emphasis* that is listed for each Gospel is the one that has traditionally been ascribed to them by the Church, which list the stations or offices of Jesus as King, Prophet, and Priest, and also as a human manifestation of the Divine Word (*Logos*) of God.

In the following Comparison Chart the Greek *Word Count* listed for each Gospel is based on the Nestle-Aland *Novum Testamentum Graece* manuscript from which the English *New American Standard Bible* (NASB) version of the four Gospels were translated. This word count will differ slightly from every other English translation (KJV, NKJV, NIV, RSV, etc.) even if they are also based on the same edition of the same Greek manuscript.

For more information about the history and the formation of the four Gospels of the New Testament, watch *Part 3* of the *Overview of The Gospels* series at:

synopticgospel.com/overview-of-the-gospels-series

5.4 - COMPARISON CHART OF THE FOUR GOSPELS

Five Column

	MATTHEW	MARK
Date	45 - 60 CE *Likely the 2nd Gospel of the four to be written.*	40 - 55 CE *Likely the 1st Gospel of the four to be written.*
Location	Possibly written in Antioch, *Turkey*.	Likely written in *Syria*, or possibly Rome.
Author	Traditionally ascribed to the apostle Matthew Levi, a wealthy tax collector from Capernaum, although it is more likely that this Gospel was written by an anonymous early Jewish convert to Christianity, and later ascribed to the apostle, which may be the case, because apart from the calling by Jesus for Matthew to become an apostle, there are no other stories in this Gospel that mention Matthew. Written in the third person, and not as a witness.	Likely written by an early Jewish convert named John who had the Roman surname of *Mark*,[3] whose *mother Mary* lived in Jerusalem,[4] and who was the *cousin of Barnabas*.[5] This John Mark was a traveling companion who accompanied both Peter and Paul, and he may have acted as a Greek interpreter or translator for Peter, who referred to Mark as *a son*.[6] While perhaps an actual son, it is more likely that Mark was converted and/or baptized into the faith by Peter, as a spiritual son. There is no indication in *The Gospel of Mark* that the author had ever met or seen Jesus, and this Gospel is written in the third person.
Audience	Written for Jewish people with Messianic expectations, to prove that Jesus is the *Messiah*[1] (Greek: *Christos* / English: *Christ* = *the Anointed One*) and King who was prophesied in the Old Testament to be sent for the salvation of the Jewish peoples.	The Gentile (non-Jewish) peoples of the Roman and Hellenistic (Greek) worlds.
Emphasis	**Jesus as the Son of David, the Messiah and King of the Jewish Peoples**	**Jesus as a suffering Servant and Prophet of God**
Focus	- seen as a bridge between Messianic expectations in the Old Testament and their fulfillment in the life of Jesus as the King of the Jews and Israel. - mentions the term *Son of David* ten times in reference to Jesus. - contains almost 200 quotations, references and allusions to the Old Testament.	- the early Galilean ministry of Jesus, and the last week of His life. - concerned with emotions, miracles, and the exorcism of demons.
Uniqueness	- with *Luke*, provides details surrounding the birth of Jesus, and a genealogy of Jesus as the *Messiah* - "*the son of David, the son of Abraham.*"[2] - with *John*, the only Gospel to use the Hebrew word: *Meshiach*[1] (*the Anointed One*) English word: *Messiah* Greek: *Christos*. - the only Gospel that mentions the term "*Kingdom of Heaven*" (*32 times*), and also the word *Church* (*3 times*).	- likely the first Gospel of the four to be written, from which *Matthew* and/or *Luke* copied or borrowed material. - explains Jewish terms, customs, and Hebrew and Aramaic words for a non-Jewish audience. - does not mention the words *Messiah, law, Samaria* or *Samaritans*.
Layout	Contents arranged in five sets of a narrative followed by a discourse (a sermon); likely used to mimic the structure of the *Torah*, the first five books of the Old Testament.	Arranged in four main sections by geographical location: Galilee - Other Journeys - Galilee Again - The Final Week In Jerusalem
Style	Rhythmic, and often poetic (in Greek).	Fast-paced action; uses the phrase "*and immediately*" more than forty times.
Length	Chapters: 28 / Verses: 1,071 Word Count: NASB - 23,534 / Greek - 18,345	Chapters: 16 / Verses: 678 - *the shortest of the four Gospels* Word Count: NASB - 14,833 / Greek - 11,304

1. Daniel 9:25 / (Deuteronomy 18:15)   2. Matthew 1:1   3. Acts 12:12, 37; 15:37   4. Acts 12:12   5. Colossians 4:10 / (Acts 12:39)   6. 1 Peter 5:13

The Synoptic Gospel

xxiii

	LUKE	**JOHN**
Date	60 - 70 CE Likely the 3rd Gospel of the four to be written.	80 - 100 CE The last of the four Gospels to be written.
Location	Likely written in Rome, or possibly Antioch (*Turkey*), or Achaea (*Greece*).	Likely written in Ephesus (*Turkey*).
Author	Luke was an educated Greek (or possibly Syrian) who was likely a new or 2nd generation Christian doctor and traveling companion of Paul, who referred to Luke as *the beloved physician*.[7] As Luke interviewed eyewitnesses to the events of the life of Jesus it is unlikely that he himself had ever met Him.[8] This Luke probably also wrote the New Testament book, *The Acts of the Apostles*, as the two books were originally bound together, and both are dedicated to "Most excellent *Theophilus*",[9] which in Greek means, *one who loves (or lover of) God*. If Theophilus was a real person, he was likely a wealthy Roman patron of Luke and/or Paul, and was possibly a high-ranking official.	Traditionally ascribed to the Jewish apostle John Zebedee, or under his authority. John and his brother James were fisherman from Capernaum, Galilee,[11] and were partners with Simon (Peter) and his brother, Andrew.[12] John refers to himself as the one *whom Jesus loved* (five times), and he is likely one of three men, with James and Peter, who made up an "inner circle" of the apostles who were closest to Jesus. John was likely the last of the apostles to die, and likely also wrote the three letters that bear his name; *1st, 2nd* and *3rd John*; and possibly also *The Book of Revelation*. Parts of this Gospel are written in the second person. For more information see *Article 3 - Why Include The Gospel of John?* on page *vi*.
Audience	Gentiles and new Christians of the Greek and Roman worlds.	Gentiles and new Christians of the Hellenistic Greek world.
Emphasis	**Jesus as a Priest in service to God**	**Jesus as the Divine Son and Word of God**
Focus	- the teachings of Jesus and salvation; to show that Jesus is the Savior of the entire world. - shows the spirituality and power of Jesus; mentions Him praying ten times, and twenty of His miracles.	- likely written to convey additional stories and details from the life of Jesus that were not already mentioned within the other Gospels, including most of the events from Jesus' travels and ministry in Judea and Jerusalem. - conveys God's love for humanity, and mentions *The Father*, *love*, *Son of God*, *life*, *light*, and *believe* more than the other three Gospels.
Uniqueness	- with *Matthew*, provides details surrounding the birth of Jesus, and a genealogy linking Him to *Adam, the Son of God*.[10] - contains historical references to the rulers of local territories. - mentions more miracles of healing, and often provides additional details. - mentions *angels*, *prayer*, and the *Holy Spirit* more than the other three Gospels. - mentions more females and women. - the only Gospel to use the words *redeem* and *redemption*. - many quotations are from the Greek *Septuagint* version of the Old Testament.	- spiritually deep theological themes; the only Gospel to identify Jesus as the *Word* (Greek: *logos*) of God, and to list His seven "*I Am...*" statements. - mentions six Jewish Feasts, including three Passovers. - does not contain any "true" parables. - mentions only eight miracles that were performed by Jesus, and calls them *signs*. - does not mention the exorcism of demons. - may address certain issues of importance within the early Church near the end of the 1st century CE, such as the nature and station of Jesus in relation to God.
Layout	Arranged in three main sections covering three periods of time; Galilee - Other Travels - The Final Week In Jerusalem	Arranged chronologically in four main sections.
Style	Precise, educated, scholarly and fast-paced (6% of this Gospel is the word "*and*").	Detailed, alliterative, and in Greek poetic.
Length	Chapters: 24 / Verses: 1,151 - *the longest of the four Gospels* Word Count: NASB - 25,794 / Greek - 19,482	Chapters: 21 / Verses: 879 Word Count: NASB - 19,519 / Greek - 15,635

[7] Colossians 4:14   [8] Luke 1:1-3   [9] Luke 1:3; Acts 1:1   [10] Luke 3:38   [11] Matthew 4:21; Mark 1:19; Luke 5:10; Acts 12:2   [12] Luke 5:10

Five Column™

The Texts of the

Four Gospel Harmony

+

Fifth Column Merger

Verse-By-Verse Edition

FIVE COLUMN

Page 1

CHAPTER 0 - PROLOGUE

	Page		Page
Act 1 - Foreword		**Act 2 - The Genealogy of Jesus**	
Scene 1 Prologue	1	Scene 1 The Genealogy of The Messiah	2
2 The Word of God	1	2 The Genealogy of The Son of God	3

CHAPTER 0 - PROLOGUE

Act 1: **Foreword**

Scene 1: Prologue

	Luke
1 Inasmuch as many have undertaken to compile an account of the things accomplished among us, just as they were handed down to us by those who from the beginning were eyewitnesses and servants of the Word,	1:1 Inasmuch as many have undertaken to compile an account of the things accomplished among us, 1:2 just as they were handed down to us by those who from the beginning were eyewitnesses and servants of the word,
2 it seemed fitting for me as well, having investigated everything carefully from the beginning, to write it out for you in consecutive order, most excellent *Theophilus*,[1] so that you may know the exact truth about the things you have been taught.	1:3 it seemed fitting for me as well, having investigated everything carefully from the beginning, to write it out for you in consecutive order, most excellent Theophilus; 1:4 so that you may know the exact truth about the things you have been taught.

1. *Greek for "one who loves God" or "lover of God"*

Scene 2: The Word of God

	John
1 In the beginning was the *Word*,[1] and the Word was with *God*,[2] and the Word was *God*.[3]	1:1 In the beginning was the Word, and the Word was with God, and the Word was God.
2 He was in the beginning with God.	1:2 He was in the beginning with God.
3 All things came into being through Him, and apart from Him nothing came into being that has come into being.	1:3 All things came into being through Him, and apart from Him nothing came into being that has come into being.
4 In Him was life, and the life was the Light of men.	1:4 In Him was life, and the life was the Light of men.
5 And the Word became flesh, and dwelt among us.	1:14~ And the Word became flesh, and dwelt among us,
6 *There was the true Light, which coming into the world, enlightens every man.*[4]	1:9 There was the true Light which, coming into the world, enlightens every man.
7 *The Light shines in the darkness,*[5] and the darkness did not comprehend it.	1:5 The Light shines in the darkness, and the darkness did not comprehend it.
8 He was in the world, and the world was made through Him, and the world did not know Him -	1:10 He was in the world, and the world was made through Him, and the world did not know Him.
9 [but] we saw His glory, glory as of the only begotten from the Father, full of grace and truth.	1:~14 [and] we saw His glory, glory as of the only begotten from the Father, full of grace and truth.

1. *Greek:* Λόγος / logos = *word, something spoken, discourse (reason, wisdom)*   2. *Greek:* Θεόν / Theon = *a God or Deity; The Supreme Deity; God The Father*
3. *Greek:* Θεὸς / Theos = *a God or Deity, Divine, Godly, God-like*   4. *Isaiah 49:6*   5. *Genesis 1:3 / Isaiah 9:2*

CHAPTER 0 - PROLOGUE

Act 2: The Genealogy of Jesus

Scene 1: The Genealogy of The Messiah

Matthew

1 The record of the genealogy of Jesus *the Messiah*,[1] the son of David, the son of Abraham:
2 Abraham was the father of Isaac,
3 Isaac the father of Jacob,
4 and Jacob the father of Judah and his brothers.
5 Judah was the father of Perez and Zerah by Tamar,
6 Perez was the father of Hezron,
7 and Hezron the father of Ram.
8 Ram was the father of Amminadab,
9 Amminadab the father of Nahshon,
10 and Nahshon the father of Salmon.
11 Salmon was the father of Boaz by Rahab,
12 Boaz was the father of Obed by Ruth,
13 and Obed the father of Jesse.
14 Jesse was the father of David the King.
15 David was the father of Solomon by Bathsheba, who had been the wife of Uriah.
16 Solomon was the father of Rehoboam,
17 Rehoboam the father of Abijah,
18 and Abijah the father of Asa.
19 Asa was the father of Jehoshaphat,
20 Jehoshaphat the father of Joram,
21 and Joram the father of Uzziah.
22 Uzziah was the father of Jotham,
23 Jotham the father of Ahaz,
24 and Ahaz the father of Hezekiah.
25 Hezekiah was the father of Manasseh,
26 Manasseh the father of Amon,
27 and Amon the father of Josiah.
28 Josiah became the father of Jeconiah and his brothers, at the time of the deportation to Babylon.
29 After the deportation to Babylon: Jeconiah became the father of Shealtiel,
30 and Shealtiel the father of Zerubbabel.
31 Zerubbabel was the father of Abihud,
32 Abihud the father of Eliakim,
33 and Eliakim the father of Azor.
34 Azor was the father of Zadok,
35 Zadok the father of Achim,
36 and Achim the father of Eliud.
37 Eliud was the father of Eleazar,
38 Eleazar the father of Matthan,
39 and Matthan the father of Jacob.
40 Jacob was the father of Joseph the husband of Mary, by whom Jesus was born, who is called the *Messiah*.[1]
41 So all <of> the generations from Abraham to David are fourteen generations;
42 <and> from David to the deportation to Babylon, <are> fourteen generations;
43 and from the deportation to Babylon to the *Messiah*,[1] <are> fourteen generations.

Matthew

1:1 The record of the genealogy of Jesus the Messiah, the son of David, the son of Abraham:
1:2 Abraham was the father of Isaac,
1:~2~ Isaac the father of Jacob,
1:~2 and Jacob the father of Judah and his brothers.
1:3 Judah was the father of Perez and Zerah by Tamar,
1:~3~ Perez was the father of Hezron,
1:~3 and Hezron the father of Ram.
1:4 Ram was the father of Amminadab,
1:~4~ Amminadab the father of Nahshon,
1:~4 and Nahshon the father of Salmon.
1:5 Salmon was the father of Boaz by Rahab,
1:~5~ Boaz was the father of Obed by Ruth,
1:~5 and Obed the father of Jesse.
1:6 Jesse was the father of David the king.
1:~6 David was the father of Solomon by Bathsheba who had been the wife of Uriah.
1:7 Solomon was the father of Rehoboam,
1:~7~ Rehoboam the father of Abijah,
1:~7 and Abijah the father of Asa.
1:8 Asa was the father of Jehoshaphat,
1:~8~ Jehoshaphat the father of Joram,
1:~8 and Joram the father of Uzziah.
1:9 Uzziah was the father of Jotham,
1:~9~ Jotham the father of Ahaz,
1:~9 and Ahaz the father of Hezekiah.
1:10 Hezekiah was the father of Manasseh,
1:~10~ Manasseh the father of Amon,
1:~10 and Amon the father of Josiah.
1:11 Josiah became the father of Jeconiah and his brothers, at the time of the deportation to Babylon.
1:12~ After the deportation to Babylon: Jeconiah became the father of Shealtiel,
1:~12 and Shealtiel the father of Zerubbabel.
1:13~ Zerubbabel was the father of Abihud,
1:~13~ Abihud the father of Eliakim,
1:~13 and Eliakim the father of Azor.
1:14~ Azor was the father of Zadok,
1:~14~ Zadok the father of Achim,
1:~14 and Achim the father of Eliud.
1:15~ Eliud was the father of Eleazar,
1:~15~ Eleazar the father of Matthan,
1:~15 and Matthan the father of Jacob.
1:16 Jacob was the father of Joseph the husband of Mary, by whom Jesus was born, who is called the Messiah.
1:17~ So all the generations from Abraham to David are fourteen generations;
1:~17~ from David to the deportation to Babylon, fourteen generations;
1:~17 and from the deportation to Babylon to the Messiah, fourteen generations.

---

1. *Hebrew:* Meshiach = *Greek:* Christos = *English:* Christ

CHAPTER 0 - PROLOGUE

Act 2: The Genealogy of Jesus

Scene 2: The Genealogy of The Son of God

Verse-By-Verse Edition

	Luke		Luke
1 <Jesus> was, as supposed, the son of Joseph,	3:~23 being, as was supposed, the son of Joseph,	28 the son of Joshua,	3:29~ the son of Joshua,
2 the son of Eli,	3:~23 the son of Eli,	29 the son of Eliezer,	3:29^{-1} the son of Eliezer,
3 the son of Matthat,	3:24~ the son of Matthat,	30 the son of Jorim,	3:29^{-2} the son of Jorim,
4 the son of Levi,	3:24^{-1} the son of Levi,	31 the son of Matthat,	3:29^{-3} the son of Matthat,
5 the son of Melchi,	3:24^{-2} the son of Melchi,	32 the son of Levi,	3:~29 the son of Levi,
6 the son of Jannai,	3:24^{-3} the son of Jannai,	33 the son of Simeon,	3:30~ the son of Simeon,
7 the son of Joseph,	3:~24 the son of Joseph,	34 the son of Judah,	3:30^{-1} the son of Judah,
8 the son of Mattathias,	3:25~ the son of Mattathias,	35 the son of Joseph,	3:30^{-2} the son of Joseph,
9 the son of Amos,	3:25^{-1} the son of Amos,	36 the son of Jonam,	3:30^{-3} the son of Jonam,
10 the son of Nahum,	3:25^{-2} the son of Nahum,	37 the son of Eliakim,	3:~30 the son of Eliakim,
11 the son of Hesli,	3:25^{-3} the son of Hesli,	38 the son of Melea,	3:31~ the son of Melea,
12 the son of Naggai,	3:~25 the son of Naggai,	39 the son of Menna,	3:31^{-1} the son of Menna,
13 the son of Maath,	3:26~ the son of Maath,	40 the son of Mattatha,	3:31^{-2} the son of Mattatha,
14 the son of Mattathias,	3:26^{-1} the son of Mattathias,	41 the son of Nathan,	3:31^{-3} the son of Nathan,
15 the son of Semein,	3:26^{-2} the son of Semein,	42 the son of David,	3:~31 the son of David,
16 the son of Josech,	3:26^{-3} the son of Josech,	43 the son of Jesse,	3:32~ the son of Jesse,
17 the son of Joda,	3:~26 the son of Joda,	44 the son of Obed,	3:32^{-1} the son of Obed,
18 the son of Joanan,	3:27~ the son of Joanan,	45 the son of Boaz,	3:32^{-2} the son of Boaz,
19 the son of Rhesa,	3:27^{-1} the son of Rhesa,	46 the son of Salmon,	3:32^{-3} the son of Salmon,
20 the son of Zerubbabel,	3:27^{-2} the son of Zerubbabel,	47 the son of Nahshon,	3:~32 the son of Nahshon,
21 the son of Shealtiel,	3:27^{-3} the son of Shealtiel,	48 the son of Amminadab,	3:33~ the son of Amminadab,
22 the son of Neri,	3:~27 the son of Neri,	49 the son of Admin,	3:33^{-1} the son of Admin,
23 the son of Melchi,	3:28~ the son of Melchi,	50 the son of Ram,	3:33^{-2} the son of Ram,
24 the son of Addi,	3:28^{-1} the son of Addi,	51 the son of Hezron,	3:33^{-3} the son of Hezron,
25 the son of Cosam,	3:28^{-2} the son of Cosam,	52 the son of Perez,	3:33^{-4} the son of Perez,
26 the son of Elmadam,	3:28^{-3} the son of Elmadam,	53 the son of Judah,	3:~33 the son of Judah,
27 the son of Er,	3:~28 the son of Er,		

continued >

CHAPTER 0 - PROLOGUE

Act 2: **The Genealogy of Jesus**

Scene 2: **The Genealogy of The Son of God**
continued

	Luke
54 the son of Jacob,	3:34~ the son of Jacob,
55 the son of Isaac,	3:34$^{~1}$ the son of Isaac,
56 the son of Abraham,	3:34$^{~2}$ the son of Abraham,
57 the son of Terah,	3:34$^{~3}$ the son of Terah,
58 the son of Nahor,	3:~34 the son of Nahor,
59 the son of Serug,	3:35~ the son of Serug,
60 the son of Reu,	3:35$^{~1}$ the son of Reu,
61 the son of Peleg,	3:35$^{~2}$ the son of Peleg,
62 the son of Heber,	3:35$^{~3}$ the son of Heber,
63 the son of Shelah,	3:~35 the son of Shelah,
64 the son of Cainan,	3:36~ the son of Cainan,
65 the son of Arphaxad,	3:36$^{~1}$ the son of Arphaxad,
66 the son of Shem,	3:36$^{~2}$ the son of Shem,
67 the son of Noah,	3:36$^{~3}$ the son of Noah,
68 the son of Lamech,	3:~36 the son of Lamech,
69 the son of Methuselah,	3:37~ the son of Methuselah,
70 the son of Enoch,	3:37$^{~1}$ the son of Enoch,
71 the son of Jared,	3:37$^{~2}$ the son of Jared,
72 the son of Mahalaleel,	3:37$^{~3}$ the son of Mahalaleel,
73 the son of Cainan,	3:~37 the son of Cainan,
74 the son of Enosh,	3:38~ the son of Enosh,
75 the son of Seth,	3:38$^{~1}$ the son of Seth,
76 the son of Adam,	3:38$^{~2}$ the son of Adam,
77 the son of God.	3:~38 the son of God.

CHAPTER 1
THE BIRTH OF JESUS

Events surrounding the Birth of Jesus.

	Page
Act 1 - The Prophecy About John	
Scene 1 The Birth of John Is Foretold To Zacharias	6
2 Elizabeth Becomes Pregnant With John	7
Act 2 - The Annunciation To Mary	
Scene 1 Gabriel Tells Mary That She Will Birth A Son	8
2 Mary Visits Elizabeth	9
Act 3 - The Birth of John	
Scene 1 The Birth and Naming of John	10
2 The Prophecy of Zacharias About John	11
Act 4 - The Birth of Jesus	
Scene 1 An Angel Solves Joseph's Dilemma	12
2 Joseph and Mary Journey To Bethlehem	12
3 The Birth of Jesus	13
4 Angelic Announcement To The Shepherds	13
5 The Naming of Jesus	14
Act 5 - Jesus Is Presented In The Temple	
Scene 1 Righteous Simeon Prophesies About Jesus	14
2 Anna The Prophetess	15
3 Return To Nazareth	15
Act 6 - To Egypt and Back	
Scene 1 King Herod and The Magi From The East	16
2 Joseph Is Warned To Flee To Egypt	17
3 Herod Orders The Death of The Male Babies	17
4 Joseph, Mary and Jesus Return From Egypt	18
Act 7 - Young Jesus in The Temple	
Scene 1 I Had To Be In My Father's House	19

MAP OF ISRAEL

Locations mentioned in this Chapter are shown with a white center.

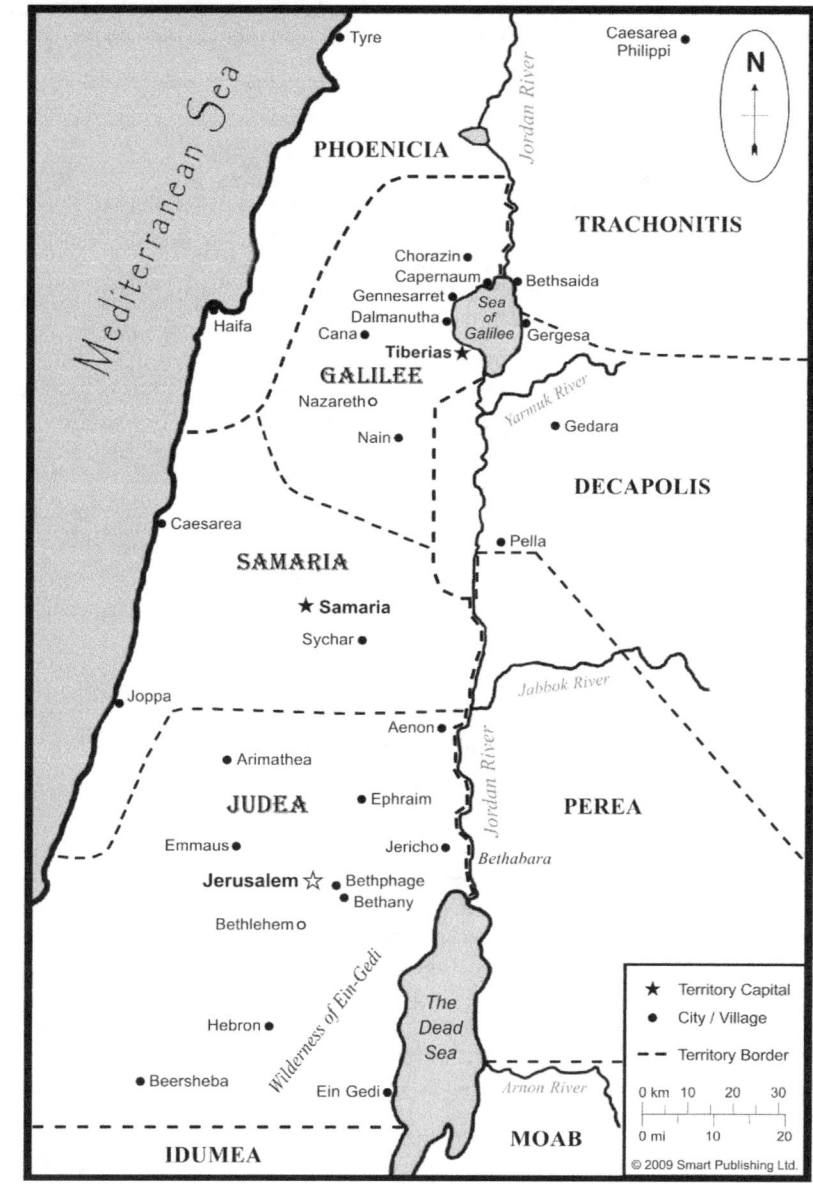

CHAPTER 1 - THE BIRTH OF JESUS	Scene 1: **The Birth of John Is Foretold To Zacharias**	Page 6
Act 1: **The Prophecy About John**	The Temple, Jerusalem, *Judea* mid June / 7 BCE	*The Unified Four Gospel Harmony*

	Mark	Luke
1 The beginning of the *gospel* [1] of Jesus *Christ*,[2] the Son of God.	*1:1* The beginning of the gospel of Jesus Christ, the Son of God.	
2 In the days of *Herod <the Great* [3] *>*, King of Judea, there was a priest of the division of *Abijah* [4] named Zacharias, [who] had a wife from the daughters of Aaron name[d] Elizabeth.		*1:5* In the days of Herod, king of Judea, there was a priest named Zacharias, of the division of Abijah; ~~and~~ [he] had a wife from the daughters of Aaron, ~~and her~~ name ~~was~~ Elizabeth.
3 They were both righteous in the sight of God, walking blamelessly in all the commandments and requirements of the Lord;		*1:6* They were both righteous in the sight of God, walking blamelessly in all the commandments and requirements of the Lord.
4 but they had no child, because Elizabeth was barren, and they were both advanced in years.		*1:7* But they had no child, because Elizabeth was barren, and they were both advanced in years.
5 Now it happened that while [Zacharias] was performing his priestly service before God, in the appointed order of his division according to the custom of the priestly office, he was chosen by lot to enter the Temple of the Lord and burn incense.		*1:8* Now it happened that while [~~he~~] was performing his priestly service before God in the appointed order of his division, *1:9* according to the custom of the priestly office, he was chosen by lot to enter the temple of the Lord and burn incense.
6 [While] the whole multitude of people were in prayer outside at the hour of the incense offering, an angel of the Lord appeared to him, standing to the right of the altar of incense.		*1:10* [~~And~~] the whole multitude of ~~the~~ people were in prayer outside at the hour of the incense offering. *1:11* ~~And~~ an angel of the Lord appeared to him, standing to the right of the altar of incense.
7 Zacharias was troubled when he saw the angel, and fear gripped him.		*1:12* Zacharias was troubled when he saw the angel, and fear gripped him.
8 But the angel said to him, "Do not be afraid, Zacharias, for your petition has been heard, and your wife Elizabeth will bear you a son; and you will give him the name *John*.[5]		*1:13* But the angel said to him, "Do not be afraid, Zacharias, for your petition has been heard, and your wife Elizabeth will bear you a son, and you will give him the name John.
9 "You will have joy and gladness, and many will rejoice at his birth, for he will be great in the sight of the Lord.		*1:14* "You will have joy and gladness, and many will rejoice at his birth. *1:15~* "For he will be great in the sight of the Lord;
10 "*He will drink no wine or liquor;* [6] and *he will be filled with the Holy Spirit while yet in his mother's womb;* [7] and He will turn many of the sons of Israel back to the Lord their God.		*1:~15* ~~and~~ he will drink no wine or liquor, and he will be filled with the Holy Spirit while yet in his mother's womb. *1:16* "And he will turn many of the sons of Israel back to the Lord their God.
11 "It is he who will go as a forerunner before Him *in the Spirit and power of Elijah, to turn the hearts of the fathers back to the children,* [8] and the disobedient to the attitude of the righteous, so as to make ready a people prepared for the Lord."		*1:17* "It is he who will go as a forerunner before Him in the spirit and power of Elijah, to turn the hearts of the fathers back to the children, and the disobedient to the attitude of the righteous, so as to make ready a people prepared for the Lord."
12 Zacharias said to the angel, "How will I know this for certain? *For I am an old man, and my wife is advanced in years.*" [9]		*1:18* Zacharias said to the angel, "How will I know this for certain? For I am an old man and my wife is advanced in years."

1. meaning "good news"   2. Hebrew: *Meshiach* = Greek: *Christos* = English: Christ   3. Herod I (73 - 4 BCE) King of Judea & Galilee (37 - 4 BCE)   4. *1 Chronicles 24:1, 8*
5. meaning God is gracious / merciful   6. Numbers 6:3   7. Jeremiah 1:5   8. Malachi 4:5-6   9. Genesis 17:17

continued >

CHAPTER 1 - THE BIRTH OF JESUS

Act 1: **The Prophecy About John**

Scene 1: **The Birth of John Is Foretold To Zacharias**
continued

The Ultimate Four Gospel Harmony

Mark	Luke
	1:19 The angel answered and said to him, "I am Gabriel, who stands in the presence of God, and I have been sent to speak to you and to bring you this good news.
	1:20 "And behold, you shall be silent and unable to speak until the day when these things take place, because you did not believe my words, which will be fulfilled in their proper time."
	1:21 The people were waiting for Zacharias, and were wondering at his delay in the temple.
	1:22 ~~But~~ when he came out, he was unable to speak to them; and they realized that he had seen a vision in the temple; [~~and~~] he kept making signs to them, and remained mute.
	1:23 When the days of his priestly service were ended, he went back home.

13 The angel answered, and said to him, *"I am Gabriel, who stands in the presence of God, and I have been sent to speak to you, and to bring you this good news.*[10]

14 *"And behold, you shall be silent and unable to speak*[11] *until the day when these things take place, because you did not believe my words, which will be fulfilled in their proper time."*

15 The people were waiting for Zacharias, and were wondering at his delay in the Temple.

16 When he came out, he was unable to speak to them, and they realized that he had seen a vision in the Temple, [because] he kept making signs to them, and remained mute.

17 When the days of his priestly service were ended, he went back home.

10. Daniel 8:16; 9:21-22   11. Ezekiel 3:26; 24:27

Scene 2: **Elizabeth Becomes Pregnant With John**

Judean hill country, *Judea*   summer / 7 BCE

	Luke
1 After these days [Zacharias'] wife Elizabeth became pregnant;	*1:24~* After these days Elizabeth [~~his~~] wife became pregnant,
2 and she kept herself in seclusion for five months, saying, "This is the way \<that\> the Lord has dealt with me in the days when He looked with favor upon me, *to take away my disgrace*[1] \<from\> among men."	*1:~24* and she kept herself in seclusion for five months, saying, *1:25* "This is the way the Lord has dealt with me in the days when He looked with favor upon me, to take away my disgrace among men."

1. Genesis 30:23

CHAPTER 1 - THE BIRTH OF JESUS

Act 2: **The Annunciation To Mary**

Scene 1: **Gabriel Tells Mary That She Will Birth A Son**

Nazareth, *Galilee*   late December / 7 BCE

A Verse-By-Verse Four Gospel Harmony

Page 8

	Luke
1 Now in the sixth month, the angel Gabriel was sent from God to a city in Galilee called Nazareth,	1:26 Now in the sixth month the angel Gabriel was sent from God to a city in Galilee called Nazareth,
2 to a virgin engaged to a man of the [house] of David whose name was Joseph; and the virgin's name was Mary.	1:27 to a virgin engaged to a man whose name was Joseph, of the [descendants]* of David; and the virgin's name was Mary.
3 Coming in, [Gabriel] said to her, "Greetings, favored one! The Lord is with you."	1:28 And coming in, [he] said to her, "Greetings, favored one! The Lord is with you."
4 But [Mary] was very perplexed at this statement, and ponder[ed] what kind of salutation this was.	1:29 But [she] was very perplexed at this statement, and kept ponder[ing] what kind of salutation this was.
5 The angel said to her, "Do not be afraid, Mary; for you have found favor with God!	1:30 The angel said to her, "Do not be afraid, Mary; for you have found favor with God.
6 "And behold, *you will conceive in your womb and bear a son; and you shall name Him Jesus.*[1]	1:31 "And behold, you will conceive in your womb and bear a son, and you shall name Him Jesus.
7 "*He will be great; and will be called the Son of the Most High!*	1:32~ "He will be great and will be called the Son of the Most High;
8 "*And the Lord God will give Him the throne of His father David, and He will reign over the house of Jacob forever, and His Kingdom will have no end.*" [2]	1:~32 and the Lord God will give Him the throne of His father David; 1:33 and He will reign over the house of Jacob forever, and His kingdom will have no end."
9 Mary said to the angel, "How can this be, since I am a virgin?"	1:34 Mary said to the angel, "How can this be, since I am a virgin?"
10 The angel answered, and said to her, "The Holy Spirit will come upon you, and the power of the Most High will overshadow you; and for that reason the Holy Child shall be called the Son of God.	1:35 The angel answered and said to her, "The Holy Spirit will come upon you, and the power of the Most High will overshadow you; and for that reason the holy Child shall be called the Son of God.
11 "And behold, even your relative Elizabeth has also conceived a son in her old age, and she who was called barren is now in her sixth month; *for nothing [is] impossible with God.*" [3]	1:36 "And behold, even your relative Elizabeth has also conceived a son in her old age; and she who was called barren is now in her sixth month. 1:37 "For nothing [will be] impossible with God."
12 Mary said, "Behold, the bondslave of the Lord! May it be done to me according to your word."	1:38~ And Mary said, "Behold, the bondslave of the Lord; may it be done to me according to your word."
13 And [Gabriel] departed from her.	1:~38 And [the angel] departed from her.

1. (Isaiah 7:14)   2. 2 Samuel 7:12-17   3. Genesis 18:14 / Jeremiah 32:17

CHAPTER 1 - THE BIRTH OF JESUS

Act 2: **The Annunciation To Mary**

Scene 2: **Mary Visits Elizabeth**

Judean hill country, *Judea*   late December / 7 BCE

Page 9

The Full Gospel United from Four

	Luke
1 [Then] Mary arose, and went in a hurry to a city [in] the hill country of Jud[ea]; and <she> entered the house of Zacharias, and greeted Elizabeth.	1:39 [Now at this time] Mary arose and went in a hurry [to] the hill country, to a city of Jud[ah], 1:40 and entered the house of Zacharias and greeted Elizabeth.
2 When Elizabeth heard Mary's greeting, the baby leaped in her womb; and Elizabeth was filled with the Holy Spirit.	1:41 When Elizabeth heard Mary's greeting, the baby leaped in her womb; and Elizabeth was filled with the Holy Spirit.
3 And she cried out with a loud voice, and said, "Blessed are you among women, and blessed is the fruit of your womb!	1:42 And she cried out with a loud voice and said, "Blessed are you among women, and blessed is the fruit of your womb!
4 "How has it happened to me, that the mother of my Lord, would come to me? For behold, when the sound of your greeting reached my ears, the baby leaped in my womb for joy.	1:43 "And how has it happened to me, that the mother of my Lord would come to me? 1:44 "For behold, when the sound of your greeting reached my ears, the baby leaped in my womb for joy.
5 "Blessed is she who believed that there would be a fulfillment of what had been spoken to her by the Lord!"	1:45 "And blessed is she who believed that there would be a fulfillment of what had been spoken to her by the Lord."
6 Mary said: "My soul exalts the Lord, and my spirit has rejoiced in God my Savior,[1] for He has had regard for the humble state of His bondslave.[2]	1:46 And Mary said: "My soul exalts the Lord, 1:47 And my spirit has rejoiced in God my Savior. 1:48~ "For He has had regard for the humble state of His bondslave;
7 "[And] behold, from this time on, all generations will count me blessed, for the Mighty One has done great things for me; and Holy is His Name!	1:~48 [for] behold, from this time on all generations will count me blessed. 1:49 "For the Mighty One has done great things for me; and holy is His name.
8 "*His mercy is upon generation after generation, toward those who fear Him.*[3]	1:50 "And His mercy is upon generation after generation toward those who fear Him.
9 "*He has done mighty deeds with His arm;*[4] He has scattered those who were proud in the thoughts of their heart.	1:51 "He has done mighty deeds with His arm; He has scattered those who were proud in the thoughts of their heart.
10 "He has brought down rulers from their thrones, and has exalted those who were humble.	1:52 "He has brought down rulers from their thrones, and has exalted those who were humble.
11 "He has filled the hungry with good things, and sent away the rich empty-handed.	1:53 "He has filled the hungry with good things; and sent away the rich empty-handed.
12 "He has given help to *Israel His servant*,[5] *in remembrance of His mercy*,[6] as He spoke to our fathers, to Abraham and his descendants, forever."	1:54 "He has given help to Israel His servant, in remembrance of His mercy, 1:55 As He spoke to our fathers, to Abraham and his descendants forever."
13 Mary stayed with [Elizabeth] about three months, and then <she> returned to her home.	1:56 And Mary stayed with [her] about three months, and then returned to her home.

1. Psalm 35:9 / Habakkuk 3:18   2. Psalm 138:6   3. Exodus 20:6 / Psalm 103:17   4. Psalm 98:1 / Isaiah 40:10   5. Isaiah 41:8   6. Psalm 98:3

CHAPTER 1 - THE BIRTH OF JESUS	Scene 1: **The Birth and Naming of John**	Page 10
Act 3: **The Birth of John**	Judean hill country, *Judea* late March / 6 BCE	*The Greatest Gospel*

	Luke
1 Now <when> the time [came] for Elizabeth to give birth, she gave birth to a son.	1:57 Now the time ~~had~~ [come] for Elizabeth to give birth, ~~and~~ she gave birth to a son.
2 Her neighbors and her relatives heard that the Lord had displayed His great mercy toward her, and they were rejoicing with her.	1:58 Her neighbors and her relatives heard that the Lord had displayed His great mercy toward her; and they were rejoicing with her.
3 And it happened that *on the eighth day they came to circumcise the child,*[1.] and they were going to [name] him Zacharias, after his father, but his mother answered and said, "No indeed, but he shall be called John."	1:59 And it happened that on the eighth day they came to circumcise the child, and they were going to [~~call~~] him Zacharias, after his father, 1:60 But his mother answered and said, "No indeed; but he shall be called John."
4 They said to her, "There is no one among your relatives who is called by that name."	1:61 ~~And~~ they said to her, "There is no one among your relatives who is called by that name."
5 And they made signs to his father, as to what he wanted him <to be> called.	1:62 And they made signs to his father, as to what he wanted him called.
6 [Zacharias] asked for a tablet, and <he> wrote as follows: "His name is John." And they were all astonished.	1:63 ~~And~~ [he] asked for a tablet and wrote as follows, "His name is John." And they were all astonished.
7 And [immediately] [the] mouth <of Zacharias> was opened, and his tongue began to speak in praise of God.	1:64 And [~~at once~~] [his] mouth was opened and his tongue ~~loosed~~, ~~and he~~ began to speak in praise of God.

1. *Genesis 17:12 / Leviticus 12:3*

CHAPTER 1 - THE BIRTH OF JESUS

Act 3: **The Birth of John**

Scene 2: **The Prophecy of Zacharias About John**

Judean hill country, *Judea*   late March / 6 BCE

Page 11

A Unified Four Gospel Harmony

	Luke
1 [John's] father Zacharias was filled with the Holy Spirit, and <he> prophesied, saying: "*Blessed be the Lord God of Israel;*[1] for He has visited us, and accomplished redemption for His people!	1:67 ~~And~~ [~~his~~] father Zacharias was filled with the Holy Spirit, and prophesied, saying: 1:68 Blessed be the Lord God of Israel, for He has visited us and accomplished redemption for His people,
2 "<He> *has raised up a horn of salvation for us in the house of David, His servant,*[2] as He spoke by the mouth of His Holy Prophets from of old:	1:69 ~~And~~ has raised up a horn of salvation for us in the house of David His servant - 1:70 as He spoke by the mouth of His holy prophets from of old -
3 "Salvation from our enemies, and from the hand of all who hate us, to show mercy toward our fathers;	1:71 Salvation from our enemies, and from the hand of all who hate us; 1:72~ To show mercy toward our fathers,
4 "and to remember His holy covenant, *the oath which He swore to Abraham our father;*[3]	1:~72 and to remember His holy covenant, 1:73 The oath which He swore to Abraham our father,
5 "to grant that we, being rescued from the hand of our enemies, might serve Him without fear, in holiness and righteousness before Him, all our days.	1:74 To grant ~~us~~ that we, being rescued from the hand of our enemies, might serve Him without fear, 1:75 in holiness and righteousness before Him all our days.
6 "And you, child, will be called the Prophet of the Most High; for *you will go on before the Lord to prepare His way;*[4]	1:76 "And you, child, will be called the prophet of the Most High; for you will go on before the Lord to prepare His ways;
7 "to give to His people the knowledge of salvation by the forgiveness of their sins, because of the tender mercy of our God, with which the Sunrise from on high will visit us;	1:77 To give to His people the knowledge of salvation by the forgiveness of their sins, 1:78 because of the tender mercy of our God, with which the Sunrise from on high will visit us,
8 "*to shine upon those who sit in darkness*[5] and the shadow of death, <and> to guide our feet into the way of peace."	1:79 to shine upon those who sit in darkness and the shadow of death, to guide our feet into the way of peace."
9 Fear came on all those living around them, and all these matters were being talked about in all the hill country of Judea.	1:65 Fear came on all those living around them; and all these matters were being talked about in all the hill country of Judea.
10 All who heard them kept them in mind, saying, "What will this child turn out to be?" for the hand of the Lord was certainly with him.	1:66 All who heard them kept them in mind, saying, "What ~~then~~ will this child turn out to be?" For the hand of the Lord was certainly with him.
11 The child continued to grow and to become strong in Spirit; and he lived in the deserts until the day of his public appearance to Israel.	1:80 ~~And~~ the child continued to grow and to become strong in spirit, and he lived in the deserts until the day of his public appearance to Israel.

1. Psalm 106:48   2. 2 Samuel 22:3 / Psalm 132:17 / Ezekiel 29:21   3. Genesis 12:2-3; 22:17-18   4. Isaiah 40:3   5. Isaiah 9:2

CHAPTER 1 - THE BIRTH OF JESUS	Scene 1: **An Angel Solves Joseph's Dilemma**	Page 12
Act 4: **The Birth of Jesus**	Nazareth, *Galilee* Spring / 6 BCE	*This Text is from the **Word-For-Word** Edition*

	Matthew
1 Now the birth of Jesus Christ was as follows: When His mother Mary had been betrothed to Joseph, before they came together, she was found to be with Child by the Holy Spirit.	1:18 Now the birth of Jesus Christ was as follows: when His mother Mary had been betrothed to Joseph, before they came together she was found to be with child by the Holy Spirit.
2 And Joseph her husband, being a righteous man, and not wanting to disgrace her, planned to *send her away*[1.] secretly.	1:19 And Joseph her husband, being a righteous man and not wanting to disgrace her, planned to send her away secretly.
3 But when he had considered this, behold, an angel of the Lord appeared to him in a dream, saying, "Joseph, son of David, do not be afraid to take Mary as your wife; for the Child who has been conceived in her is of the Holy Spirit.	1:20 But when he had considered this, behold, an angel of the Lord appeared to him in a dream, saying, "Joseph, son of David, do not be afraid to take Mary as your wife; for the Child who has been conceived in her is of the Holy Spirit."
4 "She will bear a Son; and you shall call His name Jesus, for He will save His people from their sins."	1:21 "She will bear a Son; and you shall call His name Jesus, for He will save His people from their sins."
5 Now all this took place to fulfill what was spoken by the Lord through the prophet <Isaiah>: *"Behold, the [young maiden] shall be with child, and shall bear a Son; and they shall call His name Immanuel,"*[2.] which translated means, *"God with us."*[3.]	1:22 Now all this took place to fulfill what was spoken by the Lord through the prophet: 1:23 "Behold, the [~~virgin~~]* shall be with child and shall bear a Son, and they shall call His name Immanuel," which translated means, "God with us."
6 Joseph awoke from his sleep, and did as the angel of the Lord commanded him, and took Mary as his wife;	1:24 ~~And~~ Joseph awoke from his sleep and did as the angel of the Lord commanded him, and took Mary as his wife,
7 but <he> kept her a virgin until she gave birth to a son.	1:25~ but kept her a virgin until she gave birth to a Son;

1. Deuteronomy 24:1   2. Isaiah 7:14   3. Isaiah 8:8, 10

Scene 2: **Joseph and Mary Journey To Bethlehem**

Bethlehem, *Judea*   mid September / 6 BCE

	Luke
1 In those days, a decree went out from Caesar Augustus, that a census be taken of all the inhabited earth.	2:1 ~~Now~~ in those days a decree went out from Caesar Augustus, that a census be taken of all the inhabited earth.
2 This was the first census taken while [*Quinctilius*][1.] was Governor of Syria, and everyone was on his way to register for the census, each to his own city.	2:2 This was the first census taken while [Qui~~rini~~us] was governor of Syria. 2:3 And everyone was on his way to register for the census, each to his own city.
3 In order to register, Joseph went up from the city of Nazareth [in] Galilee, to the city of David (which is called Bethlehem) [in] Judea, because he was of the house and family of David;	2:5~ in order to register 2:4 Joseph ~~also~~ went up from Galilee, [~~from~~] the city of Nazareth, [~~to~~] Judea, to the city of David which is called Bethlehem, because he was of the house and family of David,
4 along with Mary, who was engaged to him, and was with child.	2:~5 along with Mary, who was engaged to him, and was with child.

1. Publius Quinctilius Varus - Roman Governor of Syria from 7 BCE to 4 BCE

CHAPTER 1 - THE BIRTH OF JESUS

Act 4: The Birth of Jesus

Scene 3: The Birth of Jesus
Bethlehem, *Judea*   late September / 6 BCE

Four Gospels United as One

	Luke
1 While they were there, the days were completed for [Mary] to give birth; and she gave birth to her firstborn son.	2:6 While they were there, the days were completed for [her] to give birth. 2:7~ And she gave birth to her firstborn son;
2 She wrapped Him in <swaddling> cloths, and laid Him in a manger, because there was no room for them in the inn.	2:~7 and she wrapped Him in cloths, and laid Him in a manger, because there was no room for them in the inn.

Scene 4: Angelic Announcement To The Shepherds
Bethlehem, *Judea*   late September / 6 BCE

	Luke
1 In the same region there were some shepherds staying out in the fields, and keeping watch over their flock [at] night.	2:8 In the same region there were some shepherds staying out in the fields and keeping watch over their flock [by] night.
2 And an angel of the Lord suddenly stood before them, and the glory of the Lord shone around them.	2:9~ And an angel of the Lord suddenly stood before them, and the glory of the Lord shone around them;
3 They were terribly frightened, but the angel said to them, "Do not be afraid; for behold, I bring you good news of great joy, which will be for all people!	2:~9 and they were terribly frightened. 2:10 But the angel said to them, "Do not be afraid; for behold, I bring you good news of great joy which will be for all the people;
4 "For today *in the city of David,*[1.] there has been born for you a Savior,[2.] who is *Christ,*[3.] the Lord.	2:11 for today in the city of David there has been born for you a Savior, who is Christ the Lord.
5 "This will be a sign for you: you will find a baby wrapped in <swaddling> cloths, and lying in a manger."	2:12 "This will be a sign for you: you will find a baby wrapped in cloths and lying in a manger."
6 And suddenly there appeared with the angel a multitude of the Heavenly host, <who were> praising God, and saying, "Glory to God in the Highest!	2:13 And suddenly there appeared with the angel a multitude of the heavenly host praising God and saying, 2:14~ "Glory to God in the highest,
7 And on earth, peace among men with whom He is pleased."	2:~14 and on earth peace among men with whom He is pleased."
8 When the angels had gone away into heaven, the shepherds began saying to one another, "Let us go straight to Bethlehem, and see this thing that has happened, which the Lord has made known to us!"	2:15 When the angels had gone away from them into heaven, the shepherds began saying to one another, "Let us go straight to Bethlehem then, and see this thing that has happened which the Lord has made known to us.
9 So they [went] [quickly], and found their way to Mary and Joseph, and the baby, as He lay in the manger.	2:16 So they [came] [in a hurry] and found their way to Mary and Joseph, and the baby as He lay in the manger.
10 When [the shepherds] [saw] this, they made known the statement which had been told <to> them about this Child.	2:17 When [they] [had seen] this, they made known the statement which had been told them about this Child.
11 All who heard it wondered at the things which were told <to> them by the shepherds, but Mary pondered all these things, treasuring them in her heart.	2:18 And all who heard it wondered at the things which were told them by the shepherds. 2:19 But Mary treasured all these things, pondering them in her heart.
12 The shepherds went back, glorifying and praising God for all that they had heard and seen, just as [they] had been told.	2:20 The shepherds went back, glorifying and praising God for all that they had heard and seen, just as had been told [them].

1. Micah 5:2   2. (Isaiah 9:6)   3. Hebrew "Messiah" - Daniel 9:25 / (Deuteronomy 18:15)

CHAPTER 1 - THE BIRTH OF JESUS Act 4: **The Birth of Jesus**	Scene 5: **The Naming of Jesus** Judea early October / 6 BCE	Page 14 *Look for the Word-For-Word Edition*
	Matthew	**Luke**
1 When *eight days had passed, before His circumcision,*[1] *His name was called Jesus, the name given by the angel, before He was conceived in the womb.*[2]	1:~25 ~~and he~~ called His name Jesus.	2:21 ~~And~~ when eight days had passed, before His circumcision, His name was then called Jesus, the name given by the angel before He was conceived in the womb.

1. *Genesis 17:12 / Leviticus 12:3*   2. *121.6 > Matthew 1:21 / Luke 1:31*

---

1 - THE BIRTH OF JESUS Act 5: **Jesus Is Presented In The Temple**	Scene 1: **Righteous Simeon Prophesies About Jesus** The Temple, Jerusalem, *Judea* early November / 6 BCE	
		Luke
1 When *the days for their purification according to the law of Moses*[1] were completed, they brought [Jesus] up to Jerusalem, to present Him to the Lord		2:22 ~~And~~ when the days for their purification according to the law of Moses were completed, they brought [Him] up to Jerusalem to present Him to the Lord
2 (as it is written in the Law of the Lord, "Every firstborn male that opens the womb shall be called holy to the Lord"),[2]		2:23 (as it is written in the Law of the Lord, "Every firstborn male that opens the womb shall be called holy to the Lord"),
3 and to offer a sacrifice according to what was said in the Law, "A pair of turtledoves, or two young pigeons."[3]		2:24 and to offer a sacrifice according to what was said in the Law ~~of the Lord~~, "A pair of turtledoves or two young pigeons."
4 There was a man in Jerusalem whose name was Simeon, [who] was righteous and devout. <He was> looking for the consolation of Israel, and the Holy Spirit was upon him.		2:25 ~~And~~ there was a man in Jerusalem whose name was Simeon, ~~and~~ [this man] was righteous and devout, looking for the consolation of Israel; and the Holy Spirit was upon him.
5 It had been revealed to him by the Holy Spirit, that he would not see death before he had seen the Lord's Christ.		2:26 ~~And~~ it had been revealed to him by the Holy Spirit that he would not see death before he had seen the Lord's Christ.
6 He came in the Spirit into the Temple; and when the parents brought in the child Jesus to carry out for Him the custom of the Law, [Simeon] took Him into his arms, and <he> blessed God, and said,		2:27 ~~And~~ he came in the Spirit into the temple; and when the parents brought in the child Jesus, to carry out for Him the custom of the Law, 2:28 ~~then~~ [he] took Him into his arms, and blessed God, and said,
7 "Now Lord, You are releasing Your bond-servant to depart in peace, according to Your word; for my eyes have seen Your salvation, which You have prepared in the presence of all peoples; *a Light of revelation to the Gentiles,*[4] and the glory of Your people Israel!"		2:29 "Now Lord, You are releasing Your bond-servant to depart in peace, according to Your word; 2:30 For my eyes have seen Your salvation, 2:31 which You have prepared in the presence of all peoples, 2:32 a Light of revelation to the Gentiles, and the glory of Your people Israel."
8 And Simeon blessed them, and said to Mary His mother, "Behold, this Child is appointed for the fall and rise of many in Israel, and for a sign to be opposed, to the end that <the> thoughts from many hearts may be revealed.		2:34 And Simeon blessed them and said to Mary His mother, "Behold, this Child is appointed for the fall and rise of many in Israel, and for a sign to be opposed - 2:~35 to the end that thoughts from many hearts may be revealed."
9 "And a sword will pierce even your own soul."		2:35~ and a sword will pierce even your own soul -
10 His father and mother were amazed at the things which were being said about [Jesus].		2:33 ~~And~~ His father and mother were amazed at the things which were being said about [Him].

1. *Leviticus 12:2-7*   2. *Exodus 13:2, 12, 15*   3. *Leviticus 12:8*   4. *Isaiah 42:6*

CHAPTER 1 - THE BIRTH OF JESUS		
Act 5: **Jesus Is Presented In The Temple**	Scene 2: **Anna The Prophetess**	Page 15
	The Temple, Jerusalem, *Judea* early November / 6 BCE	*The Complete Four Gospel Harmony*

	Luke
1 There was a prophetess, Anna, the daughter of Phanuel, of the tribe of Asher.	2:36~ ~~And~~ there was a prophetess, Anna the daughter of Phanuel, of the tribe of Asher.
2 She was advanced in years, and had lived with her husband <for> seven years after her marriage, and then as a widow to the age of eighty-four.	2:~36 She was advanced in years and had lived with her husband seven years after her marriage, 2:37~ and then as a widow to the age of eighty-four.
3 She never left the Temple, serving night and day with fasting and prayers.	2:~37 She never left the temple, serving night and day with fastings and prayers.
4 At that very moment she came up and began giving thanks to God, and continued to speak of [Jesus] to all those who were looking for the redemption of Jerusalem.	2:38 At that very moment she came up and began giving thanks to God, and continued to speak of [~~Him~~] to all those who were looking for the redemption of Jerusalem.

Scene 3: **Return To Nazareth**

Nazareth, *Galilee*   early November / 6 BCE

	Luke
1 When they had performed everything according to the Law of the Lord, they returned to Galilee, to their own city of Nazareth.	2:39 When they had performed everything according to the Law of the Lord, they returned to Galilee, to their own city of Nazareth.
2 The Child continued to grow and become strong, increasing in wisdom; and the grace of God was upon Him.	2:40 The Child continued to grow and become strong, increasing in wisdom; and the grace of God was upon Him.

CHAPTER 1 - THE BIRTH OF JESUS

Act 6: To Egypt and Back

Scene 1: King Herod and The Magi From The East

Jerusalem, *Judea*   late autumn / 6 BCE

	Matthew
1 After Jesus was born in Bethlehem of Judea, in the days of *Herod the King,*[1.] *Magi*[2.] from the east arrived in Jerusalem, saying, "Where is He who has been born <the> King of the Jews? For we saw *His star*[3.] in the east, and have come to worship Him."	2:1 ~~Now~~ after Jesus was born in Bethlehem of Judea in the days of Herod the king, magi from the east arrived in Jerusalem, saying, 2:2 "Where is He who has been born King of the Jews? For we saw His star in the east and have come to worship Him."
2 When King Herod heard this, he was troubled, and all <of> Jerusalem with him.	2:3 When Herod ~~the~~ king heard this, he was troubled, and all Jerusalem with him.
3 Gathering together all the chief priests and scribes of the people, he inquired of them where the *Messiah*[4.] was to be born.	2:4 Gathering together all the chief priests and scribes of the people, he inquired of them where the Messiah was to be born.
4 They said to him, "In Bethlehem of Judea; for this is what has been written by the prophet:	2:5 They said to him, "In Bethlehem of Judea; for this is what has been written by the prophet:
5 *'And you, Bethlehem, land of Judah, are by no means least among the leaders of Judah; for out of you shall come forth a Ruler who will shepherd My people Israel.' "*[5.]	2:6 'And you, Bethlehem, land of Judah, are by no means least among the leaders of Judah; for out of you shall come forth a Ruler Who will shepherd My people Israel.' "
6 Then Herod secretly called the Magi, and determined from them the exact time <that> the star <had> appeared.	2:7 Then Herod secretly called the magi and determined from them the exact time the star appeared.
7 And he sent them to Bethlehem, [saying], "Go and search carefully for the Child;	2:8~ And he sent them to Bethlehem ~~and~~ [said], "Go and search carefully for the Child;
8 "and when you have found Him, report to me, so that I too may come and worship Him."	2:~8 and when you have found Him, report to me, so that I too may come and worship Him."
9 After hearing the King, [the Magi] went <on> their way; and the star, which they had seen in the east, went on before them, until it came and stood over the place where the Child was.	2:9 After hearing the king, [~~they~~] went their way; and the star, which they had seen in the east, went on before them until it came and stood over the place where the Child was.
10 When they saw the star, they rejoiced with exceeding great joy.	2:10 When they saw the star, they rejoiced exceeding~~ly~~ with great joy.
11 After coming into the house, they saw the Child, with Mary His mother; and they fell to the ground, and worshiped Him.	2:11~ After coming into the house they saw the Child with Mary His mother; and they fell to the ground and worshiped Him.
12 Then, opening their treasures, *they presented to Him gifts of gold, frankincense,*[6.] *and myrrh.*[7.]	2:~11 Then, opening their treasures, they presented to Him gifts of gold, frankincense, and myrrh.
13 Having been warned by God in a dream not to return to Herod, the Magi left for their own country by another way.	2:12 And having been warned by God in a dream not to return to Herod, the magi left for their own country by another way.

1. *Herod the Great (73 - 4 BCE) King of Judea & Galilee (37 - 4 BCE)*   2. *likely Persian / Zoroastrian astrologers*   3. *Numbers 24:17 / Isaiah 60:3*   4. *Daniel 9:25 / (Deuteronomy 18:15)*

5. *Micah 5:2 / (Numbers 24:17)*   6. *Isaiah 60:3, 6 / (Psalm 72:10)*   7. *Exodus 30:23-25*

CHAPTER 1 - THE BIRTH OF JESUS

Act 6: **To Egypt and Back**

Scene 2: Joseph Is Warned To Flee To Egypt

Nazareth, *Galilee* to Egypt   late autumn / 6 BCE

A Verse-By-Verse Four Gospel Harmony

	Matthew
1 Now when [the Magi] had gone, behold, an angel of the Lord appeared to Joseph in a dream, and said, "Get up! Take the Child and His mother, and flee to Egypt, and remain there until I tell you; for Herod is going to search for the Child to destroy Him."	2:13 Now when [~~they~~] had gone, behold, an angel of the Lord appeared to Joseph in a dream and said, "Get up! Take the Child and His mother and flee to Egypt, and remain there until I tell you; for Herod is going to search for the Child to destroy Him."
2 So Joseph got up, and took the Child and His mother while it was still night, and left for Egypt;	2:14 So Joseph got up and took the Child and His mother while it was still night, and left for Egypt.
3 <and> [they] remained there until the *death of Herod*.[1]	2:15~ [~~He~~] remained there until the death of Herod.

　　1. Herod I "The Great" - died spring (March?) 4 BCE

Scene 3: Herod Orders The Death of The Male Babies

Jerusalem, *Judea*   winter / 5 BCE

	Matthew
1 When Herod saw that he had been tricked by the Magi, he became very enraged, and <he> sent <men> <to> [slay] all the male children who were in Bethlehem, and all its vicinity; from two years old and under, according to the time which he had determined from the Magi.	2:16 ~~Then~~ when Herod saw that he had been tricked by the magi, he became very enraged, and sent ~~and~~ [slew] all the male children who were in Bethlehem and all its vicinity, from two years old and under, according to the time which he had determined from the magi.
2 Then, what had been spoken through Jeremiah the prophet was fulfilled: *"A voice was heard in Ramah, weeping and great mourning; Rachel weeping for her children, and she refused to be comforted, because they were no more."* [1]	2:17 Then what had been spoken through Jeremiah the prophet was fulfilled: 2:18 "A voice was heard in Ramah, weeping and great mourning, Rachel weeping for her children; and she refused to be comforted, because they were no more."

　　1. Jeremiah 31:15 / (Genesis 37:35)

CHAPTER 1 - THE BIRTH OF JESUS

Act 6: **To Egypt and Back**

Scene 4: **Joseph, Mary and Jesus Return From Egypt**

Egypt to Nazareth, *Galilee*   spring / 4 BCE

Page 18

Using the NASB version of The Gospels

	Matthew
1 When *Herod died*,[1.] behold, an angel of the Lord appeared to Joseph in a dream in Egypt, and said, "Get up! Take the Child and His mother, and go into the land of Israel; for those who sought the Child's life are dead."	2:19 ~~But~~ when Herod died, behold, an angel of the Lord appeared in a dream to Joseph in Egypt, and said, 2:20 "Get up, take the Child and His mother, and go into the land of Israel; for those who sought the Child's life are dead."
2 This was to fulfill what had been spoken by the Lord through the prophet: "Out of Egypt I called My Son."[2.]	2:~15 This was to fulfill what had been spoken by the Lord through the prophet: "Out of Egypt I called My Son."
3 So Joseph got up, took the Child and His mother, and came into the land of Israel.	2:21 So Joseph got up, took the Child and His mother, and came into the land of Israel.
4 But when he heard that *Archelaus*[3.] was reigning over Judea in place of his father Herod, he was afraid to go there.	2:22~ But when he heard that Archelaus was reigning over Judea in place of his father Herod, he was afraid to go there.
5 Then, after being warned by God in a dream, [Joseph] left for the region of Galilee, and <they> came and lived in a city called Nazareth.	2:~22 Then after being warned by God in a dream, [~~he~~] left for the region~~s~~ of Galilee, 2:23~ and came and lived in a city called Nazareth.
6 This was to fulfill what was spoken through the prophets: He shall be called a *Nazarene*.[4.]	2:~23 This was to fulfill what was spoken through the prophets: He shall be called a Nazarene.

1. *spring (March?) 4 BCE*   2. *Hosea 11:1 / (Numbers 23:22, 24:8)*   3. *Herod Archelaus (23 BCE - 18 CE) Ethnarch of Judea & Samaria (4 BCE - 6 CE)*   4. *source unknown*

CHAPTER 1 - THE BIRTH OF JESUS

Act 7: Young Jesus In The Temple

Scene 1: I Had To Be In My Father's House

The Temple, Jerusalem, *Judea* Passover - March / 7 CE

Page 19

NASB = New American Standard Bible

	Luke
1 Now His parents went to Jerusalem every year at the Feast of the Passover, and when [Jesus] became twelve they went up there according to the custom of the Feast.	2:41 Now His parents went to Jerusalem every year at the Feast of the Passover. 2:42 And when [He] became twelve, they went up there according to the custom of the Feast;
2 As they were returning, after spending the full number of days, the boy Jesus stayed behind in Jerusalem.	2:43~ ~~and~~ as they were returning, after spending the full number of days, the boy Jesus stayed behind in Jerusalem.
3 But His parents were unaware of it, [and] supposed Him to be in the caravan, and <they> went a day's journey.	2:~43 But His parents were unaware of it, 2:44~ [~~but~~] supposed Him to be in the caravan, and went a day's journey;
4 <When> they began looking for Him among their relatives and acquaintances, <and> did not find Him, they returned to Jerusalem looking for Him.	2:~44 ~~and~~ they began looking for Him among their relatives and acquaintances. 2:45 ~~When~~ they did not find Him, they returned to Jerusalem looking for Him.
5 After three days they found [Jesus] in the Temple, sitting in the midst of the teachers, both listening to them and asking them questions.	2:46 ~~Then~~, after three days, they found [~~Him~~] in the temple, sitting in the midst of the teachers, both listening to them and asking them questions.
6 All who heard Him were amazed at His understanding, and His answers.	2:47 ~~And~~ all who heard Him were amazed at His understanding and His answers.
7 When [His parents] saw Him, they were astonished; and His mother said to Him, "Son, why have You treated us this way? Behold, Your father and I have been anxiously looking for You!"	2:48 When [~~they~~] saw Him, they were astonished; and His mother said to Him, "Son, why have You treated us this way? Behold, Your father and I have been anxiously looking for You."
8 [Jesus] said to them, "Why were you looking for Me? Did you not know that I had to be in My Father's house?"	2:49 ~~And~~ [He] said to them, "Why ~~is it that~~ you were looking for Me? Did you not know that I had to be in My Father's house?"
9 But they did not understand [this] statement which He made to them.	2:50 But they did not understand [the] statement which He ~~had~~ made to them.
10 [Jesus] [returned] to Nazareth with them, and He [obeyed] them; and His mother treasured all these things in her heart.	2:51 ~~And~~ [He] [~~went down~~] with them ~~and came~~ to Nazareth, and He [~~continued in subjection to~~] them; and His mother treasured all these things in her heart.
11 And Jesus kept increasing in wisdom and stature, and in favor with God and men.	2:52 And Jesus kept increasing in wisdom and stature, and in favor with God and men.

CHAPTER 2
THE MESSIAH IS ANOINTED

Jesus is Baptized by John in the Jordan River.

	Page
Act 1 - John Becomes The Baptist	
Scene 1 John Begins His Ministry of Baptism	21
2 John Warns The Pharisees	22
3 The Teachings of John The Baptist	23
4 John Preaches About The Coming Messiah	23
5 John Denies That He Is The Christ or Elijah	24
Act 2 - The Baptism of Jesus	
Scene 1 John Is At First Unwilling To Baptize Jesus	25
2 Jesus Is Baptized By John In The Jordan River	26
3 John Testifies That Jesus Is The Son of God	26
Act 3 - The Messiah Is Tempted	
Scene 1 Jesus Fasts In The Wilderness For Forty Days	27
2 Satan Tries To Tempt Jesus	28

MAP OF ISRAEL

Locations mentioned in this Chapter are shown with a white center.

2 - THE MESSIAH IS ANOINTED

Act 1: John Becomes The Baptist

Scene 1: John Begins His Ministry of Baptism

Jordan River, *Judea* spring / 29 CE

One Complete Gospel United from Four

#		Matthew	Mark	Luke	John
1	In the fifteenth year of the reign of Tiberius Caesar, when Pontius Pilate was Governor of Judea, and *Herod <Antipater> was Tetrarch of Galilee,*[1.]			3:1~ ~~Now~~ in the fifteenth year of the reign of Tiberius Caesar, when Pontius Pilate was governor of Judea, and Herod was tetrarch of Galilee,	
2	and his brother Philip was Tetrarch of the region of Ituraea and Trachonitis, and Lysanias was Tetrarch of Abilene,			3:~1 and his brother Philip was tetrarch of the region of Ituraea and Trachonitis, and Lysanias was tetrarch of Abilene,	
3	in the High Priesthood of Annas and Caiaphas,			3:2~ in the high priesthood of Annas and Caiaphas,	
4	the Word of God came to John, the son of Zacharias, in the wilderness of Judea.			3:~2 the word of God came to John, the son of Zacharias, in the wilderness.	
5	John was a man sent from God, <and> He came as a witness to testify about the Light, so that all might believe through him.	3:1 Now in those days John the Baptist came, preaching in the wilderness of Judea, saying,	1:4 John the Baptist appeared in the wilderness preaching a baptism of repentance for the forgiveness of sins.		1:6 ~~There~~ came a man sent from God, ~~whose name~~ was John. 1:7 He came as a witness, to testify about the Light, so that all might believe through him.
6	He was not the Light, but he came to testify about the Light.				1:8 He was not the Light, but he came to testify about the Light.
7	And John the Baptist came into all the district[s] around the Jordan, preaching a baptism of repentance for the forgiveness of sins, saying, "Repent, for the Kingdom of Heaven is at hand!"	3:2 "Repent, for the kingdom of heaven is at hand."		3:3 And he came into all the district around the Jordan, preaching a baptism of repentance for the forgiveness of sins;	
8	For this is the one referred to, *"Behold, I send My messenger ahead of You, who will prepare Your way",*[2.]		1:2 As it is written in Isaiah the prophet: "Behold, I send My messenger ahead of You, who will prepare Your way;		
9	as it is written in the words of the book of Isaiah the prophet, when he said, *"The voice of one crying in the wilderness: 'Make ready the way of the Lord; Make His paths straight!*[3.]	3:3 For this is the one referred to by Isaiah the prophet when he said, "The voice of one crying in the wilderness, 'Make ready the way of the Lord, Make His paths straight!' "	1:3 The voice of one crying in the wilderness, 'Make ready the way of the Lord, Make His paths straight.' "	3:4 as it is written in the book of the words of Isaiah the prophet, "The voice of one crying in the wilderness, 'Make ready the way of the Lord, Make His paths straight.	
10	*"Every ravine will be filled, and every mountain and hill will be brought low; the crooked will become straight, and the rough roads smooth; and all flesh will see the salvation of God.' "*[4.]			3:5 'Every ravine will be filled, and every mountain and hill will be brought low; the crooked will become straight, and the rough roads smooth; 3:6 And all flesh will see the salvation of God.' "	

1. *Herod Antipater (aka Antipas) (20 BCE - 39 CE) Tetrarch of Galilee & Perea (4 BCE - 39 CE)*   2. *Malachi 3:1*   3. *Isaiah 40:3*   4. *Isaiah 40:4-5; 52:10*

continued >

2 - THE MESSIAH IS ANOINTED

Act 1: John Becomes The Baptist

Scene 1: John Begins His Ministry of Baptism
continued

	Matthew	Mark	Luke	John
11 Now John was clothed with a garment of camel's hair, and wore a leather belt around *his waist*;[5.] and his diet was locusts and wild honey.	3:4 Now John himself had a garment of camel's hair and a leather belt around his waist; and his food was locusts and wild honey.	1:6 John was clothed with camel's hair and wore a leather belt around his waist, and his diet was locusts and wild honey.		
12 Then all the people of Jerusalem, and all the country of Judea, and all the district around the Jordan, [were] going out to him;	3:5 Then Jerusalem was going out to him, and all Judea and all the district around the Jordan;	1:5~ And all the country of Judea was going out to him, and all the people of Jerusalem;		
13 and they were being baptized by him in the Jordan River, as they confessed their sins.	3:6 and they were being baptized by him in the Jordan River, as they confessed their sins.	1:~5 and they were being baptized by him in the Jordan River, confess~~ing~~ their sins.		

5. 2 Kings 1:8 / Zechariah 13:4

Scene 2: John Warns The Pharisees
Jordan River, *Judea*   spring / 29 CE

	Matthew	Luke
1 When [John] saw the many Pharisees and Sadducees coming out to be baptized by him, he began saying to them, "You brood of vipers! Who warned you to flee from the wrath to come?	3:7~ ~~But~~ when [~~he~~] saw many ~~of~~ the Pharisees and Sadducees coming for baptism, he said to them, "You brood of vipers, who warned you to flee from the wrath to come?	3:7 So he began saying to the crowds who were going out to be baptized by him, "You brood of vipers, who warned you to flee from the wrath to come?
2 "Therefore bear fruit in keeping with repentance;	3:8 "Therefore bear fruit in keeping with repentance;	3:8~ "Therefore bear fruits in keeping with repentance,
3 "and do not suppose that you can begin to say to yourselves, 'We have Abraham for our father'; for I say to you, that from these stones God is able to raise up children to Abraham.	3:9 and do not suppose that you can say to yourselves, 'We have Abraham for our father'; for I say to you that from these stones God is able to raise up children to Abraham.	3:~8 and do not begin to say to yourselves, 'We have Abraham for our father'; for I say to you that from these stones God is able to raise up children to Abraham.
4 "Indeed, the axe is already laid at the root of the trees, [and] every tree that does not bear good fruit is cut down, and thrown into the fire!"	3:10 "The axe is already laid at the root of the trees; [~~therefore~~] every tree that does not bear good fruit is cut down and thrown into the fire.	3:9 "Indeed the axe is already laid at the root of the trees; [~~so~~] every tree that does not bear good fruit is cut down and thrown into the fire.

2 - THE MESSIAH IS ANOINTED

Act 1: **John Becomes The Baptist**

Scene 3: **The Teachings of John The Baptist**

Jordan River, *Judea*   spring / 29 CE

The Four Gospels Unified Verse-By-Verse

#		Luke
1	The crowds were questioning [John], saying, "What shall we do?"	3:10 ~~And~~ the crowds were questioning [~~him~~], saying, "~~Then~~ what shall we do?"
2	And he would answer, and say to them, "The man who has two tunics is to share with him who has none; and he who has food is to do likewise."	3:11 And he would answer and say to them, "The man who has two tunics is to share with him who has none; and he who has food is to do likewise."
3	Some tax collectors also came to be baptized, and they [asked] him, "Teacher, what shall we do?"	3:12 ~~And~~ some tax collectors also came to be baptized, and they [~~said~~] ~~to~~ him, "Teacher, what shall we do?"
4	He said to them, "Collect no more than what you have been ordered to."	3:13 ~~And~~ he said to them, "Collect no more than what you have been ordered to."
5	<And> some soldiers were questioning [John], saying, "And what about us, what shall we do?"	3:14~ Some soldiers were questioning [~~him~~], saying, "And what about us, what shall we do?"
6	He said to them, "*Do not* take money from anyone by force, or *accuse anyone falsely;*[1] and be content with your wages."	3:~14 And he said to them, "Do not take money from anyone by force, or accuse anyone falsely, and be content with your wages."

1. Exodus 20:16; 23:1

Scene 4: **John Preaches About The Coming Messiah**

Jordan River, near Bethabara, *Perea*   summer / 29 CE

#	Matthew	Mark	Luke
1	Now while all the people were in a state of expectation, and wondering in their hearts about whether John was the Christ, [he] answered <as> he was preaching, and said to them, "As for me, I baptize you with water for repentance;	3:11~ "As for me, I baptize you with water for repentance, but He who is coming after me is mightier than I, and I am not fit to remove His sandals;	1:7 And he was preaching, and saying, "After me One is coming who is mightier than I, and I am not fit to stoop down and untie the thong of His sandals. 1:8~ "I baptized you with water;	3:15 Now while the people were in a state of expectation and all ~~were~~ wondering in their hearts about John, ~~as to~~ whether ~~he~~ was the Christ,
2	"but One is coming after me who is mightier than I, and I am not fit to stoop down and untie the thong of His sandals.			3:16~ John answered and said to them all, "As for me, I baptize you with water; but one is coming who is mightier than I, and I am not fit to untie the thong of His sandals;
3	"*He will baptize you with the Holy Spirit*[1] *and fire!*	3:~11 He will baptize you with the Holy Spirit and fire.	1:~8 but He will baptize you with the Holy Spirit."	3:~16 He will baptize you with the Holy Spirit and fire.
4	"*His winnowing fork is in His hand,*[2] *and He will thoroughly clear His threshing floor, and will gather the wheat into His barn,*	3:12~ "His winnowing fork is in His hand, and He will thoroughly clear His threshing floor; and He will gather His wheat into the barn,		3:17~ "His winnowing fork is in His hand to thoroughly clear His threshing floor, and to gather the wheat into His barn;
5	"but He will burn up the chaff with unquenchable fire."	3:~12 but He will burn up the chaff with unquenchable fire."		3:~17 but He will burn up the chaff with unquenchable fire."
6	[And] with many other exhortations [John] preached the *gospel*[3] to the people.			3:18 [~~So~~] with many other exhortations [~~he~~] preached the gospel to the people.

1. Isaiah 44:3   2. Jeremiah 15:7 / (Psalm 20:26)   3. meaning good news

2 - THE MESSIAH IS ANOINTED

Act 1: John Becomes The Baptist

Scene 5: John Denies That He Is The Christ or Elijah

Jordan River, near Bethabara, *Perea* summer / 29 CE

Page 24

The Unified Gospel

	John
1 This is the testimony of John, when the Jews sent to him priests and Levites from Jerusalem, to ask him, "Who are you?"	1:19 This is the testimony of John, when the Jews sent to him priests and Levites from Jerusalem to ask him, "Who are you?"
2 [John] confessed, and <he> did not deny, but confessed, "I am not the Christ."	1:20 And [he] confessed and did not deny, but confessed, "I am not the Christ."
3 They asked him, "What then? Are you Elijah?" And he said, "I am not."	1:21~ They asked him, "What then? Are you Elijah?" And he said, "I am not."
4 "Are you *the Prophet*?" [1.] And he answered, "No."	1:~21 Are you the Prophet? And he answered, "No."
5 Then they said to him, "Who are you, so that we may give an answer to those who sent us? What do you say about yourself?"	1:22 Then they said to him, "Who are you, so that we may give an answer to those who sent us? What do you say about yourself?"
6 [John] said, *"I am a voice of one crying in the wilderness, 'Make straight the way of the Lord,'* [2.] as Isaiah the prophet said."	1:23 [He] said, "I am a voice of one crying in the wilderness, 'Make straight the way of the Lord,' as Isaiah the prophet said."
7 [Then,] [those who] had been sent from the Pharisees asked him, "Why then are you baptizing, if you are not the Christ, nor Elijah, nor the Prophet?"	1:24 [Now] [they] had been sent from the Pharisees. 1:25 ~~They~~ asked him, ~~and said to him~~, "Why then are you baptizing, if you are not the Christ, nor Elijah, nor the Prophet?"
8 [He] answered them, saying, "I baptize in water, but among you stands One whom you do not know. It is He who comes after me, the thong of whose sandal I am not worthy to untie."	1:26 [~~John~~] answered them saying, "I baptize in water, but among you stands One whom you do not know. 1:27 "It is He who comes after me, the thong of whose sandal I am not worthy to untie."
9 These things took place in [*Bethabara*] [3.] *beyond the Jordan,* [4.] where John was baptizing.	1:28 These things took place in [Betha~~ny~~] beyond the Jordan, where John was baptizing.

1. Deuteronomy 18:15, 18 *2. Isaiah 40:3* *3. Bethany is inland, 20 km from the Jordan River* *4. Judges 7:24*

2 - THE MESSIAH IS ANOINTED	Scene 1: **John Is At First Unwilling To Baptize Jesus**	Page 25
Act 2: **The Baptism of Jesus**	Jordan River, near Bethabara, *Perea* late summer / 29 CE	*Every Gospel Deed of Jesus*

#		Matthew	Mark		John
1	In those days, Jesus arrived from Nazareth in Galilee, coming to John at the Jordan to be baptized by him.	3:13 ~~Then~~ Jesus arrived from Galilee at the Jordan coming to John, to be baptized by him.	1:9~ In those days Jesus ~~came~~ from Nazareth in Galilee		
2	[When] [John] saw Jesus coming to him, he said, "Behold, the Lamb of God who takes away the sin of the world!			1:29 [~~The next day~~] [he] saw Jesus coming to him ~~and~~ said, "Behold, the Lamb of God who takes away the sin of the world!	
3	"This is He on behalf of whom I said, 'After me comes a Man who has a higher rank than I, for He existed before me.'			1:30 "This is He on behalf of whom I said, 'After me comes a Man who has a higher rank than I, for He existed before me.'	
4	"I did not recognize Him, but so that He might be manifested to Israel, I came baptizing in water."			1:31 "I did not recognize Him, but so that He might be manifested to Israel, I came baptizing in water."	
5	John tried to prevent [Jesus], saying, "I have need to be baptized by You, and You come to me?"	3:14 ~~But~~ John tried to prevent [Him], saying, "I have need to be baptized by You, and ~~do~~ You come to me?"			
6	But Jesus said to him, "Permit it at this time; for in this way it is fitting for us to fulfill all righteousness."	3:15~ But Jesus ~~answering~~ said to him, "Permit it at this time; for in this way it is fitting for us to fulfill all righteousness.			
7	Then [John] permitted Him.	3:~15 Then [~~he~~] permitted Him.			

2 - THE MESSIAH IS ANOINTED | Scene 2: **Jesus Is Baptized By John In The Jordan River** | Page 26

Act 2: **The Baptism of Jesus** | Jordan River, near Bethabara, *Perea*   late summer / 29 CE | Youtube.com/The Greatest Gospel

	Matthew	Mark	Luke
1 When all the people were baptized, Jesus was also baptized by John in the Jordan <river>.		*1:~9* and was baptized by John in the Jordan.	*3:21* Now when all the people were baptized, Jesus was also baptized, and while He was praying, heaven was opened,
2 After being baptized, Jesus immediately came up out of the water; and while He was praying, behold, the heavens were opened,	*3:16~* After being baptized, Jesus came up immediately from the water; and behold, the heavens were opened,	*1:10~* Immediately coming up out of the water, [He] saw the heavens opening,	
3 and [John] saw the Holy Spirit of God, descending in bodily form like a dove, and lighting upon [Jesus].	*3:~16* and [he] saw the Spirit of God descending as a dove and lighting upon [Him],	*1:~10* and the Spirit descending like a dove upon [Him];	*3:22~* and the Holy Spirit descended in bodily form upon [Him] like a dove,
4 And behold, a voice came out of the heavens, <and> said, "You are My beloved Son,[1.] in You I am well-pleased!"	*3:17* and behold, a voice out of the heavens said, "This is My beloved Son, in whom I am well-pleased."	*1:11* and a voice came out of the heavens: "You are My beloved Son, in You I am well-pleased."	*3:~22* and a voice came out of heaven, "You are My beloved Son, in You I am well-pleased."

1. Psalm 2:7

Scene 3: **John Testifies That Jesus Is The Son of God**

Jordan River, near Bethabara, *Perea*   late summer / 29 CE

	John
1 John testified, and cried out, saying, "I have seen the Spirit descending as a dove out of heaven, and He remained upon [Jesus].	*1:15~* John testified about Him and cried out, saying, *1:32* John testified saying, "I have seen the Spirit descending as a dove out of heaven, and He remained upon Him.
2 "I did not recognize Him, but He who sent me to baptize in water said to me, 'He upon whom you see the Spirit descending and remaining upon Him, this is the One who baptizes in the Holy Spirit.'	*1:33* "I did not recognize Him, but He who sent me to baptize in water said to me, 'He upon whom you see the Spirit descending and remaining upon Him, this is the One who baptizes in the Holy Spirit.'
3 "I myself have seen, and have testified, that this is the Son of God!	*1:34* "I myself have seen, and have testified that this is the Son of God."
4 "This [is] He of whom I said, 'He who comes after me has a rank higher than I, for He existed before me.' "	*1:~15* "This [was] He of whom I said, 'He who comes after me has a higher rank than I, for He existed before me.' "

2 - THE MESSIAH IS ANOINTED

Act 3: The Messiah Is Tempted

Scene 1: Jesus Fasts In The Wilderness For Forty Days

Judean wilderness, *Judea*   late summer / 29 CE

Every Gospel Miracle of Jesus Christ

	Matthew	Mark	Luke
1 [When] Jesus, full of the Holy Spirit, returned from the Jordan, [He] <was> immediately impelled to go out into the wilderness, <where He> was led around by the Spirit.	4:1~ [Then] Jesus was led up by the Spirit into the wilderness	1:12 Immediately the Spirit impelled [Him] to go out into the wilderness.	4:1~ Jesus, full of the Holy Spirit, returned from the Jordan and was led around by the Spirit
2 And He was in the wilderness with the wild beasts for *forty days,*[1] being tempted by Satan, the Devil.	4:~1 to be tempted by the devil.	1:13~ And He was in the wilderness forty days being tempted by Satan; and He was with the wild beasts,	4:~1 in the wilderness for forty days, being tempted by the devil.
3 [Jesus] ate nothing during those days; and after *He had fasted <for> forty days and forty nights*[1] He became hungry.	4:2 And after He had fasted forty days and forty nights, He then became hungry.		4:2 And [He] ate nothing during those days, and when they had ended, He became hungry.

1. *Exodus 16:35, 34:28*

2 - THE MESSIAH IS ANOINTED
Act 3: The Messiah Is Tempted
Scene 2: Satan Tries To Tempt Jesus
Judean wilderness, *Judea* early autumn / 29 CE

A Four Gospel Verse-By-Verse Harmony

#		Matthew	Mark	Luke
1	[Then] the Devil came, and said to [Jesus], "If You are the Son of God, command these stones to become bread."	4:3~ [And] the ~~tempter~~ came and said to [Him], "If You are the Son of God, command ~~that~~ these stones become bread."		4:3 [And] the devil said to [Him], "If You are the Son of God, ~~tell~~ this stone to become bread."
2	But Jesus answered, and said <to> him, "It is written; 'Man shall not live on bread alone, but on every Word that proceeds out of the mouth of God.'" [1.]	4:4 But ~~He~~ answered and said, "It is written, 'Man shall not live on bread alone, but on every word that proceeds out of the mouth of God.'"		4:4 ~~And~~ Jesus answered him, "It is written, 'Man shall not live on bread alone.'"
3	Then the Devil took [Jesus] into the holy city, Jerusalem, and had Him stand on the pinnacle of the Temple.	4:5 Then the devil took [Him] into the holy city and had Him stand on the pinnacle of the temple,		4:9 ~~And he led~~ [Him] to Jerusalem and had Him stand on the pinnacle of the temple,
4	And <the Devil> said to Him, "If You are the Son of God, throw Yourself down from here, for it is written, 'He will command His angels concerning You, to guard You';	4:6~ and said to Him, "If You are the Son of God, throw Yourself down; for it is written, 'He will command His angels concerning You';		4:~9 and said to Him, "If You are the Son of God, throw Yourself down from here; 4:10 for it is written, 'He will command His angels concerning You to guard You,'
5	"and 'On their hands they will bear You up, so that You will not strike Your foot against a stone.'" [2.]	4:~6 and 'On their hands they will bear You up, so that You will not strike Your foot against a stone.'"		4:11 and, 'On their hands they will bear You up, so that You will not strike Your foot against a stone.'"
6	Jesus answered, and said to him, "On the other hand, it is <also> written, 'You shall not put the Lord your God to the test.'" [3.]	4:7 Jesus said to him, "On the other hand, it is written, 'You shall not put the Lord your God to the test.'"		4:12~ ~~And~~ Jesus answered and said to him, "It is ~~said~~, 'You shall not put the Lord your God to the test.'"
7	Again the Devil took [Jesus] up [on] a very high mountain, and showed Him all the kingdoms of the world and their glory, in a moment of time.	4:8 Again, the devil took [Him] [to] a very high mountain and showed Him all the kingdoms of the world and their glory;		4:5 ~~And he led~~ [Him] up and showed Him all the kingdoms of the world in a moment of time.
8	And the Devil said to Him, "I will give you all this domain and its glory, for it has been handed over to me, and I give it to whomever I wish.	4:9~ and ~~he~~ said to Him, "All ~~these things~~ I will give You,		4:6 And the devil said to Him, I will give You all this domain and its glory; for it has been handed over to me, and I give it to whomever I wish.
9	"Therefore, if You fall down and worship me, it shall all be Yours."	4:~9 if You fall down and worship me."		4:7 "Therefore if You worship ~~before~~ me, it shall all be Yours."
10	Then Jesus answered, and said to him, "Go, Satan! For it is written; 'You shall worship the Lord your God, and serve Him only.'" [4.]	4:10 Then Jesus said to him, Go, Satan! For it is written, 'You shall worship the Lord your God, and serve Him only.'		4:8 Jesus answered him, It is written, 'You shall worship the Lord your God and serve Him only.'
11	When the Devil had finished every temptation he left Him, until an opportune time.	4:11~ ~~Then the devil~~ left Him;		4:13 When the devil had finished every temptation, he left Him until an opportune time.
12	And behold, angels came and began to minister to [Jesus].	4:~11 and behold, angels came and began to minister to [Him].	1:~13 and ~~the~~ angels ~~were~~ ministering to [Him].	

1. Deuteronomy 8:3   2. Psalm 91:11-12   3. Deuteronomy 6:16   4. Deuteronomy 6:13;10:20

CHAPTER 3
THE FIRST YEAR OF HIS MINISTRY

Events that occurred during the First Year of The Ministry of Jesus Christ.

Act 1 - Jesus Begins His Ministry
		Page
Scene 1	Jesus Meets Andrew and Simon	30
2	Jesus Meets Philip and Nathanael	31
3	Jesus Turns Water Into Wine At A Wedding	32

Act 2 - The First Passover
Scene 1	Jesus Expels The Merchants From The Temple	33
2	A Pharisee Named Nicodemus	34
3	The Disciples of Jesus Begin Baptizing	35
4	Believe In The Son And Have Eternal Life	35

Act 3 - A Journey Through Samaria
Scene 1	King Herod Imprisons John The Baptist	36
2	The Woman At Jacob's Well	37
3	I Am The Living Water	38
4	Many Samaritans Believe In Jesus	39

Act 4 - Jesus Settles In Capernaum
Scene 1	Through Nazareth and Cana	40
2	Healing The Son of A Royal Official	40
3	Jesus Resides In Capernaum	41
4	Jesus Calls Peter and Andrew, and Others	42
5	Jesus Calls James and John	43

Act 5 - Jesus Heals Many
Scene 1	Healing A Demoniac On The Sabbath	44
2	Jesus Heals Simon Peter's Mother-in-Law	45
3	Many Come To Be Healed	45
4	Preaching And Healing Throughout Galilee	46
5	Cleansing A Leper	47
6	Resurrecting The Son of A Widow	48

Act 6 - John Enquires About Jesus
		Page
Scene 1	John Asks Jesus, "Are You The Expected One?"	49
2	John Is Elijah Who Was To Come	50
3	To What Shall I Compare This Generation?	51

Act 7 - Jesus Attends A Feast
Scene 1	Jesus Heals A Man at The Bethesda Pool	52
2	The Father And The Son	53
3	Those Who Believe My Words Will Live	54
4	My Testimony About Myself	55
5	The Parable of The Good Samaritan	56
6	Jesus Visits Martha and Mary	57

Act 8 - Events In Capernaum
Scene 1	The Man Paralyzed In A Bed	58
2	Jesus Is Accused of Blasphemy	59
3	Jesus Calls Matthew Levi	60
4	Matthew Gives A Reception For Jesus	60
5	Why Do You Not Fast?	61
6	New Cloth and Wineskins	61
7	Picking Grain On The Sabbath	62
8	Healing A Withered Hand On The Sabbath	63
9	Lord, Teach Us To Pray	63

Act 9 - The Death of John The Baptist
Scene 1	The Demand of Herodias	65
2	King Herod Has John Beheaded	65

MAP OF ISRAEL

Locations mentioned in this Chapter are shown with a white center.

3 - FIRST YEAR OF MINISTRY

Act 1: Jesus Begins His Ministry

Scene 1: Jesus Meets Andrew and Simon

Jordan River, *Judea*   early autumn / 29 CE

The Complete Gospel of Jesus Christ

	Luke	John
1 Jesus began His ministry when He was about thirty years of age.	3:23~ When He began His ministry, Jesus ~~Himself~~ was about thirty years of age,	
2 [One] day, John <the Baptist> was standing with two of his disciples; and he looked at Jesus as He walked, and said, "Behold, the Lamb of God!"		1:35 ~~Again~~ [the next] day John was standing with two of his disciples, 1:36 and he looked at Jesus as He walked, and said, "Behold, the Lamb of God!"
3 The two disciples heard [John] speak, and they followed Jesus.		1:37 The two disciples heard [him] speak, and they followed Jesus.
4 Jesus turned, and saw them following, and <He> said to them, "What do you seek?"		1:38~ ~~And~~ Jesus turned and saw them following, and said to them, "What do you seek?"
5 They said to Him, "Rabbi (which translated means "Teacher"), where are You staying?"		1:~38 They said to Him, "Rabbi (which translated means Teacher), where are You staying?"
6 He said to them, "Come, and you will see."		1:39~ He said to them, "Come, and you will see."
7 So they came and saw where [Jesus] was staying; and they stayed with Him that day, for it was about *the tenth hour.*[1]		1:~39 So they came and saw where [~~He~~] was staying; and they stayed with Him that day, for it was about the tenth hour.
8 One of the two who heard John speak, and followed [Jesus], was <named> Andrew.		1:40 One of the two who heard John speak and followed [~~Him~~], was Andrew, ~~Simon Peter's brother~~.
9 [Andrew] found his brother Simon, and said to him, "We have found the *Messiah!*"[2] (which translate[s] [as] "Christ"); <and> he brought him to Jesus.		1:41 [~~He~~] found ~~first~~ his ~~own~~ brother Simon and said to him, "We have found the Messiah" (which translate[d] [~~means~~] Christ). 1:42~ He brought him to Jesus.
10 Jesus looked at him, and said, "You are Simon, the son of John. You shall be called *Cephas*"[3] (which is translated "Peter").		1:~42 Jesus looked at him and said, "You are Simon the son of John; you shall be called Cephas" (which is translated Peter).

1. Jewish late afternoon, about 5:00 pm   2. Daniel 9:25 / (Deuteronomy 18:15)   3. Aramaic for "rock" = Greek "petra"

3 - FIRST YEAR OF MINISTRY

Act 1: **Jesus Begins His Ministry**

Scene 2: **Jesus Meets Philip and Nathanael**

Judea   early autumn / 29 CE

#		John
1	The next day Jesus purposed to go into Galilee; and He found Philip, and said to him, "Follow Me."	1:43 The next day ~~He~~ purposed to go into Galilee, and He found Philip. And Jesus said to him, "Follow Me."
2	Now Philip was from Bethsaida, the city of Andrew and Peter.	1:44 Now Philip was from Bethsaida, of the city of Andrew and Peter.
3	Philip found Nathanael, and said to him, "We have found Him of whom Moses in the Law and also the Prophets wrote - Jesus of Nazareth, the son of Joseph."	1:45 Philip found Nathanael and said to him, "We have found Him of whom Moses in the Law and also the Prophets wrote - Jesus of Nazareth, the son of Joseph."
4	Nathanael said to him, "Can anything good come out of Nazareth?"	1:46~ Nathanael said to him, "Can any good thing come out of Nazareth?"
5	Philip said to him, "Come and see!"	1:~46 Philip said to him, "Come and see."
6	<When> Jesus saw Nathanael coming to Him, <He> said, "Behold, an Israelite indeed, in whom there is no deceit."	1:47 Jesus saw Nathanael coming to Him, ~~and~~ said ~~of him~~, "Behold, an Israelite indeed, in whom there is no deceit!"
7	Nathanael said to Him, "How do You know me?"	1:48~ Nathanael said to Him, "How do You know me?"
8	Jesus answered him, "Before Philip called you, when you were under the fig tree, I saw you."	1:~48 Jesus answered ~~and said to~~ him, "Before Philip called you, when you were under the fig tree, I saw you."
9	Nathanael answered Him, "Rabbi, You are the Son of God! You are the King of Israel!"	1:49 Nathanael answered Him, "Rabbi, You are the Son of God; You are the King of Israel."
10	Jesus said to him, "You believe because I said to you that I saw you under the fig tree; you will see greater things than these.	1:50 Jesus ~~answered and~~ said to him, "Because I said to you that I saw you under the fig tree, ~~do~~ you believe? You will see greater things than these."
11	Truly, truly, I say to you, <that> you will see *the heavens opened, and the angels of God ascending and descending* [1.] [up]on the Son of Man!"	1:51 ~~And He said to him~~, "Truly, truly, I say to you, you will see the heavens opened and the angels of God ascending and descending on the Son of Man."

1. *(Genesis 28:12)*

3 - FIRST YEAR OF MINISTRY
Act 1: Jesus Begins His Ministry

Scene 3: Jesus Turns Water Into Wine At A Wedding
Cana, *Galilee*   autumn / 29 CE

	John
1 On the third day there was a wedding in Cana of Galilee.	2:1~ On the third day there was a wedding in Cana of Galilee,
2 <Mary>, the mother of Jesus was there, and Jesus and His disciples were invited to the wedding.	2:~1 ~~and~~ the mother of Jesus was there; 2:2 and ~~both~~ Jesus and His disciples were invited to the wedding.
3 When the wine ran out, [His] mother said to Jesus, "They have no wine."	2:3 When the wine ran out, [~~the~~] mother [~~of~~] Jesus said to ~~Him~~, "They have no wine."
4 [He] said to her, "Woman, what does that have to do with us? My hour has not yet come."	2:4 ~~And~~ [~~Jesus~~] said to her, "Woman, what does that have to do with us? My hour has not yet come."
5 [Mary] said to the servants, "Whatever He says to you, do it."	2:5 [~~His mother~~] said to the servants, "Whatever He says to you, do it."
6 Now there were six stone waterpots set there for the Jewish custom of purification, each [able to hold] *twenty or thirty gallons.*[1]	2:6 Now there were six stone waterpots set there for the Jewish custom of purification, [~~containing~~] twenty or thirty gallons each.
7 Jesus said to them, "Fill the pots with water." So they filled them up to the brim.	2:7 Jesus said to them, "Fill the ~~water~~pots with water." So they filled them up to the brim.
8 [Then] He said to them, "Now draw some out, and take it to the headwaiter." So they took it to him.	2:8 [~~And~~] He said to them, "Draw some out now and take it to the headwaiter." So they took it to him.
9 When the headwaiter tasted the water which had become wine, and did not know where it came from - but the servants who had drawn the water knew - [he] called the bridegroom, and said to him,	2:9 When the headwaiter tasted the water which had become wine, and did not know where it came from (but the servants who had drawn the water knew), 2:10~ [~~the headwaiter~~] called the bridegroom, and said to him,
10 "Every man serves the good wine first, and when the people have drunk freely then he serves the poorer wine; but you have kept the good wine until now!"	2:~10 "Every man serves the good wine first, and when the people have drunk freely, then he serves the poorer wine; but you have kept the good wine until now."
11 This [first] sign <which> Jesus did in Cana of Galilee manifested His glory; and His disciples believed in Him.	2:11 This [~~beginning~~] ~~of His~~ signs Jesus did in Cana of Galilee, ~~and~~ manifested His glory, and His disciples believed in Him.
12 After this, [Jesus] went down to Capernaum [with] His mother and His brothers, and His disciples, and they stayed there a few days.	2:12 After this [~~He~~] went down to Capernaum, ~~He~~ [~~and~~] His mother and His brothers and His disciples; and they stayed there a few days.

1. *approximately 90 and 130 liters*

3 - FIRST YEAR OF MINISTRY

Act 2: The First Passover

Scene 1: Jesus Expels The Merchants From The Temple

The Temple, Jerusalem, *Judea*   Passover - April / 30 CE

Every Gospel Word of Jesus Christ

	John
1 *The Passover* [1] of the Jews was near, and Jesus went up to Jerusalem.	2:13 The Passover of the Jews was near, and Jesus went up to Jerusalem.
2 In the Temple He found those who were selling <the> oxen, sheep and doves; and the money changers seated at their tables.	2:14 ~~And~~ He found in the temple those who were selling oxen ~~and~~ sheep and doves, and the money changers seated at their tables.
3 [Then] [Jesus] made a scourge of cords, and <He> drove them all out of the Temple, with the sheep and the oxen;	2:15~ [~~And~~] [~~He~~] made a scourge of cords, and drove them all out of the temple, with the sheep and the oxen;
4 and He poured out the coins of the money changers, and overturned their tables.	2:~15 and He poured out the coins of the money changers and overturned their tables;
5 And He said to those who were selling the doves, "Take these things away! Stop making My Father's house a place of business!"	2:16 and to those who were selling the doves He said, "Take these things away; stop making My Father's house a place of business."
6 His disciples remembered that it was written, *"Zeal for Your house will consume me."* [2]	2:17 His disciples remembered that it was written, "Zeal for Your house will consume me."
7 Then the Jews said to Him, "What sign do You show us as your authority for doing these things?"	2:18 The Jews then said to Him, "What sign do You show us as your authority for doing these things?"
8 Jesus answered them, "Destroy this Temple, and in three days I will raise it up."	2:19 Jesus answered them, "Destroy this temple, and in three days I will raise it up."
9 The Jews said, "It took forty-six years to build this Temple, and will You raise it up in three days?"	2:20 The Jews ~~then~~ said, "It took forty-six years to build this temple, and will You raise it up in three days?"
10 But He was speaking of the temple of His body.	2:21 But He was speaking of the temple of His body.
11 So when Jesus was raised from the dead, His disciples remembered that He <had> said this; and they believed the Scripture, and the Word which He had spoken.	2:22 So when He was raised from the dead, His disciples remembered that He said this; and they believed the Scripture and the word which Jesus had spoken.
12 Now [while] He was in Jerusalem, many believed in His Name, observing [the] signs which He was doing during the Passover Feast.	2:23 Now [when] He was in Jerusalem ~~at~~ the Passover, during ~~the~~ feast, many believed in His name, observing [~~His~~] signs which He was doing.
13 But Jesus, on His part, was not entrusting Himself to them, for He knew all men,	2:24 But Jesus, on His part, was not entrusting Himself to them, for He knew all men,
14 and because He did not need anyone to testify concerning man, [because] He Himself knew what was in man.	2:25 and because He did not need anyone to testify concerning man, [~~for~~] He Himself knew what was in man.

  1. *Deuteronomy 16:1-6*   2. *Psalm 69:9*

3 - FIRST YEAR OF MINISTRY	Scene 2: **A Pharisee Named Nicodemus**	Page 34
Act 2: **The First Passover**	Jerusalem, *Judea* Passover - April / 30 CE	*The Good News*

	John
1 Now there was a Pharisee named Nicodemus, a ruler of the Jews;	3:1 Now there was a ~~man of the~~ Pharisees, named Nicodemus, a ruler of the Jews;
2 [he] came to Jesus [at] night, and said to Him, "Rabbi, we know that You have come from God as a Teacher, for no one can do these signs that You do unless God is with him."	3:2 [~~this man~~] came to Jesus [~~by~~] night and said to Him, "Rabbi, we know that You have come from God as a teacher; for no one can do these signs that You do unless God is with him."
3 Jesus answered, and said to him, "Truly, truly, I say to you, unless one is born again, he cannot see the Kingdom of God."	3:3 Jesus answered and said to him, "Truly, truly, I say to you, unless one is born again he cannot see the kingdom of God."
4 Nicodemus said to Him, "How can a man be born when he is old? He cannot enter a second time into his mother's womb and be born, can he?"	3:4 Nicodemus said to Him, "How can a man be born when he is old? He cannot enter a second time into his mother's womb and be born, can he?"
5 Jesus answered, "Truly, truly, I say to you, unless one is born of water and the Spirit, he cannot enter into the Kingdom of God.	3:5 Jesus answered, "Truly, truly, I say to you, unless one is born of water and the Spirit he cannot enter into the kingdom of God.
6 "That which is born of the flesh is flesh, and that which is born of the Spirit is Spirit.	3:6 "That which is born of the flesh is flesh, and that which is born of the Spirit is spirit.
7 "Do not be amazed that I said to you, 'You must be born again.'	3:7 "Do not be amazed that I said to you, 'You must be born again.'
8 "The wind blows where it wishes, and you hear the sound of it but do not know where it comes from, [or] where it is going; so is everyone who is born of the Spirit."	3:8 "The wind blows where it wishes and you hear the sound of it, but do not know where it comes from [~~and~~] where it is going; so is everyone who is born of the Spirit."
9 Nicodemus said, "How can these things be?"	3:9 Nicodemus said ~~to Him~~, "How can these things be?"
10 Jesus answered him, "Are you the teacher of Israel, and do not understand these things?	3:10 Jesus answered ~~and said to~~ him, "Are you the teacher of Israel and do not understand these things?
11 "Truly, truly, I say to you, we speak of what we know, and testify of what we have seen, and you do not accept our testimony.	3:11 "Truly, truly, I say to you, we speak of what we know and testify of what we have seen, and you do not accept our testimony.
12 "If I told you earthly things and you do not believe, how will you believe if I tell you Heavenly things?	3:12 "If I told you earthly things and you do not believe, how will you believe if I tell you heavenly things?
13 "No one has ascended into Heaven but He who descended from Heaven: the Son of Man.	3:13 "No one has ascended into heaven, but He who descended from heaven: the Son of Man.
14 "As *Moses lifted up the serpent in the wilderness,*[1] even so must the Son of Man be lifted up, so that everyone who believes in Him will have eternal life.	3:14 "As Moses lifted up the serpent in the wilderness, even so must the Son of Man be lifted up; 3:15 so that whoever believes will in Him have eternal life.
15 "For God so loved the world, that He gave His only begotten Son, that whoever believes in Him shall not perish, but have eternal life.	3:16 "For God so loved the world, that He gave His only begotten Son, that whoever believes in Him shall not perish, but have eternal life.
16 "For God did not send the Son into the world to judge the world, but that the world might be saved through Him.	3:17 "For God did not send the Son into the world to judge the world, but that the world might be saved through Him.
17 "He who believes in Him is not judged;	3:18~ "He who believes in Him is not judged;
18 "<but> he who does not believe has been judged already, because he has not believed in the Name of the only begotten Son of God.	3:~18 he who does not believe has been judged already, because he has not believed in the name of the only begotten Son of God.
19 "This is the judgment: that the Light has come into the world, and men loved the darkness rather than the Light, for their deeds were evil.	3:19 "This is the judgment, that the Light has come into the world, and men loved the darkness rather than the Light, for their deeds were evil.
20 "For everyone who does evil hates the Light, and does not come to the Light, for fear that his deeds will be exposed.	3:20 "For everyone who does evil hates the Light, and does not come to the Light for fear that his deeds will be exposed.
21 "But he who practices the truth comes to the Light, so that his deeds may be manifested, as having been wrought in God."	3:21 "But he who practices the truth comes to the Light, so that his deeds may be manifested as having been wrought in God."

1. Numbers 21:9

3 - FIRST YEAR OF MINISTRY

Act 2: The First Passover

Scene 3: The Disciples of Jesus Begin Baptizing

Jordan River, Aenon, *Judea* late spring / 30 CE

	John
1 After these things, Jesus and His disciples came into the Judea[n] [countryside], and He was spending time with them there and baptizing; although Jesus Himself was not baptizing, but His disciples were.	3:22 After these things Jesus and His disciples came into the [land] of Judea, and there He was spending time with them and baptizing. 4:2 (although Jesus Himself was not baptizing, but His disciples were),
2 John was also baptizing in Aenon near Salim, because there was much water there; and <the> people were coming and being baptized, for John had not yet been thrown into prison.	3:23 John also was baptizing in Aenon near Salim, because there was much water there; and people were coming and were being baptized - 3:24 for John had not yet been thrown into prison.
3 The Lord knew that the Pharisees had heard that [He] was making and baptizing more disciples than John.	4:1 Therefore when the Lord knew that the Pharisees had heard that [Jesus] was making and baptizing more disciples than John
4 [When] a discussion arose on the part of John's disciples with a Jew about purification, they came to John, and said to him, "Rabbi, He who was with you beyond the Jordan, to whom you have testified, behold, He is baptizing, and all are coming to Him."	3:25 [Therefore there] arose a discussion on the part of John's disciples with a Jew about purification. 3:26 And they came to John and said to him, "Rabbi, He who was with you beyond the Jordan, to whom you have testified, behold, He is baptizing and all are coming to Him."
5 John answered, and said <to them>, "A man can receive nothing unless it has been given <to> him from Heaven.	3:27 John answered and said, "A man can receive nothing unless it has been given him from heaven.
6 "You yourselves are my witnesses, that I said, 'I am not the Christ,' but 'I have been sent ahead of Him.'	3:28 "You yourselves are my witnesses that I said, 'I am not the Christ,' but, 'I have been sent ahead of Him.'
7 "He who has the bride is the bridegroom; [and] the friend of the bridegroom, who stands and hears him, rejoices greatly because of the bridegroom's voice.	3:29 "He who has the bride is the bride-groom; [but] the friend of the bridegroom, who stands and hears him, rejoices greatly because of the bridegroom's voice.
8 "So this joy of mine has been made full!	3:~29 So this joy of mine has been made full.
9 "He must increase, but I must decrease."	3:30 "He must increase, but I must decrease.

Scene 4: Believe In The Son And Have Eternal Life

Jordan River, Aenon, *Judea* late spring / 30 CE

	John
1 <John said,> "He who comes from above is above all;	3:31~ "He who comes from above is above all,
2 "he who is of the earth is from the earth, and speaks of the earth.	3:~31~ he who is of the earth is from the earth and speaks of the earth.
3 "He who comes from Heaven is above all.	3:~31 He who comes from heaven is above all.
4 "What He has seen and heard, of that He testifies; and no one receives His testimony.	3:32 "What He has seen and heard, of that He testifies; and no one receives His testimony.
5 "He who has received His testimony has set his seal to this; that God is true.	3:33 "He who has received His testimony has set his seal to this, that God is true.
6 "For He whom God has sent speaks the words of God, for He gives the Spirit without measure.	3:34 "For He whom God has sent speaks the words of God; for He gives the Spirit without measure.
7 "The Father loves the Son, and has given all things into His hand.	3:35 "The Father loves the Son and has given all things into His hand.
8 "He who believes in the Son has eternal life;	3:36~ "He who believes in the Son has eternal life;
9 "but he who does not obey the Son will not see life, [and] the wrath of God <will> abide on him."	3:~36 but he who does not obey the Son will not see life, but the wrath of God abides on him."

3 - FIRST YEAR OF MINISTRY

Act 3: A Journey Through Samaria

Scene 1: King Herod Imprisons John The Baptist

Judea   late spring / 30 CE

Page 36

The Synoptic Gospel

	Matthew	Mark	Luke	John
1 Of all the wicked things which *Herod the Tetrarch* [1]. had done, [he] added this to them all: he sent and had John arrested; and he bound him, and locked him up in prison.	14:3~ ~~For when~~ Herod had John arrested, he bound hum and ~~put~~ him in prison because of Herodias, the wife of his brother Philip.	6:17 ~~For~~ Herod ~~himself~~ had sent and had John arrested and bound in prison ~~on account of~~ Herodias, the wife of his brother Philip, because he had married ~~her~~.	3:~19 and because of all the wicked things which Herod had done, 3:20 Herod also added this to them all: he locked John up in prison.	
2 For John <had> reprimanded Herod because he had married Herodias, the wife of his brother *Philip*; [2]. and <he> had been saying to Herod, "It is *not lawful for you to have your brother's wife*." [3].	14:4~ For John had been saying to ~~him~~, "It is not lawful for you to have ~~her~~."	6:18 For John had been saying to Herod, "It is not lawful for you to have your brother's wife."	3:19~ But when Herod the tetrarch was reprimanded by him because of Herodias, his brother's wife,	
3 Herodias had a grudge against [John] and wanted to put him to death, [but] Herod could not do so, for [he] was afraid of John, knowing that he was a righteous and holy man;		6:19 Herodias had a grudge against [~~him~~] and wanted to put him to death ~~and~~ could not do so; 6:20~ for [Herod] was afraid of John, knowing that he was a righteous and holy man,		
4 <and> [Herod] feared the crowd because they regarded John as a prophet, and <so> he kept him safe.	14:~5 [~~he~~] feared the crowd, because they regarded John as a prophet.	6:~20~ and he kept him safe.		
5 When [Herod] heard [John] he was very perplexed, but he enjoy[ed] listening to him.		6:~20 ~~And~~ when [~~he~~] heard [~~him~~], he was very perplexed; but he [~~used to~~] enjoy listening to him.		
6 When Jesus heard that John had been taken into custody, He withdrew <from> Judea and went into Galilee, and He had to pass through Samaria.	4:12 ~~Now~~ when Jesus heard that John had been taken into custody, He withdrew into Galilee;	1:14 ~~Now after~~ John had been taken into custody, Jesus ~~came~~ into Galilee,		4:3 He ~~left~~ Judea and went ~~away again~~ into Galilee. 4:4 And He had to pass through Samaria.

1. *Herod Antipater (aka Antipas) (20 BCE - 39 CE) Tetrarch of Galilee & Perea (4 BCE - 39 CE)*
2. *Herod Philip I (27 BCE - 34 CE) Tetrarch of Ituraea, Trachonitis, Gaulonitis & Paneas (4 BCE - 34 CE)*
3. *Leviticus 18:16; 20:21*

3 - FIRST YEAR OF MINISTRY

Act 3: A Journey Through Samaria

Scene 2: The Woman At Jacob's Well

Sychar, *Samaria*   late spring / 30 CE

Page 37

Synoptic = seeing together (as one)

	John
1 [Jesus] came to a city of Samaria called Sychar, near *the parcel of ground that Jacob gave to his son Joseph.*[1.]	4:5 ~~So~~ [He] came to a city of Samaria called Sychar, near the parcel of ground that Jacob gave to his son Joseph;
2 Jacob's well was there, [and] being wearied from His journey, Jesus was sitting by the well.	4:6~ and Jacob's well was there. [~~So~~] Jesus, being wearied from His journey, was sitting ~~thus~~ by the well.
3 [At] about *the sixth hour,*[2.] a woman of Samaria came there to draw water.	4:~6 [~~It was~~] about the sixth hour. 4:7~ There came a woman of Samaria to draw water.
4 Jesus said to her, "Give Me a drink," for His disciples had gone away into the city to buy food.	4:~7 Jesus said to her, "Give Me a drink." 4:8 For His disciples had gone away into the city to buy food.
5 The Samaritan woman said to Him, "How is it that You, being a Jew, ask me for a drink, since I am a Samaritan woman?"	4:9 ~~Therefore~~ the Samaritan woman said to Him, "How is it that You, being a Jew, ask me for a drink since I am a Samaritan woman?"
6 (For Jews have no dealings with Samaritans.)	4:~9 (For Jews have no dealings with Samaritans.)
7 Jesus answered, and said to her, "If you knew the gift of God, and who it is who says to you, 'Give Me a drink,' you would have asked Him, and He would have given you *living water.*"[3.]	4:10 Jesus answered and said to her, "If you knew the gift of God, and who it is who says to you, 'Give Me a drink,' you would have asked Him, and He would have given you living water."
8 She said to Him, "Sir, You have nothing to draw with, and the well is deep; [how] [will] You get [the] living water?	4:11 She said to Him, "Sir, You have nothing to draw with, and the well is deep; [~~where~~] ~~then~~ [~~do~~] You get [that] living water?
9 "You are not greater than our father Jacob, are You, who gave us [this] well, and drank [from] it himself, and his sons, and his cattle?"	4:12 "You are not greater than our father Jacob, are You, who gave us [the] well, and drank [of] it himself and his sons and his cattle?"

1. Genesis 33:19; Joshua 24:32   2. about noon   3. Daniel 9:25 / (Deuteronomy 18:15)

3 - **FIRST YEAR OF MINISTRY**	Scene 3: **I Am The Living Water**
Act 3: **A Journey Through Samaria**	Sychar, *Samaria* late spring / 30 CE

	John
1 Jesus answered, and said to her, "Everyone who drinks of this water will thirst again; but whoever drinks of the water that I will give him shall never thirst,	4:13 Jesus answered and said to her, "Everyone who drinks of this water will thirst again; 4:14~ but whoever drinks of the water that I will give him shall never thirst;
2 "[because] the water that I will give him will become in him a *well of water, springing up to eternal life!*" [1.]	4:~14 [but] the water that I will give him will become in him a well of water springing up to eternal life."
3 The woman said to Him, "Sir, give me this water, so <that> I will not be thirsty, nor come all the way here to draw."	4:15 The woman said to Him, "Sir, give me this water, so I will not be thirsty nor come all the way here to draw."
4 [Jesus] said to her, "Go, and call your husband <to> come here."	4:16 [He] said to her, "Go, call your husband and come here."
5 The woman answered, and said, "I have no husband."	4:17~ The woman answered and said, "I have no husband."
6 [He] said to her, "You have correctly said, 'I have no husband'; for you have had five husbands, and the one whom you [are with] now is not your husband; this you have said truly."	4:~17 [Jesus] said to her, "You have correctly said, 'I have no husband'; 4:18 for you have had five husbands, and the one whom you now [have] is not your husband; this you have said truly."
7 The woman said to [Jesus], "Sir, I perceive that You are a Prophet.	4:19 The woman said to [Him], "Sir, I perceive that You are a prophet.
8 "*Our fathers worshiped [on] this mountain,*[2.] and you people say that in *Jerusalem is the place where men ought to worship.*" [3.]	4:20 "Our fathers worshiped [in] this mountain, and you people say that in Jerusalem is the place where men ought to worship."
9 Jesus said to her, "Woman, believe Me, an hour is coming when neither [on] this mountain, nor in Jerusalem, will you worship the Father.	4:21 Jesus said to her, "Woman, believe Me, an hour is coming when neither [in] this mountain nor in Jerusalem will you worship the Father.
10 "You worship what you do not know; we worship what we know, for salvation is from the Jews.	4:22 "You worship what you do not know; we worship what we know, for salvation is from the Jews.
11 "But an hour is coming, and now is, when the true worshipers will worship the Father in Spirit and <in> truth; for such people the Father seeks to be His worshipers.	4:23 "But an hour is coming, and now is, when the true worshipers will worship the Father in spirit and truth; for such people the Father seeks to be His worshipers.
12 "God is Spirit; and those who worship Him must worship in Spirit, and truth."	4:24 "God is spirit, and those who worship Him must worship in spirit and truth."
13 The woman said to Him, "I know that <the> *Messiah* [4.] is coming (He who is called Christ); when that One comes, He will declare all things to us."	4:25 The woman said to Him, "I know that Messiah is coming (He who is called Christ); when that One comes, He will declare all things to us."
14 Jesus said to her, "I who speak to you am He."	4:26 Jesus said to her, "I who speak to you am He."
15 At this point, His disciples came, and they were amazed that He had been speaking with a woman, yet no one said, "What do You seek?" or, "Why do You speak with her?"	4:27 At this point His disciples came, and they were amazed that He had been speaking with a woman, yet no one said, "What do You seek?" or, "Why do You speak with her?"
16 So the woman left her waterpot and went into the city, and said to the men, "Come <and> see a man who told me all the things that I have done!	4:28 So the woman left her waterpot, and went into the city and said to the men, 4:29~ "Come, see a man who told me all the things that I have done;
17 "[Could] this [be] the [Messiah]?"	4:~29 this [is] not the [Christ], [is it?]"
18 <So> [the people] went out of the city, and were coming to [Jesus].	4:30 [They] went out of the city, and were coming to [Him].

1. Isaiah 44:3; (12:3) / Jeremiah 2:13 / Zechariah 13:1; 14:8   2. Genesis 12:6-7; 33:17-20 / Judges 9:6-7   3. 1 Kings 9:3 / 2 Kings 17:28 / 2 Chronicles 7:12-16 / Psalm 122:1-4 / Isaiah 2:3

3 - FIRST YEAR OF MINISTRY
Act 3: A Journey Through Samaria
Scene 4: Many Samaritans Believe In Jesus
Sychar, *Samaria*   late spring / 30 CE

	John
1 Meanwhile, [His] disciples were urging [Jesus], saying, "Rabbi, eat." But He said to them, "I have food to eat that you do not know about."	4:31 Meanwhile [the] disciples were urging [Him], saying, "Rabbi, eat." 4:32 But He said to them, "I have food to eat that you do not know about."
2 So the disciples were saying to one another, "No one brought Him anything to eat, did he?"	4:33 So the disciples were saying to one another, "No one brought Him anything to eat, did he?"
3 Jesus said to them, "My food is to do the will of Him who sent Me, and to accomplish His work.	4:34 Jesus said to them, "My food is to do the will of Him who sent Me and to accomplish His work.
4 "Do you not say, 'There are yet four months, and then comes the harvest'?	4:35~ "Do you not say, 'There are yet four months, and then comes the harvest'?
5 "Behold, I say to you, lift up your eyes and look on the fields, that they are white for harvest!	4:~35 Behold, I say to you, lift up your eyes and look on the fields, that they are white for harvest.
6 "Already he who reaps is receiving wages, and is gathering fruit for life eternal, so that he who sows and he who reaps may rejoice together.	4:36 "Already he who reaps is receiving wages and is gathering fruit for life eternal; so that he who sows and he who reaps may rejoice together.
7 "For in this case the saying is true, 'One sows, and another reaps.'	4:37 "For in this case the saying is true, 'One sows and another reaps.'
8 "I sent you to reap that for which you have not labored; others have labored, and you have entered into their labor."	4:38 "I sent you to reap that for which you have not labored; others have labored and you have entered into their labor."
9 From that city many of the Samaritans believed in Him, because of the word of the woman who testified, "He told me all the things that I have done."	4:39 From that city many of the Samaritans believed in Him because of the word of the woman who testified, "He told me all the things that I have done."
10 The Samaritans ask[ed] Jesus to stay with them, and He stayed there <for> two days.	4:40 ~~So when~~ the Samaritans ~~came to~~ Jesus, ~~they were~~ ask[~~ing~~] ~~Him~~ to stay with them; and He stayed there two days.
11 Many more believed because of His word[s];	4:41 Many more believed because of His word;
12 and they were saying to the woman, "It is no longer because of what you said that we believe, for we have heard for ourselves, and know that this One is indeed the Savior of the world!"	4:42 and they were saying to the woman, "It is no longer because of what you said that we believe, for we have heard for ourselves, and know that this One is indeed the Savior of the world."
13 After two days, [Jesus] went forth from there into Galilee, for [He] Himself testified that a prophet has no honor in his own country.	4:43 After ~~the~~ two days [~~He~~] went forth from there into Galilee. 4:44 For [~~Jesus~~] Himself testified that a prophet has no honor in his own country.

3 - FIRST YEAR OF MINISTRY

Act 4: **Jesus Settles In Capernaum**

Scene 1: **Through Nazareth and Cana**
Nazareth & Cana, *Galilee*   late spring / 30 CE

#	Matthew	Luke	John
1	Jesus returned to Galilee in the power of the Spirit, <and> the Galileans received Him, having seen all the things that He did in Jerusalem at the [Passover], for they themselves also went to the Feast;	4:14~ ~~And~~ Jesus returned to Galilee in the power of the Spirit,	4:45 ~~So when He came~~ to Galilee, the Galileans received Him, having seen all the things that He did in Jerusalem at the [~~feast~~]; for they themselves also went to the feast.
2	and news about Him spread through all the surrounding district.	4:~14 and news about Him spread through all the surrounding district.	
3	Leaving Nazareth, [Jesus] came again to Cana [in] Galilee, where He had [turned] the water <into> wine.	4:13~ ~~and~~ leaving Nazareth,	4:46~ ~~Therefore~~ [He] came again to Cana [~~of~~] Galilee where He had [~~made~~] the water wine.

Scene 2: **Healing The Son of A Royal Official**
Capernaum, *Galilee*   late spring / 30 CE

#		John
1	There was a royal official whose son was sick at Capernaum.	4:~46 ~~And~~ there was a royal official whose son was sick at Capernaum.
2	When he heard that Jesus had come out of Judea <and> into Galilee, he went to Him; and <he> implor[ed] [Jesus] to come and heal his son, [who] was at the point of death.	4:47 When he heard that Jesus had come out of Judea into Galilee, he went to Him and ~~was~~ implor[ing] [~~Him~~] to come down and heal his son; ~~for~~ [he] was at the point of death.
3	Jesus said to him, "Unless you people see signs and wonders, you simply will not believe."	4:48 ~~So~~ Jesus said to him, "Unless you people see signs and wonders, you simply will not believe."
4	The royal official said to Him, "Sir, come down before my child dies."	4:49 The royal official said to Him, "Sir, come down before my child dies."
5	Jesus said to him, "Go; your son lives!"	4:50~ Jesus said to him, "Go; your son lives."
6	The man believed the word that Jesus spoke to him, and [headed home].	4:~50 The man believed the word that Jesus spoke to him and [~~started off~~].
7	As he was going, his slaves met him, saying that his son was living.	4:51 As he was ~~now~~ going ~~down~~, his slaves met him, saying that his son was living.
8	[When] he [asked] them the hour [at which] he began to get better, they said to him, "The fever left him yesterday, at the seventh hour."	4:52 [~~So~~] he [~~inquired of~~] them the hour [when] he began to get better, ~~Then~~ they said to him, "Yesterday at the seventh hour the fever left him."
9	So the father knew that it was [the] hour in which Jesus <had> said to him, "Your son lives"; and he himself believed, and his [entire] household.	4:53 So the father knew that it was [at that] hour in which Jesus said to him, "Your son lives"; and he himself believed and his [~~whole~~] household.
10	This is [the] second sign that Jesus performed [after] He had come out of Judea <and> into Galilee.	4:54 This is ~~again~~ [a] second sign that Jesus performed [~~when~~] He had come out of Judea into Galilee.

3 - FIRST YEAR OF MINISTRY

Act 4: Jesus Settles In Capernaum

Scene 3: **Jesus Resides In Capernaum**

Capernaum, *Galilee*   late spring / 30 CE

Page 41

A United Gospel Story

	Matthew	Mark	Luke
1 [Jesus] came and settled in Capernaum, which is by the sea in the region of Zebulun and Naphtali.	*4:~13* [He] came and settled in Capernaum, which is by the sea, in the region of Zebulun and Naphtali.		
2 This was to fulfill what was spoken through Isaiah the prophet: *"The land of Zebulun and the land of Naphtali, by the way of the sea beyond the Jordan, Galilee of the Gentiles -*	*4:14* This was to fulfill what was spoken through Isaiah the prophet: *4:15* "The land of Zebulun and the land of Naphtali, by the way of the sea, beyond the Jordan, Galilee of the Gentiles -		
3 *"The people who were sitting in darkness saw a great Light; and those who were sitting in the land [of the] shadow of death, upon them a Light dawned."* [1]	*4:16* "The people who were sitting in darkness saw a great Light, and those who were sitting in the land [and] shadow of death, upon them a Light dawned."		
4 From that time, Jesus began to preach the gospel of God, and say, "The time is fulfilled and the Kingdom of Heaven is at hand; repent, and believe in the *gospel!*" [2]	*4:17* From that time Jesus began to preach and say, "Repent, for the kingdom of heaven is at hand.	*1:~14* preaching the gospel of God, *1:15* and saying, "The time is fulfilled, and the kingdom of God is at hand; repent and believe in the gospel."	
5 And He began teaching in their synagogues, and was <being> praised by all.			*4:15* And He began teaching in their synagogues and was praised by all.

1. Isaiah 9:1-2; 42:7   *2. meaning good news*

3 - FIRST YEAR OF MINISTRY	Scene 4: **Jesus Calls Peter and Andrew, and Others**		Page 42
Act 4: **Jesus Settles In Capernaum**	Sea of Galilee, near Capernaum, *Galilee* late spring / 30 CE		*A Harmonized Merger of the Four Gospels*

	Matthew	**Mark**	**Luke**
1 As Jesus was walking by the Sea of Galilee, He saw <the> two brothers, Simon who was called Peter, and Andrew his brother, casting a net into the sea, for they were fishermen.	4:18 ~~Now~~ as Jesus was walking by the Sea of Galilee, He saw two brothers, Simon who was called Peter, and Andrew his brother, casting a net into the sea; for they were fishermen.	1:16 As ~~He~~ was ~~going~~ ~~along~~ by the Sea of Galilee, He saw Simon and Andrew, ~~the~~ brother ~~of Simon~~, casting a net in the sea; for they were fishermen.	
2 [Later], [Jesus] was standing by the [sea], and the crowd was pressing around Him, and listening to the Word of God.			5:1 [~~Now~~] ~~it happened that while~~ the crowd was pressing around Him and listening to the word of God, [He] was standing by the [lake] ~~of Gennesaret~~;
3 And He saw two boats lying at the [shore]; but the fishermen had gotten out of them, and were washing their nets.			5:2 and He saw two boats lying at the [~~edge of the lake~~]; but the fishermen had gotten out of them and were washing their nets.
4 [Jesus] got into Simon's boat, and asked him to [move] a little way from the land, [then] He sat down and began teaching the people from the boat.			5:3 [~~And~~] [He] got into ~~one of the~~ boats, ~~which was~~ Simon's, and asked him to [~~put out~~] a little way from the land. [~~And~~] He sat down and began teaching the people from the boat.
5 When He had finished speaking, [Jesus] said to Simon, "Put out into the deep water, and let down your nets for a catch."			5:4 When He had finished speaking, [He] said to Simon, "Put out into the deep water and let down your nets for a catch."
6 Simon answered, and said, "Master, we <have> worked hard all night and caught nothing; but I will do as You say, and let down the nets."			5:5 Simon answered and said, "Master, we worked hard all night and caught nothing, but I will do as You say and let down the nets."
7 When they had done this, they enclosed a great quantity of fish, and their nets began to break.			5:6 When they had done this, they enclosed a great quantity of fish, and their nets began to break;
8 So they signaled their partners in the other boat for them to come and help; and they came and filled both of the boats, so that they began to sink.			5:7 so they signaled ~~to~~ their partners in the other boat for them to come and help ~~them~~. And they came and filled both of the boats, so that they began to sink.
9 When Simon Peter saw [this], he fell down at Jesus' feet, saying, "Go away from me Lord, for I am a sinful man,"			5:8 ~~But~~ when Simon Peter saw [~~that~~], he fell down at Jesus' feet, saying, "Go away from me Lord, for I am a sinful man!"
10 for amazement had seized him and all <of> his companions, because of the [amount] of fish which they had [caught].			5:9 For amazement had seized him and all his companions because of the [~~catch~~] of fish which they had [~~taken~~];
11 Jesus said to them, "Follow Me, and do not fear; from now on I will make you become fishers of men!"	4:19~ ~~And He~~ said to them, "Follow Me, and I will make you fishers of men."	1:17 ~~And~~ Jesus said to them, "Follow Me, and I will make you become fishers of men."	5:~10 ~~And~~ Jesus said to ~~Simon~~, "Do not fear, from now on you ~~will~~ be ~~catching~~ men.
12 Immediately they left their nets, and followed Him.	4:20 Immediately they left their nets and followed Him.	1:18 Immediately they left their nets and followed Him.	

3 - FIRST YEAR OF MINISTRY

Act 4: **Jesus Settles In Capernaum**

Scene 5: **Jesus Calls James and John**

Sea of Galilee, near Capernaum, *Galilee*   late spring / 30 CE

Quotations and references are italicized

	Matthew	Mark	Luke
1 Going on a little farther from there, [Jesus] saw two other brothers; James, the son of Zebedee, and John his brother, who were partners with Simon.	4:21~ Going on from there [He] saw two other brothers, James the son of Zebedee, and John his brother,	1:19~ Going a little farther, [He] saw James the son of Zebedee, and John his brother,	5:10~ and so also were James and John, sons of Zebedee, who were partners with Simon.
2 [They] were in the boat with their father Zebedee, mending the nets.	4:~21~ in the boat with Zebedee their father, mending their nets;	1:~19 [who] were also in the boat mending the nets.	
3 [Jesus] called them, and when they had brought their boats to land, immediately they left everything, and their father in the boat with the hired servants, and <they> went away and followed Him.	4:~21 and [He] called them. 4:22~ Immediately they left the boat and their father, and followed Him.	1:20 Immediately [He] called them; and they left their father Zebedee in the boat with the hired servants, and went away to follow Him.	5:11 When they had brought their boats to land, they left everything and flowed Him.

	Mark	Luke
3 - **FIRST YEAR OF MINISTRY** Act 5: **Jesus Heals Many** Scene 1: **Healing A Demoniac On The Sabbath** Capernaum, *Galilee* a Sabbath, summer / 30 CE		Page 44 **FIVE COLUMN**

#		Mark	Luke
1	They went into Capernaum, and on the Sabbath [Jesus] entered the synagogue, and began to teach them.	1:21 They went into Capernaum; and ~~immediately~~ on the Sabbath [He] entered the synagogue and began to teach.	4:31 And ~~He came down~~ to Capernaum, ~~a city of Galilee~~, and ~~He was~~ teaching them on the Sabbath;
2	They were amazed at His teaching, for He was teaching them as one having authority, and not as the scribes.	1:22 They were amazed at His teaching; for He was teaching them as one having authority, and not as the scribes.	4:32 ~~and~~ they were amazed at His teaching, for ~~His message~~ was ~~with~~ authority.
3	Just then, there was a man in the synagogue possessed by the unclean spirit of a demon.	1:23~ Just then there was a man in ~~their~~ synagogue ~~with an~~ unclean spirit;	4:33~ In the synagogue there was a man possessed by the spirit of ~~an~~ unclean demon,
4	And he cried out with a loud voice, saying, "Let us alone!	1:~23 and he cried out, saying,	4:~33 and he cried out with a loud voice, 4:34~ "Let us alone!
5	"What business do we have with each other, Jesus of Nazareth? Have You come to destroy us?	1:24~ "What business do we have with each other, Jesus of Nazareth? Have You come to destroy us?	4:~34~ What business do we have with each other, Jesus of Nazareth? Have You come to destroy us?
6	"I know who You are - the Holy One of God!"	1:~24 I know who You are - the Holy One of God!"	4:~34 I know who You are - the Holy One of God!"
7	But Jesus rebuked him, saying, "Be quiet, and come out of him."	1:25 ~~And~~ Jesus rebuked him, saying, "Be quiet, and come out of him!"	4:35~ But Jesus rebuked him, saying, "Be quiet, and come out of him!"
8	When the demon had thrown [the man] down <and> into convulsions in the midst of the people, the unclean spirit cried out with a loud voice, and came out of him without [hurting] him.	1:26 Throw~~ing~~ [him] into convulsions, the unclean spirit cried out with a loud voice and came out of him.	4:~35 ~~And~~ when the demon had thrown [him] down in the midst of the people, ~~he~~ came out of him without ~~doing~~ him ~~any~~ [harm].
9	And they were all amazed, and began talking among themselves, <and> saying, "What is this message?	1:27~ They were all amazed, ~~so that they debated~~ among themselves, saying, "What is this?	4:36~ And amaze~~ment came upon them~~ all, and they began talking ~~with one another~~ saying, "What is this message?
10	"A new teaching with authority! For with authority and power He commands even the unclean spirits, and they obey Him, and come out!"	1:~27 A new teaching with authority! He commands even the unclean spirits, and they obey Him."	4:~36 For with authority and power He commands the unclean spirits and ~~they~~ come out."
11	Then [Jesus] got up, and left the synagogue.		4:38~ Then [~~He~~] got up and left the synagogue,
12	And immediately the news about Him spread everywhere, into every locality in all the district[s] surrounding Galilee.	1:28 Immediately the news about Him spread everywhere into all the surrounding district ~~of~~ Galilee.	4:37 And the ~~report~~ about Him ~~was~~ spread~~ing~~ into every locality in the surrounding district.

3 - FIRST YEAR OF MINISTRY

Act 5: **Jesus Heals Many**

Scene 2: **Jesus Heals Simon Peter's Mother-in-Law**

Capernaum, *Galilee* a Sabbath, summer / 30 CE

Verse-By-Verse Edition

#		Matthew	Mark	Luke
1	After they came out of the synagogue, they entered the house of Simon and Andrew, with James and John.		1:29 ~~And~~ ~~immediately~~ after they came out of the synagogue, they ~~came into~~ the house of Simon and Andrew, with James and John.	4:38~ ~~and~~ entered Simon~~'s~~ ~~home~~.
2	When Jesus came into Peter's home, He saw his mother-in-law lying sick in bed <and> suffering from a high fever.	8:14 When Jesus came into Peter's home, He saw his mother-in-law lying sick in bed ~~with~~ a fever.	1:30~ ~~Now~~ Simon's mother-in-law ~~was~~ lying sick ~~with~~ a fever;	4:~38~ ~~Now Simon's~~ mother-in-law ~~was~~ suffering from a high fever,
3	Immediately they spoke to Jesus, and asked Him to help her.		1:~30 and immediately they spoke to Jesus ~~about~~ ~~her~~.	4:~38 and ~~they~~ asked Him to help her.
4	He came to her, and standing over her, He [took] her by the hand, <and> raised her up.	8:15~ He ~~touched~~ her hand,	1:31~ ~~And~~ He came to her and raised her up, [taking] her by the hand,	4:39~ And standing over her,
5	<Then> He rebuked the fever, and it left her; and she immediately got up and waited on them.	8:~15 and ~~the fever~~ left her; and she got up and waited on ~~Him~~.	1:~31 and ~~the fever~~ left her, and she waited on them.	4:~39 He rebuked the fever, and it left her; and she immediately got up and waited on them.

Scene 3: **Many Come To Be Healed**

Capernaum, *Galilee* Saturday evening, summer / 30 CE

#		Matthew	Mark	Luke
1	When evening came, after the sun had set, they began bringing to Him all who were ill with various diseases, and many who were demon-possessed; and the whole city [was] gathered at the door.	8:16~ When evening came, they ~~brought~~ to Him many who were demon-possessed;	1:32 When evening came, after the sun had set, they began bringing to Him all who were ill and ~~those~~ who were demon-possessed. 1:34~1 with various diseases, 1:33 And the whole city [had] gathered at the door.	4:40~ ~~While~~ the sun ~~was~~ setting, all ~~those who had~~ any who were ~~sick~~ with various diseases ~~brought~~ ~~them~~ to Him;
2	Laying His hands on each one of them, [Jesus] healed all who were ill, and He cast out the spirits with a word.	8:~16 and He cast out the spirits with a word, ~~and~~ healed all who were ill.	1:34~ And [He] healed many who were ill 1:34~2 and cast out ~~many~~ ~~demons~~;	4:~40 and laying His hands on each one of them, [He] ~~was~~ healing ~~them~~.
3	This was to fulfill what was spoken through Isaiah the prophet: *"He Himself took our infirmities, and carried away our diseases."* [1]	8:17 This was to fulfill what was spoken through Isaiah the prophet: "He Himself took our infirmities and carried away our diseases."		
4	Demons were also coming out of many, shouting, "You are the Son of God!"			4:41~ Demons also were coming out of many, shouting, "You are the Son of God!"
5	But rebuking them, [Jesus] would not allow the demons to speak, because they knew [that] He was the Christ.		1:~34 and [He] ~~was~~ not ~~permitting~~ the demons to speak, because they knew ~~who~~ He was.	4:~41 But rebuking them, [He] would not allow ~~them~~ to speak, because they knew ~~Him~~ ~~to be~~ the Christ.

1. *Isaiah 53:4*

3 - FIRST YEAR OF MINISTRY

Act 5: Jesus Heals Many

Scene 4: **Preaching And Healing Throughout Galilee**

Galilee   a Sunday, summer / 30 CE

Matthew is the longest Gospel

	Matthew	Mark	Luke
1 Early the <next> morning, while it was still dark, Jesus got up, left the house, and went away to a secluded place, and was praying there.		*1:35* In the early morning, while it was still dark, Jesus got up, left the house, and went away to a secluded place, and was praying there.	*4:42~* When day came, Jesus left and went to a secluded place;
2 The crowds were searching for Him, <and when> Simon and his companions found Him, they said to Him, "Everyone is looking for You."		*1:36* Simon and his companions searched for Him; *1:37* they found Him, and said to Him, "Everyone is looking for You."	*4:~42~* and the crowds were searching for Him,
3 <The crowds> came and tried to keep Him from going away from them, but He said to them, "I must go to the other cities <and> towns nearby, so that I may preach the Kingdom of God there also; for I was sent for this purpose."		*1:38* He said to them, "Let us go somewhere else to the towns nearby, so that I may preach there also; for that is what I came for.	*4:~42* and came to Him and tried to keep Him from going away from them. *4:43* But He said to them, "I must preach the kingdom of God to the other cities also, for I was sent for this purpose.
4 So Jesus was going throughout all of Galilee, teaching in their synagogues, and proclaiming the gospel of the Kingdom;	*4:23~* Jesus was going throughout all Galilee, teaching in their synagogues and proclaiming the gospel of the kingdom,	*1:39~* And He went into their synagogues throughout all Galilee, preaching	*4:44* So He kept on preaching in the synagogues of Judea.
5 and casting out the demons, and healing every kind of disease and every kind of sickness among the people.	*4:~23* and healing every kind of disease and every kind of sickness among the people.	*1:~39* and casting out the demons.	
6 The news about [Jesus] spread throughout all <of> Syria, and they brought to Him all who were ill, <and> those suffering with various diseases and pains, demoniacs, epileptics, <and> paralytics and He healed them.	*4:24* The news about [Him] spread throughout all Syria; and they brought to Him all who were ill, those suffering with various diseases and pains, demoniacs, epileptics, paralytics; and He healed them.		
7 Large crowds followed Him from Galilee and the Decapolis, and from Jerusalem and Judea, and beyond the Jordan.	*4:25* Large crowds followed Him from Galilee and the Decapolis and Jerusalem and Judea and from beyond the Jordan.		

3 - FIRST YEAR OF MINISTRY	Scene 5: **Cleansing A Leper**		Page 47
Act 5: **Jesus Heals Many**	Galilee summer / 30 CE		*The Four Gospels Harmoniously United*

	Matthew	Mark	Luke
1 While He was in one of the cities, there was a man covered with leprosy; and when he saw Jesus, he came and bowed down on his knees before Him, and implored Him, saying, "Lord, if You are willing, You can make me clean!"	8:2 ~~And~~ a leper came ~~to Him~~ and bowed down before Him, and ~~said~~, "Lord, if You are willing, You can make me clean."	1:40 ~~And~~ a leper came ~~to Jesus~~, ~~beseeching~~ Him and ~~falling~~ on his knees before Him, and saying, "If You are willing, You can make me clean."	5:12 While He was in one of the cities, ~~behold~~, there was a man covered with leprosy; and when he saw Jesus, he ~~fell~~ on his ~~face~~ and implored Him, saying, "Lord, if You are willing, You can make me clean."
2 Moved with compassion, Jesus stretched out His hand and touched him, and said, "I am willing; be cleansed."	8:3~ Jesus stretched out His hand and touched him, sa~~ying~~, "I am willing; be cleansed."	1:41 Moved with compassion, Jesus stretched out His hand and touched him, and said ~~to him~~, |"I am willing; be cleansed."	5:13~ ~~And He~~ stretched out His hand and touched him, sa~~ying~~, "I am willing; be cleansed."
3 Immediately the leprosy left [the man], and he was cleansed.	8:~3 ~~And~~ immediately ~~his~~ leprosy was cleansed.	1:42 Immediately the leprosy left [~~him~~] and he was cleansed.	5:~13 ~~And~~ immediately the leprosy left [~~him~~].
4 Jesus sent Him away, and sternly ordered him, [saying], "See that you tell no one; but go, and show yourself to the priest, and *present the offering for your cleansing that Moses commanded,*[1] as a testimony to them."	8:4 ~~And~~ Jesus [said] ~~to him~~, "See that you tell no one; but go, show yourself to the priest and present the offering that Moses commanded, as a testimony to them."	1:43 ~~And He~~ sternly ~~warn~~ed him and ~~immediately~~ sent him away, 1:44 ~~and He~~ [said] ~~to him~~, "See that you ~~say nothing to any~~one; but go, show yourself to the priest and offer for your cleansing ~~what~~ Moses commanded, as a testimony to them."	5:14 ~~And He~~ ordered him ~~to~~ tell no one, "But go and show yourself to the priest and ~~make an~~ offering for your cleansing, ~~just as~~ Moses commanded as a testimony to them."
5 But [the man] went out and began to proclaim it freely, and the news about [Jesus] was spreading around even farther.		1:45~ But [he] went out and began to proclaim it freely and ~~to~~ spread the news around,	5:15~ ~~But~~ the news about [~~Him~~] was spreading even farther,
6 And large crowds were gathering to Him from everywhere, to hear Him, and to be healed of their sicknesses;		1:~45 and ~~they~~ were ~~com~~ing to Him from everywhere.	5:~15 and large crowds were gathering to hear Him and to be healed of their sicknesses.
7 to such an extent that Jesus could no longer publicly enter a city, but stayed out in <the> unpopulated areas, <where> [He] would often slip away <in>to the wilderness and pray.		1:~45 to such an extent that Jesus could no longer publicly enter a city, but stayed out in unpopulated areas;	5:16 ~~But~~ [Jesus] ~~Himself~~ would often slip away to the wilderness and pray.

1. *Leviticus 14:1-32*

3 - FIRST YEAR OF MINISTRY

Act 5: **Jesus Heals Many**

Scene 6: **Resurrecting The Son of A Widow**

Nain, *Galilee*   summer / 30 CE

Get the 552 page **Word-For-Word** Edition

	Luke
1 Soon afterwards [Jesus] went to a city called Nain; and His disciples were going along with Him, accompanied by a large crowd.	7:11 Soon afterwards [He] went to a city called Nain; and His disciples were going along with Him, accompanied by a large crowd.
2 As He approached the gate of the city, a dead man was being carried out, the only son of his mother.	7:12~ Now as He approached the gate of the city, a dead man was being carried out, the only son of his mother,
3 She was a widow, and a sizeable crowd from the city was with her.	7:~12 and she was a widow; and a sizeable crowd from the city was with her.
4 When the Lord saw her, He felt compassion for her, and said to her, "Do not weep."	7:13 When the Lord saw her, He felt compassion for her, and said to her, "Do not weep."
5 [Then] He came up and touched the coffin, and the bearers came to a halt.	7:14~ [And] He came up and touched the coffin; and the bearers came to a halt.
6 [Jesus] said, "Young man, I say to you, arise!" <and> the dead man sat up, and began to speak.	7:~14 And [He] said, "Young man, I say to you, arise!" 7:15~ The dead man sat up and began to speak.
7 Jesus gave him back to his mother, <and> fear gripped them all.	7:~15 And Jesus gave him back to his mother. 7:16~ Fear gripped them all,
8 And they began glorifying God, saying, "A great prophet has arisen among us!" and, "God has visited His people!"	7:~16 and they began glorifying God, saying, "A great prophet has arisen among us!" and, "God has visited His people!"
9 This report concerning [Jesus] went out all over Judea, and in[to] all <of> the surrounding district.	7:17 This report concerning [Him] went out all over Judea and in all the surrounding district.
10 <Then> the disciples of John <the Baptist> reported to him about all these things.	7:18 The disciples of John reported to him about all these things.

3 - FIRST YEAR OF MINISTRY
Act 6: John Enquires About Jesus

Scene 1: John Asks Jesus, "Are You The Expected One?"
Capernaum, *Galilee*   summer / 30 CE

Through The Gospel - Verse-By-Verse

	Matthew	Luke
1 When John, while imprisoned, heard of the works of Christ, he summon[ed] two of his disciples, <and> sent them to the Lord, saying, "Are You the Expected One, or do we look for someone else?"	11:2 ~~Now~~ when John, while imprisoned, heard of the works of Christ, he sent ~~word by~~ his disciples	7:19 Summon[~~ing~~] two of his disciples, ~~John~~ sent them to the Lord, saying, "Are You the Expected One, or do we look for someone else?
2 When the men came to [Jesus], they said to Him, "John the Baptist has sent us to ask You, 'Are you the Expected One, or shall we look for someone else?' "	11:3 ~~and~~ said to Him, "Are You the Expected One, or shall we look for someone else?	7:20 When the men came to [~~Him~~], they said, "John the Baptist has sent us to You, ~~to~~ ask, 'Are You the Expected One, or ~~do~~ we look for someone else?' "
3 At that very time [Jesus] cured many people of diseases and afflictions, and evil spirits; and He gave sight to many who were blind.		7:21 At that very time [~~He~~] cured many people of diseases and afflictions and evil spirits; and He gave sight to many who were blind.
4 He answered, and said to them, "Go and report to John what you see and hear: *the blind receive sight and the lame walk, the lepers are cleansed and the deaf hear, the dead are raised up,*[1] *and the poor have the gospel preached to them.*[2]	11:4 ~~Jesus~~ answered and said to them, "Go and report to John what you hear and see: 11:5 the blind receive sight and the lame walk, the lepers are cleansed and the deaf hear, the dead are raised up, and the poor have the gospel preached to them.	7:22 ~~And~~ He answered and said to them, "Go and report to John what you ~~have~~ ~~seen~~ and ~~heard~~: the blind receive sight, the lame walk, the lepers are cleansed, and the deaf hear, the dead are raised up, the poor have the gospel preached to them.
5 "And blessed is he who does not take offense at Me."	11:6 "And blessed is he who does not take offense at Me."	7:23 "Blessed is he who does not take offense at Me."

1. Isaiah 29:18; 35:5-6   2. Isaiah 61:1

3 - FIRST YEAR OF MINISTRY

Act 6: **John Enquires About Jesus**

Scene 2: **John Is Elijah Who Was To Come**

Capernaum, *Galilee*   summer / 30 CE

The United Gospel   Page 50

	Matthew	Luke
1 When the messengers of John had left, Jesus began to speak to the crowds about John.	11:7~ ~~As these men were going away~~, Jesus began to speak to the crowds about John,	7:24~ When the messengers of John had left, ~~He~~ began to speak to the crowds about John,
2 <He asked them,> "What did you go out into the wilderness to see? A reed shaken by the wind?	11:~7 "What did you go out into the wilderness to see? A reed shaken by the wind?	7:24 "What did you go out into the wilderness to see? A reed shaken by the wind?
3 "But what did you go out to see? A man dressed in soft clothing?	11:8~ "But what did you go out to see? A man dressed in soft clothing?	7:25~ "But what did you go out to see? A man dressed in soft clothing?
4 "Those who are splendidly [dress]ed [in] soft clothing, and live in luxury, are found in royal palaces.	11:~8 Those who [~~wear~~] soft clothing are in ~~kings'~~ palaces!	7:~25 Those who are splendidly [~~cloth~~]ed and live in luxury are found in royal palaces!
5 "But what did you go out to see? A prophet? Yes, I tell you, and one who is more than a Prophet.	11:9 "But what did you go out to see? A prophet? Yes, I tell you, and one who is more than a prophet.	7:26 "But what did you go out to see? A prophet? Yes, I ~~say to~~ you, and one who is more than a prophet.
6 "This is the One about whom it is written, *'Behold, I send My messenger ahead of You, who will prepare Your way before You.'* [1]	11:10 "This is the one about whom it is written, 'Behold, I send My messenger ahead of You, who will prepare Your way before You.'	7:27 "This is the one about whom it is written, 'Behold, I send My messenger ahead of You, who will prepare Your way before You.'
7 "Truly I say to you, among those born of women there has not arisen anyone greater than John the Baptist!	11:11~ "Truly I say to you, among those born of women there has not arisen anyone greater than John the Baptist!	7:28~ "I say to you, among those born of women there is ~~no~~ one greater than John;
8 "Yet the one who is least in the Kingdom of Heaven is greater than he.	11:~11 Yet the one who is least in the kingdom of heaven is greater than he.	7:~28 yet ~~he~~ who is least in the kingdom of ~~God~~ is greater than he."
9 "From the days of John the Baptist until now, the Kingdom of Heaven suffers violence, and violent men take it by force;	11:12 "From the days of John the Baptist until now the kingdom of heaven suffers violence, and violent men take it by force.	
10 "for all the prophets, and the Law, prophesied until John.	11:13 "For all the prophets and the Law prophesied until John.	
11 "And if you are willing to accept it, John himself is Elijah who was to come.	11:14 "And if you are willing to accept it, John himself is Elijah who was to come.	
12 "He who has ears to hear, let him hear!"	11:15 "He who has ears to hear, let him hear.	
13 When all the people and the tax collectors heard this, they acknowledged God's justice, having been baptized with the baptism of John.		7:29 When all the people and the tax collectors heard this, they acknowledged God's justice, having been baptized with the baptism of John.
14 But the Pharisees and the lawyers rejected God's purpose for themselves, not having been baptized by John.		7:30 But the Pharisees and the lawyers rejected God's purpose for themselves, not having been baptized by John.

1. Malachi 3:1

3 - FIRST YEAR OF MINISTRY

Act 6: **John Enquires About Jesus**

Scene 3: **To What Shall I Compare This Generation?**

Capernaum, *Galilee*   summer / 30 CE

Page 51

Mark is the shortest, and likely written first

	Matthew	Luke
1 <Then Jesus said,> "To what shall I compare the men of this generation, and what are they like?	*11:16~* "~~But~~ to what shall I compare this generation?	*7:31* "To what ~~then~~ shall I compare the men of this generation, and what are they like?
2 "They are like children sitting in the market place, who call out to one another, and say, 'We played the flute for you, and you did not dance; we sang a dirge, and you did not weep.'	*11:~16* ~~It is~~ like children sitting in the market place~~s~~, who call out to ~~the~~ other ~~children~~, *11:17* and say, 'We played the flute for you, and you did not dance; we sang a dirge, and you did not ~~mourn~~.'	*7:32* "They are like children who sit in the market place ~~and~~ call to one another, and ~~they~~ say, 'We played the flute for you, and you did not dance; we sang a dirge, and you did not weep.'
3 "For John the Baptist has come neither eating bread nor drinking wine, and they say, 'He has a demon!'	*11:18* "For John ~~came~~ neither eating nor drinking, and they say, 'He has a demon!'	*7:33* "For John the Baptist has come eating ~~no~~ bread ~~and~~ drinking ~~no~~ wine, and ~~you~~ say, 'He has a demon!'
4 "The Son of Man has come eating and drinking, and you say, 'Behold, a gluttonous man and a drunkard, a friend of tax collectors and sinners.'	*11:19~* "The Son of Man ~~came~~ eating and drinking, and ~~they~~ say, 'Behold, a gluttonous man and a drunkard, a friend of tax collectors and sinners!'	*7:34* "The Son of Man has come eating and drinking, and you say, 'Behold, a gluttonous man and a drunkard, a friend of tax collectors and sinners!'
5 "Yet wisdom is vindicated by all <of> her deeds."	*11:~19* Yet wisdom is vindicated by her deeds."	*7:35* "Yet wisdom is vindicated by all her ~~children~~."

3 - FIRST YEAR OF MINISTRY

Act 7: **Jesus Attends A Feast**

Scene 1: **Jesus Heals A Man at The Bethesda Pool**

Bethesda Pool, Jerusalem, *Judea*   a Sabbath, summer / 30 CE

The Greatest Story Ever Told

	John
1 After [this], there was a feast of the Jews, and Jesus went up to Jerusalem.	5:1 After [these things] there was a feast of the Jews, and Jesus went up to Jerusalem.
2 Now there is in Jerusalem by the sheep gate a pool, which in Hebrew is called *Bethesda*,[1.] having five porticoes.	5:2 Now there is in Jerusalem by the sheep gate a pool, which is called in Hebrew Bethesda, having five porticoes.
3 In these lay a multitude of those who were sick, blind, lame, and withered.	5:3~ In these lay a multitude of those who were sick, blind, lame, and withered,
4 <They were> waiting for the mov[ement] of the waters, for an angel of the Lord went down at certain seasons into the pool, and stirred up the water; <and> whoever then first stepped in after the stirring up of the water was made well from whatever disease with which he was afflicted.	5:~3 {waiting for the mov[ing] of the waters; 5:4 for an angel of the Lord went down at certain seasons into the pool and stirred up the water; whoever then first, after the stirring up of the water, stepped in was made well from whatever disease with which he was afflicted.}
5 A man was there who had been ill for thirty-eight years.	5:5 A man was there who had been ill for thirty-eight years.
6 When Jesus saw him lying there, and knew that he had been in that condition <for> a long time, He said to him, "Do you wish to get well?"	5:6 When Jesus saw him lying there, and knew that he had already been a long time in that condition, He said to him, "Do you wish to get well?"
7 The sick man answered, "Sir, I have no [one] to put me into the pool when the water is stirred up, but while I am coming, another steps down before me."	5:7 The sick man answered Him, "Sir, I have no [man] to put me into the pool when the water is stirred up, but while I am coming, another steps down before me."
8 Jesus said to him, "Get up, pick up your pallet, and walk."	5:8 Jesus said to him, "Get up, pick up your pallet and walk."
9 Immediately the man became well, and <he> picked up his pallet, and began to walk.	5:9~ Immediately the man became well, and picked up his pallet and began to walk.
10 Now it was the Sabbath on that day, so the Jews were saying to the man who was cured, "*It is the Sabbath, and it is not permissible for you to carry your pallet.*"[2.]	5:~9 Now it was the Sabbath on that day. 5:10 So the Jews were saying to the man who was cured, "It is the Sabbath, and it is not permissible for you to carry your pallet."
11 But he answered them, "He who made me well was the one who said to me, 'Pick up your pallet, and walk.'"	5:11 But he answered them, "He who made me well was the one who said to me, 'Pick up your pallet and walk.'"
12 They asked him, "Who is the man who said to you, 'Pick up your pallet and walk'?" But the man who was healed did not know who it was, for Jesus had slipped away <into> [the] crowd.	5:12 They asked him, "Who is the man who said to you, 'Pick up your pallet and walk'?" 5:13 But the man who was healed did not know who it was, for Jesus had slipped away while there was [a] crowd in that place.
13 Afterward, Jesus found him in the Temple, and said to him, "Behold, you have become well. Do not sin anymore, so that nothing worse happens to you."	5:14 Afterward Jesus found him in the temple and said to him, "Behold, you have become well; do not sin anymore, so that nothing worse happens to you."

1. Hebrew meaning House of "Mercy", "Kindness" or "Grace"   2. Exodus 20:8-10; 31:15 / Deuteronomy 5:12-14 / Jeremiah 17:21-22

3 - FIRST YEAR OF MINISTRY | Scene 2: **The Father And The Son**

Act 7: **Jesus Attends A Feast** — Jerusalem, *Judea*   a Sabbath, summer / 30 CE

The Unified Gospel Story of Jesus

	John
1 The man went away and told the Jews that it was Jesus who had made him well.	5:15 The man went away, and told the Jews that it was Jesus who had made him well.
2 [So] the Jews were persecuting Jesus, because He was doing these things on the Sabbath.	5:16 [For this reason] the Jews were persecuting Jesus, because He was doing these things on the Sabbath.
3 But [Jesus] answered them, "My Father is working until now, and I Myself am working."	5:17 But [He] answered them, "My Father is working until now, and I Myself am working."
4 [So] the Jews were seeking all the more to kill [Jesus], because not only was He breaking the Sabbath, but <He> was also calling God His own Father, <thus> making Himself equal with God.	5:18 [For this reason therefore] the Jews were seeking all the more to kill [Him], because He not only was breaking the Sabbath, but also was calling God His own Father, making Himself equal with God.
5 [But] Jesus answered, and [said] to them, "Truly, truly, I say to you, the Son can do nothing of Himself, unless it is something <that> He sees the Father <is> doing;	5:19~ [Therefore] Jesus answered and was [saying] to them, "Truly, truly, I say to you, the Son can do nothing of Himself, unless it is something He sees the Father doing;
6 "for whatever the Father does, these things the Son also does, in <the> [same] [way].	5:~19 for whatever the Father does, these things the Son also does in [like] [manner].
7 "For the Father loves the Son, and shows Him all <of the> things that He Himself is doing;	5:20 "For the Father loves the Son, and shows Him all things that He Himself is doing;
8 "and the Father will show Him greater works than these, so that you will marvel!	5:~20 and the Father will show Him greater works than these, so that you will marvel.
9 "For just as the Father raises the dead, and gives them life, even so the Son also gives life to whom He wishes.	5:21 "For just as the Father raises the dead and gives them life, even so the Son also gives life to whom He wishes.
10 "For the Father <does> not judge anyone, but He has given all judgment to the Son, so that all will honor the Son, even as they honor the Father.	5:22 "For not even the Father judges anyone, but He has given all judgment to the Son, 5:23~ so that all will honor the Son even as they honor the Father.
11 "He who does not honor the Son does not honor the Father who sent Him."	5:~23 He who does not honor the Son does not honor the Father who sent Him."

3 - FIRST YEAR OF MINISTRY	Scene 3: **Those Who Believe My Words Will Live**	Page 54
Act 7: **Jesus Attends A Feast**	Jerusalem, *Judea* a Sabbath, summer / 30 CE	*The Full Gospel*

	John
1 "Truly, truly, I say to you, he who hears My word[s], and believes Him who sent Me, has eternal life, and does not come into judgment, but has passed out of death <and> into life.	5:24 "Truly, truly, I say to you, he who hears My word, and believes Him who sent Me, has eternal life, and does not come into judgment, but has passed out of death into life.
2 "Truly, truly, I say to you, <that> an hour is coming, and now is, when the dead will hear the voice of the Son of God, and those who hear will live.	5:25 "Truly, truly, I say to you, an hour is coming and now is, when the dead will hear the voice of the Son of God, and those who hear will live.
3 "For just as the Father has life in Himself, even so He gave the Son to also have life in Himself;	5:26 "For just as the Father has life in Himself, even so He gave to the Son also to have life in Himself;
4 "and *because He is the Son of Man, He gave Him authority to execute judgment.*[1.]	5:27 and He gave Him authority to execute judgment, because He is the Son of Man.
5 "Do not marvel at this, *for an hour is coming in which all who are in the tombs will hear His voice, and will come forth;*[2.]	5:28 "Do not marvel at this; for an hour is coming, in which all who are in the tombs will hear His voice, 5:29~ and will come forth;
6 "*those who did good deeds to a resurrection of life,*	5:~29~ those who did ~~the~~ good deeds to a resurrection of life,
7 "<and> *those who committed evil deeds, to a resurrection of judgment.*[3.]	5:~29 those who committed ~~the~~ evil deeds to a resurrection of judgment.
8 "I can do nothing on My own initiative. As I hear, I judge; and My judgment is just, because I do not seek My own will, but the will of Him who sent Me."	5:30 "I can do nothing on My own initiative. As I hear, I judge; and My judgment is just, because I do not seek My own will, but the will of Him who sent Me."

1. Daniel 7:13-14   2. Isaiah 26:29   3. Daniel 12:2

Scene 4: My Testimony About Myself

3 - FIRST YEAR OF MINISTRY
Act 7: **Jesus Attends A Feast**
Jerusalem, *Judea* — a Sabbath, summer / 30 CE

#	Merged	John
1	"If I alone testify about Myself, My testimony is not true.	5:31 "If I alone testify about Myself, My testimony is not true.
2	"There is another who testifies of Me, and I know that the testimony which He gives about Me is true.	5:32 "There is another who testifies of Me, and I know that the testimony which He gives about Me is true.
3	"You have sent to John, and he has testified to the truth.	5:33 "You have sent to John, and he has testified to the truth.
4	"But the testimony which I receive is not from man, but I say these things so that you may be saved.	5:34 "But the testimony which I receive is not from man, but I say these things so that you may be saved.
5	"[John] was the lamp that was burning and shining, and you were willing to rejoice for a while in his Light.	5:35 "[~~He~~] was the lamp that was burning and ~~was~~ shining and you were willing to rejoice for a while in his light.
6	"But the testimony which I have is greater than the testimony of John;	5:36~ "But the testimony which I have is greater than the testimony of John;
7	"for the works which the Father has given Me to accomplish - the very works that I do - testify about Me, that the Father has sent Me.	5:~36 for the works which the Father has given Me to accomplish - the very works that I do - testify about Me, that the Father has sent Me.
8	"And the Father who sent Me, He has testified of Me.	5:37~ "And the Father who sent Me, He has testified of Me.
9	"You have neither heard His voice at any time, nor seen His form.	5:~37 You have neither heard His voice at any time nor seen His form.
10	"You do not have His Word abiding in you, for you do not believe Him whom He <has> sent.	5:38 "You do not have His word abiding in you, for you do not believe Him whom He sent.
11	"You search the Scriptures because you think that in them you have eternal life; it is these that testify about Me;	5:39 "You search the Scriptures because you think that in them you have eternal life; it is these that testify about Me;
12	"and <yet> you are unwilling to come to Me, so that you may have life.	5:40 and you are unwilling to come to Me so that you may have life.
13	"I do not receive glory from men;	5:41 "I do not receive glory from men;
14	"but I know you, that you do not have the love of God in yourselves.	5:42 but I know you, that you do not have the love of God in yourselves.
15	"I have come in My Father's Name, and you do not receive Me;	5:43~ "I have come in My Father's name, and you do not receive Me;
16	"<but> if another comes in his own name, you will receive him.	5:~43 if another comes in his own name, you will receive him.
17	"How can you believe, when you receive glory from one another, and you do not seek the glory that is from The One and only God?	5:44 "How can you believe, when you receive glory from one another and you do not seek the glory that is from the one and only God?
18	"Do not think that I will accuse you before The Father; the One who accuses you is Moses, in whom you have set your hope.	5:45 "Do not think that I will accuse you before the Father; the one who accuses you is Moses, in whom you have set your hope.
19	"For if you believed Moses, you would believe Me, for *he wrote about Me*.[1]	5:46 "For if you believed Moses, you would believe Me, for he wrote about Me.
20	"But if you do not believe his writings, how will you believe My words?"	5:47 "But if you do not believe his writings, how will you believe My words?"

1. Deuteronomy 18:15, 18

	3 - FIRST YEAR OF MINISTRY	Scene 5: **The Parable of The Good Samaritan**	Page 56

Act 7: **Jesus Attends A Feast** — Jerusalem, *Judea* — a Sabbath, summer / 30 CE — *The Four Gospels United as One*

		Luke
1	A lawyer stood up, and put [Jesus] to the test, saying, "Teacher, what shall I do to inherit eternal life?"	10:25 ~~And~~ a lawyer stood up and put [~~Him~~] to the test, saying, "Teacher, what shall I do to inherit eternal life?
2	[Jesus] said to him, "What is written in the Law? How does it read to you?"	10:26 ~~And~~ [~~He~~] said to him, "What is written in the Law? How does it read to you?"
3	He answered, *"You shall love the Lord your God with all your heart, and with all your soul, and with all your strength, and with all your mind;* [1.]	10:27~ ~~And~~ he answered, "You shall love the Lord your God with all your heart, and with all your soul, and with all your strength, and with all your mind;
4	"and *your neighbor as yourself."* [2.]	10:~27 and your neighbor as yourself."
5	[Jesus] said to him, "You have answered correctly. Do this and you will live."	10:28 ~~And~~ [~~He~~] said to him, "You have answered correctly; do this and you will live."
6	But wishing to justify himself, [the lawyer] said to [Him], "And who is my neighbor?"	10:29 But wishing to justify himself, [~~he~~] said to [~~Jesus~~], "And who is my neighbor?"
7	Jesus replied, and said, "A man was going down from Jerusalem to Jericho, and <he> fell among robbers; and they stripped him and beat him, and went away leaving him half dead.	10:30 Jesus replied and said, "A man was going down from Jerusalem to Jericho, and fell among robbers, and they stripped him and beat him, and went away leaving him half dead.
8	"By chance a priest was [traveling] on that road, and when he saw [the wounded man], he passed by on the other side.	10:31 "~~And~~ by chance a priest was [~~going~~] ~~down~~ on that road, and when he saw [~~him~~], he passed by on the other side.
9	"Likewise a Levite, when he came to the place and saw him, <he> also passed by on the other side.	10:32 "Likewise a Levite also, when he came to the place and saw him, passed by on the other side.
10	"But a Samaritan who was on a journey came upon him; and when he saw him he felt compassion, and <he> came to him, and bandaged up his wounds, pouring oil and wine on them.	10:33 "But a Samaritan, who was on a journey, came upon him; and when he saw him, he felt compassion, 10:34~ and came to him and bandaged up his wounds, pouring oil and wine on them;
11	"[Then] he put him on his own beast, and brought him to [the] inn, and took care of him.	10:~34 [~~and~~] he put him on his own beast, and brought him to [~~an~~] inn and took care of him.
12	"On the next day, he took out two denarii and gave them to the innkeeper, and said, 'Take care of him; and whatever more you spend, I will repay you when I return.'	10:35 "On the next day he took out two denarii and gave them to the innkeeper and said, 'Take care of him; and whatever more you spend, when I return I will repay you.'
13	"Which of these three do you think proved to be a neighbor to the man who fell into the robbers' hands?"	10:36 "Which of these three do you think proved to be a neighbor to the man who fell into the robbers' hands?"
14	[The lawyer] said, "The one who showed mercy toward him."	10:37~ ~~And~~ [~~he~~] said, "The one who showed mercy toward him."
15	Then Jesus said to him, "Go, and do the same."	10:~37 Then Jesus said to him, "Go and do the same."

1. Deuteronomy 6:5-6; 10:12; 30:6   2. Leviticus 19:18, 34

3 - FIRST YEAR OF MINISTRY

Act 7: **Jesus Attends A Feast**

Scene 6: **Jesus Visits Martha and Mary**

Bethany, *Judea*   summer / 30 BCE

93% of Mark is paralleled in the other three

	Luke
1 As they were traveling [Jesus] entered a village, and a woman named Martha welcomed Him into her home.	10:38 ~~Now~~ as they were traveling ~~along~~, [He] entered a village; and a woman named Martha welcomed Him into her home.
2 She had a sister [nam]ed Mary, who was seated at the Lord's feet, <and> listening to His word[s].	10:39 She had a sister [~~call~~]ed Mary, who was seated at the Lord's feet, listening to His word.
3 But Martha was distracted with all <of> her preparations; and she came to [Jesus], and said, "Lord, do You not care that my sister has left me to do all <of> the serving alone? Tell her to help me!"	10:40 But Martha was distracted with all her preparations; and she came ~~up~~ to [Him] and said, "Lord, do You not care that my sister has left me to do all the serving alone? ~~Then~~ tell her to help me."
4 But the Lord answered, and said to her, "Martha, Martha, you are worried and bothered about so many things, but only one thing is necessary;	10:41 But the Lord answered and said to her, "Martha, Martha, you are worried and bothered about so many things; 10:42~ but only one thing is necessary,
5 "for Mary has chosen the good part, which shall not be taken away from her."	10:~42 for Mary has chosen the good part, which shall not be taken away from her."

3 - **FIRST YEAR OF MINISTRY**

Act 8: **Events In Capernaum**

Scene 1: **The Man Paralyzed In A Bed**
Capernaum, *Galilee*   summer / 30 CE

A Unified Harmony of The Gospels

	Matthew	Mark	Luke
1 When [Jesus] [returned] to Capernaum several days [later], it was heard that He was at home, and so many [had] gathered together that there was no longer <any> room, not even near the door.		2:1 When [He] [had come back] to Capernaum several days [afterward], it was heard that He was at home. 2:2~ And many [were] gathered together, so that there was no longer room, not even near the door; and	5:17~ One day
2 He was speaking the Word to them, and there were some Pharisees and teachers of the law sitting there who had come from every village of Galilee and Judea, and from Jerusalem.		2:~2 He was speaking the word to them.	5:~17~ He was teaching and there were some Pharisees and teachers of the law sitting there, who had come from every village of Galilee and Judea and from Jerusalem;
3 The power of the Lord was present for Him to perform healing, and they brought to Him a man who was paralyzed, lying on a bed carried by four men.	9:2~ And they brought to Him a paralytic lying on a bed.	2:3 And they came bringing to Him a paralytic, carried by four men.	5:~17 and the power of the Lord was present for Him to perform healing. 5:18~ And some men were carrying a man who was paralyzed; on a bed
4 They were trying to bring him in and to set him down in front of [Jesus], but being unable <to> find any way to bring him in because of the crowd, they went up on <to> the roof, <and> removed the [tiles] above Him.		2:4~ Being unable to get to Him because of the crowd, they removed the [roof] above Him;	5:~18 and they were trying to bring him in and to set him down in front of [Him]. 5:19~ But not finding any way to bring him in because of the crowd, they went up on the roof
5 When they had dug an opening, they let the paralytic down through the tiles with the stretcher on which <he> was lying, into the middle of the crowd, in front of Jesus.		2:~4 and when they had dug an opening, they let down the pallet on which the paralytic was lying.	5:~19 and let him down through the tiles with his stretcher, into the middle of the crowd, in front of Jesus.
6 Seeing their faith, Jesus said to the paralytic, "Take courage, son; your sins are forgiven."	9:~2 Seeing their faith, Jesus said to the paralytic, "Take courage, son; your sins are forgiven."	2:5 And Jesus seeing their faith said to the paralytic, "Son, your sins are forgiven."	5:20 Seeing their faith, He said, "Friend, your sins are forgiven you."

	3 - **FIRST YEAR OF MINISTRY**	Scene 2: **Jesus Is Accused of Blasphemy**	Page 59
	Act 8: **Events In Capernaum**	Capernaum, *Galilee* summer / 30 CE	*The United Gospel Verse-By-Verse*

#		Matthew	Mark	Luke
1	Some of the scribes and Pharisees <who> were sitting there began to reason in their hearts, <and> say to themselves, "Why does this man speak that way? This fellow is blaspheming!	9:3 ~~And~~ some of the scribes said to themselves, "This fellow blasphem~~es~~."	2:6 ~~But~~ some of the scribes were sitting there ~~and~~ reasoning in their hearts, 2:7~ "Why does this man speak that way? ~~He~~ is blaspheming;	5:21~ The scribes and ~~the~~ Pharisees began to reason, say~~ing~~,
2	"Who is this man who speaks blasphemies? *Who can forgive sins, but God alone?*" [1]		2:~7 who can forgive sins but God alone?"	5:~21 "Who is this man who speaks blasphemies? Who can forgive sins, but God alone?"
3	Immediately Jesus <was> aware in His Spirit that they were reasoning [this] way within themselves; <and He> answered, and said to them, "Why are you thinking evil about these things in your hearts?	9:4 ~~And~~ Jesus ~~knowing~~ ~~their~~ ~~thoughts~~ said, "Why are you thinking evil in your hearts?	2:8 Immediately Jesus, aware in His spirit that they were reasoning [that] way within themselves, said to them, "Why are you ~~reasoning~~ about these things in your hearts?	5:22 ~~But~~ Jesus, aware ~~of~~ ~~their~~ reasonings, answered and said to them, "Why are you ~~reasoning~~ in your hearts?
4	Which is easier to say? 'Your sins are forgiven', or to say, 'Get up, and pick up your pallet, and walk'?	9:5 "Which is easier, to say, 'Your sins are forgiven,' or to say, 'Get up, and walk'?	2:9 "Which is easier, to say ~~to the paralytic~~, 'Your sins are forgiven'; or to say, 'Get up, and pick up your pallet and walk'?	5:23 "Which is easier, to say, 'Your sins ~~have~~ ~~been~~ forgiven ~~you~~,' or to say, 'Get up, and walk'?
5	"But, so that you may know that the Son of Man has authority on earth to forgive sins," He then said to the paralytic, "I say to you, get up, and pick up your pallet, and go home."	9:6 "But so that you may know that the Son of Man has authority on earth to forgive sins" - then He said to the paralytic, "Get up, pick up your ~~bed~~ and go home."	2:10 "But so that you may know that the Son of Man has authority on earth to forgive sins" - He said to the paralytic, 2:11 "I say to you, get up, pick up your pallet and go home."	5:24 "But, so that you may know that the Son of Man has authority on earth to forgive sins" - He said to the paralytic - "I say to you, get up, and pick up your ~~stretcher~~ and go home."
6	And immediately [the man] got up before them, and picked up what he had been lying on, and went home, glorifying God in the sight of everyone.	9:7 And [he] got up and went home.	2:12~ And immediately [he] got up and picked up ~~the pallet~~ and went ~~out~~ in the sight of everyone,	5:25 Immediately [he] got up before them, and picked up what he had been lying on, and went home glorifying God.
7	When the crowds saw this, they were all struck with astonishment, and <they> began glorifying God, who had given such authority to men.	9:8 ~~But~~ when the crowds saw this, they were ~~awe~~struck, and ~~glori~~fied God, who had given such authority to men.	2:~12~ ~~so that~~ they were all ~~amazed~~ and ~~were~~ glorifying God,	5:26~ They were all struck with astonishment and began glorifying God;
8	And they were filled with [awe], saying, "We have seen remarkable things today. We have never seen anything like this!"		2:~12 saying, "We have never seen anything like this."	5:~26 and they were filled with [~~fear~~], saying, "We have seen remarkable things today."
9	[Jesus] went out by the seashore; and all the people were coming to Him, and He was teaching them.		2:13 ~~And~~ [He] went out ~~again~~ by the seashore; and all the people were coming to Him, and He was teaching them.	

1. Isaiah 43:25

3 - FIRST YEAR OF MINISTRY

Act 8: **Events In Capernaum**

Scene 3: **Jesus Calls Matthew Levi**

Capernaum, *Galilee*   summer / 30 CE

The Story of The Life of Jesus

	Matthew	Mark	Luke
1 After that, Jesus went on from there, and as He passed by He noticed a tax collector named Matthew Levi sitting in the tax collector's booth; and He said to him, "Follow Me."	9:9~ As Jesus went on from there, He saw a man called Matthew, sitting in the tax collector's booth; and He said to him, "Follow Me!"	2:14~ As He passed by, He saw Levi the son of Alphaeus [1.] sitting in the tax booth, and He said to him, "Follow Me!"	5:27 After that He went out and noticed a tax collector named Levi sitting in the tax booth, and He said to him, "Follow Me."
2 [Matthew] got up, left everything behind, and began to follow [Jesus].	9:~9 And [he] got up and followed [Him].	2:~14 And [he] got up and followed [Him].	5:28 And [he] left everything behind, and got up and began to follow [Him].

1. James, not Matthew, is the son of Alphaeus - Matthew 10:3 / Mark 3:18 / Luke 6:15 / Acts 1:13, unless both men had a father named Alphaeus, or Alphaeus was the father of both James and also Matthew Levi

Scene 4: **Matthew Gives A Reception For Jesus**

Capernaum, *Galilee*   summer / 30 CE

	Matthew	Mark	Luke
1 Then [Matthew] gave a [large] reception for [Jesus] in his house.	9:10~ Then in the house	2:~15~ in his house,	5:29~ And [Levi] gave a [big] reception for [Him] in his house;
2 And as Jesus was reclining at the table, behold, a great crowd of many tax collectors and sinners came, and were dining with Jesus and His disciples; for there were many of them, and they were following Him.	9:~10 it happened that as Jesus was reclining at the table behold, many tax collectors and sinners came and were dining with Jesus and His disciples.	2:15~ And it happened that He was reclining at the table 2:~15 and many tax collectors and sinners were dining with Jesus and His disciples; for there were many of them, and they were following Him.	5:~29 and there was a great crowd of tax collectors and other people who were reclining at the table with them.
3 When the Pharisees and their scribes saw that [Jesus] was eating with the tax collectors and sinners, they began grumbling, <and> said to His disciples, "Why is your Teacher eating and drinking with the tax collectors and sinners?"	9:11 When the Pharisees saw this, they said to His disciples, "Why is your Teacher eating with the tax collectors and sinners?"	2:16 When the scribes of the Pharisees saw that [He] was eating with the sinners and tax collectors, they said to His disciples, "Why is He eating and drinking with tax collectors and sinners?"	5:30 The Pharisees and their scribes began grumbling at His disciples, saying, "Why do you eat and drink with the tax collectors and sinners?
4 When Jesus heard this, He answered and said to them, "It is not those who are healthy who need a physician, but those who are sick.	9:12 But when Jesus heard this, He said, "It is not those who are healthy who need a physician, but those who are sick.	2:17~ And hearing this, Jesus said to them, "It is not those who are healthy who need a physician, but those who are sick;	5:31 And Jesus answered and said to them, "It is not those who are well who need a physician, but those who are sick.
5 "But go and learn what this means: '*I desire compassion, and not sacrifice,*' [1.]	9:13~ "But go and learn what this means: 'I desire compassion, and not sacrifice,'		
6 "for I have not come to call the righteous, but sinners, to repentance."	9:~13 for I did not come to call the righteous, but sinners."	2:~17 I did not come to call the righteous, but sinners."	5:32 "I have not come to call the righteous but sinners to repentance."

1. Hosea 6:6 / Micah 6:6-8

3 - FIRST YEAR OF MINISTRY
Act 8: **Events In Capernaum**

Scene 5: **Why Do You Not Fast?**
Capernaum, *Galilee*   summer / 30 CE

Luke also wrote The Book of Acts

	Matthew	Mark	Luke
1	The disciples of John <the Baptist> and the Pharisees were fasting, and [John's disciples] came to [Jesus], and said to Him, "[We] often fast and offer prayers, <and> the disciples of the Pharisees also do the same.	9:14~ ~~Then~~ the disciples of John came to [~~Him~~], ~~asking~~,	2:18~ John's disciples and the Pharisees were fasting; and [~~they~~] came and said to Him,	5:33~ And [~~they~~] said to Him, "[~~The disciples of John~~] often fast and offer prayers, the disciples of the Pharisees also do the same,
2	"Why do we and the disciples of the Pharisees fast, but Your disciples eat and drink, <and> do not fast?"	9:~14 "Why do we and the Pharisees fast, but Your disciples do not fast?"	2:~18 "Why do ~~John's disciples~~ and the disciples of the Pharisees fast, but Your disciples do not fast?"	5:~33 but Yours eat and drink."
3	Jesus said to them, "While the bridegroom is with them, the attendants of the bridegroom cannot fast, can they?	9:15~ ~~And~~ Jesus said to them, "The attendants of the bridegroom cannot ~~mourn as long as~~ the bridegroom is with them, can they?	2:19~ ~~And~~ Jesus said to them, "While the bridegroom is with them, the attendants of the bridegroom cannot fast, can they?	5:34 ~~And~~ Jesus said to them, "~~You~~ cannot ~~make~~ the attendants of the bridegroom fast while the bridegroom is with them, can ~~you~~?
4	"So long as they have the bridegroom with them, they cannot fast; but the days will come when the bridegroom is taken away from them, and then they will fast in those days."	9:~15 But the days will come when the bridegroom is taken away from them, and then they will fast."	2:~19 So long as they have the bridegroom with them, they cannot fast. 2:20 "But the days will come when the bridegroom is taken away from them, and then they will fast in ~~that~~ day."	5:35 "But the days will come; ~~and~~ when the bridegroom is taken away from them, then they will fast in those days."

Scene 6: **New Cloth and Wineskins**
Capernaum, *Galilee*   summer / 30 CE

	Matthew	Mark	Luke
1	[Jesus] also [told] them a parable: "No one tears a piece of unshrunk cloth from a new garment and sews it on an old garment, otherwise the new piece will not match the old; and <when> the new patch pulls away from the <old> garment a worse tear results.	9:16~ ~~But~~ no one ~~puts~~ a ~~patch~~ of unshrunk cloth on an old garment; ~~for~~ the patch pulls away from the garment, ~~and~~ a worse tear results.	2:21 "No one sews a ~~patch~~ of unshrunk cloth on an old garment; otherwise the patch pulls away from it, the new ~~from the old~~, ~~and~~ a worse tear results.	5:36 And [He] was also [telling] them a parable: "No one tears a piece of cloth from a new garment and ~~puts~~ it on an old garment; otherwise ~~he will both tear~~ the new, and ~~the~~ piece ~~from the~~ new will not match the old.
2	"Nor do people put new wine into old wineskins, otherwise the new wine will burst the wineskins, and it will be spilled out [and] lost; and the skins will be ruined as well.	9:17~ "Nor do people put new wine into old wineskins; otherwise the wineskins burst, and the ~~wine pours~~ out and the ~~wineskins are~~ ruined;	2:22~ "~~No one~~ puts new wine into old wineskins; otherwise the wine will burst the skins, and ~~the~~ wine ~~[is]~~ lost and the skins as well;	5:37 "~~And no one~~ puts new wine into old wineskins; otherwise the new wine will burst the skins and it will be spilled out, and the skins will be ruined.
3	"But new wine must be put into fresh wineskins, and <then> both are preserved.	9:~17 but ~~they~~ put new wine into fresh wineskins, and both are preserved."	2:~22 but ~~one~~ puts new wine into fresh wineskins."	5:38 "But new wine must be put into fresh wineskins.
4	"And no one after drinking old wine wishes for new, for he says, 'The old is [better].'"			5:39 "And no one, after drinking old wine wishes for new; for he says, 'The old is [~~good enough~~].'"

continued >

3 - FIRST YEAR OF MINISTRY

Act 8: Events In Capernaum

Scene 7: Picking Grain On The Sabbath
continued

The Unified Gospel Story of Jesus Christ

	Matthew	Mark	Luke
1 It happened that Jesus was passing through some grainfields on the Sabbath; and <as> His disciples began to make their way along <they> became hungry, and <they> began to pick the heads of grain, rubbing them in their hands, and eating the grain.	12:1 ~~At that time~~ Jesus ~~went~~ through ~~the~~ grainfields on the Sabbath; and His disciples became hungry and began to pick the heads of grain and eat.	2:23 ~~And~~ it happened that He was passing through ~~the~~ grainfields on the Sabbath; and His disciples began to make their way along ~~while~~ picking the heads of grain.	6:1 ~~Now~~ it happened that He was passing through some grainfields on a Sabbath; and His disciples ~~were~~ picking the heads of grain, rubbing them in their hands, and eating the grain.
2 When some of the Pharisees saw this, they said to [Jesus], "Look, why are Your disciples *doing what is not lawful to do on the Sabbath?"* [1]	12:2 ~~But~~ when the Pharisees saw this, they said to [Him], "Look, Your disciples do what is not lawful to do on a Sabbath.	2:24 The Pharisees ~~were~~ saying to [Him], "Look, why are ~~they~~ doing what is not lawful on the Sabbath?	6:2 ~~But~~ some of the Pharisees said, "Why ~~do you~~ do what is not lawful on the Sabbath?
3 Jesus answering them, said, "Have you never read what David did when he was in need, and he and his companions who were with him became hungry;	12:3 ~~But~~ He said ~~to~~ them, "Have you ~~not~~ read what David did when he became hungry, he and his companions,	2:25 ~~And~~ He said ~~to~~ them, "Have you never read what David did when he was in need and he and his companions became hungry;	6:3 ~~And~~ Jesus answering them said, "Have you ~~not even~~ read what David did when he was hungry, he and ~~those~~ who were with him,
4 *"how he entered the house of God in the time of Abiathar the High Priest, and took and ate the consecrated bread,*[2] *and he also gave it to his companions,*	12:4~ how he entered the house of God, and ~~they~~ ate the consecrated bread,	2:26~ how he entered the house of God in the time of Abiathar the high priest, and ate the consecrated bread, 2:~26 and he also gave it to ~~those who were with him?"~~	6:4~ how he entered the house of God, and took and ate the consecrated bread 6:~4 and gave it to his companions?"
5 *"which was not lawful for him to eat, nor for those with him, <or> anyone except for the priests alone?*[3]	12:~4 which was not lawful for him to eat nor for those with him, ~~but~~ for the priests alone?	2:~26 which ~~is~~ not lawful for anyone to eat except the priests,	6:~4~ which ~~is~~ not lawful for and to eat except the priests alone,
6 "Or have you not read in the Law, that *on the Sabbath the priests in the Temple break the Sabbath, and are innocent?* [4]	12:5 "Or have you not read in the Law, that on the Sabbath the priests in the temple break the Sabbath and are innocent?		
7 "But I say to you that something greater than the Temple is here.	12:6 "But I say to you that something greater than the temple is here.		
8 "[And] if you had known what this means, '*I desire mercy, and not sacrifice,*' [5] you would not have condemned the innocent."	12:7 "[~~But~~] if you had known what this means, 'I desire compassion, and not a sacrifice,' you would not have condemned the innocent.		
9 And Jesus said to them, "*The Sabbath was made for man, and not man for the Sabbath.*[6]		2:27 Jesus said to them, "The Sabbath was made for man, and not man for the Sabbath.	6:5~ And ~~He was~~ saying to them,
10 "[Therefore,] the Son of Man is Lord, even of the Sabbath."	12:8 "[~~For~~] the Son of Man is Lord of the Sabbath."	2:28 "[~~So~~] the Son of Man is Lord even of the Sabbath."	6:~5 "The Son of Man is Lord of the Sabbath."

1. *Exodus 20:8-10; 31:15 / Deuteronomy 5:12-14*   2. *1 Samuel 21:6*   3. *Exodus 29:33 / Leviticus 24:5-9*   4. *Numbers 28:9-10*   5. *Hosea 6:6*   6. *Exodus 20:10 / Deuteronomy 5:14*

3 - FIRST YEAR OF MINISTRY

Act 8: Events In Capernaum

Scene 8: Healing A Withered Hand On The Sabbath

Galilee   a Sabbath, late summer / 30 CE

	Matthew	Mark	Luke
1 Departing from there, [Jesus] entered into their synagogue, and was teaching; and a man was there whose right hand was withered.	12:9 Departing from there, [He] ~~went~~ into their synagogue. 12:10~ And a man was there whose hand was withered.	3:1 [He] entered ~~again~~ into a synagogue; and a man was there whose hand was withered.	6:6 ~~On another Sabbath~~ [He] entered the synagogue and was teaching; and ~~there~~ was a man there whose right hand was withered.
2 The scribes and the Pharisees were watching [Jesus] closely, to see if He would heal him on the Sabbath, so that they might find reason to accuse Him.	12:~10 so that they might accuse Him	3:2 ~~They~~ were watching [Him] to see if He would heal him on the Sabbath, so that they might accuse Him.	6:7 The scribes and the Pharisees were watching [Him] closely to see if He ~~healed~~ on the Sabbath, so that they might find reason to accuse Him.
3 And they questioned Jesus, asking, "Is it lawful to heal on the Sabbath?"	12:~10~ And they questioned Jesus, asking, "Is it lawful to heal on the Sabbath?"		
4 But [Jesus] knew what they were thinking, and He said to the man with the withered hand, "Get up, and come forward." And [the man] he got up, and came forward.		3:3 He said to the man with the withered hand, "Get up and come forward!"	6:8 But [He] knew what they were thinking, and He said to the man with the withered hand, "Get up and come forward!" And [he] got up and came forward.
5 And Jesus said to them, "I ask you, is it lawful to do good or to do harm on the Sabbath, to save a life or to destroy it?" But they kept silent.		3:4 And ~~He~~ said to them, "Is it lawful to do good or to do harm on the Sabbath, to save a life or to ~~kill~~?" But they kept silent.	6:9 And Jesus said to them, "I ask you, is it lawful to do good or to do harm on the Sabbath, to save a life or to destroy it?
6 And [Jesus] said to them, "What man is there among you who has a sheep, and if it falls into a pit on the Sabbath, will he not take hold of it, and lift it out?	12:11 And [He] said to them, "What man is there among you who has a sheep, and if it falls into a pit on the Sabbath, will he not take hold of it and lift it out?		
7 "How much more valuable is a man than a sheep!	12:12~ "How much more valuable ~~then~~ is a man than a sheep!		
8 "So then, it is lawful to do good on the Sabbath."	12:~12 So then, it is lawful to do good on the Sabbath."		
9 Then looking around at them all with anger, grieved at their hardness of heart, [Jesus] said to the man, "Stretch out your hand."	12:13~ Then [He] said to the man, "Stretch out your hand!"	3:5~ ~~After~~ looking around at them with anger, grieved at their hardness of heart, [He] said to the man, "Stretch out your hand."	6:10~ ~~After~~ looking around at them all, [He] said to him, "Stretch out your hand!"
10 He stretched it out, and his hand was restored to normal, like the other.	12:~13 He stretched it out, and ~~it~~ was restored to normal, like the other.	3:~5 ~~And~~ he stretched it out, and his hand was restored.	6:~10 ~~And~~ he ~~did so~~; and his hand was restored.
11 But [the Pharisees] were filled with rage, and <they> discussed together what they might do to Jesus.			6:11 But [they themselves] were filled with rage, and discussed together what they might do to Jesus.
12 [They] went out and immediately began conspiring with the Herodians against Him, as to how they might destroy Him.	12:14 ~~But~~ [the Pharisees] went out and ~~conspired~~ against Him, as to how they might destroy Him.	3:6 [The Pharisees] went out and immediately began conspiring with the Herodians against Him, as to how they might destroy Him.	
13 Jesus, aware of this, withdrew from there to the sea, with His disciples.	12:15~ ~~But~~ Jesus, aware of this, withdrew from there.	3:7~ Jesus withdrew to the sea with His disciples;	
14 A great multitude followed Him; and He told His disciples that a boat should stand ready, [in case] [the people] [should] crowd Him.	12:~15 ~~Many~~ followed Him,	3:~7 ~~and~~ a great multitude followed; 3:9 And He told His disciples that a boat should stand ready for Him ~~because of the crowd~~, [so that] [they] [would] ~~not~~ crowd Him;	

3 - FIRST YEAR OF MINISTRY

Act 8: **Events In Capernaum**

Scene 9: **Lord, Teach Us To Pray**

Galilee   late summer / 30 BCE

A Four Gospel Verse-By-Verse Harmony

	Luke
1 It happened that while Jesus was praying in a certain place, after He had finished, one of His disciples said to Him, "Lord, teach us to pray, just as John taught his disciples."	11:1 It happened that while Jesus was praying in a certain place, after He had finished, one of His disciples said to Him, "Lord, teach us to pray just as John ~~also~~ taught his disciples."
2 [Jesus] said to them, "When you pray, say: 'Father, [Holy] [is] Your Name! Your Kingdom come.	11:2 ~~And~~ [He] said to them, "When you pray, say: 'Father, [~~hallowed~~] [be] Your name. Your kingdom come.
3 "*Give us each day our daily bread*;[1]	11:3 'Give us each day our daily bread.
4 "and forgive us our sins, [as] we forgive everyone who is indebted to us.	11:4~ 'And forgive us our sins, [~~for~~] we ~~ourselves also~~ forgive everyone who is indebted to us.
5 "And lead us not into temptation.' "	11:~4 And lead us not into temptation.' "

1. Proverb 30:8

3 - FIRST YEAR OF MINISTRY
Act 9: The Death of John The Baptist

Scene 1: **The Demand of Herodias**
Jerusalem, Judea late summer / 30 CE

Seeing the Four Gospels as One

	Matthew	Mark
1 [The] day came <for John the Baptist> when <King> Herod[1] on his birthday gave a banquet for his lords and military commanders, and the leading men of Galilee.	14:6~ ~~But~~ when Herod's birthday came,	6:21 [A] ~~strategic~~ day came when Herod on his birthday gave a banquet for his lords and military commanders and the leading men of Galilee;
2 When the daughter of Herodias came in and danced before them, she pleased Herod and his dinner guests so much, that [he] said to [her], "Ask me for whatever you want, and I will give it to you!"	14:~6 the daughter of Herodias danced before them ~~and~~ pleased Herod, 14:7~ so much that	6:22 ~~and~~ when the daughter of Herodias ~~herself~~ came in and danced, she pleased Herod and his dinner guests; ~~and~~ [the king] said to [~~the girl~~], "Ask me for whatever you want and I will give it to you."
3 And [the King] swore an oath to her; "Whatever you ask of me, I will give to you, up to half of my kingdom."[2]	14:~7 [he] ~~promised~~ ~~with~~ an oath to give ~~her~~ whatever ~~she~~ asked.	6:23 And [he] swore to her, "Whatever you ask of me, I will give ~~it~~ to you; up to half of my kingdom."
4 [The girl] went out, and said to her mother, "What shall I ask for?" And [Herodias] said, "The head of John the Baptist!"		6:24 ~~And~~ [~~she~~] went out and said to her mother, "What shall I ask for?" And [~~she~~] said, "The head of John the Baptist."
5 Having been prompted by her mother, [the girl] immediately came in a hurry to the King, and said, "I want you to give me here at once the head of John the Baptist, on a platter."	14:8 Having been prompted by her mother, ~~she~~ said, "Give me here on a platter the head of John the Baptist."	6:25 Immediately [~~she~~] came in a hurry to the king and ~~asked~~, ~~saying~~, "I want you to give me at once the head of John the Baptist on a platter."
6 And although [Herod] was very grieved, yet because of his oaths, and because of his dinner guests, [the king] was unwilling to refuse her, <and> [he] commanded it to be given.	14:9 Although [he] was grieved, [~~the king~~] commanded it to be given because of his oaths, and because of his dinner guests.	6:26 And although [~~the king~~] was very ~~sorry~~, yet because of his oaths and because of his dinner guests, [he] was unwilling to refuse her.

1. Herod Antipater (aka Antipas) (20 BCE - 39 CE) Tetrarch of Galilee & Perea (4 BCE - 39 CE)   2. Esther 5:3, 6; 7:2

Scene 2: **King Herod Has John Beheaded**
Jerusalem, Judea late summer / 30 CE

	Matthew	Mark	John
1 Immediately King <Herod> sent an executioner [to] behead John in the prison; and <he> commanded him to bring back his head.	14:10 [~~He~~] sent [~~and had~~] John behead~~ed~~ in the prison.	6:27~ Immediately ~~the~~ king sent an executioner 6:~27 [~~and had~~] him behead~~ed~~ in the prison, 6:27⁻¹ and commanded him to bring back his head.	
2 [The executioner] went, and brought [John's] head on a platter, and gave it to the girl, and she gave it to her mother.	14:11 And [his] head ~~was~~ brought on a platter and ~~given~~ to the girl, and she ~~brought~~ it to her mother.	6:27⁻² ~~And~~ [he] went 6:28 and brought [his] head on a platter, and gave it to the girl; and ~~the girl~~ gave it to her mother.	
3 When [John's] disciples heard about this, they came and took his body away, and laid it in a tomb; [then] they went and reported <this> to Jesus.	14:12 ~~His disciples~~ came and took away ~~the~~ body and ~~buried~~ it; [~~and~~] they went and reported to Jesus.	6:29 When [his] disciples heard about this, they came and took away his body and laid it in a tomb.	
4 When Jesus heard about John, He withdrew from there in a boat to a secluded place by Himself, [on] the other side of the Sea of Galilee, [near] Tiberias.	14:13~ ~~Now~~ when Jesus heard about John, He withdrew from there in a boat to a secluded place by Himself;		6:1 ~~After these things~~ Jesus ~~went away~~ [to] the other side of the Sea of Galilee ([~~or~~] Tiberias).

CHAPTER 4
THE SECOND YEAR OF HIS MINISTRY

Events that occurred during the Second Year of The Ministry of Jesus Christ.

	Page
Act 1 - Jesus Chooses Twelve Apostles	
Scene 1 Miracles of Healing	68
2 Jesus Appoints Twelve Apostles	69
Act 2 - The Sermon On The Mount	
Scene 1 The Beatitudes	70
2 You Are The Salt of The Earth	71
3 You Are The Light of The World	72
4 The Eye Is The Lamp of The Body	72
5 I Have Come To Fulfill The Law	73
6 Forgive Your Brother	73
7 Settle With Your Opponent	74
8 On Adultery and Divorce	74
9 Make No Oath By Heaven or Earth	75
Act 3 - The Sermon On True Wealth	
Scene 1 Give To Everyone Who Asks of You	75
2 Love Your Enemy	76
3 When You Give To The Poor	76
4 When You Pray	77
5 The Lord's Prayer	77
6 When You Fast	78
7 Life Is Not About Possessions	78
8 Store Up Treasure In Heaven	79
9 Do Not Worry About Food or Clothing	80
Act 4 - The Sermon On Spiritual Fruit	
Scene 1 On Judging Another Person	81
2 Seek, and You Will Find	82
3 The Fruit of False Prophets	83
4 Build On The Solid Foundation of The Word	84
5 Jesus Finishes His Sermon	84

	Page
Act 5 - Events In Galilee	
Scene 1 Healing a Centurion's Servant	85
2 Perfumed Feet In The Home of A Pharisee	86
3 Preaching The Kingdom of God	87
4 Jesus Denounces The Unrepentant Cities	87
5 Come to Me - My Burden Is Light	88
Act 6 - On Good and Evil Spirits	
Scene 1 You Heal By Beelzebul	89
2 How Can Satan Cast Out Satan?	90
3 The Unforgivable Sin	91
4 On Good and Evil	91
5 A Wicked Generation Seeks A Sign	92
6 On Unclean Spirits	92
7 Woe To You Pharisees!	93
8 Woe To You Lawyers As Well!	93
9 Who Are My Mother and My Brothers?	94
Act 7 - Parables About The Kingdom	
Scene 1 The Parable of The Sower a)	95
2 Why Do You Speak To Them In Parables?	96
3 The Parable of The Sower b) Explained	97
4 The Parable of The Tares a)	98
5 The Kingdom of Heaven Is Like A Mustard Seed	99
6 More Parables About The Kingdom of Heaven	100
7 The Parable of The Tares b) Explained	101

	Page
Act 8 - Mighty Miracles	
Scene 1 Jesus Calms The Stormy Sea	102
2 A Demon-Possessed Man Named Legion	103
3 Jesus Sends The Demons Into The Swine	104
4 Jairus Implores Jesus To Heal His Daughter a)	105
5 A Woman Is Healed of Her Hemorrhage	106
6 Jesus Heals The Daughter of Jairus b)	107
7 Two Blind Men and A Mute Demon	108
8 Reading In His Hometown On The Sabbath	109
9 The Nazarenes Take Offense At Jesus	110
Act 9 - Jesus Sends The Apostles	
Scene 1 Jesus Sends His Twelve Apostles To Preach	111
2 Jesus Instructs The Apostles	112
3 Peace, To Those Who Receive You	112
4 I Send You Out As Sheep Among Wolves	113
5 You Will Be Persecuted, But Do Not Fear	114
6 Whoever Confesses The Son of Man	115
7 I Have Not Come To Bring Peace	115
8 He Who Is Worthy of Me	116
9 The Apostles Go Out and Preach The Gospel	116

The Gospel Story of The Life of Jesus

MAP OF ISRAEL

Locations mentioned in this Chapter are shown with a white center.

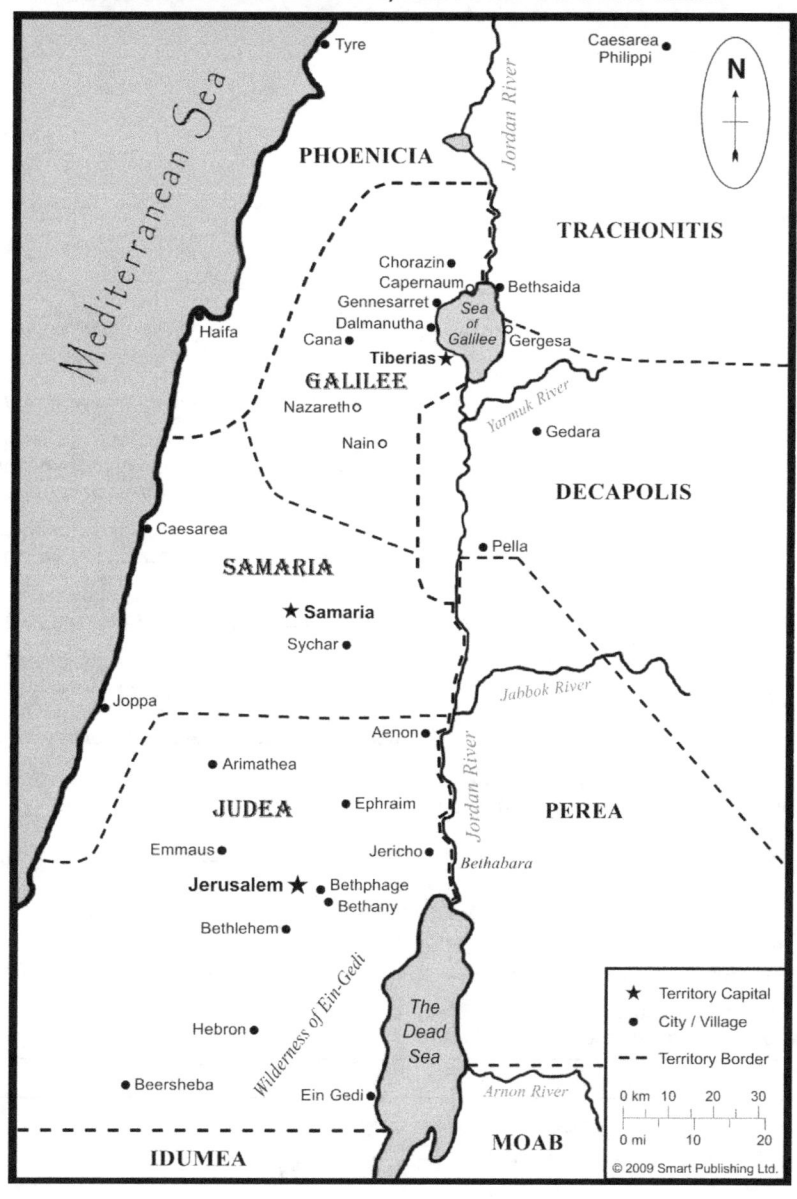

3 - FIRST YEAR OF MINISTRY

Act 1: **Jesus Chooses Twelve Apostles**

Scene 1: **Miracles of Healing**

Capernaum, *Galilee*   spring / 31 CE

The Complete Verse-By-Verse Gospel Harmony

	Matthew	Mark	Luke
1 A great number of people heard of all that [Jesus] was doing, and came to Him.		*3:~8* a great number of people heard of all that [He] was doing and came to Him.	
2 All those who had afflictions pressed around Him, in order to touch Him, for power was coming from Him and healing them all; and those who were troubled with unclean spirits were being cured.	*12:~15* and ~~He~~ healed them all,	*3:10* ~~for~~ He ~~had~~ healed ~~many, with the result that~~ all those who had afflictions pressed around Him in order to touch Him.	*6:~18* and those who were troubled with unclean spirits were being cured. *6:19* ~~And~~ all ~~the people were trying~~ to touch Him, for power was coming from Him and healing them all.
3 Whenever the unclean spirits saw [Jesus], they would fall down before Him, and shout, "You are the Son of God!" and He <would> earnestly warn them not to tell who He was.	*12:16* and warn~~ed~~ them not to tell who He was.	*3:11* Whenever the unclean spirits saw [Him], they would fall down before Him and shout, "You are the Son of God!" *3:12* And He earnestly warn~~ed~~ them not to tell who He was.	
4 This was to fulfill what was spoken through Isaiah the prophet: *"Behold, My Servant whom I have chosen; My Beloved in whom My Soul is well-pleased!*	*12:17* This was to fulfill what was spoken through Isaiah the prophet: *12:18~* "Behold, My Servant whom I have chosen; My Beloved in whom My soul is well-pleased;		
5 *"I will put My Spirit upon Him, and He shall proclaim justice to the Gentiles.*	*12:~18* I will put My Spirit upon Him, and He shall proclaim justice to the Gentiles.		
6 *"He will not quarrel, nor cry out; nor will anyone hear His voice in the streets.*	*12:19* "He will not quarrel, nor cry out; nor will anyone hear His voice in the streets.		
7 *"A battered reed He will not break off, and a smoldering wick He will not put out, until He leads justice to victory.*	*12:20* "A battered reed He will not break off, and a smoldering wick He will not put out, until He leads justice to victory.		
8 *"And in His Name the Gentiles will hope."* [1]	*12:21* "And in His name the Gentiles will hope."		

1. Isaiah 42:1-4

4 - SECOND YEAR OF MINISTRY
Act 1: Jesus Chooses Twelve Apostles

Scene 2: Jesus Appoints Twelve Apostles
Mount Eremos, near Capernaum, Galilee   spring / 31 CE

The United Gospel Story of Jesus Christ

#		Matthew	Mark	Luke	John
1	When Jesus saw the crowds, He went up on the mountain to pray; and He spent the whole night in prayer to God.	5:1~ When Jesus saw the crowds, He went up on the mountain;	3:13~ ~~And~~ He went up on the mountain	6:12 ~~It was at this time that~~ He went ~~off to~~ the mountain to pray, and He spent the whole night in prayer to God.	
2	When day came, He called His disciples, and summoned to Himself those whom He wanted.		3:~13~ and summoned those whom He Himself wanted,	6:13~ ~~And~~ when day came, He called His disciples to Him	
3	After He sat down, they came to Him; and He appointed twelve of them, whom He [called] *apostles*,[1.]	5:~1 and after He sat down, ~~His disciples~~ came to Him.	3:~13 ~~and~~ they came to Him. 3:14~ And He appointed twelve,	6:~13 and ~~chose~~ twelve of them, whom He ~~also~~ [named] ~~as~~ apostles:	
4	so that they would be with Him, and that He could send them out to preach, and to have authority to cast out the demons.		3:~14 so that they would be with Him and that He could send them out to preach, 3:15 and to have authority to cast out the demons.		
5	Now the names of the twelve apostles are these: The first <is> Simon, <the son of John>,[2.] to whom [Jesus] also gave the name Peter (*Cephas*[3.]);	10:2~ Now the names of the twelve apostles are these: The first, Simon, who ~~is called~~ Peter,	3:16 Simon (to whom [~~He~~] gave the name Peter),	6:14~ Simon, whom [~~He~~] also ~~named~~ Peter,	
6	and Andrew his brother;	10:2~1 and Andrew his brother;	3:18~ and Andrew	6:14~1 and Andrew his brother;	
7	and James, the son of Zebedee;	10:2~2 and James the son of Zebedee,	3:17~ and James the son of Zebedee,	6:14~2 and James	
8	and John his brother (to them He gave the name Boanerges, which means, "Sons of Thunder");	10:~2 and John his brother;	3:~17 and John ~~the~~ brother ~~of James~~ (to them He gave the name Boanerges, which means, "Sons of Thunder");	6:14~3 and John;	
9	and Philip, who was from Bethsaida in Galilee;	10:3~ Philip	3:18~1 and Philip,	6:14~4 and Philip	12:~21~ who was from Bethsaida [of] Galilee,
10	and *Bartholomew*[4.] [from] Cana in Galilee;	10:3~1 and Bartholomew;	3:18~2 and Bartholomew,	6:~14 and Bartholomew;	21:2~3 [of] Cana in Galilee
11	and Matthew <*Levi*>,[5.] the tax collector <*from Capernaum*>;[6.]	10:3~3 and Matthew the tax collector;	3:18~3 and Matthew,	6:15~ and Matthew	
12	and Thomas, <who is> called *Didymus*[7.] <(which means "twin")>;	10:3~2 Thomas	3:18~4 and Thomas,	6:15~1 and Thomas;	20:24 / 21:2 called Didymus,
13	and James, the son of Alphaeus;	10:3~4 James the son of Alphaeus,	3:18~5 and James the son of Alphaeus,	6:15~2 James the son of Alphaeus,	
14	and Judas Thaddaeus, the son of James;	10:~3 and Thaddaeus;	3:18~6 and Thaddaeus;	6:16~ Judas the son of James,	
15	and Simon <*Iscariot*>,[8.] who was called the Zealot;	10:4~ Simon the Zealot,	3:~18 and Simon the Zealot;	6:~15 and Simon who was called the Zealot;	
16	and Judas Iscariot, <*the son of Simon*>,[8.] the one who [would] betray Him.	10:~4 and Judas Iscariot, the one who betrayed Him.	3:19 and Judas Iscariot, who betrayed Him.	6:~16 and Judas Iscariot, who [~~became~~] ~~a traitor~~.	

1. meaning "one who is sent"   2. Hebrew "Barjonah"(TSG 531.6 / Matthew 16:17) / John 1:42; 21:15-17   3. Aramaic for "rock" = Greek "petra" - John 1:42
4. may also be Nathanael: John 1:45-49; 21:2 / Acts 1:13   5. Mark 2:14 / Luke 5:27   6. Mark 2:1-14   7. Greek for twin or double   8. John 6:71; 13:2, 26

	Matthew	Mark	Luke
1 Jesus came down with [the apostles], and stood on a level place [where] there was a large crowd of His disciples.			6:17~ Jesus came down with [them] and stood on a level place; [and] there was a large crowd of His disciples,
2 And a great throng of people <was there> from Galilee, and from Jerusalem and all <of> Judea, and from Idumea, and beyond the Jordan, and the coastal region[s] of Tyre and Sidon, who had come to hear [Jesus], and to be healed of their diseases.		3:~7 from Galilee followed and also from Judea, 3:8~ and from Jerusalem, and from Idumea, and beyond the Jordan, and the vicinity of Tyre and Sidon,	6:~17 and a great throng of people from all Judea and Jerusalem and the coastal region of Tyre and Sidon 6:18~ who had come to hear [Him] and to be healed of their diseases;
3 Turning His gaze toward His disciples, [Jesus] opened His mouth, and began to teach them, saying,	5:2 [He] opened His mouth and began to teach them, saying,		6:20~ And turning His gaze toward His disciples, [He] began to say,
4 "Blessed are you who are poor, for yours is the Kingdom of God.			6:~20 "Blessed are you who are poor, for yours is the kingdom of God.
5 "Blessed are the poor in spirit, for theirs is the Kingdom of Heaven.	5:3 "Blessed are the poor in spirit, for theirs is the kingdom of heaven.		
6 "Blessed are those who mourn, for they shall be comforted.	5:4 "Blessed are those who mourn, for they shall be comforted.		
7 *Blessed are the gentle, for they shall inherit the earth.*[1.]	5:5 "Blessed are the gentle, for they shall inherit the earth.		
8 "Blessed are you who hunger and thirst for righteousness now, for you shall be satisfied.	5:6 "Blessed are those who hunger and thirst for righteousness, for they shall be satisfied.		6:21 "Blessed are you who hunger now, for you shall be satisfied.
9 "Blessed are you who weep now, for you shall laugh.			6:~21 "Blessed are you who weep now, for you shall laugh.
10 *Blessed are the merciful, for they shall receive mercy.*[2.]	5:7 "Blessed are the merciful, for they shall receive mercy.		
11 "Blessed are the pure in heart, for they shall see God.	5:8 "Blessed are the pure in heart, for they shall see God.		
12 "Blessed are the peacemakers, for they shall be called sons of God.	5:9 "Blessed are the peacemakers, for they shall be called sons of God.		
13 "Blessed are those who have been persecuted for the sake of righteousness, for theirs is the Kingdom of Heaven.	5:10 "Blessed are those who have been persecuted for the sake of righteousness, for theirs is the kingdom of heaven.		
14 "Blessed are you when people insult you, and men hate you, and persecute you, and scorn your name, and falsely say all kinds of evil <things> against you, because of Me, the Son of Man.	5:11 "Blessed are you when people insult you and persecute you, and falsely say all kinds of evil against you because of Me.		6:22 "Blessed are you when men hate you, and ostracize you, and insult you, and scorn your name as evil, for the sake of the Son of Man.
15 "Rejoice and be glad in that day, and leap for joy; for behold, your reward in Heaven is great; for in the same way their fathers persecuted the prophets who were before you.	5:12 "Rejoice and be glad, for your reward in heaven is great; for in the same way they persecuted the prophets who were before you."		6:23 "Be glad in that day and leap for joy, for behold, your reward is great in heaven. For in the same way their fathers used to treat the prophets.

1. Psalm 37:11   2. Psalm 41:1

continued >

4 - SECOND YEAR OF MINISTRY

Act 2: The Sermon On The Mount

Scene 1: **The Beatitudes**
continued

	Matthew	Mark	Luke
16 "But woe to you who are rich <now>, for you are receiving your comfort in full.			6:24 "But woe to you who are rich, for you are receiving your comfort in full.
17 "Woe to you who are well-fed now, for you shall be hungry.			6:25~ "Woe to you who are well-fed now, for you shall be hungry.
18 "Woe to you who laugh now, for you shall mourn and weep.			6:~25 Woe to you who laugh now, for you shall mourn and weep.
19 "Woe to you when all men speak well of you, for their fathers used to treat the false prophets in the same way."			6:26 "Woe to you when all men speak well of you, for their fathers used to treat the false prophets in the same way."

Scene 2: **You Are The Salt of The Earth**

Mount Eremos, near Capernaum, *Galilee*   spring / 31 CE

	Matthew	Mark	Luke
1 "You are the salt of the earth, [and] salt is good;	5:13~ "You are the salt of the earth;	9:50~ "Salt is good;	14:34~ "[~~Therefore~~], salt is good;
2 "but if the salt has become unsalty <and> tasteless, with what will it be seasoned? How can it be made salty again?	5:~13~ but if the salt has become tasteless, how can it be made salty again?	9:~50~ but if the salt becomes unsalty, ~~with what will you~~ make it salty again?	14:~34 but if ~~even~~ salt has become tasteless, with what will it be seasoned?
3 "It is useless for either the soil or the manure pile, [and] is no longer good for anything except to be thrown out, and trampled under foot by men.	5:~13 [~~It~~] is no longer good for anything, except to be thrown out and trampled under foot by men.		14:35~ "It is useless either for the soil or ~~for~~ the manure pile; ~~it is~~ thrown out.
4 "Have salt in yourselves, and be at peace with one another.		9:~50 Have salt in yourselves, and be at peace with one another."	
5 "If anyone has ears to hear, let [them] hear."		4:23 "If anyone has ears to hear, let [~~him~~] hear."	14:~35 ~~He who~~ has ears to hear, let [~~him~~] hear."

4 - SECOND YEAR OF MINISTRY

Act 2: The Sermon On The Mount

Scene 3: **You Are The Light of The World**

Mount Eremos, near Capernaum, *Galilee*   spring / 31 CE

The Complete Gospel presented Verse-By-Verse

	Matthew	Mark	Luke 8:16-17	Luke 11:33
1	And [Jesus] [said] to them, "You are the light of the world!	5:14~ "You are the light of the world.	4:21~ And [He] ~~was~~ [saying] to them,		
2	"A city set on a hill cannot be hidden,	5:~14 A city set on a hill cannot be hidden;			
3	"[and] no one after lighting a lamp covers it over with a basket, or puts it under a bed <or> away in a cellar,	5:15~ [nor] ~~does~~ anyone light a lamp ~~and put~~ it ~~under~~ a basket,	4:~21~ A lamp ~~is not brought to be put~~ ~~under~~ a basket, ~~is~~ it or under a bed?	8:16~ "[Now] no one after lighting a lamp covers it over with a ~~container~~, or puts it under a bed;	11:33~ "No one, after lighting a lamp puts it away in a cellar ~~nor under~~ a basket,
4	"but it is put on a lampstand, and it gives light to all who are in the house, so that those who enter may see the light.	5:~15 but on ~~the~~ lampstand, and it gives light to all who are in the house.	4:~21 Is it ~~not brought to be~~ put on ~~the~~ lampstand?	8:~16 but [he] ~~puts~~ ~~it~~ on a lampstand, so that those who ~~come in~~ may see the light.	11:~33 but on ~~the~~ lampstand, so that those who enter may see the light.
5	"<Therefore>, let your light shine before men in such a way that they may see your good works, and glorify your Father who is in Heaven.	5:16 "Let your light shine before men in such a way that they may see your good works, and glorify your Father who is in heaven.			
6	"For nothing is hidden except to be revealed [and] become evident; nor has anything been secret that will not come to light and be known."		4:22 "For nothing is hidden, except to be revealed; nor has anything been secret ~~but~~ that ~~it would~~ come to light.	8:17 "For nothing is hidden [that will not] become evident, nor anything secret that will not be known and come to light.	

Scene 4: **The Eye Is The Lamp of The Body**

Mount Eremos, near Capernaum, *Galilee*   spring / 31 CE

	Matthew	Luke
1	"The eye is the lamp of the body, so if your eye is clear <then> your whole body will also be full of light;	6:22 "The eye is the lamp of the body; so ~~then~~ if your eye is clear, your whole body will also be full of light.	11:34~ "The eye is the lamp of ~~your~~ body; ~~when~~ your eye is clear, your whole body also ~~is~~ full of light;
2	"but if your eye is bad, <then> your whole body will also be full of darkness.	6:23~ "But if your eye is bad, your whole body will be full of darkness.	11:~34 but ~~when it~~ is bad, your body also ~~is~~ full of darkness.
3	"If the light that is in you is darkness, great is [that] darkness!	6:~23 If ~~then~~ the light that is in you is darkness, ~~how~~ great is [the] darkness!	
4	"Watch out then, that the light in you is not darkness.		11:35 "Then watch out that the light in you is not darkness.
5	"Therefore, if your whole body is full of light, with no dark part in it, it will be wholly illumined, as when the lamp illumines you with its rays."		11:36 "If therefore your whole body is full of light, with no dark part in it, it will be wholly illumined, as when the lamp illumines you with its rays."

4 - SECOND YEAR OF MINISTRY
Act 2: **The Sermon On The Mount**

Scene 5: I Have Come To Fulfill The Law
Mount Eremos, near Capernaum, *Galilee*   spring / 31 CE

John's Gospel was the last written

		Matthew
1	"Do not think that I came to abolish the Law, or the Prophets; I did not come to abolish, but to fulfill.	5:17 "Do not think that I came to abolish the Law or the Prophets; I did not come to abolish but to fulfill.
2	"For truly I say to you, until heaven and earth pass away, not the smallest letter or stroke shall pass from the Law, until [everything] is [fulfilled].	5:18 "For truly I say to you, until heaven and earth pass away, not the smallest letter or stroke shall pass from the Law until [all] is [accomplished].
3	"Whoever then annuls one of the least of these commandments, and teaches others to do the same, shall be called least in the Kingdom of Heaven;	5:19~ "Whoever then annuls one of the least of these commandments, and teaches others to do the same, shall be called least in the kingdom of heaven;
4	"but whoever keeps <them>, and teaches them, [they] shall be called great in the Kingdom of Heaven.	5:~19 but whoever keeps and teaches them, [he] shall be called great in the kingdom of heaven.
5	"For I say to you, that unless your righteousness surpasses that of the scribes and <the> Pharisees, you will not enter the Kingdom of Heaven."	5:20 "For I say to you that unless your righteousness surpasses that of the scribes and Pharisees, you will not enter the kingdom of heaven.

Scene 6: Forgive Your Brother

		Matthew
1	"You have heard that the ancients were told, *'You shall not commit murder'* [1]	5:21~ "You have heard that the ancients were told, 'You shall not commit murder'
2	"and 'Whoever commits murder shall be liable to the court.'	5:~21 and 'Whoever commits murder shall be liable to the court.'
3	"But I say to you that everyone who is angry with his brother shall be guilty before the court;	5:22~ "But I say to you that everyone who is angry with his brother shall be guilty before the court;
4	"and whoever says to his brother, 'You good-for-nothing,' shall be guilty before the supreme court;	5:~22~ and whoever says to his brother, 'You good-for-nothing,' shall be guilty before the supreme court;
5	"and whoever says, 'You fool,' shall be guilty enough to go into the fiery hell!	5:~22 and whoever says, 'You fool,' shall be guilty enough to go into the fiery hell.
6	"Therefore, if you are presenting your offering at the altar, and there remember that your brother has something against you, leave your offering there before the altar, and go;	5:23 "Therefore if you are presenting your offering at the altar, and there remember that your brother has something against you, 5:24~ leave your offering there before the altar and go;
7	"first be reconciled to your brother, and then come and present your offering."	5:~24 first be reconciled to your brother, and then come and present your offering.

1. *Exodus 20:13 / Deuteronomy 5:17*

4 - SECOND YEAR OF MINISTRY
Act 2: **The Sermon On The Mount**

Scene 7: **Settle With Your Opponent**
Mount Eremos, near Capernaum, *Galilee*   spring / 31 CE

Page 74
A Verse-By-Verse Unified Gospel

		Matthew	**Luke**
1	"Why do you not on your own initiative judge what is right?		*12:57* "~~And~~ why do you not ~~even~~ on your own initiative judge what is right?
2	"For while you are going with your opponent at law to appear before the magistrate, make an effort to settle quickly with him on the way there, so that he may not drag you before the judge,	*5:25~* "Make ~~friends~~ quickly with your opponent at law while you are with him on the way, so that ~~your opponent~~ may not ~~hand~~ you ~~over to~~ the judge,	*12:58~* "For while you are going with your opponent to appear before the magistrate, on ~~your~~ way there make an effort to settle with him, so that he may not drag you before the judge,
3	"and the judge turn you over to the officer, and the officer throw you into prison.	*5:~25* and the judge to the officer, ~~and~~ you ~~be thrown~~ into prison.	*12:~58* and the judge turn you over to the officer, and the officer throw you into prison.
4	"Truly I say to you, <that> you will not get out of there until you have paid the very last cent."	*5:26* "Truly I say to you, you will not ~~come~~ out of there until you have paid ~~up~~ the last cent.	*12:59* "I say to you, you will not get out of there until you have paid the very last cent."

Scene 8: **On Adultery and Divorce**

		Matthew
1	"You have heard that it was said, *'You shall not commit adultery';* [1]	*5:27* "You have heard that it was said, 'You shall not commit adultery';
2	"but I say to you, that everyone who looks at a woman with lust for her, has already committed adultery with her in his heart.	*5:28* but I say to you that everyone who looks at a woman with lust for her has already committed adultery with her in his heart.
3	"If your right eye makes you stumble, tear it out and throw it from you, for it is better for you to lose one of the parts of your body, than for your whole body to be thrown into hell.	*5:29* "If your right eye makes you stumble, tear it out and throw it from you; for it is better for you to lose one of the parts of your body, than for your whole body to be thrown into hell.
4	"If your right hand makes you stumble, cut it off and throw it from you, for it is better for you to lose one of the parts of your body, than for your whole body to go into hell.	*5:30* "If your right hand makes you stumble, cut it off and throw it from you; for it is better for you to lose one of the parts of your body, than for your whole body to go into hell.
5	"It was said, *'Whoever sends his wife away, let him give her a certificate of divorce';* [2]	*5:31* "It was said, 'Whoever sends his wife away, let him give her a certificate of divorce';
6	"but I say to you, that everyone who divorces his wife, except for the reason of unchastity, makes her commit adultery;	*5:32* but I say to you that everyone who divorces his wife, except for the reason of unchastity, makes her commit adultery;
7	"and whoever marries a divorced woman commits adultery."	*5:~32* and whoever marries a divorced woman commits adultery.

1. *Exodus 20:14 / Deuteronomy 5:18*   2. *Deuteronomy 24:1*

4 - SECOND YEAR OF MINISTRY	Scene 9: **Make No Oath By Heaven or Earth**	
Act 2: **The Sermon On The Mount**	Mount Eremos, near Capernaum, *Galilee* spring / 31 CE	*A Complete Account from the Four Gospels*

	Matthew
1 "Again, you have heard that the ancients were told, *'You shall not make false vows, but shall fulfill your vows to the Lord.'* [1.]	5:33 "Again, you have heard that the ancients were told, 'You shall not make false vows, but shall fulfill your vows to the Lord.'
2 "But I say to you, make no oath at all; either by Heaven, for it is the throne of God, or by *the earth, for it is the footstool of His feet,*[2.]	5:34 "But I say to you, make no oath at all, either by heaven, for it is the throne of God, 5:35~ or by the earth, for it is the footstool of His feet,
3 "or by *Jerusalem, for it is the city of the great King.*[3.]	5:~35 or by Jerusalem, for it is the city of the great King.
4 "Nor shall you make an oath by your head, for you cannot make one hair white or black.	5:36 "Nor shall you make an oath by your head, for you cannot make one hair white or black.
5 "But let your statement be 'Yes' or 'No', <because> anything [more than] these [leads] [to] evil."	5:37 "But let your statement be, 'Yes, yes' or 'No, no'; anything [beyond] these [is] [of] evil.

1. *Numbers 30:2 / Leviticus 19:12 / Deuteronomy 23:23*   2. *Isaiah 66:1*   3. *Psalm 48:1-2*

---

4 - SECOND YEAR OF MINISTRY	Scene 1: **Give To Everyone Who Asks of You**	
Act 3: **The Sermon On True Wealth**	Mount Eremos, near Capernaum, *Galilee* spring / 31 CE	

	Matthew	Luke
1 "You have heard that it was said, *'An eye for an eye, and a tooth for a tooth;'*[1.] but I say to you, do not resist an evil person;	5:38 "You have heard that it was said, an eye for an eye, and a tooth for a tooth.' 5:39~ "But I say to you, do not resist an evil person;	
2 "[and] *whoever slaps you on your right cheek, turn* <and> *offer the other to him also.*[2.]	5:~39 [but whoever slaps you on your right cheek, turn the other to him also.	6:29~ "Whoever hits you on the cheek, offer the other to him also;
3 "If anyone wants to sue you, and take away your shirt, do not withhold your shirt from him - <and> let him have your coat also!	5:40 "If anyone wants to sue you and take your shirt, let him have your coat also.	6:~29 and whoever takes away your coat, do not withhold your shirt from him either
4 "Whoever forces you to go one mile, go with him two.	5:41 "Whoever forces you to go one mile, go with him two.	
5 "Give to everyone who asks of you, and do not turn away from [the one] who wants to borrow from you;	5:42 "Give to him who asks of you, and do not turn away from [him] who wants to borrow from you.	6:30~ "Give to everyone who asks of you,
6 "and whoever takes away what is yours, do not demand it back.		6:~30 and whoever takes away what is yours, do not demand it back.
7 "If you lend to those from whom you expect to receive, what credit is that to you? Even sinners lend to sinners in order to receive back the same amount.		6:34 "If you lend to those from whom you expect to receive, what credit is that to you? Even sinners lend to sinners in order to receive back the same amount.
8 "Give, and it will be given to you. They will pour into your lap a good measure - pressed down, shaken together, and running over.		6:38~ "Give, and it will be given to you. They will pour into your lap a good measure - pressed down, shaken together, and running over.
9 "For by your standard of measure, it will be measured to you in return."		6:~38 For by your standard of measure it will be measured to you in return."

1. *Exodus 21:24 / Leviticus 24:20 / Deuteronomy 19:21*   2. *Isaiah 50:6*

4 - SECOND YEAR OF MINISTRY
Act 3: The Sermon On True Wealth

Scene 2: Love Your Enemy
Mount Eremos, near Capernaum, *Galilee*   spring / 31 CE

The Ultimate Gospel

	Matthew	Luke
1 "You have heard that it was said, 'You *shall love your neighbor*[1] and hate your enemy.'	5:43 "You have heard that it was said, 'You shall love your neighbor and hate your enemy.'	
2 "But I say to you who hear; love your enemies, <and> do good to those who hate you;	5:44~ "But I say to you, love your enemies	6:27 "But I say to you who hear, love your enemies, do good to those who hate you,
3 "bless those who curse you, and pray for those who mistreat you.	5:~44 and pray for those who ~~persecute~~ you,	6:28 bless those who curse you, pray for those who mistreat you.
4 "If you greet only your brothers, what more are you doing than others? Do not even the Gentiles do the same?	5:47 "If you greet only your brothers, what more are you doing than others? Do not even the Gentiles do the same?	
5 "<And> if you <only> do good to those who do good to you, what credit is that to you? For even sinners do the same.		6:33 "If you do good to those who do good to you, what credit is that to you? For even sinners do the same.
6 "But love your enemies, and do good;		6:35~ "But love your enemies, and do good,
7 "and lend, expecting nothing in return, and your reward will be great, [for] you will be sons of the Most High, your Father who is in Heaven;	5:45~ [~~so that~~] you ~~may~~ be sons of your Father who is in heaven;	6:~35 and lend, expecting nothing in return; and your reward will be great, [~~and~~] you will be sons of the Most High;
8 "for He Himself is kind to evil and ungrateful men, [and] He *causes His sun to rise on the good and the evil,*[2] and <He> sends rain [to] the righteous and the unrighteous.	5:~45 [~~for~~] He causes His sun to rise on the evil and the good, and sends rain [~~on~~] the righteous and the unrighteous.	6:~35 for He Himself is kind to ungrateful and evil men.
9 "<Therefore,> be merciful, just as your Father is merciful.		6:36 "Be merciful, just as your Father is merciful.
10 "If you love those who love you, what credit is that to you? What reward do you have? Do not even the tax collectors do the same?	5:46 "~~For~~ if you love those who love you, what reward do you have? Do not even the tax collectors do the same?	6:32~ "If you love those who love you, what credit is that to you?
11 "For even sinners love those who love them.		6:~32 For even sinners love those who love them.
12 "Therefore *you are to be perfect,*[3] as your Heavenly Father is perfect."	5:48 "Therefore you are to be perfect, as your heavenly Father is perfect.	

1. Leviticus 19:18   2. Job 25:3   3. Genesis 17:1

Scene 3: When You Give To The Poor
Mount Eremos, near Capernaum, *Galilee*   spring / 31 CE

	Matthew
1 "Beware of practicing your righteousness to be noticed by men, otherwise you <will> have no reward with your Father who is in Heaven.	6:1 "Beware of practicing your righteous-ness ~~before~~ men to be noticed by ~~them~~; otherwise you have no reward with your Father who is in heaven.
2 "So when you give to the poor, do not sound a trumpet before you, as the hypocrites do in the synagogues and in the streets, so that they may be honored by men. Truly I say to you, they have their reward in full.	6:2 "So when you give to the poor, do not sound a trumpet before you, as the hypocrites do in the synagogues and in the streets, so that they may be honored by men. Truly I say to you, they have their reward in full.
3 "But when you give to the poor, do not let your left hand know what your right hand is doing, so that your giving will be in secret;	6:3 "But when you give to the poor, do not let your left hand know what your right hand is doing, 6:4~ so that your giving will be in secret;
4 "and your Father, who sees what is done in secret, will reward you."	6:~4 and your Father who sees what is done in secret will reward you.

| 4 - SECOND YEAR OF MINISTRY | Scene 4: **When You Pray** | Page 77 |
| Act 3: **The Sermon On True Wealth** | Mount Eremos, near Capernaum, *Galilee*　　spring / 31 CE | *The Unified Four Gospel Merger* |

	Matthew
1　"When you pray, you are not to be like the hypocrites, for they love to stand and pray in the synagogues and on the street corners, so that they may be seen by men. Truly I say to you, they have their reward in full.	6:5　"When you pray, you are not to be like the hypocrites; for they love to stand and pray in the synagogues and on the street corners so that they may be seen by men. Truly I say to you, they have their reward in full.
2　"But when you pray, go into your room <and> close [the] door, and pray to your Father who is in secret; and your Father, who sees what is done in secret, will reward you.	6:6　"But ~~you~~, when you pray, go into your ~~inner~~ room, close [~~your~~] door and pray to your Father who is in secret, and your Father who sees what is done in secret will reward you.
3　"And when you are praying, do not use meaningless repetition as the Gentiles do, for they suppose that they will be heard for their many words, so do not be like them;	6:7　"And when you are praying, do not use meaningless repetition as the Gentiles do, for they suppose that they will be heard for their many words.　6:8~　"So do not be like them;
4　"for your Father knows what you need before you ask Him."	6:~8　for your Father knows what you need before you ask Him.

Scene 5: **The Lord's Prayer**
Mount Eremos, near Capernaum, *Galilee*　　spring / 31 CE

	Matthew	**Mark**
1　"Pray, then, in this way: Our Father who is in Heaven, [Holy] [is] Your Name.	6:9　"Pray, then, in this way: 'Our Father who is in heaven, [~~Hallowed~~] [~~be~~] Your name.	
2　"Your Kingdom come, <and> *Your will be done, on earth as it is in Heaven.*[1.]	6:10　'Your kingdom come. Your will be done, on earth as it is in heaven.	
3　"*Give us this day our daily bread,*[2.]	6:11　'Give us this day our daily bread.	
4　"and forgive us our debts, as we also have forgiven our debtors.	6:12　'And forgive us our debts, as we also have forgiven our debtors.	
5　"And do not lead us into temptation, but deliver us from evil,	6:13~　'And do not lead us into temptation, but deliver us from evil.	
6　"for Yours is the Kingdom, and the power, and the glory, forever. Amen.	6:~13　[For Yours is the kingdom and the power and the glory forever. Amen.]'	
7　"Whenever you stand praying, if you have anything against anyone, forgive others for their transgressions, so that your Father who is in Heaven will also forgive you your transgressions.	6:14~　"~~For~~ if you forgive others for their transgressions, your heaven~~ly~~ Father will also forgive you.	11:25　"Whenever you stand praying, forgive, if you have anything against anyone, so that your Father who is in heaven will also forgive you your transgressions.
8　"But if you do not forgive others, then neither will your Father who is in Heaven forgive your transgressions."	6:15　"But if you do not forgive others, then your Father will ~~not~~ forgive your transgressions.	11:26　{But if you do not forgive, neither will your Father who is in heaven forgive your transgressions."}

1. Psalm 103:20-21　　2. Proverb 30:8

4 - SECOND YEAR OF MINISTRY

Act 3: **The Sermon On True Wealth**

Scene 6: **When You Fast**

Mount Eremos, near Capernaum, *Galilee* spring / 31 CE

Look for **The Red Letter Gospel**

	Matthew
1 "Whenever you fast, do not put on a gloomy face as the hypocrites do, for they neglect their appearance so that they will be noticed by men when they are fasting. Truly I say to you, they have their reward in full.	*6:16* "Whenever you fast, do not put on a gloomy face as the hypocrites do, for they neglect their appearance so that they will be noticed by men when they are fasting. Truly I say to you, they have their reward in full.
2 "But you, when you fast, anoint your head and wash your face, so that your fasting will not be noticed by men, but by your Father who is in secret;	*6:17* "But you, when you fast, anoint your head and wash your face *6:18~* so that your fasting will not be noticed by men, but by your Father who is in secret;
3 "and your Father, who sees what is done in secret, will reward you."	*6:~18* and your Father who sees what is done in secret will reward you.

Scene 7: **Life Is Not About Possessions**

Mount Eremos, near Capernaum, *Galilee* spring / 31 CE

	Luke
1 Someone in the crowd said to [Jesus], "Teacher, tell my brother to divide the family inheritance with me."	*12:13* Someone in the crowd said to [~~Him~~], "Teacher, tell my brother to divide the family inheritance with me."
2 [Jesus] said to him, "Man, who appointed Me a judge or arbitrator over you?"	*12:14* ~~But~~ [He] said to him, "Man, who appointed Me a judge or arbitrator over you?"
3 Then He said to them, "Beware, and be on your guard against every form of greed; for not even when one has an abundance does his life consist of his possessions."	*12:15* Then He said to them, "Beware, and be on your guard against every form of greed; for not even when one has an abundance does his life consist of his possessions."
4 And He told them a parable, saying, "The land of a rich man was very productive, and he began reasoning to himself, saying, 'What shall I do, since I have no place to store my crops?'	*12:16* And He told them a parable, saying, "The land of a rich man was very productive. *12:17* "And he began reasoning to himself, saying, 'What shall I do, since I have no place to store my crops?'
5 Then he said, 'This is what I will do: I will tear down my barns, and build larger ones, and there I will store all my grain and my goods.	*12:18* "Then he said, 'This is what I will do: I will tear down my barns and build larger ones, and there I will store all my grain and my goods.
6 "And I will say to my soul, "Soul, you have many goods laid up for many years to come; eat, drink, and be merry!" '	*12:19* 'And I will say to my soul, "Soul, you have many goods laid up for many years to come; eat, drink and be merry." '
7 "But God said to him, 'You fool! This very night your soul is required of you; and now who will own what you have prepared?'	*12:20* "But God said to him, 'You fool! This very night your soul is required of you; and now who will own what you have prepared?'
8 "So is the man who stores up treasure for himself, and is not rich toward God."	*12:21* "So is the man who stores up treasure for himself, and is not rich toward God."

4 - SECOND YEAR OF MINISTRY

Act 3: The Sermon On True Wealth

Scene 8: **Store Up Treasure In Heaven**

Mount Eremos, near Capernaum, *Galilee*   spring / 31 CE

Page 79

The Greatest Four Gospel Harmony & Merger

	Matthew	Luke
1 *"Do not store up for yourselves treasures on earth,*[1] *where moth and rust destroy, and where thieves break in and steal.*	6:19 "Do not store up for yourselves treasures on earth, where moth and rust destroy, and where thieves break in and steal.	
2 "But sell your possessions, and give to charity; make yourselves money belts which do not wear out.	6:20~ "But	12:33~ "Sell your possessions and give to charity; make yourselves money belts which do not wear out,
3 "Store up for yourselves an unfailing treasure in Heaven, where neither moth nor rust destroys, and where thieves do not break in or steal;	6:~20 store up for yourselves treasures in heaven, where neither moth nor rust destroys, and where thieves do not break in or steal;	12:~33 an unfailing treasure in heaven, where ~~no thief~~ ~~comes~~ ~~near~~ nor moth destroys.
4 "for where your treasure is, there your heart will be also."	6:21 for where your treasure is, there your heart will be also.	12:34 "For where your treasure is, there your heart will be also.

1. *(Proverb 23:4)*

4 - SECOND YEAR OF MINISTRY
Act 3: The Sermon On True Wealth

Scene 9: Do Not Worry About Food or Clothing
Mount Eremos, near Capernaum, *Galilee* spring / 31 CE

synopticgospel.com

	Matthew	Luke
1 And [Jesus] said, "For this reason I say to you, do not worry about your life, as to what you will eat, or what you will drink, nor for your body, as to what you will put on; for life is more than food, and the body <is> more than clothing.	6:25 "For this reason I say to you, do not ~~be~~ ~~worried~~ about your life, as to what you will eat or what you will drink; nor for your body, as to what you will put on. Is ~~not~~ life more than food, and the body more than clothing?	12:22 And [He] said ~~to His disciples~~, "For this reason I say to you, do not worry about your life, as to what you will eat; nor for your body, as to what you will put on. 12:23 "For life is more than food, and the body more than clothing.
2 "Consider the birds of the air, for they do not sow nor reap; they have no storeroom, <and> nor <do they> gather into barns; and yet God, your Heavenly Father, feeds them.	6:26~ "~~Look at~~ the birds of the air, ~~that~~ they do not sow, nor reap nor gather into barns, and yet your heavenly Father feeds them.	12:24~ "Consider the ~~ravens~~, for they ~~neither~~ sow nor reap; they have no storeroom nor barn, and yet God feeds them;
3 "You are much more valuable than the birds!	6:~26 Are you ~~not~~ ~~worth~~ much more than ~~they~~?	12:~24 ~~how~~ much more valuable you are than the birds!
4 "And which of you by worrying can add a single hour to [your] life's span?	6:27 "And ~~who~~ of you by ~~being~~ ~~worried~~ can add a single hour to [his] life?	12:25 "And which of you by worrying can add a single hour to [his] life's span?
5 "If then, you cannot do even a very little thing, why do you worry about other matters?		12:26 "If then you cannot do even a very little thing, why do you worry about other matters?
6 "And why are you worried about clothing? Observe the lilies of the field, <and> consider how they grow;	6:28~ "And why are you worried about clothing? Observe how the lilies of the field grow;	12:27~ "Consider the lilies, how they grow;
7 "they do not toil, nor do they spin, yet I say to you, that not even Solomon, in all his glory, clothed himself like one of these.	6:~28 they do not toil nor do they spin, 6:29 yet I say to you that not even Solomon in all his glory clothed himself like one of these.	12:~27 they ~~neither~~ toil nor spin; ~~but I~~ ~~tell~~ you, not even Solomon in all his glory clothed himself like one of these.
8 "But if God so clothes the grass in the field, which is alive today and tomorrow is thrown into the furnace, how much more will He clothe you, you men of little faith!	6:30 "But if God so clothes the grass ~~of~~ the field, which is alive today and tomorrow is thrown into the furnace, will He ~~not~~ much more clothe you? You of little faith!	12:28 But if God so clothes the grass in the field, which is alive today and tomorrow is thrown into the furnace, how much more will He clothe you? You men of little faith!
9 "<So> then, do not say, 'What will we eat?' and 'What will we drink?' or 'What will we wear for clothing?' and do not <be> [anxious];	6:31 "Do not [~~worry~~] then say~~ing~~, 'What will we eat?' ~~or~~ 'What will we drink?' or 'What will we wear for clothing?'	12:29 "[~~And~~] do not ~~seek~~ what ~~you~~ will eat and what ~~you~~ will drink, and do not ~~keep~~ [worrying].
10 "for the nations of the world eagerly seek all these things, [and] your Heavenly Father knows that you need [them].	6:32 "For the ~~Gentiles~~ eagerly seek all these things; [for] your heavenly Father knows that you need [~~all~~ ~~these~~ ~~things~~].	12:30 "For all these things the nations of the world eagerly seek; [~~but~~] your Father knows that you need [~~these~~ ~~things~~].
11 "But seek first His Kingdom, and His righteousness, and all these things will be added to you.	6:33 "But seek first His kingdom and His righteousness, and all these things will be added to you.	12:31 "But seek His kingdom, and these things will be added to you.
12 "Do not be afraid, little flock, for your Father has gladly chosen to give you the Kingdom!		12:32 "Do not be afraid, little flock, for your Father has chosen gladly to give you the kingdom.
13 "So do not worry about tomorrow, for tomorrow will care for itself,	6:34~ "So do not worry about tomorrow; for tomorrow will care for itself.	
14 "<because> each day has enough trouble of its own."	6:~34 Each day has enough trouble of its own."	

| 4 - SECOND YEAR OF MINISTRY | Scene 1: **On Judging Another Person** | Page 81 |
| Act 4: **The Sermon on Spiritual Fruit** | Mount Eremos, near Capernaum, *Galilee*   spring / 31 CE | *The United Gospel Story* |

	Matthew	**Luke**
1 "Do not judge, and you will not be judged; do not condemn, and you will not be condemned; pardon, and you will be pardoned.	7:1 "Do not judge ~~so that~~ you will not be judged.	6:37 "Do not judge, and you will not be judged; ~~and~~ do not condemn, and you will not be condemned; pardon, and you will be pardoned.
2 "For in the way <that> you judge, you will be judged, and by your standard of measure, it will be measured to you.	7:2 "For in the way you judge, you will be judged; and by your standard of measure, it will be measured to you.	
3 "Why do you look at the speck that is in your brother's eye, but do not notice the log that is in your own eye?	7:3 "Why do you look at the speck that is in your brother's eye, but do not notice the log that is in your own eye?	6:41 "Why do you look at the speck that is in your brother's eye, but do not notice the log that is in your own eye?
4 "Or how can you say to your brother, 'Brother, let me take out the speck that is in your eye,' when behold, you yourself do not see the log that is in your own eye?	7:4 "Or how can you say to your brother, 'Let me take the speck out ~~of~~ your eye,' ~~and~~ behold, the log is in your own eye?	6:42 "Or how can you say to your brother, 'Brother, let me take out the speck that is in your eye,' when you yourself do not see the log that is in your own eye?
5 "You hypocrite! First take the log out of your own eye, and then you will see clearly to take out the speck that is in your brother's eye."	7:5 "You hypocrite, first take the log out of your own eye, and then you will see clearly to take the speck out ~~of~~ your brother's eye.	6:~42 You hypocrite, first take the log out of your own eye, and then you will see clearly to take out the speck that is in your brother's eye.
6 And He also spoke a parable to them: "A blind man cannot guide a blind man, can he? Will they not both fall into a pit?"		6:39 And He also spoke a parable to them: "A blind man cannot guide a blind man, can he? Will they not both fall into a pit?

4 - SECOND YEAR OF MINISTRY
Act 4: The Sermon on Spiritual Fruit

Scene 2: **Ask, and It Will Be Given To You**

Mount Eremos, near Capernaum, *Galilee*   spring / 31 CE

The Four Gospels Combined as One

	Matthew	Luke
1 Then [Jesus] said to them, "Suppose <that> one of you goes to a friend at midnight, and says to him, 'Friend, lend me three loaves, for a friend of mine has come to me [on] a journey, and I have nothing to [give] him';		11:5 Then [He] said to them, "Suppose one of you has a friend, and goes to him at midnight and says to him, "Friend, lend me three loaves; 11:6 for a friend of mine has come to me [from] a journey, and I have nothing to [set before] him";
2 "[but] from inside he answers, and says, 'Do not bother me; the door [is] shut, and my children and I are in bed; I cannot get up and give you anything.'		11:7 [and] from inside he answers and says, 'Do not bother me; the door [has already been] shut and my children and I are in bed; I cannot get up and give you anything."
3 "I tell you, even though he will not get up and give him anything because he is his friend, yet because of his persistence he will get up and give him as much as he needs.		11:8 "I tell you, even though he will not get up and give him anything because he is his friend, yet because of his persistence he will get up and give him as much as he needs.
4 "So I say to you: Ask, and it will be given to you; seek, and you will find; knock, and it will be opened to you!	7:7 "Ask, and it will be given to you; seek, and you will find; knock, and it will be opened to you.	11:9 "So I say to you, ask, and it will be given to you; seek, and you will find; knock, and it will be opened to you.
5 "For everyone who asks, receives; and *he who seeks finds;* [1.] and to him who knocks, it will be opened.	7:8 "For everyone who asks receives, and he who seeks finds, and to him who knocks it will be opened.	11:10 "For everyone who asks, receives; and he who seeks finds, and to him who knocks it will be opened.
6 "Now suppose one of you fathers is asked by his son for a fish; he will not give him a snake instead of a fish, will he?	7:10 "Or if he asks for a fish, he will not give him a snake, will he?	11:11 "Now suppose one of you fathers is asked by his son for a fish; he will not give him a snake, instead of a fish, will he?
7 "Or what man when asked for a loaf, will give him a stone?	7:9 "Or what man is there among you who, when his son asks for a loaf, will give him a stone?	11:12 "Or if he is asked for an egg, he will not give him a scorpion, will he?
8 "If you then, being evil, know how to give good gifts to your children, how much more will your Heavenly Father give the Holy Spirit <and> what is good to those who ask Him.	7:11 "If you then, being evil, know how to give good gifts to your children, how much more will your Father who is in heaven give what is good to those who ask Him!	11:13 "If you then, being evil, know how to give good gifts to your children, how much more will your heavenly Father give the Holy Spirit to those who ask Him?"
9 "In everything therefore, treat other people the same way <that> you want them to treat you; for this is the Law, and the Prophets.	7:12 "In everything, therefore, treat people the same way you want them to treat you, for this is the Law and the Prophets.	6:31 "Treat others the same way you want them to treat you.
10 "Enter through the narrow gate; for the gate is wide, and the way is broad, that leads to destruction, and there are many who enter through it.	7:13 "Enter through the narrow gate; for the gate is wide and the way is broad that leads to destruction, and there are many who enter through it.	
11 "[But] the gate is small, and the way is narrow that leads to life, and there are few who find it."	7:14 "[For] the gate is small and the way is narrow that leads to life, and there are few who find it.	

1. Proverb 8:17

4 - SECOND YEAR OF MINISTRY
Act 4: **The Sermon on Spiritual Fruit**

Scene 3: **The Fruit of False Prophets**
Mount Eremos, near Capernaum, *Galilee* spring / 31 CE

	Matthew	Luke
1 "Do not give what is holy to dogs, and do not throw your pearls before swine, [because] they will trample them under their feet, and <then> turn and tear you to pieces.	7:6 "Do not give what is holy to dogs, and do not throw your pearls before swine, [~~or~~] they will trample them under their feet, and turn and tear you to pieces.	
2 "*Beware of the false prophets* [1] who come to you in sheep's clothing, but inwardly are ravenous wolves!	7:15 "Beware of the false prophets, who come to you in sheep's clothing, but inwardly are ravenous wolves.	
3 "You will know them by their fruits, for each tree is known by its fruit.	7:16~ "You will know them by their fruits.	6:44~ "For each tree is known by its ~~own~~ fruit.
4 "For men do not gather figs from thorns, nor do they pick grapes from a briar bush.	7:~16 Grapes ~~are~~ not gather~~ed~~ from thorn bush~~es~~ nor figs from thistles, ~~are they~~?	6:~44 For men do not gather figs from thorns, nor do they pick grapes from a briar bush.
5 "So every good tree bears good fruit, but the bad tree bears bad fruit.	7:17 "So every good tree bears good fruit, but the bad tree bears bad fruit.	
6 "For there is no good tree which produces bad fruit, <and> nor on the other hand, can a bad tree produce good fruit.	7:18 "A good tree ~~cannot~~ produce bad fruit, nor can a bad tree produce good fruit.	6:43 "For there is no good tree which produces bad fruit, nor on the other hand, a bad tree ~~which~~ produce~~s~~ good fruit.
7 "So then, you will know them by their fruits.	7:20 "So then, you will know them by their fruits.	
8 "Every tree that does not bear good fruit is cut down, and thrown into the fire."	7:19 "Every tree that does not bear good fruit is cut down and thrown into the fire.	

1. *Jeremiah 23:16*

4 - SECOND YEAR OF MINISTRY
Act 4: **The Sermon on Spiritual Fruit**

Scene 4: **Build On The Solid Foundation of The Word**

Mount Eremos, near Capernaum, *Galilee*   spring / 31 CE

A Verse-By-Verse Gospel Harmony

	Matthew	Luke
1 "Not everyone who says to Me, 'Lord, Lord,' will enter the Kingdom of Heaven, but [the one] who does the will of My Father who is in Heaven will enter.	7:21 "Not everyone who says to Me, 'Lord, Lord,' will enter the kingdom of heaven, but [he] who does the will of My Father who is in heaven will enter.	
2 "Many will say to Me on that day, 'Lord, Lord, did we not prophesy in Your Name, and in Your Name cast out demons, and in Your Name perform many miracles?'	7:22 "Many will say to Me on that day, 'Lord, Lord, did we not prophesy in Your name, and in Your name cast out demons, and in Your name perform many miracles?'	
3 "Then I will declare to them, 'Why do you call Me, "Lord, Lord," and do not do what I say?	7:23~ ~~And~~ then I will declare to them,	6:46 "Why do you call Me, 'Lord, Lord,' and do not do what I say?
4 "I never knew you. *Depart from Me, you who practice lawlessness!* [1.]	7:~23 'I never knew you; depart from Me, you who practice lawlessness.'	
5 "Therefore, everyone who comes to Me, and hears these Words of Mine, and acts on them, I will show you whom he may be compared to: He is like a wise man building a house, who dug deep, and laid a foundation on the rock.	7:24 "Therefore everyone who hears these words of Mine and acts on them, may be compared to ~~a~~ wise man ~~who~~ built ~~his~~ house on the rock.	6:47 "Everyone who comes to Me and hears M~~y~~ words and acts on them, I will show you whom he ~~is like~~: 6:48~ he is like a man building a house, who dug deep and laid a foundation on the rock;
6 "And when the rains fell and the floods came, the winds blew, and the torrent burst <and> slammed against that house; and yet <the storm> could not shake it, and it did not fall, because it had been founded on the rock.	7:25 "~~And~~ the rain fell, and the floods came, ~~and~~ the winds blew and slammed against that house; and yet could not shake it, and it did not fall, ~~for~~ it had been founded on the rock.	6:~48 and when ~~a~~ flood ~~occurred~~, the torrent burst against that house and could not shake it, because it had been ~~well~~ ~~built~~.
7 "But the one who hears these words of Mine, and does not act on them accordingly, is like a foolish man who built his house on the sand, without any foundation.	7:26 "~~Every~~one who hears these words of Mine and does not act on them, ~~will be~~ like a foolish man who built his house on the sand.	6:49~ "But the one who ~~has heard~~ and ~~has~~ not act~~ed~~ accordingly, is like a man who built ~~a~~ house on the ~~ground~~ without any foundation;
8 "The rain[s] fell, and the floods came, and the winds blew, and the torrent burst and slammed against that house, and immediately it collapsed - and great was the ruin of that house."	7:27 "The rain fell, and the floods came, and the winds blew and slammed against that house; and it ~~fell~~ - and great was its ~~fall~~."	6:~49 and the torrent burst against ~~it~~ and immediately it collapsed, and the ruin of that house was great."

1. Psalm 6:8

Scene 5: **Jesus Finishes His Sermon**

Mount Eremos, near Capernaum, *Galilee*   spring / 31 CE

	Matthew	Luke
1 When Jesus had finished all <of> His discourse in the hearing of the people, the crowds were amazed at His teaching, for He was teaching them as one having authority, and not as their scribes.	7:28 When Jesus had finished ~~these words~~, the crowds were amazed at His teaching; 7:29 for He was teaching them as one having authority, and not as their scribes.	7:1~ When ~~He~~ had ~~complet~~ed all His discourse in the hearing of the people,
2 When Jesus came down from the mountain, large crowds followed Him, <and> He went to Capernaum.	8:1 When Jesus came down from the mountain, large crowds followed Him.	7:~1 He went to Capernaum.

4 - SECOND YEAR OF MINISTRY	Scene 1: **Healing A Centurion's Servant**	Page 85
Act 5: **Events In Galilee**	Capernaum, *Galilee* spring / 31 CE	*All the Gospel Deeds of Jesus*

	Matthew	**Luke**
1 When Jesus entered Capernaum, a centurion, who[se] highly regarded slave was sick and about to die, heard about [Him].	8:5~ ~~And~~ when Jesus entered Capernaum, a centurion	7:2 ~~And~~ a centurion~~'s~~ slave, who ~~was~~ highly regarded ~~by him~~, was sick and about to die. 7:3~ ~~When he~~ heard about [~~Jesus~~],
2 <And> he sent some Jewish elders <to> ask [Jesus] to come and save the life of his slave, <who> [was] lying at home paralyzed, <and> [terribly] tormented.	8:6 ~~and saying, "Lord, my servant~~ [is] lying paralyzed at home, [~~fearfully~~] tormented."	7:~3 he sent some Jewish elders ask~~ing~~ [Him] to come and save the life of his slave.
3 When [the elders] came to Jesus, they earnestly implored Him, saying, "He is worthy for You to grant this to him, for he loves our nation, and it was he who built our synagogue."	8:~5 came to [Him], implor~~ing~~ Him,	7:4 When [~~they~~] came to Jesus, they earnestly implored Him, saying, "He is worthy for You to grant this to him; 7:5 for he loves our nation and it was he who built ~~us~~ our synagogue."
4 Jesus said, "I will come and heal him," [and] [He] started on His way with them.	8:7 Jesus said ~~to him~~, "I will come and heal him."	7:6~ [~~Now~~] [~~Jesus~~] started on His way with them;
5 When [Jesus] was not far from the house, the centurion said to Him, "Lord, do not trouble yourself further, for I am not worthy for You to come under my roof, <and> for this reason I did not even consider myself worthy to come to You; but *just say the word, and my servant will be healed;* [1.]	8:8 ~~But~~ the centurion said "Lord, I am not worthy for You to come under my roof, but just say the word, and my servant will be healed.	7:~6 ~~and~~ when [He] was not far from the house, the centurion ~~sent friends~~, say~~ing~~ to Him "Lord, do not trouble Yourself further, for I am not worthy for You to come under my roof; 7:7 for this reason I did not even con-sider myself worthy to come to You, but just say the word, and my servant will be healed.
6 "for I also am a man placed under authority, with soldiers under me; and I say to this one, 'Go!' and he goes, and to another, 'Come here,' and he comes, and to my slave, 'Do this,' and he does it."	8:9 "For I also am a man under authority, with soldiers under me; and I say to this one, 'Go!' and he goes, and to another, 'Come!' and he comes, and to my slave, 'Do this!' and he does it."	7:8 "For I also am a man placed under authority, with soldiers under me; and I say to this one, 'Go!' and he goes, and to another, 'Come!' and he comes, and to my slave, 'Do this!' and he does it."
7 When Jesus heard this, He marveled at him; and <He> turned and said to the crowd that was following, "Truly I say to you, I have not found even in Israel anyone with such great faith!	8:10 ~~Now~~ when Jesus heard this, He marveled and said to ~~those who were~~ following, "Truly I say to you, I have not found such great faith with anyone in Israel.	7:9 ~~Now~~ when Jesus heard this, He marveled at him, and turned and said to the crowd that was following ~~Him~~, "I say to you, not even in Israel have I found such great faith.
8 "I say to you, that many will come from <the> east and <the> west, and recline at the table with Abraham, Isaac and Jacob, in the Kingdom of Heaven;	8:11 "I say to you that many will come from east and west, and recline at the table with Abraham, Isaac and Jacob in the kingdom of heaven;	
9 "but the sons of the Kingdom will be cast out into the outer darkness; in that place there will be weeping, and gnashing of teeth."	8:12 but the sons of the kingdom will be cast out into the outer darkness; in that place there will be weeping and gnashing of teeth."	
10 [Then] Jesus said to the centurion, "Go; it shall be done for you as you have believed."	8:13~ [~~And~~] Jesus said to the centurion, "Go; it shall be done for you as you have believed."	
11 And the servant was healed <at> that very moment.	8:~13 And the servant was healed that very moment.	
12 When those who had been sent returned to the house, they found the slave in good health.		7:10 When those who had been sent returned to the house, they found the slave in good health.

1. (Psalm 107:20)

4 - SECOND YEAR OF MINISTRY
Act 5: Events In Galilee

Scene 2: Perfumed Feet In The Home of A Pharisee
Capernaum, *Galilee*   summer / 31 CE

The Complete Gospel

	Luke
1 Now one of the Pharisees [invited] [Jesus] to dine with him, and He entered the Pharisee's house, and reclined at the table.	7:36 Now one of the Pharisees [was requesting] [Him] to dine with him, and He entered the Pharisee's house and reclined at the table.
2 There was a woman in the city who was a sinner, and when she learned that [Jesus] was reclining at the table in the Pharisee's house, she brought an alabaster vial of perfume,	7:37 And there was a woman in the city who was a sinner; and when she learned that [He] was reclining at the table in the Pharisee's house, she brought an alabaster vial of perfume,
3 and standing behind [Jesus], weeping at His feet, she began to wet His feet with her tears, and wiping them with the hair of her head, and kissing His feet, and anointing them with the perfume.	7:38 and standing behind [Him] at His feet, weeping, she began to wet His feet with her tears, and kept wiping them with the hair of her head, and kissing His feet and anointing them with the perfume.
4 When the Pharisee who had invited [Jesus] saw this, he said to himself, "If this man were a prophet, He would know who and what sort of person this woman is who is touching Him; that she is a sinner."	7:39 Now when the Pharisee who had invited [Him] saw this, he said to himself, "If this man were a prophet He would know who and what sort of person this woman is who is touching Him, that she is a sinner."
5 Jesus [said to] him, "Simon, I have something to say to you." He replied, "Say it, Teacher."	7:40 And Jesus [answered] him, "Simon, I have something to say to you." And he replied, "Say it, teacher."
6 "A moneylender had two debtors: one owed five hundred denarii, and the other fifty.	7:41 "A moneylender had two debtors: one owed five hundred denarii, and the other fifty.
7 "When they were unable to repay, he graciously forgave them both. So which of them will love him more?"	7:42 "When they were unable to repay, he graciously forgave them both. So which of them will love him more?"
8 Simon answered, and said, "I suppose the one whom he forgave more."	7:43~ Simon answered and said, "I suppose the one whom he forgave more."
9 [Jesus] said to him, "You have judged correctly."	7:~43 And [He] said to him, "You have judged correctly."
10 Turning toward the woman, [Jesus] said to Simon, "Do you see this woman?	7:44~ Turning toward the woman, [He] said to Simon, "Do you see this woman?
11 "<When> I entered your house, you gave Me no water for My feet; but she has wet My feet with her tears, and wiped them with her hair.	7:~44 I entered your house; you gave Me no water for My feet, but she has wet My feet with her tears and wiped them with her hair.
12 "You gave Me no kiss; but she, since the time <that> I came in, has not ceased to kiss My feet.	7:45 "You gave Me no kiss; but she, since the time I came in, has not ceased to kiss My feet.
13 "You did not anoint My head with oil, but she <has> anointed My feet with perfume!	7:46 "You did not anoint My head with oil, but she anointed My feet with perfume.
14 "For this reason, I say to you, <that> her sins, which are many, have been forgiven, for she loved much;	7:47~ "For this reason I say to you, her sins, which are many, have been forgiven, for she loved much;
15 "but he who is forgiven little, loves little."	7:~47 but he who is forgiven little, loves little."
16 Then [Jesus] said to [the woman], "Your sins have been forgiven."	7:48 Then [He] said to [her], "Your sins have been forgiven."
17 Those who were reclining at the table with Him began to say to themselves, "Who is this man who forgives sins?"	7:49 Those who were reclining at the table with Him began to say to themselves, "Who is this man who even forgives sins?"
18 And [Jesus] said to [her], "Your faith has saved you. Go in peace."	7:50 And [He] said to [the woman], "Your faith has saved you; go in peace."

4 - SECOND YEAR OF MINISTRY

Act 5: Events In Galilee

Scene 3: Preaching The Kingdom Of God
Galilee   summer / 31 CE

Page 87

FIVE COLUMN

	Luke
1 Soon afterwards, [Jesus] began going around from one city and village to another, proclaiming and preaching the Kingdom of God.	8:1~ Soon afterwards, [He] began going around from one city and village to another, proclaiming and preaching the kingdom of God.
2 The twelve <apostles> were with Him, and also some women who had been healed of evil spirits and sicknesses: Mary who was called Magdalene, from whom seven demons had gone out; and Joanna the wife of Chuza, Herod's steward; and Susanna;	8:~1 The twelve were with Him, 8:2 and also some women who had been healed of evil spirits and sicknesses: Mary who was called Magdalene, from whom seven demons had gone out, 8:3~ and Joanna the wife of Chuza, Herod's steward, and Susanna,
3 and many others who were contributing to their support out of their private means.	8:~3 and many others who were contributing to their support out of their private means.

Scene 4: Jesus Denounces The Unrepentant Cities
Galilee   summer / 31 CE

	Matthew	Luke
1 Then [Jesus] began to denounce the cities in which most of His miracles were done, because they did not repent.	11:20 Then [He] began to denounce the cities in which most of His miracles were done, because they did not repent.	
2 "Woe to you, Chorazin! Woe to you, Bethsaida! For if the miracles had been performed in Tyre and Sidon which occurred in you, they would have repented long ago, sitting in sackcloth and ashes.	11:21 "Woe to you, Chorazin! Woe to you, Bethsaida! For if the miracles had ~~occurred~~ in Tyre and Sidon which occurred in you, they would have repented long ago in sackcloth and ashes.	10:13 "Woe to you, Chorazin! Woe to you, Bethsaida! For if the miracles had been performed in Tyre and Sidon which occurred in you, they would have repented long ago sitting in sackcloth and ashes.
3 "Nevertheless, I say to you, <that> it will be more tolerable for Tyre and Sidon in the day of judgment, than for you!	11:22 "Nevertheless I say to you, it will be more tolerable for Tyre and Sidon in the day of judgment than for you.	10:14 "~~But~~ it will be more tolerable for Tyre and Sidon in the judgment than for you.
4 "And you, Capernaum, *you will not be exalted to Heaven - you will be brought down to Hades;* [1.] for if the miracles had occurred in Sodom which occurred in you, it would have remained to this day.	11:23 "And you, Capernaum, will not be exalted to heaven, ~~will~~ you? You will ~~descend~~ to Hades; for if the miracles had occurred in Sodom which occurred in you, it would have remained to this day.	10:15 "And you, Capernaum, will not be exalted to heaven, ~~will~~ you? You will be brought down to Hades!
5 "Nevertheless, I say to you, that it will be more tolerable for the land of Sodom in the day of judgment, than for you."	11:24 "Nevertheless I say to you that it will be more tolerable for the land of Sodom in the day of judgment, than for you."	10:12 "I say to you, it will be more tolerable in ~~that~~ day for Sodom than for ~~that city~~.

1. Isaiah 14:13, 15

4 - SECOND YEAR OF MINISTRY

Act 5: Events In Galilee

Scene 5: Come To Me - My Burden Is Light

Galilee   summer / 31 CE

The Greatest Gospel

	Matthew	Luke
1 At that time, Jesus rejoiced greatly in the Holy Spirit, and said, "I praise You, O Father, Lord of Heaven and earth, that You have hidden these things from the wise and intelligent, and *have revealed them to infants.*[1]	11:25 At that time Jesus said, "I praise You, father, Lord of heaven and earth, that You have hidden these things from the wise and intelligent and have revealed them to infants.	10:21~ At that ~~very~~ time ~~He~~ rejoiced greatly in the Holy Spirit, and said, "I praise You, O Father, Lord of heaven and earth, that You have hidden these things from the wise and intelligent and have revealed them to infants.
2 "Yes, Father, for this way was well-pleasing in Your sight.	11:26 "Yes, father, for this way was well-pleasing in Your sight.	10:~21 Yes, father, for this way was well-pleasing in Your sight.
3 "All things have been handed over to Me by My Father;	11:27~ "All things have been handed over to Me by My Father;	10:22~ "All things have been handed over to Me by My Father,
4 "and no one knows who the Son is except the Father, and nor does anyone know who the Father is except the Son,	11:~27~ and no one knows the Son except the Father; nor does anyone know the Father except the Son,	10:~22~ and no one knows who the Son is except the Father, and who the Father is except the Son,
5 "and anyone to whom the Son wills to reveal Him.	11:~27 and anyone to whom the Son wills to reveal Him.	10:~22 and anyone to whom the Son wills to reveal Him."
6 "Come to Me, all who are heavy-laden and weary, and I will give you rest.	11:28 "Come to Me, all who are weary and heavy-laden, and I will give you rest.	
7 "Take My yoke upon you, and learn from Me, for I am gentle and humble in heart, and *you will find rest for your souls;*[2] for My yoke is easy, and My burden is light."	11:29 "Take My yoke upon you and learn from Me, for I am gentle and humble in heart, and you will find rest for your souls. 11:30 "For My yoke is easy and My burden is light."	

1. (Psalm 8:2)   2. Jeremiah 6:16

4 - SECOND YEAR OF MINISTRY
Act 6: On Good and Evil Spirits

Scene 1: You Heal By Beelzebul
Capernaum, *Galilee* summer / 31 CE

Page 89
All the Gospel Miracles of Jesus

	Matthew	Mark	Luke
1 [When] [Jesus] came home, the crowd gathered <together> again, to such an extent that they could not even eat a meal.		3:20 [And] [He] came home, and the crowd gathered again, to such an extent that they could not even eat a meal.	
2 When His own people heard this, they went to take custody of Him, for they were saying, "He has lost His senses!"		3:21 When His own people heard of this, they went out to take custody of Him; for they were saying, "He has lost His senses."	
3 Then a demon-possessed man who was blind and mute was brought to Jesus; and He cast out [the] demon <and> healed him, so that the mute man spoke and saw.	12:22 Then a demon-possessed man who was blind and mute was brought to Jesus, and He healed him, so that the mute man spoke and saw.		11:14~ And He was casting out [a] demon, and it was mute; when the demon had gone out, the mute man spoke;
4 All the crowds were amazed, and were saying, "This man cannot be the Son of David, can he?"	12:23 All the crowds were amazed, and were saying, "This man cannot be the Son of David, can he?"		11:~14 and the crowds were amazed.
5 But when the Pharisees <and> the scribes who [had come] down from Jerusalem heard this, some of them were saying, "He is possessed by Beelzebul!";	12:24~ But when the Pharisees heard this, they said, 12:24^{-2} Beelzebul	3:22~ The scribes who [came] down from Jerusalem were saying, "He is possessed by Beelzebul",	11:15~ But some of them said, 11:15^{-2} Beelzebul,
6 and "This man casts out the demons only by the ruler of the demons."	12:24^{-1} "This man casts out demons only by 12:~24 the ruler of the demons."	3:~22 and "He casts out the demons by the ruler of the demons."	11:15^{-1} "He casts out demons by 11:~15 the ruler of the demons."
7 Others test[ed] [Jesus] <by> demanding a sign <out> of Heaven from Him.			11:16 Others, to test [Him], were demanding of Him a sign from heaven.

4 - SECOND YEAR OF MINISTRY

Act 6: On Good and Evil Spirits

Scene 2: How Can Satan Cast Out Satan?

Capernaum, *Galilee* summer / 31 CE

The Good News of Jesus Christ

#		Matthew	Mark	Luke
1	Knowing their thoughts, Jesus called them to Himself, and began speaking to them in parables.	*12:25~* ~~And~~ knowing their thoughts Jesus	*3:23~* ~~And~~ He called them to Himself and began speaking to them in parables,	*11:17⁻¹* kn~~e~~w their thoughts
2	He said to them, "How can Satan cast out Satan?	*12:25⁻¹* said to them,	*3:~23* "How can Satan cast out Satan?	*11:17~* ~~But~~ He *11:17⁻²* ~~and~~ said to them,
3	"If any kingdom is divided against itself that kingdom cannot stand, <and> is laid waste.	*12:25⁻²* "Any kingdom divided against itself is laid waste;	*3:24* "If ~~a~~ kingdom is divided against itself, that kingdom cannot stand.	*11:17⁻³* "Any kingdom divided against itself is laid waste;
4	"And if any house or city is divided against itself, [it] will not be able to stand, <and> falls.	*12:~25* and any city or house divided against itself will not stand.	*3:25* "If a house is divided against itself, [~~that house~~] will not be able to stand.	*11:~17* and ~~a~~ house divided against itself falls.
5	"<So>, if Satan has risen up against himself, and casts out Satan, he also is divided against himself. How then will his kingdom stand? He cannot stand, but is finished!	*12:26* "If Satan casts out Satan, he is divided against himself; how then will his kingdom stand?	*3:26* "If Satan has risen up against himself and is divided, he cannot stand, but ~~he~~ is finished!	*11:18* "If Satan also is divided against himself, how will his kingdom stand?
6	"You say that I cast out demons by Beelzebul; and if I cast out demons by Beelzebul, by whom do your sons cast them out? So for this reason, they will be your judges.	*12:27* "If I by Beelzebul cast out demons, by whom do your sons cast them out? For this reason they will be your judges.		*11:~18* ~~For~~ you say that I cast out demons by Beelzebul. *11:19* "And if I by Beelzebul cast out demons, by whom do your sons cast them out? So they will be your judges.
7	"But if I cast out demons by the Spirit of God, then the Kingdom of God has come upon you!	*12:28* "But if I cast out demons by the Spirit of God, then the kingdom of God has come upon you.		*11:20* "But if I cast out demons by the ~~finger~~ of God, then the kingdom of God has come upon you.
8	"When a strong man, fully armed, guards his own house, his possessions are undisturbed.			*11:21* "When a strong man, fully armed, guards his own house, his possessions are undisturbed.
9	"But when someone stronger than he attacks him, and overpowers him, he takes away from him all his armor on which he had relied, and distributes his plunder.			*11:22* "But when someone stronger than he attacks him and overpowers him, he takes away from him all his armor on which he had relied and distributes his plunder.
10	"But no one can enter the strong man's house <to> plunder and carry off his property unless he first binds the strong man, and then he will plunder his house."	*12:29* "~~Or how~~ can ~~any~~one enter the strong man's house and carry off his property, unless he first binds the strong man? And then he will plunder his house.	*3:27* "But no one can enter the strong man's house ~~and~~ plunder his property unless he first binds the strong man, and then he will plunder his house.	

4 - SECOND YEAR OF MINISTRY

Act 6: On Good and Evil Spirits

Scene 3: **The Unforgivable Sin**
Capernaum, *Galilee*   summer / 31 CE

Page 91

90% of John is non-synoptic (unique)

#		Matthew	Mark	Luke
1	"He who is not with Me is against Me, and he who does not gather with Me scatters.	12:30 "He who is not with Me is against Me; and he who does not gather with Me scatters.		11:23 "He who is not with Me is against Me; and he who does not gather with Me scatters.
2	"Therefore, truly I say to you, all sins, and whatever blasphemies people utter, shall be forgiven the sons of men;	12:31~ "Therefore I say to you, ~~any sin and~~ blasphem~~y~~ shall be forgiven people,	3:28 "Truly I say to you, all sins shall be forgiven the sons of men, and whatever ~~they~~ utter;	
3	"but whoever blasphemes against the Holy Spirit is guilty of an eternal sin, <and> shall never be forgiven.	12:~31 but blasphem~~y~~ against the Spirit shall ~~not~~ be forgiven.	3:29 but whoever blasphemes against the Holy Spirit never ~~has forgiveness, but~~ is guilty of an eternal sin" -	
4	"Whoever speaks a word against the Son of Man, it shall be forgiven him;	12:32~ "Whoever speaks a word against the Son of Man, it shall be forgiven him;		12:10~ "~~And everyone~~ who speaks a word against the Son of Man, it ~~will~~ be forgiven him;
5	"but whoever blasphemes against the Holy Spirit, it will not be forgiven him, either in this age, or in the age to come" -	12:~32 but whoever ~~speaks~~ against the Holy Spirit, it ~~shall~~ not be forgiven him, either in this age or in the age to come.		12:~10 but ~~he~~ who blasphemes against the Holy Spirit, it will not be forgiven him.
6	because they were saying, "He has an unclean spirit."		3:30 because they were saying, "He has an unclean spirit."	

Scene 4: **On Good and Evil**
Capernaum, *Galilee*   summer / 31 CE

#		Matthew	Luke
1	"Either make the tree good and its fruit good, or make the tree bad and its fruit bad; for the tree is known by its fruit.	12:33 "Either make the tree good and its fruit good, or make the tree bad and its fruit bad; for the tree is known by its fruit.	
2	"You brood of vipers, how can you, being evil, speak what is good?	12:34~ "You brood of vipers, how can you, being evil, speak what is good?	
3	"The good man, out of the good treasure of his heart, brings forth what is good; and the evil man, out of his evil treasure, brings forth what is evil; for the mouth speaks of that which fills the heart.	12:35 "The good man brings out of ~~his~~ good treasure what is good; and the evil man brings out of his evil treasure what is evil. 12:~34 For the mouth speaks ~~out~~ of that which fills the heart.	6:45 "The good man out of the good treasure of his heart brings forth what is good; and the evil man out of ~~the~~ evil treasure brings forth what is evil; for ~~his~~ mouth speaks ~~from~~ that which fills ~~his~~ heart.
4	"I tell you that in the day of judgment, people shall give an accounting for every careless word that they speak;	12:36 "~~But~~ I tell you that every careless word that people speak, they shall give an accounting for ~~it~~ in the day of judgment.	
5	"for by your words you will be justified, and by your words you will be condemned."	12:37 "For by your words you will be justified, and by your words you will be condemned."	

4 - SECOND YEAR OF MINISTRY
Act 6: On Good and Evil Spirits

Scene 5: A Wicked Generation Seeks A Sign
Capernaum, *Galilee*   summer / 31 CE

This Text is from the Word-For-Word Edition

	Matthew	Luke
1 Then some of the scribes and Pharisees said to [Jesus], "Teacher, we want to see a sign from You!"	*12:38* Then some of the scribes and Pharisees said to [~~Him~~], "Teacher, we want to see a sign from You."	
2 As the crowds were increasing, [Jesus] answered, and said to them, "This generation is an evil and adulterous generation <because> it seeks for a sign; and yet no sign will be given to it, but the sign of Jonah the prophet.	*12:39* ~~But~~ [~~He~~] answered and said to them, "An evil and adulterous generation ~~craves~~ for a sign; and yet no sign will be given to it but the sign of Jonah the prophet;	*11:29* As the crowds were increasing, [~~He~~] ~~began to~~ say, "This generation is ~~a wicked~~ generation; it seeks for a sign, and yet no sign will be given to it but the sign of Jonah.
3 "For just as *Jonah was three days and three nights in the belly of the sea monster,*[1.] *<and> became a sign to the Ninevites,*[2.] so will the Son of Man be to this generation - three days and three nights in the heart of the earth.	*12:40* for just as Jonah was three days and three nights in the belly of the sea monster, so will the Son of Man be three days and three nights in the heart of the earth.	*11:30* "For just as Jonah became a sign to the Ninevites, so will the Son of Man be to this generation.
4 "The men of Nineveh will stand up with this generation at the judgment, and <they> will condemn it, because *they repented at the preaching of Jonah;*[3.]	*12:41* "The men of Nineveh will stand up with this generation at the judgment, and will condemn it because they repented at the preaching of Jonah;	*11:32~* "The men of Nineveh will stand up with this generation at the judgment and condemn it, because they repented at the preaching of Jonah;
5 "and behold, something greater than Jonah is here!	*12:~41* and behold, something greater than Jonah is here.	*11:~32* and behold, something greater than Jonah is here.
6 "The Queen of the South will rise up with the men of this generation at the judgment, and condemn them, because *she came from the ends of the earth to hear the wisdom of Solomon;*[4.]	*12:42~* "The Queen of the South will rise up with this generation at the judgment and ~~will~~ condemn ~~it~~, because she came from the ends of the earth to hear the wisdom of Solomon;	*11:31~* "The Queen of the South will rise up with the men of this generation at the judgment, and condemn them, because she came from the ends of the earth to hear the wisdom of Solomon;
7 "and behold, something greater than Solomon is here."	*12:42* and behold, something greater than Solomon is here.	*11:~31* and behold, something greater than Solomon is here.

1. *Jonah 1:17*   2. *Jonah 3:3-5*   3. *Jonah 3:5*   4. *1 Kings 10:1-13 / 2 Chronicles 9:1-12*

Scene 6: On Unclean Spirits

	Matthew	Luke
1 "Now when the unclean spirit goes out of a man, it passes through waterless places seeking rest, and does not find any.	*12:43* "Now when the unclean spirit goes out of a man, it passes through waterless places seeking rest, and does not find it.	*11:24~* "When the unclean spirit goes out of a man, it passes through waterless places seeking rest, and not ~~finding~~ any,
2 "Then it says, 'I will return to my house from which I came'; and when it comes, it finds it unoccupied, swept, and put in order.	*12:44* "Then it says, 'I will return to my house from which I came'; and when it comes, it finds it unoccupied, swept, and put in order.	*11:~24* it says, 'I will return to my house from which I came.' *11:25* And when it comes, it finds it swept and put in order.
3 "Then it goes and takes along with it seven other spirits more evil than itself, and they go in, and live there; and the last state of that man becomes worse than the first.	*12:45~* "Then it goes and takes along with it seven other spirits more ~~wicked~~ than itself, and they go in and live there; and the last state of that man becomes worse than the first.	*11:26* "Then it goes and takes along seven other spirits more evil than itself, and they go in and live there; and the last state of that man becomes worse than the first."
4 "That is the way it will also be with this evil generation."	*12:~45* That is the way it will also be with this evil generation."	
5 While Jesus was saying these things, one of the women in the crowd raised her voice, and said to Him, "Blessed is the womb that bore You, and the breasts at which You nursed!"		*11:27* While Jesus was saying these things, one of the women in the crowd raised her voice, and said to Him, "Blessed is the womb that bore You and the breasts at which You nursed."
6 But He said, "On the contrary; Blessed are those who hear the Word of God, and observe it!"		*11:28* But He said, "On the contrary, blessed are those who hear the word of God and observe it."

4 - SECOND YEAR OF MINISTRY	Scene 7: **Woe To You Pharisees!**	Page 93
Act 6: **On Good and Evil Spirits**	Capernaum, *Galilee* summer / 31 CE	*All the Gospel Teachings of Jesus*

Scene 7: Woe To You Pharisees!

Capernaum, *Galilee*   summer / 31 CE

	Luke
1 When He had spoken, a Pharisee asked [Jesus] to have lunch with him; and He went in, and reclined at the table.	11:37 ~~Now~~ when He had spoken, a Pharisee asked [~~Him~~] to have lunch with him; and He went in, and reclined at the table.
2 The Pharisee was surprised that [Jesus] had not first ceremonially washed before the meal.	11:38 ~~When~~ the Pharisee ~~saw it, he~~ was surprised that [He] had not first ceremonially washed before the meal.
3 But the Lord said to him, "Now you Pharisees clean the outside of the cup and the platter, but inside of you, you are full of robbery and wickedness.	11:39 But the Lord said to him, "Now you Pharisees clean the outside of the cup and ~~of~~ the platter; but inside of you, you are full of robbery and wickedness.
4 "You foolish ones! Did He who made the outside not also make the inside?	11:40 "You foolish ones, did not He who made the outside make the inside also?
5 "[So] give that which is within as charity, and then all things are clean for you.	11:41 "~~But~~ give that which is within as charity, and then all things are clean for you.
6 "But woe to you Pharisees! For you pay tithe of mint and rue, and every kind of garden herb, and yet disregard justice, and the love of God; these are the things <that> you should have done, without neglecting the others!	11:42 "But woe to you Pharisees! For you pay tithe of mint and rue and every kind of garden herb, and yet disregard justice and the love of God; ~~but~~ these are the things you should have done without neglecting the others.
7 "Woe to you Pharisees! For you love the chief seats in the synagogues, and the respectful greetings in the market places.	11:43 "Woe to you Pharisees! For you love the chief seats in the synagogues and the respectful greetings in the market places.
8 "Woe to you! For you are like concealed tombs, and the people who walk over them are unaware of it."	11:44 "Woe to you! For you are like concealed tombs, and the people who walk over them are unaware of it."

Scene 8: Woe To You Lawyers As Well!

	Luke
1 One of the lawyers said to [Jesus] in reply, "Teacher, when You say this, You insult us too."	11:45 One of the lawyers said to [~~Him~~] in reply, "Teacher, when You say this, You insult us too."
2 [So] [Jesus] said, "Woe to you lawyers as well! For you weigh men down with burdens <that are> hard to bear, while you yourselves will not touch the burdens with even one of your fingers!	11:46 [~~But~~] [~~He~~] said, "Woe to you lawyers as well! For you weigh men down with burdens hard to bear, while you yourselves will not even touch the burdens with one of your fingers.
3 "Woe to you lawyers! For you have taken away the key of knowledge;	11:52~ "Woe to you lawyers! For you have taken away the key of knowledge;
4 "you yourselves did not enter, and you hindered those who were entering."	11:~52 you yourselves did not enter, and you hindered those who were entering."
5 [Then] the scribes and the Pharisees began to be very hostile, and to question Him closely on many subjects, plotting to catch Him in something <that> He might say.	11:53 [~~When~~] ~~He left there~~, the scribes and the Pharisees began to be very hostile and to question Him closely on many subjects, 11:54 plotting [~~against Him~~] to catch Him in something He might say.
6 Under these circumstances, after so many thousands of people had gathered together that they were stepping on one another, [Jesus] began saying to His disciples, "Beware of the leaven of the Pharisees, which is hypocrisy."	12:1 Under these circumstances, after so many thousands of people had gathered together that they were stepping on one another, [~~He~~] began saying to His disciples ~~first of all~~, "Beware of the leaven of the Pharisees, which is hypocrisy."

4 - SECOND YEAR OF MINISTRY

Act 6: On Good and Evil Spirits

Scene 9: Who Are My Mother and My Brothers?

Capernaum, *Galilee*   summer / 31 CE

The Four Gospels Unified Verse-By-Verse

Page 94

	Matthew	Mark	Luke
1 While [Jesus] was still speaking to the crowds, behold, His mother and brothers arrived, and were standing outside, unable to get to Him because of the crowd.	12:46~ While [He] was still speaking to the crowds, behold, His mother and brothers were standing outside,	3:31~ ~~Then~~ His mother and ~~His~~ brothers arrived, and standing outside	8:19 And His mother and brothers ~~came to Him~~, and ~~they~~ were unable to get to Him because of the crowd.
2 Seeking to speak to Him, they sent word, and called Him.	12:~46 seeking to speak to Him.	3:~31 they sent word ~~to Him~~ and called Him.	
3 A crowd was sitting around [Jesus], and someone reported to Him, "Behold, Your mother and Your brothers are standing outside, wishing to speak to you."	12:47 Someone ~~said~~ to Him, "Behold, Your mother and Your brothers are standing outside ~~seek~~ing to speak to You."	3:32 A crowd was sitting around [~~Him~~], and ~~they~~ ~~said~~ to Him, "Behold, Your mother and Your brothers are outside ~~looking for~~ You."	8:20 And ~~it was~~ reported to Him, "Your mother and Your brothers are standing outside, wishing to ~~see~~ You.
4 But Jesus answered the one who was telling Him, and said, "Who is My mother, and who are My brothers?"	12:48 But Jesus answered the one who was telling Him and said, "Who is My mother and who are My brothers?"	3:33 Answer~~ing~~ ~~them~~, He said, "Who ~~are~~ My mother and My brothers?"	8:21~ But ~~He~~ answered
5 Looking about at those who were sitting around Him, <Jesus> stretch[ed] out His hand toward His disciples, and said, "Behold My mother, and My brothers!	12:49 ~~And~~ stretch[ing] out His hand toward His disciples, ~~He~~ said, "Behold My mother and My brothers!	3:34 Looking about at those who were sitting around Him, ~~He~~ said, "Behold My mother and My brothers!	8:~21~ and said ~~to them~~,
6 "My mother and My brothers are these who hear the Word of God, and do it.			8:~21 My mother and My brothers are these who hear the word of God and do it.
7 "For whoever does the will of God, My Father who is in Heaven, he is My brother, and sister, and mother."	12:50 "For whoever does the will of My Father who is in heaven, he is My brother and sister and mother."	3:35 "For whoever does the will of God, he is My brother and sister and mother."	

4 - SECOND YEAR OF MINISTRY
Act 7: **Parables About The Kingdom**

Scene 1: **The Parable of The Sower a)**
Sea of Galilee, Capernaum, *Galilee*   summer / 31 CE

All The Gospel Words of Jesus

	Matthew	Mark	Luke
1 That day Jesus went out of the house, and was sitting by the sea.	13:1 That day Jesus went out of the house and was sitting by the sea.	4:1~1 by the sea.	
2 He began to teach again, and such a very large crowd was journeying from the various cities and gathering to Him, that He got into a boat in the sea, and sat down.	13:2~ And large crowds gathered to Him, so He got into a boat and sat down,	4:1~ He began to teach again 4:1~2 And such a very large crowd gathered to Him that He got into a boat in the sea and sat down;	8:4~ When a large crowd was coming together and those from the various cities were journeying to Him,
3 The whole crowd was standing on the beach by the sea, and He was teaching them many things in parables.	13:~2 and the whole crowd was standing on the beach. 13:~3 And He spoke many things to them in parables,	4:~1 and the whole crowd was by the sea on the land. 4:2~ And He was teaching them many things in parables,	8:~4 He spoke by way of a parable:
4 In His teaching <He> was saying to them, "Listen to this! Behold, the sower went out to sow his seed;	13:~3 saying, "Behold, the sower went out to sow;	4:~2 and was saying to them in His teaching, 4:3 "Listen to this! Behold, the sower went out to sow;	8:5~ "The sower went out to sow his seed;
5 "and as he sowed, some seeds fell beside the road, and [they] [were] trampled under foot, and the birds of the air came and ate them up.	13:4 and as he sowed, some seeds fell beside the road, and the birds came and ate them up.	4:4 as he was sowing, some seed fell beside the road, and the birds came and ate it up.	8:~5 and as he sowed, some fell beside the road, and [it] [was] trampled under foot and the birds of the air ate it up.
6 "Other seed[s] fell on rocky ground, where they did not have much soil; and immediately they sprang up because they had no depth of soil.	13:5 "Others fell on the rocky places, where they did not have much soil; and immediately they sprang up, because they had no depth of soil.	4:5 "Other seed fell on the rocky ground where it did not have much soil; and immediately it sprang up because it had no depth of soil.	8:6~ "Other seed fell on rocky soil,
7 "But as soon as they grew up, after the sun had risen, they were scorched, and because they had no root they withered away.	13:6 "But when the sun had risen, they were scorched; and because they had no root, they withered away.	4:6 "And after the sun had risen, it was scorched; and because it had no root, it withered away.	8:~6 and as soon as it grew up, it withered away, because it had no moisture.
8 "Other seed fell among the thorns, and the thorns grew up with [them], and choked them out, and [they] yielded no crop.	13:7 "Others fell among the thorns, and the thorns came up and choked them out.	4:7 "Other seed fell among the thorns, and the thorns came up and choked it, and it yielded no crop.	8:7 "Other seed fell among the thorns; and the thorns grew up with it and choked it out.
9 "Other seeds fell on the good soil, and as they grew up and increased they yielded a crop; and some produced thirty, some sixty, and some a hundred times as [much]."	13:8 "And others fell on the good soil and yielded a crop, some a hundredfold, some sixty, and some thirty.	4:8 "Other seeds fell [into] the good soil, and as they grew up and increased, they yielded a crop and produced thirty, sixty, and a hundredfold."	8:8~ "Other seed fell i[into] the good soil, and grew up, and produced a crop a hundred times as [great]."
10 As [Jesus] was saying these things, He would call out, "He who has ears to hear, let him hear!"	13:9 "He who has ears, let him hear."	4:9 And [He] was saying, "He who has ears to hear, let him hear."	8:~8 As [He] said these things, He would call out, "He who has ears to hear, let him hear."

4 - SECOND YEAR OF MINISTRY

Act 7: Parables About The Kingdom

Scene 2: **Why Do You Speak To Them In Parables?**

Capernaum, *Galilee*   summer / 31 CE

Page 96

The Four Gospels Unified as One

	Matthew	Mark	Luke
1	As soon as [Jesus] was alone, His disciples, along with the twelve, came and [asked] Him, "Why do You speak to them in parables?" <and they> began questioning Him as to what this parable meant.	*13:10* ~~And the~~ disciples came and [~~said to~~] Him, "Why do You speak to them in parables?"	*4:10* As soon as [~~He~~] was alone, His ~~followers~~, along with the twelve, began ~~asking~~ Him ~~about~~ the parables.	*8:9* His disciples began questioning Him as to what this parable meant.
2	Turning to the disciples, Jesus answered them privately, and said, "To you it has been granted to know the mysteries of the Kingdom of Heaven, but to the rest who are outside, it has not been granted.	*13:11* Jesus answered them, "To you it has been granted to know the mysteries of the kingdom of heaven, but to ~~them~~ it has not been granted.	*4:11~* And ~~He was saying to~~ them, "To you has been ~~given~~ the mystery of the kingdom of ~~God~~, but ~~those~~ who are outside ~~get~~	*10:23~* Turning to the disciples, ~~He said~~ privately, *8:10~* And ~~He~~ said, "To you it has been granted to know the mysteries of the kingdom of ~~God~~, but to the rest
3	"Therefore, I speak everything to them in parables, so that while seeing they may see and not perceive, and while hearing they may hear, and not understand.	*13:13* "Therefore I speak to them in parables; ~~because~~ while seeing they ~~do~~ not ~~see~~, and while hearing they ~~do not~~ hear, nor ~~do they~~ understand.	*4:~11* everything in parables, *4:12~* so that while seeing, they may see and not perceive, and while hearing, they may hear and not understand,	*8:~10* ~~it is~~ in parables so that seeing they ~~may~~ not ~~see~~, and hearing they may not understand.
4	"In their case, the prophecy of Isaiah is being fulfilled, which says, *'You will keep on hearing, but will not understand; you will keep on seeing, but will not perceive;*	*13:14* "In their case the prophecy of Isaiah is being fulfilled, which says, 'You will keep on hearing, but will not understand; you will keep on seeing, but will not perceive;		
5	*"for the heart of this people has become dull; with their ears they scarcely hear, and they have closed their eyes,*	*13:15~* For the heart of this people has become dull, with their ears they scarcely hear, and they have closed their eyes,		
6	*"otherwise they would see with their eyes, hear with their ears, and understand with their heart, and return,* and be forgiven, *and I would heal them.'* [1]	*13:~15* otherwise they would see with their eyes, hear with their ears, and understand with their heart and return, and I would heal them.'	*4:~12* otherwise they ~~might~~ return and be forgiven."	
7	"But blessed are your eyes, because they see the things you see; and your ears, because they hear!	*13:16* "But blessed are your eyes, because they see; and your ears, because they hear.		*10:~23* "Blessed are ~~the~~ eyes ~~which~~ see the things you see,
8	"For truly I say to you, that many prophets, kings and righteous men, desired to see the things which you see, and <they> did not see them; and to hear the things which you hear, and <they> did not hear them."	*13:17* "For truly I say to you that many prophets and righteous men desired to see ~~what~~ you see, and did not see ~~it~~, and to hear ~~what~~ you hear, and did not hear ~~it~~.		*10:24* for I say to you, that many prophets ~~and~~ kings ~~wished~~ to see the things which you see, and did not see them, and to hear the things which you hear, and did not hear them."
9	And He said to them, "Do you not understand this parable? How will you understand all the parables?"		*4:13* And He said to them, "Do you not understand this parable? How will you understand all the parables?	

1. Isaiah 6:9-10; 43:8

4 - SECOND YEAR OF MINISTRY
Act 7: **Parables About The Kingdom**

Scene 3: **The Parable of The Sower b) Explained**
Capernaum, *Galilee*   summer / 31 CE

A United Harmony of the Four Gospels

	Matthew	Mark	Luke
1 "Hear then the parable of the sower: The sower sows the [seed], <and> the seed is the Word of God.	13:18 "Hear then the parable of the sower.	4:14 "The sower sows the [word].	8:11 "Now the parable is this: the seed is the word of God.
2 "Those who are beside the road where the seed is sown are the ones who have heard; and when they hear the Word of the Kingdom, and do not understand it, the immediately the evil one - Satan, the Devil - comes, and takes away the Word which has been sown in their heart, so that they will not believe, and be saved.	13:19 "When anyone hears the word of the kingdom and does not understand it, the evil one comes and snatches away what has been sown in his heart. This is the one on whom seed was sown beside the road.	4:15 " These are the ones who are beside the road where the word is sown; and when they hear, immediately Satan comes and takes away the word which has been sown in them.	8:12 "Those beside the road are those who have heard; the devil comes and takes away the word from their heart, so that they will not believe and be saved.
3 "In a similar way are the ones on whom seed was sown on the rocky soil; these are [the ones] who, when they hear the Word, <they> immediately receive it with joy; and yet, they have no firm root in themselves, [and] are only temporary;	13:20~ "The one on whom seed was sown on the rocky places, this is the man who hears the word and immediately receives it with joy; 13:21~ yet he has no firm root in himself, [but] is only temporary,	4:16 "In a similar way these are the ones on whom seed was sown on the rocky places, who, when they hear the word, immediately receive it with joy; 4:17~ and they have no firm root in themselves, [but] are only temporary;	8:13~ "Those on the rocky soil are [those] who, when they hear, receive the word with joy; and these have no firm root;
4 "they believe for a while, and then in time of temptation, <or> when affliction or persecution arises because of the Word, they immediately fall away.	13:~21 and when affliction or persecution arises because of the word, immediately he falls away.	4:~17 then, when affliction or persecution arises because of the word, immediately they fall away.	8:~13 they believe for a while, and in time of temptation fall away.
5 "Others are the ones on whom the seed was sown which fell among the thorns; these are the ones who have heard the Word, but as they go on their way, the worries of the world, and the deceitfulness of wealth and riches, and the desire for <the> pleasures of this life and other things, enter in and choke the Word, and it becomes unfruitful, <and> they bring no fruit to maturity.	13:22 "And the one on whom seed was sown among the thorns, this is the man who hears the word, and the worry of the world and the deceitfulness of wealth choke the word, and it becomes unfruitful.	4:18 "And others are the ones on whom seed was sown among the thorns; these are the ones who have heard the word, 4:19 but the worries of the world, and the deceitfulness of riches, and the desires for other things enter in and choke the word, and it becomes unfruitful.	8:14 "The seed which fell among the thorns, these are the ones who have heard, and as they go on their way they are choked with worries and riches and pleasures of this life, and bring no fruit to maturity.
6 "And the ones on whom the seed was sown in the good soil are the ones who hear the Word in a good and honest heart; and <they> understand it, and accept it, and hold it fast, and indeed bear fruit with perseverance; and <they> bring forth, some thirty, some sixty, and some a hundred [times as much]."	13:23 "And the one on whom seed was sown on the good soil, this is the man who hears the word and understands it; who indeed bears fruit and brings forth, some a hundred[fold], some sixty, and some thirty."	4:20 "And those are the ones on whom seed was sown on the good soil; and they hear the word and accept it and bear fruit, thirty, sixty, and a hundred[fold]."	8:15 "But the seed in the good soil, these are the ones who have heard the word in an honest and good heart, and hold it fast, and bear fruit with perseverance.
7 And [Jesus] [said] to them, "So take care what you listen to, <and> how you listen!		4:24~ And [He] [was saying] to them, "Take care what you listen to.	8:18~ "So take care how you listen;
8 "By your standard of measure it will be measured to you, and [even] more will be given <to> you.		4:~24 By your standard of measure it will be measured to you; and more will be given you [besides].	
9 "For whoever has, to him more shall be given, and he will have an abundance;	13:12~ "For whoever has, to him more shall be given, and he will have an abundance;	4:25~ For whoever has, to him more shall be given;	8:~18~ for whoever has, to him more shall be given;
10 "but whoever does not have, even what he thinks he has shall be taken away from him."	13:~12 but whoever does not have, even what he has shall be taken away from him.	4:~25 and whoever does not have, even what he has shall be taken away from him."	8:~18 and whoever does not have, even what he thinks he has shall be taken away from him."

4 - SECOND YEAR OF MINISTRY
Act 7: **Parables About The Kingdom**

Scene 4: **The Parable of The Tares a)**
Capernaum, *Galilee*   summer / 31 CE

Verse-By-Verse Edition

		Matthew	Mark
1	[Jesus] [said], "The Kingdom of God is like a man who casts seed upon the soil, and he goes to bed at night and gets up by day; and the seed sprouts and grows - how, he himself does not know.		4:26 And [He] [was saying], "The kingdom of God is like a man who casts seed upon the soil; 4:27 and he goes to bed at night and gets up by day, and the seed sprouts and grows - how, he himself does not know.
2	"The soil produces crops by itself; first the blade, then the head, then the mature grain in the head.		4:28 "The soil produces crops by itself; first the blade, then the head, then the mature grain in the head.
3	"[And] when the crop permits, he immediately [uses] the sickle, because the harvest has come."		4:29 "[But] when the crop permits, he immediately [puts in] the sickle, because the harvest has come."
4	[He] presented another parable to them, saying, "The Kingdom of Heaven may be compared to a man who sowed good seed in his field.	13:24 [Jesus] presented another parable to them, saying, "The kingdom of heaven may be compared to a man who sowed good seed in his field.	
5	"But while his men were sleeping, his enemy came and sowed tares among the wheat, and went away.	13:25 "But while his men were sleeping, his enemy came and sowed tares among the wheat, and went away.	
6	"<Later,> when the wheat sprouted and bore grain, then the tares also became evident.	13:26 "But when the wheat sprouted and bore grain, then the tares became evident also.	
7	"The slaves of the landowner came to him, and said, 'Sir, did you not sow good seed in your field? How then does it have tares?'	13:27 "The slaves of the landowner came and said to him, 'Sir, did you not sow good seed in your field? How then does it have tares?'	
8	"He said to them, 'An enemy has done this.'	13:28~ "And he said to them, 'An enemy has done this!'	
9	"[His] slaves said, 'Do you want us to go and gather them up?'	13:~28 [The] slaves said to him, 'Do you want us, then, to go and gather them up?'	
10	"But he said, 'No; for while you are gathering up the tares, you may <also> uproot the wheat with them.	13:29 "But he said, 'No; for while you are gathering up the tares, you may uproot the wheat with them.	
11	"Allow both to grow together until the harvest, and in the time of the harvest I will say to the reapers, "First gather up the tares, and bind them in bundles to burn them up; but gather the wheat into my barn."'"	13:30 'Allow both to grow together until the harvest; and in the time of the harvest I will say to the reapers, "First gather up the tares and bind them in bundles to burn them up; but gather the wheat into my barn."'"	

4 - SECOND YEAR OF MINISTRY
Act 7: Parables About The Kingdom

Scene 5: The Kingdom of Heaven Is Like A Mustard Seed
Capernaum, *Galilee* summer / 31 CE

Page 99

The Four Gospels Harmoniously Unified

	Matthew	Mark	Luke
1 [Jesus] presented another parable to them, and said, "What is the Kingdom of God like, and to what shall I compare it?	13:31~ [He] presented another parable to them, s~~aying~~,	4:30 And ~~He~~ said, "~~How shall we picture~~ the kingdom of God, ~~or by~~ what ~~parable~~ shall ~~we present~~ it?	13:18 ~~So He was~~ saying, "What is the kingdom of God like, and to what shall I compare it?
2 "The Kingdom of Heaven is like a mustard seed, which a man took and sowed in his garden.	13:~31 "The kingdom of heaven is like a mustard seed, which a man took and sowed in his ~~field~~;	4:31~ "~~It~~ is like a mustard seed, which,	13:19 "~~It~~ is like a mustard seed, which a man took and ~~threw~~ into his ~~own~~ garden;
3 "When sown upon the soil, it is smaller than all the other seeds, *but when it is full grown it is larger than all the garden plants, and forms large branches and becomes a tree, so that the birds of the air can come and nest in its branches."* [1]	13:32 ~~and this~~ is smaller than all other seeds, but when it is full grown, it is larger than the garden plants and becomes a tree, so that the birds of the air come and nest in its branches."	4:~31 when sown upon the soil, ~~though~~ it is smaller than all the seeds ~~that are upon the soil~~, 4:32 ~~yet~~ when it is ~~sown~~, it grows ~~up~~ and becomes larger than all the garden plants and forms large branches; so that the birds of the air can nest ~~under~~ its ~~shade~~."	13:~19 ~~and~~ it grew and became a tree, ~~and~~ the birds of the air nested in its branches."

1. *Ezekiel 17:23; 31:6*

4 - SECOND YEAR OF MINISTRY
Act 7: Parables About The Kingdom

Scene 6: More Parables About The Kingdom of Heaven
Capernaum, *Galilee*   summer / 31 CE

	Matthew	Mark	Luke
1	Again [Jesus] said, "To what shall I compare the Kingdom of God?" <and> He spoke another parable to them:	13:33~ He spoke another parable to them,		13:20 And again [He] said, "To what shall I compare the kingdom of God?
2	"The Kingdom of Heaven is like leaven, which a woman took and hid in three [measures] of flour, until it was all leavened.	13:~33 "The kingdom of heaven is like leaven, which a woman took and hid in three [pecks] of flour until it was all leavened."		13:21 "It is like leaven, which a woman took and hid in three [pecks] of flour until it was all leavened."
3	"The Kingdom of Heaven is like a treasure hidden in the field, which a man found and <then> hid again; and [for] <the> joy [of] it, he goes and sells all that he has, and buys that field.	13:44 "The kingdom of heaven is like a treasure hidden in the field, which a man found and hid again; and from joy over it he goes and sells all that he has and buys that field.		
4	"Again, the Kingdom of Heaven is like a merchant seeking fine pearls, and upon finding one pearl of great value, he went and sold all that he had, and bought it.	13:45 "Again, the kingdom of heaven is like a merchant seeking fine pearls, 13:46 and upon finding one pearl of great value, he went and sold all that he had and bought it.		
5	"Again, the Kingdom of Heaven is like a dragnet <that is> cast into the sea, and gather[ed] every kind of fish; and when [the net] was filled, they drew it up on <to> the beach.	13:47 "Again, the kingdom of heaven is like a dragnet cast into the sea, and gather[ing] fish of every kind; 13:48~ and when [it] was filled, they drew it up on the beach;		
6	"[Then] they sat down, and <they> gathered the good fish into containers, but the bad <ones> they threw away.	13:~48 [and] they sat down and gathered the good fish into containers, but the bad they threw away.		
7	"So it will be at the end of the age; the angels will come forth and take out the wicked from among the righteous, and <they> will throw them into the furnace of fire; in that place there will be weeping, and gnashing of teeth."	13:49 "So it will be at the end of the age; the angels will come forth and take out the wicked from among the righteous, 13:50 and will throw them into the furnace of fire; in that place there will be weeping and gnashing of teeth.		
8	<Jesus asked them,> "Have you understood all these things?" They said to Him, "Yes."	13:51 "Have you understood all these things?" They said to Him, "Yes."		
9	[Then] [He] said to them, "Therefore every scribe who has become a disciple of the Kingdom of Heaven is like [the] head of a household, who brings out his treasure <of both> old things and new."	13:52 [And] [Jesus] said to them, "Therefore every scribe who has become a disciple of the kingdom of heaven is like [a] head of a household, who brings out of his treasure things new and old."		
10	With many such parables Jesus was speaking the Word to the crowds, [as much] as they were able to hear it; and He did not speak to them without a parable,	13:34 All these things Jesus spoke to the crowds in parables, and He did not speak to them without a parable.	4:33 With many such parables He was speaking the word to them, [so far] as they were able to hear it; 4:34~ and He did not speak to them without a parable;	
11	but He was explaining everything privately to His disciples.		4:~34 but He was explaining everything privately to His own disciples.	

continued >

4 - SECOND YEAR OF MINISTRY
Act 7: **Parables About The Kingdom**

Scene 6: **More Parables About The Kingdom of Heaven**
continued

Gospel = God-spell or Good News

Matthew	Mark	Luke
12 This was to fulfill what was spoken through the prophet: *"I will open My mouth in parables; I will utter things hidden since the foundation of the world!"* [1]	13:35 This was to fulfill what was spoken through the prophet: "I will open My mouth in parables; I will utter things hidden since the foundation of the world."	
13 Then [Jesus] left the crowds, and went into the house.	13:36~ Then [He] left the crowds and went into the house.	

1. Psalm 78:2-3

Scene 7: **The Parable of The Tares b) Explained**
Capernaum, *Galilee*   summer / 31 CE

	Matthew
1 [The] disciples [of Jesus] came to Him, and said, "Explain to us the parable of the tares of the field."	13:~36 And [His] disciples came to Him and said, "Explain to us the parable of the tares of the field."
2 He said, "The One who sows the good seed is the Son of Man, and the field is the world.	13:37 And He said, "The one who sows the good seed is the Son of Man, 13:38~ and the field is the world;
3 "As for the good seed, these are the sons of the Kingdom;	13:~38~ and as for the good seed, these are the sons of the kingdom;
4 "and the tares are the sons of the evil one, and the enemy who sowed them is the Devil.	13:~38 and the tares are the sons of the evil one; 13:39~ and the enemy who sowed them is the devil,
5 "The harvest is the end of the age, and the reapers are angels.	13:~39 and the harvest is the end of the age; and the reapers are angels.
6 "So just as the tares are gathered up, and burned with fire, so shall it be at the end of the age:	13:40 "So just as the tares are gathered up and burned with fire, so shall it be at the end of the age.
7 "The Son of Man will send forth His angels, and they will gather out of His Kingdom all <of the> stumbling blocks, and those who commit lawlessness, and <they> will throw them into the furnace of fire; in that place there will be weeping, and gnashing of teeth.	13:41 "The Son of Man will send forth His angels, and they will gather out of His kingdom all stumbling blocks, and those who commit lawlessness, 13:42 and will throw them into the furnace of fire; in that place there will be weeping and gnashing of teeth.
8 "Then *the righteous will shine forth as the sun* [1] in the Kingdom of their Father.	13:43~ "Then the righteous will shine forth as the sun in the kingdom of their Father.
9 "He who has ears, let him hear."	13:~43 He who has ears, let him hear.
10 When Jesus had finished these parables, He departed from there.	13:53 When Jesus had finished these parables, He departed from there.

1. Daniel 12:3

4 - SECOND YEAR OF MINISTRY

Act 8: Mighty Miracles

Scene 1: Jesus Calms The Stormy Sea

Sea of Galilee, *Galilee* summer / 31 CE

Youtube.com/TheGreatestGospel

#		Matthew	Mark	Luke
1	On one of those days, when evening came, a crowd <was gathered> around Jesus, <so> He gave orders to depart, and said to [His apostles], "Let us go over to the other side of the sea."	8:18 ~~Now~~ when Jesus ~~saw~~ a crowd around ~~Him~~, He gave orders to depart to the other side of the sea.	4:35 On ~~that~~ day, when evening came, He said to [~~them~~], "Let us go over to the other side."	8:22 ~~Now~~ on one of those days 8:~22 and ~~He~~ said to [~~them~~], "Let us go over to the other side of the ~~lake~~."
2	Leaving the crowd, Jesus got into the boat, <and> His [apostles] followed Him.	8:23 ~~When~~ ~~He~~ got into the boat, His [~~disciples~~] followed Him.	4:36~ Leaving the crowd, ~~they~~ ~~took~~ Him ~~along with them~~ in the boat, ~~just as He was~~;	8:~22 Jesus ~~and His disciples~~ got into ~~a~~ boat,
3	[When] they launched out other boats were with [them], [and] as they were sailing along, Jesus fell asleep on the cushion in the stern.	8:~24 ~~but~~ Jesus ~~Himself~~ ~~was~~ asleep.	4:36~ ~~and~~ other boats were with [~~Him~~]. 4:38~ Jesus ~~Himself~~ ~~was~~ in the stern, asleep on the cushion;	8:~22 [So] they launched out. 8:23~ [But] as they were sailing along ~~He~~ fell asleep;
4	And behold, a great storm arose, <and> a fierce gale of wind descended [up]on the sea, so that the waves were breaking over the boat.	8:24~ And behold, ~~there~~ arose a great storm on the sea, so that 8:24⁻² ~~covered with~~ the waves;	4:37~ And ~~there~~ arose a fierce gale of wind, ~~and~~ the waves were breaking over the boat so ~~much~~ that	8:~23~ and a fierce gale of wind descended on the ~~lake~~,
5	The boat was filling up, and they began to be in danger;	8:24⁻¹ the boat was ~~being~~	4:~37 the boat was ~~already~~ filling up.	8:~23 and they began ~~to be~~ ~~swamped~~ ~~and~~ to be in danger.
6	[so] they came to Jesus, and *woke Him up,*[1] and said to Him, "Master, Master! Save us Lord, we are perishing!"	8:25 [And] they came to ~~Him~~ and woke Him, sa~~ying~~, "Save us, Lord; we are perishing!"	4:~38 [and] they woke Him and said to Him, "~~Teacher~~, ~~do You not care that~~ we are perishing?"	8:24~ They came to Jesus and woke Him up, sa~~ying~~, "Master, Master, we are perishing!"
7	He said to them, "Why are you afraid, you men of little faith?"	8:26~ He said to them, "Why are you afraid, you men of little faith?"	4:~40~ "Why are you afraid?	
8	Then [Jesus] got up and rebuked the winds, and <He> said to the sea, "Hush, be still."	8:~26~ Then [He] got up and rebuked the winds and the sea,	4:39~ And [He] got up and rebuked the wind and said to the sea, "Hush, be still."	8:~24~ ~~And~~ [He] got up and rebuked the wind and
9	And the wind died down, and *the surging waves stopped, and it became perfectly calm.*[2]	8:~26 and it became perfectly calm.	4:~39 And the wind died down and it became perfectly calm.	8:~24 the surging waves, and ~~they~~ stopped, and it became calm.
10	And He said to them, "Do you still no[t] have faith?"		4:40~ And He said to them, 4:~40 "Do you still have no faith?"	8:25~ And He said to them, "~~Where is your~~ faith?"
11	The men were very amazed and fearful, and <they> said to one another, "What kind of a man is this, that He commands even the winds and the sea, and they obey Him?"	8:27 The men were amazed, and said, "What kind of a man is this, that even the winds and the sea obey Him?"	4:41 ~~They~~ ~~became~~ very ~~much afraid~~ and said to one another, "~~Who then~~ is this, that even the wind and the sea obey Him?"	8:~25 ~~They~~ were fearful and amazed sa~~ying~~ to one another, "~~Who then~~ is this, that He commands even the winds and the ~~water~~, and they obey Him?"

1. (Psalm 44:23)   2. Psalm 65:7; 89:9; 107:29

4 - SECOND YEAR OF MINISTRY
Act 8: Mighty Miracles
Scene 2: A Demon-Possessed Man Named Legion
Gergesa, *Decapolis* summer / 31 CE

Four Gospels United in Harmony — Page 103

#		Matthew	Mark	Luke
1	They sailed to the country of the Gerasenes, which is opposite Galilee, [on] the other side of the sea.	8:28~ ~~When~~ He ~~came~~ [to] the other side ~~into~~ the country of the ~~Ga~~darenes,	5:1 They ~~came~~ [to] the other side of the sea, ~~into~~ the country of the Gerasenes.	8:26 ~~Then~~ they sailed to the country of the Gerasenes, which is opposite Galilee.
2	When [Jesus] got out of the boat <and> came onto the land, He was immediately met by a man from the city, as [he] [was] coming out from the tombs.	8:28~1 ~~two men~~ 8:28~3 met Him as [they] [were] coming out ~~of~~ the tombs.	5:2~ When [He] got out of the boat, immediately a man from the tombs 5:~2 met Him,	8:27~ ~~And~~ when [He] came ~~out~~ onto the land, He was met by a man from the city
3	[He] was possessed with demons, and had not put on any clothing for a long time.	8:28~2 [~~who~~] were demon-possessed	5:~2 ~~with an unclean spirit~~	8:~27 [~~who~~] was possessed with demons; and ~~who~~ had not put on any clothing for a long time,
4	He was not living in a house, but had his dwelling among the tombs; for the demon[s] had seized him many times, and <would> drive <him> into the desert.		5:3~ ~~and~~ he had his dwelling among the tombs.	8:~27 ~~and~~ was not living in a house, but ~~in~~ the tombs. 8:29~1 For ~~it~~ had seized him many times; 8:~29 and ~~be~~ driven ~~by~~ the demon into the desert.
5	He was kept under guard, [but] no one was able to bind him anymore, <not> even with a chain, because he had often been bound with shackles and chains, [but] he would [tear] apart the shackles, and [break] [his] chains in pieces; and no one was strong enough to subdue him.		5:~3 [And] no one was able to bind him anymore, even with a chain; 5:4 because he had often been bound with shackles and chains, ~~and~~ [the] chains ~~had been~~ [torn] apart ~~by him~~ and the shackles [broken] in pieces, and no one was strong enough to subdue him.	8:29~2 ~~and~~ he was bound with chains and shackles ~~and~~ kept under guard, [and yet] he would break ~~his~~ ~~bonds~~
6	Constantly, night and day, he was screaming among the tombs and in the mountains, and gashing himself with stones; <and> [He] [was] so extremely violent that no one could pass by that way.	8:~28 [They] [were] so extremely violent that no one could pass by that way.	5:5 Constantly, night and day, he was screaming among the tombs and in the mountains, and gashing himself with stones.	
7	Seeing Jesus from a distance, he ran up and bowed down before Him; and [he] cried out with a loud voice, saying, "What business do we have with each other, Jesus, Son of the Most High God?	8:29~ And [they] cried out, saying, "What business do we have with each other, son of God?	5:6 Seeing Jesus from a distance, he ran up and bowed down before Him; 5:7~ and ~~shouting~~ with a loud voice, ~~he said,~~ "What business do we have with each other, Jesus, son of the Most High God?	8:28~ Seeing Jesus, he cried out and ~~fell~~ before Him, ~~and~~ said ~~in~~ a loud voice, "What business do we have with each other, Jesus, son of the Most High God?
8	"Have You come here to torment us before the time? I beg You by God, do not torment me!"	8:~29 Have You come here to torment us before the time?"	5:~7 I ~~implore~~ You by God, do not torment me!"	8:~28 I beg You, do not torment me."
9	for [Jesus] had commanded the unclean spirit, saying, "Come out of the man!"		5:8 For [He] had ~~been~~ saying ~~to him,~~ "Come out of the man, ~~you~~ unclean spirit!"	8:29 For [He] had commanded the unclean spirit ~~to~~ come out of the man.
10	Jesus asked him, "What is your name?"		5:9~ ~~And~~ He ~~was~~ asking him, "What is your name?"	8:30~ ~~And~~ Jesus asked him, "What is your name?"
11	He said, "My name is Legion, for we are many;" for many demons had entered <into> him.		5:~9 And he said ~~to Him,~~ "My name is Legion; for we are many."	8:~30 And he said, Legion; for many demons had entered him.
12	And they began imploring [Jesus] earnestly not to send them into the abyss.		5:10 And he began ~~to~~ implore [Him] earnestly not to send them ~~out of~~ the ~~country~~.	8:31 They ~~were~~ imploring [Him] not to ~~command~~ them ~~to go away~~ into the abyss.

	4 - SECOND YEAR OF MINISTRY Act 8: **Mighty Miracles**	Scene 3: **Jesus Sends The Demons Into The Swine** Gergesa, *Decapolis* summer / 31 CE		*The Verse-By-Verse Four Gospel Harmony*
	Matthew		**Mark**	**Luke**
1	Now there was a large herd of many swine feeding nearby on the mountain, and the demons began to implore [Jesus] to permit them to enter <into> the swine,	8:30 Now there was a herd of many swine feeding ~~at a distance from them~~. 8:31~ The demons began to ~~entreat~~ [~~Him~~],	5:11 Now there was a large herd of swine feeding nearby on the mountain. 5:12~ The demons implored [~~Him~~],	8:32~ Now there was a herd of many swine feeding ~~there~~ on the mountain; and the demons implored [~~Him~~] to permit them to enter the swine.
2	saying, "If You are going to cast us out, send us into the herd of swine, so that we may enter <into> them."	8:~31 saying, "If You are going to cast us out, send us into the herd of swine."	5:12 saying, "Send us into the swine so that we may enter them."	
3	Jesus gave them permission, and He said to them, "Go!"	8:32~ And He said to them, "Go!"	5:13~ Jesus gave them permission.	8:~32 ~~And He~~ gave them permission.
4	[Then] the unclean spirits came out of the man, and entered into the swine;	8:~32~ [And] ~~they~~ came out and ~~went~~ into the swine,	5:~13~ [And] ~~coming~~ out, the unclean spirits entered the swine;	8:33~ [And] the ~~demons~~ came out of the man and entered the swine;
5	and the whole herd, about two thousand of them, rushed down the steep bank <and> into the sea, and drowned in the waters.	8:~32 and the whole herd rushed down the steep bank into the sea and ~~perish~~ed in the waters.	5:~13 and the herd rushed down the steep bank into the sea, about two thousand of them; and ~~they were~~ drowned in the ~~sea~~.	8:~33 and the herd rushed down the steep bank into the ~~lake~~ and ~~was~~ drowned.
6	When their herdsmen saw what had happened they ran away; and <they> went and reported everything in the city, and out in the country, including what had happened to the demoniac.	8:33 ~~The~~ herdsmen ran away, and went ~~to~~ the city and reported everything including what had happened to the demoniacs.	5:14~ Their herdsmen ran away and reported ~~it~~ in the city and in the country.	8:34 When ~~the~~ herdsmen saw what had happened, they ran away and reported ~~it~~ in the city and out in the country.
7	And behold, the whole city came out to see what had happened, <and> to meet Jesus.	8:34~ And behold, the whole city came out to meet Jesus;	5:~14 And the ~~people~~ came to see what ~~it was~~ that had happened.	8:35~ The ~~people went~~ out to see what had happened;
8	They came to Jesus, and observed the man from whom the demons had gone out sitting down at the feet of Jesus, clothed, and in his right mind - the very man who had had the "legion" - and they became frightened.		5:15 They came to Jesus and observed the man who had ~~been~~ demon-~~possessed~~ sitting down, clothed and in his right mind, the very man who had had the "legion"; and they became frightened.	8:~35 ~~and~~ they came to Jesus, and ~~found~~ the man from whom the demons had gone out, sitting down, at the feet of Jesus, clothed and in his right mind; and they became frightened.
9	Those who had seen it described to them how the demon-possessed man had been made well, and all about the swine.		5:16 Those who had seen it described to them how ~~it had happened to~~ the demon-possessed man, and all about the swine.	8:36 Those who had seen it ~~reported~~ to them how the man ~~who was~~ demon-possessed had been made well.
10	When they saw [Jesus], all the people of the country of the Gerasenes and the surrounding district began to ask Him to leave their region, for they were gripped with great fear.	8:~34 ~~and~~ when they saw [~~Him~~], ~~they implored~~ Him to leave their region.	5:17 And ~~they~~ began to ~~implore~~ Him to leave their region.	8:37~ ~~And~~ all the people of the country of the Gerasenes and the surrounding district ask~~ed~~ Him to leave ~~them~~, for they were gripped with great fear;
11	As [Jesus] was getting into the boat [to] return, the man from whom the demons had gone out was begging Him that he might accompany Him.		5:18 As [He] was getting into the boat, the man who had ~~been~~ demon-~~possessed~~ was ~~imploring~~ Him that he might accompany Him.	8:~37 ~~and~~ [He] g~~o~~t into ~~a~~ boat [~~and~~] return~~ed~~. 8:38~ ~~But~~ the man from whom the demons had gone out was begging Him that he might accompany Him;

continued >

4 - SECOND YEAR OF MINISTRY

Act 8: **Mighty Miracles**

Scene 3: **Jesus Sends The Demons Into The Swine**

continued

All of the Gospel Events in Order

	Matthew	Mark	Luke
12 but [Jesus] did not let him, [and] He sent him away, saying, "Go, <and> return to your home, and report to your people what great things God has done for you, and how He had mercy on you."		5:19 And [He] did not let him, [but] He said to him, "Go home to your people and report to them what great things the Lord has done for you, and how He had mercy on you."	8:~38 but [He] sent him away, saying, 8:39~ "Return to your house and describe what great things God has done for you."
13 So [the man] went away, and began to proclaim throughout the whole city <and> in Decapolis what great things Jesus had done for him; and everyone was amazed.		5:20 And [he] went away and began to proclaim in Decapolis what great things Jesus had done for him; and everyone was amazed.	8:~39 So [he] went away, proclaiming throughout the whole city what great things Jesus had done for him.

Scene 4: **Jairus Implores Jesus To Heal His Daughter a)**

Capernaum, *Galilee*   summer / 31 CE

	Matthew	Mark	Luke
1 [After] getting into the boat, Jesus crossed over to the other side <of> the sea, and came to His own city.	9:1~ Getting into a boat, Jesus crossed over the sea and came to His own city.	5:21~ [When] Jesus had crossed over again in the boat to the other side,	
2 As [He] returned, the people welcomed Him, <and> a large crowd gathered around Him, for they had all been waiting for Him, so He stayed by the seashore.		5:~21 a large crowd gathered around Him; and so He stayed by the seashore.	8:40 And as [Jesus] returned, the people welcomed Him, for they had all been waiting for Him.
3 While [Jesus] was [speak]ing to them, a synagogue official named Jairus came, [who] had an only daughter about twelve years old, [who] was dying.	9:18~ While [He] was [say]ing these things to them, a synagogue official came	5:22~ One of the synagogue officials named Jairus came up, 5:~42~ for she was twelve years old.	8:41~ And there came an official of the synagogue; a man named Jairus, 8:42~ for [he] had an only daughter, about twelve years old, and [she] was dying.
4 Seeing [Jesus], [Jairus] bowed down at His feet, and began to earnestly implore Him to come to his house, saying, "My little daughter is at the point of death; but please, come and lay Your hand on her, so that she will get well, and live!"	9:~18 and bowed down before Him, and said, "My daughter has just died; but come and lay Your hand on her, and she will live."	5:~22 and on seeing [Him], fell at His feet 5:23 and implored Him earnestly, saying, "My little daughter is at the point of death; please come and lay Your hands on her, so that she will get well and live."	8:~41 and [he] fell at Jesus' feet, and began to implore Him to come to his house;
5 Jesus got up and began to follow him, and so did His [apostles].	9:19 Jesus got up and began to follow him, and so did His [disciples].		

4 - SECOND YEAR OF MINISTRY
Act 8: **Mighty Miracles**

Scene 5: **A Woman Is Healed of Her Hemorrhage**
Capernaum, *Galilee*   summer / 31 CE

A Harmonized Unity of The Gospels

#		Matthew	Mark	Luke
1	As [Jesus] went off with [Jairus], a large crowd was following Him, and pressing in on Him.		5:24 ~~And~~ [He] went off with [him]; ~~and~~ a large crowd was following Him and pressing in on Him.	8:~42 ~~But~~ as [He] went, ~~the~~ crowds ~~were~~ pressing ~~against~~ Him.
2	And a woman <was there> who had been suffering from a hemorrhage for twelve years, and could not be healed by anyone.	9:20~ And a woman who had been suffering from a hemorrhage for twelve years,	5:25 A woman who ~~had~~ had a hemorrhage for twelve years,	8:43 And a woman who had a hemorrhage for twelve years, and could not be healed by anyone,
3	<She> had endured much at the hands of many physicians, and had spent all that she had, and was not helped at all, but rather had grown worse.		5:26 ~~and~~ had endured much at the hands of many physicians, and had spent all that she had and was not helped at all, but rather had grown worse -	
4	After hearing about Jesus, she came up in the crowd behind Him, and touched the fringe of His cloak; for she thought to herself, "If I just touch His garment, I will get well."	9:~20 came up behind Him and touched the fringe of His cloak; 9:21 for she ~~was saying~~ to herself, "If I ~~only~~ touch His garment, I will get well."	5:27 after hearing about Jesus, she came up in the crowd behind Him and touched His cloak. 5:28 For she thought, "If I just touch His garment, I will get well."	8:44~ came up behind Him and touched the fringe of His cloak,
5	At once her hemorrhage stopped, <and> the flow of her blood was dried up; and she felt in her body that she was healed of her affliction.	9:~22 At once ~~the woman~~ was ~~made well~~.	5:29 ~~Immediately~~ the flow of her blood was dried up; and she felt in her body that she was healed of her affliction.	8:~44 ~~and immediately~~ her hemorrhage stopped.
6	Immediately Jesus, perceiving that power had gone forth from Him, turned around in the crowd, and said, "Who is the one who touched My garments?"		5:30 Immediately Jesus, perceiving ~~in Himself~~ that ~~the~~ power ~~proceeding~~ from Him had gone forth, turned around in the crowd and said, "Who touched My garments?"	8:45~ And ~~Jesus~~ said, "Who is the one who touched Me?"
7	While they were all denying it, Peter said to Him, "Master, You see the people are crowding and pressing in on You, and You say, 'Who touched Me?' "		5:31 ~~And His disciples~~ said to Him, "You see the ~~crowd~~ pressing in on You, and You say, 'Who touched Me?'"	8:~45 ~~And~~ while they were all denying Peter said, "Master, the people are crowding and pressing in on You."
8	But Jesus said, "Someone did touch Me, for I [am] aware that power [has] gone out of Me."			8:46 But Jesus said, "Someone did touch Me, for I [was] aware that power [had] gone out of Me."
9	And He turned to see the woman who had done this.	9:22~ ~~But Jesus~~ turning and ~~seeing her~~	5:32 And He ~~looked around~~ to see the woman who had done this.	
10	When the woman saw that she had not escaped notice, she came <in> fear and trembling, and fell down before Him.		5:33~ ~~But~~ the woman fear[ing] and trembling, ~~aware of what~~ had ~~happened to her~~, came and fell down before Him,	8:47~ When the woman saw that she had not escaped notice, she came trembling and fell down before Him,
11	And <she> told Him the whole truth, and declared in the presence of all the people the reason why she had touched Him, and how she had been immediately healed.		5:~33 and told Him the whole truth.	8:~47 and declared in the presence of all the people the reason why she had touched Him, and how she had been immediately healed.
12	[Jesus] said to her, "Daughter, take courage. Your faith has made you well.	9:~22~ said, "Daughter, take courage; your faith has made you well."	5:34~ ~~And~~ [He] said to her, "Daughter, your faith has made you well;	8:48~ ~~And~~ [He] said to her, "Daughter, your faith has made you well;
13	"Go in peace, and be healed of your affliction."		5:~34 go in peace and be healed of your affliction."	8:~48 go in peace."

4 - SECOND YEAR OF MINISTRY
Act 8: Mighty Miracles

Scene 6: Jesus Heals The Daughter of Jairus b)
Capernaum, *Galilee*   summer / 31 CE

A Verse-By-Verse Four Gospel Merger

#		Matthew	Mark	Luke
1	While He was still speaking, someone from the house of the synagogue official came, saying, "Your daughter has died; do not trouble the Teacher anymore."		5:35 While He was still speaking, ~~they~~ came from the house of the synagogue official, saying, "Your daughter has died; ~~why~~ trouble the Teacher anymore?	8:49 While He was still speaking, someone came from the house of the synagogue official, saying, "Your daughter has died; do not trouble the Teacher anymore.
2	When Jesus overheard this, He said to [Jairus], "Do not be afraid any longer; only believe, and she will be made well."		5:36 ~~But~~ Jesus, overhearing ~~what was being spoken~~, said to [~~the synagogue official~~], "Do not be afraid any longer, only believe.	8:50 ~~But~~ when Jesus heard this, He ~~answered~~ [~~him~~], "Do not be afraid any longer; only believe, and she will be made well."
3	And He did not allow anyone to accompany Him, except Peter and James, and John, the brother of James.		5:37 And He allowed ~~no~~ one to accompany Him, except Peter and James and John the brother of James.	8:~51~ He did not allow anyone to ~~enter with~~ Him, except Peter and John and James,
4	When they came to the synagogue official's house, [Jesus] saw a commotion, <with> flute-players and the crowd <of> people in noisy disorder, all loudly weeping and wailing, <and> lamenting for [the girl].	9:23 When ~~Jesus~~ came ~~into~~ the official's house, ~~and~~ saw ~~the~~ flute-players and the crowd in noisy disorder,	5:38 They came to the house ~~of the~~ synagogue official; ~~and~~ [He] saw a commotion, and people loudly weeping and wailing.	8:51~ When ~~He~~ came to the house, 8:52~ ~~Now they were~~ all weeping and lamenting for [~~her~~];
5	Entering in, [Jesus] said to them, "Why make a commotion and weep? Stop weeping, <and> leave - for the girl has not died, but is asleep."	9:24~ [He] said, "Leave; for the girl has not died, but is asleep.	5:39 ~~And~~ entering in, [He] said to them, "Why make a commotion and weep? The ~~child~~ has not died, but is asleep."	8:~52 but [He] said, "Stop weeping, for ~~she~~ has not died, but is asleep."
6	And they began laughing at Him, knowing that she had died.	9:~24 And they began laughing at Him.	5:40~ They began laughing at Him.	8:53 And they began laughing at Him, knowing that she had died.
7	When the crowd had been sent out, [Jesus] took along the girl's father and mother, and His own companions, and entered the room where the child was.	9:25~ ~~But~~ when the crowd had been sent out, He entered	5:~40 ~~But putting them all~~ out, [He] took along the ~~child~~'s father and mother and His own companions, and entered the room where the child was.	8:~51 ~~and~~ the girl's father and mother.
8	<Then> He took her by the hand, and called to her, saying, "Talitha kum!" which translated means, "Little girl, arise!"	9:~25~ ~~and~~ took her by the hand,	5:41 ~~Taking the child~~ by the hand, He ~~said to her~~, "Talitha kum!" (which translated means, Little girl, ~~I say to you~~, ~~get up~~!).	8:54 He, ~~however~~, took her by the hand and called saying, "~~Child~~, arise!"
9	Immediately her spirit returned, and the girl got up, and began to walk.	9:~25 and the girl got up.	5:42~ Immediately the girl got up and began to walk,	8:55~ ~~And~~ her spirit returned, and ~~she~~ got up immediately;
10	Her parents were completely astounded, but [Jesus] gave them strict orders to tell no one about what had happened; and that <she> should be given something to eat.		5:~42 ~~And immediately they~~ were completely astounded. 5:43 And [He] gave them strict orders ~~that~~ no one ~~should know~~ about this, and ~~He said~~ that something should be given ~~her~~ to eat.	8:56 Her parents were ~~amazed~~; but [He] ~~instructed~~ them to tell no one what had happened. 8:~55 and ~~He gave orders for~~ something be given ~~to her~~ to eat.
11	This news spread throughout all that land.	9:26 This news spread throughout all that land.		

4 - SECOND YEAR OF MINISTRY

Act 8: **Mighty Miracles**

Scene 7: **Two Blind Men and A Mute Demon**

Capernaum, *Galilee* summer / 31 CE

The Gospel

	Matthew
1 As Jesus went on from there, two blind men followed Him, crying out, "Have mercy on us, son of David!"	9:27 As Jesus went on from there, two blind men followed Him, crying out, "Have mercy on us, son of David!"
2 When He entered the house, the blind men came up to Him, and Jesus said to them, "Do you believe that I am able to do this?"	9:28~ When He entered the house, the blind men came up to Him, and Jesus said to them, "Do you believe that I am able to do this?"
3 They said to Him, "Yes, Lord."	9:~28 They said to Him, "Yes, Lord."
4 Then <Jesus> touched their eyes, <and> [said], "It shall be done to you according to your faith." And their eyes were opened.	9:29 Then He touched their eyes, [saying], "It shall be done to you according to your faith." 9:30~ And their eyes were opened.
5 Jesus sternly warned them: "See that no one knows about this."	9:~30 And Jesus sternly warned them: "See that no one knows about this!"
6 But they went out and spread the news about Him throughout all that land.	9:31 But they went out and spread the news about Him throughout all that land.
7 As they were going, a mute, demon-possessed man was brought to [Jesus].	9:32 As they were going out, a mute, demon- possessed man was brought to [Him].
8 After the demon was cast out, the mute man spoke; and the crowds were amazed, and were saying, "Nothing like this has ever been seen in Israel!"	9:33 After the demon was cast out, the mute man spoke; and the crowds were amazed, and were saying, "Nothing like this has ever been seen in Israel."
9 But the Pharisees were saying, "He casts out the demons by the ruler of the demons."	9:34 But the Pharisees were saying, "He casts out the demons by the ruler of the demons."

4 - SECOND YEAR OF MINISTRY

Act 8: **Mighty Miracles**

Scene 8: **Reading In His Hometown On The Sabbath**

Capernaum, *Galilee*   summer / 31 CE

	Matthew	Mark	Luke
1 Jesus came to Nazareth, His hometown where He had been brought up, and His disciples followed Him.	13:54~ He came to His hometown	6:1 Jesus ~~went out from there and~~ came ~~into~~ His hometown; and His disciples followed Him.	4:16~ ~~And~~ He came to Nazareth, where He had been brought up;
2 When the Sabbath came, as was His custom, He entered the synagogue, and began to teach.	13:~54~ ~~in their~~ synagogue, and began teaching ~~them~~	6:2~ When the Sabbath came ~~He~~ began to teach ~~in~~ the synagogue;	4:~16~ ~~and~~ as was His custom, He entered the synagogue ~~on~~ the Sabbath
3 <He> stood up to read, and the book of the prophet Isaiah was handed to Him.			4:~16 ~~and~~ stood up to read. 4:17~ ~~And~~ the book of the prophet Isaiah was handed to Him.
4 He opened the book, and found the place where it [is] written, *"The Spirit of the Lord is upon Me, because He <has> anointed Me to preach the gospel to the poor.*			4:~17 ~~And~~ He opened the book and found the place where it [~~was~~] written, 4:18~ "The Spirit of the Lord is upon Me, because He anointed Me to preach the gospel to the poor.
5 *"He has sent Me to proclaim release to the captives, and recovery of sight to the blind, to set free those who are oppressed, <and> to proclaim the favorable year of the Lord."* [1]			4:~18 He has sent Me to proclaim release to the captives, and recovery of sight to the blind, to set free those who are oppressed, 4:19 To proclaim the favorable year of the Lord."
6 [Then] [Jesus] closed the book, gave it back to the attendant, and sat down; and the eyes of [everyone] in the synagogue were fixed on Him.			4:20 [~~And~~] [~~He~~] closed the book, gave it back to the attendant and sat down; and the eyes of [~~all~~] in the synagogue were fixed on Him.
7 And He [said] to them, "Today, this Scripture has been fulfilled in your hearing."			4:21 And He ~~began to~~ [say] to them, "Today this Scripture has been fulfilled in your hearing."

1. Isaiah 61:1-2 (49:8; 58:6)

Scene 9: **The Nazarenes Take Offense At Jesus**

Nazareth, *Galilee*   a Sabbath, late summer / 31 CE

	Matthew	Mark	Luke
1 The many listeners were astonished, and said, "Where did this man get these things, and what is this wisdom given to Him; and such miracles as these performed by His hands?"	13:~54 ~~so that~~ they were astonished, and said, "Where did this man get this wisdom and these mirac~~ulous~~ ~~powers~~?	6:~2 ~~and~~ the many listeners were astonished, sa~~ying~~, "Where did this man get these things, and what is this wisdom given to Him, and such miracles as these performed by His hands?	
2 <While> all were speaking well of Him, and wondering at the gracious words which were falling from His lips, they were saying, "Is this not the carpenter, Joseph's son?	13:55~ "Is not this the carpenter~~'s~~ son?	6:3~ "Is not this the carpenter,	4:22 ~~And~~ all were speaking well of Him, and wondering at the gracious words which were falling from His lips; ~~and~~ they were saying, "Is this not Joseph's son?"
3 "Is not His mother Mary; and His brothers: James and Joseph, and Judas and Simon?	13:~55 Is not His mother ~~called~~ Mary, and His brothers, James and Joseph and Simon and Judas?	6:3~1 ~~the son of~~ Mary, and brother ~~of~~ James and Jose~~s~~ and Judas and Simon?	
4 "And are not all <of> His sisters here with us?	13:56~ "And His sisters, are ~~they~~ not all with us?	6:3~2 Are not His sisters here with us?"	

4 - SECOND YEAR OF MINISTRY	Scene 9: **The Nazarenes Take Offense At Jesus**		Page 110
Act 8: **Mighty Miracles**	Capernaum, *Galilee* summer / 31 CE		*The Texts of the Four Gospels Combined*

	Matthew	Mark	Luke
5 Where then did this man get all these things?" And they took offense at Him.	13:~56 Where then did this man get all these things?" 13:57~ And they took offense at Him.	6:~3 And they took offense at Him.	
6 [So] Jesus said to them, "A prophet is not without honor, except in his hometown, and among his own relatives, and in his own household.	13:~57 [But] Jesus said to them, "A prophet is not without honor except in his hometown and |in his own household."	6:4 Jesus said to them, "A prophet is not without honor except in his hometown and among his own relatives and in his own household."	
7 "Truly I say to you, <that> no prophet is welcome in his hometown."			4:24 ~~And He said~~, "Truly I say to you, no prophet is welcome in his hometown.
8 And He said to them, "No doubt you will quote this proverb to Me, 'Physician, heal yourself!			4:23~ And He said to them, "No doubt you will quote this proverb to Me, 'Physician, heal yourself!
9 "Whatever we heard <that> was done at Capernaum, do here in your hometown as well.'			4:~23 Whatever we heard was done at Capernaum, do here in your hometown as well.' "
10 "But I say to you in truth, <that> there were many widows in Israel *in the days of Elijah, when the sky was shut up for three years and six months,* [and] *a great famine came over all the land;*			4:25 "But I say to you in truth, there were many widows in Israel in the days of Elijah, when the sky was shut up for three years and six months, [~~when~~] a great famine came over all the land;
11 "*and yet Elijah was sent to none of them, but only to Zarephath in the land of Sidon, a woman who was a widow.*[1]			4:26 and yet Elijah was sent to none of them, but only to Zarephath, in the land of Sidon, ~~to~~ a woman who was a widow.
12 "And there were *many lepers in Israel in the time of Elisha the prophet, and none of them was cleansed, but only Naaman the Syrian."*[2]			4:27 "And there were many lepers in Israel in the time of Elisha the prophet; and none of them was cleansed, but only Naaman the Syrian."
13 All the people in the synagogue were filled with rage as they heard these things;			4:28 ~~And~~ all the people in the synagogue were filled with rage as they heard these things;
14 and they got up and drove [Jesus] out of the city, and led Him to the brow of the hill on which their city had been built, in order to throw Him down the cliff; but passing through their midst, He went <on> His way.			4:29 and they got up and drove [~~Him~~] out of the city, and led Him to the brow of the hill on which their city had been built, in order to throw Him down the cliff. 4:30 But passing through their midst, He went His way.
15 And He did not do many miracles there, because of their unbelief, except that He laid His hands on a few sick people, and healed them.	13:58 And He did not do many miracles there because of their unbelief.	6:5 And He ~~could~~ do no miracle there except that He laid His hands on a few sick people and healed them.	
16 And He wondered at their unbelief.		6:6~ And He wondered at their unbelief.	

1. *1 Kings 17:9*   2. *2 Kings 5:1-14*

4 - SECOND YEAR OF MINISTRY

Act 9: Jesus Sends The Apostles

Scene 1: Jesus Sends His Twelve Apostles To Preach

Capernaum, *Galilee*   late summer / 31 CE

The Unified Four Gospels - Verse-By-Verse — Page 111

	Matthew	Mark	Luke
1 Jesus was going through all the cities and villages, teaching in their synagogues and proclaiming the gospel of the Kingdom,	9:35~ Jesus was going through all the cities and villages, teaching in their synagogues and proclaiming the gospel of the kingdom,	6:~6 ~~And He~~ was going ~~around the~~ villages teaching.	
2 and healing every kind of disease, and every kind of sickness.	9:~35 and healing every kind of disease and every kind of sickness.		
3 Seeing the people, He felt compassion for them, because they were distressed and dispirited, *like sheep without a shepherd.*[1]	9:36 Seeing the people, He felt compassion for them, because they were distressed and dispirited like sheep without a shepherd.		
4 [And] He said to His disciples, "The harvest is plentiful, but the workers are few; therefore beseech the lord of the harvest to send out workers into his harvest."	9:37 [~~Then~~] He said to His disciples, "The harvest is plentiful, but the workers are few. 9:38 "Therefore beseech the Lord of the harvest to send out workers into His harvest."		
5 [Then] Jesus summoned His twelve [apostles]; and \<He\> gave them power and authority over all \<of\> the unclean spirits, to cast out the demons, and to heal every kind of disease, and every kind of sickness.	10:1 Jesus summoned His twelve [~~disciples~~] and gave them authority over unclean spirits, to cast ~~them~~ out, and to heal every kind of disease and every kind of sickness.	6:7~ [~~And~~] ~~He~~ summoned ~~the~~ twelve 6:~7 and gave them authority over the unclean spirits;	9:1 [~~And~~] ~~He called the~~ twelve ~~together~~, and gave them power and authority over all the demons and to heal disease~~s~~.
6 And He began to send them out in pairs, to proclaim the Kingdom of God, and to perform healing.		6:~7~ and began to send them out in pairs,	9:2 And He sent them out to proclaim the kingdom of God and to perform healing.

1. Numbers 27:17

4 - SECOND YEAR OF MINISTRY

Act 9: Jesus Sends The Apostles

Scene 2: Jesus Instructs The Apostles
Capernaum, *Galilee*   late summer / 31 CE

The Good News

	Matthew	Mark	Luke
1 Jesus sent [the] twelve out after instructing them: "Do not go [to] the Gentiles, and do not enter any city of the Samaritans, but rather go to the lost sheep of the house of Israel.	10:5 [These] twelve Jesus sent out after instructing them: "Do not go [in the way of] the Gentiles, and do not enter any city of the Samaritans; 10:6 but rather go to the lost sheep of the house of Israel.	6:8~ and He instructed them	9:3~ And He said to them,
2 "And as you go, preach, saying, 'The Kingdom of Heaven is at hand!'	10:7 "And as you go, preach, saying, 'The kingdom of heaven is at hand.'		
3 "Heal the sick, raise the dead, cleanse the lepers, <and> cast out <the> demons.	10:8~ "Heal the sick, raise the dead, cleanse the lepers, cast out demons.		
4 "Freely you received, freely give.	10:~8 Freely you received, freely give.		
5 "Take nothing for your journey - neither a staff or a bag, nor bread or money.	10:10~ or a bag for your journey, or a staff;	6:~8~ that they should take nothing for their journey, except a mere staff - no bread, no bag, no money	9:~3~ "Take nothing for your journey, neither a staff, nor a bag, nor bread, nor money;
6 "Do not acquire gold or silver, or copper for your belt, but wear sandals, and do not even have two tunics, for the worker is worthy of his support."	10:9 "Do not acquire gold, or silver, or copper for your money belts, 10:~10 or even two coats, or sandals, for the worker is worthy of his support.	6:~8 in their belt - 6:9 but to wear sandals; and He added, "Do not put on two tunics."	9:~3 and do not even have two tunics apiece.

Scene 3: Peace, To Those Who Receive You
Capernaum, *Galilee*   late summer / 31 CE

	Matthew	Mark	Luke
1 [Jesus] said to them, "Whatever city or village you enter, inquire who is worthy in it, and stay at [their] house until you leave that city.	10:11 "And whatever city or village you enter, inquire who is worthy in it, and stay at [his] house until you leave that city.	6:10 And [He] said to them, "Wherever you enter a house, stay there until you leave town.	9:4 "Whatever house you enter, stay there until you leave that city.
2 "As you enter the house, give it your greeting.	10:12 "As you enter the house, give it your greeting.		
3 "If the house[hold] is worthy, let your peace [come upon] it; but if it is not worthy, <let> your peace [return to] you.	10:13 "If the house is worthy, [give] it your blessing of peace. But if it is not worthy, [take back] your blessing of peace.		
4 "As for those who do not receive you, nor heed your words, as you go out from that house or city shake the dust off the soles of your feet, as a testimony against them.	10:14 "Whoever does not receive you, nor heed your words, as you go out of that house or that city, shake the dust off your feet.	6:11 "Any place that does not receive you or listen to you, as you go out from there, shake the dust off the soles of your feet for a testimony against them."	9:5 "And as for those who do not receive you, as you go out from that city, shake the dust off your feet as a testimony against them."
5 "Truly I say to you, it will be more tolerable for the land of Sodom and Gomorrah in the day of judgment, than for that city!"	10:15 "Truly I say to you, it will be more tolerable for the land of Sodom and Gomorrah in the day of judgment than for that city.		

4 - SECOND YEAR OF MINISTRY
Act 9: Jesus Sends The Apostles

Scene 4: I Send You Out As Sheep Among Wolves
Capernaum, *Galilee* — late summer / 31 CE

	Matthew	Luke
1 "Behold, I send you out as sheep in the midst of wolves, so be <as> shrewd as serpents, and <as> innocent as doves.	10:16 "Behold, I send you out as sheep in the midst of wolves; so be shrewd as serpents and innocent as doves.	
2 "But beware of men, for they will hand you over to the courts, and scourge you in their synagogues.	10:17 "But beware of men, for they will hand you over to the courts and scourge you in their synagogues;	
3 "You will even be brought before governors and kings for My sake, as a testimony to them, and to the Gentiles.	10:18 ~~and~~ you will even be brought before governors and kings for My sake, as a testimony to them and to the Gentiles.	
4 "[So] when they bring you before the synagogues, and hand you over <to> the authorities and rulers, do not worry about how or what you are to speak in your defense, or what you are to say, for the Holy Spirit *will teach you in that very hour what you are to say*,[1.]	10:19 "[~~But~~] when they hand you over, do not worry about how or what you are to say; for ~~it~~ will ~~be given~~ you in that hour what you are to say.	12:11 "When they bring you before the synagogues and the rulers and ~~the~~ authorities, do not worry about how or what you are to speak in your defense, or what you are to say; 12:12 for the Holy Spirit will teach you in that very hour what you ~~ought~~ to say."
5 "for it is not you who speak, but it is the Spirit of your Father who speaks [through] you."	10:20 "For it is not you who speak, but it is the Spirit of your Father who speaks [~~in~~] you.	

1. *Exodus 4:12*

4 - SECOND YEAR OF MINISTRY	Scene 5: **You Will Be Persecuted, But Do Not Fear**	Page 114
Act 9: **Jesus Sends The Apostles**	Capernaum, *Galilee* late summer / 31 CE	*A Complete Four Gospel Harmony*

	Matthew	Luke
1 "Brother will betray brother to death, and a father his child; and children will rise up against parents, and cause them to be put to death.[1]	10:21 "Brother will betray brother to death, and a father his child; and children will rise up against parents and cause them to be put to death.	
2 "You will be hated by all because of My Name, but it is the one who has endured to the end who will be saved.	10:22 "You will be hated by all because of My name, but it is the one who has endured to the end who will be saved.	
3 "Whenever they persecute you in one city, flee to the next, for truly I say to you, <that> you will not finish going through the cities of Israel until the Son of Man comes.	10:23 "~~But~~ whenever they persecute you in one city, flee to the next; for truly I say to you, you will not finish going through the cities of Israel until the Son of Man comes.	
4 "A disciple is not above his teacher, <and> nor <is> a slave above his master; but everyone, after he has been fully trained, will be like his teacher.	10:24 "A disciple is not above his teacher, nor a slave above his master.	6:40 "A ~~pupil~~ is not above his teacher; but everyone, after he has been fully trained, will be like his teacher.
5 "It is enough for the disciple that he become like his teacher, and the slave like his master.	10:25~ "It is enough for the disciple that he become like his teacher, and the slave like his master.	
6 "If they have called the head of the house Beelzebul, how much more will they malign the members of his household!	10:~25 If they have called the head of the house Beelzebul, how much more will they malign the members of his household!	
7 "Therefore do not fear them, for there is nothing concealed that will not be revealed, or hidden that will not be known.	10:26 "Therefore do not fear them, for there is nothing concealed that will not be revealed, or hidden that will not be known.	12:2 "~~But~~ there is nothing ~~covered up~~ that will not be revealed, ~~and~~ hidden that will not be known.
8 "Accordingly, whatever I tell you in the darkness, speak in the light; and what you hear whispered in your ear, proclaim upon the housetops!	10:27 "What I tell you in the darkness, speak in the light; and what you hear whispered in your ear, proclaim upon the housetops.	12:3 "Accordingly, whatever you ~~have said~~ in the dark ~~will be heard~~ in the light, and what you ~~have~~ whispered in ~~the inner rooms will be~~ proclaim~~ed~~ upon the housetops.
9 "I say to you, My friends, do not be afraid of those who kill the body, and after that have no more that they can do, [because] <they> are unable to kill the soul.	10:28~ "Do not ~~fear~~ those who kill the body [but] are unable to kill the soul;	12:4 "I say to you, My friends, do not be afraid of those who kill the body and after that have no more that they can do.
10 "But rather I will warn you whom to fear: Fear the One who, after He has killed, has authority to cast into hell, <and> is able to destroy both body and soul. Yes, I tell you, fear Him!	10:~28 but rather fear ~~Him~~ who is able to destroy both soul and body in hell.	12:5 "But I will warn you whom to fear: fear the One who, after He has killed, has authority to cast into hell; yes, I tell you, fear Him!
11 "Are not five sparrows sold for a cent? And yet not one of them is forgotten [by] God, <or> fall[s] to the ground apart from your Father.	10:29 "Are not ~~two~~ sparrows sold for a cent? And yet not one of them ~~will~~ fall to the ground apart from your Father.	12:6 "Are not five sparrows ~~sold~~ for ~~two~~ cents? Yet not one of them is forgotten [~~before~~] God.
12 "But indeed, the very hairs of your head are all numbered, so do not fear, you are more valuable than many sparrows."	10:30 "But the very hairs of your head are all numbered. 10:31 "So do not fear; you are more valuable than many sparrows.	12:7 "Indeed, the very hairs of your head are all numbered. Do not fear; you are more valuable than many sparrows.

1. Micah 7:6

4 - SECOND YEAR OF MINISTRY

Act 9: **Jesus Sends The Apostles**

Scene 6: **Whoever Confesses The Son of Man**
Capernaum, *Galilee*   late summer / 31 CE

Page 115

Matthew is the longest Gospel

	Matthew	Luke
1 "Therefore I say to you: Everyone who confesses Me before men, I, the Son of Man, will also confess him before the angels of God, <and> My Father who is in Heaven.	10:32 "Therefore everyone who confesses Me before men, I will also confess him before My Father who is in heaven.	12:8 "~~And~~ I say to you, everyone who confesses Me before men, the Son of Man will confess him also before the angels of God;
2 "But whoever denies Me before men, I will also deny him before the angels of God, <and> My Father who is in Heaven."	10:33 "But whoever denies Me before men, I will also deny him before My Father who is in heaven.	12:9 but ~~he~~ who denies Me before men will ~~be denied~~ before the angels of God.

Scene 7: **I Have Not Come To Bring Peace**
Capernaum, *Galilee*   late summer / 31 CE

	Matthew	Luke
1 "I have come to cast fire upon the earth, and how I wish <that> it were already kindled.		12:49 "I have come to cast fire upon the earth; and how I wish it were already kindled!
2 "But I have a baptism to undergo, and I am distressed until it is accomplished.		12:50 "But I have a baptism to undergo, and ~~how~~ distressed I am until it is accomplished!
3 "Do you think that I came to bring peace on the earth? I tell you, no, but rather division, <for> I did not come to bring peace, but a sword!	10:34 "Do ~~not~~ think that I came to bring peace on the earth; I did not come to bring peace, but a sword.	12:51 "Do you ~~suppose~~ that I came to ~~grant~~ peace on earth? I tell you, no, but rather division;
4 "I [have come] to set a son against his father, and <a> father against <his> son.	10:35~ "~~For~~ I [came] to set a ~~man~~ against his father,	12:~53~ father against son and son against father,
5 "From now on, five members in one household will be divided, three against two, and two against three.		12:52 ~~for~~ from now on five members in one household will be divided, three against two and two against three.
6 "They will be divided mother against daughter, and a daughter against her mother; mother-in-law against daughter-in-law, and a daughter-in-law against her mother-in-law;	10:~35 and a daughter against her mother, and a daughter-in-law against her mother-in-law;	12:53~ "They will be divided, 12:~53 mother against daughter and daughter against mother, mother-in-law against daughter-in-law and daughter-in-law against mother-in-law."
7 "and *a man's enemies will be the members of his <own> household.*" [1]	10:36 and a man's enemies will be the members of his household.	

1. Micah 7:6

4 - SECOND YEAR OF MINISTRY

Act 9: Jesus Sends The Apostles

Scene 8: He Who Is Worthy of Me
Capernaum, Galilee   late summer / 31 CE

	Matthew
1 "He who loves \<his\> father or \<his\> mother more than Me, is not worthy of Me; and he who loves \<his\> son or daughter more than Me, is not worthy of Me.	10:37 "He who loves father or mother more than Me is not worthy of Me; and he who loves son or daughter more than Me is not worthy of Me.
2 "And he who does not take his cross, and follow after Me, is not worthy of Me.	10:38 "And he who does not take his cross and follow after Me is not worthy of Me.
3 "He who has found his life will lose it; and he who has lost his life for My sake, will find it.	10:39 "He who has found his life will lose it, and he who has lost his life for My sake will find it.
4 "He who receives you receives Me; and he who receives Me, receives Him who sent Me.	10:40 "He who receives you receives Me, and he who receives Me receives Him who sent Me.
5 "He who receives a prophet in the name of a prophet, shall receive a prophet's reward;	10:41~ "He who receives a prophet in the name of a prophet shall receive a prophet's reward;
6 "and he who receives a righteous man in the name of a righteous man, shall receive a righteous man's reward.	10:~41 and he who receives a righteous man in the name of a righteous man shall receive a righteous man's reward.
7 "And whoever in the name of a disciple, gives \<the\> [least] of [My disciples] even a cup of cold water to drink, truly I say to you, he shall not lose his reward."	10:42 "And whoever in the name of a disciple gives to [one of these] [little] ones even a cup of cold water to drink, truly I say to you, he shall not lose his reward."
8 When Jesus had finished giving instructions to His twelve [apostles] He departed from there, to teach and preach in their cities.	11:1 When Jesus had finished giving instructions to His twelve [discip]les, He departed from there to teach and preach in their cities.

Scene 9: The Apostles Go Out and Preach The Gospel
Capernaum, Galilee   late summer / 31 CE

	Mark	Luke
1 [The twelve apostles] depart[ed], and began going throughout the villages, preaching the *gospel*[1.] that men should repent.	6:12 [They] went out and preached that men should repent.	9:6~ Depart[ing], [they] began going throughout the villages, preaching the gospel
2 And they were casting out many demons, and anointing many sick people with oil, and healing them everywhere.	6:13 And they were casting out many demons and were anointing with oil many sick people and healing them.	9:~6 and healing everywhere.

1. "Good News"

CHAPTER 5
THE THIRD YEAR OF HIS MINISTRY

Events that occurred during the Third Year of The Ministry of Jesus Christ.

Act 1 - The Bread of Life
		Page
Scene 1	The Apostles Return	118
2	Jesus Feeds A Crowd of Five Thousand	119
3	Jesus Walks On The Sea of Galilee	121
4	Peter Joins Jesus On The Sea	122
5	Healing In Gennesaret	122
6	I Am The Bread of Life	123
7	The Will of The Father	124
8	Eat My Flesh, and Drink My Blood	125
9	Some Disciples Stumble At This	126

Act 2 - In Galilee, and Beyond
Scene 1	Eating With Unwashed Hands	127
2	The Things From The Heart Defile The Man	128
3	The Wisdom of A Canaanite Woman	129
4	Jesus Restores The Hearing of A Deaf Man	130
5	Jesus Feeds Four Thousand People	131
6	The Pharisees and Sadducees Seek A Sign	132
7	Beware Of The Leaven of The Pharisees	133
8	Healing A Blind Man at Bethsaida	134
9	Healing A Crippled Woman on The Sabbath	134

Act 3 - A Trip To Trachonitis
Scene 1	Who Do The People Say That I Am?	135
2	Jesus Rebukes Peter	136
3	If Anyone Wishes To Follow Me	137
4	Jesus Is Transfigured With Moses and Elijah	138
5	Why Must Elijah Come First?	139
6	Jesus Cures A Demon-Possessed Boy	140
7	Why Could We Not Drive Out The Demon?	141
8	Follow Me	142

Act 4 - Return To Capernaum
		Page
Scene 1	Jesus Foreshadows His Death and Resurrection	143
2	Paying The Poll-Tax	143
3	The Greatest In The Kingdom of Heaven	144
4	Do Not Cause The Children To Stumble	145
5	On Stumbling Blocks and Hell Fire	145
6	If Your Brother Sins	146
7	On Forgiveness and The Unforgiving Slave	147
8	He Who Is Not Against Us Is For Us	148

Act 5 - Jesus Sends Seventy Disciples
Scene 1	The Trials Of Discipleship	149
2	Jesus Sends Seventy Disciples To Preach	149
3	King Herod Is Perplexed About Jesus	150

Act 6 - On Dining Etiquette
Scene 1	A Sabbath Meal With Pharisees	150
2	Do Not Take The Place of Honor	151
3	Invite The Poor, and Be Blessed	151
4	The Seventy Disciples Return	151

Act 7 - A Collection of Parables
Scene 1	The Joy Over One Sinner Who Repents	152
2	The Prodigal Son	153
3	Rejoice! Your Lost Brother Has Been Found	154
4	The Shrewd Manager	155
5	He Who Is Faithful With Little Things	156
6	Lazarus and The Rich Man	157
7	Pray, and Don't Lose Heart	158
8	The Pharisee and The Tax Collector	158

MAP OF ISRAEL

Locations mentioned in this Chapter are shown with a white center.

5 - THIRD YEAR OF MINISTRY

Act 1: The Bread of Life

Scene 1: The Apostles Return

Galilee — early spring / 32 CE

Look for the Word-For-Word Edition

	Matthew	Mark	Luke	John
1 When the apostles returned, Jesus went up on the mountain, and there He sat down with [them]; and they gave Him an account of all that they had done and taught.		6:30 The apostles ~~gathered together~~ with Jesus; and they ~~reported to~~ Him all that they had done and taught.	9:10~ When the apostles returned, they gave an account ~~to~~ Him of all that they had done.	6:3 ~~Then~~ Jesus went up on the mountain, and there He sat down with [~~His disciples~~].
2 [Then] He said to them, "Come away by yourselves to a secluded place, and rest <for> a while." For there were many people coming and going, and they did not even have time to eat.		6:31 [~~And~~] He said to them, "Come away by yourselves to a secluded place and rest a while." (For there were many people coming and going, and they did not even have time to eat.)		
3 Taking Him with them, they went away in the boat, <and> withdrew to a secluded place by themselves, <near> a city called Bethsaida.		6:32 They went away in the boat to a secluded place by themselves.	9:~10 Taking them with Him, He withdrew by ~~Himself~~ to a city called Bethsaida.	
4 But the crowds were aware of this, <because> the people saw them going, and many recognized them; and a large crowd followed Him, because they saw the signs which He was performing on those who were sick.	14:13⁻¹ ~~and when~~ the ~~people heard~~ of this, 14:13⁻³ followed Him	6:33~ The people saw them going, and many recognized them and	9:11~ But the crowds were aware of this and followed Him;	6:2 A large crowd followed Him, because they saw the signs which He was performing on those who were sick.
5 <So> they ran there together on foot from all <of> the cities, and [arrived] [before] them.	14:13⁻² they 14:~13 on foot from the cities.	6:~33 ran there together on foot from all the cities, and [~~got there~~] [~~ahead of~~] them.		
6 When Jesus went ashore, He saw [the] large crowd; and He felt compassion for them, because *they were like sheep without a shepherd.*[1]	14:14~ When ~~He~~ went ashore, He saw [a] large crowd, and felt compassion for them	6:34~ When Jesus went ashore, He saw [a] large crowd, and He felt compassion for them because they were like sheep without a shepherd;		
7 He welcom[ed] them, and began speaking to them about the Kingdom of God, <and> to teach them many things;		6:~34 and ~~He~~ began to teach them many things.	9:~11~ and welcom[~~ing~~] them, ~~He~~ began speaking to them about the kingdom of God	
8 and <He> cur[ed] those who <were> sick <and> had need of healing.	14:~14 and ~~healed~~ ~~their sick~~.		9:~11 and cur[~~ing~~] those who had need of healing.	

1. *Numbers 27:17*

5 - THIRD YEAR OF MINISTRY

Act 1: The Bread of Life

Scene 2: Jesus Feeds A Crowd of Five Thousand
near Tiberias, *Galilee* April / 32 CE

The Unified Gospel Story

#	Unified	Matthew	Mark	Luke	John
1	When it was evening, and the day was ending, His twelve [apostles] came to [Jesus], and said, "We are here in a desolate place and the hour is already late, so send the crowds away, that they may go into the surrounding countryside and villages, and find lodging, and buy themselves something to eat."	14:15 When it was evening, ~~the~~ [disciples] came to [Him] and said, "~~This~~ place ~~is~~ desolate and the hour is already late; so send the crowds away, that they may go into ~~the~~ villages and buy ~~food for~~ themselves."	6:35 When it was ~~already quite late~~, His [disciples] came to [Him] and said, "~~This~~ place ~~is~~ desolate and ~~it is~~ already ~~quite~~ late; 6:36 so send ~~them~~ away that they may go into the surrounding countryside and villages and buy themselves something to eat."	9:12 ~~Now~~ the day was ending, and the twelve came and said to [Him], "Send the crowd away, that they may go into the surrounding villages and countryside and find lodging and ~~get~~ something to eat; ~~for~~ here we are in a desolate place."	
2	But Jesus answered, <and> said to them, "They do not need to go away - you give them something to eat."	14:16 But Jesus said to them, "They do not need to go away; you give them something to eat!"	6:37~ But ~~He~~ answered them, "You give them something to eat!"	9:13 But ~~He~~ said to them, "You give them something to eat!"	
3	Now the Feast of Passover was near, [so] Jesus, seeing [the] large crowd, said to Philip, "Where are we to buy bread, so that these may eat?"				6:4 Now the Passover, ~~the feast of the Jews~~, was near. 6:5 [~~Therefore~~] Jesus, ~~lifting up His eyes and~~ seeing ~~that~~ [a] large crowd ~~was coming to Him~~, said to Philip, "Where are we to buy bread, so that these may eat?"
4	[Jesus] [said] this to test [Philip], [because] He Himself knew what He was intending to do.				6:6 This [He] was [saying] to test [him], [for] He Himself knew what He was intending to do.
5	Philip answered Him, "Two hundred denari worth of bread is not sufficient for everyone to receive <even> a little."				6:7 Philip answered Him, "Two hundred denarii worth of bread is not sufficient ~~for them~~, for everyone to receive a little."
6	And they said to [Jesus], "Shall we go and buy bread for all these people?"		6:~37 And they said to [Him], "Shall we go and ~~spend two hundred denari on~~ bread ~~and give them something to eat~~?"	9:~13 ~~unless perhaps~~ we go and buy ~~food~~ for all these people."	
7	He said to them, "How many loaves do you have? Go <and> look."		6:38~ ~~And~~ He said to them, "How many loaves do you have? Go look!"		
8	When they found out, Andrew, Simon Peter's brother, said to Him, "There is a lad here who has five barley loaves and two fish; but what are these for so many people?"	14:17 ~~They~~ said to Him, "~~We have only~~ here five loaves and two fish."	6:~38 ~~And~~ when they found out, ~~they~~ said, "Five, and two fish."	9:~13 ~~And~~ they said, "~~We have no more than~~ five loaves and two fish,	6:8 ~~One of His disciples~~, Andrew, Simon Peter's brother, said to Him, 6:9 "There is a lad here who has five barley loaves and two fish, but what are these for so many people?"
9	[Jesus] said, "Bring them here to Me."	14:18 ~~And~~ [He] said, "Bring them here to Me."			
10	[Then] He said to His [apostles], "Have the people sit down to eat, in groups of about fifty each."	14:19~ ~~Ordering~~ the people ~~to~~ sit down	6:39~ [~~And~~] He ~~commanded them all to~~ sit down ~~by~~ groups	9:~14 [~~And~~] He said to His [disciples], "Have ~~them~~ sit down to eat in groups of about fifty each."	6:10~ ~~Jesus~~ said, "Have the people sit down."

continued >

5 - **THIRD YEAR OF MINISTRY**

Act 1: **The Bread of Life**

Scene 2: **Jesus Feeds A Crowd of Five Thousand**
continued

The Four Gospels Harmoniously United

	Matthew	Mark	Luke	John
11 Now there was much grass [there], so they all sat down on the green grass in groups of hundreds, and of fifties.	14:19⁻¹ on the grass	6:40~ They sat down 6:~39 on the green grass. 6:~40 in groups of hundreds and of fifties.	9:15 They ~~did so and had them~~ all sit down.	6:~10~ Now there was much grass [in ~~the place~~]. So ~~the men~~ sat down,
12 Then Jesus took the five loaves and the two fish; and looking up to heaven, He [gave] thanks, blessed the food, and broke the loaves.	14:19⁻² ~~He~~ took the five loaves and the two fish, and looking up ~~toward~~ heaven, He blessed the food, and ~~breaking~~ the loaves	6:41~ ~~And He~~ took the five loaves and the two fish, and looking up ~~toward~~ heaven, He blessed the food and broke the loaves	9:16~ Then ~~He~~ took the five loaves and the two fish, and looking up to heaven, He blessed ~~them~~, and broke ~~them~~,	6:11~ Jesus then took the loaves, ~~and~~ having [given] thanks,
13 And He kept giving them to the [apostles], and [they] [served] then to the crowds [of] people who were seated.	14:~19 He gave them to the [~~disciples~~], and [~~the disciples~~]-[~~gave~~] them to the crowds,	6:~41~ and He kept giving them to the [disciples] [~~to set before~~] ~~them~~;	9:~16 and kept giving them to the [disciples] [~~to set before~~] [~~the~~] ~~people~~.	6:~11~ He ~~distributed to those~~ who were seated;
14 Likewise, He also divided up the two fish among them all, as much as they wanted; and *they all ate and were satisfied.*¹·	14:20~ and they all ate and were satisfied.	6:~41 ~~and~~ He divided up the two fish among them all. 6:42 They all ate and were satisfied,	9:17 And they all ate and were satisfied;	6:~11 likewise also ~~of the~~ fish as much as they wanted.
15 When [the people] were filled, [Jesus] said to His [apostles], "Gather up the leftover fragments, so that nothing will be lost."				6:12 When [~~they~~] were filled, [He] said to His [~~disciples~~], "Gather up the leftover fragments so that nothing will be lost."
16 So they picked up the broken pieces which were left over from the five barley loaves and the <two> fish by those who had eaten, and filled twelve baskets full.	14:~20 They picked up what ~~was~~ left over ~~of~~ the broken pieces, twelve full baskets.	6:43 and they picked up twelve full baskets of the broken pieces, and ~~also of~~ the fish.	9:~17 ~~and~~ the broken pieces which ~~they~~ had left over ~~were~~ picked up, twelve baskets full.	6:13 So they ~~gathered them~~ up, and filled twelve baskets ~~with fragments~~ from the five barley loaves which were left over by those who had eaten.
17 There were in number about five thousand men who ate the loaves, besides women and children.	14:21 There were about five thousand men who ate, besides women and children.	6:44 There were five thousand men who ate the loaves.	9:~14 (~~For~~ there were about five thousand men).	6:~10 in number about five thousand
18 When the people saw the sign which [Jesus] had performed, they said, "Truly, this is the Prophet who is to come into the world!"				6:14 ~~Therefore~~ when the people saw the sign which [He] had performed, they said, "This is truly the Prophet who is to come into the world."

1. 2 Kings 4:43-44

5 - **THIRD YEAR OF MINISTRY**

Act 1: **The Bread of Life**

Scene 3: **Jesus Walks On The Sea of Galilee**
Sea of Galilee, *Galilee*   spring / 32 CE

Page 121

A Verse-By-Verse Harmony of The Four Gospels

#		Matthew	Mark	John
1	Jesus, perceiving that [the people] were intending to come and take Him by force [and] make Him King, immediately made His [apostles] [go] down to the sea, get into the boat, and go ahead of Him to Capernaum, [on] the other side.	14:22~ Immediately He made the [disciples] get into the boat and go ahead of Him [to] the other side,	6:45~ Immediately Jesus made His [disciples] get into the boat and go ahead of Him [to] the other side,	6:15~ So Jesus, perceiving that [they] were intending to come and take Him by force [to] make Him king, 6:~16 His [disciples] [went] down to the sea, 6:17 and after getting into a boat, 6:17~2 to Capernaum.
2	<So> they started to cross the sea, while He Himself was sending the crowds away.	14:~22 while He sent the crowds away.	6:~45 while He Himself was sending the crowd away.	6:17~1 they started to cross the sea
3	After [Jesus] had bid the crowds farewell, <and> sent <them> away, He withdrew <and> went up on the mountain again, to pray alone, by Himself.	14:23~ After [He] had sent the crowds away He went up on the mountain by Himself to pray;	6:46 After bidding them farewell, He left for the mountain to pray.	6:~15 withdrew again to the mountain by Himself alone. 6:17~3 It had already become dark,
4	When evening came, and it had become dark, the boat was already a long distance from the land, in the middle of the sea, and Jesus had not yet come to them, <but> was <still> there alone on the land.	14:~23 and when it was evening, He was there alone. 14:~24~ already a long distance from the land,	6:47 When it was evening, the boat was in the middle of the sea, and He was alone on the land.	6:16~ Now when evening came, 6:~17 and Jesus had not yet come to them.
5	The sea began to be stirred up, [and] the boat was <being> battered by the waves, because a strong wind was blowing against them.	14:24~ [But] the boat was 14:~24 battered by the waves, for the wind was contrary.	6:48~1 for the wind was against them,	6:18 The sea began to be stirred up because a strong wind was blowing.
6	Then, when they had rowed about *three or four miles*,[1] in the *fourth watch*[2] of the night, [Jesus] came to them, walking on the sea.	14:25 And in the fourth watch of the night [He] came to them, walking on the sea.	6:48~2 at about the fourth watch of the night [He] came to them, walking on the sea;	6:19~ Then, when they had rowed about three or four miles,
7	Seeing them straining at the oars, He intended to pass by them.		6:48~ Seeing them straining at the oars, 6:~48 and He intended to pass by them.	
8	When the [apostles] saw Jesus walking on the sea, and drawing near to the boat, they supposed that it was a ghost and they were terrified; and <they> cried out in fear, for they all saw Him.	14:26 When the [disciples] saw Him walking on the sea, they were terrified, and said, "It is a ghost!" And they cried out in fear.	6:49 But when they saw Him walking on the sea, they supposed that it was a ghost, and cried out; 6:50~ for they all saw Him and were terrified.	6~:19 they saw Jesus walking on the sea and drawing near to the boat; and they were frightened.
9	Immediately Jesus spoke to them, and said, "Take courage, it is I! Do not be afraid."	14:27 But immediately Jesus spoke to them, saying, "Take courage, it is I; do not be afraid."	6:~50 But immediately He spoke with them and said to them, "Take courage; it is I, do not be afraid."	6:20 But He said to them, "It is I; do not be afraid."

1. Approximately 5 to 6 km   *2. Roman time: 3 to 6 am*

5 - **THIRD YEAR OF MINISTRY**

Act 1: **The Bread of Life**

Scene 4: **Peter Joins Jesus On The Sea**

Sea of Galilee, *Galilee*   spring / 32 CE

The Gospel Story of Jesus Christ

	Matthew	Mark	John
1 Peter said to [Jesus], "Lord, if it is You, command me to come to You on the water." [Jesus] said <to him>, "Come."	14:28 Peter said to [~~Him~~], "Lord, if it is You, command me to come to You on the water." 14:29~ ~~And~~ [~~He~~] said, "Come!"		
2 [So] Peter got out of the boat, and walked on the water, and came toward Jesus.	14:~29 [~~And~~] Peter got out of the boat, and walked on the water and came toward Jesus.		
3 But <upon> seeing the wind he became frightened, and beg[an] to sink; <and> he cried out, "Lord, save me!"	14:30 But seeing the wind, he became frightened, and beg[~~inning~~] to sink, he cried out, "Lord, save me!"		
4 Immediately Jesus stretched out His hand, and took hold of [Peter], and said to him, "You of little faith, why did you doubt?"	14:31 Immediately Jesus stretched out His hand and took hold of [~~him~~], and said to him, "You of little faith, why did you doubt?"		
5 So they were willing to receive [Jesus] into the boat.			6:21~ So they were willing to receive [~~Him~~] into the boat,
6 When He got into the boat the wind stopped,[1] and immediately the boat was at the land to which they were going.	14:32 When ~~they~~ got into the boat, the wind stopped.	6:51~ ~~Then~~ He got into the boat ~~with them~~, and the wind stopped;	6:~21 and immediately the boat was at the land to which they were going.
7 They were utterly astonished, for they had not gained any insight from the incident of the loaves, but their heart was hardened.		6:~51 ~~and~~ they were utterly astonished, 6:52 for they had not gained any insight from the incident of the loaves, but their heart was hardened.	
8 And those who were in the boat worshiped [Jesus], saying, "You are certainly God's Son!"	14:33 And those who were in the boat worshiped [~~Him~~], saying, "You are certainly God's Son!"		

1. *Psalm 107:29*

Scene 5: **Healing In Gennesaret**

Gennesaret, *Galilee*   spring / 32 CE

	Matthew	Mark
1 When they had crossed over they came to land at Gennesaret, and moored to the shore.	14:34 When they had crossed over, they came to land at Gennesaret.	6:53 When they had crossed over they came to land at Gennesaret, and moored to the shore.
2 When they got out of the boat, immediately the people of that place recognized [Jesus], and they sent word into all [the] surrounding district;	14:35~ ~~And~~ when the ~~men~~ of that place recognized [~~Him~~], they sent word into all [~~that~~] surrounding district	6:54 When they got out of the boat, immediately the people recognized [~~Him~~], 6:55~ and ~~ran about~~ [~~that~~] ~~whole~~ ~~country~~
3 and <they> began to carry on their pallets all who were sick, to the place they heard <that> [Jesus] was.	14:~35 and ~~brought~~ to ~~Him~~ all who were sick;	6:~55 and began to carry ~~here and there~~ on their pallets ~~those~~ who were sick, to the place they heard [~~He~~] was.
4 <And> wherever He [went in] <the> villages or <the> cities or <the> countryside, they were laying the sick in the market places, and imploring Him that they might just touch the fringe of His cloak; and as many as touched it were cured.	14:36 and ~~they~~ implored Him that they might just touch the fringe of His cloak; and as many as touched it were cured.	6:56 Wherever He [~~entered~~] villages, or cities, or countryside, they were laying the sick in the market places, and imploring Him that they might just touch the fringe of His cloak; and as many as touched it were ~~being~~ cured.

5 - THIRD YEAR OF MINISTRY

Act 1: The Bread of Life

Scene 6: I Am The Bread of Life

Capernaum, *Galilee*   spring / 32 CE

	John
1 The next day, the crowd that stood on the other side of the sea saw that there was [only] one small boat there, and that [the] [apostles] of Jesus had gone away in the boat with[out] <Him>.	6:22 The next day the crowd that stood on the other side of the sea saw that there was ~~no other~~ small boat there, [except] one, and that Jesus had ~~not entered~~ with ~~His disciples into~~ the boat, ~~but that~~ [His] [disciples] had gone away ~~alone~~.
2 Other small boats came there from Tiberias, near the place where they ate the bread, after the Lord had given thanks.	6:23 There came other small boats from Tiberias near ~~to~~ the place where they ate the bread after the Lord had given thanks.
3 When the crowd seeking Jesus saw that [He] was not there, nor His [apostles], they got into [their] boats, and [crossed] <the sea> to Capernaum.	6:24 ~~So~~ when the crowd saw that [~~Jesus~~] was not there, nor His [~~disciples~~], they ~~themselves~~ got into [the] ~~small~~ boats, and [~~came~~] to Capernaum seeking Jesus.
4 When they found [Jesus] on the other side of the sea, they said to Him, "Rabbi, when did You get here?"	6:25 When they found [~~Him~~] on the other side of the sea, they said to Him, "Rabbi, when did You get here?"
5 Jesus answered, and said, "Truly, truly, I say to you, you seek Me not because you saw signs, but because you ate of the loaves, and were filled.	6:26 Jesus answered ~~them~~ and said, "Truly, truly, I say to you, you seek Me, not because you saw signs, but because you ate of the loaves and were filled.
6 "Do not work for the food which perishes, but for the food which endures to eternal life, which the Son of Man will give to you; for on Him The Father, God, has set His seal."	6:27 "Do not work for the food which perishes, but for the food which endures to eternal life, which the Son of Man will give to you; for on Him the Father, God, has set His seal."
7 Therefore they said to Him, "What shall we do, so that we may work the works of God?"	6:28 Therefore they said to Him, "What shall we do, so that we may work the works of God?"
8 Jesus answered, and said to them, "This is the work of God; that you believe in Him whom He has sent."	6:29 Jesus answered and said to them, "This is the work of God, that you believe in Him whom He has sent."
9 So they said to Him, "What do You do for a sign, so that we may see, and believe You? What work do You perform?	6:30 So they said to Him, "What ~~then~~ do You do for a sign, so that we may see, and believe You? What work do You perform?
10 "Our fathers ate manna in the wilderness, as it is written, *'He gave them bread out of Heaven to eat.'* "[1]	6:31 "Our fathers ate ~~the~~ manna in the wilderness; as it is written, 'He gave them bread out of heaven to eat.' "
11 Jesus said to them, "Truly, truly, I say to you, it is not Moses who has given you the bread out of Heaven, but it is My Father who gives you the true bread out of Heaven.	6:32 Jesus ~~then~~ said to them, "Truly, truly, I say to you, it is not Moses who has given you the bread out of heaven, but it is My Father who gives you the true bread out of heaven.
12 "For the bread of God is that which comes down out of Heaven, and gives life to the world."	6:33 "For the bread of God is that which comes down out of heaven, and gives life to the world."
13 They said to Him, "Lord, always give us this bread!"	6:34 ~~Then~~ they said to Him, "Lord, always give us this bread."
14 Jesus said to them, "I am the bread of life; he who comes to Me will not hunger, and he who believes in Me will never thirst.	6:35 Jesus said to them, "I am the bread of life; he who comes to Me will not hunger, and he who believes in Me will never thirst.
15 "But I [say] to you, that you have seen Me, and yet do not believe."	6:36 "But I [~~said~~] to you that you have seen Me, and yet do not believe.

1. Exodus 16:14-15, 31 / Nehemiah 9:15 / Psalm 78:24

5 - THIRD YEAR OF MINISTRY	Scene 7: **The Will of The Father**	Page 124
Act 1: **The Bread of Life**	Capernaum, *Galilee*　　spring / 32 CE	*Four Gospels United as One*

		John
1	"All that The Father gives <to> Me will come to Me, and the one who comes to Me I will certainly not cast out;	6:37 "All that the Father gives Me will come to Me, and the one who comes to Me I will certainly not cast out.
2	"for I have not come down from Heaven to do My own will, but <to do> the will of Him who sent Me.	6:38 "For I have come down from heaven, not to do My own will, but the will of Him who sent Me.
3	"This is the will of Him who sent Me, that of all that He has given Me I lose nothing, but raise it up on the last day.	6:39 "This is the will of Him who sent Me, that of all that He has given Me I lose nothing, but raise it up on the last day.
4	"For this is the will of My Father, that everyone who beholds the Son, and believes in Him, will have eternal life,	6:40 "For this is the will of My Father, that everyone who beholds the Son and believes in Him will have eternal life,
5	"and I Myself will raise him up on the last day."	6:~40 and I Myself will raise him up on the last day."
6	Therefore the Jews were grumbling about [Jesus], because He said, "I am the bread that came down out of Heaven."	6:41 Therefore the Jews were grumbling about [~~Him~~], because He said, "I am the bread that came down out of heaven."
7	<And> they were saying, "Is this not Jesus, the son of Joseph, whose father and mother we know? How does He now say, 'I have come down out of Heaven'?"	6:42 They were saying, "Is not this Jesus, the son of Joseph, whose father and mother we know? How does He now say, 'I have come down out of heaven'?"
8	Jesus answered, and said to them, "Do not grumble among yourselves. No one can come to Me unless The Father who sent Me draws him; and I will raise him up on the last day.	6:43 Jesus answered and said to them, "Do not grumble among yourselves. 6:44 "No one can come to Me unless the Father who sent Me draws him; and I will raise him up on the last day.
9	"It is written in the prophets, 'And they shall all be taught of God.' [1.]	6:45~ "It is written in the prophets, 'And they shall all be taught of God.'
10	"Everyone who has heard, and learned from The Father, comes to Me.	6:~45 Everyone who has heard and learned from the Father, comes to Me.
11	"Not that anyone has seen The Father, except the One who is from God, He has seen The Father.	6:46 "Not that anyone has seen the Father, except the One who is from God; He has seen the Father.
12	"Truly, truly, I say to you, he who believes has eternal life!	6:47 "Truly, truly, I say to you, he who believes has eternal life.
13	"I am the bread of life.	6:48 "I am the bread of life.
14	"Your fathers ate the manna in the wilderness, and they died.	6:49 "Your fathers ate the manna in the wilderness, and they died.
15	"This is the bread which comes down out of Heaven, so that one may eat of it, and not die."	6:50 "This is the bread which comes down out of heaven, so that one may eat of it and not die.

1. Isaiah 54:13

5 - **THIRD YEAR OF MINISTRY**	Scene 8: **Eat My Flesh, and Drink My Blood**	Page 125
Act 1: **The Bread of Life**	Capernaum, *Galilee* spring / 32 CE	*A Harmonious Gospel Merger*

		John
1	<Jesus said,> "I am the living bread that came down out of Heaven; if anyone eats of this bread, he will live forever;	6:51~ "I am the living bread that came down out of heaven; if anyone eats of this bread, he will live forever;
2	"and the bread which I will give for the life of the world is My flesh."	6:~51 and the bread ~~also~~ which I will give for the life of the world is My flesh."
3	Then the Jews began to argue with one another, saying, "How can this man give us His flesh to eat?"	6:52 Then the Jews began to argue with one another, saying, "How can this man give us His flesh to eat?"
4	So Jesus said to them, "Truly, truly, I say to you, unless you eat the flesh of the Son of Man, and drink His blood, you have no life in yourselves.	6:53 So Jesus said to them, "Truly, truly, I say to you, unless you eat the flesh of the Son of Man and drink His blood, you have no life in yourselves.
5	"He who eats My flesh, and drinks My blood, has eternal life, and I will raise him up on the last day.	6:54 "He who eats My flesh and drinks My blood has eternal life, and I will raise him up on the last day.
6	"For My flesh is true food, and My blood is true drink.	6:55 "For My flesh is true food, and My blood is true drink.
7	"He who eats My flesh, and drinks My blood, abides in Me, and I in him.	6:56 "He who eats My flesh and drinks My blood abides in Me, and I in him.
8	"As the living Father <has> sent Me, and I live because of the Father, so he who eats Me will also live because of Me.	6:57 "As the living Father sent Me, and I live because of the Father, so he who eats Me, ~~he~~ also will live because of Me.
9	"This is the bread which came down out of Heaven, not as the fathers ate and died; he who eats this bread will live forever."	6:58 "This is the bread which came down out of heaven; not as the fathers ate and died; he who eats this bread will live forever."
10	[Jesus] said these things in the synagogue, as He taught in Capernaum.	6:59 These things [~~He~~] said in the synagogue as He taught in Capernaum.

5 - THIRD YEAR OF MINISTRY

Act 1: **The Bread of Life**

Scene 9: **Some Disciples Stumble At This**

Capernaum, *Galilee* spring / 32 CE

A United Four Gospel Harmony

	John
1 When they heard this, many of His disciples said, "This is a difficult statement; who [is able] to [hear] it?"	6:60 ~~Therefore~~ many of His disciples, when they heard this said, "This is a difficult statement; who [~~can~~] [~~listen~~] to it?"
2 Jesus, [aware] that His disciples grumbled at this, said to them, "Does this cause you to stumble? What then, if you see the Son of Man ascending to where He was before?	6:61 ~~But~~ Jesus, [~~conscious~~] that His disciples grumbled at this, said to them, "Does this cause you to stumble? 6:62 "What then if you see the Son of Man ascending to where He was before?
3 "It is the Spirit who gives life, the flesh <does> [not] [benefit].	6:63~ "It is the Spirit who gives life; the flesh [~~profits~~] [nothing];
4 "The words that I have spoken to you are Spirit, and <they> are life.	6:~63 the words that I have spoken to you are spirit and are life.
5 "But there are some of you who do not believe." For Jesus knew from the beginning [the ones] who did not believe, and who it was that would betray Him.	6:64 "But there are some of you who do not believe." For Jesus knew from the beginning who [~~they were who~~] did not believe, and who it was that would betray Him.
6 And He was saying, "For this reason I said to you that no one can come to Me, unless it has been granted <to> [them] from The Father."	6:65 And He was saying, "For this reason I ~~have~~ said to you, that no one can come to Me unless it has been granted [~~him~~] from the Father."
7 As a result of this, many of His disciples withdrew, and were not walking with Him anymore.	6:66 As a result of this many of His disciples withdrew and were not walking with Him anymore.
8 So Jesus said to the twelve, "You do not also want to go away, do you?"	6:67 So Jesus said to the twelve, "You do not want to go away also, do you?"
9 Simon Peter answered Him, "Lord, to whom shall we go? You have <the> words of eternal life!	6:68 Simon Peter answered Him, "Lord, to whom shall we go? You have words of eternal life.
10 "We have believed, and have come to know, that You are the Holy One of God."	6:69 "We have believed and have come to know that You are the Holy One of God."
11 Jesus answered them, "Did I Myself not choose the twelve <of> you, and yet one of you is a devil?"	6:70 Jesus answered them, "Did I Myself not choose you, the twelve, and yet one of you is a devil?"
12 Now He meant Judas, the son of Simon Iscariot, for he, one of the twelve, was going to betray Him.	6:71 Now He meant Judas the son of Simon Iscariot, for he, one of the twelve, was going to betray Him.

5 - THIRD YEAR OF MINISTRY	Scene 1: **Eating With Unwashed Hands**	Page 127
Act 2: **In Galilee, and Beyond**	Capernaum, *Galilee* summer / 32 CE	*Quotations and references are italicized*

	Matthew	Mark
1 Then some Pharisees and scribes came from Jerusalem, <and> gathered around Jesus.	15:1~ Then some Pharisees and scribes came to Jesus from Jerusalem	7:1 ~~The~~ Pharisees and some ~~of the~~ scribes gathered around ~~Him when they had come~~ from Jerusalem,
2 And <they> [saw] that some of His disciples were eating their bread with impure hands, that is, unwashed.		7:2 and [~~had seen~~] that some of His disciples were eating their bread with impure hands, that is, unwashed.
3 The Pharisees and the scribes asked [Jesus], "Why do Your disciples not walk according to the tradition of the elders?	15:~1 ~~and~~ said, 15:2~ "Why do Your disciples ~~break~~ the tradition of the elders?	7:5~ The Pharisees and the scribes asked [Him], "Why do Your disciples not walk according to the tradition of the elders,
4 "For they do not wash their hands when they eat bread, but <they> eat their bread with impure hands."	15:~2 For they do not wash their hands when they eat bread."	7:~5 but eat their bread with impure hands?"
5 (For the Pharisees and all the Jews do not eat unless they carefully wash their hands, thus observing the traditions of the elders;		7:3 (For the Pharisees and all the Jews do not eat unless they carefully wash their hands, thus observing the traditions of the elders;
6 and when they come <in> from the market place they do not eat unless they <first> cleanse themselves;		7:4~ and when they come from the market place, they do not eat unless they cleanse themselves;
7 and there are many other things which they observe, such as the washing of cups and pitchers, copper pots and <dining couches>.)		7:~4 and there are many other things which they ~~have received in order to~~ observe, such as the washing of cups and pitchers and copper pots.)
8 [Jesus] answered, and said to them, "Why do you yourselves transgress the commandment of God, to [keep] the tradition of men?	15:3 ~~And~~ [He] answered and said to them, "Why do you yourselves transgress the commandment of God [~~for the sake~~] of ~~your~~ tradition?	7:8 "~~Neglecting~~ the commandment of God, ~~you~~ [hold] ~~to~~ the tradition of men."
9 "<For> you are experts at setting aside the commandment of God, in order to keep your tradition.		7:9 ~~He was also saying to them,~~ "You are experts at setting aside the commandment of God in order to keep your tradition.
10 "For [through] Moses, God said, *'Honor your father and your mother';* [1.] and, *'He who speaks evil of <his> father or <his> mother is to be put to death.'* [2.]	15:4 "For God said, *'Honor your father and your mother,'* and, *'He who speaks evil of father or mother is to be put to death.'*	7:10 "For Moses said, *'Honor your father and your mother';* and, *'He who speaks evil of father or mother, is to be put to death';*
11 "But you say, 'Whoever says to his father or his mother, "Whatever I have that would help you is Corban," ' ([which means] [it] has been given to God) , <so> you no longer permit him to do anything <to> honor his father, or his mother.	15:5 "But you say, 'Whoever says to his father or his mother, "Whatever I have that would help you has been given to God," 15:6~ he ~~is not~~ to honor his father or his mother.'	7:11 but you say, '~~If a man~~ says to his father or his mother, whatever I have that would help you is Corban ([~~that is to say~~], given to God),' 7:12 you no longer permit him to do anything ~~for~~ his father or his mother;
12 "And by this you invalidate the Word of God for the sake of your tradition, which you have handed down; and you do many things such as that."	15:~6 And by this you invalidate~~d~~ the word of God for the sake of your tradition.	7:13 ~~thus~~ invalidat~~ing~~ the word of God ~~by~~ your tradition which you have handed down; and you do many things such as that."
13 And He said to them, "You hypocrites! Rightly did Isaiah prophesy of you, as it is written: *'This people honors Me with their lips, but their heart is far away from Me. But in vain do they worship Me, teaching as doctrines the precepts of men!' "* [3.]	15:7 "You hypocrites, rightly did Isaiah prophesy of you: 15:8 *'This people honors Me with their lips, but their heart is far away from Me.* 15:9 *'But in vain do they worship Me, teaching as doctrines the precepts of men.'*	7:6 And He said to them, "Rightly did Isaiah prophesy of you hypocrites, as it is written: *'This people honors Me with their lips, but their heart is far away from Me.* 7:7 *'But in vain do they worship Me, teaching as doctrines the precepts of men.'*

1. Exodus 20:12 / Deuteronomy 5:16   2. Exodus 21:17 / Proverb 20:20   3. Isaiah 29:13

continued >

5 - THIRD YEAR OF MINISTRY Act 2: **In Galilee, and Beyond**	Scene 1: **Eating With Unwashed Hands** *continued*	*The Complete Gospel Story*

	Matthew	**Mark**
14 After Jesus called the crowd to Him[self], He again began saying to them, "Listen to Me, all of you - hear and understand! There is nothing outside the man which can defile him if it goes into him.	15:10 After Jesus called the crowd to Him, He said to them, "Hear and understand.	7:14 After ~~He~~ called the crowd to Him again, He began saying to them, "Listen to Me, all of you, and understand: 7:15~ there is nothing outside the man which can defile him if it goes into him;
15 "It is not what enters into the mouth that defiles the man, but the things which proceed out of the mouth are what defile the man.	15:11 "It is not what enters into the mouth that defiles the man, but what proceeds out of the mouth, ~~this~~ defiles the man."	7:~15 but the things which proceed out of the ~~man~~ are what defile the man.
16 "If anyone has ears to hear, let him hear!"		7:16 {"If anyone has ears to hear, let him hear."}
17 Then [His] [apostles] came and said to [Jesus], "Do You know that the Pharisees were offended when they heard this statement?"	15:12 Then [the] [~~disciples~~] came and said to [~~Him~~], "Do You know that the Pharisees were offended when they heard this statement?"	
18 "But He answered, and said, "Every plant which My Heavenly Father did not plant, shall be uprooted.	15:13 But He answered and said, "Every plant which My heavenly Father did not plant shall be uprooted.	
19 "[Leave] them alone, they are <the> blind guides of the blind;	15:14~ "[~~Let~~] them alone; they are blind guides of the blind.	
20 "and if a blind man guides a blind man both will fall into a pit."	15:~14 And if a blind man guides a blind man, both will fall into a pit."	

Scene 2: **The Things From The Heart Defile The Man**

Capernaum, Galilee   summer / 32 CE

	Matthew	**Mark**
1 When [Jesus] left the crowd and entered the house, His disciples questioned Him, <and> Peter said, "Explain the parable to us."	15:15 Peter said ~~to Him~~, "Explain the parable to us."	7:17 When [He] ~~had~~ left the crowd and entered the house, His disciples questioned Him ~~about~~ the parable.
2 Jesus said to them, "Are you still so lacking in understanding also?	15:16 Jesus said, "Are you still lacking in understanding also?	7:18~ ~~And He~~ said to them, "Are you so lacking in understanding also?
3 "Do you not understand that [any]thing that goes into the mouth from outside cannot defile [a man] because it does not go into his heart, but <it> passes into the stomach and is eliminated, thus [purifying] all foods.	15:17 "Do you not understand that [~~every~~]thing that goes into the mouth passes into the stomach, and is eliminated?	7:~18 Do you not understand that ~~whatever~~ goes into the ~~man~~ from outside cannot defile [him], 7:19 because it does not go into his heart, but into ~~his~~ stomach, and is eliminated?" (Thus ~~He declared~~ all foods [~~clean~~])*
4 "The things which proceed out of the mouth come from the heart, and those [are] what defile [a] man.	15:18 "~~But~~ the things ~~that~~ proceed out of the mouth come from the heart, and those defile [~~the~~] man.	7:20 ~~And He was saying~~, "~~That~~ which proceeds out of the ~~man~~, ~~that~~ [is] what defiles [~~the~~] man.
5 "For *from within, out of the heart of men, come evil thoughts;* [1.] pride, envy, false witness, slander, foolishness and wickedness; deeds of coveting as well as deceit, sensuality, fornications, adulteries, thefts and murders.	15:19 "For out of the heart come evil thoughts, murders, adulteries, fornications, thefts, false witness, slander~~s~~.	7:21 "For from within, out of the heart of men, ~~proceed the~~ evil thoughts, fornications, thefts, murders, adulteries, 7:22 deeds of coveting and wickedness, as well as deceit, sensuality, envy, slander, pride, ~~and~~ foolishness.
6 "All these are the evil things which proceed from within and defile [a] man;	15:20~ "These are the things which defile [~~the~~] man;	7:23 "All these evil things proceed from within and defile [~~the~~] man."
7 "but to eat with unwashed hands does not defile [him]."	15:~20 but to eat with unwashed hands does not defile [~~the man~~]."	

1. Genesis 6:5

	Scene 3: **The Wisdom of A Canaanite Woman**	
5 - THIRD YEAR OF MINISTRY	District of Tyre near Sidon, *Phoenicia* summer / 32 CE	
Act 2: **In Galilee, and Beyond**		*The Four Gospels United in Harmony*

	Matthew	**Mark**
1 Jesus got up and went away from there, and withdrew to the district of Tyre and Sidon.	15:21 Jesus went away from there, and withdrew ~~into~~ the district of Tyre and Sidon.	7:24~ Jesus got up and went away from there to the ~~region~~ of Tyre.
2 He entered a house, and wanted no one to know of it, <and> yet He could not escape notice.		7:~24 And ~~when~~ He ~~had~~ entered a house, ~~He~~ wanted no one to know of it; yet He could not escape notice.
3 After hearing of [Jesus], a Canaanite woman of the Syrophoenician race from that region came out, whose little daughter had an unclean spirit.	15:22~ ~~And~~ a Canaanite woman from that region came out	7:25~ ~~But~~ after hearing of [Him], ~~a woman~~ whose little daughter had an unclean spirit 7:26~ ~~Now the~~ woman ~~was~~ a ~~Gentile~~, of the Syrophoenician race.
4 Immediately <she> came and fell at His feet, and began to cry out, saying, "Have mercy on me, Lord, son of David! My daughter is cruelly demon-possessed."	15:~22 and began to cry out, saying, "Have mercy on me, Lord, son of David; my daughter is cruelly demon-possessed."	7:~25 immediately came and fell at His feet.
5 And she kept asking [Jesus] to cast the demon out of her daughter, but He did not answer her a word.	15:23~ But He did not answer her a word.	7:~26 And she kept asking [Him] to cast the demon out of her daughter.
6 His disciples came and implored Him, saying, "Send her away, because she keeps shouting at us."	15:~23 ~~And~~ His disciples came and implored Him, saying, "Send her away, because she keeps shouting at us."	
7 But [Jesus] answered, and said, "I was sent only to the lost sheep of the house of Israel."	15:24 But [He] answered and said, "I was sent only to the lost sheep of the house of Israel."	
8 [Then] she bow[ed] down before Him, <and> [said], "Lord, help me!"	15:25 [But] she ~~came and began to~~ bow down before Him, [saying], "Lord, help me!"	
9 He answered her, "Let the children be satisfied first; for it is not good to take the children's bread, and throw it to the dogs."	15:26 ~~And~~ He answered ~~and said~~, It is not good to take the children's bread and throw it to the dogs."	7:27 ~~And~~ He ~~was~~ ~~saying~~ it is not good to take the children's bread and throw it to the dogs."
10 She said to Him, "Yes, Lord, but even the dogs under the table feed on the children's crumbs, which fall from their master's table."	15:27 But she said, "Yes, Lord; but even the dogs feed on the crumbs which fall from their masters' table."	7:28 ~~But~~ she ~~answered and~~ said to Him, "Yes, Lord, but even the dogs under the table feed on the children's crumbs."
11 Then Jesus said to her, "O woman, your faith is great! Because of this answer it shall be done for you as you wish. Go; the demon has gone out of your daughter."	15:28~ Then Jesus said to her, "O woman, your faith is great; it shall be done for you as you wish.	7:29 ~~And~~ He said to her, "Because of this answer go; the demon has gone out of your daughter.
12 And her daughter was healed at once.	15:~28 And her daughter was healed at once.	
13 Going back to her home, [the woman] found the child lying on the bed, the demon having left.		7:30 ~~And~~ going back to her home, [~~she~~] found the child lying on the bed, the demon having left.

5 - THIRD YEAR OF MINISTRY
Act 2: In Galilee, and Beyond

Scene 4: Jesus Restores The Hearing of A Deaf Man
Decapolis   summer / 32 CE

	Matthew	Mark
1 Departing from there, Jesus [passed] through Sidon; and <leaving> the [district] of Tyre <He> [traveled] to the Sea of Galilee, within the region of Decapolis.	*15:29~* Departing from there, Jesus [went along by] the Sea of Galilee,	*7:31* Again He went out from the [region] of Tyre, and [came] through Sidon to the Sea of Galilee, within the region of Decapolis
2 Having gone up on the mountain, [Jesus] was sitting there; and large crowds came to Him, bringing with them those who were lame, crippled, blind, mute, and many others; and they laid them down at His feet, and He healed them.	*15:~29* and having gone up on the mountain, [He] was sitting there. *15:30* And large crowds came to Him, bringing with them those who were lame, crippled, blind, mute, and many others, and they laid them down at His feet; and He healed them.	
3 They brought to Him one who was deaf and spoke with difficulty, and they implored Him to lay His hand on him.		*7:32* They brought to Him one who was deaf and spoke with difficulty, and they implored Him to lay His hand on him.
4 Jesus took him by himself, aside from the crowd, and put His fingers into [the man's] ears.		*7:33~* Jesus took him aside from the crowd, by himself, and put His fingers into [his] ears,
5 After spitting, [Jesus] touched his tongue with the saliva; and looking up to heaven with a deep sigh, He said to him, "Ephphatha!" that is, "Be opened!"		*7:~33* and after spitting, [He] touched his tongue with the saliva; *7:34* and looking up to heaven with a deep sigh, He said to him, "Ephphatha!" that is, "Be opened!"
6 And <immediately> his ears were opened, and the impediment of his tongue was removed, and he began <to> speak [clearly].		*7:35* And his ears were opened, and the impediment of his tongue was removed, and he began speaking [plainly].
7 The crowd marveled as they saw the mute speaking, the crippled restored, the lame walking, and the blind seeing.	*15:31~* So the crowd marveled as they saw the mute speaking, the crippled restored, and the lame walking, and the blind seeing;	
8 <And> they were utterly astonished, saying, "He has done all things well. He makes even the deaf to hear, and the mute to speak!"		*7:37* They were utterly astonished, saying, "He has done all things well; He makes even the deaf to hear and the mute to speak."
9 And they glorified the God of Israel.	*15:~31* and they glorified the God of Israel.	
10 [Jesus] gave them orders not to tell anyone; but the more He ordered them, the more widely they continued to proclaim it.		*7:36* And [He] gave them orders not to tell anyone; but the more He ordered them, the more widely they continued to proclaim it.

5 - THIRD YEAR OF MINISTRY
Act 2: **In Galilee, and Beyond**

Scene 5: **Jesus Feeds Four Thousand People**
Decapolis summer / 32 CE

	Matthew	Mark
1 In those days, there was again a large crowd, and they had nothing to eat.		8:1~ In those days, when there was again a large crowd and they had nothing to eat,
2 Jesus called His [apostles] to Him, and said, "I feel compassion for the people, because they have now remained with Me <for> three days, and have nothing to eat.	15:32~ And Jesus called His [disciples] to Him, and said, "I feel compassion for the people, because they have remained with Me now three days and have nothing to eat;	8:~1 Jesus called His [disciples] and said to them, 8:2 "I feel compassion for the people because they have remained with Me now three days and have nothing to eat.
3 I do not want to send them away hungry to their homes, for some of them have come from a great distance, and they might faint on the way."	15:~32 and I do not want to send them away hungry, for they might faint on the way."	8:3 "If I send them away hungry to their homes, they will faint on the way; and some of them have come from a great distance."
4 His [apostles] said to Him, "Where will we be able to find enough loaves <of> bread here in this desolate place, to satisfy such a large crowd <of> people?"	15:33 The [disciples] said to Him, "Where would we get so many loaves in this desolate place to satisfy such a large crowd?"	8:4 And His [disciples] answered Him, "Where will anyone be able to find enough bread here in this desolate place to satisfy these people?"
5 Jesus ask[ed] them, "How many loaves do you have?" They said, "Seven."	15:34~ And Jesus said to them, "How many loaves do you have?" And they said, "Seven,	8:5 And He was ask[ing] them, "How many loaves do you have?" And they said, "Seven."
6 [Then] [Jesus] directed the people to sit down on the ground, and taking the seven loaves, He gave thanks, and broke them.	15:35 [And] [He] directed the people to sit down on the ground; 15:36~ and He took the seven loaves and the fish; and giving thanks, He broke them	8:6~ [And] [He] directed the people to sit down on the ground; and taking the seven loaves, He gave thanks and broke them
7 <Then He> started giving them to His [apostles] to serve, and they served them to the people.	15:~36 and started giving them to the [disciples], and the disciples gave them to the people.	8:~6 and started giving them to His [disciples] to serve to them, and they served them to the people.
8 They also had a few small fish, and after [Jesus] had blessed them, He ordered these to be served as well.	15:~34 and a few small fish."	8:7 They also had a few small fish; and after [He] had blessed them, He ordered these to be served as well.
9 *They all ate and were satisfied*;[1] and they picked up seven large baskets full of the broken pieces [that] [were] left over.	15:37 And they all ate and were satisfied, and they picked up [what] [was] left over of the broken pieces, seven large baskets full.	8:8 And they ate and were satisfied; and they picked up seven large baskets full of [what] [was] left over of the broken pieces.
10 There were about four thousand men who ate, besides women and children; and <then> [Jesus] sent them away.	15:38 And those who ate were four thousand men, besides women and children.	8:9 About four thousand were there; and [He] sent them away.

1. *2 Kings 4:43-44*

5 - THIRD YEAR OF MINISTRY

Act 2: **In Galilee, and Beyond**

Scene 6: **The Pharisees and Sadducees Seek A Sign**

Dalmanutha, *Galilee* summer / 32 CE

Page 132

The Good News Gospel

	Matthew	Mark	Luke
1 [After] sending the crowds away, Jesus got into the boat with His disciples, and came to the district of Dalmanutha, <in> the region of Magadan.	15:39 [And] sending away the crowds, Jesus got into the boat and came to the region of Magadan.	8:10 And Immediately He entered the boat with His disciples and came to the district of Dalmanutha.	
2 The Pharisees and Sadducees came and began to argue with [Jesus]; and to test Him, <they> asked Him to show them a sign from Heaven.	16:1 The Pharisees and Sadducees came up, and testing Jesus, asked Him to show them a sign from heaven.	8:11 The Pharisees came out and began to argue with [Him], seeking from Him a sign from heaven, to test Him.	
3 Sighing deeply in His spirit, He said to them, "Why does this generation seek for a sign?	16:2~ But He replied to them,	8:12~ Sighing deeply in His spirit, He said, "Why does this generation seek for a sign?	12:54~ And He was also saying to the crowds,
4 "When you see a cloud rising in the west, immediately you say, 'A shower is coming,' and so it turns out;	16:~2 "When it is evening, you say, 'It will be fair weather, for the sky is red.'		12:~54 "When you see a cloud rising in the west, immediately you say, 'A shower is coming,' and so it turns out.
5 "and when a south wind is blowing, you say, 'It will be hot today,' and it turns out that way.	16:3~ "And in the morning, 'There will be a storm today, for the sky is red and threatening.'		12:55 "And when you see a south wind blowing, you say, 'It will be a hot day,' and it turns out that way.
6 "You hypocrites! You know how to analyze the appearance of the earth and the sky, but why can you not discern the signs of this present time?	16:~3 Do you know how to discern the appearance of the sky, but cannot discern the signs of the times?		12:56 "You hypocrites! You know how to analyze the appearance of the earth and the sky, but why do you not analyze this present time?
7 "Truly I say to you, an evil and adulterous generation seeks [for] a sign;	16:4~ "An evil and adulterous generation seeks [after] a sign;	8:~12 Truly I say to you,	
8 "and no sign will be given to this generation, except the sign of *Jonah*." [1]	16:~4 and a sign will not be given it, except the sign of Jonah."	8:~12 no sign will be given to this generation."	

1. *Jonah 1:17; 3:3-5*

5 - THIRD YEAR OF MINISTRY

Act 2: In Galilee, and Beyond

Scene 7: Beware Of The Leaven of The Pharisees

Sea of Galilee, *Galilee*   summer / 32 CE

A Unified Four Gospel Merger

	Matthew	**Mark**
1 Leaving them, [Jesus] embarked [with] [His] [apostles], and <they> [crossed] to the other side of the sea.	16:~4 And [He] left them and went away. 16:5~ [And] [the] [disciples] [came] to the other side of the sea,	8:13 Leaving them, [He] again embarked and [went away] to the other side.
2 They had forgotten to bring any bread, and did not have more than one loaf in the boat with them.	16:~5 but they had forgotten to bring any bread.	8:14 And they had forgotten to take bread, and did not have more than one loaf in the boat with them.
3 Jesus was giving orders to them, saying, "Watch out! Beware of the leaven of the Pharisees and <of the> Sadducees, and the leaven of Herod!"	16:6 And Jesus said to them, "Watch out and beware of the leaven of the Pharisees and Sadducees.	8:15 And He was giving orders to them, saying, "Watch out! Beware of the leaven of the Pharisees and the leaven of Herod."
4 <So> they began to discuss with one another the fact that they had no bread, saying, "He said that because we did not bring any bread."	16:7 They began to discuss this among themselves saying, "He said that because we did not bring any bread."	8:16 They began to discuss with one another the fact that they had no bread.
5 But Jesus, aware of this, said to them, "You men of little faith! Why do you discuss the fact that you have no bread?	16:8 But Jesus, aware of this, said, "You men of little faith, why do you discuss among yourselves that you have no bread?	8:17~ And Jesus, aware of this, said to them, "Why do you discuss the fact that you have no bread?
6 "Do you not yet see or understand? Do you have a hardened heart?	16:9~ "Do you not yet understand	8:~17 Do you not yet see or understand? Do you have a hardened heart?
7 "Having eyes, do you not see? And having ears, do you not hear?		8:18~ "Having eyes, do you not see? And having ears, do you not hear?
8 "Do you not remember when I broke the five loaves for the five thousand? And how many baskets full of broken pieces <did> you pick up?" They said to Him, "Twelve."	16:~9 or remember the five loaves of the five thousand, and how many baskets full you picked up?	8:~18 And do you not remember, 8:19 when I broke the five loaves for the five thousand, how many baskets full of broken pieces you picked up?" They said to Him, "Twelve."
9 "Or when I broke the seven loaves for the four thousand, and how many large baskets full of broken pieces did you pick up?" They said, "Seven."	16:10 "Or the seven loaves of the four thousand, and how many large baskets full you picked up?	8:20 "When I broke the seven for the four thousand, how many large baskets full of broken pieces did you pick up?" And they said to Him, "Seven."
10 [Then] He [said] to them, "<So> how is it that you do not yet understand, that I did not speak to you concerning bread, but <to> beware of the leaven of the Pharisees, and <of the> Sadducees?"	16:11 "How is it that you do not understand that I did not speak to you concerning bread? But beware of the leaven of the Pharisees and Sadducees."	8:21 [And] He was [saying] to them, "Do you not yet understand?"
11 Then they understood that He did not say to beware of the leaven of bread, but of the teaching[s] of the Pharisees, and <the> Sadducees.	16:12 Then they understood that He did not say to beware of the leaven of bread, but of the teaching of the Pharisees and Sadducees.	

| 5 - THIRD YEAR OF MINISTRY | Scene 8: **Healing A Blind Man at Bethsaida** | Page 134 |
| Act 2: **In Galilee, and Beyond** | Bethsaida, *Trachonitis*   summer / 32 CE | *The Four Gospels United as One* |

	Mark
1 [When] they came to Bethsaida, they brought a blind man to Jesus, and implored Him to touch him.	8:22 [And] they came to Bethsaida. And they brought a blind man to Jesus and implored Him to touch him.
2 Taking the blind man by the hand, [Jesus] brought him out of the village.	8:23~ Taking the blind man by the hand, [He] brought him out of the village;
3 [Then] after spitting on his eyes, and laying His hands on him, [Jesus] asked him, "Do you see anything?"	8:~23 [and] after spitting on his eyes and laying His hands on him, [He] asked him, "Do you see anything?"
4 He looked up, and said, "I see men! [But] I see them like trees, walking around."	8:24 And he looked up and said, "I see men, [for] I see them like trees, walking around."
5 Again [Jesus] laid His hands on [the man's] eyes; and <when> he looked intently, [he] was restored, and began to see everything clearly.	8:25 Then again [He] laid His hands on [his] eyes; and he looked intently [and] was restored, and began to see everything clearly.
6 And [Jesus] sent him to his home, saying, "Do not enter the village."	8:26 And [He] sent him to his home, saying, "Do not even enter the village."

Scene 9: **Healing A Crippled Woman on The Sabbath**

Bethsaida, *Trachonitis*   a Sabbath, summer / 32 CE

	Luke
1 [Jesus] was teaching in one of the synagogues on the Sabbath, and a woman was there who for eighteen years had a sickness caused by a spirit, [who] was bent [over], and could not straighten up at all.	13:10 And [He] was teaching in one of the synagogues on the Sabbath. 13:11 And there was a woman who for eighteen years had had a sickness caused by a spirit; and [she] was bent [double], and could not straighten up at all.
2 When Jesus saw her, He called her over, and said to her, "Woman, you are freed from your sickness."	13:12 When Jesus saw her, He called her over and said to her, "Woman, you are freed from your sickness."
3 [Then] He laid His hands on her, and immediately she was made erect again, and began glorifying God.	13:13 [And] He laid His hands on her; and immediately she was made erect again and began glorifying God.
4 But the synagogue official, indignant because Jesus had healed on the Sabbath, began saying to the crowd, "There are six days in which work should be done, so come during them and get healed, and not on the Sabbath day!"	13:14 But the synagogue official, indignant because Jesus had healed on the Sabbath, began saying to the crowd in response, "There are six days in which work should be done; so come during them and get healed, and not on the Sabbath day."
5 But the Lord answered him, and said, "You hypocrites! Does not each of you on the Sabbath untie his ox or his donkey from the stall, and lead him away to water him?	13:15 But the Lord answered him and said, "You hypocrites, does not each of you on the Sabbath untie his ox or his donkey from the stall and lead him away to water him?
6 "And this woman, a daughter of Abraham as she is, whom Satan has bound for eighteen long years, should she not have been released from this bond on the Sabbath day?"	13:16 "And this woman, a daughter of Abraham as she is, whom Satan has bound for eighteen long years, should she not have been released from this bond on the Sabbath day?"
7 As [Jesus] said this, His opponents were being humiliated; and the entire crowd was rejoicing over all <of> the glorious things being done by Him.	13:17 As [He] said this, all His opponents were being humiliated; and the entire crowd was rejoicing over all the glorious things being done by Him.

5 - THIRD YEAR OF MINISTRY

Act 3: A Trip To Trachonitis

Scene 1: Who Do The People Say That I Am?

Caesarea Philippi, *Trachonitis*   summer / 32 CE

The Harmonious Gospel

	Matthew	Mark	Luke
1 Jesus went out with His disciples, <and> came to the villages in the district of Caesarea Philippi.	*16:~13* ~~Now when~~ Jesus came ~~into~~ the district of Caesarea Philippi,	*8:27~* Jesus went out, ~~along~~ with His disciples, to the villages of Caesarea Philippi;	
2 On the way, it happened that while He was praying alone with [His] [apostles], He questioned them saying, "Who do the people say that I am?"	*16:~13* He ~~was asking His disciples~~, "Who do people say that the ~~Son of Man is~~?"	*8:~27* ~~and~~ on the way He questioned ~~His disciples~~, saying ~~to them~~, "Who do people say that I am?"	*9:18* ~~And~~ it happened that while He was praying alone, [the] [disciples] ~~were~~ with ~~Him~~, ~~and~~ He questioned them, saying, "Who do the people say that I am?"
3 They answered Him, saying, "Some say John the Baptist, and others say Elijah; but still others, that Jeremiah, or one of the prophets of old, has risen again."	*16:14* And they said "Some say John the Baptist; and others, Elijah; but still others, Jeremiah, or one of the prophets."	*8:28* They ~~told~~ Him, saying, "John the Baptist; and others say Elijah; but others, one of the prophets."	*9:19* They answered ~~and~~ said, "John the Baptist, and others say Elijah; but others, that one of the prophets of old has risen again."
4 [Jesus] continued questioning them, and [asked], "But who do you say that I am?"	*16:15* He [said] ~~to them~~, "But who do you say that I am?"	*8:~29* ~~And~~ [He] continued ~~by~~ questioning them, "But who do you say that I am?"	*9:20~* And He [said] ~~to them~~, "But who do you say that I am?"
5 Simon Peter answered, and said to Him, "You are the Christ, the Son of the living God."	*16:16* Simon Peter answered, "You are the Christ, the Son of the living God."	*8:~29* Peter answered and said to Him, "You are the Christ."	*9:~20* ~~And~~ Peter answered and said, "The Christ of God."
6 Jesus said to him, "Blessed are you, Simon *Barjona*,[1] because flesh and blood did not reveal this to you, but My Father who is in Heaven.	*16:17* ~~And~~ Jesus said to him, "Blessed are you, Simon Barjona, because flesh and blood did not reveal this to you, but My Father who is in heaven.		
7 "I also say to you that you are Peter, and upon this rock I will build My Church; and the gates of Hades will not overpower it!	*16:18* "I also say to you that you are Peter, and upon this rock I will build My church; and the gates of Hades will not overpower it.		
8 "I will give you the keys of the Kingdom of Heaven; and whatever you bind on earth [will be] bound in Heaven, and whatever you loose on earth [will be] loosed in Heaven."	*16:19* "I will give you the keys of the kingdom of heaven; and whatever you bind on earth [~~shall have been~~] bound in heaven, and whatever you loose on earth [~~shall have been~~] loosed in heaven."		
9 Then He warned the [apostles], and instructed them that they should not tell anyone that He was the Christ.	*16:20* Then He warned the [~~disciples~~] that they should tell ~~no~~ one that He was the Christ.	*8:30* ~~And~~ He warned ~~them to~~ tell ~~no~~ one ~~about Him~~.	*9:21* ~~But~~ He warned ~~them~~ and instructed them not ~~to~~ tell ~~this to~~ anyone,

5 - THIRD YEAR OF MINISTRY

Act 3: **A Trip To Trachonitis**

Scene 2: **Jesus Rebukes Peter**

Caesarea Philippi, *Trachonitis* summer / 32 CE

FIVE COLUMN

	Matthew	Mark	Luke
1 From that time, Jesus began to teach His disciples that He must go to Jerusalem, saying, "The Son of Man must suffer many things, and be rejected by the elders, and the chief priests and the scribes, and be killed; and on the third day be raised up again."	16:21 From that time Jesus began to ~~show~~ His disciples that He must go to Jerusalem, ~~and~~ suffer many things ~~from~~ the elders and chief priests and scribes, and be killed, and be raised up on the third day.	8:31 ~~And He~~ began to teach ~~them that~~ the Son of Man must suffer many things and be rejected by the elders and the chief priests and the scribes, and be killed, and ~~after~~ three days ~~rise~~ again.	9:22 saying, "The Son of Man must suffer many things and be rejected by the elders and chief priests and scribes, and be killed, and be raised up on the third day."
2 He was stating the matter plainly, [but] Peter took Him aside, and began to rebuke Him, saying, "God forbid it, Lord! This shall never happen to You."	16:22 Peter took Him aside and began to rebuke Him, saying, "God forbid it, Lord! This shall never happen to You."	8:32 ~~And~~ He was stating the matter plainly. [And] Peter took Him aside and began to rebuke Him.	
3 [Jesus] turned around, and seeing His [apostles] He rebuked Peter, and said, "Get behind Me, Satan!	16:23~ ~~But~~ [He] turned and said to Peter, "Get behind Me, satan!	8:33~ ~~But~~ turning around and seeing His [~~disciples~~], He rebuked Peter and said, "Get behind Me, Satan;	
4 "You are a stumbling block to Me, for you are not setting your mind on God's interests, but <on> man's."	16:~23 You are a stumbling block to Me; for you are not setting your mind on God's interests, but man's."	8:~33 for you are not setting your mind on God's interests, but man's."	

5 - THIRD YEAR OF MINISTRY

Act 3: A Trip To Trachonitis

Scene 3: If Anyone Wishes To Follow Me

Caesarea Philippi, *Trachonitis*   summer / 32 CE

Page 137

Get the 552 page **Word-For-Word** *Edition*

	Matthew	Mark	Luke
1 Then Jesus summoned the crowd with His disciples, and <He> said to them all, "If anyone wishes to come after Me, he must deny himself, and take up his cross [every day], and follow Me.	16:24 Then Jesus said to ~~His disciples~~, "If anyone wishes to come after Me, he must deny himself, and take up his cross and follow Me.	8:34 ~~And~~ He summoned the crowd with His disciples, and said to them, "If anyone wishes to come after Me, he must deny himself, and take up his cross and follow Me.	9:23 ~~And~~ ~~He~~ ~~was~~ saying to them all, "If anyone wishes to come after Me, he must deny himself, and take up his cross [daily] and follow Me.
2 "For whoever wishes to save his life will lose it; but whoever loses his life for My sake, and the gospel's, he is the one who will save it.	16:25 "For whoever wishes to save his life will lose it; but whoever loses his life for My sake will ~~find~~ it.	8:35 "For whoever wishes to save his life will lose it, but whoever loses his life for My sake and the gospel's will save it.	9:24 "For whoever wishes to save his life will lose it, but whoever loses his life for My sake, he is the one who will save it.
3 "For what will it profit a man if he gains the whole world <but> loses himself, and forfeits his soul?	16:26~ "For what will it profit a man if he gains the whole world and forfeits his soul?	8:36 "For what ~~does~~ it profit a man ~~to~~ gain the whole world, and forfeit his soul?	9:25 "For what ~~is~~ a man profit~~ed~~ if he gains the whole world, and loses ~~or~~ forfeits himself?
4 "What will a man give in exchange for his soul?	16:~26 ~~Or~~ what will a man give in exchange for his soul?	8:37 ~~For~~ what will a man give in exchange for his soul?	
5 "For whoever is ashamed of Me and My words in this sinful and adulterous generation, the Son of Man will also be ashamed of him when He comes in His glory, and the glory of His Father, with the holy angels.		8:38 "For whoever is ashamed of Me and My words in this adulterous and sinful generation, the Son of Man will also be ashamed of him when He comes in the glory of His Father with the holy angels."	9:26 "For whoever is ashamed of Me and My words, the Son of Man will be ashamed of him when He comes in His glory, and the glory of ~~the~~ Father ~~and~~ ~~of~~ the holy angels.
6 "For the Son of Man is going to come in the glory of His Father with His angels, and then <He> will repay every man according to his deeds."	16:27 "For the Son of Man is going to come in the glory of His Father with His angels, and will then repay every man according to his deeds."		
7 And Jesus [said] to them, "Truly I say to you, <that> there are some of those who are standing here who will not taste death until they see the Son of Man coming in the Kingdom of God, after it has come with power!"	16:28 "Truly I say to you, there are some of those who are standing here who will not taste death until they see the Son of Man coming in ~~His~~ kingdom."	9:1 And Jesus [~~was~~ ~~saying~~] to them, "Truly I say to you, there are some of those who are standing here who will not taste death until they see the kingdom of God after it has come with power."	9:27 "~~But~~ I say to you ~~truthfully~~, there are some of those standing here who will not taste death until they see the kingdom of God."

	5 - THIRD YEAR OF MINISTRY	Scene 4: **Jesus Is Transfigured With Moses and Elijah**		
	Act 3: **A Trip To Trachonitis**	Mount Hermon, *Trachonitis* summer / 32 CE		*Using the NASB version of The Gospels*

	Matthew	**Mark**	**Luke**
1 Six days later, Jesus took Peter and James, and John his brother, and led them up on a high mountain, to pray by themselves.	17:1 Six days later Jesus took ~~with Him~~ Peter and James and John his brother, and led them up on a high mountain by themselves.	9:2~ Six days later, Jesus took ~~with Him~~ Peter and James and John, and ~~brought~~ them up on a high mountain by themselves.	9:28 ~~Some~~ eight days ~~after these sayings~~, ~~He~~ took along Peter and John and James, and ~~went~~ up on ~~the~~ mountain to pray.
2 While [Jesus] was praying, He was transfigured before them; and the appearance of His face became different, <and> shone like the sun,	17:2 ~~And~~ He was transfigured before them; and His face shone like the sun,	9:~2 ~~And~~ He was transfigured before them;	9:29~ ~~And~~ while [He] was praying, the appearance of His face became different,
3 and His garments became radiant and exceedingly white, and gleaming as light - as no launderer on earth can whiten them.	17:~2 and His garments became ~~as~~ white as light.	9:3 and His garments became radiant and exceedingly white, as no launderer on earth can whiten them.	9:~29 and His ~~clothing~~ became white and gleaming.
4 And behold, two men, Moses along with Elijah, appeared to them, and they were talking with Jesus.	17:3 And behold, Moses ~~and~~ Elijah appeared to them, talking with ~~Him~~.	9:4 Elijah appeared to them along ~~with~~ Moses; and they were talking with Jesus.	9:30 And behold, two men ~~were~~ talking with ~~Him~~; and they were Moses ~~and~~ Elijah,
5 Appearing in glory, [they] were speaking of His departure, which He was about to [fulfill] at Jerusalem.			9:31 [who], appearing in glory, were speaking of His departure which He was about to [accomplish] at Jerusalem.
6 Now Peter and his companions had been overcome with sleep, but when they were fully awake they saw His glory, and the two men standing with Him.			9:32 Now Peter and his companions had been overcome with sleep; but when they were fully awake, they saw His glory and the two men standing with Him.
7 As [they] were leaving, Peter said to Jesus, "Master, it is good for us to be here! If you wish, let us make three tabernacles; one for You, and one for Moses, and one for Elijah"	17:4 Peter said to Jesus, "~~Lord~~, it is good for us to be here; if You wish, ~~I will~~ make three tabernacles ~~here~~, one for You, and one for Moses, and one for Elijah."	9:5 Peter said to Jesus, "~~Rabbi~~, it is good for us to be here; let us make three tabernacles, one for You, and one for Moses, and one for Elijah."	9:33~ ~~And~~ as [these] were leaving ~~Him~~, Peter said to Jesus, "Master, it is good for us to be here; let us make three tabernacles: one for You, and one for Moses, and one for Elijah"
8 - not realizing what he was saying, for he did not know what to answer, for they [were] terrified.		9:6 For he did not know what to answer; for they [became] terrified.	9:~33 - not realizing what he was saying.
9 While [Peter] was still speaking, a bright cloud formed, and began to overshadow them; and they were afraid as they entered the cloud.	17:5~ While [he] was still speaking, a bright cloud overshadow~~ed~~ them,	9:7~ ~~Then~~ a cloud formed, overshadow~~ing~~ them,	9:34 While [he] was ~~saying this~~, a cloud formed and began to overshadow them; and they were afraid as they entered the cloud.
10 And behold, a voice came out of the cloud, <and> said, "This is My beloved Son, My Chosen One with whom I am well-pleased. Listen to Him."	17:~5 and behold, a voice out of the cloud said, "This is My beloved Son, with whom I am well-pleased; listen to Him!"	9:~7 and a voice came out of the cloud, "This is My beloved Son, listen to Him!"	9:35 ~~Then~~ a voice came out of the cloud, s~~aying~~, "This is My Son, My Chosen One; listen to Him!"
11 When the [apostles] heard the voice they fell face down to the ground, and were terrified.	17:6 When the [~~disciples~~] heard ~~this~~, they fell face down to the ground and were terrified.		9:36~ ~~And~~ when the voice ~~had spoken~~,
12 Jesus came to them, and touched them, and said, "Get up, and do not be afraid."	17:7 ~~And~~ Jesus came to them and touched them and said, "Get up, and do not be afraid."		
13 And lifting up their eyes they looked around, and saw no one with them anymore, except Jesus Himself alone.	17:8 And lifting up their eyes, they saw no one except Jesus Himself alone.	9:8 ~~All at once~~ they looked around and saw no one with them anymore, except Jesus alone.	9:~36~ Jesus ~~was found~~ alone.

continued >

5 - THIRD YEAR OF MINISTRY

Act 3: **A Trip To Trachonitis**

Scene 4: **Jesus Is Transfigured With Moses and Elijah**
continued

	Matthew	Mark	Luke
14 As they were coming down from the mountain, Jesus commanded them not to relate to anyone what they had seen, saying, "Tell the vision to no one, until the Son of Man has risen from the dead."	17:9 As they were coming down from the mountain, Jesus commanded them, saying, "Tell the vision to no one until the Son of Man has risen from the dead."	9:9 As they were coming down from the mountain, ~~He gave~~ them ~~orders~~ not to relate to anyone what they had seen, until the Son of Man ~~rose~~ from the dead.	
15 They seized upon that statement, discussing with one another what "rising from the dead" meant.		9:10 They seized upon that statement, discussing with one another what rising from the dead meant.	

Scene 5: **Why Must Elijah Come First?**

Mount Hermon, *Trachonitis*   summer / 32 CE

	Matthew	Mark	Luke
1 [The three apostles] asked [Jesus], "Why is it that the scribes say that *Elijah must come first?*"[1.]	17:10 ~~And~~ [~~His disciples~~] asked [~~Him~~], "Why ~~then do~~ the scribes say that Elijah must come first?	9:11 [~~They~~] asked [~~Him~~], ~~saying~~, "Why is it that the scribes say that Elijah must come first?	
2 He answered, and said to them, "Elijah does come first, and will restore all things.	17:11 ~~And~~ He answered and said, "Elijah ~~is coming~~ and will restore all things;	9:12~ ~~And~~ He said to them, "Elijah does first come and restore all things.	
3 "And yet, how is it written of the Son of Man, that *He will suffer many things, and be treated with contempt?*[2.]		9:~12 And yet how is it written of the Son of Man that He will suffer many things and be treated with contempt?	
4 "But I say to you that Elijah has indeed already come, and they did not recognize him; but they did to him whatever they wished, just as it is written of him.	17:12~ but I say to you that Elijah already came, and they did not recognize him, but did to him whatever they wished.	9:13 "But I say to you that Elijah has indeed come, ~~and~~ they did to him whatever they wished, just as it is written of him."	
5 "So also is the Son of Man going to suffer at their hands."	17:~12 So also the Son of Man is going to suffer at their hands."		
6 Then the [apostles] understood that He had spoken to them about John the Baptist.	17:13 Then the [~~disciples~~] understood that He had spoken to them about John the Baptist.		
7 And they kept silent, and reported to no one in those days any of the things which they had seen.			9:~36 And they kept silent, and reported to no one in those days any of the things which they had seen.

1. Malachi 4:5   2. Isaiah 53:3

5 - **THIRD YEAR OF MINISTRY**	Scene 6: **Jesus Cures A Demon-Possessed Boy**	Page 140
Act 3: **A Trip To Trachonitis**	near Mount Hermon, *Trachonitis* summer / 32 CE	*The Gospel of Jesus Christ*

	Matthew	Mark	Luke
1 The next day, when they <had> [come] down from the mountain <and> back to the [apostles], they saw a large crowd around them, and some scribes arguing with them.		9:14 When they [came] back to the [disciples], they saw a large crowd around them, and some scribes arguing with them.	9:37~ On the next day, when they [came] down from the mountain, a large crowd
2 When the crowd saw [Jesus] they were amazed, and immediately began running up to greet Him.		9:15 Immediately, when the entire crowd saw [Him], they were amazed and began running up to greet Him.	9:~37 met Him.
3 When <Jesus> came to the crowd, He asked [His apostles], "What are you discussing with them?"	17:14~ When they came to the crowd,	9:16 And He asked [them], "What are you discussing with them?"	
4 A man from the crowd came up to Jesus, and falling on his knees before Him, answered saying, "Teacher, I brought You my son. I beg you to have mercy on [him], for he is my only boy.	17:~14 a man came up to Jesus, falling on his knees before Him and saying, 17:15~ "Lord, have mercy on my son, for	9:17~ And one of the crowd answered Him, "Teacher, I brought You my son,	9:38 And a man from the crowd shouted, saying, "Teacher, I beg You to look at my son, for he is my only boy,
5 "He is a lunatic and is very ill, possessed [by] a spirit which makes him mute; and it has often thrown him into both the fire and the water, to destroy him.	17:~15 he is a lunatic and is very ill; for he often falls into the fire and often into the water.	9:~17 possessed [with] a spirit which makes him mute; 9:22~ "It has often thrown him both into the fire and into the water to destroy him.	
6 "Whenever it seizes him he suddenly screams, and it slams him to the ground, and throws him into a convulsion; and he foams at the mouth, and grinds his teeth, and stiffens out;		9:18~ and whenever it seizes him, it slams him to the ground and he foams at the mouth, and grinds his teeth and stiffens out.	9:39~ and a spirit seizes him, and he suddenly screams, and it throws him into a convulsion with foaming at the mouth;
7 "and only with difficulty does it leave him, mauling him as it [goes].			9:~39 and only with difficulty does it leave him, mauling him as it [leaves].
8 "I brought him to your disciples, <and> begged [them] to cast it out, [but] they could not cure him."	17:16 "I brought him to Your disciples, [and] they could not cure him."	9:~18 I told [Your disciples] to cast it out, [and] they could not do it."	9:40 "I begged [Your disciples] to cast it out, [and] they could not."
9 Jesus answered, and said, "O you unbelieving and perverted generation! How long shall I be with you, and how long shall I put up with you?	17:17~ And Jesus answered and said, "You unbelieving and perverted generation, how long shall I be with you? How long shall I put up with you?	9:19~ And He answered them and said, "O unbelieving generation, how long shall I be with you? How long shall I put up with you?	9:41~ And Jesus answered and said, "You unbelieving and perverted generation, how long shall I be with you and put up with you?
10 "Bring your son here to Me."	17:~17 Bring him here to Me."	9:~19 Bring him to Me!"	9:~41 Bring your son here."
11 They brought the boy to Him; <and> while he was approaching, immediately when he saw [Jesus] the demon slammed [the boy] to the ground, and threw him into a convulsion; <and> he began rolling around, and foaming at the mouth.		9:20 They brought the boy to Him. When he saw [Him], immediately the spirit threw him into a convulsion, and falling to the ground, he began rolling around and foaming at the mouth.	9:42~ While he was still approaching, the demon slammed [him] to the ground and threw him into a convulsion.
12 [Jesus] asked his father, "How long has this been happening to him?"		9:21~ And [He] asked his father, "How long has this been happening to him?"	
13 He said, "From childhood. But if You can do anything, take pity on us, and help us."		9:~21 And he said, "From childhood. 9:~22 But if You can do anything, take pity on us and help us!"	

continued >

5 - THIRD YEAR OF MINISTRY

Act 3: **A Trip To Trachonitis**

Scene 6: **Jesus Cures A Demon-Possessed Boy**
continued

The Four Gospels Unified - Verse-By-Verse

	Matthew	Mark	Luke
14 Jesus said to him, " 'If You can?' All things are possible to [the one] who believes."		9:23 ~~And~~ Jesus said to him, " 'If You can?' All things are possible to [~~him~~] who believes."	
15 Immediately the boy's father cried out, and said, "I do believe! Help my [lack of faith]."		9:24 Immediately the boy's father cried out and said, "I do believe; help my [~~unbelief~~]."	
16 When Jesus saw that a crowd was rapidly gathering, He rebuked the unclean spirit, saying, "You deaf and mute spirit, I command you: Come out of him, and do not enter him again!"	17:18~ ~~And Jesus~~ rebuked ~~him~~,	9:25 When Jesus saw that a crowd was rapidly gathering, He rebuked the unclean spirit, saying, ~~to it~~, "You deaf and mute spirit, I command you, come out of him and do not enter him again."	9:42~1 ~~But~~ Jesus rebuked the unclean spirit,
17 After crying out, and throwing him into terrible convulsions, the demon came out of him, and the boy was cured at once; [but] [he] became so much like a corpse that most of them said, "He is dead."	17:~18 and the demon came out of him, and the boy was cured at once.	9:26 After crying out and throwing him into terrible convulsions, ~~it~~ came out; [and] [the boy] became so much like a corpse that most of them said, "He is dead!"	9:42~2 and ~~heal~~ed the boy
18 But Jesus took him by the hand, raised him up, and gave him back to his father.		9:27 But Jesus took him by the hand ~~and~~ raised him; ~~and he got~~ up.	9:~42 and gave him back to his father.
19 And they were all amazed at the greatness of God; [and] everyone was marveling at all that [Jesus] was doing.			9:43~ And they were all amazed at the greatness of God. [~~But~~] ~~while~~ everyone was marveling at all that [~~He~~] was doing

Scene 7: **Why Could We Not Drive Out The Demon?**

Trachonitis   summer / 32 CE

	Matthew	Mark	Luke
1 When [Jesus] [entered] the house, His [apostles] began questioning Him privately, and [asked], "Why could we not drive out [the demon]?"	17:19 ~~Then the~~ [disciples] ~~came to Jesus~~ privately and [~~said~~], "Why could we not drive [~~it~~] out?	9:28 When [He] [~~came into~~] the house, His [disciples] began questioning Him privately, "Why could we not drive [~~it~~] out?"	
2 He said to them, "Because of the littleness of your faith."	17:20~ ~~And~~ He said to them, "Because of the littleness of your faith."		
3 The apostles said to the Lord, "Increase our faith!"			17:5 The apostles said to the Lord, "Increase our faith!"
4 [Jesus] [replied], "Truly I say to you, if you had faith the size of a mustard seed, you would say to this mountain, 'Be uprooted, and move from here to there' and it would obey you and move; and nothing will be impossible [for] you."	17:~20 ~~for~~ truly I say to you, if you ha~~ve~~ faith the size of a mustard seed, you ~~will~~ say to this mountain, 'Move from here to there,' and ~~it will~~ move; and nothing will be impossible [~~to~~] you.		17:6 ~~And~~ [the Lord] [~~said~~], If you had faith ~~like~~ a mustard seed, you would say to this ~~mulberry tree~~, 'Be uprooted and ~~be planted in the sea~~'; and it would obey you.
5 [Then] He said to them, "But this kind does not go out by anything except prayer and fasting."	17:21 {"But this kind does not go out except ~~by~~ prayer and fasting."}	9:29 [And] He said to them, "This kind ~~cannot come~~ out by anything ~~but~~ prayer."	

5 - THIRD YEAR OF MINISTRY

Act 3: **A Trip To Trachonitis**

Scene 8: **Follow Me**
Galilee   summer / 32 CE

	Matthew	Mark	Luke
1 From there they went out and began to go through Galilee, and [Jesus] did not want anyone to know about it.		9:30 From there they went out and began to go through Galilee, and [He] did not want anyone to know about it.	
2 As they were going along the road a scribe came, and said to [Jesus], "Teacher, I will follow You, wherever You go."	8:19 ~~Then~~ a scribe came and said to [~~Him~~], "Teacher, I will follow You wherever You go."		9:57 As they were going along the road, ~~someone~~ said to Him, "I will follow You wherever You go."
3 Jesus said to him, "The foxes have holes, and the birds of the air have nests, but the Son of Man has nowhere to lay His head."	8:20 Jesus said to him, "The foxes have holes and the birds of the air have nests, but the Son of Man has nowhere to lay His head."		9:58 ~~And~~ Jesus said to him, "The foxes have holes and the birds of the air have nests, but the Son of Man has nowhere to lay His head."
4 [Then] [Jesus] said to another of the disciples, "Follow Me." But he said, "Lord, permit me first to go and bury my father."	8:21 Another of the disciples said ~~to Him~~, "Lord, permit me first to go and bury my father."		9:59 [And] [He] said to another "Follow Me!" But he said, "Lord, permit me first to go and bury my father."
5 Jesus said to him, "Follow Me, and allow the dead to bury their own dead.	8:22 ~~But~~ Jesus said to him, "Follow Me, and allow the dead to bury their own dead.		9:60~ ~~But~~ He said to him, "Allow the dead to bury their own dead;
6 "But as for you, go and proclaim everywhere the Kingdom of God."			9:~60 but as for you, go and proclaim everywhere the kingdom of God."
7 Another said, "I will follow You, Lord, but first, permit me to say good-bye to those at home."			9:61 Another ~~also~~ said, "I will follow You, Lord; but first permit me to say good-bye to those at home."
8 But Jesus said to him, "No one, after putting his hand to the plow, and looking back, is fit for the Kingdom of God."			9:62 But Jesus said to him, "No one, after putting his hand to the plow and looking back, is fit for the kingdom of God."

5 - THIRD YEAR OF MINISTRY
Act 4: Return To Capernaum

Scene 1: Jesus Foreshadows His Death and Resurrection
Galilee summer / 32 CE

The Unified Gospel Story of Jesus

	Matthew	Mark	Luke
1 While they were [travel]ing [through] Galilee, Jesus was teaching His disciples; and <He> said to them, "Let these words sink into your ears; for the Son of Man is going to be delivered into the hands of men, and they will kill Him;	17:22 ~~And~~ while they were [~~gather~~]ing ~~together~~ [in] Galilee Jesus said to them, "The Son of Man is going to be delivered into the hands of men; 17:23~ and they will kill Him,	9:31~ ~~For He~~ was teaching His disciples and ~~telling~~ them, "The Son of Man is to be delivered into the hands of men, and they will kill Him;	9:~43 ~~He~~ said to ~~His disciples~~, 9:44 "Let these words sink into your ears; for the Son of Man is going to be delivered into the hands of men."
2 "and when He has been killed, He will be raised on the third day."	17:~23~ and He will be raised on the third day."	9:~31 and when He has been killed, He will ~~rise~~ ~~three~~ days ~~later~~."	
3 But they did not understand this statement, [because] it was concealed from them so that they would not perceive it;		9:32~ But they did not understand this statement,	9:~45 But they did not understand this statement, [~~and~~] it was concealed from them so that they would not perceive it;
4 and they were afraid to ask Him about this statement, and were deeply grieved.	17:~23 And ~~they~~ were deeply grieved.	9:~32 and they were afraid to ask Him.	9:~45 and they were afraid to ask Him about this statement.

Scene 2: Paying The Poll-Tax
Capernaum, Galilee summer / 32 CE

	Matthew	Mark
1 When they came to Capernaum, those who collected the two-drachma tax came to Peter, and said, "Does your Teacher not pay the two-drachma tax?" He said, "Yes."	17:24 When they came to Capernaum, those who collected the two-drachma tax came to Peter and said, "Does your teacher not pay the two-drachma tax?" 17:25~ He said, "Yes."	9:33~ They came to Capernaum;
2 When [Peter] came into the house, Jesus spoke to him first, saying, "What do you think, Simon? From whom do the kings of the earth collect customs [and] poll-tax; from their sons, or from strangers?"	17:~25 ~~And~~ when [~~he~~] came into the house, Jesus spoke to him first, saying, "What do you think, Simon? From whom do the kings of the earth collect customs [~~or~~] poll-tax, from their sons or from strangers?"	
3 When Peter said, "From strangers," Jesus said to him, "Then the sons are exempt.	17:26 When Peter said, "From strangers," Jesus said to him, "Then the sons are exempt.	
4 "However, so that we do not offend them, go to the sea and throw in a hook, and take the first fish that comes up; and when you open its mouth, you will find a shekel.	17:27~ "However, so that we do not offend them, go to the sea and throw in a hook, and take the first fish that comes up; and when you open its mouth, you will find a shekel.	
5 "Take that, and give it to them, for you and Me."	17:~27 Take that and give it to them for you and Me."	

5 - THIRD YEAR OF MINISTRY	Scene 3: **The Greatest In The Kingdom of Heaven**
Act 4: **Return To Capernaum**	Capernaum, *Galilee* summer / 32 CE

	Matthew	Mark	Luke
1 When [Jesus] was in the house, He began to question [the apostles], <and He asked them,> "What were you discussing on the way?"		9:~33 ~~and~~ when [~~He~~] was in the house, He began to question [~~them~~], "What were you discussing on the way?"	
2 But they kept silent, for on the way they had discussed with one another as to which of them was the greatest, <and> an argument <had> started among them.		9:34 But they kept silent, for on the way they had discussed with one another which of them was the greatest.	9:46 An argument started among them as to which of them ~~might be~~ the greatest.
3 [They] [asked] Jesus, "Who then, is <the> greatest in the Kingdom of Heaven?"	18:1 ~~At that time~~ [the disciples] ~~came to~~ Jesus and [said], "Who then is greatest in the kingdom of heaven?"		
4 Knowing what they were thinking in their heart[s], Jesus [sat] down, called the twelve, and said to them, "If anyone wants to be first, he shall be <the> last of all, and <the> servant of all."		9:35 [Sitting] down, ~~He~~ called the twelve and said to them, "If anyone wants to be first, he shall be last of all and servant of all."	9:47~ ~~But~~ Jesus, knowing what they were thinking in their heart,
5 And He called a child to Himself, and stood him by His side.	18:2 And He called a child to Himself and ~~set~~ him ~~before them~~,	9:36~ ~~Taking~~ a child, He ~~set~~ him ~~before them~~,	9:~47 ~~took~~ a child and stood him by His side,
6 Taking him in His arms, [Jesus] said to them, "Truly I say to you, unless you are converted and become like children, you will not enter the Kingdom of Heaven; for the one who is least among all of you, this is the one who is great.	18:3 ~~and~~ said, "Truly I say to you, unless you are converted and become like children, you will not enter the kingdom of heaven.	9:~36 ~~and~~ taking him in His arms, [He] said to them,	9:48 ~~and~~ said to them, 9:~48 for the one who is least among all of you, this is the one who is great."
7 "Whoever then humbles himself as this child, he is the greatest in the Kingdom of Heaven.	18:4 "Whoever then humbles himself as this child, he is the greatest in the kingdom of heaven.		
8 "Whoever receives one child like this in My Name receives Me;	18:5 "~~And~~ whoever receives one ~~such~~ child in My name receives Me;	9:37~ "Whoever receives one child like this in My name receives Me;	9:48~1 Whoever receives this child in My name receives Me,
9 "and whoever receives Me, receives Him who sent Me."		9:~37 and whoever receives Me ~~does not~~ receive ~~Me, but~~ Him who sent Me.	9:48~2 and whoever receives Me receives Him who sent Me;

5 - THIRD YEAR OF MINISTRY

Act 4: Return To Capernaum

Scene 4: Do Not Cause The Children To Stumble
Capernaum, Galilee   summer / 32 CE

Mark is the shortest, and likely written first

	Matthew	Mark	Luke
1	"See that you do not despise one of these little ones, for I say to you that their angels in Heaven continually see the face of My Father who is in Heaven.	18:10 "See that you do not despise one of these little ones, for I say to you that their angels in heaven continually see the face of My Father who is in heaven.		
2	"Whoever causes one of these little ones who believe in Me to stumble, it would be better for him if a heavy millstone were hung around his neck, and he were thrown into the sea, and drowned in [its] depth.	18:6 but whoever causes one of these little ones who believe in Me to stumble, it would be better for him to have a heavy millstone hung around his neck, and to be drowned in [the] depth.	9:42 "Whoever causes one of these little ones who believe to stumble, it would be better for him if, with a heavy millstone hung around his neck, he had been cast into the sea.	17:2 "It would be better for him if a millstone were hung around his neck and he were thrown into the sea, than that he would cause one of these little ones to stumble.
3	"So it is the will of your Father who is in Heaven that not one of these little ones perish."	18:14 "So it is not the will of your Father who is in heaven that one of these little ones perish.		

Scene 5: On Stumbling Blocks and Hell Fire

	Matthew	Mark	Luke
1	[Jesus] said to His disciples, "Woe to the world because of its stumbling blocks, for it is inevitable that stumbling blocks come, but woe to [the] [person] through whom they come.	18:7 "Woe to the world because of its stumbling blocks! For it is inevitable that stumbling blocks come; but woe to [that] [man] through whom the stumbling block comes!		17:1 [He] said to His disciples, "It is inevitable that stumbling blocks come, but woe to [him] through whom they come!"
2	"If your hand causes you to stumble, cut it off and throw it from you; <for> it is better for you to enter life crippled, than having your two hands to go into hell; into the eternal, unquenchable fire;	18:8~ "If your hand 18:8~2 causes you to stumble, cut it off and throw it from you; it is better for you to enter life crippled 18:8~4 than to have two hands 18:~8 the eternal fire.	9:43 "If your hand causes you to stumble, cut it off; it is better for you to enter life crippled, than, having your two hands, to go into hell, into the unquenchable fire,	
3	"where their worm does not die, and the fire is not quenched.¹		9:44 {where their worm does not die, and the fire is not quenched.}	
4	"Or if your foot causes you to stumble, cut it off! It is better for you to enter life lame, than <to> [have] your two feet and be cast into hell.	18:8~1 or your foot 18:8~3 or lame, 18:8~5 or two feet and be cast into	9:45 If your foot causes you to stumble, cut it off; it is better for you to enter life lame, than, [having] your two feet, to be cast into hell,	
			9:46 {where their worm does not die, and the fire is not quenched.}	
5	"If your eye causes you to stumble, pluck it out and throw it from you! It is better for you to enter <into> life <in> the Kingdom of God with one eye, than to have two eyes and be cast into the fiery hell;	18:9 "If your eye causes you to stumble, pluck it out and throw it from you. It is better for you to enter life with one eye, than to have two eyes and be cast into the fiery hell.	9:47 "If your eye causes you to stumble, throw it out; it is better for you to enter the kingdom of God with one eye, than, having two eyes, to be cast into hell,	
6	"where their worm does not die, and the fire is not quenched.¹		9:48 where their worm does not die, and the fire is not quenched.	
7	"For everyone will be salted with fire."		9:49 "For everyone will be salted with fire.	

1. *Isaiah 66:24 / (Jeremiah 7:20)*

5 - THIRD YEAR OF MINISTRY

Act 4: **Return To Capernaum**

Scene 6: **If Your Brother Sins**

Capernaum, *Galilee* summer / 32 CE

The Greatest Gospel

	Matthew	Luke
1 "Be on your guard! If your brother sins, go and show him his fault, <and> rebuke him in private.	18:15~ "If your brother sins, go and show him his fault in private	17:3~ "Be on your guard! If your brother sins, rebuke him;
2 "If he listens to you, and repents, forgive him; you have won your brother.	18:~15 if he listens to you, you have won your brother.	17:~3 and ~~if he~~ repents, forgive him.
3 "And if he sins against you seven times a day, and returns to you seven times, saying, 'I repent', forgive him.		17:4 "And if he sins against you seven times a day, and returns to you seven times, saying, 'I repent,' forgive him."
4 "But if he does not listen to you, take one or two more with you, *so that by the mouth of two or three witnesses every fact may be confirmed.*[1]	18:16 "But if he does not listen to you, take one or two more with you, so that by the mouth of two or three witnesses every fact may be confirmed.	
5 "If he refuses to listen to them, tell it to the Church;	18:17~ "If he refuses to listen to them, tell it to the church;	
6 "and if he refuses to listen even to the Church let him be to you as a Gentile and a tax collector.	18:~17 and if he refuses to listen even to the church, let him be to you as a Gentile and a tax collector.	
7 "<For> truly I say to you, whatever you bind on earth shall [be] bound in Heaven, and whatever you loose on earth shall [be] loosed in Heaven.	18:18 "Truly I say to you, whatever you bind on earth shall ~~have~~ [been] bound in heaven; and whatever you loose on earth shall ~~have~~ [been] loosed in heaven.	
8 "Again I say to you, that if two of you on earth agree about anything that they may ask, it shall be done for them by My Father who is in Heaven;	18:19 "Again I say to you, that if two of you agree on earth about anything that they may ask, it shall be done for them by My Father who is in heaven.	
9 "for where two or three have gathered together in My Name, I am there in their midst."	18:20 "For where two or three have gathered together in My name, I am there in their midst."	

1. Deuteronomy 19:15

5 - THIRD YEAR OF MINISTRY

Act 4: Return To Capernaum

Scene 7: On Forgiveness and The Unforgiving Slave

Capernaum, *Galilee*   summer / 32 CE

Page 147

Gospel = God-spell or Good News

	Matthew
1 Peter said to [Jesus], "Lord, how often shall my brother sin against me, and I forgive him? Up to seven times?"	18:21 ~~Then~~ Peter ~~came and~~ said to [~~Him~~], "Lord, how often shall my brother sin against me and I forgive him? Up to seven times?"
2 Jesus said to him, "I do not say to you up to seven times, but up to seventy times seven.	18:22 Jesus said to him, "I do not say to you, up to seven times, but up to seventy times seven.
3 "For this reason the Kingdom of Heaven may be compared to a king who wished to settle accounts with his slaves.	18:23 "For this reason the kingdom of heaven may be compared to a king who wished to settle accounts with his slaves.
4 "When he [began] to settle them, one who owed him ten thousand talents was brought to him.	18:24 "When he [~~had begun~~] to settle them, one who owed him ten thousand talents was brought to him.
5 "But since he did not have the means to repay, his lord commanded him to be sold, along with his wife and children, and all that he had, and repayment to be made.	18:25 "But since he did not have the means to repay, his lord commanded him to be sold, along with his wife and children and all that he had, and repayment to be made.
6 "So the slave fell to the ground, and prostrated himself before him, saying, 'Have patience with me, and I will repay you everything!'	18:26 "So the slave fell to the ground and prostrated himself before him, saying, 'Have patience with me and I will repay you everything.'
7 "And the lord of that slave felt compassion, and <he> forgave him the debt, and released him.	18:27 "And the lord of that slave felt compassion and released him and forgave him the debt.
8 "But that slave went out and found one of his fellow slaves who owed him a hundred denarii, and he seized him, and began to choke him, saying, 'Pay back what you owe!'	18:28 "But that slave went out and found one of his fellow slaves who owed him a hundred denarii; and he seized him and began to choke him, saying, 'Pay back what you owe.'
9 "So his fellow slave fell to the ground, and began to plead with him, saying, 'Have patience with me, and I will repay you.'	18:29 "So his fellow slave fell to the ground and began to plead with him, saying, 'Have patience with me and I will repay you.'
10 "But he was unwilling, and <he> went and threw him in prison, until he should pay back what [he] owed.	18:30 "But he was unwilling and went and threw him in prison until he should pay back what [~~was~~] owed.
11 "When [the other] slaves saw what had happened, they were deeply grieved, and <they> came and reported [it] to their lord.	18:31 "~~So~~ when [~~his fellow~~] slaves saw what had happened, they were deeply grieved and came and reported to their lord [~~all that had happened~~].
12 "His lord summon[ed] him, <and> said, 'You wicked slave! I forgave you all that debt because you pleaded with me.	18:32 "~~Then~~ summon[~~ing~~] him, his lord said ~~to him~~, 'You wicked slave, I forgave you all that debt because you pleaded with me.
13 "Should you not also have had mercy on your fellow slave, in the same way that I had mercy on you?'	18:33 'Should you not also have had mercy on your fellow slave, in the same way that I had mercy on you?'
14 "And his lord, moved with anger, handed him over to the torturers, until he [repaid] all that <he> owed.	18:34 "And his lord, moved with anger, handed him over to the torturers until he ~~should~~ [repay] all that ~~was~~ owed ~~him~~.
15 "My Heavenly Father will also do the same to you, if each of you does not forgive his brother from your heart."	18:35 "My heavenly Father will also do the same to you, if each of you does not forgive his brother from your heart."

5 - THIRD YEAR OF MINISTRY

Act 4: Return To Capernaum

Scene 8: He Who Is Not Against Us Is For Us

Capernaum, *Galilee*   summer / 32 CE

Verse-By-Verse Edition

	Mark	Luke
1 <The apostle> John said to [Jesus], "Master, we saw someone casting out demons in Your Name, and we tried to prevent him because he was not following along with us."	9:38 John said to [Him], "~~Teacher~~, we saw someone casting out demons in Your name, and we tried to prevent him because he was not following us."	9:49 John ~~answered and~~ said, "Master, we saw someone casting out demons in Your name; and we tried to prevent him because he ~~does~~ not follow along with us."
2 But Jesus said, "Do not hinder him, for there is no one who will perform a miracle in My Name, and [then] be able to speak evil of Me.	9:39 But Jesus said, "Do not hinder him, for there is no one who will perform a miracle in My name, and be able [~~soon afterward~~] to speak evil of Me.	9:50~ But Jesus said ~~to him~~, "Do not hinder him;
3 "He who is not against us is for us.	9:40 "~~For~~ he who is not against us is for us.	9:~50 ~~for~~ he who is not against ~~you~~ is for ~~you~~."
4 "[And] whoever gives you a cup of water to drink, because of your name as <a> follower of Christ, truly I say to you, he will not lose his reward."	9:41 "[~~For~~] whoever gives you a cup of water to drink because of your name as ~~followers~~ of Christ, truly I say to you, he will not lose his reward.	

5 - THIRD YEAR OF MINISTRY
Act 5: Jesus Sends Seventy Disciples

Scene 1: The Trials Of Discipleship
Galilee — summer / 32 CE

	Luke
1 Now large crowds were [traveling] with [Jesus], and He turned to them, and said, "If anyone comes to Me, and does not hate his own father and mother, and wife and children, and brothers and sisters, and even his own life, he cannot be My disciple.	14:25 Now large crowds were [~~going along~~] with [~~Him~~]; and He turned and said to them, 14:26 "If anyone comes to Me, and does not hate his own father and mother and wife and children and brothers and sisters, ~~yes~~, and even his own life, he cannot be My disciple.
2 "Whoever does not carry his own cross, and come after Me, cannot be My disciple.	14:27 "Whoever does not carry his own cross and come after Me cannot be My disciple.
3 "For which one of you, when he wants to build a tower, does not first sit down and calculate the cost, to see if he has enough to complete it?	14:28 "For which one of you, when he wants to build a tower, does not first sit down and calculate the cost to see if he has enough to complete it?
4 "Otherwise, when he has laid a foundation, and is not able to finish, all who observe it [will] ridicule him, saying, 'This man began to build, and was not able to finish!'	14:29 "Otherwise, when he has laid a foundation and is not able to finish, all who observe it [~~begin to~~] ridicule him, 14:30 saying, 'This man began to build and was not able to finish.'
5 "Or what king, when he sets out to meet another king in battle, will not first sit down and consider whether he is strong enough with ten thousand men to encounter the one coming against him with twenty thousand?	14:31 "Or what king, when he sets out to meet another king in battle, will not first sit down and consider whether he is strong enough with ten thousand men to encounter the one coming against him with twenty thousand?
6 "[Otherwise], while the other is still far away, he sends a delegation, and asks for terms of peace.	14:32 "[~~Or else~~], while the other is still far away, he sends a delegation and asks for terms of peace.
7 "So then, none of you can be My disciple, who does not give up all <of> his own possessions."	14:33 "So then, none of you can be My disciple who does not give up all his own possessions.

Scene 2: Jesus Sends Seventy Disciples To Preach

	Luke
1 After this, the Lord appointed seventy [disciples]; and <He> sent them <out> in pairs ahead of Him, to every city and place where He Himself was going to come.	10:1 ~~Now~~ after this the Lord appointed seventy [~~others~~], and sent them in pairs ahead of Him to every city and place where He Himself was going to come.
2 And He [said] to them, "The harvest is plentiful, but the laborers are few; therefore beseech the Lord of the harvest to send <more> laborers out into His harvest.	10:2 And He was [~~saying~~] to them, "The harvest is plentiful, but the laborers are few; therefore beseech the Lord of the harvest to send out laborers into His harvest.
3 "Go! Behold, I send you out as lambs in the midst of wolves.	10:3 "Go; behold, I send you out as lambs in the midst of wolves.
4 "Carry no money belt, no bag, no shoes; and greet no one on the way.	10:4 "Carry no money belt, no bag, no shoes; and greet no one on the way.
5 "Whatever house you enter, first say, 'Peace be to this house!'	10:5 "Whatever house you enter, first say, 'Peace be to this house.'
6 "If a man of peace is there, your peace will rest on him; but if not, it will return to you.	10:6 "If a man of peace is there, your peace will rest on him; but if not, it will return to you.
7 "Stay in that house, eating and drinking what they give you, for the laborer is worthy of his wages.	10:7~ "Stay in that house, eating and drinking what they give you; for the laborer is worthy of his wages.
8 "Do not keep moving from house to house, <and> [which]ever city you enter and they receive you, eat what is set before you;	10:~7 Do not keep moving from house to house. 10:8 "[~~What~~]ever city you enter and they receive you, eat what is set before you;
9 "and heal those in it who are sick, and say to them, 'The Kingdom of God has come near to you!'	10:9 and heal those in it who are sick, and say to them, 'The kingdom of God has come near to you.'
10 "But [which]ever city you enter and they do not receive you, go out into its streets and say, 'Even the dust of your city, which clings to our feet, we wipe off in protest against you!	10:10 "But [~~what~~]ever city you enter and they do not receive you, go out into its streets and say, 10:11~ 'Even the dust of your city which clings to our feet we wipe off in protest against you;
11 "[And] be sure of this, that the Kingdom of God has come near.'	10:~11 [~~yet~~] be sure of this, that the kingdom of God has come near.'
12 "The one who listens to you listens to Me, and the one who rejects you rejects Me;	10:16~ "The one who listens to you listens to Me, and the one who rejects you rejects Me;
13 "and he who rejects Me, rejects the One who sent Me."	10:~16 and he who rejects Me rejects the One who sent Me."

5 - THIRD YEAR OF MINISTRY
Act 5: Jesus Sends Seventy Disciples

Scene 3: King Herod Is Perplexed About Jesus
Jerusalem, *Judea* summer / 32 CE

Matthew	Mark	Luke

1 At that time, *King Herod,*[1] the Tetrarch <of Galilee>, heard the news about Jesus, for His name had become well known.
  — 14:1 At that time Herod the tetrarch heard the news about Jesus,
  — 6:14~ ~~And~~ King Herod heard ~~of it~~, for His name had become well known;
  — 9:7~ ~~Now~~ Herod the tetrarch heard ~~of all that was happening~~;

2 And he was greatly perplexed, because people were saying, "This is John the Baptist! He has risen from the dead, and that is why these miraculous powers are at work in him."
  — 14:2 ~~and~~ said ~~to his servants~~, "This is John the Baptist; he has risen from the dead, and that is why miraculous powers are at work in him."
  — 6:~14 ~~and~~ people were saying, "John the Baptist has risen from the dead, and that is why these miraculous powers are at work in Him."
  — 9:~7 and he was greatly perplexed, because ~~it was said by some that~~ John had risen from the dead,

3 But some were saying, "He is Elijah", and others that He is a prophet, <or that> one of the prophets of old had risen again.
  — 6:15 But ~~others~~ were saying, "He is Elijah." And others ~~were saying~~, "He is a prophet, ~~like~~ one of the prophets of old."
  — 9:8 ~~and by~~ some ~~that~~ Elijah ~~had appeared~~, and ~~by~~ others that one of the prophets of old had risen again.

4 But Herod said, "I myself had John beheaded, [so] who is this man about whom I hear such things?"
  — 6:16 But ~~when~~ Herod ~~heard of it, he kept~~ saying, "John, ~~whom~~ I beheaded, ~~has risen!~~"
  — 9:9~ Herod said, "I myself had John beheaded; [but] who is this man about whom I hear such things?"

5 And he [wanted] to see [Jesus].
  — 9:~9 And he [~~kept trying~~] to see [~~Him~~].

1. Herod Antipater (aka Antipas) (20 BCE - 39 CE) Tetrarch of Galilee & Perea (4 BCE - 39 CE)

5 - THIRD YEAR OF MINISTRY
Act 6: On Dining Etiquette

Scene 1: A Sabbath Meal With Pharisees
Capernaum, *Galilee* a Sabbath, summer / 32 CE

	Luke
1 When [Jesus] went into the house of one of the leaders of the Pharisees on the Sabbath to eat bread, they were watching Him closely.	14:1 ~~It happened that~~ when [He] went into the house of one of the leaders of the Pharisees on the Sabbath to eat bread, they were watching Him closely.
2 There in front of [Jesus] was a man suffering from dropsy, and [He] [ask]ed the lawyers and <the> Pharisees, "Is it lawful to heal on the Sabbath, or not?" But they kept silent.	14:2 ~~And~~ there in front of [~~Him~~] was a man suffering from dropsy. 14:3 And [~~Jesus~~] [~~answer~~]ed ~~and spoke to~~ the lawyers and Pharisees, ~~saying~~, "Is it lawful to heal on the Sabbath, or not?" 14:4~ But they kept silent.
3 [Then] [Jesus] took hold of [the man], and healed him, and sent him away.	14:~4 [~~And~~] [~~He~~] took hold of [~~him~~] and healed him, and sent him away.
4 And He said to them, "Which of you will have a son or an ox fall into a well on [the] Sabbath day, and not immediately pull him out?"	14:5 And He said to them, "Which ~~one~~ of you will have a son or an ox fall into a well, and ~~will~~ not immediately pull him out on [a] Sabbath day?"
5 And they could make no reply to this.	14:6 And they could make no reply to this.

5 - THIRD YEAR OF MINISTRY	Scene 2: **Do Not Take The Place of Honor**	Page 151
Act 6: **On Dining Etiquette**	Jerusalem, *Judea* summer / 32 CE	*Synoptic = seeing together (as one)*

Scene 2: Do Not Take The Place of Honor
Jerusalem, *Judea*   summer / 32 CE

	Luke
1 [Then] [Jesus] began speaking a parable to the invited guests, when He noticed how they [were] picking out the places of honor at the table.	14:7~ [And] [He] began speaking a parable to the invited guests when He noticed how they [had been] picking out the places of honor at the table,
2 <He> [said] to them, "When you are invited to a wedding feast, do not take the place of honor, for someone more distinguished than you may have been invited, and [the one] who invited you will come and say to you, 'Give your place to this man,' and then in disgrace you <will> proceed to occupy the last place.	14:~7 [saying] to them, 14:8 "When you are invited by someone to a wedding feast, do not take the place of honor, for someone more distinguished than you may have been invited by him, 14:9 and [he] who invited you both will come and say to you, 'Give your place to this man,' and then in disgrace you proceed to occupy the last place.
3 "But when you are invited, go and recline at the last place, so that when the one who invited you comes, [they] may say to you, 'Friend, move up higher', <and> then you will have honor in the sight of all who are at the table with you.	14:10 "But when you are invited, go and recline at the last place, so that when the one who has invited you comes, [he] may say to you, 'Friend, move up higher'; then you will have honor in the sight of all who are at the table with you.
4 "For everyone who exalts himself will be humbled, and he who humbles himself will be exalted."	14:11 "For everyone who exalts himself will be humbled, and he who humbles himself will be exalted."

Scene 3: Invite The Poor, and Be Blessed

	Luke
1 [Jesus] went on to say to the one who had invited Him, "When you give a luncheon or a dinner do not invite your friends or your brothers, or your relatives or rich neighbors, otherwise they may also invite you in return, and that will be your repayment.	14:12 And [He] also went on to say to the one who had invited Him, "When you give a luncheon or a dinner, do not invite your friends or your brothers or your relatives or rich neighbors, otherwise they may also invite you in return and that will be your repayment.
2 "But when you give a reception invite the poor, the crippled, the lame, <and> the blind, and you will be blessed;	14:13 "But when you give a reception, invite the poor, the crippled, the lame, the blind, 14:14~ and you will be blessed,
3 "<for> since they do not have the means to repay you, you will be repaid at the resurrection of the righteous."	14:~14 since they do not have the means to repay you; for you will be repaid at the resurrection of the righteous."
4 "When one of those reclining at the table with [Jesus] heard this, he said to Him, "Blessed is everyone who will eat bread in the Kingdom of God!"	14:15 When one of those who were reclining at the table with [Him] heard this, he said to Him, "Blessed is everyone who will eat bread in the kingdom of God!"

Scene 4: The Seventy Disciples Return
Capernaum, *Galilee*   summer / 32 CE

	Luke
1 The seventy <disciples> returned with joy, saying, "Lord, even the demons are subject to us in Your Name!"	10:17 The seventy returned with joy, saying, "Lord, even the demons are subject to us in Your name."
2 [Jesus] said to them, "I [saw] Satan fall[ing] like lightning from Heaven!	10:18 And [He] said to them, "I [was watching] Satan fall from heaven like lightning.
3 "Behold, I have given you authority to tread on serpents and scorpions, and over all the power of the enemy; and nothing will injure you.	10:19 "Behold, I have given you authority to tread on serpents and scorpions, and over all the power of the enemy, and nothing will injure you.
4 "Nevertheless, do not rejoice in this - that the spirits are subject to you - but rejoice that your names are recorded in Heaven."	10:20 "Nevertheless do not rejoice in this, that the spirits are subject to you, but rejoice that your names are recorded in heaven."

5 - **THIRD YEAR OF MINISTRY** Act 7: **A Collection of Parables**	Scene 1: **The Joy Over One Sinner Who Repents** Capernaum, *Galilee* summer / 32 CE	Page 152 *The Story of The Life of Jesus*

	Matthew	Luke
1 Now all the tax collectors and the sinners were coming near [Jesus] to listen to Him, <and> both the Pharisees and the scribes began to grumble, saying, "This man receives sinners, and eats with them."		15:1 Now all the tax collectors and the sinners were coming near [Him] to listen to Him. 15:2 Both the Pharisees and the scribes began to grumble, saying, "This man receives sinners and eats with them."
2 So [Jesus] told them this parable, saying, "What do you think? What man among you, if he has a hundred sheep, and one of them has gone astray, does not leave the ninety-nine in the open pasture, and go <and> search for the one which is lost, until he finds it?	18:12 "What do you think? ~~If any~~ man has a hundred sheep, and one of them has gone astray, does ~~he~~ not leave the ninety-nine ~~on~~ the ~~mountains~~ and go ~~and~~ search for the one ~~that is straying~~?	15:3 So [He] told them this parable, saying, 15:4 "What man among you, if he has a hundred sheep and has ~~lost~~ one of them, does not leave the ninety-nine in the open pasture and go ~~after~~ the one which is lost until he finds it?
3 "<And> when he has found it, truly I say to you, he lays it on his shoulders, <and> rejoices over it more than over the ninety-nine which have not gone astray.	18:13 "~~If it turns out that~~ he ~~finds~~ it, truly I say to you, ~~he~~ rejoices over it more than over the ninety-nine which have not gone astray.	15:5 "When he has found it, he lays it on his shoulders, rejoic~~ing~~.
4 "And when he comes home, he calls together his friends and his neighbors, saying to them, 'Rejoice with me, for I have found my sheep which was lost!'		15:6 "And when he comes home, he calls together his friends and his neighbors, saying to them, 'Rejoice with me, for I have found my sheep which was lost!'
5 "I tell you, in the same way there will be more joy in Heaven over one sinner who repents, than over ninety-nine righteous persons who need no repentance.		15:7 "I tell you ~~that~~ in the same way, there will be more joy in heaven over one sinner who repents than over ninety-nine righteous persons who need no repentance.
6 "Or what woman, if she has ten silver coins and loses one coin, does not light a lamp and sweep the house, and search carefully until she finds it?		15:8 "Or what woman, if she has ten silver coins and loses one coin, does not light a lamp and sweep the house and search carefully until she finds it?
7 "<And> when she has found it, she calls together her friends and neighbors, saying, 'Rejoice with me, for I have found the coin which I had lost!'		15:9 "When she has found it, she calls together her friends and neighbors, saying, 'Rejoice with me, for I have found the coin which I had lost!'
8 "I tell you, in the same way there is joy in the presence of the angels of God over one sinner who repents.		15:10 "In the same way, I tell you, there is joy in the presence of the angels of God over one sinner who repents."
9 "For the Son of Man has come to save that which was lost."	18:11 {"For the Son of Man has come to save that which was lost."}	

5 - THIRD YEAR OF MINISTRY	Scene 2: **The Prodigal Son**
Act 7: **A Collection of Parables**	Capernaum, *Galilee* summer / 32 CE

Luke

1. [Then] [Jesus] said, "A man had two sons. The younger of them said to his father, 'Father, give me the share of the estate that falls to me.' So [the man] divided his wealth between them.
2. "Not many days later, the younger son gathered everything together, and went on a journey to a distant country, and there he squandered his estate with loose living.
3. "Now when he had spent everything, a severe famine occurred in that country, and he began to be impoverished.
4. "So he went and hired himself out to one of the citizens of that country, [who] sent him into his fields to feed swine.
5. "No one was giving anything to him, and he would have gladly filled his stomach with the pods that the swine were eating.
6. "When he came to his senses, he said, 'How many of my father's hired men have more than enough bread, [while] I am here dying [from] hunger?
7. "I will get up and go to my father, and <I> will say to him, "Father, I have sinned against Heaven, and in your sight.
8. "I am no longer worthy to be called your son; make me as one of your hired men."'
9. "So he got up, and [went] to his father.
10. "While he was still a long way off, his father saw him, and felt compassion for him; and <he> ran and embraced him, and kissed him.
11. "The son said to him, 'Father, I have sinned against Heaven and in your sight. I am no longer worthy to be called your son.'
12. "But the father said to his slaves, 'Quickly! Bring out the best robe, and put it on him; and put a ring on his hand, and sandals on his feet.
13. "And bring the fattened calf, kill it, and let us eat and celebrate! For this son of mine was dead, and has come to life again; he was lost, and has been found!'
14. "And they began to celebrate."

15:11 [And] [He] said, "A man had two sons. 15:12 "The younger of them said to his father, 'Father, give me the share of the estate that falls to me.' So [he] divided his wealth between them.

15:13 "And not many days later, the younger son gathered everything together and went on a journey into a distant country, and there he squandered his estate with loose living.

15:14 "Now when he had spent everything, a severe famine occurred in that country, and he began to be impoverished.

15:15 "So he went and hired himself out to one of the citizens of that country, and [he] sent him into his fields to feed swine.

15:16 "And he would have gladly filled his stomach with the pods that the swine were eating, and no one was giving anything to him.

15:17 "But when he came to his senses, he said, 'How many of my father's hired men have more than enough bread, [but] I am dying here [with] hunger!

15:18 'I will get up and go to my father, and will say to him, "Father, I have sinned against heaven, and in your sight;

15:19 I am no longer worthy to be called your son; make me as one of your hired men."'

15:20~ "So he got up and [came] to his father.

15:~20 But while he was still a long way off, his father saw him and felt compassion for him, and ran and embraced him and kissed him.

15:21 "And the son said to him, 'Father, I have sinned against heaven and in your sight; I am no longer worthy to be called your son.'

15:22 "But the father said to his slaves, 'Quickly bring out the best robe and put it on him, and put a ring on his hand and sandals on his feet;

15:23 and bring the fattened calf, kill it, and let us eat and celebrate; 15:24~ for this son of mine was dead and has come to life again; he was lost and has been found.'

15:~24 And they began to celebrate.

5 - THIRD YEAR OF MINISTRY
Act 7: A Collection of Parables

Scene 3: Rejoice! Your Lost Brother Has Been Found
Capernaum, *Galilee*   summer / 32 CE

Luke

1 "Now his older son was in the field, and when he approached the house he heard music and dancing; [so] he summoned one of the servants, and [asked them] what [was happening].

2 "[The servant] said to him, 'Your brother has come, and your father has killed the fattened calf, because he has received him back safe and sound.'

3 "[Then] [the son] became angry, and <he> was not willing to go in; [so] his father came out, and began pleading with him.

4 "But he answered, and said to his father, 'Look! For so many years I have been serving you, and I have never neglected a command of yours, and yet you have never given me <even> a young goat so that I might celebrate with my friends.

5 "But when this son of yours [comes], who has devoured your wealth with prostitutes, you kill the fattened calf for him!'

6 "[His father] said to him, 'Son, you have always been with me, and all that is mine is yours.

7 "But we had to celebrate and rejoice, for your brother was dead, and has begun to live; <he> was lost, and has been found!' "

15:25 "Now his older son was in the field, and when he ~~came and~~ approached the house, he heard music and dancing. 15:26 "[And] he summoned one of the servants and [~~began inquiring~~] what [~~these things could be~~].

15:27 "~~And~~ [he] said to him, 'Your brother has come, and your father has killed the fattened calf because he has received him back safe and sound.'

15:28 "[~~But~~] [he] became angry and was not willing to go in; [~~and~~] his father came out and began pleading with him.

15:29 "But he answered and said to his father, 'Look! For so many years I have been serving you and I have never neglected a command of yours; and yet you have never given me a young goat, so that I might celebrate with my friends;

15:30 but when this son of yours [~~came~~], who has devoured your wealth with prostitutes, you kill~~ed~~ the fattened calf for him.'

15:31 "~~And~~ [he] said to him, 'Son, you have always been with me, and all that is mine is yours.

15:32 'But we had to celebrate and rejoice, for this brother ~~of yours~~ was dead and has begun to live, ~~and~~ was lost and has been found.' "

Scene 4: The Shrewd Manager

Capernaum, Galilee — summer / 32 CE

5 - THIRD YEAR OF MINISTRY
Act 7: **A Collection of Parables**

	Luke
1 [Jesus] also [said] to [His] disciples, "There was a rich man who had a manager, and this manager was reported to him as squandering his possessions.	16:1 ~~Now~~ [He] ~~was~~ also [~~saying~~] to [~~the~~] disciples, "There was a rich man who had a manager, and this manager was reported to him as squandering his possessions.
2 "[So] he called [the manager], and said to him, 'What is this I hear about you? Give an accounting of your management, for you can no longer be <the> manager.'	16:2 "[~~And~~] he called [~~him~~] and said to him, 'What is this I hear about you? Give an accounting of your management, for you can no longer be manager.'
3 "The manager said to himself, 'What shall I do, since my master is taking the management away from me? I am not strong enough to dig, <and> I am ashamed to beg.	16:3 "The manager said to himself, 'What shall I do, since my master is taking the management away from me? I am not strong enough to dig; I am ashamed to beg.
4 "I know what I shall do, so that when I am removed from the management people will welcome me into their homes.'	16:4 'I know what I shall do, so that when I am removed from the management people will welcome me into their homes.'
5 "[Then] He summoned each of his master's debtors;	16:5~ "[~~And~~] he summoned each ~~one~~ of his master's debtors,
6 "and he [said] to the first, 'How much do you owe my master?' He said, 'A hundred measures of oil.'	16:~5 and he [~~began saying~~] to the first, 'How much do you owe my master?' 16:~6 "~~And~~ he said, 'A hundred measures of oil.'
7 "[The manager] said to him, 'Take your bill sit down, and quickly write fifty.'	16:6~ ~~And~~ [he] said to him, 'Take your bill, ~~and~~ sit down quickly and write fifty.'
8 "Then he said to another, 'How much do you owe?' He said, 'A hundred measures of wheat.'	16:7 "Then he said to another, '~~And~~ how much do you owe?' ~~And~~ he said, 'A hundred measures of wheat.'
9 "[The manager] said to him, 'Take your bill, and write eighty.'	16:~7 [~~He~~] said to him, 'Take your bill, and write eighty.'
10 "And [the rich man] praised the unrighteous manager, because he had acted shrewdly;	16:8~ "And [~~his master~~] praised the unrighteous manager because he had acted shrewdly;
11 "for the sons of this age are more shrewd in relation to [each other], than <are> the sons of light.	16:~8 for the sons of this age are more shrewd in relation to [~~their own kind~~] than the sons of light.
12 "[So] I say to you, make friends for yourselves by means of the wealth of unrighteousness, so that when it fails they will receive you into the eternal [abode]."	16:9 "[~~And~~] I say to you, make friends for yourselves by means of the wealth of unrighteousness, so that when it fails, they will receive you into the eternal [~~dwellings~~].

	Matthew	Luke
1 "He who is faithful in a very little thing is faithful also in much;		*16:10~* "He who is faithful in a very little thing is faithful also in much;
2 "and he who is unrighteous in a very little thing is also unrighteous in much.		*16:~10* and he who is unrighteous in a very little thing is unrighteous also in much.
3 "Therefore, if you have not been faithful in the use of unrighteous wealth, who will entrust you [with] true riches?		*16:11* "Therefore if you have not been faithful in the use of unrighteous wealth, who will entrust ~~the~~ true riches [to] you?
4 "And if you have not been faithful [with] that which is another's, who will give you that which is your own?		*16:12* "And if you have not been faithful [~~in the use of~~] that which is another's, who will give you that which is your own?
5 "No one can serve two masters, for either he will hate the one and love the other, or he will be devoted to one and despise the other.	*6:24~* "No one can serve two masters; for either he will hate the one and love the other, or he will be devoted to one and despise the other.	*16:13~* "No ~~servant~~ can serve two masters; for either he will hate the one and love the other, or ~~else~~ he will be devoted to one and despise the other.
6 "You cannot serve God and wealth."	*6:~24* You cannot serve God and wealth.	*16:~13* You cannot serve God and wealth."
7 Now the Pharisees, who [are] lovers of money, were listening to all these things, and scoffing at Him.		*16:14* Now the Pharisees, who [~~were~~] lovers of money, were listening to all these things and ~~were~~ scoffing at Him.
8 [Jesus] said to them, "You are those who justify yourselves in the sight of men, but God knows your hearts;		*16:15~* ~~And~~ [He] said to them, "You are those who justify yourselves in the sight of men, but God knows your hearts;
9 "for that which is highly esteemed among men is detestable in the sight of God.		*16:~15* for that which is highly esteemed among men is detestable in the sight of God.
10 "The Law and the Prophets were proclaimed until John, <and> since that time the gospel of the Kingdom of God has been preached, and everyone is forcing his way into it.		*16:16* "The Law and the Prophets were proclaimed until John; since that time the gospel of the kingdom of God has been preached, and everyone is forcing his way into it.
11 "But it is easier for heaven and <the> earth to pass away, than for one stroke of a letter of the Law to fail."		*16:17* "But it is easier for heaven and earth to pass away than for one stroke of a letter of the Law to fail.

	Luke
1 <Then Jesus said>, "There was a rich man, and he habitually dressed in purple and fine linen, joyously living in splendor every day.	16:19 "~~Now~~ there was a rich man, and he habitually dressed in purple and fine linen, joyously living in splendor every day.
2 "And a poor man named Lazarus was laid at his gate, covered with sores, and longing to be fed with the crumbs which were falling from the rich man's table; [and] even the dogs were coming and licking his sores.	16:20 "And a poor man named Lazarus was laid at his gate, covered with sores, 16:21 and longing to be fed with the crumbs which were falling from the rich man's table; [~~besides~~], even the dogs were coming and licking his sores.
3 "Now the poor man died, and was carried away by the angels to Abraham's bosom; and the rich man also died, and was buried.	16:22 "Now the poor man died and was carried away by the angels to Abraham's bosom; and the rich man also died and was buried.
4 "In Hades, [the rich man] lifted up his eyes, and saw Abraham far away, and Lazarus in his bosom.	16:23~ "In Hades [~~he~~] lifted up his eyes, 16:~23 and saw Abraham far away and Lazarus in his bosom.
5 "Being in torment, he cried out, and said, 'Father Abraham, have mercy on me, and send Lazarus so that he may dip the tip of his finger in water, and cool off my tongue, for I am in agony in this flame!'	16:~23~ being in torment, 16:24 "~~And~~ he cried out and said, 'Father Abraham, have mercy on me, and send Lazarus so that he may dip the tip of his finger in water and cool off my tongue, for I am in agony in this flame.'
6 "But Abraham said, 'Child, remember that during your life you received your good things, and likewise Lazarus bad things; but now he is being comforted here, and you are in agony.	16:25 "But Abraham said, 'Child, remember that during your life you received your good things, and likewise Lazarus bad things; but now he is being comforted here, and you are in agony.
7 "And besides all <of> this, there is a great chasm between us and you, so that those who wish to [go] from here to you [are] not able, and none may cross over from there to us.'	16:26 'And besides all this, between us and you there is a great chasm ~~fixed~~, so that those who wish to [~~come~~] ~~over~~ from here to you [~~will~~] not ~~be~~ able, and ~~that~~ none may cross over from there to us.'
8 "[The rich man] said, 'Then I beg you, father, that you send [Lazarus] to my father's house, for I have five brothers, in order that he may warn them, so that they will not also come to this place of torment.'	16:27 "~~And~~ [~~he~~] said, 'Then I beg you, father, that you send [~~him~~] to my father's house for I have five brothers - 16:28 in order that he may warn them, so that they will not also come to this place of torment.'
9 "But Abraham said, 'They have Moses and the Prophets; let them hear them.'	16:29 "But Abraham said, 'They have Moses and the Prophets; let them hear them.'
10 "He said, 'No, father Abraham, but if someone goes to them from the dead, they will repent!'	16:30 "~~But~~ he said, 'No, father Abraham, but if someone goes to them from the dead, they will repent!'
11 "But [Abraham] said to him, 'If they do not listen to Moses and the Prophets <then> they will not be persuaded, even if someone rises from the dead.' "	16:31 "But [~~he~~] said to him, 'If they do not listen to Moses and the Prophets, they will not be persuaded even if someone rises from the dead.' "

5 - THIRD YEAR OF MINISTRY	Scene 7: **Pray, and Don't Lose Heart**
Act 7: **A Collection of Parables**	Capernaum, *Galilee* summer / 32 CE

The Full Gospel Story

	Luke
1 [Jesus] [told] them a parable, to show that at all times they [should] pray, and not lose heart, saying, "In a certain city there was a judge who did not fear God, and <he> did not respect man.	18:1 ~~Now~~ [He] [~~was telling~~] them a parable to show that at all times they [~~ought to~~] pray and not ~~to~~ lose heart, saying, 18:2 "In a certain city there was a judge who did not fear God and did not respect man.
2 "<And> there was a widow in that city [who] kept coming to him, <and> saying, 'Give me legal protection from my opponent!'	18:3 "There was a widow in that city, ~~and~~ [she] kept coming to him, saying, 'Give me legal protection from my opponent.'
3 "For a while he was unwilling, but [later] he said to himself, 'Even though I do not fear God nor respect man, yet because this widow bothers me I will give her legal protection, otherwise by continually coming, she will wear me out.' "	18:4 "For a while he was unwilling; but [~~afterward~~] he said to himself, 'Even though I do not fear God nor respect man, 18:5 yet because this widow bothers me, I will give her legal protection, otherwise by continually coming she will wear me out.' "
4 And [Jesus] said, "Hear what the unrighteous judge said.	18:6 And [~~the Lord~~] said, "Hear what the unrighteous judge said;
5 "Will God not bring about justice for His elect who cry to Him day and night, [or] will He delay [helping] them?	18:7 ~~now~~, will not God bring about justice for His elect who cry to Him day and night, [~~and~~] will He delay [~~long over~~] them?
6 "I tell you that He will bring about justice for them quickly!	18:8~ "I tell you that He will bring about justice for them quickly.
7 "However, when the Son of Man comes, will He find faith on the earth?"	18:~8 However, when the Son of Man comes, will He find faith on the earth?"

Scene 8: **The Pharisee and The Tax Collector**

Capernaum, *Galilee*   summer / 32 CE

	Luke
1 [Jesus] also told this parable to some people who trusted in themselves that they were righteous, and <who> viewed others with contempt:	18:9 ~~And~~ [He] also told this parable to some people who trusted in themselves that they were righteous, and viewed others with contempt:
2 "Two men went up into the Temple to pray, one a Pharisee, and the other a tax collector.	18:10 "Two men went up into the temple to pray, one a Pharisee and the other a tax collector.
3 "The Pharisee stood, and was praying this to himself: 'God, I thank You that I am not like other people: swindlers, unjust, adulterers, or even like this tax collector.	18:11 "The Pharisee stood and was praying this to himself: 'God, I thank You that I am not like other people: swindlers, unjust, adulterers, or even like this tax collector.
4 "I fast twice a week, <and> I pay tithes of all that I get.'	18:12 'I fast twice a week; I pay tithes of all that I get.'
5 "But the tax collector, standing some distance away, was unwilling even to lift up his eyes to Heaven, but <he> was beating his breast, <and> saying, 'God, be merciful to me, the sinner.'	18:13 "But the tax collector, standing some distance away, was even unwilling to lift up his eyes to heaven, but was beating his breast, saying, 'God, be merciful to me, the sinner!'
6 "I tell you <that> this man went to his house justified, rather than the other; for everyone who exalts himself will be humbled, but he who humbles himself will be exalted."	18:14 "I tell you, this man went to his house justified rather than the other; for everyone who exalts himself will be humbled, but he who humbles himself will be exalted."

CHAPTER 6
THE FINAL YEAR OF HIS MINISTRY

Events that occurred during the Final Year of The Ministry of Jesus Christ.

Act 1 - The Feast of Tabernacles (Booths)

		Page
Scene 1	His Brothers Did Not Believe In Him	161
2	Why Do You Seek To Kill Me?	162
3	Where I Am Going You Cannot Come	163
4	Come To Me, and Drink	164
5	The Pharisees Are Divided	164

Act 2 - Discussions In The Temple

		Page
Scene 1	Jesus Forgives An Adulteress	165
2	My Testimony and Judgment Is True	166
3	You Are From Below, I Am From Above	167
4	Abraham Is Our Father	168
5	Your Father Is The Devil	169
6	You Have A Demon!	170

Act 3 - Healing A Man Born Blind

		Page
Scene 1	Jesus Cures A Man Who Was Born Blind	171
2	The Pharisees Question The Man & His Parents	172
3	They Question The Man A Second Time	173
4	Do You Believe In The Son of Man?	173

Act 4 - The Good Shepherd

		Page
Scene 1	I Am The Door Of The Sheep	174
2	I Am The Good Shepherd	174
3	I Lay Down My Life To Take It Again	175
4	Repent And Bear Fruit, or Perish	175

Act 5 - The Feast of Dedication

		Page
Scene 1	Depart From Me, All You Evildoers!	176
2	I And The Father Are One	177
3	The Jews Try To Stone Jesus For Blasphemy	177

Act 6 - The Resurrection of Lazarus

		Page
Scene 1	Jesus Hears That Lazarus Has Died	178
2	I Am The Resurrection and The Life	179
3	Mary Goes To Meet Jesus	179
4	Jesus Calls Lazarus Forth From The Tomb	180
5	The Pharisees Plot To Kill Jesus	181

Act 7 - Further Teachings

		Page
Scene 1	Teachings On Divorce	182
2	Teachings On Adultery	183
3	A Word About Eunuchs	183
4	Let The Children Come To Me	184
5	What Must I Do To Obtain Eternal Life?	185
6	It Is Hard For The Wealthy To Enter The Kingdom	186
7	What Will There Be For Us?	187
8	The Generous Landowner	188
9	The Unworthy Slaves	188

Act 8 - The Road To Jerusalem

		Page
Scene 1	Shall We Command Fire From Heaven?	189
2	The Ten Lepers of Samaria	189
3	What Will Happen To The Son of Man	190
4	To Sit On My Right and On My Left	191
5	The Greatest Is The One Who Serves	191
6	Jesus Restores The Sight of Bartimaeus	192
7	The Salvation of Zaccheus	193
8	The Parable of The Good and Faithful Servants	194

Act 9 - Anointed For Burial

		Page
Scene 1	Mary Anoints Jesus With Perfume	196
2	The Disciples Question The Waste	197

MAP OF ISRAEL

Locations mentioned in this Chapter are shown with a white center.

6 - THE FINAL YEAR

Act 1: **The Feast of Tabernacles**

Scene 1: **His Brothers Did Not Believe In Him**

Galilee   October / 32 CE

	John
1 Jesus was walking in Galilee, for He was unwilling to walk in Judea, because the Jews were seeking to kill Him.	7:1 ~~After these things~~ Jesus was walking in Galilee, for He was unwilling to walk in Judea because the Jews were seeking to kill Him.
2 Now [the Feast of [*Tabernacles*] [1.] was near, therefore His brothers said to [Jesus], "Leave here and go into Judea, so that Your disciples may see [the] works which You are doing, for no one does anything in secret when he seeks to be known publicly.	7:2 Now ~~the feast of the Jews~~, the Feast of [~~Booths~~], was near. 7:3 Therefore His brothers said to [~~Him~~], "Leave here and go into Judea, so that Your disciples ~~also~~ may see [~~Your~~] works which You are doing. 7:4~ "For no one does anything in secret when he ~~himself~~ seeks to be known publicly.
3 "If You do these things, show Yourself to the world."	7:~4 If You do these things, show Yourself to the world."
4 For His brothers [did] not believ[e] in Him.	7:5 For not ~~even~~ His brothers [~~were~~] believ[~~ing~~] in Him.
5 Jesus said to them, "My time is not yet here, but your time is always opportune.	7:6 ~~So~~ Jesus said to them, "My time is not yet here, but your time is always opportune.
6 "The world cannot hate you, but it hates Me, because I testify that its deeds are evil.	7:7 "The world cannot hate you, but it hates Me because I testify ~~of it~~, that its deeds are evil.
7 "You go to the feast; I [will] not go to this Feast yet, because My time has not come."	7:8 "Go ~~up~~ to the feast you~~rselves~~; I [~~do~~] not go ~~up~~ to this feast because My time has not yet [~~fully~~] come."
8 Having said these things to them, [Jesus] stayed in Galilee.	7:9 Having said these things to them, [~~He~~] stayed in Galilee.

1. Leviticus 23:34 / also known as "Booths"

6 - THE FINAL YEAR Act 1: **The Feast of Tabernacles**	Scene 2: **Why Do You Seek To Kill Me?** The Temple, Jerusalem, *Judea* Feast of Tabernacles, October / 32 CE

Page 162

The Gospel of Good News

	John
1 When His brothers had gone up to the feast, then [Jesus] Himself also went up, not publicly, but in secret.	7:10 ~~But~~ when His brothers had gone up to the feast, then [He] Himself also went up, not publicly, but ~~as if~~, in secret.
2 So the Jews were seeking Him at the feast, and saying, "Where is He?"	7:11 So the Jews were seeking Him at the feast and ~~were~~ saying, "Where is He?"
3 There was much grumbling among the crowds concerning Him. Some were saying, "He is a good man," <but> others were saying, "No, on the contrary, He leads the people astray."	7:12 There was much grumbling among the crowds concerning Him; some were saying, "He is a good man"; others were saying, "No, on the contrary, He leads the people astray."
4 Yet no one was speaking openly of Him for fear of the Jews.	7:13 Yet no one was speaking openly of Him for fear of the Jews.
5 When it was the *mid[dle] of the Feast*,[1] Jesus went up into the Temple, and began to teach.	7:14 ~~But~~ when it was ~~now~~ the mid[st] of the feast Jesus went up into the temple, and began to teach.
6 The Jews were astonished, saying, "Having never been educated, how has this man become learned?"	7:15 The Jews ~~then~~ were astonished, saying, "How has this man become learned, having never been educated?"
7 So Jesus answered them, and said, "My teaching is not Mine, but His who sent Me.	7:16 So Jesus answered them and said, "My teaching is not Mine, but His who sent Me.
8 "If anyone is willing to do His will, he will know of the teaching, whether it is of God, or whether I speak from Myself.	7:17 "If anyone is willing to do His will, he will know of the teaching, whether it is of God or whether I speak from Myself.
9 "He who speaks from himself seeks his own glory;	7:18~ "He who speaks from himself seeks his own glory;
10 "but He who is seeking the glory of the One who sent Him is true, and there is no unrighteousness in Him.	7:~18 but He who is seeking the glory of the One who sent Him, ~~He~~ is true, and there is no unrighteousness in Him.
11 "Did not *Moses give you the Law?*[2] And yet none of you carries out the Law.	7:19~ "Did not Moses give you the Law, and yet none of you carries out the Law?
12 "Why do you seek to kill Me?"	7:~19 Why do you seek to kill Me?"
13 The crowd answered, "You have a demon! Who seeks to kill You?"	7:20 The crowd answered, "You have a demon! Who seeks to kill You?"
14 Jesus answered them, "I did one deed, and you all marvel.	7:21 Jesus answered them, "I did one deed, and you all marvel.
15 "For this reason *Moses has given you circumcision*[3] - not [that] it is from Moses, but from *the fathers*[4] - and on the Sabbath you circumcise a man.	7:22 "For this reason Moses has given you circumcision (not [~~because~~] it is from Moses, but from the fathers), and on the Sabbath you circumcise a man.
16 "If a man receives circumcision on the Sabbath, so that the Law of Moses will not be broken, are you angry with Me because I made an entire man well on the Sabbath?	7:23 "If a man receives circumcision on the Sabbath so that the Law of Moses will not be broken, are you angry with Me because I made an entire man well on the Sabbath?
17 "Do not judge according to appearance, but judge with righteous judgment."	7:24 "Do not judge according to appearance, but judge with righteous judgment."

1. seven day Feast   2. Exodus 20:1-17 / Deuteronomy 5:1-22; 33:4   3. Leviticus 12:3   4. Genesis 17:9-14

6 - THE FINAL YEAR

Act 1: The Feast of Tabernacles

Scene 3: **Where I Am Going You Cannot Come**

The Temple, Jerusalem, *Judea* — Feast of Tabernacles, October / 32 CE

The Complete Verse-By-Verse Gospel Harmony

		John
1	Some of the people [from] Jerusalem were saying, "Is this not the man whom they are seeking to kill?	7:25 ~~So~~ some of the people [of] Jerusalem were saying, "Is this not the man whom they are seeking to kill?
2	"Look, He is speaking publicly, and they are <not> saying [any]thing to Him. The rulers do not really know that this is the Christ, do they?	7:26 "Look, He is speaking publicly, and they are saying [~~no~~]thing to Him. The rulers do not really know that this is the Christ, do they?
3	"We know where this man is from, but whenever the Christ may come, no one knows where He is from."	7:27 "~~However~~, we know where this man is from; but whenever the Christ may come, no one knows where He is from."
4	[Therefore], Jesus cried out <while> teaching in the Temple, and [said], "You both know Me, and <you> know where I am from.	7:28~ [~~Then~~] Jesus cried out in the temple, teaching and [~~saying~~], "You both know Me and know where I am from;
5	"And I have not come [for] Myself, but He who sent Me is true, whom you do not know.	7:~28 and I have not come [~~of~~] Myself, but He who sent Me is true, whom you do not know.
6	"<But> I know Him, because I am from Him, and He sent Me."	7:29 "I know Him, because I am from Him, and He sent Me."
7	So they were seeking to seize [Jesus], [but] no man laid his hand on Him, because His hour had not yet come.	7:30 So they were seeking to seize [~~Him~~]; [~~and~~] no man laid his hand on Him, because His hour had not yet come.
8	Many [in] the crowd believed in Him, and were saying, "When the Christ comes, He will not perform more signs than this man has, will He?"	7:31 ~~But~~ many [~~of~~] the crowd believed in Him; and ~~they~~ were saying, "When the Christ comes, He will not perform more signs ~~than those which~~ this man has, will He?"
9	<When> the Pharisees heard the crowd muttering these things about [Jesus], [they] and the chief priests sent [attendants] to seize Him.	7:32 The Pharisees heard the crowd muttering these things about [~~Him~~], and the chief priests and [~~the Pharisees~~] sent [~~officers~~]* to seize Him.
10	Therefore Jesus said, "For a little while longer I am with you, <and> then I go to Him who sent Me.	7:33 Therefore Jesus said, "For a little while longer I am with you, then I go to Him who sent Me.
11	"*You will seek Me, and will not find Me*;¹ and where I am you cannot come."	7:34 "You will seek Me, and will not find Me; and where I am, you cannot come."
12	The Jews then said to one another, "Where does this man intend to go, that we will not find Him?	7:35~ The Jews then said to one another, "Where does this man intend to go that we will not find Him?
13	"Is He intending to go [in]to the Dispersion among the Greeks, and teach [them]?	7:~35 He is ~~not~~ intending to go to the Dispersion among the Greeks, and teach [~~the Greeks~~], ~~is He~~?
14	"What is this statement that He said; 'You will seek Me and will not find Me; and where I am you cannot come'?"	7:36 "What is this statement that He said, 'You will seek Me, and will not find Me; and where I am, you cannot come'?"

1. *Hosea 5:6*

6 - THE FINAL YEAR

Act 1: The Feast of Tabernacles

Scene 4: Come To Me, and Drink

The Temple, Jerusalem, *Judea* Feast of Tabernacles, October / 32 CE

A Full Four Gospel Merged Harmony

	John
1 Now on the last day, the great day of the Feast, Jesus stood and cried out, "If anyone is thirsty, let him come to Me and drink!	7:37 Now on the last day, the great day of the feast, Jesus stood and cried out, ~~saying~~, "If anyone is thirsty, let him come to Me and drink.
2 "He who believes in Me, as the Scripture <has> said, *'From his innermost being will flow rivers of living water.'* "[1.]	7:38 "He who believes in Me, as the Scripture said, 'From his innermost being will flow rivers of living water.' "
3 This Jesus spoke of The Spirit, whom those who believed in Him were to receive; for The Spirit [had] not yet <been> given, because He was not yet glorified.	7:39 ~~But~~ this He spoke of the Spirit, whom those who believed in Him were to receive; for the Spirit [~~was~~] not yet given, because Jesus was not yet glorified.
4 Some of the people therefore, when they heard these words, were saying, "This is certainly *the Prophet*,"[2.] <and> others were saying, "This is *the Christ*."[3.]	7:40 Some of the people therefore, when they heard these words, were saying, "This certainly is the Prophet." 7:41~ Others were saying, "This is the Christ."
5 Still others were saying, "Surely the Christ is not going to come from Galilee, is He? Has not the Scripture said that the Christ comes from *the descendants of David*,[4.] and from *Bethlehem*,[5.] *the village where David was*?"[6.]	7:~41 Still others were saying, "Surely the Christ is not going to come from Galilee, is He? 7:42 "Has not the Scripture said that the Christ comes from the descendants of David, and from Bethlehem, the village where David was?"
6 So a division occurred in the crowd because of Him. Some of them wanted to seize [Jesus], but no one laid hands on Him.	7:43 So a division occurred in the crowd because of Him. 7:44 Some of them wanted to seize [~~Him~~], but no one laid hands on Him.

1. (Isaiah 44:3, 43:20, 55:1)   2. Deuteronomy 18:15, 18   3. Messiah - Daniel 9:25   4. Jeremiah 23:5 / (Psalm 132:11) / (Isaiah 11:1)   4. Micah 5:2   5. 1 Samuel 16:1

Scene 5: The Pharisees Are Divided

The Temple, Jerusalem, *Judea*   Feast of Tabernacles, October / 32 CE

	John
1 The [Temple attendants] [went] to the chief priests and <the> Pharisees, [who] [asked] them, "Why did you not bring Him?"	7:45 The [~~officers~~]* ~~then~~ [came] to the chief priests and Pharisees, ~~and~~ [they] [~~said to~~] them, "Why did you not bring Him?"
2 The [attendants] answered, "Never has a man spoken the way <that> this man speaks."	7:46 The [~~officers~~]* answered, "Never has a man spoken the way this man speaks."
3 The Pharisees [said to] them, "You have not also been led astray, have you? No one of the rulers or Pharisees has believed in Him, has he?	7:47 The Pharisees ~~then~~ [~~answered~~] them, "You have not also been led astray, have you? 7:48 "No one of the rulers or Pharisees has believed in Him, has he?
4 "But this crowd, which does not know the Law, is accursed!"	7:49 "But this crowd which does not know the Law is accursed."
5 Nicodemus, who [had come] to [Jesus] before, being one of them, said, "Our Law does not judge a man unless it first hears from him, and knows what he is doing, does it?"	7:50 Nicodemus (~~he~~ who [came] to [Him] before, being one of them) said ~~to them~~, 7:51 "Our Law does not judge a man unless it first hears from him and knows what he is doing, does it?"
6 They answered him, "You are not also from Galilee, are you? Search and see, that no prophet arises out of Galilee."	7:52 They answered him, "You are not also from Galilee, are you? Search, and see that no prophet arises out of Galilee."
7 Everyone went to his home, but Jesus went to the Mount of Olives.	7:53 {Everyone went to his home. 8:1 But Jesus went to the Mount of Olives.}

6 - THE FINAL YEAR

Act 2: **Discussions In The Temple**

Scene 1: **Jesus Forgives An Adulteress**

The Temple, Jerusalem, *Judea*   October / 32 CE

The Complete Gospel of Jesus

	John
1 Early in the morning, [Jesus] came again into the Temple, and all the people were coming to Him, so He sat down, and began to teach them.	8:2 {Early in the morning [He] came again into the temple, and all the people were coming to Him; and He sat down and began to teach them.
2 The scribes and the Pharisees brought a woman <who was> caught [committing] *adultery*;[1.] and having set her in the center of the court[yard], they said to Him, "Teacher, this woman has been caught in *adultery*,[1.] in the very act.	8:3 The scribes and the Pharisees brought a woman caught [in] adultery, and having set her in the center of the court, they said to Him, 8:4 "Teacher, this woman has been caught in adultery, in the very act.
3 "Now in the Law, Moses commanded us to *stone such women*;[2.] what then, do You say?"	8:5 "Now in the Law Moses commanded us to stone such women; what then do You say?"
4 They were saying this <to> test Him, so that they might have grounds [to] accus[e] Him.	8:6~ They were saying this, testing Him, so that they might have grounds [for] accus[ing] Him.
5 But Jesus stooped down, and wrote on the ground with His finger.	8:~6 But Jesus stooped down and with His finger wrote on the ground.
6 When they persisted in asking Him, He straightened up, and said to them, "He who is without sin among you, let him be the first to throw a stone at her."	8:7 But when they persisted in asking Him, He straightened up, and said to them, "He who is without sin among you, let him be the first to throw a stone at her."
7 Again He stooped down, and wrote on the ground.	8:8 Again He stooped down and wrote on the ground.
8 When they heard it, <being convicted by their conscience,> they began to go out one by one, beginning with the older ones; and He was left alone [with] the woman where she was, in the [middle] of the court[yard].	8:9 When they heard it, they began to go out one by one, beginning with the older ones, and He was left alone, [and] the woman, where she was, in the [center] of the court.
9 Straightening up, Jesus said to her, "Woman, where are they? Did no one condemn you?" She said, "No one, Lord."	8:10 Straightening up, Jesus said to her, "Woman, where are they? Did no one condemn you?" 8:11~ She said, "No one, Lord."
10 And Jesus said, "I do not condemn you, either. Go, <and> from now on, sin no more."	8:~11 And Jesus said, "I do not condemn you, either. Go. From now on sin no more."}

1. Exodus 20:14 / Deuteronomy 5:18   2. Leviticus 20:10

6 - THE FINAL YEAR

Act 2: Discussions In The Temple

Scene 2: My Testimony and Judgment Is True

The Temple, Jerusalem, *Judea*   October / 32 CE

John

1 Again Jesus spoke to them, saying, "I am the Light of the world. He who follows Me will not walk in darkness, but will have the Light of life."

2 The Pharisees said to Him, "You are testifying about Yourself; Your testimony is not true."

3 Jesus answered, and said to them, "Even if I testify about Myself, My testimony is true, for I know where I [have come] from, and where I am going;

4 "but you do not know where I come from, or where I am going.

5 "You judge according to the flesh, <but> I am not judging anyone.

6 "But even if I do judge, My judgment is true, for I am not alone in it, but I and The Father who sent Me.

7 "In your law it [is] written that *the testimony of two men is true.*[1]

8 "I am He who testifies about Myself, and The Father who sent Me testifies about Me."

9 So they [said] to Him, "Where is Your Father?"

10 Jesus answered, "You know neither Me, nor My Father. If you knew Me, you would know My Father also."

11 These words [Jesus] spoke in the treasury, as He taught in the Temple; and no one seized Him, because His hour had not yet come.

---

1. *Deuteronomy 17:6; 19:15*

8:12 ~~Then~~ Jesus again spoke to them, saying, "I am the Light of the world; he who follows Me will not walk in ~~the~~ darkness, but will have the Light of life."

8:13 ~~So~~ the Pharisees said to Him, "You are testifying about Yourself; Your testimony is not true."

8:14~ Jesus answered and said to them, "Even if I testify about Myself, My testimony is true, for I know where I [~~came~~] from and where I am going;

8:~14 but you do not know where I come from or where I am going.

8:15 "You judge according to the flesh; I am not judging anyone.

8:16 "But even if I do judge, My judgment is true; for I am not alone in it, but I and the Father who sent Me.

8:17 "~~Even~~ in your law it [~~has been~~] written that the testimony of two men is true.

8:18 "I am He who testifies about Myself, and the Father who sent Me testifies about Me."

8:19~ So they ~~were~~ [~~saying~~] to Him, "Where is Your Father?"

8:~19 Jesus answered, "You know neither Me nor My Father; if you knew Me, you would know My Father also."

8:20 These words [~~He~~] spoke in the treasury, as He taught in the temple; and no one seized Him, because His hour had not yet come.

6 - THE FINAL YEAR

Act 2: **Discussions In The Temple**

Scene 3: **You Are From Below, I Am From Above**

The Temple Treasury, Jerusalem, *Judea*   October / 32 CE

Every Gospel Deed of Jesus

	John
1 Then [Jesus] said to them again, "I go away, and you will seek Me; and <you> will die in your sin[s].	8:21~ Then [He] said again to them, "I go away, and you will seek Me, and will die in your sin;
2 "Where I am going, you cannot come."	8:~21 where I am going, you cannot come."
3 So the Jews were saying, "Surely He will not kill Himself, will He, since He says, 'Where I am going, you cannot come'?"	8:22 So the Jews were saying, "Surely He will not kill Himself, will He, since He says, 'Where I am going, you cannot come'?"
4 [Then] [Jesus] [said] to them, "You are from below, I am from above. You are of this world, I am not of this world.	8:23 [And] [He] [was saying] to them, You are from below, I am from above; you are of this world, I am not of this world.
5 "Therefore I said to you that you will die in your sins, [because] [if] you <do not> believe that I am He, you will die in your sins."	8:24 "Therefore I said to you that you will die in your sins; [for] [unless] you believe that I am He, you will die in your sins."
6 So they [said] to Him, "Who are You?"	8:25~ So they [were saying] to Him, "Who are You?"
7 Jesus said to them, "What have I been saying to you from the beginning?	8:~25 Jesus said to them, "What have I been saying to you from the beginning?
8 "I have many things to speak and to judge concerning you, but He who sent Me is true, and the things which I heard from Him, these I speak to the world."	8:26 "I have many things to speak and to judge concerning you, but He who sent Me is true; and the things which I heard from Him, these I speak to the world."
9 They did not realize that He [was] speaking to them about The Father, so Jesus said, "When you lift up the Son of Man, then you will know that I am He;	8:27 They did not realize that He [had been] speaking to them about the Father. 8:28~ So Jesus said, "When you lift up the Son of Man, then you will know that I am He,
10 "and <that> I do nothing on My own initiative, but I speak these things as The Father <has> taught Me.	8:~28 and I do nothing on My own initiative, but I speak these things as the Father taught Me.
11 "And He who sent Me is with Me; He has not left Me alone, for I always do the things that are pleasing to Him."	8:29 "And He who sent Me is with Me; He has not left Me alone, for I always do the things that are pleasing to Him."
12 As [Jesus] spoke these things many came to believe in Him.	8:30 As [He] spoke these things, many came to believe in Him.

6 - THE FINAL YEAR

Act 2: Discussions In The Temple

Scene 4: Abraham Is Our Father
The Temple, Jerusalem, *Judea*   October / 32 CE

Page 168

The Complete Gospel United from Four

	John
1 Jesus [said] to those Jews who had believed <in> Him, "If you [abide] in My Word, you are truly [My] disciples;	8:31 ~~So~~ Jesus [~~was saying~~] to those Jews who had believed Him, "If you [~~continue~~] in My word, then you are truly disciples [~~of Mine~~];
2 "and you will know the truth, and the truth will make you free."	8:32 and you will know the truth, and the truth will make you free."
3 They answered Him, "We are Abraham's descendants, and have never been enslaved to anyone. How [can] You say, 'You will become free'?"	8:33 They answered Him, "We are Abraham's descendants and have never yet been enslaved to anyone; how [~~is it that~~] You say, 'You will become free'?"
4 Jesus answered them, "Truly, truly, I say to you, everyone who commits sin is the slave of sin.	8:34 Jesus answered them, "Truly, truly, I say to you, everyone who commits sin is the slave of sin.
5 "The slave does not remain in the house forever, <but> the son does remain forever.	8:35 "The slave does not remain in the house forever; the son does remain forever.
6 "So if the Son [sets] you free, you will really be free.	8:36 "So if the Son [~~makes~~] you free, you will be free [~~indeed~~].
7 "I know that you are Abraham's descendants, yet you seek to kill Me, because My Word has no place in you.	8:37 "I know that you are Abraham's descendants; yet you seek to kill Me, because My word has no place in you.
8 "I speak the things which I have seen with My Father, [and] you do the things which you heard from your father."	8:38 "I speak the things which I have seen with My Father; [~~therefore~~] you ~~also~~ do the things which you heard from your father."
9 They said to Him, "Abraham is our father."	8:39~ They ~~answered and~~ said to Him, "Abraham is our father."
10 Jesus said to them, "If you are Abraham's children, <then> do the deeds of Abraham.	8:~39 Jesus said to them, "If you are Abraham's children, do the deeds of Abraham.
11 "But as it is, you are seeking to kill Me, a man who has told you the truth which I heard from God; this Abraham did not do. You are doing the deeds of your father."	8:40 "But as it is, you are seeking to kill Me, a man who has told you the truth, which I heard from God; this Abraham did not do. 8:41~ "You are doing the deeds of your father."
12 They said to Him, "We [have] not <been> born [through] fornication; *we have one Father: God.*" [1]	8:~41 They said to Him, "We [~~were~~] not born [~~of~~] fornication; we have one Father: God."
13 Jesus said to them, "If God were your Father you would love Me, [because] I have come from God;	8:42~ Jesus said to them, "If God were your Father, you would love Me, [~~for~~] I ~~proceeded forth and~~ have come from God,
14 "[and] I have not come [for Myself], but He sent Me."	8:~42 [~~for~~] I have not ~~even~~ come [~~on My~~ ~~own initiative~~],* but He sent Me."

1. Isaiah 63:16

Scene 5: Your Father Is The Devil

The Temple, Jerusalem, Judea — October / 32 CE

	John
1 <Jesus said to them>, "Why do you not understand what I am saying? It is because you cannot hear My Word.	8:43 "Why do you not understand what I am saying? It is because you cannot hear My word.
2 "You are of your father the Devil, and you want to do the desires of your father.	8:44~ "You are of your father the devil, and you want to do the desires of your father.
3 "He was a murderer from the beginning, and <he> does not stand in the truth, because there is no truth in him.	8:~44~ He was a murderer from the beginning, and does not stand in the truth because there is no truth in him.
4 "Whenever he speaks a lie, he speaks from his own nature, for he is a liar, and the father of lies.	8:~44 Whenever he speaks a lie, he speaks from his own nature, for he is a liar and the father of lies.
5 "But because I speak the truth, you do not believe Me.	8:45 "But because I speak the truth, you do not believe Me.
6 "Which one of you convicts Me of sin?	8:46~ "Which one of you convicts Me of sin?
7 "If I <am> speak[ing] <the> truth, why do you not believe Me?	8:~46 If I speak truth, why do you not believe Me?
8 "He who is of God hears the Words of God;	8:47~ "He who is of God hears the words of God;
9 "<and> for this reason you do not hear them, because you are not of God."	8:~47 for this reason you do not hear them, because you are not of God."

6 - THE FINAL YEAR

Act 2: Discussions In The Temple

Scene 6: You Have A Demon!

The Temple, Jerusalem, *Judea*   October / 32 CE

The Full Gospel

	John
1 The Jews answered, and said to Him, "Do we not rightly say that You are a Samaritan, and <that You> have a demon?"	8:48 The Jews answered and said to Him, "Do we not say rightly that You are a Samaritan and have a demon?"
2 Jesus answered, "I do not have a demon; but I honor My Father, and you dishonor Me.	8:49 Jesus answered, "I do not have a demon; but I honor My Father, and you dishonor Me.
3 "I do not seek My <own> glory; there is One who seeks and judges.	8:50 "~~But~~ I do not seek My glory; there is One who seeks and judges.
4 "Truly, truly, I say to you, if anyone keeps My Word, he will [not] see death <in this age>."	8:51 "Truly, truly, I say to you, if anyone keeps My word he will [never] see death." *
5 The Jews said to Him, "Now we know that You have a demon! *Abraham died, and the prophets also*; [1.] and You say, 'If anyone keeps My Word, he will [not] taste death <in this age>.'	8:52 The Jews said to Him, "Now we know that You have a demon. Abraham died, and the prophets also; and You say, 'If anyone keeps My word, he will [~~never~~] taste ~~of~~ death.'
6 "Surely You are not greater than our father Abraham, who died? The prophets [also] died. Whom do You make Yourself out to be?"	8:53 "Surely You are not greater than our father Abraham, who died? The prophets died [~~too~~]; Whom do You make Yourself out to be?"
7 Jesus answered, "If I glorify Myself, My glory is nothing; it is My Father who glorifies Me, of whom you say, 'He is our God'.	8:54 Jesus answered, "If I glorify Myself, My glory is nothing; it is My Father who glorifies Me, of whom you say, 'He is our God';
8 "And you have not come to know Him, but I know Him; and if I say that I do not know Him <then> I [will] be a liar like you.	8:55~ and you have not come to know Him, but I know Him; and if I say that I do not know Him, I will be a liar like you,
9 "But I do know Him, and <I> keep His Word.	8:~55 but I do know Him and keep His word.
10 "Your father Abraham rejoiced to see My day, and he saw it, and was glad."	8:56 "Your father Abraham rejoiced to see My day, and he saw it and was glad."
11 So the Jews said to Him, "You are not yet fifty years old, and You have seen Abraham?"	8:57 So the Jews said to Him, "You are not yet fifty years old, and have You seen Abraham?"
12 Jesus said to them, "Truly, truly, I say to you, <that> before Abraham was born, *I am*." [2.]	8:58 Jesus said to them, "Truly, truly, I say to you, before Abraham was born, I am."
13 Therefore they picked up stones to throw at Jesus, but [He] hid Himself, and went out of the Temple.	8:59 Therefore they picked up stones to throw at [Him], but Jesus hid Himself and went out of the temple.

1. Genesis 25:8 / Zechariah 1:5   2. Exodus 3:14 / (Micah 5:2)

6 - THE FINAL YEAR

Act 3: Healing A Man Born Blind

Scene 1: Jesus Cures A Man Who Was Born Blind

Jerusalem, *Judea* a Sabbath, October / 32 CE

	John
1 As [Jesus] passed by, He saw a man <who had been> [born] blind, and His disciples asked Him, "Rabbi, who sinned, this man or his parents, that he would be born blind?"	9:1 As [He] passed by, He saw a man blind from [birth]. 9:2 And His disciples asked Him, "Rabbi, who sinned, this man or his parents, that he would be born blind?"
2 Jesus answered, "It was neither that this man sinned, nor his parents, but it was so that the works of God might be displayed in him.	9:3 Jesus answered, "It was neither that this man sinned, nor his parents; but it was so that the works of God might be displayed in him.
3 "We must work the works of Him who sent Me [while] it is day, <because> night is coming when no one can work.	9:4 "We must work the works of Him who sent Me [as long as] it is day; night is coming when no one can work.
4 "While I am in the world, I am the Light of the world."	9:5 "While I am in the world, I am the Light of the world."
5 When [Jesus] had said this, He spat on the ground, and made clay of the spittle, and applied the clay to <the> eyes [of the blind man].	9:6 When [He] had said this, He spat on the ground, and made clay of the spittle, and applied the clay to [his] eyes,
6 And <Jesus> said to him, "Go, <and> wash in the pool of Siloam" (which is translated as *sent*).	9:7~ and said to him, "Go, wash in the pool of Siloam" (which is translated, sent).
7 So [the man] went away and washed, and <he> came back seeing.	9:~7 So [he] went away and washed, and came back seeing.
8 Therefore the neighbors, and those who [had] [seen] him as a beggar, were saying, "Is this not the one who used to sit and beg?"	9:8 Therefore the neighbors, and those who [previously] [saw] him as a beggar, were saying, "Is not this the one who used to sit and beg?
9 [Some] were saying, "This is he," [and] others were saying, "No, but he is like him."	9:9~ [Others] were saying, "This is he," [still] others were saying, "No, but he is like him."
10 He <himself> kept saying, "I am the one!"	9:~9 He kept saying, "I am the one."
11 So they were saying to him, "How were your eyes opened?"	9:10 So they were saying to him, "How then were your eyes opened?"
12 He answered, "The man who is called Jesus made clay, and anointed my eyes; and <He> said to me, 'Go to Siloam, and wash.'	9:11~ He answered, "The man who is called Jesus made clay, and anointed my eyes, and said to me, 'Go to Siloam and wash';
13 "So I went away and washed, and I received sight!"	9:~11 so I went away and washed, and I received sight."
14 They [asked] him, "Where is He?" He said, "I do not know."	9:12 They [said to] him, "Where is He?" He said, "I do not know."

6 - THE FINAL YEAR
Act 3: **Healing A Man Born Blind**

Scene 2: **The Pharisees Question The Man and His Parents**
Jerusalem, *Judea*   a Sabbath, October / 32 CE

A Unified Verse-By-Verse Gospel Harmony

	John
1 Now it was a Sabbath on the day when Jesus made the clay, and opened [the] eyes <of> the man who [had been born] blind, <so> they brought <him> to the Pharisees.	9:14 Now it was a Sabbath on the day when Jesus made the clay and opened [his] eyes. 9:13 They brought to the Pharisees the man who [was formerly] blind.
2 [When] the Pharisees ask[ed] him how he <had> received his sight, he said to them, "[Jesus] applied clay to my eyes, and I washed, and <now> I see."	9:15 [Then] the Pharisees also were ask[ing] him again how he received his sight. And he said to them, "[He] applied clay to my eyes, and I washed, and I see."
3 Therefore, some of the Pharisees were saying, "This man is not from God, because He does not keep the Sabbath."	9:16~ Therefore some of the Pharisees were saying, "This man is not from God, because He does not keep the Sabbath."
4 But others were saying, "How can a man who is a sinner perform such signs?" And there was a division among them.	9:~16 But others were saying, "How can a man who is a sinner perform such signs?" And there was a division among them.
5 So they said to the man again, "What do you say about Him, since He opened your eyes?" He said, "He is a prophet."	9:17 So they said to the blind man again, "What do you say about Him, since He opened your eyes?" And he said, "He is a prophet."
6 The Jews did not believe that he had been <born> blind and had received sight, until they called the [man's] parents, and questioned them, saying, "Is this is your son, <and> was <he> was born blind? How then, does he now see?"	9:18 The Jews then did not believe it of him, that he had been blind and had received sight, until they called the parents [of the very one] who had received his sight, 9:19 and questioned them, saying, "Is this your son, who you say was born blind? Then how does he now see?"
7 His parents answered them, and said, "We know that this is our son, and that he was born blind; but how he now sees, we do not know; or who opened his eyes, we do not know.	9:20 His parents answered them and said, "We know that this is our son, and that he was born blind; 9:21~ but how he now sees, we do not know; or who opened his eyes, we do not know.
8 "He is of age; ask him, <and> he will speak for himself."	9:~21 Ask him; he is of age, he will speak for himself."
9 His parents said this because they were afraid of the Jews, for the Jews had agreed that if anyone confessed [Jesus] to be <the> Christ, he was to be put out of the synagogue.	9:22 His parents said this because they were afraid of the Jews, for the Jews had already agreed that if anyone confessed [Him] to be Christ, he was to be put out of the synagogue.
10 For this reason his parents said, "He is of age; ask him."	9:23 For this reason his parents said, "He is of age; ask him."

6 - THE FINAL YEAR
Act 3: **Healing A Man Born Blind**

Scene 3: **They Question The Man A Second Time**
Jerusalem, *Judea*   a Sabbath, October / 32 CE

Page 173
Every Gospel Word of Jesus Christ

	John
1 So <for> a second time [the Pharisees] called the man who had been <born> blind, and <they> said to him, "Give glory to God! We know that this man <Jesus> is a sinner."	9:24 So a second time [they] called the man who had been blind, and said to him, "Give glory to God; we know that this man is a sinner.
2 [The man] answered, "Whether He is a sinner, I do not know. One thing I do know, <is> that though I was blind, now I see."	9:25 He then answered, "Whether He is a sinner, I do not know; one thing I do know, that though I was blind, now I see."
3 So they said to him, "What did He do to you? How did He open your eyes?"	9:26 So they said to him, "What did He do to you? How did He open your eyes?"
4 He answered them, "I told you already, and you did not listen; why do you want to hear it again? Do you [also] want to become His disciples?"	9:27 He answered them, "I told you already and you did not listen; why do you want to hear it again? You do not want to become His disciples [too], do you?"
5 [The Pharisees] reviled him, and said, "You are His disciple, but we are disciples of Moses!	9:28 [They] reviled him and said, "You are His disciple, but we are disciples of Moses.
6 We know that *God has spoken to Moses*,[1] but as for this man, we do not know where He is from."	9:29 "We know that God has spoken to Moses, but as for this man, we do not know where He is from."
7 The man answered them, "Well, here is an amazing thing, that you do not know where He is from, and yet He opened my eyes!	9:30 The man answered and said to them, "Well, here is an amazing thing, that you do not know where He is from, and yet He opened my eyes.
8 "We know that *God does not hear sinners*,[2] but if anyone is God-fearing and does His will, He hears [them].	9:31 "We know that God does not hear sinners; but if anyone is God-fearing and does His will, He hears [him].
9 "Since the beginning of time, it has never been heard that anyone opened the eyes of a person born blind.	9:32 "Since the beginning of time it has never been heard that anyone opened the eyes of a person born blind.
10 "If this man were not from God, He could do nothing."	9:33 "If this man were not from God, He could do nothing."
11 They answered him, "You were born entirely in sins, and are you teaching us?" So they put him out.	9:34 They answered him, "You were born entirely in sins, and are you teaching us?" So they put him out.

1. Exodus 3:4 / Numbers 12:6-8   2. Zechariah 7:13

Scene 4: **Do You Believe In The Son of Man?**

	John
1 Jesus heard that they had put him out; and finding him, [Jesus] [asked], "Do you believe in the Son of Man?"	9:35 Jesus heard that they had put him out, and finding him, [He] [said], "Do you believe in the Son of Man?"
2 [The man] answered, "Who is He, Lord, that I may believe in Him?"	9:36 [He] answered, "Who is He, Lord, that I may believe in Him?"
3 Jesus said to him, "You have both seen Him, and He is the One who is talking with you."	9:37 Jesus said to him, "You have both seen Him, and He is the one who is talking with you."
4 He said, "Lord, I believe!" And he worshiped Him.	9:38 And he said, "Lord, I believe." And he worshiped Him.
5 Jesus said, "For judgment I came into this world, so that those who do not see may see, and that those who see may become blind."	9:39 And Jesus said, "For judgment I came into this world, so that those who do not see may see, and that those who see may become blind."
6 The Pharisees who were with [Jesus] heard these things, and <they> said to Him, "Are we [also] blind?"	9:40 Those of the Pharisees who were with [Him] heard these things and said to Him, "We are not blind [too], are we?"
7 Jesus said to them, "If you were blind you would have no sin, but since you say, 'We see,' your sin remains."	9:41 Jesus said to them, "If you were blind you would have no sin; but since you say, 'We see,' your sin remains.

6 - THE FINAL YEAR
Act 4: **The Good Shepherd**

Scene 1: **I Am The Door Of The Sheep**
Jerusalem, *Judea*   a Sabbath, October / 32 CE

Page 174
synopticgospel.com

John

1 "Truly, truly, I say to you, he who does not enter into the fold of the sheep by the door, but climbs [in] some other way, is a thief and a robber.

2 "But he who enters by the door is [the] shepherd of the sheep.

3 "To him the doorkeeper opens; and the sheep hear his voice, and he calls [them] by name, and leads them out.

4 "When he puts [them] [out], he goes ahead of them, and the sheep follow him because they know his voice.

5 "They will not follow a stranger, but will flee from him, because they do not know the voice of strangers."

6 Jesus spoke this figure of speech to them, but they did not understand what He [was] saying.

7 So Jesus said to them again, "Truly, truly, I say to you, I am the door of the sheep.

8 "All who came before Me [were] thieves and [bandits], [and] the sheep did not hear them.

9 "I am the door. If anyone enters through Me, he will be saved, and will go in and out, and find pasture.

10 "The thief comes only to steal, and kill, and destroy; <but> I [have come] <so> that they may have life, and have it abundantly."

10:1 "Truly, truly, I say to you, he who does not enter by the door into the fold of the sheep, but climbs [up] some other way, ~~he~~ is a thief and a robber.

10:2 "But he who enters by the door is [a] shepherd of the sheep.

10:3 "To him the doorkeeper opens, and the sheep hear his voice, and he calls [~~his own sheep~~] by name and leads them out.

10:4 "When he puts [~~forth~~] [~~all his own~~], he goes ahead of them, and the sheep follow him because they know his voice.

10:5 "A stranger they ~~simply~~ will not follow, but will flee from him, because they do not know the voice of strangers."

10:6 This figure of speech Jesus spoke to them, but they did not understand what ~~those things were which~~ He [~~had been~~] saying ~~to them~~.

10:7 So Jesus said to them again, "Truly, truly, I say to you, I am the door of the sheep.

10:8 "All who came before Me [~~are~~] thieves and [~~robbers~~], [~~but~~] the sheep did not hear them.

10:9 "I am the door; if anyone enters through Me, he will be saved, and will go in and out and find pasture.

10:10 "The thief comes only to steal and kill and destroy; I [came] that they may have life, and have it abundantly."

Scene 2: **I Am The Good Shepherd**
Jerusalem, *Judea*   a Sabbath, October / 32 CE

John

1 "*I am the good shepherd*; [1.] the good shepherd lays down His life for the sheep.

2 "He who is a hired hand, and is not a shepherd [nor] the owner of the sheep, <when he> sees the wolf coming <he> leaves the sheep and flees; and the wolf scatters [the sheep], and snatches them.

3 "He flees because he is a hired hand, and is not <really> concerned about the sheep.

4 "I am the good shepherd, and I know My own, and My own know Me, even as The Father knows Me, and I know The Father;

5 "and I lay down My life for the sheep.

6 "<And> I *have other sheep which are not of this fold,*[2.] and I must bring them also.

7 "They will hear My voice, and they will become one flock, with one shepherd."

10:11 "I am the good shepherd; the good shepherd lays down His life for the sheep.

10:12 "He who is a hired hand, and not a shepherd, ~~who~~ is [not] the owner of the sheep, sees the wolf coming, ~~and~~ leaves the sheep and flees, and the wolf snatches [~~them~~] and scatters them.

10:13 "He flees because he is a hired hand and is not concerned about the sheep.

10:14 "I am the good shepherd, and I know My own and My own know Me, 10:15~ even as the Father knows Me and I know the Father;

10:~15 and I lay down My life for the sheep.

10:16~ "I have other sheep, which are not of this fold; I must bring them also,

10:~16 and they will hear My voice, and they will become one flock with one shepherd."

1. Isaiah 40:10-11   2. Isaiah 56:8

6 - THE FINAL YEAR	Scene 3: **I Lay Down My Life To Take It Again**	
Act 4: **The Good Shepherd**	Jerusalem, *Judea* a Sabbath, October / 32 CE	*The United Gospel Story*

	John
1 "For this reason The Father loves Me, because I lay down My life so that I may take it again.	10:17 "For this reason the Father loves Me, because I lay down My life so that I may take it again.
2 "No one has taken it from Me, but I lay it down on My own initiative.	10:18~ "No one has taken it ~~away~~ from Me, but I lay it down on My own initiative.
3 "I have authority to lay it down, and I have authority to take it up again. This commandment I received from My Father."	10:~18 I have authority to lay it down, and I have authority to take it up again. This commandment I received from My Father."
4 A division occurred again among the Jews because of these words. Many of them were saying, "He has a demon and is insane! Why do you listen to Him?"	10:19 A division occurred again among the Jews because of these words. 10:20 Many of them were saying, "He has a demon and is insane. Why do you listen to Him?"
5 Others were saying, "These are not the sayings of one <who is> demon-possessed.	10:21~ Others were saying, "These are not the sayings of one demon-possessed.
6 "*A demon cannot open the eyes of the blind,*[1.] can he?"	10:~21 A demon cannot open the eyes of the blind, can he?"

1. *Exodus 4:11*

Scene 4: **Repent And Bear Fruit, or Perish**

Jerusalem, *Judea* a Sabbath, October / 32 CE

	Luke
1 Now on the same occasion there were some present who reported to [Jesus] about the Galileans whose blood Pilate had mixed with their sacrifices.	13:1 Now on the same occasion there were some present who reported to [~~Him~~] about the Galileans whose blood Pilate had mixed with their sacrifices.
2 Jesus said to them, "Do you suppose that these Galileans were greater sinners than all other Galileans, because they suffered this fate?	13:2 ~~And~~ Jesus said to them, "Do you suppose that these Galileans were greater sinners than all other Galileans because they suffered this fate?
3 "I tell you, no; but unless you repent, you will all likewise perish.	13:3 "I tell you, no, but unless you repent, you will all likewise perish.
4 "Or do you suppose that those eighteen on whom the tower in Siloam fell and killed, were worse culprits than all the men who live in Jerusalem?	13:4 "Or do you suppose that those eighteen on whom the tower in Siloam fell and killed ~~them~~ were worse culprits than all the men who live in Jerusalem?
5 "I tell you, no; but unless you repent, you will all likewise perish!"	13:5 "I tell you, no, but unless you repent, you will all likewise perish."
6 [Then] [Jesus] began telling this parable: "A man had a fig tree which had been planted in his vineyard, and he came looking for fruit on it, and did not find any.	13:6 [~~And~~] [He] began telling this parable: "A man had a fig tree which had been planted in his vineyard; and he came looking for fruit on it and did not find any.
7 "He said to the keeper <of the> vineyard, 'Behold, for three years I have come looking for fruit on this fig tree without finding any. Cut it down. Why does it even use up the ground?'	13:7 "~~And~~ he said to the vineyard-keeper, 'Behold, for three years I have come looking for fruit on this fig tree without finding any. Cut it down! Why does it even use up the ground?'
8 "[The vine-keeper] answered him, 'Let it alone, sir, for this year [also], until I dig around it and put in fertilizer; and if it bears fruit next year, fine; but if not, <I will> cut it down.' "	13:8 "[~~And~~] [he] answered ~~and said to~~ him, 'Let it alone, sir, for this year [~~too~~], until I dig around it and put in fertilizer; 13:9 and if it bears fruit next year, fine; but if not, cut it down.' "

6 - THE FINAL YEAR

Act 5: The Feast of Dedication

Scene 1: Depart From Me, All You Evildoers!

Galilee — December / 32 CE

Page 176

A Harmony of the Four Gospels

	Luke	John
1 The Feast of the Dedication [was near], and [Jesus] was passing through from one city and village to another, teaching, and proceeding on His way to Jerusalem.	13:22 And [He] was passing through from one city and village to another, teaching, and proceeding on His way to Jerusalem	10:22 [At that time] the Feast of the Dedication ~~took place at~~ Jerusalem;
2 Someone said to Him, "Lord, are there just a few who are being saved?"	13:23~ ~~And~~ someone said to Him, "Lord, are there just a few who are being saved?"	
3 [Jesus] said to them, "Strive to enter through the narrow door, for many I tell you, will seek to enter, and will not be able.	13:~23 ~~And~~ [He] said to them, 13:24 "Strive to enter through the narrow door; for many, I tell you, will seek to enter and will not be able.	
4 "[When] the head of the house gets up and shuts the door, then you [will] stand outside, and knock on the door, saying, 'Lord, open up to us!'	13:25~ "[~~Once~~] the head of the house gets up and shuts the door, and you [~~begin to~~] stand outside and knock on the door, saying, 'Lord, open up to us!'	
5 "[And] He will answer, and say to you, 'I do not know where you are from.'	13:~25 [~~then~~] He will answer and say to you, 'I do not know where you are from.'	
6 "Then you will say, 'We ate and drank in Your presence, and You taught in our streets';	13:26 "Then you will ~~begin to~~ say, 'We ate and drank in Your presence, and You taught in our streets';	
7 "and He will say, 'I tell you, I do not know where you are from. *Depart from Me, all you evildoers!*' [1.]	13:27 and He will say, 'I tell you, I do not know where you are from; depart from Me, all you evildoers.'	
8 "In that place there will be weeping, and gnashing of teeth, when you see Abraham and Isaac and Jacob, and all the prophets in the Kingdom of God, but yourselves being thrown out.	13:28 "In that place there will be weeping and gnashing of teeth when you see Abraham and Isaac and Jacob and all the prophets in the Kingdom of God, but yourselves being thrown out.	
9 "They will come from <the> east and <the> west, and from <the> north and south, and will recline at the table in the Kingdom of God.	13:29 "~~And~~ they will come from east and west and from north and south, and will recline at the table in the kingdom of God.	
10 "And behold, some who are last will be first, and some who are first will be last."	13:30 "And behold, some are last who will be first and some are first who will be last."	
11 At that time, some Pharisees approached <Jesus>, <and> [said] to Him, "Leave here <and> go away, for *Herod* [2.] wants to kill You."	13:31 ~~Just~~ at that time some Pharisees approached, [~~saying~~] to Him, "Go away, leave here, for Herod wants to kill You."	
12 [But] [Jesus] said to them, "Go and tell that fox: 'Behold, I cast out demons and perform cures today and tomorrow, and the third day I reach My goal.'	13:32 [~~And~~] [He] said to them, "Go and tell that fox, 'Behold, I cast out demons and perform cures today and tomorrow, and the third day I reach My goal.'	
13 "Nevertheless, I must journey on today and tomorrow, and the next day, for it cannot be that a prophet would perish outside of Jerusalem."	13:33 "Nevertheless I must journey on today and tomorrow and the next day; for it cannot be that a prophet would perish outside of Jerusalem.	

1. Psalm 6:8   2. Herod Antipater (aka Antipas) (20 BCE - 39 CE) Tetrarch of Galilee & Perea (4 BCE - 39 CE)

6 - THE FINAL YEAR | Scene 2: **I And The Father Are One**

Act 5: **The Feast of Dedication** | The Temple, Jerusalem, *Judea* — Feast of Dedication, December / 32 CE | *Luke also wrote The Book of Acts*

	John
1 It was winter, and Jesus was walking in the Temple, in the portico of Solomon.	*10:23* it was winter, and Jesus was walking in the temple in the portico of Solomon.
2 The Jews gathered around Him, and were saying to Him, "How long will You keep us in suspense? If You are the Christ, tell us plainly."	*10:24* The Jews ~~then~~ gathered around Him, and were saying to Him, "How long will You keep us in suspense? If You are the Christ, tell us plainly."
3 Jesus answered them, "I told you, and you do not believe.	*10:25~* Jesus answered them, "I told you, and you do not believe;
4 "The works that I do in My Father's Name, these testify of Me; but you do not believe, because you are not of My sheep.	*10:~25* the works that I do in My Father's name, these testify of Me. *10:26* "But you do not believe because you are not of My sheep.
5 "My sheep hear My voice, and I know them, and they follow Me.	*10:27* "My sheep hear My voice, and I know them, and they follow Me;
6 "I give eternal life to them, and they will never perish; and no one will snatch them out of My hand.	*10:28* ~~and~~ I give eternal life to them, and they will never perish; and no one will snatch them out of My hand.
7 "My Father, who has given them to Me, is greater than all, and no one is able to snatch them out of The Father's hand.	*10:29* "My Father, who has given them to Me, is greater than all; and no one is able to snatch them out of the Father's hand.
8 "I and The Father are One."	*10:30* "I and the Father are one."

Scene 3: The Jews Try To Stone Jesus For Blasphemy

	John
1 The Jews picked up stones again to stone [Jesus].	*10:31* The Jews picked up stones again to stone [~~Him~~].
2 [He] [said to] them, "I showed you many good works from The Father; for which of them are you stoning Me?"	*10:32* [~~Jesus~~] [answered] them, "I showed you many good works from the Father; for which of them are you stoning Me?"
3 The Jews answered Him, "We do not stone you for a god work, but for blasphemy - because You, being a man, make Yourself out to be God."	*10:33* The Jews answered Him, "For a good work we do not stone You, but for blasphemy; ~~and~~ because You, being a man, make Yourself out to be God."
4 Jesus answered them, "Has it not been written in your Law, *'I said, you are gods'*? [1.]	*10:34* Jesus answered them, "Has it not been written in your Law, 'I said, you are gods'?
5 "If he called them gods to whom the Word of God came, and the Scripture cannot be broken, do you say of Him whom the Father sanctified and sent into the world, 'You are blaspheming,' because I said, 'I am the Son of God'?	*10:35* "If he called them gods, to whom the word of God came (and the Scripture cannot be broken), *10:36* do you say of Him, whom the Father sanctified and sent into the world, 'You are blaspheming,' because I said, 'I am the Son of God'?
6 "If I do not do the works of My Father, <then> do not believe Me;	*10:37* "If I do not do the works of My Father, do not believe Me;
7 "but if I do them, <even> though you do not believe Me, believe the works, so that you may know and understand that The Father is in Me, and <that> I <am> in The Father."	*10:38* but if I do them, though you do not believe Me, believe the works, so that you may know and understand that the Father is in Me, and I in the Father."
8 Therefore they were seeking again to seize [Jesus], [but] He eluded their grasp.	*10:39* Therefore they were seeking again to seize [~~Him~~], [~~and~~] He eluded their grasp.
9 And He went away again beyond the Jordan, to the place where John was first baptizing, and He stay[ed] there.	*10:40* And He went away again beyond the Jordan to the place where John was first baptizing, and He ~~was~~ stay[~~ing~~] there.
10 Many came to [Jesus], and <they> were saying, "While John performed no sign, yet everything <that> [he] said about this man was true!"	*10:41* Many came to [~~Him~~] and were saying, "While John performed no sign, yet everything [~~John~~] said about this man was true."
11 <And> many believed in [Jesus] there.	*10:42* Many believed in [~~Him~~] there.

1. Psalm 82:6

6 - THE FINAL YEAR

Act 6: The Resurrection of Lazarus

Scene 1: Jesus Hears That Lazarus Has Died

Galilee   winter / 33 CE

The Four Gospels Combined as One

#		John
1	Now Lazarus, [from] the village of Bethany, was sick.	11:1~ Now a ~~certain man was sick~~, Lazarus [~~of~~] Bethany, the village of 11:~2 was sick.
2	<He was the> brother <of> Martha, and her sister Mary.	11:~1 Mary and her sister Martha. 11:~2~ ~~whose~~ brother ~~Lazarus~~
3	So the sisters sent word to [Jesus], saying, "Lord, he whom You love is sick."	11:3 So the sisters sent word to [~~Him~~], saying, "Lord, he whom You love is sick."
4	When Jesus heard this, He said, "This sickness is not to end in death, but for the glory of God, so that the Son of God may be glorified by it."	11:4 ~~But~~ when Jesus heard this, He said, "This sickness is not to end in death, but for the glory of God, so that the Son of God may be glorified by it."
5	Now Jesus loved Martha and her sister, and Lazarus, [yet] when He heard that [Lazarus] was sick, He stayed <for> two [more] days in the place where He was.	11:5 Now Jesus loved Martha and her sister and Lazarus. 11:6 [~~So~~] when He heard that [~~he~~] was sick, He ~~then~~ stayed two days [~~longer~~] in the place where He was.
6	After [two days], [Jesus] said to [His] [apostles], "Let us go to Judea again."	11:7 ~~Then~~ after [two days] [~~He~~] said to [~~the~~] [~~disciples~~], "Let us go to Judea again."
7	The [apostles] said to Him, "Rabbi, the Jews were just now seeking to stone You, and You are going there again?"	11:8 The [~~disciples~~] said to Him, "Rabbi, the Jews were just now seeking to stone You, and are You going there again?"
8	Jesus answered, "Are there not twelve hours in the day? If anyone walks in the day he does not stumble, because he sees the light of this world.	11:9 Jesus answered, "Are there not twelve hours in the day? If anyone walks in the day, he does not stumble, because he sees the light of this world.
9	"But if anyone walks in the night he stumbles, because the light is not in him."	11:10 "But if anyone walks in the night, he stumbles, because the light is not in him."
10	[Then] [Jesus] said to them, "Our friend Lazarus has fallen asleep, [and] I go so that I may waken him."	11:11 ~~This~~ [He] said, ~~and~~ [~~after that~~] ~~He~~ said to them, "Our friend Lazarus has fallen asleep; [~~but~~] I go, so that I may awaken him ~~out of sleep~~."
11	The [apostles] said to Him, "Lord, if he has fallen asleep, he will recover."	11:12 The [~~disciples~~] ~~then~~ said to Him, "Lord, if he has fallen asleep, he will recover."
12	Now they thought that Jesus was speaking of literal sleep, but He had spoken of his death.	11:13 Now Jesus had spoken of his death, but they thought that He was speaking of literal sleep.
13	So Jesus said to them plainly, "Lazarus is dead; and I am glad for your sakes that I was not there, so that you may believe.	11:14 So Jesus ~~then~~ said to them plainly, "Lazarus is dead, 11:15~ and I am glad for your sakes that I was not there, so that you may believe;
14	"[Now], let us go to him."	11:~15 [~~but~~] let us go to him."
15	[Then] Thomas, who is called *Didymus*,[1] said to his fellow [apostles], "Let us also go, so that we may die with Him!"	11:16 [~~Therefore~~] Thomas, who is called Didymus, said to his fellow [~~disciples~~], "Let us also go, so that we may die with Him."

1. Greek for "twin"

6 - THE FINAL YEAR
Act 6: The Resurrection of Lazarus

Scene 2: I Am The Resurrection and The Life
Bethany, *Judea*   winter / 33 CE

FIVE COLUMN

	John
1 Many [came] to console Martha and Mary concerning their brother; [but] when Martha heard that Jesus was coming she went to meet Him, [while] Mary stayed at the house.	11:19 ~~and~~ many ~~of the Jews~~ [had come] to Martha and Mary, ~~to~~ console ~~them~~ concerning their brother. 11:20 Martha [~~therefore~~], when she heard that Jesus was coming, went to meet Him, [~~but~~] Mary stayed at the house.
2 Bethany was near Jerusalem, about *two miles*[1] [away].	11:18 ~~Now~~ Bethany was near Jerusalem, about two miles [~~off~~];
3 <When they met,> Martha said to Jesus, "Lord, if You had been here, my brother would not have died.	11:21 Martha ~~then~~ said to Jesus, "Lord, if You had been here, my brother would not have died.
4 "<Yet> even now, I know that whatever You ask of God, God will give You."	11:22 "Even now I know that whatever You ask of God, God will give You."
5 Jesus said to her, "Your brother will rise again."	11:23 Jesus said to her, "Your brother will rise again."
6 Martha said, "I know that he will rise again, in the resurrection on the last day."	11:24 Martha said ~~to Him~~, "I know that he will rise again in the resurrection on the last day."
7 Jesus said to her, "I am the resurrection, and the life.	11:25~ Jesus said to her, "I am the resurrection and the life;
8 "He who believes in Me will live, even if he dies; and everyone who lives and believes in Me will never die.	11:~25 he who believes in Me will live even if he dies, 11:26~ and everyone who lives and believes in Me will never die.
9 "Do you believe this?"	11:~26 Do you believe this?"
10 She said to Him, "Yes, Lord. I have believed that You are the Christ, the Son of God, even He who comes into the world."	11:27 She said to Him, "Yes, Lord; I have believed that You are the Christ, the Son of God, even He who comes into the world."
11 [After] [Martha] had said this, she went and secretly called her sister Mary, saying, "The Teacher is here, and is calling for you."	11:28 [When] [she] had said this, she went ~~away~~ and called Mary her sister, saying secretly, "The Teacher is here and is calling for you."
12 When [Mary] heard [this] she got up quickly, and [went] to Him.	11:29 ~~And~~ when [she] heard [it], she got up quickly and [~~was coming~~] to Him.
13 When [those] who were consoling Mary in the house saw that [she] got up quickly and went out, they followed her, supposing that she was going to the tomb, to weep there.	11:31 ~~Then~~ [the Jews] who were ~~with her~~ in the house, and consoling [her], when ~~they~~ saw that Mary got up quickly and went out, they followed her, supposing that she was going to the tomb to weep there.

1. *approximately 3.2 km*

Scene 3: Mary Goes To Meet Jesus
Bethany, *Judea*   winter / 33 CE

	John
1 Now Jesus had not yet come into the village, but was still in the place where Martha <had> met Him.	11:30 Now Jesus had not yet come into the village, but was still in the place where Martha met Him.
2 When Mary came to where Jesus was, she fell at His feet, saying, "Lord, if You had been here, my brother would not have died."	11:32 ~~Therefore~~, when Mary came where Jesus was, she ~~saw Him, and~~ fell at His feet, saying to ~~Him~~, "Lord, if You had been here, my brother would not have died."
3 When Jesus saw her weeping, and the Jews who came with her also weeping, He was deeply moved in spirit, and troubled.	11:33 When Jesus ~~therefore~~ saw her weeping, and the Jews who came with her also weeping, He was deeply moved in spirit and ~~was~~ troubled,
4 <He> [asked], "Where have you laid him?" They said to Him, "Lord, come and see."	11:34 ~~and~~ [said], "Where have you laid him?" They said to Him, "Lord, come and see."
5 Jesus wept, so the Jews were saying, "See how He loved him!"	11:35 Jesus wept. 11:36 So the Jews were saying, "See how He loved him!"
6 But some of them said, "Could not this man, who opened the eyes of the blind man, <not> also have kept [Lazarus] from dying?"	11:37 But some of them said, "Could not this man, who opened the eyes of the blind man, have kept [~~this man~~] also from dying?"

6 - THE FINAL YEAR	Scene 4: **Jesus Calls Lazarus Forth From The Tomb**
Act 6: **The Resurrection of Lazarus**	Bethany, *Judea* winter / 33 CE

*This Text is from the **Word-For-Word** Edition*

	John
1 When Jesus [arrived], He found that [Lazarus] had already been in the tomb <for> four days.	11:17 So when Jesus [came], He found that [he] had already been in the tomb four days.
2 <The tomb> was a cave, and <there> was a stone lying against it.	11:~38 Now [it] was a cave, and a stone was lying against it.
3 Being again deeply moved within, Jesus came to the tomb, <and> said, "Remove the stone."	11:38~ So Jesus, again being deeply moved within, came to the tomb. 11:39~ Jesus said, "Remove the stone."
4 Martha, the sister of the deceased, said to Him, "Lord, by this time there will be a stench, for he has been dead <for> four days."	11:~39 Martha, the sister of the deceased, said to Him, "Lord, by this time there will be a stench, for he has been dead four days."
5 Jesus said to her, "Did I not say to you that if you believe you will see the glory of God?" So they removed the stone.	11:40 Jesus said to her, "Did I not say to you that if you believe, you will see the glory of God?" 11:41~ So they removed the stone.
6 Then Jesus raised His eyes, and said, "Father, I thank You that You have heard Me.	11:~41 Then Jesus raised His eyes, and said, "Father, I thank You that You have heard Me.
7 "I [know] that You always hear Me, but because of the people standing around I said it, so that they may believe that You sent Me."	11:42 "I [knew] that You always hear Me; but because of the people standing around I said it, so that they may believe that You sent Me."
8 [After] [Jesus] had said [this], He cried out with a loud voice, "Lazarus, come forth!"	11:43 [When] [He] had said [these things], He cried out with a loud voice, "Lazarus, come forth."
9 <And> the man who had died came forth, bound hand and foot with wrappings, and a cloth was wrapped around his face.	11:44~ The man who had died came forth, bound hand and foot with wrappings, and his face was wrapped around with a cloth.
10 Jesus said to them, "Unbind him, and let him go."	11:~44 Jesus said to them, "Unbind him, and let him go."
11 Many of the Jews who [had come] to Mary saw what [Jesus] [did], and <they> believed in Him;	11:45 Therefore many of the Jews who [came] to Mary, and saw what [He] [had done], believed in Him.
12 but some of them went to the Pharisees, and told them [what] Jesus had done.	11:46 But some of them went to the Pharisees and told them [the things which] [Jesus] had done.

6 - THE FINAL YEAR

Act 6: The Resurrection of Lazarus

Scene 5: The Pharisees Plot To Kill Jesus

Jerusalem, *Judea* winter / 33 CE

	John
1 [Then] the chief priests and the Pharisees [gathered] [the] *Council*[1.] <together>, and <they> were saying, "What are we doing? For this man is performing many signs.	11:47 [~~Therefore~~] the chief priests and the Pharisees [~~convened~~] [a] council, and were saying, "What are we doing? For this man is performing many signs.
2 "If we let Him go on like this, all men will believe in Him, and <then> the Romans will come and take away both our place, and our nation."	11:48 "If we let Him go on like this, all men will believe in Him, and the Romans will come and take away both our place and our nation."
3 But one of them, Caiaphas, who was <the> High Priest that year, said to them, "You know nothing at all; nor do you take into account that it is expedient for [us] that one man die for the people, and that the whole nation not perish."	11:49 But one of them, Caiaphas, who was high priest that year, said to them, "You know nothing at all, 11:50 nor do you take into account that it is expedient for [~~you~~] that one man die for the people, and that the whole nation not perish."
4 Now he did not say this on his own initiative, but being <the> High Priest that year, he <had> prophesied that Jesus was going to die for the nation;	11:51 Now he did not say this on his own initiative, but being high priest that year, he prophesied that Jesus was going to die for the nation,
5 and not only for the nation, but in order that He might also gather together into one the children of God who are scattered abroad.	11:52 and not for the nation only, but in order that He might also gather together into one the children of God who are scattered abroad.
6 So from that day, they planned together to kill [Jesus].	11:53 So from that day ~~on~~ they planned together to kill [Him].
7 Therefore He no longer continued to walk publicly among the Jews, but <He> went away from there to a city called Ephraim, in the country near the wilderness, and He stayed there with [His] [apostles].	11:54 Therefore ~~Jesus~~ no longer continued to walk publicly among the Jews, but went away from there to the country near the wilderness, into a city called Ephraim; and there He stayed with [~~the~~] [~~disciples~~].

[1.] *Hebrew word* sanhedrin *means "sitting together" or "council"*

6 - THE FINAL YEAR Act 7: **Further Teachings**	Scene 1: **Teachings On Divorce** Judea early spring / 33 CE	Page 182 *The Gospel of Jesus Christ*

	Matthew	Mark
1 When Jesus [arrived] in the region of Judea beyond the Jordan, large crowds gathered <together> <and> followed Him again;	19:1 When Jesus had finished these words, He departed from Galilee and [came] into the region of Judea beyond the Jordan; 19:2~ and large crowds followed Him,	10:1~ Getting up, He went from there to the region of Judea and beyond the Jordan; crowds gathered around Him again,
2 and according to His custom, He once more began to teach them, and He healed them.	19:~2 and He healed them there.	10:~1 and, according to His custom, He once more began to teach them.
3 <Then> some Pharisees came to Jesus, and testing Him <they> began to question Him, asking, "Is it lawful for a man to divorce his wife, for any reason?"	19:3 Some Pharisees came to Jesus, testing Him, and asking, "Is it lawful for a man to divorce his wife for any reason at all?"	10:2 Some Pharisees came up to Jesus, testing Him, and began to question Him whether it was lawful for a man to divorce a wife.
4 He answered, and said to them, "What did Moses command you?"	19:4~ And He answered and said,	10:3 And He answered and said to them, "What did Moses command you?"
5 They said, "*Moses permitted a man to write [his wife] a certificate of divorce, and send her away.*" [1]	19:7 They said to Him, "Why then did Moses command to give [her] a certificate of divorce and send her away?"	10:4 They said, "Moses permitted a man to write a certificate of divorce and send her away."
6 Jesus said to them, "Because of your hardness of heart Moses wrote you this commandment, <which> permitted you to divorce your wives; but from the beginning, it has not been this way.	19:8 He said to them, "Because of your hardness of heart Moses permitted you to divorce your wives; but from the beginning it has not been this way.	10:5 But Jesus said to them, "Because of your hardness of heart he wrote you this commandment. 10:6~ "But
7 "Have you not read that *from the beginning of creation, God who created them made them male and female,* [2]	19:4 "Have you not read that He who created them from the beginning made them male and female,	10:~6 from the beginning of creation, God made them male and female.
8 "and said, '*For this reason a man shall leave his father and mother and be joined to his wife, and the two shall become one flesh*'? [3] So they are no longer two, but one flesh.	19:5 and said, 'For this reason a man shall leave his father and mother and be joined to his wife, and the two shall become one flesh'? 19:6~ "So they are no longer two, but one flesh.	10:7 "For this reason a man shall leave his father and mother, 10:8 and the two shall become one flesh; so they are no longer two, but one flesh.
9 "What therefore God has joined together, let no man separate."	19:~6 What therefore God has joined together, let no man separate."	10:9 "What therefore God has joined together, let no man separate."

     1. *Deuteronomy 24:1, 3*   2. *Genesis 1:27; 5:2*   3. *Genesis 2:24*

6 - THE FINAL YEAR
Act 7: **Further Teachings**

Scene 2: **Teachings On Adultery**
Judea   early spring / 33 CE

Page 183
The Unified Four Gospel Merger

	Matthew	Mark	Luke
1 In the house, [His] disciples began questioning [Jesus] about this.		10:10 In the house [the] disciples began questioning [Him] about this again.	
2 He said to them, "Everyone who divorces his wife, except for immorality, and marries another woman, commits adultery against her.	19:9 "And I say to you, whoever divorces his wife, except for immorality, and marries another woman commits adultery."	10:11 And He said to them, "Whoever divorces his wife and marries another woman commits adultery against her;	
3 "And if [a woman] divorces her husband, and marries another man, she is committing adultery.		10:12 and if [she herself] divorces her husband and marries another man, she is committing adultery."	
4 "And he who marries one who is divorced from a husband commits adultery."			16:~18 and he who marries one who is divorced from a husband commits adultery.
5 The disciples said to [Jesus], "If the relationship of [a] man with his wife is like this, it is better not to marry."	19:10 The disciples said to [Him], "If the relationship of [the] man with his wife is like this, it is better not to marry."		
6 [Jesus] said to them, "Not all men can accept this statement, but only those to whom it has been given."	19:11 But [He] said to them, "Not all men can accept this statement, but only those to whom it has been given.		

Scene 3: **A Word About Eunuchs**

	Matthew
1 <And Jesus said,> "There are eunuchs who were born that way from their mother's womb, and there are eunuchs who were made eunuchs by men,	19:12~ "For there are eunuchs who were born that way from their mother's womb; and there are eunuchs who were made eunuchs by men;
2 "and there are also eunuchs who made themselves eunuchs for the sake of the Kingdom of Heaven.	19:~12~ and there are also eunuchs who made themselves eunuchs for the sake of the kingdom of heaven.
3 "Let he who is able to accept this, accept it."	19:~12 He who is able to accept this, let him accept it."

6 - THE FINAL YEAR

Act 7: **Further Teachings**

Scene 4: **Let The Children Come To Me**

Judea   early spring / 33 CE

Page 184

A Verse-By-Verse Four Gospel Harmony

	Matthew	Mark	Luke
1 Then they were bringing some children <and> even their babies to [Jesus], so that He might touch them, and pray.	19:13~ Then some children were br~~ought~~ to [Him] so that He might ~~lay His hands on~~ them and pray.	10:13~ ~~And~~ they were bringing children to [Him] so that He might touch them;	18:15~ ~~And~~ they were bringing even their babies to [Him] so that He ~~would~~ touch them;
2 When the disciples saw it, they began rebuking them;	19:~13 ~~and~~ the disciples rebuk~~ed~~ them.	10:~13 ~~but~~ the disciples rebuk~~ed~~ them.	18:~15 ~~but~~ when the disciples saw it, they began rebuking them.
3 but when Jesus saw this, He was indignant, and <He> said to them, "Permit the children, and do not hinder them from coming to Me; for the Kingdom of Heaven belongs to such as these!	19:14 But Jesus said, "~~Let~~ the children ~~alone~~, and do not hinder them from coming to Me; for the kingdom of heaven belongs to such as these."	10:14 But when Jesus saw this, He was indignant and said to them, "Permit the children ~~to~~ come to Me; do not hinder them; for the kingdom of God belongs to such as these.	18:16 But Jesus ~~called for~~ them, saying, "Permit the children ~~to~~ come to Me, and do not hinder them, for the kingdom of ~~God~~ belongs to such as these.
4 "Truly I say to you, whoever does not receive the Kingdom of God like a child, will not enter it at all."		10:15 "Truly I say to you, whoever does not receive the kingdom of God like a child will not enter it at all."	18:17 "Truly I say to you, whoever does not receive the kingdom of God like a child will not enter it at all."
5 [Then] [Jesus] took [the young children] in His arms, and <He> began blessing them.		10:16~ [And] [He] took [them] in His arms and began blessing them,	
6 After laying His hands on them, He departed from there.	19:15 After laying His hands on them, He departed from there.	10:~16 laying His hands on them.	

6 - THE FINAL YEAR	Scene 5: **What Must I Do To Obtain Eternal Life?**		Page 185
Act 7: **Further Teachings**	Judea early spring / 33 CE		Seeing the Four Gospels as One

	Matthew	Mark	Luke
1 As [Jesus] was setting out on a journey, a <young> ruler came up and knelt before Him, and questioned Him, saying, "Good Teacher, what shall I do that I may obtain eternal life?"	19:16 ~~And~~ ~~someone~~ came ~~to Him~~ and ~~said~~, "Teacher, what ~~good thing~~ shall I do that I may obtain eternal life?"	10:17 As [He] was setting out on a journey, a ~~man~~ ran up ~~to Him~~ and knelt before Him, and ~~asked~~ Him, "Good Teacher, what shall I do ~~to inherit~~ eternal life?	18:18 A ruler questioned Him, saying, "Good Teacher, what shall I do ~~to inherit~~ eternal life?
2 Jesus said to him, "Why do you call Me good? There is only One who is good; no one is good except God alone.[1]	19:17~ ~~And~~ He said to him, "Why ~~are~~ you ~~asking~~ Me ~~about what is~~ good? There is only One who is good;	10:18 ~~And~~ Jesus said to him, "Why do you call Me good? No one is good except God alone.	18:19 ~~And~~ Jesus said to him, "Why do you call Me good? No one is good except God alone.
3 "But if you wish to enter into life, keep the commandments."	19:~17 but if you wish to enter into life, keep the commandments."		
4 He said to Him, "Which ones?"	19:18~ ~~Then~~ he said to Him, "Which ones?"		
5 Jesus said, "You know the commandments: Do not commit murder;[2]	19:18~1 ~~And~~ Jesus said, "~~You shall~~ not commit murder;	10:19 "You know the commandments, 'Do not murder,	18:20 "You know the commandments, 18:20~2 do not murder,
6 "Do not commit adultery;[3]	19:18~2 ~~You shall~~ not commit adultery;	10:19~1 do not commit adultery,	18:20~1 'Do not commit adultery,
7 "Do not steal;[4]	19:18~3 ~~shall~~ not steal;	10:19~2 do not steal,	18:20~3 do not steal,
8 "Do not bear false witness;[5]	19:~18 ~~You shall~~ not bear false witness;	10:19~3 do not bear false witness,	18:20~4 do not bear false witness,
9 "Do not defraud;[6]		10:19~4 do not defraud,	
10 "Honor your father and <your> mother;[7]	19:19~ Honor your father and mother;	10:~19 Honor your father and mother.' "	18:~20 Honor your father and mother.' "
11 "and, You shall love your neighbor as yourself."[8]	19:~19 and You shall love your neighbor as yourself."		
12 The young [ruler] said to Him, "Teacher, I have kept all these things from my youth up. What am I still lacking?	19:20 The young [~~man~~] said to Him, "All these things I have kept; what am I still lacking?"	10:20 ~~And~~ [he] said to Him, "Teacher, I have kept all these things from my youth up."	18:21 ~~And~~ [he] said, "All these things I have kept from my youth."
13 When Jesus heard this, He felt a love for him, and said to him, "One thing <that> you still lack, if you wish to be complete; go and sell all that you possess, and distribute it to the poor, and you will have treasure in Heaven;	19:21~ Jesus said to him, "If you wish to be complete, go and sell ~~your~~ possessions and ~~give~~ to the poor, and you will have treasure in heaven;	10:21~ ~~Looking at him~~, Jesus felt a love for him and said to him, "One thing you lack: go and sell all you possess and ~~give~~ to the poor, and you will have treasure in heaven;	18:22~ When Jesus heard this, He said to him, "One thing you still lack; sell all that you possess and distribute it to the poor, and you ~~shall~~ have treasure in heaven;
14 "and come, follow Me."	19:~21 and come, follow Me."	10:~21 and come, follow Me."	18:~22 and come, follow Me."
15 But when the young [ruler] heard these words he became very sad; and he went away grieving, for he was one who owned much property, <and was> extremely rich.	19:22 But when the young [~~man~~] heard ~~this statement~~, he went away grieving; for he was one who owned much property.	10:22 But ~~at~~ these words he ~~was~~ saddened, and he went away grieving, for he was one who owned much property.	18:23 But when [he] ~~had~~ heard these ~~things~~, he became very sad, for he was extremely rich.

1. 1 Samuel 2:2   2. Exodus 20:13 / Deuteronomy 5:17   3. Exodus 20:14 / Deuteronomy 5:18 / Leviticus 18:20; 20:10   4. Exodus 20:15 / Deuteronomy 5:19

5. Exodus 20:16 / Deuteronomy 5:20   6. Exodus 20:17 / Deuteronomy 5:21 / Leviticus 19:13   7. Exodus 20:12 / Deuteronomy 5:16 / Leviticus 20:9   8. Leviticus 19:18

	6 - THE FINAL YEAR	Scene 6: **It Is Hard For The Wealthy To Enter The Kingdom**		
	Act 7: **Further Teachings**	Judea early spring / 33 CE		

	Matthew	**Mark**	**Luke**
1 Jesus looked around, and said to His disciples, "How hard it is for those who are wealthy to enter the Kingdom of God!	19:23~ ~~And~~ Jesus said to His disciples,	10:23 ~~And~~ Jesus, look~~ing~~ around, said to His disciples, "How hard it ~~will be~~ for those who are wealthy to enter the kingdom of God!	18:24 ~~And~~ Jesus looked ~~at him~~ and said, "How hard it is for those who are wealthy to enter the kingdom of God!
2 "Truly I say to you, it is hard for a rich man to enter the Kingdom of Heaven."	19:~23 Truly I say to you, it is hard for a rich man to enter the kingdom of heaven.		
3 The disciples were amazed at His words, [so] Jesus said to them again, "Children, how hard it is to enter the Kingdom of God.		10:24 The disciples were amazed at His words. [But] Jesus ~~answered~~ again ~~and~~ said to them, "Children, how hard it is to enter the kingdom of God!	
4 "Again I say to you, it is easier for a camel to go through the eye of a needle, than for a rich man to enter the Kingdom of God."	19:24 "Again I say to you, it is easier for a camel to go through the eye of a needle, than for a rich man to enter the kingdom of God."	10:25 "It is easier for a camel to go through the eye of a needle than for a rich man to enter the kingdom of God."	18:25 "~~For~~ it is easier for a camel to go through the eye of a needle than for a rich man to enter the kingdom of God."
5 When the disciples heard this, they were even more astonished; and <they> said to Him, "Then who can be saved?"	19:25 When the disciples heard this, they were ~~very~~ astonished and said, "Then who can be saved?"	10:26 They were even more astonished and said to Him, "Then who can be saved?"	18:26 They ~~who~~ heard ~~it~~ said, "Then who can be saved?"
6 Looking at them, Jesus said, "With people this is impossible, but not with God, for *all things are possible with God."* [1.]	19:26 ~~And~~ looking at them Jesus said ~~to them~~, "With people this is impossible, ~~but~~ all things are possible with God."	10:27 Looking at them, Jesus said, "With people it is impossible, but not with God; for all things are possible with God."	18:27 ~~But He~~ said, "~~The things that are~~ impossible with people are possible with God."

1. Jeremiah 32:17

6 - THE FINAL YEAR
Act 7: Further Teachings
Scene 7: What Will There Be For Us?
Judea — early spring / 33 CE

#		Matthew	Mark	Luke
1	Then Peter said to [Jesus], "Behold, we have left our own homes <and> everything, and followed You; what then, will there be for us?"	19:27 Then Peter said to [Him], "Behold, we have left everything and followed You; what then will there be for us?"	10:28 Peter ~~began to~~ say to [Him], "Behold, we have left everything and followed You."	18:28 Peter said, "Behold, we have left our own homes and followed You."
2	Jesus said to them, "Truly, I say to you who have followed Me, in the regeneration, when the Son of Man will sit on His glorious throne, <then> you also shall sit upon twelve thrones, judging the twelve tribes of Israel.	19:28 ~~And~~ Jesus said to them, "Truly I say to you, ~~that you~~ who have followed Me, in the regeneration when the Son of Man will sit on His glorious throne, you also shall sit upon twelve thrones, judging the twelve tribes of Israel.	10:29~ Jesus said,	18:29~ ~~And He~~ said to them,
3	"<And> I say to you, <that> there is no one who has left house or farm, or wife or brothers or sisters, or father or mother or children, for the sake <of the> gospel of the Kingdom of God, and for My sake, who will not receive many times as much;	19:29~ ~~And every~~one who has left house~~s~~ or brothers or sisters or father or mother or children or farms for My ~~name's~~ sake, will receive many times as much,	10:~29 "~~Truly~~ I say to you, there is no one who has left house or brothers or sisters or father or mother or children or farms, for My sake and for the gospel's sake, 10:30~ ~~but that he~~ will receive ~~a hundred~~ times as much	18:29~2 "~~Truly~~ I say to you, there is no one who has left house or wife or brothers or father or mother or children for the sake of the kingdom of God, 18:30~ who will not receive many times as much
4	"now, in the present age - houses and farms, and brothers and sisters, and mothers and children, along with persecutions -		10:~30~ now in the present age, houses and brothers and sisters and mothers and children and farms, along with persecutions;	18:~30~ ~~at this~~ time
5	"and in the age to come, <they> will inherit eternal life.	19:~29 and will inherit eternal life.	10:~30 and in the age to come, eternal life.	18:~30 and in the age to come, eternal life."
6	"But many who are <the> first will be <the> last, and the last <will be> first."	19:30 "But many who are first will be last; and the last, first."	10:31 "But many who are first will be last, and the last, first."	

6 - THE FINAL YEAR
Act 7: Further Teachings

Scene 8: The Generous Landowner
Judea   early spring / 33 CE

	Matthew
1 <Jesus said,> "The Kingdom of Heaven is like a landowner who went out early in the morning to hire laborers for his vineyard.	20:1 "~~For~~ the kingdom of heaven is like a landowner who went out early in the morning to hire laborers for his vineyard.
2 "When he had agreed with the laborers for a denarius for the day, he sent them into his vineyard.	20:2 "When he had agreed with the laborers for a denarius for the day, he sent them into his vineyard.
3 "<At> about the third hour, he went out and saw others standing idle in the market place; and he said to [them], 'You also go into the vineyard, and whatever is right I will give you.' And so they went.	20:3 "~~And~~ he went out about the third hour and saw others standing idle in the market place; 20:4 and to [those] he said, 'You also go into the vineyard, and whatever is right I will give you.' And so they went.
4 "Again he went out about the sixth <hour> and the ninth hour, and did the same thing.	20:5 "Again he went out about the sixth and the ninth hour, and did the same thing.
5 "[At] about the eleventh hour, he went out and found others standing around, and he said to them, 'Why have you been standing here idle all day long?'	20:6 "[~~And~~] about the eleventh hour he went out and found others standing around; and he said to them, 'Why have you been standing here idle all day long?'
6 "They said to him, 'Because no one hired us.' He said to them, 'You too go into the vineyard.'	20:7 "They said to him, 'Because no one hired us.' He said to them, 'You go into the vineyard too.'
7 "When evening came, the vineyard owner said to his foreman, 'Call the laborers, and pay them their wages, beginning with the last group to the first.'	20:8 "When evening came, the owner ~~of the~~ vineyard said to his foreman, 'Call the laborers and pay them their wages, beginning with the last group to the first.'
8 "When those hired about the eleventh hour came, [they] each received a denarius.	20:9 "When those hired about the eleventh hour came, each [~~one~~] received a denarius.
9 "When those <who were> hired first came, they thought that they would receive more, but each of them also received a denarius.	20:10 "When those hired first came, they thought that they would receive more; but each of them also received a denarius.
10 "When they received it, they grumbled at the landowner, saying, 'These last men have worked only one hour, and you have made them equal to us who have borne the burden, and the scorching heat of the day.'	20:11 "When they received it, they grumbled at the landowner, 20:12 saying, 'These last men have worked only one hour, and you have made them equal to us who have borne the burden and the scorching heat of the day.'
11 "But he answered, and said to them, 'Friend, I am doing you no wrong. Did you not agree with me for a denarius? Take what is yours and go;	20:13 "But he answered and said to ~~one of~~ them, 'Friend, I am doing you no wrong; did you not agree with me for a denarius? 20:14~ 'Take what is yours and go,
12 "but I wish to give to this last man the same as to you.	20:~14 but I wish to give to this last man the same as to you.
13 "Is it not lawful for me to do what I wish with what is my own? Or is your eye envious because I am generous?'	20:15 'Is it not lawful for me to do what I wish with what is my own? Or is your eye envious because I am generous?'
14 "So the last shall be first, and the first last."	20:16 "So the last shall be first, and the first last."

Scene 9: The Unworthy Slaves

	Luke
1 "Which of you having a slave plowing, or tending sheep, will say to him when he has come in from the field, 'Come immediately, and sit down to eat'?	17:7 "Which of you, having a slave plowing or tending sheep, will say to him when he has come in from the field, 'Come immediately and sit down to eat'?
2 "But will he not say to him, 'Prepare something for me to eat, and properly clothe yourself, and serve me while I eat and drink; and <then> afterward you may eat and drink'?	17:8 "But will he not say to him, 'Prepare something for me to eat, and properly clothe yourself and serve me while I eat and drink; and afterward you may eat and drink'?
3 "He does not thank the slave because he did the things which were commanded, does he?	17:9 "He does not thank the slave because he did the things which were commanded, does he?
4 "So you too, when you do all the things which are commanded <of> you, say, 'We are unworthy slaves, <for> we have done only [what] we [should] have done.'"	17:10 "So you too, when you do all the things which are commanded you, say, 'We are unworthy slaves; we have done only [~~that which~~] we [~~ought to~~] have done.'"

6 - THE FINAL YEAR

Act 8: **The Road To Jerusalem**

Scene 1: **Shall We Command Fire From Heaven?**

Samaria late March / 33 CE

A Complete Account from the Four Gospels

	Luke
1 When the days were approaching for His ascension, [Jesus] was determined to go to Jerusalem, and He sent messengers ahead of Him.	9:51 When the days were approaching for His ascension, [He] was determined to go to Jerusalem; 9:52~ and He sent messengers ~~on~~ ahead of Him,
2 They went and entered a village of the Samaritans, to make arrangements for [Jesus], but [the Samaritans] did not receive Him, because He was traveling to Jerusalem.	9:~52 ~~and~~ they went and entered a village of the Samaritans to make arrangements for [Him]. 9:53 But [~~they~~] did not receive Him, because He was traveling to~~ward~~ Jerusalem.
3 When His [apostles] James and John saw this, they said, "Lord, do You want us to command fire to come down from heaven, and consume them?"	9:54 When His [~~disciples~~] James and John saw this, they said, "Lord, do You want us to command fire to come down from heaven and consume them?"
4 But [Jesus] turned and rebuked them, and said, "You do not know what kind of spirit you are of -	9:55 But [He] turned and rebuked them, {and said, "You do not know what kind of spirit you are of;
5 "for the Son of Man did not come to destroy men's lives, but to save them."	9:56~ for the Son of Man did not come to destroy men's lives, but to save them."}
6 And they went on to another village.	9:~56 And they went on to another village.

Scene 2: **The Ten Lepers of Samaria**

Samaria late March / 33 CE

	Luke
1 While on the way to Jerusalem, [Jesus] was passing [from] Galilee into Samaria.	17:11 While [He] ~~was~~ on the way to Jerusalem, He was passing [~~between~~] Samaria ~~and~~ Galilee.
2 As He entered a village, ten leprous men who stood at a distance met Him; and they raised their voices, saying, "Jesus, Master! Have mercy on us!"	17:12 As He entered a village, ten leprous men who stood at a distance met Him; 17:13 and they raised their voices, saying, "Jesus, Master, have mercy on us!"
3 When [Jesus] saw them, He said to them, "Go, and show yourselves to the priests."	17:14~ When [He] saw them, He said to them, "Go and show yourselves to the priests."
4 And as they were going, they were cleansed.	17:~14 And as they were going, they were cleansed.
5 When one of them saw that he had been healed, he [re]turned, glorifying God with a loud voice.	17:15 ~~Now~~ one of them, when he saw that he had been healed, turned [~~back~~], glorifying God with a loud voice,
6 And he <came and> fell on his face at [Jesus'] feet, <and> [gave] thanks to Him. And he was a Samaritan.	17:16 and he fell on his face at [His] feet, [~~giving~~] thanks to Him. And he was a Samaritan.
7 Jesus said, "Were there not ten cleansed? But where are the <other> nine?	17:17 ~~Then~~ Jesus ~~answered and~~ said, "Were there not ten cleansed? But the nine - where are ~~they~~?
8 "<Did> no one return to give glory to God, except this foreigner?"	17:18 "[~~Was~~] no one ~~found who~~ returned to give glory to God, except this foreigner?"
9 And [Jesus] said to him, "Stand up and go. Your faith has made you well."	17:19 And [He] said to him, "Stand up and go; your faith has made you well."

6 - THE FINAL YEAR

Act 8: **The Road To Jerusalem**

Scene 3: **What Will Happen To The Son of Man**

Samaria late March / 33 CE

Page 190

A Full Four Gospel Merged Harmony

	Matthew	Mark	Luke
1 On the road to Jerusalem, Jesus was walking ahead of them. They were amazed, and those who followed were fearful.	20:17~ As ~~Jesus was about to go up~~ to Jerusalem,	10:32~ ~~They were~~ on the road ~~going up~~ to Jerusalem, ~~and~~ Jesus was walking ~~on~~ ahead of them; ~~and~~ they were amazed, and those who followed were fearful.	
2 On the way, [Jesus] took the twelve [apostles] aside by themselves, and <He> began to tell them again what was going to happen to Him.	20:~17~ and on the way [He] took the twelve [disciples] aside by themselves,	10:~32 ~~And~~ again [He] took the twelve aside and began to tell them what was going to happen to Him,	18:31~ ~~Then~~ [He] took the twelve aside
3 He said, "Behold, we are going up to Jerusalem, and all the things which are written through the prophets about the Son of Man will be accomplished.	20:17 He said ~~to them~~, 20:18~ "Behold, we are going up to Jerusalem;	10:33~ ~~saying~~, "Behold, we are going up to Jerusalem,	18:~31 ~~and~~ said ~~to them~~, "Behold, we are going up to Jerusalem, and all things which are written through the prophets about the Son of Man will be accomplished.
4 "[He] will be delivered to the chief priests and the scribes, and they will condemn Him to death.	20:~18 and [the Son of Man] will be delivered to the chief priests and scribes, and they will condemn Him to death,	10:33~ and [the Son of Man] will be delivered to the chief priests and the scribes; and they will condemn Him to death, and	
5 "[Then] <they> will hand Him over to the Gentiles, [who] will mock and mistreat Him, and spit on Him, and scourge Him; and after they have scourged Him, they will crucify Him, and kill Him;	20:19~ [and] will hand Him over to the Gentiles ~~to~~ mock and scourge ~~and~~ crucify Him,	10:33 [and] will hand Him over to the Gentiles. 10:34~ "[~~They~~] will mock Him and spit on Him, and scourge Him and kill Him,	18:32 "~~For He~~ will ~~be~~ hand~~ed~~ over to the Gentiles, ~~and~~ will ~~be~~ mock~~ed~~ and mistreat~~ed~~ and spit ~~upon~~, 18:33~ and after they have scourged Him, they will kill Him;
6 "and on the third day He will rise again."	20:~19 and on the third day He will ~~be raised up~~."	10:~34 and ~~three~~ days ~~later~~ He will rise again."	18:~33 and the third day He will rise again."
7 But the [apostles] understood none of these things, [because] the meaning of this statement was hidden from them, and they did not [understand] the things that [He] said.			18:34 But the [~~disciples~~] understood none of these things, [and] the meaning of this statement was hidden from them, and they did not [~~comprehend~~] the things that [~~were~~] said.

6 - THE FINAL YEAR

Act 8: **The Road To Jerusalem**

Scene 4: **To Sit On My Right and On My Left**

Samaria late March / 33 CE

All of the Gospel Events in Order

	Matthew	Mark
1 Then the mother of James and John, the two sons of Zebedee, came up to Jesus with her sons, bowing down, and making a request of Him.	20:20 Then the mother of the sons of Zebedee came to Jesus with her sons, bowing down and making a request of Him,	10:35~ James and John, the two sons of Zebedee, came up to Jesus,
2 <They> [said], "Teacher, we want You to do for us whatever we ask of You."		10:~35 [saying], "Teacher, we want You to do for us whatever we ask of You."
3 He said <to them>, "What do you want Me to do for you?"	20:21~ ~~And~~ He said ~~to her~~, "What do you ~~wish~~?"	10:36 ~~And~~ He said ~~to them~~, "What do you want Me to do for you?"
4 They said, "Grant <us> that in Your Kingdom we may sit in Your glory, one on Your right, and one on Your left."	20:~21 ~~She~~ said ~~to Him~~, "~~Command~~ that in Your kingdom ~~these two sons of mine~~ may sit one on Your right and one on Your left."	10:37 They said ~~to Him~~, "Grant that we may sit one on Your right and one on Your left, in Your glory."
5 But Jesus answered, <and> said to them, "You do not know what you are asking. Are you able to drink the cup that I am about to drink; or to be baptized with the baptism with which I am baptized?"	20:22 But Jesus answered, "You do not know what you are asking. Are you able to drink the cup that I am about to drink?"	10:38 But Jesus said to them, "You do not know what you are asking. Are you able to drink the cup that I drink, or to be baptized with the baptism with which I am baptized?"
6 They said to Him, "We are able."	20:~22 They said to Him, "We are able."	10:39~ They said to Him, "We are able."
7 [So] Jesus said to them, "<Then> the cup that I drink you shall drink, and you shall be baptized with the baptism with which I am baptized.	20:23~ He said to them, "~~My~~ cup you shall drink;	10:~39 [And] Jesus said to them, "The cup that I drink you shall drink; and you shall be baptized with the baptism with which I am baptized.
8 "But to sit on My right and on My left, this is not Mine to give, but it is for those for whom it has been prepared by my Father."	20:~23 but to sit on My right and on My left, this is not Mine to give, but it is for those for whom it has been prepared by My Father."	10:40 "But to sit on My right ~~or~~ on My left, this is not Mine to give; but it is for those for whom it has been prepared."
9 Hearing this, the ten began to feel indignant with the two brothers, James and John.	20:24 ~~And~~ hearing this, the ten ~~became~~ indignant with the two brothers.	10:41 Hearing this, the ten began to feel indignant with James and John.

Scene 5: **The Greatest Is The One Who Serves**

Samaria late March / 33 CE

	Matthew	Mark
1 Jesus called them to Himself, and said to them, "You know that those who are recognized as the rulers of the Gentiles lord it over them, and their great men exercise authority over them.	20:25 ~~But~~ Jesus called them to Himself and said, the rulers of the Gentiles lord it over them, and their great men exercise authority over them.	10:42 Calling them to Himself, Jesus said to them, "You know that those who are recognized as rulers of the Gentiles lord it over them; and their great men exercise authority over them.
2 "But it is not this way among you; [for] whoever wishes to become great among you shall be your servant, and whoever wishes to be first among you, shall be [the] slave of all,	20:26 "It is not this way among you, [~~but~~] whoever wishes to become great among you shall be your servant, 20:27~ and whoever wishes to be first among you shall be [~~your~~] slave;	10:43 "But it is not this way among you, [~~but~~] whoever wishes to become great among you shall be your servant, 10:44 and whoever wishes to be first among you shall be slave of all.
3 "For even the Son of Man did not come to be served, but to serve, and to give His life <as> a ransom for many."	20:28 ~~just as~~ the Son of Man did not come to be served, but to serve, and to give His life a ransom for many."	10:45 "For even the Son of Man did not come to be served, but to serve, and to give His life a ransom for many."

6 - THE FINAL YEAR

Act 8: **The Road To Jerusalem**

Scene 6: **Jesus Restores The Sight of Bartimaeus**

Jericho, *Judea*   late March / 33 CE

Look for The Red Letter Gospel

	Matthew	Mark	Luke
1 As Jesus was approaching Jericho with His disciples, and a large crowd follow[ing] Him, a blind beggar named Bartimaeus, the son of Timaeus, was sitting by the road begging.	20:29 As ~~they were~~ leaving Jericho, a large crowd follow[ed] Him. 20:30~ ~~And~~ two blind ~~men~~ sitting by the road,	10:46 ~~Then they came to Jericho.~~ And as He was leaving Jericho with His disciples and a large crowd, a blind beggar named Bartimaeus, the son of Timaeus, was sitting by the road.	18:35 As Jesus was approaching Jericho, a blind ~~man~~ was sitting by the road begging.
2 Hearing a crowd going by, he began to inquire what this was. They told him that Jesus of Nazareth was passing by.	20:30~2 was passing by,	10:~47~ ~~the Nazarene~~,	18:36 ~~Now~~ hearing a crowd going by, he began to inquire what this was. 18:37 They told him that Jesus of Nazareth was passing by.
3 When he heard that it was Jesus, [Bartimaeus] began to cry out, <and> say, "Lord Jesus, son of David, have mercy on me!"	20:30~1 ~~hearing~~ that Jesus 20:~30 cried out, "Lord, have mercy on ~~us~~, son of David!"	10:47~ When he heard that it was Jesus 10:~47 [he] began to cry out and say, "Jesus, son of David, have mercy on me!"	18:38 And [he] ~~called~~ out, saying, "Jesus, son of David, have mercy on me!"
4 Those who led the way were sternly telling him to be quiet, but he kept crying out all the more, "Lord! Son of David! Have mercy on me!"	20:31 ~~The crowd~~ sternly ~~told them~~ to be quiet, but ~~they~~ cried out all the more, "Lord, son of David, have mercy on ~~us~~!"	10:48 ~~Many~~ were sternly telling him to be quiet, but he kept crying out all the more, "Son of David, have mercy on me!"	18:39 Those who led the way were sternly telling him to be quiet; but he kept crying out all the more, "Son of David, have mercy on me!"
5 Jesus stopped, and said, "Call him here."	20:32~ ~~And~~ Jesus stopped and call~~ed them~~,	10:49~ ~~And~~ Jesus stopped and said, "Call him here."	18:40~ ~~And~~ Jesus stopped and ~~commanded that he be brought to~~ Him;
6 So they called the blind man, saying to him, "Take courage <and> stand up, He is calling for you."		10:~49 So they called the blind man, saying to him, "Take courage, stand up! He is calling for you."	
7 Throwing aside his cloak, he jumped up and came to Jesus.		10:50 Throwing aside his cloak, he jumped up and came to Jesus.	
8 When [Bartimaeus] came near, Jesus [asked] him, "What do you want Me to do for you?"	20:~32 and said, "What do you want Me to do for you?"	10:51~ ~~And answering~~ him, Jesus ~~said~~, "What do you want Me to do for you?"	18:~40 and when [he] came near, He [questioned] him, 18:41~ "What do you want Me to do for you?"
9 The blind man said, "Lord, I want to regain my sight."	20:33 ~~They~~ said ~~to Him~~, "Lord, ~~we~~ want ~~our eyes to be opened~~."	10:~51 And the blind man said ~~to Him~~, "~~Rabboni~~, I want to regain my sight!"	18:~41 ~~And~~ he said, "Lord, I want to regain my sight!"
10 Moved with compassion, Jesus touched [his] eyes, and said to him, "Go, receive your sight. Your faith has made you well."	20:34~ Moved with compassion, Jesus touched [~~their~~] eyes;	10:52 And ~~Jesus~~ said to him, "Go; your faith has made you well."	18:42 And ~~Jesus~~ said to him, "Receive your sight; your faith has made you well."
11 Immediately [Bartimaeus] regained his sight, and <he> began following [Jesus] on the road, glorifying God.	20:~34 ~~and~~ immediately [~~they~~] regained ~~their~~ sight and followed [Him].	10:52 Immediately [~~he~~] regained his sight and began following [Him] on the road.	18:43~ Immediately [~~he~~] regained his sight and began following [Him], glorifying God;
12 When all the people saw it, they gave praise to God.			18:~43 ~~and~~ when all the people saw it, they gave praise to God.

6 - THE FINAL YEAR Act 8: **The Road To Jerusalem**	Scene 7: **The Salvation of Zaccheus** Jericho, *Judea* late March / 33 CE

The Full Gospel United from Four

	Luke
1 <As> [Jesus] was passing through Jericho, a rich, chief tax collector name[d] Zaccheus was trying to see who Jesus was, [but] <he> was unable <to> because of the crowd, <and> [because] he was small in stature.	*19:1* [He] ~~entered~~ Jericho ~~and~~ was passing through. *19:2* ~~And there was a man called by the~~ name ~~of~~ Zaccheus; ~~he was~~ a chief tax collector ~~and he was~~ rich. *19:3* ~~Zaccheus~~ was trying to see who Jesus was, [and] was unable because of the crowd, [~~for~~] he was small in stature.
2 So he ran ahead, and climbed up into a sycamore tree in order to see [Jesus], [who] was about to pass [by] that way.	*19:4* So he ran ~~on~~ ahead and climbed up into a sycamore tree in order to see [Him], ~~for~~ [He] was about to pass [through] that way.
3 When Jesus came to the place, He looked up, and said to him, "Zaccheus, hurry and come down, for today I must stay at your house."	*19:5* When Jesus came to the place, He looked up and said to him, "Zaccheus, hurry and come down, for today I must stay at your house."
4 [Zaccheus] hurried and came down, and <he> gladly received [Jesus].	*19:6* ~~And~~ [he] hurried and came down and received [~~Him~~] gladly.
5 When [the crowd] saw it, they all began to grumble, saying, "He has gone to be the guest of a man who is a sinner."	*19:7* When [~~they~~] saw it, they all began to grumble, saying, "He has gone to be the guest of a man who is a sinner."
6 Zaccheus stopped, and said to the Lord, "Behold Lord, half of my possessions I will give to the poor;	*19:8~* Zaccheus stopped and said to the Lord, "Behold, Lord, half of my possessions I will give to the poor,
7 "and if I have defrauded anyone of anything, I will give <them> back four times as much."	*19:~8* and if I have defrauded anyone of anything, I will give back four times as much."
8 Jesus said to him, "Today salvation has come to this house, because he is also a son of Abraham;	*19:9* ~~And~~ Jesus said to him, "Today salvation has come to this house, because he, [~~too~~], is a son of Abraham.
9 "for the Son of Man has come to seek and to save that which was lost."	*19:10* For the Son of Man has come to seek and to save that which was lost."

6 - THE FINAL YEAR	Scene 8: **The Parable of The Good and Faithful Servants**	Page 194
Act 8: **The Road To Jerusalem**	Judea late March / 33 CE	A Complete Four Gospel Harmony

	Matthew	Luke
1 While they were listening to these things, Jesus [told] <them> a parable, because He was near Jerusalem, and they supposed that the Kingdom of God was going to appear immediately.		19:11 While they were listening to these things, Jesus ~~went on to~~ [tell] a parable, because He was near Jerusalem, and they supposed that the kingdom of God was going to appear immediately.
2 He said, "It is just like a nobleman about to go on a journey to a distant country, to receive a Kingdom for himself, and then return.	25:14~ "~~For~~ it is just like a man about to go on a journey,	19:12 ~~So~~ He said, "A nobleman ~~went~~ to a distant country to receive a kingdom for himself, and then return.
3 "And he called his slaves, and entrusted his possessions to them.	25:~14 ~~who~~ called his ~~own~~ slaves and entrusted his possessions to them.	19:13~ "And he called ~~ten of~~ his slaves, and
4 "To one <of them> he gave five <gold> [coins], <and> to another <he gave> two <gold coins>, and to another one <coin>, each according to his ability.	25:15~ "To one he gave five [talents], to another, two, and to another, one, each according to his ~~own~~ ability;	19:~13~ gave ~~them ten~~ [minas]
5 "And <he> said to them, 'Do business with this until I come back,' and went on his journey.	25:~15 and ~~he~~ went on his journey.	19:~13 and said to them, 'Do business with this until I come back.'
6 "But his citizens hated him, and <they> sent a delegation after him, saying, 'We do not want this man to reign over us!'		19:14 "But his citizens hated him and sent a delegation after him, saying, 'We do not want this man to reign over us.'
7 "Immediately the one who had received the five <gold> [coins] went and traded with them, and <he> gained five more <gold> [coins].	25:16 "Immediately the one who had received the five [talents] went and traded with them, and gained five more [talents].	
8 "In the same manner, the one who had received the two <gold> [coins] gained two more.	25:17 "In the same manner the one who had received the two [talents] gained two more.	
9 "But he who received the one [coin] went away, and <he> dug a hole in the ground, and hid his master's money.	25:18 "But he who received the one [talents] went away, and dug a hole in the ground and hid his master's money.	
10 "After a long time, the master of those slaves receiv[ed] the kingdom, and returned.	25:19~ "~~Now~~ after a long time the master of those slaves ~~came~~ and	19:15~ "~~When~~ he returned, ~~after~~ receiv[ing] the kingdom,
11 "<Then> he ordered that [the] slaves to whom he had given the money be called to him, so that he might know what business they had done, <and to> settle accounts with them.	25:~19 settled accounts with them.	19:~15 he ordered that [these] slaves, to whom he had given the money, be called to him so that he might know what business they had done.
12 "The one who had received the five <gold> [coins] came, and brought five more <gold> [coins], saying, 'Master, you entrusted five <gold> [coins] to me, <and> see, I have gained five more [coins].'	25:20 "The one who had received the five [talents] came ~~up~~ and brought five more [talents], saying, 'Master, you entrusted five [talents] to me. See, I have gained five more [talents].'	19:16 "The ~~first appeared~~ saying, 'Master, ~~your~~ [mina] ~~has made ten minas~~ more.'
13 "His master said to him, 'Well done, good and faithful slave! Because you have been faithful with a few little things, I will put you in charge of many things; you are to be in authority over ten cities. Enter into the joy of your master!'	25:21 "His master said to him, 'Well done, good and faithful slave. You ~~were~~ faithful with a few things, I will put you in charge of many things; enter into the joy of your master.'	19:17 "~~And he~~ said to him, 'Well done, good slave, because you have been faithful ~~in~~ a ~~very~~ little thing, you are to be in authority over ten cities.'
14 "The second [slave], who had received the two <gold> [coins] came and said, 'Master, you entrusted two <gold> [coins] to me. See, I have gained two more [coins]!'	25:22 "~~Also the~~ [one] who had received the two [talents] came ~~up~~ and said, 'Master, you entrusted two [talents] to me. See I have gained two more [talents].'	19:18 "The second came, sa~~ying~~, '~~Your~~ [mina], master, ha~~s made five minas~~.'

continued >

6 - THE FINAL YEAR

Act 8: **The Road To Jerusalem**

Scene 8: **The Parable of The Good and Faithful Servants**
continued

Page 195

The Gospel Story of Jesus Christ

	Matthew	Luke
15 "His master said to him, 'Well done, good and faithful slave! You were faithful with a few things, I will put you in charge of many things; you are to be over five cities. Enter into the joy of your master!'	25:23 "His master said to him, 'Well done, good and faithful slave. You were faithful with a few things, I will put you in charge of many things; enter into the joy of your master.'	19:19 ~~And he~~ said to him ~~also~~, '~~And~~ you are to be over five cities.'
16 "[When] the one who had received the one <gold> [coin] came, <he> said, 'Master, I knew you to be a hard <and> exacting man; you reap what you did not sow, and gather where you did not lay down; I knew you to be a hard man and I was afraid of you, and <so I> hid your [money] in the ground.	25:24 "[And] the one ~~also~~ who had received the one [talent] came ~~up and~~ said, 'Master, I knew you to be a hard man, ~~reaping~~ where you did not sow and gathering where you ~~scattered no seed~~. 25:25~ And I was afraid, and ~~went away and~~ hid your [talent] in the ground.	19:20~ "~~Another~~ came, ~~saying~~, 'Master, 19:21 ~~for~~ I was afraid of you, ~~because~~ you ~~are an~~ exacting man; you ~~take up~~ what you did not lay down ~~and~~ reap what you did not sow.'
17 "See, you have what is yours. Here is your [coin], which I kept [hidden] in a handkerchief.'	25:~25 See, you have what is yours.'	19:~20 here is your [mina], which I kept [~~put away~~] in a handkerchief;
18 "But his master answered, and said to him, 'By your own words I will judge you, wicked, lazy, <and> worthless slave!	25:26~ "But his master answered and said to him, 'You wicked, lazy slave,	19:22~ "~~He~~ said to him, 'By your own words I will judge you, you worthless slave.
19 '[If] you knew that I am an exacting man, reaping where I did not sow, and taking up what I did not lay down, then you [should] have put my money in the bank, and on my arrival I would have received my money back with interest.'	25:~26 you knew that I reap where I did not sow and ~~gather where~~ I ~~scattered no seed~~. 25:27 'Then you [~~ought to~~] have put my money in the bank, and on my arrival I would have received my money back with interest.	19:~22 [Did] you ~~know~~ that I am an exacting man, taking up what I did not lay down and reaping ~~what~~ I did not sow? 19:23 'Then ~~why did~~ you ~~not~~ put my money in the bank, and ~~having come~~, I would have ~~collected it~~ with interest?'
20 "Then he said to the bystanders, 'Take the <gold> [coin] away from him, and give it to the one who has the ten [coins].'	25:28 'Therefore take away the [talent] from him, and give it to the one who has the ten [talents].'	19:24 "Then he said to the bystanders, 'Take the [mina] away from him and give it to the one who has the ten [minas].'
21 "They said to him, '<But> master, he has ten <gold> [coins] already.'		19:25 "~~And~~ they said to him, 'Master, he has ten [minas] already.'
22 "<But He said,> 'I tell you that to everyone who has, more shall be given, and he will have an abundance.	25:29~ ~~For~~ to everyone who has, more shall be given, and he will have an abundance;	19:26~ "I tell you that to everyone who has, more shall be given,
23 "But from the one who does not have, even what he does have shall be taken away <from him>.	25:~29 but from the one who does not have, even what he does have shall be taken away.	19:~26 but from the one who does not have, even what he does have shall be taken away.
24 "Throw [that] worthless slave out into the outer darkness; in that place there will be weeping, and gnashing of teeth.	25:30 "Throw out [the] worthless slave into the outer darkness; in that place there will be weeping and gnashing of teeth.	
25 "[And] these enemies of mine, who did not want me to reign over them, bring them here, and slay them in my presence.' "		19:27 "[~~But~~] these enemies of mine, who did not want me to reign over them, bring them here and slay them in my presence."
26 After [Jesus] said these things, He [continued] on to Jerusalem.		19:28 After [He] ~~had~~ said these things, He [~~was going~~] on ~~ahead, going up~~ to Jerusalem.

6 - THE FINAL YEAR

Act 9: Anointed For Burial

Scene 1: Mary Anoints Jesus With Perfume
Bethany, *Judea* Saturday evening, March 28th / 33 CE

	Matthew	Mark	John
1 Now the Passover was near, and many [from] the country went up to Jerusalem to purify themselves before the [feast].			11:55 Now the Passover ~~of the Jews~~ was near, and many went up to Jerusalem [~~out of~~] the country before the [~~Passover~~] to purify themselves.
2 They were [looking] for Jesus, and were saying to one another as they stood in the Temple, "What do you think? Will He come to the feast at all?"			11:56 ~~So~~ they were [~~seeking~~] for Jesus, and were saying to one another as they stood in the temple, "What do you think; ~~that~~ He will ~~not~~ come to the feast at all?
3 Now the chief priests and the Pharisees had given orders, that if anyone knew where [Jesus] was he was to report it, so that they might seize Him.			11:57 Now the chief priests and the Pharisees had given orders that if anyone knew where [~~He~~] was, he was to report it, so that they might seize Him.
4 Jesus therefore, six days before the Passover, came to Bethany where Lazarus was, whom [He] had raised from the dead.			12:1 Jesus, therefore, six days before the Passover, came to Bethany where Lazarus was, whom [~~Jesus~~] had raised from the dead.
5 While Jesus was in Bethany, they made a supper <for> Him at the home of Simon the leper.	26:6 ~~Now when~~ Jesus was in Bethany, at the home of Simon the leper,	14:3~ While ~~He~~ was in Bethany at the home of Simon the leper,	12:2~ ~~So~~ they made Him a supper ~~there~~,
6 Martha was serving, and Lazarus was one of those reclining at the table with Him.		14:~3~ ~~and~~ reclining at the table,	12:~2 and Martha was serving; ~~but~~ Lazarus was one of those reclining at the table with Him.
7 <Then> Mary came to [Jesus] with an alabaster vial <of> a pound of very costly perfume of pure nard; and she broke the vial, and poured it over His head as He reclined at the table.	26:7 ~~a woman~~ came to [Him] with an alabaster vial of very costly perfume, and she poured it ~~on~~ His head as He reclined at the table.	14:~3 ~~there~~ came ~~a woman~~ with an alabaster vial of very costly perfume of pure nard; and she broke the vial and poured it over His head.	12:3~ Mary ~~then took~~ a pound of very costly perfume of pure nard,
8 [Then] <she> anointed [His] feet, and wiped His feet with her hair; and the house was filled with the fragrance of the perfume.			12:~3 [~~and~~] anointed ~~the~~ feet [~~of Jesus~~] and wiped His feet with her hair; and the house was filled with the fragrance of the perfume.
			11:2~ ~~It was the Mary who anointed the Lord with ointment, and wiped His feet with her hair,~~

6 - THE FINAL YEAR

Act 9: Anointed For Burial

Scene 2: The Disciples Question The Waste
Bethany, *Judea* Saturday evening, March 28th / 33 CE

	Matthew	Mark	John
1 When some <of> the [apostles] saw this, they were indignant, and said to one another, "Why has this perfume been wasted, for [it] might have been sold for a high price?" And they were scolding her.	26:8 But the [disciples] were indignant when they saw this, and said, "Why this waste? 26:9~ "For [this perfume] might have been sold for a high price	14:4 But some were indignantly remarking to one another, "Why has this perfume been wasted? 14:5~ "For [this perfume] might have been sold for 14:~5 And they were scolding her.	
2 Judas Iscariot, [the] [apostle] who was intending to betray [Jesus], said, "Why was this perfume not sold for over three hundred denarii, and the money given to the poor?"	26:~9 and the money given to the poor."	14:~5~ over three hundred denarii, and the money given to the poor."	12:4 Judas Iscariot, [one of His] [disciples], who was intending to betray [Him], said, 12:5 "Why was this perfume not sold for three hundred denarii and given to poor people?"
3 Now he said this not because he was concerned about the poor <people>, but because he was a thief, and as he had the money box, he used to pilfer what was put into it.			12:6 Now he said this, not because he was concerned about the poor, but because he was a thief, and as he had the money box, he used to pilfer what was put into it.
4 But Jesus, aware of this, said to them, "[Leave] her alone, [and] [let] [her] keep it.	26:10~ But Jesus, aware of this, said to them,	14:6~ But Jesus said, "[Let] her alone;	12:7~ Therefore Jesus said, "[Let] her alone, [so that] [she] [may] keep it
5 "Why do you bother the woman? For she has done a good deed to Me.	6:~10 "Why do you bother the woman? For she has done a good deed to Me.	14:~6 why do you bother her? She has done a good deed to Me.	
6 "For *you always have the poor with you,*[1] and whenever you wish you can do good to them; but you do not always have Me.	26:11 "For you always have the poor with you; but you do not always have Me.	14:7 "For you always have the poor with you, and whenever you wish you can do good to them; but you do not always have Me.	12:8 "For you always have the poor with you, but you do not always have Me."
7 "She has done what she could, for when she poured this perfume she anointed My body, to prepare Me beforehand, for the day of My burial.	26:12 "For when she poured this perfume on My body, she did it to prepare Me for burial.	14:8 "She has done what she could; she has anointed My body beforehand for the burial.	12:~7 for the day of My burial.
8 "Truly I say to you, wherever this gospel is preached in the whole world, what this woman has done will also be spoken of, in memory of her."	26:13 "Truly I say to you, wherever this gospel is preached in the whole world, what this woman has done will also be spoken of in memory of her."	14:9 "Truly I say to you, wherever the gospel is preached in the whole world, what this woman has done will also be spoken of in memory of her."	
9 <When> the large crowd learned that [Jesus] was there, they came not only for [His] sake, but <so> that they might also see Lazarus, whom He <had> raised from the dead.			12:9 The large crowd of the Jews then learned that [He] was there; and they came, not for [Jesus'] sake only, but that they might also see Lazarus, whom He raised from the dead.
10 [So] the chief priests planned to also put Lazarus to death, because on account of him many of the Jews were going away, and believing in Jesus.			12:10 [But] the chief priests planned to put Lazarus to death also; 12:11 because on account of him many of the Jews were going away and were believing in Jesus.

1. *Deuteronomy 15:11*

CHAPTER 7
THE FINAL WEEK

Events that occurred during the Final Week of The Life and Ministry of Jesus Christ.

Act 1 - Sunday - Arrival In Jerusalem

	Page
Scene 1 The Lord Has Need of Your Donkey	200
2 Jesus Rides On The Colt	201
3 The Approach To Jerusalem	201
4 Hosanna, To The Son of David!	202
5 Jesus Weeps For Jerusalem	203
6 Jesus Enters Jerusalem	203
7 Jesus Cleanses The Temple, The Final Time	204
8 Healing In The Temple	204

Act 2 - Monday

	Page
Scene 1 Jesus Curses A Fig Tree	205
2 Who Gave You This Authority?	206
3 Who Did The Will of His Father?	207
4 The Parable of The Evil Vine-Growers	208
5 To Serve Me, You Must Follow Me	209
6 A Voice From Heaven	210
7 Believe In The Light	210
8 Believe In Me, and The One Who Sent Me	211

Act 3 - Tuesday

	Page
Scene 1 Be Prepared For The Wedding Feast	212
2 The Pharisees Plot To Trap Jesus	213
3 Is It Lawful To Pay Taxes To Caesar?	213
4 In The Next Life, Whose Wife Will She Be?	214
5 The Greatest Commandment	215

Act 4 - Wednesday - Woe to The Pharisees

	Page
Scene 1 How Is The Christ The Son of David?	216
2 Beware Of The Scribes and The Pharisees	217
3 The Hypocrisy Of The Scribes and The Pharisees	218
4 First, Clean The Inside of The Cup	219
5 You Shed The Blood of The Prophets	219
6 A Second Lament For Jerusalem	220
7 The Greatest Contributor To The Treasury	220

Act 5 - Wednesday - The End of The Age

	Page
Scene 1 The Temple Will Be Destroyed	221
2 The Signs of The End of The Age	222
3 Your Testimony When They Persecute You	223
4 You Will Be Hated Because Of My Name	223
5 Do Not Turn Back!	224
6 False Christs Will Arise	225
7 Signs In The Sun, Moon and Stars	226

Act 6 - Wednesday - The Return

	Page
Scene 1 The Parable of The Fig Tree	227
2 One Will Be Taken, and The Other Will Be Left	228
3 Be On The Alert!	229
4 Be Dressed In Readiness	230
5 The Lamps of The Ten Virgins	231
6 Separating The Sheep From The Goats	232
7 Judas Plots With The Jews To Betray Jesus	233

Act 7 - Thursday - The Last Supper

	Page
Scene 1 Preparing The Venue	234
2 The Last Supper Begins	235
3 Jesus Washes His Apostles' Feet	236
4 One Of You Will Betray Me	237
5 Judas Is Revealed	238
6 The Blood of The New Covenant	239
7 My New Commandment: Love One Another	239
8 Peter, You Will Deny Me Three Times	240
9 Two Swords Are Enough	241

Act 8 - The Holy Spirit and The Father

	Page
Scene 1 I Am The Way, and The Truth, and The Life	242
2 The Holy Spirit Helper	243
3 I Go Away, and I Will Come To You	244
4 Abide In My Love, and Bear Fruit	244
5 My Commandment Again: Love One Another	245
6 The World Hates Me and My Father	245
7 More About The Holy Spirit of Truth	246
8 I Am Going To The Father	247
9 Jesus Prays To The Father	248

MAP OF JERUSALEM

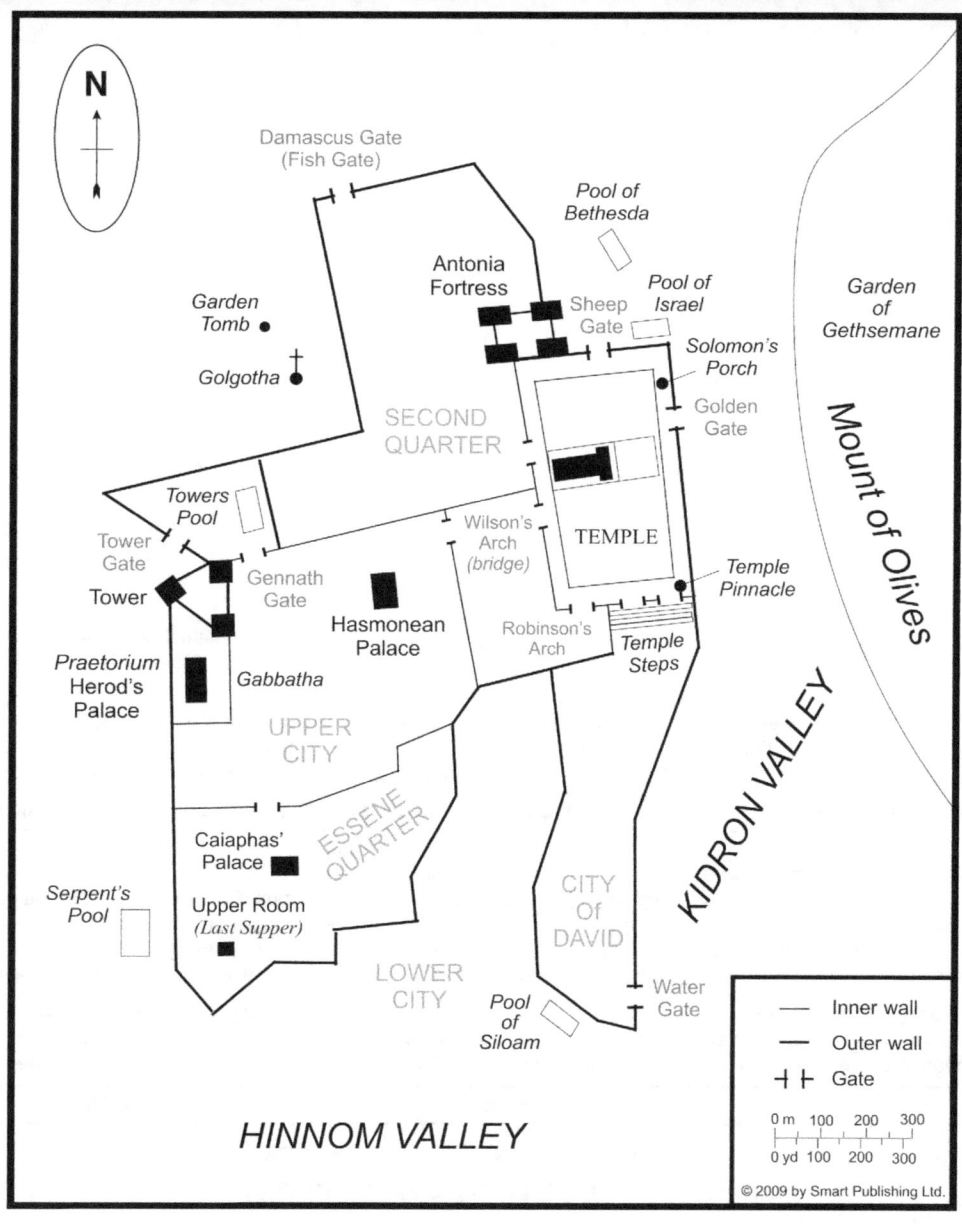

7 - THE FINAL WEEK
Act 1: Sunday - Arrival In Jerusalem

Scene 1: The Lord Has Need of Your Donkey
Bethphage, *Judea* Sunday, March 29th / 33 CE

Verse-By-Verse Edition

	Matthew	Mark	Luke	John
1	The next day, they approached Jerusalem <from> Bethany, and [came] to Bethphage, near the Mount of Olives.	21:1~ ~~When~~ they ~~had~~ approached Jerusalem and [~~had come~~] to Bethphage, ~~at~~ the Mount of Olives,	11:1~ ~~As~~ they approached Jerusalem, ~~at~~ Bethphage ~~and~~ Bethany, near the Mount of Olives,	19:29~ ~~When~~ He approached Bethphage ~~and~~ Bethany, near the mount ~~that is called~~ Olivet	12:12~ ~~On~~ the next day
2	Jesus sent two of His [apostles], and said to them, "Go into the village ahead of you; and immediately as you enter you will find a donkey tied there, and a colt with her, on which no one has ever yet sat.	21:~1 ~~then~~ Jesus sent two [~~disciples~~], 21:2~ ~~saying~~ to them, "Go into the village ~~opposite~~ you, and immediately you will find a donkey tied there and a colt with her;	11:~1 He sent two of His [~~disciples~~], 11:2~ and said to them, "Go into the village ~~opposite~~ you, and immediately as you enter ~~it~~ you will find a ~~colt~~ tied there, on which no one yet has ever sat;	19:~29 ~~He~~ sent two of ~~the~~ [~~disciples~~], 19:30~ ~~saying~~, "Go into the village ahead of you; there, as you enter, you will find a ~~colt~~ tied on which no one yet has ever sat;	
3	"Untie it, and bring it here to Me.	21:~2 untie ~~them~~ and bring ~~them~~ to Me.	11:~2 untie it and bring it here.	19:~30 untie it and bring it here.	
4	"<And> if anyone asks you, 'Why are you untying it?' you shall say, 'The Lord has need of it,' and he will immediately send it back here."	21:3 "If anyone ~~says anything to~~ you, you shall say, 'The Lord has need of ~~them~~,' and immediately he will send ~~them~~."	11:3 "If anyone ~~says to~~ you, 'Why are you ~~doing this~~?' you say, 'The Lord has need of it'; and immediately he will send it back here."	19:31 "If anyone asks you, 'Why are you untying it?' you shall say, 'The Lord has need of it.' "	
5	The <two> [apostles] went and did just as Jesus had instructed them.	21:6 The [~~disciples~~] went and did just as Jesus had instructed them,			

7 — THE FINAL WEEK

Act 1: Sunday - Arrival In Jerusalem

Scene 2: Jesus Rides On The Colt

Bethphage, *Judea* Sunday, March 29th / 33 CE

The Four Gospels Harmoniously Unified

	Matthew	Mark	Luke	John
1 So those who were sent went, and <they> found a colt outside in the street, tied at the door just as [Jesus] had told them, and they untied it.		11:4 They went ~~away~~ and found a colt tied at the door, outside in the street; and they untied it.	19:32 So those who were sent ~~away~~ and found ~~it~~ just as [He] had told them.	
2 As they were untying the colt, its owners said to them, "What are you doing? Why are you untying the colt?"		11:5 ~~Some of the bystanders were~~ sa~~ying~~ to them, "What are you doing, untying the colt?	19:33 As they were untying the colt, its owners said to them, "Why are you untying the colt?"	
3 [The apostles] spoke to them just as Jesus had told them, <and> said, "The Lord has need of it;" and they gave them permission.		11:6 ~~They~~ spoke to them just as Jesus had told them, and they gave them permission.	19:34 ~~They~~ said, "The Lord has need of it."	
4 <So> they brought the young donkey to Jesus, and they laid their coats on it, and He sat on it.	21:7 ~~and~~ brought the donkey ~~and the colt~~, and laid their coats on ~~them~~; and He sat on ~~the coats~~.	11:7 They brought the ~~colt~~ to Jesus and ~~put~~ their coats on it; and He sat on it.	19:35 They brought ~~it~~ to Jesus, and they ~~threw~~ their coats on ~~the colt~~ and ~~put Jesus~~ on it.	12:14~ Jesus, ~~finding~~ a young donkey, sat on it;
5 This took place to fulfill what was spoken through the prophets, as it is written: "Say to the daughter of Zion; 'Fear not,[1] behold, your King is coming to you, gentle, and mounted on a donkey, even on a colt, the foal of a beast of burden.' "[2]	21:4 This took place to fulfill what was spoken through the prophet: 21:5 "Say to the daughter of Zion, 'Behold your King is coming to you, Gentle, and mounted on a donkey, even on a colt, the foal of a beast of burden.' "			12:~14 as it is written, 12:15 "Fear not, daughter of Zion; behold, your King is coming, ~~seat~~ed on a donkey~~'s~~ colt."

1. 1. Isaiah 62:11   2. Zechariah 9:9

Scene 3: The Approach To Jerusalem

Bethphage, *Judea* Sunday, March 29th / 33 CE

	Matthew	Mark	Luke	John
1 When the large crowd who had come to the feast heard that Jesus was coming to Jerusalem, <they> went out to meet Him.				12:~12 the large crowd who had come to the feast, when ~~they~~ heard that Jesus was coming to Jerusalem, 12:13~1 ~~and~~ went out to meet Him,
2 As He was going, many [in] the crowd were spreading their coats on the road, and *others took leafy branches which they had cut from the palm trees,*[1] and <they> spread them [on] the road.	21:8 ~~Most [of]~~ the crowd spread their coats ~~in~~ the road, and others ~~were~~ cut~~ting~~ branches from the trees and spread~~ing~~ them [in] the road.	11:8 ~~And~~ many spread their coats ~~in~~ the road, and others spread leafy branches which they had cut from the ~~fields~~.	19:36 As He was going, ~~they~~ were spreading their coats on the road.	12:13~ took ~~the~~ branches ~~of~~ the palm trees

1. Leviticus 23:40

7 – THE FINAL WEEK

Act 1: Sunday –
Arrival In Jerusalem

Scene 4: Hosanna, To The Son of David!

Bethphage, *Judea*   Sunday, March 29th / 33 CE

Page 202

Look for the Word-For-Word Edition

	Matthew	Mark	Luke	John
1 As [Jesus] was approaching near the descent of the Mount of Olives, the whole crowd of [His] disciples began to praise God joyfully with a loud voice, for all the miracles which they had seen.			19:37 As ~~soon as~~ [He] was approaching, near the descent of the Mount of Olives, the whole crowd of [~~the~~] disciples began to praise God joyfully with a loud voice for all the miracles which they had seen,	
2 Those who went ahead of Him, and those who followed, began to shout, "*Hosanna*,[1.] to the son of David!	21:9~ ~~The crowds going~~ ahead of Him, and those who followed, ~~were~~ shout~~ing~~, "Hosanna to the Son of David;	11:9~ Those who went ~~in front~~ and those who followed ~~were~~ shout~~ing~~: "Hosanna!	19:38~ shout~~ing~~:	12:13[13~2] ~~and~~ began to shout, Hosanna!
3 "*Blessed is He who comes in the Name of the Lord*,[2.] even the King of Israel!	21:~9~ blessed is He who comes in the name of the Lord;	11:~9 Blessed is He who comes in the name of the Lord;	19:~38~ "Blessed is ~~the King~~ who comes in the name of the Lord;	12:~13 Blessed is He who comes in the name of the Lord, even the King of Israel.
4 "Blessed is the coming kingdom of our father David!		11:10~ Blessed is the coming kingdom of our father David;		
5 "Peace in Heaven, and Hosanna in the highest!"	21:~9 Hosanna in the highest!"	11:~10 Hosanna in the highest!"	19:~38 peace in heaven and ~~glory~~ in the highest!"	
6 Some of the Pharisees in the crowd said to [Jesus], "Teacher, rebuke Your disciples!"			19:39 Some of the Pharisees in the crowd said to [~~Him~~], "Teacher, rebuke Your disciples."	
7 But [He] answered, "I tell you, if these become silent, <then> *the stones will cry out!*"[3.]			19:40 But [~~Jesus~~] answered, "I tell you, if these become silent, the stones will cry out!"	
8 These things His disciples did not understand at first, but when Jesus was glorified then they remembered that these things were written of Him, and that they had done these things to Him.				12:16 These things His disciples did not understand at ~~the~~ first; but when Jesus was glorified, then they remembered that these things were written of Him, and that they had done these things to Him.
9 So the people who were with [Jesus] when He called Lazarus out of the tomb, and raised him from the dead, continued to testify about Him.				12:17 So the people, who were with [~~Him~~] when He called Lazarus out of the tomb and raised him from the dead, continued to testify about Him.
10 For this reason also the people went [to] [meet] Him, because they heard that He had performed this sign.				12:18 For this reason also the people went [~~and~~] [met] Him, because they heard that He had performed this sign.
11 So the Pharisees said to one another, "You see that you are not doing any good; look, the <whole> world has gone after Him."				12:19 So the Pharisees said to one another, "You see that you are not doing any good; look, the world has gone after Him."

1. *means: save / rescue / Savior*   2. *Psalm 118:26*   3. *(Habakkuk 2:11)*

7 - THE FINAL WEEK
Act 1: **Sunday -
Arrival In Jerusalem**

Scene 5: **Jesus Weeps For Jerusalem**

Bethphage, *Judea*   Sunday, March 29th / 33 CE

A United Gospel Story

	Luke
1 [As] [Jesus] approached Jerusalem and saw the city, He wept over it, saying, "If [only] you had known in this day the things which make for peace. But now they have been hidden from your eyes.	19:41 [When] [He] approached Jerusalem, He saw the city and wept over it, 19:42 saying, "If you had known in this day, [even] you, the things which make for peace! But now they have been hidden from your eyes.
2 "For the days will come upon you, when your enemies will throw up a barricade against you, and surround you, and hem you in on every side;	19:43 "For the days will come upon you when your enemies will throw up a barricade against you, and surround you and hem you in on every side,
3 "and they will level you to the ground, and your children within you; and they will not leave in you one stone upon another,	19:44~ and they will level you to the ground and your children within you, and they will not leave in you one stone upon another,
4 "because you did not recognize the time of your visitation."	19:~44 because you did not recognize the time of your visitation."

Scene 6: **Jesus Enters Jerusalem**

Jerusalem, *Judea*   Sunday, March 29th / 33 CE

	Matthew	Mark
1 When they came to Jerusalem, Jesus entered [the city]; <and> all the [people] [were] stirred, <and> saying, "Who is this?"	21:10 When He had entered Jerusalem, all the [city] [was] stirred, saying, "Who is this?"	11:11~ Jesus entered [Jerusalem] 11:15~ Then they came to Jerusalem.
2 And the crowds were saying, "This is the Prophet Jesus, from Nazareth in Galilee."	21:11 And the crowds were saying, "This is the prophet Jesus, from Nazareth in Galilee."	

7 - THE FINAL WEEK
Act 1: Sunday - Arrival In Jerusalem

Scene 7: Jesus Cleanses The Temple, The Final Time
The Temple, Jerusalem, *Judea* — Sunday, March 29th / 33 CE

The Four Gospels United as One — Page 204

	Matthew	Mark	Luke
		11:~11~ ~~and came into the temple~~;	
1 Jesus entered the Temple, and began to drive out all those who were buying and selling in the Temple.	*21:12~* ~~And~~ Jesus entered the temple and ~~drove~~ out all those who were buying and selling in the temple,	*11:~15~* ~~And~~ He entered the temple and began to drive out those who were buying and selling in the temple,	*19:45* Jesus entered the temple and began to drive out those who were selling.
2 <He> overturned the tables of the money changers, and the seats of those who were selling doves; and He would not permit anyone to carry merchandise through the Temple.	*21:~12* ~~and~~ overturned the tables of the money changers and the seats of those who were selling doves.	*11:~15* ~~and~~ overturned the tables of the money changers and the seats of those who were selling doves; *11:16* and He would not permit anyone to carry merchandise through the temple.	
3 [Then] [Jesus] began to teach, and said to them, "It is written, '*My house shall be called a house of prayer for all the nations*',[1.] but *you have made it a robbers' den!*"[2.]	*21:13* [And] [He] said to them, "It is written, 'My house shall be called a house of prayer for all the nations'; but ~~you are~~ making it a robbers' den."	*11:17* [And] [He] began to teach and ~~say~~ to them, "Is it ~~not~~ written, 'My house shall be called a house of prayer for all the nations'? But you have made it a robbers' den."	*19:46* ~~saying~~ to them, "It is written, '~~And~~ My house shall be a house of prayer,' but you have made it a robbers' den."
4 <When> the chief priests and the scribes heard this, <they> began seeking how to destroy Him;[3.] [but] they were afraid of Him, for the whole crowd was astonished at His teaching.		*11:18* The chief priests and the scribes heard this, ~~and~~ began seeking how to destroy Him; [for] they were afraid of Him, for the whole crowd was astonished at His teaching.	

1. Isaiah 56:7   2. Jeremiah 7:11   3. Psalm 2:2

Scene 8: Healing In The Temple
The Temple, Jerusalem, *Judea* — Sunday, March 29th / 33 CE

	Matthew	Mark
1 The blind and the lame came to [Jesus] in the Temple, and He healed them.	*21:14* ~~And~~ the blind and the lame came to [~~Him~~] in the temple, and He healed them.	
2 But when the chief priests and the scribes saw the wonderful things that He had done, and the children in the Temple who were shouting, "Hosanna to the Son of David!" they became indignant, and said to Him, "Do You hear what these children are saying?"	*21:15* But when the chief priests and the scribes saw the wonderful things that He had done, and the children who were shouting in the temple, "Hosanna to the Son of David," they became indignant *21:16~* and said to Him, "Do You hear what these children are saying?"	
3 Jesus said to them, "Yes. Have you never read, '*Out of the mouth of infants and nursing babies You have prepared praise for Yourself*'?"[1.]	*21:~16* ~~And~~ Jesus said to them, "Yes; have you never read, 'Out of the mouth of infants and nursing babies You have prepared praise for Yourself'?"	
4 Then, after looking around at everything, since it was late, [Jesus] left with the twelve; and <they> went out of the city to Bethany, and spent the night there.	*21:17* ~~And~~ [He] left ~~them~~ and went out of the city to Bethany, and spent the night there.	*11:~11* ~~and~~ after looking around at everything, [~~He~~] left ~~for~~ Bethany with the twelve, since it was ~~already~~ late.

1. Psalm 8:2

7 - THE FINAL WEEK

Act 2: Monday

Scene 1: Jesus Curses A Fig Tree

east of Jerusalem, *Judea*   Monday, March 30th / 33 CE

John's Gospel was the last written

		Matthew	**Mark**
1	The next day, they left Bethany in the morning, <and> [were] returning to the city.	21:18~ Now in the morning, when He [was] returning to the city,	11:12~ On the next day, when they had left Bethany, 11:~20~ in the morning
2	[Jesus] became hungry, <and> seeing a lone fig tree in leaf at a distance by the road, He went to see if perhaps He would find any [fruit] on it.	21:~18 [He] became hungry. 21:19~ Seeing a lone fig tree by the road,	11:~12 He became hungry. 11:13~ Seeing a fig tree in leaf, at a distance He went to see if perhaps He would find any[thing] on it;
3	When He came to [the tree], He found nothing on it but only leaves, for it was not the season for figs.	21:19~1 He came to [it] and found nothing on it except leaves only;	11:~13 and when He came to [it], He found nothing but leaves, for it was not the season for figs.
4	[Jesus] said to it, "May no one ever eat fruit from you again!" And His [apostles] were listening.	21:19~2 and [He] said to it, "[No longer] shall there ever be any fruit from you."	11:14 [He] said to it, "May no one ever eat fruit from you again!" And His [disciples] were listening.
5	As they were passing by, they saw the fig tree withered from the roots up.	21:~19 And at once the fig tree withered.	11:20~ As they were passing by 11:~20 they saw the fig tree withered from the roots up.
6	Peter said to [Jesus], "Rabbi, look, the fig tree which You cursed has withered!"		11:21 Peter said to [Him], "Rabbi, look, the fig tree which You cursed has withered."
7	Seeing this, [His] [apostles] were amazed, and asked, "How did the fig tree wither all at once?"	21:20 Seeing this, [the] [disciples] were amazed and asked, "How did the fig tree wither all at once?"	
8	Jesus answered, and said to them, "Have faith in God.	21:21~ And Jesus answered and said to them,	11:22 And Jesus answered saying to them, "Have faith in God.
9	"Truly I say to you, if you have faith, and do not doubt, you will not only do what was done to [this] fig tree, but even if you say to this mountain, 'Be taken up and cast into the sea,' and do not doubt in [your] heart, but believe that what [you] say is going to happen, <then> it will be granted <to> [you], <and> it will happen.	21:~21 "Truly I say to you, if you have faith and do not doubt, you will not only do what was done to [the] fig tree, but even if you say to this mountain, 'Be taken up and cast into the sea,' it will happen.	11:23 "Truly I say to you, whoever says to this mountain, 'Be taken up and cast into the sea,' and does not doubt in [his] heart, but believes that what [he] says is going to happen, it will be granted [him].
10	"Therefore I say to you, all things for which you ask in prayer, believing that you will receive them, they will be granted <to> you."	21:22 "And all things you ask in prayer, believing, you will receive."	11:24 "Therefore I say to you, all things for which you pray and ask, believe that you have received them, and they will be granted you.

7 - THE FINAL WEEK

Act 2: **Monday**

Scene 2: **Who Gave You This Authority?**

The Temple, Jerusalem, *Judea*   Monday, March 30th / 33 CE

The Good News Gospel

	Matthew	Mark	Luke
1 When they came to Jerusalem, [Jesus] entered the Temple, <and> was teaching the people.	21:23~ When [He] entered the Temple, 21:23⁻² teaching,	11:27~ They came ~~again~~ to Jerusalem. ~~And~~ [He] was ~~walking in~~ the temple,	20:1~ ~~On one of the days~~ 20:1⁻² teaching the people ~~in~~ the temple
2 While He was preaching the gospel, the chief priests and the scribes, with the elders of the people, came <and> confronted Him.	21:23⁻¹ the chief priests ~~and~~ the elders of the people came ~~to Him~~ while He was	11:~27 the chief priests and the scribes ~~and~~ the elders came ~~to Him~~,	20:1⁻¹ while He was 20:~1 ~~and~~ preaching the gospel, the chief priests and the scribes with the elders confronted Him,
3 And they began saying to Him, "Tell us, by what authority are You doing these things; or who is the one who gave You [the] authority to do these things?"	21:~23 and ~~said~~, "By what authority are You doing these things, ~~and~~ who gave You [this] authority?"	11:28 and began saying to Him, "By what authority are You doing these things, or who gave You [this] authority to do these things?"	20:2 and they ~~spoke~~ saying to Him, "Tell us by what authority You are doing these things, or who is the one who gave You [this] authority?"
4 Jesus answered, and said to them, "I will also ask you a question, which if you answer Me, then I will tell you by what authority I do these things.	21:24 Jesus said to them, "I will also ask you ~~one thing~~, which if you ~~tell~~ Me, I will ~~also~~ tell you by what authority I do these things.	11:29 ~~And~~ Jesus said to them, "I will ask you ~~one~~ question, ~~and~~ you answer Me, ~~and~~ then I will tell you by what authority I do these things.	20:3 Jesus answered and said to them, "I will also ask you a question, ~~and~~ you ~~tell~~ Me:
5 "The baptism of John was from what source - from Heaven, or from men? Answer Me."	21:25~ "The baptism of John was from what source, from heaven or from men?"	11:30 "Was the baptism of John from heaven, or from men? Answer Me."	20:4 "Was the baptism of John from heaven or from men?"
6 They began reasoning among themselves, saying, "If we say, 'From Heaven,' He will say to us, 'Then why did you not believe him?'	21:~25 And they began reasoning among themselves, saying, "If we say, 'From heaven,' He will say to us, 'Then why did you not believe him?'	11:31 They began reasoning among themselves, saying, "If we say, 'From heaven,' He will say, 'Then why did you not believe him?'	20:5 They reason~~ed~~ among themselves, saying, "If we say, 'From heaven,' He will say, 'Why did you not believe him?'
7 "But if we say, 'From men,' we fear <that> the people will stone us to death, for they are all convinced that John was a real prophet."	21:26 "But if we say, 'From men,' we fear the people; for they all ~~regard~~ John ~~as~~ a prophet."	11:32 "But ~~shall~~ we say, 'From men,'? - ~~they were afraid of~~ the people, for ~~everyone considered~~ John ~~to have been~~ a real prophet.	20:6 "But if we say, 'From men,' all the people will stone us to death, for they are convinced that John was a prophet."
8 So they answered Jesus, <and> said, "We do not know where it came from."	21:27~ ~~And~~ answer~~ing~~ Jesus, ~~they~~ said, "We do not know."	11:33~ Answer~~ing~~ Jesus, ~~they~~ said, "We do not know."	20:7 So they answered ~~that they~~ did not know where it came from.
9 And Jesus said to them, "<Then> neither will I tell you by what authority I do these things."	21:~27 ~~He also~~ said to them, "Neither will I tell you by what authority I do these things."	11:~33 And Jesus said to them, "~~Nor~~ will I tell you by what authority I do these things."	20:8 And Jesus said to them, "~~Nor~~ will I tell you by what authority I do these things."

7 - THE FINAL WEEK

Act 2: **Monday**

Scene 3: Who Did The Will of His Father?

The Temple, Jerusalem, *Judea* Monday, March 30th / 33 CE

	Matthew
1 "What do you think? A man had two sons, and he came to the first <one>, and said, 'Son, go work today in the vineyard.'	21:28 "~~But~~ what do you think? A man had two sons, and he came to the first and said, 'Son, go work today in the vineyard.'
2 "He answered, 'I will not'; but afterward he regretted it, and went.	21:29 "~~And~~ he answered, 'I will not'; but afterward he regretted it and went.
3 "<Then> the man came to [his] second <son>, and <he> said the same thing.	21:30~ "The man came to [~~the~~] second and said the same thing;
4 "[The son] answered, 'I will, sir', but he did not go.	21:~30 ~~and~~ [he] answered, 'I will, sir'; but he did not go.
5 "Which of the two did the will of his father?" They said, "The first."	21:31~ "Which of the two did the will of his father?" They said, "The first."
6 Jesus said to them, "Truly I say to you, that the tax collectors and prostitutes will get into the Kingdom of God before you;	21:~31 Jesus said to them, "Truly I say to you that the tax collectors and prostitutes will get into the kingdom of God before you.
7 "for John came to you in the way of righteousness, and you did not believe him; but the tax collectors and prostitutes did believe him;	21:32~ "For John came to you in the way of righteousness and you did not believe him; but the tax collectors and prostitutes did believe him;
8 "and you, seeing this, did not even feel remorse afterward, so as to believe him."	21:~32 and you, seeing this, did not even feel remorse afterward so as to believe him.

7 - THE FINAL WEEK
Act 2: Monday

Scene 4: The Parable of The Evil Vine-Growers
The Temple, Jerusalem, *Judea* Monday, March 30th / 33 CE

The Verse-By-Verse Four Gospel Harmony

	Matthew	Mark	Luke
1	[Then] [Jesus] began to tell them <a> parable: "Listen to this: There was a landowner who planted a vineyard, and <he> put a wall around it, and dug a vat under the wine press, and built a tower.	21:33~ "Listen to another parable. There was a landowner who planted a vineyard and put a wall around it and dug a wine press in it, and built a tower,	12:1~ [And] [He] began to speak to them in parables: "A man planted a vineyard and put a wall around it, and dug a vat under the wine press and built a tower,	20:9~ [And] [He] began to tell [the people] this parable: "A man planted a vineyard
2	"[Then] <he> rented it out to vine-growers, and went <away> on a journey for a long time.	21:~33 [and] rented it out to vine-growers and went on a journey.	12:~1 [and] rented it out to vine-growers and went on a journey.	20:~9 [and] rented it out to vine-growers, and went on a journey for a long time.
3	"At the harvest time, [the landowner] sent a slave to the vine-growers, so that they would give him some of the produce of the vineyard.	21:34 "When the harvest time approached [he] sent his slaves to the vine-growers to receive his produce.	12:2 "At the harvest time [he] sent a slave to the vine-growers, in order to receive some of the produce of the vineyard from the vine-growers.	20:10 "At the harvest time [he] sent a slave to the vine-growers, so that they would give him some of the produce of the vineyard;
4	"But the vine-growers took [the] slave and beat him, and sent him away empty-handed.	21:35~ "The vine-growers took [his] slaves and beat one,	12:3 "They took him, and beat him and sent him away empty-handed.	20:~10 but the vine-growers beat him and sent him away empty-handed.
5	"Again [the landowner] proceeded to send another slave, and they also beat him, wounded him in the head, treated him shamefully, and sent him away empty-handed.		12:4 "Again [he] sent them another slave, and they wounded him in the head, and treated him shamefully.	20:11 "And [he] proceeded to send another slave; and they beat him also and treated him shamefully and sent him away empty-handed.
6	"[So] [the landowner] [sent] a third <slave>, and this one they also wounded, and cast out.	21:~35 a third.		20:12 "[And] he [proceeded to] send a third; and this one also they wounded and cast out.
7	"And he sent another, and that one they stoned and killed.	21:~35~ and killed another, and stoned	12:5~ "And he sent another, and that one they killed;	
8	"[Then] [the landowner] sent [a] large group of slaves, and they did the same thing to them, beating some and killing others.	21:36 "[Again] [he] sent another group of slaves larger than the first; and they did the same thing to them.	12:~5 and so with many others, beating some and killing others.	
9	"The owner of the vineyard said, 'What shall I do?'			20:13~ "The owner of the vineyard said, 'What shall I do?
10	"He had one more to send, a beloved son; [so] last of all he sent his son to them, saying, 'I will send my beloved son, perhaps they will respect him.'	21:37 "[But] afterward he sent his son to them saying, 'They will respect my son.'	12:6 "He had one more to send, a beloved son; he sent him to them, last of all saying, 'They will respect my son.'	20:~13 I will send my beloved son; perhaps they will respect him.'
11	"But when the vine-growers saw the son, they reasoned among themselves, <and> said to one another, 'This is the heir; come, let us kill him and seize his inheritance, so that [it] will be ours!'	21:38 "But when the vine-growers saw the son, they said among themselves, 'This is the heir; come, let us kill him and seize his inheritance.'	12:7 "But those vine-growers said to one another, 'This is the heir; come, let us kill him, and [the inheritance] will be ours!'	20:14 "But when the vine-growers saw him, they reasoned with one another, saying, 'This is the heir; let us kill him so that [the inheritance] will be ours.'
12	"So they took [the son], and threw him out of the vineyard, and killed him.	21:39 "They took [him], and threw him out of the vineyard and killed him.	12:8 "They took [him], and killed him and threw him out of the vineyard.	20:15~ "So they threw him out of the vineyard and killed him.
13	"Therefore, when the owner of the vineyard comes, what will he do to those vine-growers?	21:40 "Therefore when the owner of the vineyard comes, what will he do to those vine-growers?"	12:9~ "What will the owner of the vineyard do?	20:~15 What, then, will the owner of the vineyard do to them?
14	"He will come and destroy those wretches, and <then he> will rent out the vineyard to other vine-growers, who will pay him the proceeds at the proper seasons."	21:41 "He will bring those wretches to a wretched end, and will rent out the vineyard to other vine-growers who will pay him the proceeds at the proper seasons."	12:~9 "He will come and destroy the vine-growers, and will give the vineyard to others.	20:16~ "He will come and destroy these vine-growers and will give the vineyard to others."

continued >

7 - THE FINAL WEEK	Scene 4: **The Parable of The Evil Vine-Growers**	Page 209
Act 2: **Monday**	continued	*The Gospel of Good News*

	Matthew	Mark	Luke
15 When [the people] heard it, they said to [Jesus], "May it never be!"	*21:41~* They said to [Him],		*20:~16* When [they] heard it, they said, "May it never be!"
16 But [He] looked at them, and said, "What then is this that is written; have you never read this Scripture?	*21:42~* [Jesus] said to them, "Did you never read in the Scriptures,	*12:10~* "Have you not even read this Scripture:	*20:17~* But [Jesus] looked at them and said, "What then is this that is written:
17 'The stone which the builders rejected [has become] the chief corner stone. This came about from the Lord, and it is marvelous in our eyes'.[1]	*21:~42* 'The stone which the builders rejected, this became the chief corner stone; this came about from the Lord, and it is marvelous in our eyes'?	*12:10* 'The stone which the builders rejected, this became the chief corner stone; *12:11* This came about from the Lord, and it is marvelous in our eyes'?"	*20:~17* 'The stone which the builders rejected, this became the chief corner stone'?
18 "Therefore, I say to you, \<that> the Kingdom of God will be taken away from you, and given to a people producing the fruit of it."	*21:43* "Therefore I say to you, the kingdom of God will be taken away from you and given to a people, producing the fruit of it.		
19 "And, 'Everyone who falls on that stone will be broken to pieces; but on whomever it falls, it will scatter [them] like dust!' "[2]	*21:44* "And he who falls on this stone will be broken to pieces; but on whomever it falls, it will scatter [him] like dust."		*20:18* "Everyone who falls on that stone will be broken to pieces; but on whomever it falls, it will scatter [him] like dust."
20 When the scribes, the chief priests, and the Pharisees heard this parable, they understood that [Jesus] was speaking against them, and they tried to lay hands on Him that very hour;	*21:45* When the chief priests and the Pharisees heard His parables, they understood that [He] was speaking about them.	*12:12~* And they were *12:~12* for they understood that [He] spoke the parable against them.	*20:19~* The scribes and the chief priests tried to lay hands on Him that very hour, *20:~19* for they understood that [He] was speaking this parable against them.
21 [but] when they sought to seize Him they feared the people, because they considered Him to be a prophet.	*21:46* When they sought to seize Him, they feared the people, because they considered Him to be a prophet.	*12:~12* seeking to seize Him, and [yet] they feared the people,	*20:~19* [and] they feared the people;

1. Psalm 118:22-23   2. Isaiah 8:14-15

Scene 5: **To Serve Me, You Must Follow Me**

	John
1 [Then] some Greeks \<from> among those who were going up to worship at the feast came to Philip, and \<they> [said] to him, "Sir, we wish to see Jesus."	*12:20* [Now] there were some Greeks among those who were going up to worship at the feast; *12:21* [these] then came to Philip, and began to ask him, [saying], "Sir, we wish to see Jesus."
2 Philip [went] and told Andrew, \<and> [the two of them] came and told Jesus.	*12:22* Philip [came] and told Andrew; [Andrew and Philip] came and told Jesus.
3 Jesus [said] \<to> them, "The hour has come for the Son of Man to be glorified!	*12:23* And Jesus [answered] them, saying, "The hour has come for the Son of Man to be glorified.
4 "Truly, truly, I say to you, unless a grain of wheat falls into the earth and dies, it remains alone; but if it dies, it bears much fruit.	*12:24* "Truly, truly, I say to you, unless a grain of wheat falls into the earth and dies, it remains alone; but if it dies, it bears much fruit.
5 "[The one] who loves his life \<will> lose it; and he who hates his life in this world, will keep it [and] [live] eternal[ly].	*12:25* "[He] who loves his life loses it, and he who hates his life in this world will keep it [to] [life] eternal.
6 "If anyone serves Me, he must follow Me; and where I am, there My servant will be also.	*12:26* "If anyone serves Me, he must follow Me; and where I am, there My servant will be also;
7 "If anyone serves Me, the Father will honor him."	*12:~26* if anyone serves Me, the Father will honor him."

7 - THE FINAL WEEK

Act 2: **Monday**

Scene 6: A Voice From Heaven

The Temple, Jerusalem, *Judea*   Monday, March 30th / 33 CE

A Complete Four Gospel Merger

Page 210

	John
1 "Now My soul has become troubled. And what shall I say, 'Father, save Me from this hour'? But I <have> [come for] this hour.	12:27 "Now My soul has become troubled; and what shall I say, 'Father, save Me from this hour'? But for this purpose I [came to] this hour.
2 "Father, glorify Your Name!"	12:28~ "Father, glorify Your name."
3 Then a voice came out of heaven: "I have both glorified it, and will glorify it again."	12:~28 Then a voice came out of heaven: "I have both glorified it, and will glorify it again."
4 So the crowd of people who stood by and heard it were saying that it had thundered; others were saying, "An angel has spoken to Him."	12:29 So the crowd of people who stood by and heard it were saying that it had thundered; others were saying, "An angel has spoken to Him."
5 Jesus answered, and said, "This voice has not come for My sake, but for your sakes.	12:30 Jesus answered and said, "This voice has not come for My sake, but for your sakes.
6 "Now judgment is upon this world, <and> now the ruler of this world will be cast out!	12:31 "Now judgment is upon this world; now the ruler of this world will be cast out.
7 "And I, if *I am lifted up from the earth, will draw all men to Myself.*" [1]	12:32 "And I, if I am lifted up from the earth, will draw all men to Myself."
8 [Jesus] was saying this to indicate the kind of death by which He was <going> to die.	12:33 But [He] was saying this to indicate the kind of death by which He was to die.

1. (Numbers 21:8)

Scene 7: Believe In The Light

The Temple, Jerusalem, *Judea*   Monday, March 30th / 33 CE

	John
1 The crowd answered [Jesus], "*We have heard out of the Law that the Christ is to remain forever,*[1] [so] how can You say, 'The Son of Man must be lifted up'?	12:34~ The crowd then answered [Him], "We have heard out of the Law that the Christ is to remain forever; [and] how can You say, 'The Son of Man must be lifted up'?
2 "Who is this Son of Man?"	12:~34 Who is this Son of Man?"
3 Jesus said to them, "For a little while longer the Light is among you;	12:35~ So Jesus said to them, "For a little while longer the Light is among you.
4 "walk while you have the Light, so that the darkness will not overtake you.	12:~35~ Walk while you have the Light, so that darkness will not overtake you;
5 "He who walks in darkness does not know where he goes.	12:~35 he who walks in the darkness does not know where he goes.
6 "While you have the Light, believe in the Light, so that you may become sons of Light."	12:36~ "While you have the Light, believe in the Light, so that you may become sons of Light."
7 <After> Jesus spoke these things, He went away, and hid Himself from them, [because] [al]though He had performed so many signs before them, they [did] not believe in Him.	12:~36 These things Jesus spoke, and He went away and hid Himself from them. 12:37 [But] though He had performed so many signs before them, yet they [were] not believing in Him.
8 This was to fulfill the word which Isaiah the prophet spoke: "*Lord, who has believed our report? And to whom has the arm of the Lord been revealed?*"[2]	12:38 This was to fulfill the word of Isaiah the prophet which he spoke: "Lord, who has believed our report? And to whom has the arm of the Lord been revealed?"
9 For this reason they could not believe, for Isaiah [also] said, "*He has blinded their eyes, and He hardened their heart, so that they would not see with their eyes, and perceive with their heart, and [return], and I <would> heal them.*"[3]	12:39 For this reason they could not believe, for Isaiah said [again], 12:40 "He has blinded their eyes and He hardened their heart, so that they would not see with their eyes and perceive with their heart, and [be converted]* and I heal them."
10 These things Isaiah said because he saw His glory, and spoke of Him.	12:41 These things Isaiah said because he saw His glory, and he spoke of Him.
11 Nevertheless, many of the rulers [also] believed in [Jesus], but because of the Pharisees they were not confessing Him, for fear that they would be put out of the synagogue; for they loved the approval of men [more] than the approval of God.	12:42 Nevertheless many [even] of the rulers believed in [Him], but because of the Pharisees they were not confessing Him, for fear that they would be put out of the synagogue; 12:43 for they loved the approval of men [rather] than the approval of God.

1. Micah 4:7   2. Isaiah 53:1   3. Isaiah 6:9-10 / (Ezekiel 12:2)

7 - THE FINAL WEEK

Act 2: Monday

Scene 8: Believe In Me, and The One Who Sent Me

The Temple, Jerusalem, *Judea* Monday, March 30th / 33 CE

	Luke	John
1 Jesus cried out, and said, "He who believes in Me, does not believe in Me, but in Him who sent Me.		*12:44* ~~And~~ Jesus cried out and said, "He who believes in Me, does not believe in Me but in Him who sent Me.
2 "He who sees Me, sees the One who sent Me.		*12:45* "He who sees Me sees the One who sent Me.
3 "I have come as Light into the world, so that everyone who believes in Me will not remain in darkness.		*12:46* "I have come as Light into the world, so that everyone who believes in Me will not remain in darkness.
4 "If anyone hears My sayings, and does not keep them, I do not judge him; for I did not come to judge the world, but to save the world.		*12:47* "If anyone hears My sayings and does not keep them, I do not judge him; for I did not come to judge the world, but to save the world.
5 "He who rejects Me, and does not receive My sayings, has one who judges him - the Word <which> I spoke is what will judge him, [on] the last day.		*12:48* "He who rejects Me and does not receive My sayings, has one who judges him; the word I spoke is what will judge him [~~at~~] the last day.
6 "For I did not speak on My own initiative, but *The Father Himself who sent Me has given Me a commandment as to what to say, and what to speak.*[1]		*12:49* "For I did not speak on My own initiative, but the Father Himself who sent Me has given Me a commandment as to what to say and what to speak.
7 "I know that His commandment is eternal life, therefore the things <that> I speak, I speak just as The Father has told Me."		*12:50* "I know that His commandment is eternal life; therefore the things I speak, I speak just as the Father has told Me."
8 [Jesus] was teaching daily in the Temple, [and] the chief priests and the scribes, and the leading men among the people were trying to destroy Him;	*19:47* ~~And~~ [He] was teaching daily in the temple; [~~but~~] the chief priests and the scribes and the leading men among the people were trying to destroy Him,	
9 [but] they could not find anything that they might do <to Him>, [because] all the people were hanging on to every word <that> He said.	*19:48* [~~and~~] they could not find anything that they might do, [~~for~~] all the people were hanging on to every word He said.	

1. *Deuteronomy 18:18-19*

---

7 - THE FINAL WEEK

Act 3: Tuesday

Scene 1: Be Prepared For The Wedding Feast

The Temple, Jerusalem, *Judea* Tuesday, March 31st / 33 CE

	Matthew	Luke
1 Having been questioned by the Pharisees as to when the Kingdom of God was coming, [Jesus] answered them, and said, "The Kingdom of God is not coming with signs to be observed; nor will they say, 'Look, here it is!' or, 'There it is!' for behold, the kingdom of God is in your midst."		*17:20* ~~Now~~ having been questioned by the Pharisees as to when the kingdom of God was coming, [He] answered them and said, "The kingdom of God is not coming with signs to be observed; *17:21* nor will they say, 'Look, here it is!' or, 'There it is!' for behold, the kingdom of God is in your midst."
2 <Then> He spoke to them in parables again, saying, "The Kingdom of Heaven may be compared to a king who gave a big wedding feast for his son, and he invited many <guests>.	*22:1* ~~Jesus~~ spoke to them again in parables, saying, *22:2* "The kingdom of heaven may be compared to a king who gave a wedding feast for his son.	*14:16* ~~But~~ He said to ~~him~~, "A ~~man was giving~~ a big ~~dinner~~, and he invited many;
3 "At the dinner hour, he sent out his slaves to say to those who had been invited, 'Come to the wedding feast, for everything is ready now.'	*22:3~* "~~And~~ he sent out his slaves to ~~call~~ those who had been invited to the wedding feast,	*14:17* ~~and~~ at the dinner hour he sent his slave to say to those who had been invited, 'Come; for everything is ready now.'

continued >

7 - THE FINAL WEEK Act 3: **Tuesday**	Scene 1: **Be Prepared For The Wedding Feast** *continued*	Page 212 *The Ultimate Gospel Story*

	Matthew	Luke
4 "But they paid no attention, and <they> went <on> their way, and were unwilling to come.	22:~3 and ~~they~~ were unwilling to come. 22:~5~ "But they paid no attention and went their way,	
5 "Again [the king] sent out other slaves saying, 'Tell those who have been invited, "Behold, I have prepared my dinner; my oxen and my fattened livestock are all butchered, and everything is ready. Come to the wedding feast!" '	22:4 "Again [~~he~~] sent out other slaves saying, 'Tell those who have been invited, "Behold, I have prepared my dinner; my oxen and my fattened livestock are all butchered and everything is ready; come to the wedding feast." '	
6 "But they all began to make excuses. The first one said, 'I have bought a piece of land, and I need to go and look at it; please consider me excused.'	22:~5~ one to ~~his own~~ farm,	14:18 "But they all ~~alike~~ began to make excuses. The first one said ~~to him~~, 'I have bought a piece of land and I need to go ~~out~~ and look at it; please consider me excused.'
7 "Another one said, 'I have bought five yoke of oxen, and I am going to try them out; please consider me excused.'		14:19 "Another one said, 'I have bought five yoke of oxen, and I am going to try them out; please consider me excused.'
8 "Another one said, 'I have married a wife, and for that reason I cannot come;' <and> another <went> to his business.	22:~5 another to his business,	14:20 "Another one said, 'I have married a wife, and for that reason I cannot come.'
9 "The rest seized his slaves, and mistreated them, and killed them.	22:6 and the rest seized his slaves and mistreated them and killed them.	
10 "[When] the slave came back and reported this to his master, the king became enraged; and he sent his armies [who] destroyed those murderers, and set their city on fire.	22:7 "~~But~~ the king ~~was~~ enraged, and he sent his armies [~~and~~] destroyed those murderers and set their city on fire.	14:21~ "[And] the slave came back and reported this to his master. ~~Then~~ the ~~head of the household~~ became ~~angry~~
11 "Then [the king] said to his slaves, 'The wedding is ready, but those who were invited [are] not worthy; therefore, go out at once into the streets and <the> lanes of the city, and invite the poor and <the> crippled, and <the> blind and <the> lame, here to the wedding feast.'	22:8 "Then [~~he~~] said to his slaves, 'The wedding is ready, but those who were invited [~~were~~] not worthy. 22:9 'Go therefore to the ~~main highways~~, ~~and as many as you find there~~, invite to the wedding feast.'	14:~21 and said to his slave, 'Go out at once into the streets and lanes of the city and ~~bring in~~ here the poor and crippled and blind and lame.'
12 "The slave said, 'Master, what you commanded has been done, and there is still room.'		14:22 "~~And~~ the slave said, 'Master, what you commanded has been done, and still there is room.'
13 "The [king] said to the slave, 'Go out into the highways and along the hedges, and compel them to come in, so that my house may be filled; for I tell you, none of those who were invited, shall taste my dinner.'		14:23 "~~And~~ the [~~master~~] said to the slave, 'Go out into the highways and along the hedges, and compel them to come in, so that my house may be filled. 14:24 'For I tell you, none of those ~~men~~ who were invited shall taste ~~of~~ my dinner.' "
14 "[His] slaves went out into the streets, and gathered together all <that> they found, both good and evil, and the wedding hall was filled with dinner guests.	22:10 "[~~Those~~] slaves went out into the streets and gathered together all they found, both evil and good; and the wedding hall was filled with dinner guests.	
15 "When the king came in to look over the dinner guests, he saw a man there who was not dressed in wedding clothes, and he said to him, 'Friend, how did you come in here without wedding clothes?' And the man was speechless.	22:11 "~~But~~ when the king came in to look over the dinner guests, he saw a man there who was not dressed in wedding clothes, 22:12 and he said to him, 'Friend, how did you come in here without wedding clothes?' And the man was speechless.	
16 "Then the king said to the servants, 'Bind him hand and foot, and throw him into the outer darkness; in that place there will be weeping, and gnashing of teeth!'	22:13 "Then the king said to the servants, 'Bind him hand and foot, and throw him into the outer darkness; in that place there will be weeping and gnashing of teeth.'	
17 "For many are called, but few are chosen."	22:14 "For many are called, but few are chosen."	

7 - THE FINAL WEEK	Scene 2: **The Pharisees Plot To Trap Jesus**		
Act 3: **Tuesday**	Jerusalem, *Judea* Tuesday, March 31st / 33 CE		

	Matthew	Mark	Luke
1 Then the Pharisees left [Jesus] and went away, and <they> plotted together how they might trap Him in what He said. So they watched Him.	22:15 Then the Pharisees went and plotted together how they might trap Him in what He said.	12:~12 ~~And so~~ they left [~~Him~~] and went away.	20:20~ So they watched Him,
2 Then they sent spies to Him - some of their disciples who pretended to be righteous, along with the Herodians - in order that they might catch Him in some statement, so that they could deliver Him to the rule and authority of the Governor.	22:16~ ~~And~~ they sent their disciples to Him, along with the Herodians,	12:13 Then they sent some of ~~the Pharisees and~~ Herodians to Him in order ~~to~~ trap Him in ~~a~~ statement.	20:~20 ~~and~~ sent spies who pretended to be righteous, in order that they might catch Him in some statement, so that they could deliver Him to the rule and ~~the~~ authority of the governor.

Scene 3: Is It Lawful To Pay Taxes To Caesar?

The Temple, Jerusalem, *Judea*   Tuesday, March 31st / 33 CE

	Matthew	Mark	Luke
1 [The spies] came to [Jesus], and <they> questioned Him, saying, "Teacher, we know that You are truthful, and <that You> speak and teach correctly, and teach the way of God in truth, <because You> defer to no one, and are not partial to any.	22:~16 saying, "Teacher, we know that You are truthful and teach the way of God in truth, ~~and~~ defer to n one; ~~for~~ You are not partial to any.	12:14~ [they] came and said to [Him], "Teacher, we know that You are truthful and defer to no one; ~~for~~ You are not partial to any, ~~but~~ teach the way of God in truth.	20:21 [they] questioned Him, saying, "Teacher, we know that You speak and teach correctly, and You are not partial to any, ~~but~~ teach the way of God in truth.
2 "Tell us then, what do you think? Is it lawful for us to pay taxes to Caesar, or not? Shall we pay, or shall we not pay?"	22:17 "Tell us then, what do You think? Is it lawful to ~~give~~ a poll-tax to Caesar, or not?"	12:~14 Is it lawful to pay ~~a poll-~~tax to Caesar, or not? 12:15~ "Shall we pay or shall we not pay?"	20:22 "Is it lawful for us to pay taxes to Caesar, or not?"
3 But Jesus, knowing their hypocrisy perceived their malice, and said to them, "Why are you testing Me, you hypocrites? Show Me the coin used for the poll-tax."	22:18 But Jesus perceived their malice, and said, "Why are you testing Me, you hypocrites?" 22:19~ "Show Me the coin used for the poll-tax."	12:~15 But He, knowing their hypocrisy, said to them, "Why are you testing Me? ~~Bring~~ Me a denarius ~~to look at~~."	20:23 But ~~He detected~~ their ~~trickery~~ and said to them, 20:24~ "Show Me ~~a denarius~~.
4 They brought Him a denarius; and He asked them, "Whose likeness and inscription does it have?"	22:~19 ~~And~~ they brought Him a denarius. 22:20 And He said to them, "Whose likeness and inscription ~~is this~~?"	12:16~ They brought ~~one~~. And He said to them, "Whose likeness and inscription ~~is this~~?"	20:~24 Whose likeness and inscription does it have?"
5 They said to Him, "Caesar's."	22:21 They said to Him, "Caesar's."	12:~16 ~~And~~ they said to Him, "Caesar's."	20:~24 They said, "Caesar's."
6 Then Jesus said to them, "Then render to Caesar the things that are Caesar's, and to God the things that are God's."	22:~21 Then ~~He~~ said to them, "Then render to Caesar the things that are Caesar's; and to God the things that are God's."	12:~17 ~~And~~ Jesus said to them, "Render to Caesar the things that are Caesar's, and to God the things that are God's."	20:25 ~~And He~~ said to them, "Then render to Caesar the things that are Caesar's, and to God the things that are God's."
7 Hearing this, they were amazed at His answer, [and] became silent.	22:22 ~~And~~ hearing this, they were amazed,	12:~17 ~~And~~ they were amazed at ~~Him~~.	20:~26 ~~and being~~ amazed at His answer, [~~they~~] became silent.
8 And [being] unable to catch Him in a saying in the presence of the people, they [left] Him, and went away.	22:~22 and [~~leaving~~] Him, they went away.		20:~26 And ~~they~~ [were] unable to catch Him in a saying in the presence of the people;

The Four Gospels Harmoniously United

7 - THE FINAL WEEK

Act 3: Tuesday

Scene 4: In The Next Life, Whose Wife Will She Be?

Jerusalem, *Judea*   Tuesday, March 31st / 33 CE

The Unified Gospel Verse-By-Verse

#	Unified	Matthew	Mark	Luke
1	On that day, some of the Sadducees (who say that there is no resurrection) came to Jesus, and began <to> question Him, saying, "Teacher, Moses wrote for us that *if a man dies and leaves behind a wife, and is childless, his brother, as next of kin should marry his wife, and raise up children for his brother.*[1]	22:23 On that day some Sadducees (who say there is no resurrection) came to Jesus and questioned Him, 22:24 ~~asking~~, "Teacher, Moses said, 'If a man dies having no children, his brother as next of kin ~~shall~~ marry his wife, and raise up children for his brother.'	12:18 Some Sadducees (who say that there is no resurrection) came to Jesus, and began questioning Him, saying, 12:19 "Teacher, Moses wrote for us that if a man's brother dies and leaves behind a wife and ~~leaves~~ no child, his brother should marry ~~the~~ wife and raise up children ~~to~~ his brother.	20:27 ~~Now there~~ came to ~~Him~~ some of the Sadducees (who say that there is no resurrection) 20:28 and ~~they~~ questioned Him, saying, "Teacher, Moses wrote for us that if a man's ~~brother~~ dies ~~having~~ a wife, and ~~he~~ is childless, his brother should marry ~~the~~ wife and raise up children ~~to~~ his brother.
2	"Now there were seven brothers; and the first <one> married a wife, and died; and having no children <he> left his wife to his brother.	22:25 "Now there were seven brothers ~~with us~~; and the first married and died, and having no children left his wife to his brother;	12:20 "There were seven brothers; and the first ~~took~~ a wife, and died ~~leaving~~ no children.	20:29 "Now there were seven brothers; and the first ~~took~~ a wife and died ~~childless~~;
3	"So the second [brother] married her, and <he also> died leaving behind no children; and the third <one> likewise married her, and so in the same way all seven died, leaving no children.	22:26 so ~~also~~ the second, and the third, ~~down to the~~ seven~~th~~.	12:21 "The second [one] married her, and died leaving behind no children; and the third likewise; 12:22~ and so all seven ~~left~~ no children.	20:30 ~~and~~ the second 20:31 and the third married her; and in the same way all seven died, leaving no children.
4	"Finally, last of all, the woman died.	22:27 "Last of all, the woman died.	12:~22 Last of all the woman died ~~also~~.	20:32 "Finally the woman died ~~also~~.
5	"In the resurrection therefore, when they rise again, which one of the seven will she be <the> wife <of>, for all seven had married her?"	22:28 "In the resurrection, therefore, ~~whose~~ wife of the seven will she be? For ~~they~~ all had married her."	12:23 "In the resurrection, when they rise again, which one's wife will she be? For all seven had married her."	20:33 "In the resurrection therefore, which one's wife will she be? For all seven had married her."
6	Jesus answered, and said to them, "You are mistaken, [because] you do not understand the Scriptures, nor the power of God.	22:29 ~~But~~ Jesus answered and said to them, "You are mistaken, not understand~~ing~~ the Scriptures nor the power of God.	12:24 Jesus said to them, "~~Is this not the reason~~ you are mistaken, [that] you do not understand the Scriptures or the power of God?	20:34~ Jesus said to them,
7	"The sons of this age marry and are given in marriage, but those who are considered worthy to attain to that age and the resurrection, when they rise from the dead, they neither marry nor are <they> given in marriage;	22:30 ~~For in~~ the resurrection they neither marry nor are given in marriage,	12:25 ~~For~~ when they rise from the dead, they neither marry nor are given in marriage,	20:~34 "The sons of this age marry and are given in marriage, 20:35 but those who are considered worthy to attain to that age and the resurrection from the dead, neither marry nor are given in marriage;
8	"[because] they cannot die anymore, because they are like angels in Heaven, and are sons of God, being sons of the resurrection.	22:~30 ~~but~~ are like angels in heaven.	12:~25 ~~but~~ are like angels in heaven.	20:36 [for] they cannot even die anymore, because they are like angels, and are sons of God, being sons of the resurrection.
9	"But regarding the fact that the dead are raised, have you not read the passage about the burning bush in the book of Moses, where God [said] to him, *'I am the God of Abraham, and the God of Isaac, and the God of Jacob'?*[2]	22:31 "But regarding the ~~resurrection of~~ the dead, have you not read ~~what~~ [was spoken] to ~~you~~ by God: 22:32~ 'I am the God of Abraham, and the God of Isaac, and the God of Jacob'?	12:26 "But regarding the fact that the dead ~~rise again~~ have you not read in the book of Moses, ~~in~~ the passage about the burning bush, ~~how~~ God [spoke] to him, ~~saying~~, 'I am the God of Abraham, and the God of Isaac, and the God of Jacob'?	20:37 "But that the dead are raised, ~~even~~ Moses ~~showed in~~ the passage about the burning bush, where he [calls] ~~the Lord~~ the God of Abraham, and the God of Isaac, and the God of Jacob'?
10	"Now He is not the God of the dead, but of the living, for all live to Him. You are greatly mistaken."	22:~32 He is not the God of the dead but of the living."	12:27 "He is not the God of the dead, but of the living; you are greatly mistaken."	20:38 "Now He is not the God of the dead but of the living; for all live to Him."
11	When the crowds heard this, they were astonished at His teaching.	22:33 When the crowds heard this, they were astonished at His teaching.		

1. Deuteronomy 25:5-6   *2. Exodus 3:6, 14-15 / (Genesis 26:24)*

continued >

| 7 - THE FINAL WEEK | Scene 4: **In The Next Life, Whose Wife Will She Be?** |
| Act 3: **Tuesday** | continued |

	Matthew	Mark	Luke
12 Some of the scribes said, "Teacher, You have spoken well;" for they did not have <the> courage to question [Jesus] any longer about anything.			20:39 Some of the scribes ~~answered and~~ said, "Teacher, You have spoken well." 20:40 For they did not have courage to question [Him] any longer about anything.

Scene 5: The Greatest Commandment

The Temple, Jerusalem, *Judea*   Tuesday, March 31st / 33 CE

	Matthew	Mark	Luke
1 When the Pharisees heard that Jesus had silenced the Sadducees, they gathered themselves together.	22:34 ~~But~~ when the Pharisees heard that Jesus had silenced the Sadducees, they gathered themselves together.		
2 One of the scribes, a lawyer, came and heard them arguing, and recognizing that [Jesus] had answered them well, <he> asked Him a question, <to> test Him.	22:35 One of ~~them~~, a lawyer, asked Him a question, ~~testing~~ Him,	12:28~ One of the scribes came and heard them arguing, and recognizing that [He] had answered them well, asked Him,	
3 <He asked,> "Teacher, [what] is the great commandment in the Law? [Which] commandment is the foremost of all?"	22:36 "Teacher, [which] is the great commandment in the Law?"	12:~28 "[~~What~~] commandment is the foremost of all?"	
4 Jesus answered, "The foremost is: 'Hear, O Israel! The Lord our God is One Lord;'1.	22:37~ ~~And He said to him,~~	12:29 Jesus answered, "The foremost is, 'Hear, O Israel! The Lord our God is one Lord;	
5 "and 'you shall love the Lord your God with all your heart, and with all your soul, and with all your mind, and with all your strength.'2.	22:~37 "'You shall love the Lord your God with all your heart, and with all your soul, and with all your mind,	12:30 and you shall love the Lord your God with all your heart, and with all your soul, and with all your mind, and with all your strength.'	
6 "This is the great and foremost commandment.	22:38 "This is the great and foremost commandment.		
7 "<And> the second, is this: 'You shall love your neighbor as yourself.'3.	22:39 "The second is ~~like it~~, 'You shall love your neighbor as yourself.'	12:31~ "The second is this, 'You shall love your neighbor as yourself.'	
8 "There is no other commandment greater than these, <because> on these two commandments depend the whole Law, and the Prophets."	22:40 "On these two commandments depend the whole Law and the Prophets."	12:~31 There is no other commandment greater than these."	
9 The scribe said to Him, "Right, Teacher! You have truly stated that *He is One, and <that> there is no one else besides Him;*4.		12:32 The scribe said to Him, "Right, teacher; You have truly stated that He is One, and there is no one else besides Him;	
10 "and <that> to love Him with all [your] heart, and with all [your mind], and with all [your] strength,2. and to love one's neighbor as [your]self,3. is <worth> much more than all burnt offerings and sacrifices."5.		12:33 and to love Him with all [the] heart and with all [~~the understanding~~] and with all [the] strength, and to love one's neighbor as [~~him~~]self, is much more than all burnt offerings and sacrifices."	

1. Deuteronomy 6:4   2. Deuteronomy 6:5; 10:12; 30:6   3. Leviticus 19:18, 34   4. Deuteronomy 4:35 / Isaiah 45:21   5. Hosea 6:6

continued >

7 - THE FINAL WEEK
Act 3: Tuesday

Scene 5: The Greatest Commandment
continued

	Matthew	Mark	Luke
11 When Jesus saw that he had answered intelligently, He said to him, "You are not far from the Kingdom of God."		*12:34~* When Jesus saw that he had answered intelligently, He said to him, "You are not far from the kingdom of God."	
12 After that, no one would venture to ask [Jesus] any more questions.		*12:~34* After that, no one would venture to ask [Him] any more questions.	
13 Now during the day He was teaching in the Temple, but when evening came they would go out of the city, and spend the night on the Mount [of] Olive[s].		*11:19* When evening came, they would go out of the city.	*21:37* Now during the day He was teaching in the temple, but at evening He would go out and spend the night on the mount [that is called] Olive[t].

---

7 - THE FINAL WEEK
Act 4: Wednesday - Woe to The Pharisees

Scene 1: How Is The Christ The Son of David?
The Temple, Jerusalem, *Judea*   Wednesday, April 1st / 33 CE

	Matthew	Mark	Luke
1 All the people would get up early in the morning, and come to the Temple to listen to [Jesus].			*21:38* And all the people would get up early in the morning to come to Him in the temple to listen to [Him].
2 As He taught in the Temple, while the Pharisees were gathered together, Jesus asked them a question: "What do you think about the Christ; whose son is He?"	*22:41* Now while the Pharisees were gathered together, Jesus asked them a question: *22:42~* "What do you think about the Christ, whose son is He?"	*12:~35~* as He taught in the temple,	
3 They said to Him, "The son of David."	*22:~42* They said to Him, "The son of David."		
4 Then Jesus said to them, "How is it that the scribes say that the Christ is David's son?	*22:43~* He said to them, "Then how does	*12:35~* And Jesus began to say, *12:~35* "How is it that the scribes say that the Christ is the son of David?	*20:41* Then He said to them, "How is it that they say the Christ is David's son?
5 "For in the book of Psalms, David himself in the Holy Spirit calls Him 'Lord,' saying, *'The Lord said to my Lord, "Sit at My right hand, until I make Your enemies a footstool beneath Your feet."'* [1]	*22:~43* David in the Spirit call Him 'Lord,' saying, *22:44* 'The Lord said to my Lord, "Sit at My right hand, until I put Your enemies beneath Your feet"'?	*12:36* "David himself said in the Holy Spirit, 'The Lord said to my Lord, "Sit at My right hand, until I put Your enemies beneath Your feet."'	*20:42* "For David himself says in the book of Psalms, 'The Lord said to my Lord, "Sit at My right hand, *20:43* until I make Your enemies a footstool for Your feet."'
6 "Therefore, if David himself calls Him 'Lord,' how is He his son?"	*22:45* "If David then calls Him 'Lord,' how is He his son?"	*12:37~* "David himself calls Him 'Lord'; so in what sense is He his son?"	*20:44* "Therefore David calls Him 'Lord,' and how is He his son?"
7 The large crowd enjoyed listening to [Jesus], <but> no one was able to answer Him a word, <and> nor did anyone dare to ask Him another question from that day on.	*22:46* No one was able to answer Him a word, nor did anyone dare from that day on to ask Him another question.	*12:~37* And the large crowd enjoyed listening to [Him].	

1. Psalm 110:1

7 - THE FINAL WEEK
Act 4: Wednesday - Woe To The Pharisees

Scene 2: Beware Of The Scribes and The Pharisees
The Temple, Jerusalem, *Judea*   Wednesday, April 1st / 33 CE

A Verse-By-Verse Harmony of The Four Gospels

#	Matthew	Mark	Luke
1	While the crowds <of> people were listening, Jesus spoke to His disciples.	23:1 ~~Then~~ Jesus spoke ~~to~~ the crowds ~~and~~ to His disciples,		20:45 ~~And~~ while ~~all the~~ people were listening, ~~He~~ said to ~~the~~ disciples,
2	In His teaching He was saying, "The scribes and the Pharisees have seated themselves in the chair of Moses, therefore all that they tell you, do and observe;	23:2 saying: "The scribes and the Pharisees have seated themselves in the chair of Moses; 23:3~ therefore all that they tell you, do and observe,	12:38~ In His teaching He was saying:	
3	"but do not do according to their deeds, for they say things, and do not do them.	23:~3 but do not do according to their deeds; for they say things and do not do them.		
4	"They tie up heavy burdens, and lay them on men's shoulders, but they themselves are unwilling to move them with so much as a finger.	23:4 "They tie up heavy burdens and lay them on men's shoulders, but they themselves are unwilling to move them with so much as a finger.		
5	"They do all their deeds to be noticed by men, for they broaden their phylacteries, and lengthen the tassels of their garments.	23:5 ~~But~~ they do all their deeds to be noticed by men; for they broaden their phylacteries and lengthen the tassels of their garments.		
6	"<So> beware of the scribes who like to walk around in long robes, and love respectful greetings in the market places, and the chief seats in the synagogues, the places of honor at banquets, and being called Rabbi by men.	23:6 ~~They~~ love the place of honor at banquets and the chief seats in the synagogues, 23:7 and respectful greetings in the market places, and being called Rabbi by men.	12:~38 Beware of the scribes who like to walk around in long robes, and ~~like~~ respectful greetings in the market places, 12:39 and chief seats in the synagogues and places of honor at banquets,	20:46 "Beware of the scribes, who like to walk around in long robes, and love respectful greetings in the market places, and chief seats in the synagogues and places of honor at banquets,
7	"But do not be called Rabbi; for One is your Teacher, and you are all brothers.	23:8 "But do not be called Rabbi; for One is your Teacher, and you are all brothers.		
8	"Do not call anyone on earth your father, for you [have] One Father, who is in Heaven.	23:9 "Do not call anyone on earth your father; for One [is] ~~your~~ Father, ~~He~~ who is in heaven.		
9	"Do not be called leaders; for One is your Leader, that is, Christ.	23:10 "Do not be called leaders; for One is your Leader, that is, Christ.		
10	"The greatest among you shall be your servant, <and> whoever exalts himself shall be humbled, and whoever humbles himself shall be exalted.	23:11 ~~But~~ the greatest among you shall be your servant. 23:12 "Whoever exalts himself shall be humbled; and whoever humbles himself shall be exalted.		
11	"But woe to you, scribes and Pharisees! Hypocrites, because you shut off the Kingdom of Heaven from people; for you yourselves do not enter in, <and> nor do you allow those who are entering to go in."	23:13 "But woe to you, scribes and Pharisees, hypocrites, because you shut off the kingdom of heaven from people; for you do not enter in yourselves, nor do you allow those who are entering to go in.		

7 - THE FINAL WEEK Act 4: **Wednesday -** **Woe To The Pharisees**	Scene 3: **The Hypocrisy Of The Scribes and The Pharisees** The Temple, Jerusalem, *Judea* Wednesday, April 1st / 33 CE		Page 218 *A Four Gospel Harmony*
	Matthew	**Mark**	**Luke**
1 "Woe to you, scribes and Pharisees! Hypocrites, because you devour widows' houses, and for appearance's sake you make long prayers; therefore you will receive greater condemnation!	23:14 {"Woe to you, scribes and Pharisees, hypocrites, because you devour widows' houses, and for a ~~pretense~~ you make long prayers; therefore you will receive greater condemnation.}	12:40 ~~who~~ devour widows' houses, and for appearance's sake ~~offer~~ long prayers; ~~these~~ will receive greater condemnation.	20:47 ~~who~~ devour widows' houses, and for appearance's sake ~~offer~~ long prayers. ~~These~~ will receive greater condemnation."
2 "Woe to you, scribes and Pharisees! Hypocrites, because you travel around on land and sea to make one proselyte; and when he becomes one, you make him twice as much a son of hell as yourselves!	23:15 "Woe to you, scribes and Pharisees, hypocrites, because you travel around on sea and land to make one proselyte; and when he becomes one, you make him twice as much a son of hell as yourselves.		
3 "Woe to you, blind guides who say, 'Whoever swears by the Temple, that is nothing, but whoever swears by the gold of the Temple is obligated.'	23:16 "Woe to you, blind guides, who say, 'Whoever swears by the temple, that is nothing; but whoever swears by the gold of the temple is obligated.'		
4 "You fools and blind men! Which is more important; the gold, or the Temple that sanctified the gold?	23:17 "You fools and blind men! Which is more important, the gold or the temple that sanctified the gold?		
5 "And <you say,> 'Whoever swears by the altar, that is nothing, but whoever swears by the offering on it, he is obligated.'	23:18 "And, 'Whoever swears by the altar, that is nothing, but whoever swears by the offering on it, he is obligated.'		
6 "You blind men! Which is more important; the offering, or *the altar that sanctifies the offering?* [1]	23:19 "You blind men, which is more important, the offering, or the altar that sanctifies the offering?		
7 "Therefore, whoever swears by the altar, swears by both the altar and by everything on it.	23:20 "Therefore, whoever swears by the altar, swears both by the altar and by everything on it.		
8 "And whoever swears by the Temple, swears by both the Temple and by Him who dwells within it.	23:21 "And whoever swears by the temple, swears both by the temple and by Him who dwells within it.		
9 "And whoever swears by Heaven, swears by both the throne of God, and by Him who sits upon it.	23:22 "And whoever swears by heaven, swears both by the throne of God and by Him who sits upon it.		
10 "Woe to you, scribes and Pharisees, hypocrites! For you tithe mint and dill and cummin, and have neglected the weightier provisions of the law: justice and mercy and faithfulness.	23:23~ "Woe to you, scribes and Pharisees, hypocrites! For you tithe mint and dill and cummin, and have neglected the weightier provisions of the law: justice and mercy and faithfulness;		
11 "These are the things you should have done, without neglecting the others.	23:~23 these are the things you should have done without neglecting the others.		
12 "You blind guides who strain out a gnat, and swallow a camel!"	23:24 "You blind guides, who strain out a gnat and swallow a camel!		

1. *Exodus 29:37; 30:29*

7 - THE FINAL WEEK	Scene 4: **First, Clean The Inside of The Cup**	Page 219
Act 4: **Wednesday -**	The Temple, Jerusalem, *Judea* Wednesday, April 1st / 33 CE	
Woe To The Pharisees		*The Greatest Four Gospel Harmony & Merger*

	Matthew
1 "Woe to you, scribes and Pharisees! Hypocrites, [because] you clean the outside of the cup and of the dish, but inside [you] are full of robbery and self-indulgence!	23:25 "Woe to you, scribes and Pharisees, hypocrites! [For] you clean the outside of the cup and of the dish, but inside [they] are full of robbery and self-indulgence.
2 "You blind Pharisee! First clean the inside of the cup and the dish, so that the outside of it may become clean also.	23:26 "You blind Pharisee, first clean the inside of the cup and of the dish, so that the outside of it may become clean also.
3 "Woe to you, scribes and Pharisees! Hypocrites, [because] you are like whitewashed tombs, which on the outside appear beautiful, but inside they are full of dead men's bones, and all uncleanness.	23:27 "Woe to you, scribes and Pharisees, hypocrites! [For] you are like whitewashed tombs which on the outside appear beautiful, but inside they are full of dead men's bones and all uncleanness.
4 "So you too appear outwardly righteous to men, but in[side] you are full of hypocrisy and lawlessness."	23:28 "So you, too, outwardly appear righteous to men, but in[wardly] you are full of hypocrisy and lawlessness.

Scene 5: **You Shed The Blood of The Prophets**

The Temple, Jerusalem, *Judea* Wednesday, April 1st / 33 CE

	Matthew	Luke
1 "Woe to you, scribes and Pharisees! Hypocrites, [because] you build the tombs of the prophets, and adorn the monuments of the righteous, and it was your fathers who killed them!	23:29 "Woe to you, scribes and Pharisees, hypocrites! [For] you build the tombs of the prophets and adorn the monuments of the righteous,	11:47 "Woe to you! [For] you build the tombs of the prophets, and it was your fathers who killed them.
2 "<You> say, 'If we had been living in the days of our fathers, we would not have been partners with them in shedding the blood of the prophets.'	23:30 and say, 'If we had been living in the days of our fathers, we would not have been partners with them in shedding the blood of the prophets.'	
3 "So you are witnesses, <and> testify against yourselves, that you are <the> sons of those who murdered the prophets, and <that you> approve <of> the deeds of your fathers, because it was they who killed them, and you build their tombs!	23:31 "So you testify against yourselves, that you are sons of those who murdered the prophets.	11:48 "So you are witnesses and approve the deeds of your fathers; because it was they who killed them, and you build their tombs.
4 "For this reason, the wisdom of God said, 'Behold, I am sending to you prophets and apostles, wise men and scribes; some of them you will scourge in your synagogues, and persecute from city to city.	23:34~ "Therefore, behold, I am sending you prophets and wise men and scribes; and some of them you will scourge in your synagogues, and 23:~34 persecute from city to city,	11:49~ "For this reason also the wisdom of God said, 'I will send to them prophets and apostles, 11:~49 persecute,
5 "Some of them you will kill, and some [you] will crucify, so that upon this generation may fall the guilt of all the righteous blood of all the prophets shed on the earth, since the foundation of the world;	23:~34 some of them you will kill and crucify, 23:35 so that upon you may fall the guilt of all the righteous blood shed on the earth	11:~49 and some of them they will kill and some [they] will 11:50 so that the blood of all the prophets, shed since the foundation of the world, may be charged against this generation,
6 "from *the blood of righteous Able,*[1] *to the blood of Zechariah, the son of Berechiah, whom you murdered [beside] the altar <in> the House of God.'*[2]	23:~35 from the blood of righteous Abel to the blood of Zechariah, the son of Berechiah, whom you murdered [between] the temple [and] the altar.	11:51~ from the blood of Abel to the blood of Zechariah, who was killed between the altar and the house of God;
7 "Yes, truly I say to you, all these things will be charged against this generation. Fill up, then, the measure of the guilt of your fathers!	23:36 "Truly I say to you, all these things will come upon this generation. 23:32 "Fill up, then, the measure of the guilt of your fathers.	11:~51 yes, I tell you, it shall be charged against this generation.'
8 "You serpents! You brood of vipers! How will you escape the sentence of hell?"	23:33 "You serpents, you brood of vipers, how will you escape the sentence of hell?	

1. Genesis 4:8   2. (2 Chronicles 24:20-21)

7 - THE FINAL WEEK
Act 4: Wednesday - Woe To The Pharisees

Scene 6: A Second Lament For Jerusalem
The Temple, Jerusalem, *Judea* Wednesday, April 1st / 33 CE

The United Gospel of Jesus Christ

	Matthew	Luke
1 "O Jerusalem, Jerusalem, the city that kills the prophets, and stones those who are sent to her!	23:37~ "Jerusalem, Jerusalem, ~~who~~ kills the prophets and stones those who are sent to her!	13:34~ "O Jerusalem, Jerusalem, the city that kills the prophets and stones those sent to her!
2 "How often I wanted to gather your children together, just the way <that> a hen gathers her brood <of> chicks under her wings; [but] you were unwilling, and you would not have it.	23:~37 How often I wanted to gather your children together, the way a hen gathers her chicks under her wings, [~~and~~] you were unwilling.	13:~34 How often I wanted to gather your children together, just ~~as~~ a hen gathers her brood under her wings, and you would not have it!
3 "Behold, your house is being left to you desolate.	23:38 "Behold, your house is being left to you desolate!	13:35~ "Behold, your house is left to you desolate;
4 "And I say to you, <that> you will not see Me from now on, until the time comes when you say, 'Blessed is He who comes in the Name of the Lord!' " [1].	23:39 "~~For~~ I say to you, from now on you will not see Me until you say, 'Blessed is He who comes in the name of the Lord!' "	13:~35 and I say to you, you will not see Me until the time comes when you say, 'Blessed is He who comes in the name of the Lord!' "

1. Psalm 118:26

Scene 7: The Greatest Contributor To The Treasury
The Temple, Jerusalem, *Judea* Wednesday, April 1st / 33 CE

	Mark	Luke
1 [Jesus] sat down opposite the treasury, and began observing how the people were putting <their> money into the treasury.	12:41~ ~~And~~ [He] sat down opposite the treasury, and began observing how the people were putting money into the treasury;	21:1~ And ~~He looked up~~ 21:~1 into the treasury.
2 <He> saw the many rich people putting in their large sums, and He saw a poor widow [come] and put in two small copper coins, which amount to a cent.	12:~41 ~~and~~ many rich people ~~were~~ putting in large sums. 12:42 A poor widow [~~came~~] and put in two small copper coins, which amount to a cent.	21:~1 ~~and~~ saw the rich putting their ~~gifts~~ 21:2 And He saw a poor widow putt~~ing~~ in two small copper coins.
3 Calling His disciples to Him, [Jesus] said to them, "Truly I say to you, <that> this poor widow put in to the treasury more than all of the <other> contributors; for they all put into the offering out of their surplus, but she, out of her poverty, put in all she owned, all that she had to live on."	12:43 Calling His disciples to Him, [He] said to them, "Truly I say to you, this poor widow put in more than all the contributors to the treasury; 12:44 for they all put in out of their surplus, but she, out of her poverty, put in all she owned, all she had to live on."	21:3 ~~And~~ [He] said, "Truly I say to you, this poor widow put in more than all of ~~them~~; 21:4 for they all out of their surplus put into the offering; but she out of her poverty put in all that she had to live on."

7 - THE FINAL WEEK
Act 5: Wednesday - The End of The Age

Scene 1: The Temple Will Be Destroyed

The Temple, Jerusalem, *Judea*   Wednesday, April 1st / 33 CE

Page 221

90% of John is non-synoptic (unique)

	Matthew	Mark	Luke
1 Jesus came out of the Temple and was [leaving], when some <of> His [apostles] [began] talking about the Temple, <and saying> that it was adorned with beautiful stones and votive gifts.	24:1 Jesus came out ~~from~~ the temple and was going away when His [~~disciples~~] ~~came up to point out~~ the temple ~~buildings to Him~~.	13:1~ ~~As~~ ~~He~~ ~~was~~ ~~going~~ out of the temple,	21:5~ ~~And~~ ~~while~~ some [~~were~~] talking about the temple, that it was adorned with beautiful stones and votive gifts,
2 One of [them] said to [Jesus], "Teacher, behold! What wonderful stones, and what wonderful buildings!"		13:~1 one of [~~His disciples~~] said to [~~Him~~], "Teacher, behold what wonderful stones and what wonderful buildings!"	
3 Jesus said to them, "As for all these great buildings which you are looking at, truly, I say to you, the days will come [when] there will not be left one stone upon another here, which will not be torn down."	24:2 And ~~He~~ said to them, "~~Do you not see~~ all these ~~things~~? Truly I say to you, not one stone here will be left upon another, which will not be torn down."	13:2 ~~And~~ Jesus said to ~~him~~, "~~Do you see~~ these great buildings? Not one stone will be left upon another which will not be torn down."	21:~5 ~~He~~ said, 21:6 "As for these ~~things~~ which you are looking at, the days will come [in which] there will not be left one stone upon another which will not be torn down."

7 - THE FINAL WEEK
Act 5: Wednesday - The End of The Age

Scene 2: The Signs of The End of The Age
Mount of Olives, Jerusalem, *Judea* Wednesday, April 1st / 33 CE

The Ultimate Gospel

	Matthew	Mark	Luke
1 As [Jesus] was sitting on the Mount of Olives, opposite the Temple, [His] [apostles] Peter, James, John and Andrew came to Him, <and they> questioned Him privately, saying, "Teacher, tell us when will these things happen,	24:3~ As [He] was sitting on the Mount of Olives, [the] [disciples] came to Him privately, saying, "Tell us, when will these things happen,	13:3 As [He] was sitting on the Mount of Olives opposite the temple, Peter and James and John and Andrew were questioning Him privately, 13:4~ "Tell us, when will these things be,	21:7~ They questioned Him, saying, "Teacher, when therefore will these things happen?
2 "and what will be the sign of Your coming, and of the end of the age, when all these things are going to take place?"	24:~3 and what will be the sign of Your coming, and of the end of the age?	13:~4 and what will be the sign when all these things are going to be fulfilled?"	21:~7 And what will be the sign when these things are about to take place?"
3 Jesus answered, and began to say to them, "See to it that no one misleads you, for many will come in My Name, saying, 'I am the Christ!' and, 'The time is near!' and will mislead many, <so> do not go after them."	24:4 And Jesus answered and said to them, "See to it that no one misleads you. 24:5 "For many will come in My name, saying, 'I am the Christ,' and will mislead many.	13:5 And Jesus began to say to them, "See to it that no one misleads you. 13:6 "Many will come in My name, saying, 'I am He!' and will mislead many.	21:8 And He said, "See to it that you are not misled; for many will come in My name, saying, 'I am He,' and, 'The time is near.' Do not go after them.
4 Then [Jesus] continued by saying to them, "You will be hearing of wars and rumors of wars. When you hear of wars and disturbances do not be frightened, for these things must take place first, but the end does not follow immediately.	24:6 "You will be hearing of wars and rumors of wars. See that you are not frightened, for these things must take place, but that is not yet the end.	13:7 "When you hear of wars and rumors of wars, do not be frightened; these things must take place; but that is not yet the end.	21:10~ Then [He] continued by saying to them, 21:9 "When you hear of wars and disturbances, do not be terrified; for these things must take place first, but the end does not follow immediately."
5 "For nation will rise up against nation, and kingdom against kingdom; in various places there will be great earthquakes and famines, and plagues;	24:7 "For nation will rise against nation, and kingdom against kingdom, in various places there will be famines and earthquakes	13:8~ "For nation will rise up against nation, and kingdom against kingdom, there will be earthquakes in various places; there will also be famines.	21:~10 "Nation will rise against nation and kingdom against kingdom, 21:11~ and there will be great earth-quakes, and in various places plagues and famines;
6 "and there will also be terrors, and great signs from heaven.			21:~11 and there will be great earth-quakes, and in various places plagues and famines; and there will be terrors and great signs from heaven.
7 "But all these things are [only] the beginning of birth pangs."	24:8 "But all these things are [merely] the beginning of birth pangs.	13:~8 These things are [merely] the beginning of birth pangs.	

7 - THE FINAL WEEK
Act 5: **Wednesday -
The End of The Age**

Scene 3: **Your Testimony When They Persecute You**

Mount of Olives, Jerusalem, *Judea*   Wednesday, April 1st / 33 CE

Page 223

A United Harmony of the Four Gospels

	Matthew	Mark	Luke
1 "Be on your guard, [because] before all <of> these things, they will lay their hands on you, and <they> will persecute you.		13:9~ "But be on your guard;	21:12~ "[But] before all these things, they will lay their hands on you and will persecute you,
2 "Then they will deliver you to tribulation [in] the courts, and you will be flogged in the synagogues and prisons.	24:9~ Then they will deliver you to tribulation,	13:~9 for they will deliver you [to] the courts, and you will be flogged in the synagogues,	21:~12 delivering you to the synagogues and prisons,
3 "<And they> will bring you <to stand> before governors and kings, for My sake. [This] will lead to an opportunity for your testimony to them.		13:~9 and you will stand before governors and kings for My sake as a testimony to them.	21:~12 bringing you before kings and governors for My name's sake. 21:13 "[It] will lead to an opportunity for your testimony.
4 "<So> when they arrest you and hand you over, do not worry beforehand about what you are to say, but say whatever is given <to> you in that <very> hour; for it is not you who speaks, but it is the Holy Spirit.		13:11 "When they arrest you and hand you over, do not worry beforehand about what you are to say, but say whatever is given you in that hour; for it is not you who speak, but it is the Holy Spirit.	
5 "So [do] not prepare <a> defens[e] for [yourself] beforehand, for I will give you [speech] and wisdom which none of your opponents will be able to resist, or refute."			21:14 "So [make up your minds] not to prepare beforehand to [defend] [yourselves]; 21:15 for I will give you [utterance] and wisdom which none of your opponents will be able to resist or refute.

Scene 4: **You Will Be Hated Because Of My Name**

	Matthew	Mark	Luke
1 "Many false prophets will arise and mislead many; <and> because lawlessness [has] increased, most people's love will grow cold.	24:11 "Many false prophets will arise and will mislead many. 24:12 "Because lawlessness [is] increased, most people's love will grow cold.		
2 "At that time, many will fall away, and hate one another, and you will be betrayed.	24:10 "At that time many will fall away and will betray one another and hate one another.		21:16~ "But you will be betrayed
3 "Brother will betray brother to death, and a father his child; and children will rise up against <their> parents, and relatives, and friends;		13:12 "Brother will betray brother to death, and a father his child; and children will rise up against parents	21:~16 even by parents, and brothers and relatives and friends,
4 "and they will put some of you to death.	24:~9 and will kill you,	13:~12 and have them put to death.	21:~16 and they will put some of you to death,
5 "You will be hated by all because of My Name, <and> yet not [one] hair of your head will perish.	24:~9 and you will be hated by all nations because of My name.	13:13~ "You will be hated by all because of My name,	21:17 and you will be hated by all because of My name. 21:18 "Yet not [a] hair of your head will perish.
6 "By your endurance you will gain your lives, [and] the one who endures to the end will be saved.	24:13 "[But] the one who endures to the end, he will be saved.	13:~13 [but] the one who endures to the end, he will be saved.	21:19 "By your endurance you will gain your lives.
7 "This gospel of the Kingdom must first be preached in the whole world, as a testimony to all the nations, and then the end will come."	24:14 "This gospel of the kingdom shall be preached in the whole world as a testimony to all the nations, and then the end will come.	13:10 "The gospel must first be preached to all the nations.	

7 - THE FINAL WEEK
Act 5: Wednesday - The End of The Age

Scene 5: Do Not Turn Back!
Mount of Olives, Jerusalem, *Judea* Wednesday, April 1st / 33 CE

	Matthew	Mark	Luke
1 "When you see Jerusalem surrounded by armies, then recognize that her desolation is near.			21:20 "~~But~~ when you see Jerusalem surrounded by armies, then recognize that her desolation is near.
2 "[And] when you see *the abomination of desolation, which was spoken of [by] Daniel the prophet, standing in the Holy Place*[1] where it should not be (let the reader understand), then those who are in Judea must flee to the mountains, and those who are in the city must leave, and those who are in the country must not enter the city,	24:15 "[~~Therefore~~] when you see the abomination of desolation which was spoken of [~~through~~] Daniel the prophet, standing in the holy place (let the reader understand), 24:16 then those who are in Judea must flee to the mountains.	13:14 "[~~But~~] when you see the abomination of desolation standing where it should not be (let the reader understand), then those who are in Judea must flee to the mountains.	21:21 "Then those who are in Judea must flee to the mountains, and those who are in ~~the midst of~~ the city must leave, and those who are in the country must not enter the city;
3 "because these are days of vengeance, so that all <the> things which are written will be fulfilled.			21:22 because these are days of vengeance, so that all things which are written will be fulfilled.
4 "On that day, the one who is on the housetop, and whose goods are in the house, must not go down or go in to get anything out of his house.	24:17 "Who~~ever~~ is on the housetop must not go down to get ~~the~~ things out ~~that are in~~ his house.	13:15 "The one who is on the housetop must not go down, or go in to get anything out of his house;	17:31~ "On that day, the one who is on the housetop and whose goods are in the house must not go down to ~~take them~~ out;
5 "And likewise, whoever is in the field must not turn back to get his coat.	24:18 "Whoever is in the field must not turn back to get his ~~cloak~~.	13:16 ~~and the one~~ who is in the field must not turn back to get his coat.	17:~31 and likewise ~~the one~~ who is in the field must not turn back.
6 "Remember Lot's wife; whoever seeks to keep his life will lose it, and whoever loses his life will preserve it.			17:32 "Remember Lot's wife. 17:33 "Whoever seeks to keep his life will lose it, and whoever loses his life will preserve it.
7 "But woe to those who are pregnant, and to those who are nursing babies in those days, for there will be great distress upon the land, and wrath to this people!	24:19 "But woe to those who are pregnant and to those who are nursing babies in those days!	13:17 "But woe to those who are pregnant and to those who are nursing babies in those days!	21:23 "Woe to those who are pregnant and to those who are nursing babies in those days; for there will be great distress upon the land and wrath to this people;
8 "They will fall by the edge of the sword, and be led captive into all the nations;			21:24~ ~~and~~ they will fall by the edge of the sword, and ~~will~~ be led captive into all the nations;
9 "and *Jerusalem will be trampled under foot by the Gentiles, until the times of the Gentiles are fulfilled.*[2]			21:~24 and Jerusalem will be trampled under foot by the Gentiles until the times of the Gentiles are fulfilled.
10 "But pray that your flight may not happen in the winter, or on a Sabbath;	24:20 "But pray that your flight ~~will~~ not ~~be~~ in the winter, or on a Sabbath.	13:18 "But pray that ~~it~~ may not happen in the winter.	
11 "*for those days will be a time of great tribulation, such as has not occurred since the beginning*[3] *of the creation of the world which God created until now, nor ever will.*	24:21 "For ~~then there~~ will be a great tribulation, such as has not occurred since the beginning of the world until now, nor ever will.	13:19 "For those days will be a time of tribulation such as has not occurred since the beginning of the creation which God created until now, ~~and never will~~.	
12 "<And> unless the Lord had shortened those days, no life would have been saved; but for the sake of the elect whom He chose, those days will be cut short."	24:22 "Unless those days had ~~been cut~~ short, no life would have been saved; but for the sake of the elect those days will be cut short.	13:20 "Unless the Lord had shortened those days, no life would have been saved; but for the sake of the elect, whom He chose, ~~He~~ shorten~~ed~~ the days.	

1. Daniel (9:27); 11:31; 12:11   2. Daniel 9:27, 12:7   3. Daniel (9:26); 12:1 / (Jeremiah 30:7)

7 - THE FINAL WEEK
Act 5: Wednesday - The End of The Age

Scene 6: False Christs Will Arise

Mount of Olives, Jerusalem, *Judea* Wednesday, April 1st / 33 CE

The Unified Gospel Story

#		Matthew	Mark	Luke
1	[Then] [Jesus] said to the [apostles], "The days will come when you will long to see one of the days of the Son of Man, and you will not see it.			17:22 [And] [He] said to the [~~disciples~~], "The days will come when you will long to see one of the days of the Son of Man, and you will not see it.
2	"And then if anyone says to you, 'Behold, here is the Christ,' or 'Look, He is there!' do not believe him, <and> do not go and run away after them;	24:23 "Then if anyone says to you, 'Behold, here is the Christ,' or 'There He is,' do not believe him.	13:21 "And then if anyone says to you, 'Behold, here is the Christ'; or '~~Behold~~, He is there'; do not believe him;	17:23 "~~They will~~ say to you, '~~Look~~ there! Look here!' Do not go away, and ~~do not~~ run after them.
3	"for false Christs and false prophets will arise, and will show signs and wonders, so as to lead astray if possible, even the elect.	24:24 "For false Christs and false prophets will arise and will show great signs and wonders, so as to mislead, if possible, even the elect.	13:22 for false Christs and false prophets will arise, and will show signs and wonders, ~~in order~~ to lead astray, if possible, the elect.	
4	"But take heed! Behold, I have told you everything in advance.	24:25 "Behold, I have told you in advance.	13:23 "But take heed; behold, I have told you everything in advance.	
5	"So if they say to you, 'Behold, He is in the wilderness,' do not go out; or, 'Behold, He is in the inner rooms,' do not believe them.	24:26 "So if they say to you, 'Behold, He is in the wilderness,' do not go out, or, 'Behold, He is in the inner rooms,' do not believe them.		
6	"For just as the lightning comes from the east, and flashes even to the west, so will the coming of the Son of Man be in His day."	24:27 "For just as the lightning comes from the east and flashes even to the west, so will the coming of the Son of Man be.		17:24 "For just ~~like~~ the lightning, ~~when it~~ flashes ~~out of one part of~~ the sky, ~~shines~~ to the ~~other part of the sky~~, so will the Son of Man be in His day.

7 - THE FINAL WEEK
Act 5: Wednesday - The End of The Age

Scene 7: Signs In The Sun, Moon and Stars

Mount of Olives, Jerusalem, *Judea* Wednesday, April 1st / 33 CE

#	Matthew	Mark	Luke
1	"Immediately after the tribulation of those days, there will be signs in <the> sun, <and the> moon, and <the> stars.	24:29~ "~~But~~ immediately after the tribulation of those days	13:24~ "~~But in~~ those days, after ~~that~~ tribulation,	21:25~ "There will be signs in sun ~~and~~ moon and stars,
2	"*The sun will be darkened, and the moon will not give its light;* [1]	24:~29 the sun will be darkened, and the moon will not give its light,	13:~24 the sun will be darkened and the moon will not give its light,	
3	"*and the stars will be falling from heaven, for the powers that are in the heavens will be shaken.* [2]	24:~29 and the stars will fall from ~~the sky, and~~ the powers ~~of~~ the heavens will be shaken.	13:25 and the stars will be falling from heaven, ~~and~~ the powers that are in the heavens will be shaken.	21:~26 for the powers ~~of~~ the heavens will be shaken.
4	"And on the earth, dismay among nations <who are> perplex[ed] at the roaring of the sea and the waves, <with> men fainting from fear [at] the expectation of the things which are coming upon the world.			21:~25 and on the earth dismay among nations, ~~in~~ perplex[ity] at the roaring of the sea and the waves, 21:26~ men fainting from fear [and] the expectation of the things which are coming upon the world;
5	"Then the sign of the Son of Man will appear in the sky, and *all the tribes of the earth will mourn.*	24:30~ "~~And~~ then the sign of the Son of Man will appear in the sky, and ~~then~~ all the tribes of the earth will mourn,		
6	"*And they will see the Son of Man coming in the clouds* [3] *of* [heaven], *with great power and glory!*	24:~30 and they will see the Son of Man coming ~~on~~ the clouds of [~~the sky~~]* with power and great glory.	13:26 "[~~Then~~] they will see the Son of Man coming in clouds with power and great glory.	21:27 "[~~Then~~] they will see the Son of Man coming in ~~a~~ cloud with power and great glory.
7	"Then He will send forth His angels with a great trumpet, and they will gather together His elect from the four winds, from the farthest end of the earth to the farthest end of Heaven.	24:31 "~~And~~ He will send forth His angels with a great trumpet and they will gather together His elect from the four winds, from ~~one~~ end of the ~~sky~~ to the ~~other~~.	13:27 "~~And~~ then He will send forth ~~the~~ angels, and will gather together His elect from the four winds, from the farthest end of the earth to the farthest end of heaven.	
8	"But when <you see> these things begin to take place, straighten up, and lift up your heads, because your redemption is drawing near!"			21:28 "But when these things begin to take place, straighten up and lift up your heads, because your redemption is drawing near."

1. Ecclesiastes 12:2 / Isaiah 13:10 / Ezekiel 32:7-8 / Joel 2:10; 3:15 / Zephaniah 1:15   2. Daniel 8:10 / (Revelation 12:3-9)   3. Revelation 1:7 / (Daniel 7:13)

7 - THE FINAL WEEK

Act 6: Wednesday - The Return

Scene 1: The Parable of The Fig Tree

Mount of Olives, Jerusalem, *Judea* Wednesday, April 1st / 33 CE

All the Gospel Deeds of Jesus

	Matthew	Mark	Luke
1	Then [Jesus] [said] <to> them, "Now learn a parable. behold the fig and all the trees: as soon as it puts forth its leaves you see it, and know for yourselves that summer is now near.	24:32 "Now learn ~~the~~ parable ~~from~~ the fig ~~tree: when its branch has already become tender and~~ puts forth its leaves, you know that summer is near;	13:28 "Now learn ~~the~~ parable ~~from~~ the fig ~~tree: when its branch has already become tender and~~ puts forth its leaves, you know that summer is near;	21:29 Then [He] [told] them a parable: "Behold the fig ~~tree~~ and all the trees; 21:30 as soon as ~~they~~ put forth leaves, you see it and know for yourselves that summer is now near.
2	"Even so, when you see all these things happening, recognize that the Kingdom of God is near, <and> He <is> right at the door.	24:33 so, ~~you too~~, when you see all these things, recognize that He is near, right at the door.	13:29 "Even so, ~~you too~~, when you see these things happening, recognize that He is near, right at the door.	21:31 "So ~~you also~~, when you see these things happening, recognize that the kingdom of God is near.
3	"Truly I say to you, this generation will not pass away until all these things take place.	24:34 "Truly I say to you, this generation will not pass away until all these things take place.	13:30 "Truly I say to you, this generation will not pass away until all these things take place.	21:32 "Truly I say to you, this generation will not pass away until all things take place.
4	*"Heaven and earth will pass away, but My words will not pass away.*[1]	24:35 "Heaven and earth will pass away, but My words will not pass away.	13:31 "Heaven and earth will pass away, but My words will not pass away.	21:33 "Heaven and earth will pass away, but My words will not pass away.
5	"But of that day and hour, no one knows - not even the angels in Heaven, nor the Son - but The Father alone.	24:36 "But of that day and hour no one knows, not even the angels ~~of~~ heaven, nor the Son, but the Father alone.	13:32 "But of that day or hour no one knows, not even the angels in heaven, nor the Son, but the Father alone.	
6	"But first, He must suffer many things, and be rejected by this generation.			17:25 "But first He must suffer many things and be rejected by this generation.
7	"For the coming of the Son of Man will be just like it happened in *the days of Noah*;[2] for in those days before the flood, they were eating and they were drinking, <and> they were marrying and being given in marriage, until the day that Noah entered the ark.	24:37 "For the coming of the Son of Man will be just like the days of Noah. 24:38 "For ~~as~~ in those days before the flood they were eating and drinking, marrying and giv~~ing~~ in marriage, until the day that Noah entered the ark,		17:26 "~~And~~ just as it happened in the days of Noah, ~~so it will be also in the days of the~~ Son of Man: 17:27~ they were eating, they were drinking, they were marrying, ~~they were~~ being given in marriage, until the day that Noah entered the ark,
8	"And they did not understand until the flood came, and took them all away.	24:39~ and they did not understand until the flood came and took them all ~~away~~;		17:~27 ~~and~~ the flood came and ~~destroyed~~ them all.
9	"The same [thing] happened in *the days of Lot*:[3] They were eating <and> they were drinking, they were buying <and> they were selling, they were planting <and> they were building;			17:28 "[It] ~~was~~ the same ~~as~~ happened in the days of Lot: they were eating, they were drinking, they were buying, they were selling, they were planting, they were building;
10	"but on the day that Lot went out from Sodom, it rained fire and brimstone from heaven, and destroyed them all.			17:29 but on the day that Lot went out from Sodom it rained fire and brimstone from heaven and destroyed them all.
11	"So it will be just the same, on the day that the Son of Man is revealed."	24:~39 so will the ~~coming of~~ the Son of Man be.		17:30 "It will be just the same on the day that the Son of Man is revealed.

1. (Isaiah 40:8)   2. Genesis 7:6 – 9:29   3. Genesis 19:1-29

7 - THE FINAL WEEK

Act 6: Wednesday - The Return

Scene 2: One Will Be Taken, and The Other Will Be Left

Mount of Olives, Jerusalem, *Judea*   Wednesday, April 1st / 33 CE

	Matthew	Mark	Luke
1 "I tell you, on that night there will be two <people> in one bed; one will be taken, and the other will be left.			*17:34* "I tell you, on that night there will be two in one bed; one will be taken and the other will be left.
2 "There will be two men in the field; one will be taken, and the other will be left.	*24:40* "~~Then~~ there will be two men in the field; one will be taken and ~~one~~ will be left.		*17:36* {"Two men will be in the field; one will be taken and the other will be left."}
3 "Two women will be grinding at the same mill; one will be taken, and the other will be left."	*24:41* "Two women will be grinding at the mill; one will be taken and ~~one~~ will be left.		*17:35* "~~There~~ will be two women grinding at the same ~~place~~; one will be taken and the other will be left.
4 They [asked] Him, "Where, Lord?"			*17:37~* ~~And answering~~ they [~~said to~~] Him, "Where, Lord?"
5 [Jesus] said, "Wherever the corpse is, there the vultures will also be gathered.	*24:28* "Wherever the corpse is, there the vultures will gather.		*17:~37* ~~And~~ [He] said ~~to them~~, "Where the ~~body~~ is, there the vultures will also be gathered.
6 "Therefore take heed, <and> keep on the alert, for you do not know when the appointed day <of> your Lord will come."	*24:42* "Therefore ~~be~~ on the alert, for you do not know ~~which~~ day your Lord ~~is coming~~.	*13:33* "Take heed, keep on the alert; for you do not know when the appointed ~~time~~ will come.	

7 - THE FINAL WEEK

Act 6: Wednesday - The Return

Scene 3: Be On The Alert!

Mount of Olives, Jerusalem, *Judea* Wednesday, April 1st / 33 CE

All the Gospel Miracles of Jesus

	Matthew	Mark	Luke
1 "Be on guard, so that your hearts will not be weighed down with dissipation and drunkenness, and the worries of <this> life, and that day come [up]on you suddenly like a trap; for it will come upon all those who dwell on the face of all the earth.			21:34 "Be on guard, so that your hearts will not be weighted down with dissipation and drunkenness and the worries of life, and that day will not come on you suddenly like a trap; 21:35 for it will come upon all those who dwell on the face of all the earth.
2 "It is like a man going away on a journey, who upon leaving his house <he> put[s] his slaves in charge, assigning to each one his task; [and] <he> commanded the doorkeeper to stay on the alert.		13:34 "It is like a man away on a journey, who upon leaving his house and put[ting] his slaves in charge, assigning to each one his task, [also] commanded the doorkeeper to stay on the alert.	
3 "But be sure of this, that if the head of the house had known at what hour of the night the thief was coming, he would have been on the alert, and <he> would not have allowed his house to be broken into.	24:43 "But be sure of this, that if the head of the house had known at what time of the night the thief was coming, he would have been on the alert and would not have allowed his house to be broken into.		12:39 "But be sure of this, that if the head of the house had known at what hour the thief was coming, he would not have allowed his house to be broken into.
4 "Therefore, be on the alert! For you do not know when the master of the house is coming, whether in the evening, at midnight, or when the rooster crows, or in the morning - in case he should come suddenly, and find you asleep.		13:35 "Therefore, be on the alert - for you do not know when the master of the house is coming, whether in the evening, at midnight, or when the rooster crows, or in the morning - 13:36 in case he should come suddenly and find you asleep.	
5 "For this reason you also must be ready, for the Son of Man is coming at an hour when you do not expect <that> He will.	24:44 "For this reason you also must be ready; for the Son of Man is coming at an hour when you do not think He will.		12:40 "You too, be ready; for the Son of Man is coming at an hour that you do not expect."
6 "[So] keep on the alert at all times, praying that you may have <the> strength to escape <of> all these things that are about to take place, and to stand before the Son of Man.			21:36 "[But] keep on the alert at all times, praying that you may have strength to escape all these things that are about to take place, and to stand before the Son of Man."
7 "What I say to you, I say to all: 'Be on the alert!' "		13:37 "What I say to you I say to all, 'Be on the alert!' "	

7 - THE FINAL WEEK

Act 6: Wednesday - The Return

Scene 4: **Be Dressed In Readiness**

Mount of Olives, Jerusalem, *Judea* Wednesday, April 1st / 33 CE

The Texts of the Four Gospels Combined

		Matthew	Luke
1	"Be dressed in readiness, and keep your lamps lit!		*12:35* "Be dressed in readiness, and keep your lamps lit.
2	"Be like men who are waiting for their master when he returns from the wedding feast, so that they may immediately open the door to him when he comes and knocks.		*12:36* "Be like men who are waiting for their master when he returns from the wedding feast, so that they may immediately open the door to him when he comes and knocks.
3	"Blessed are those slaves whom the master will find on the alert when he comes!		*12:37~* "Blessed are those slaves whom the master will find on the alert when he comes;
4	"Truly I say to you, that he will gird himself to serve, and have them recline at the table; and \<he himself\> will come and wait on them.		*12:~37* truly I say to you, that he will gird himself to serve, and have them recline at the table, and will come ~~up~~ and wait on them.
5	"So whether he comes in the second watch, or even in the third, and finds them [ready], blessed are those slaves!"		*12:38* "Whether he comes in the second watch, or even in the third, and finds them [~~so~~], blessed are those slaves.
6	Peter said, "Lord, are You addressing this parable to us, or to everyone else as well?"		*12:41* Peter said, "Lord, are You addressing this parable to us, or to everyone else as well?"
7	[Jesus] said, "Who then is the faithful and sensible steward, whom his master will put in charge of his household servants, to give them their food \<and\> rations at the proper time?	*24:45* "Who then is the faithful and sensible ~~slave~~ whom his master put in charge of his household to give them their ~~food~~ at the proper time?	*12:42* ~~And~~ [~~the Lord~~] said, "Who then is the faithful and sensible steward, whom his master will put in charge of his servants, to give them their rations at the proper time?
8	"Blessed is that slave whom his master \<will\> find so doing when he comes! Truly I say to you, that he will put him in charge of all his possessions.	*24:46* "Blessed is that slave whom his master finds so doing when he comes. *24:47* "Truly I say to you that he will put him in charge of all his possessions.	*12:43* "Blessed is that slave whom his master finds so doing when he comes. *12:44* "Truly I say to you that he will put him in charge of all his possessions.
9	"But if that evil slave says in his heart, 'My master will not be coming for a long time', and \<he\> begins to beat his fellow slaves, both men and women, and to eat and get drunk with drunkards,	*24:48* "But if that evil slave says in his heart, 'My master ~~is~~ not coming for a long time,' *24:49* and begins to beat his fellow slaves and eat ~~and drink~~ with drunkards;	*12:45* "But if that slave says in his heart, 'My master will be a long time ~~in~~ coming,' and begins to beat ~~the~~ slaves, both men and women, and to eat ~~and drink~~ and get drunk;
10	"\<then\> the master of that slave will come on a day when he does not expect him, and at an hour which he does not know, and \<he\> will cut him in pieces, and assign him a place with the hypocrites, \<and the\> unbelievers; in that place there will be weeping, and gnashing of teeth.	*24:50* the master of that slave will come on a day when he does not expect him and at an hour which he does not know, *24:51* and will cut him in pieces and assign him a place with the hypocrites; in that place there will be weeping and gnashing of teeth.	*12:46* the master of that slave will come on a day when he does not expect him and at an hour he does not know, and will cut him in pieces, and assign him a place with ~~the~~ unbelievers.
11	"And that slave who knew his master's will, and did not get ready, or act in accord[ance] with [it], will receive many lashes;		*12:47* "And that slave who knew his master's will and did not get ready or act in accord with [~~his will~~], will receive many lashes,
12	"but the one who did not know it, and committed deeds worthy of a flogging, will receive [only] \<a\> few.		*12:48~* but the one who did not know it, and committed deeds worthy of a flogging, will receive [~~but~~] few.
13	"From everyone who has been given much, much will be required; and to whom they entrusted much, of him they will ask all the more."		*12:~48* From everyone who has been given much, much will be required; and to whom they entrusted much, of him they will ask all the more."

7 - THE FINAL WEEK

Act 6: **Wednesday - The Return**

Scene 5: **The Lamps of The Ten Virgins**

Mount of Olives, Jerusalem, *Judea*   Wednesday, April 1st / 33 CE

All the Gospel Teachings of Jesus

	Matthew
1 "[At that time,] the Kingdom of Heaven [may] be compar[ed] to ten virgins, who took their lamps, and went out to meet the bridegroom.	25:1 "[Then] the kingdom of heaven [will] be compar[able] to ten virgins, who took their lamps and went out to meet the bridegroom.
2 "Five of them were foolish and five were prudent; for when the foolish took their lamps, they took no oil with them, but the prudent took oil in flasks along with their lamps.	25:2 "Five of them were foolish, and five were prudent. 25:3 "For when the foolish took their lamps, they took no oil with them, 25:4 but the prudent took oil in flasks along with their lamps.
3 "Now while the bridegroom was delaying, they all got drowsy, and began to sleep.	25:5 "Now while the bridegroom was delaying, they all got drowsy and began to sleep.
4 "But at midnight there was a shout, 'Behold, the bridegroom! Come out to meet him!'	25:6 "But at midnight there was a shout, 'Behold, the bridegroom! Come out to meet him.'
5 "[When] [the ten] virgins rose and trimmed their lamps, the foolish said to the prudent, 'Give us some of your oil, for our lamps are going out!'	25:7 "[Then] [all those] virgins rose and trimmed their lamps. 25:8 "The foolish said to the prudent, 'Give us some of your oil, for our lamps are going out.'
6 "But the prudent answered, 'No, there will not be enough for us and you too. Go instead to the dealers, and buy some for yourselves.'	25:9 "But the prudent answered, 'No, there will not be enough for us and you too; go instead to the dealers and buy some for yourselves.'
7 "While they were going away to make the purchase the bridegroom came, and those who were ready went in with him to the wedding feast; and the door was shut.	25:10 "And while they were going away to make the purchase, the bridegroom came, and those who were ready went in with him to the wedding feast; and the door was shut.
8 "Later, the other virgins also came, saying, 'Lord, lord, open up [to] us!' But he answered, 'Truly I say to you, I do not know you.'	25:11 "Later the other virgins also came, saying, 'Lord, lord, open up [for] us.' 25:12 "But he answered, 'Truly I say to you, I do not know you.'
9 "Be on the alert then, [because] you do not know the day, or the hour."	25:13 "Be on the alert then, [for] you do not know the day nor the hour.

7 - THE FINAL WEEK

Act 6: Wednesday - The Return

Scene 6: Separating The Sheep From The Goats

Mount of Olives, Jerusalem, *Judea* Wednesday, April 1st / 33 CE

	Matthew	Mark	Luke
1	"When the Son of Man comes in His glory, and all the angels with Him, then He will sit on His glorious throne.	25:31 "~~But~~ when the Son of Man comes in His glory, and all the angels with Him, then He will sit on His glorious throne.		
2	"All the nations will be gathered before Him, and He will separate them one from another, as the shepherd separates the sheep from the goats;	25:32 "All the nations will be gathered before Him; and He will separate them from one another, as the shepherd separates the sheep from the goats;		
3	"and He will put the sheep on His right, and the goats on the left.	25:33 and He will put the sheep on His right, and the goats on the left.		
4	"Then the King will say to those on His right, 'Come, you who are blessed of My Father, inherit the Kingdom prepared for you from the foundation of the world!	25:34 "Then the King will say to those on His right, 'Come, you who are blessed of My Father, inherit the kingdom prepared for you from the foundation of the world.		
5	"For I was hungry, and you gave Me something to eat; I was thirsty, and you gave Me something to drink; I was a stranger, and you invited Me in; I was sick, and you visited Me; I was in prison, and you came to Me.'	25:35 For I was hungry, and you gave Me something to eat; I was thirsty, and you gave Me something to drink; I was a stranger, and you invited Me in; 25:36 I was sick, and you visited Me; I was in prison, and you came to Me.'		
6	"Then the righteous will answer Him, 'Lord, when did we see You hungry, and feed You; or thirsty, and give You something to drink?	25:37 "Then the righteous will answer Him, 'Lord, when did we see You hungry, and feed You, or thirsty, and give You something to drink?		
7	"When did we see You a stranger, and invite You in; or naked, and clothe You?	25:38 '~~And~~ when did we see You a stranger, and invite You in, or naked, and clothe You?		
8	"<Or> when did we see You sick or in prison, and come to You?'	25:39 'When did we see You sick, or in prison, and come to You?'		
9	"The King will answer, and say to them, 'Truly I say to you, to the extent that you did it to one of these brothers of Mine, even the least of them, you did it to Me.'	25:40 "The King will answer and say to them, 'Truly I say to you, to the extent that you did it to one of these brothers of Mine, even the least of them, you did it to Me.'		
10	"Then He will say to those on His left, *'Depart from Me accursed ones,*[1] *into the eternal fire which has been prepared for the Devil and his angels!*	25:41 "Then He will ~~also~~ say to those on His left, 'Depart from Me, accursed ones, into the eternal fire which has been prepared for the devil and his angels;		
11	"For I was hungry, and you gave Me nothing to eat; I was thirsty, and you gave Me nothing to drink;	25:42 for I was hungry, and you gave Me nothing to eat; I was thirsty, and you gave Me nothing to drink;		
12	"I was a stranger, and you did not invite Me in; naked, and you did not clothe Me; sick and in prison, and you did not visit Me.'	25:43 I was a stranger, and you did not invite Me in; naked, and you did not clothe Me; sick, and in prison, and you did not visit Me.'		
13	"Then they will [say], 'Lord, when did we see You hungry or thirsty, or a stranger, or naked, or sick, or in prison, and did not take care of You?'	25:44 "Then they ~~themselves also~~ will [answer], 'Lord, when did we see You hungry, or thirsty, or a stranger, or naked, or sick, or in prison, and did not take care of You?'		
14	"[And] He will answer them, 'Truly I say to you, <that> to the extent that you did not do it to one of the least of these, you did not do it to Me.'	25:45 "[~~Then~~] He will answer them, 'Truly I say to you, to the extent that you did not do it to one of the least of these, you did not do it to Me.'		

 1. *Psalm 6:8; 119:115*

continued >

7 - THE FINAL WEEK	Scene 6: **Separating The Sheep From The Goats**		Page 233
Act 6: **Wednesday - The Return**	*continued*		*All the Gospel Words of Jesus*

	Matthew	Mark	Luke
15 "These will go away into eternal punishment, but the righteous into eternal life."	25:46 "These will go away into eternal punishment, but the righteous into eternal life."		
16 When Jesus had finished all <of> these words, He said to His [apostles], "You know that the Feast of Unleavened Bread and the Passover [are] two days away, and the Son of Man is <going> to be handed over for crucifixion."	26:1 When Jesus had finished all these words, He said to His [disciples], 26:2 "You know that after two days the Passover [is] coming, and the Son of Man is to be handed over for crucifixion."	14:1~ Now the Passover and Unleavened Bread [were] two days away;	22:1 Now the Feast of Unleavened Bread, which is called the Passover, [was] approaching.

Scene 7: **Judas Plots With The Jews To Betray Jesus**

The Temple, Jerusalem, *Judea*   Wednesday, April 1st / 33 CE

	Matthew	Mark	Luke	John
1 The chief priests and the scribes, [with] the elders of the people, were gathered together in the court of the High Priest, named Caiaphas; and they plotted together seeking how they might seize Jesus by stealth, and put Him to death.	26:3 Then the chief priests [and] the elders of the people were gathered together in the court of the high priest, named Caiaphas; 26:4 and they plotted together to seize Jesus by stealth and kill Him.	14:~1 and the chief priests and the scribes were seeking how to seize Him by stealth and kill Him;	22:2~ The chief priests and the scribes were seeking how they might put Him to death;	
2 But they were afraid of the people, <and> [said], "Not during the festival, otherwise a riot might occur."	26:5 But they were [saying], "Not during the festival, otherwise a riot might occur among the people."	14:2 for they were [saying], "Not during the festival, otherwise there might be a riot of the people."	22:~2 for they were afraid of the people.	
3 Then Satan entered into the heart of one of the twelve, Judas, the son of Simon Iscariot.	26:14~ Then one of the twelve, named Judas Iscariot,	14:10~ Then Judas Iscariot, who was one of the twelve,	22:3 And Satan entered into Judas who was called Iscariot, belonging to the number of the twelve.	13:2~ During supper, the devil having already put into the heart of Judas Iscariot, the son of Simon,
4 And he went to the chief priests to discuss how he might betray [Jesus] to them.	26:~14 went to the chief priests	14:~10 went off to the chief priests in order to betray [Him] to them.	22:4 And he went away and discussed with the chief priests and officers how he might betray [Him] to them.	13:~2 to betray [Him],
5 <Judas> said, "What will you give me to betray Him to you?"	26:15~ and said, "What are you willing to give me to betray Him to you?"			
6 They were glad when they heard this, and agreed to give him money; and *they weighed out thirty pieces of silver to him.*[1]	26:~15 And they weighed out thirty pieces of silver to him.	14:11~ They were glad when they heard this, and promised to give him money.	22:5 They were glad and agreed to give him money.	
7 So [Judas] consented, and from then on he began looking for a good opportunity to betray Jesus to them, [away] from the crowd.	26:16 From then on he began looking for a good opportunity to betray Jesus.	14:~11 And he began seeking how to betray Him at an opportune time.	22:6 So [he] consented, and began seeking a good opportunity to betray Him to them [apart] from the crowd.	

1. Zechariah 11:12

7 - THE FINAL WEEK

Act 7: Thursday - The Last Supper

Scene 1: Preparing The Venue

Jerusalem, *Judea* Thursday, April 2nd / 33 CE

Page 234

A Four Gospel Verse-By-Verse Harmony

	Matthew	Mark	Luke	John
1	Now on the first day of Unleavened Bread, on which the Passover lamb was to be sacrificed, His [apostles] came to Jesus, and asked him, "Where do you want us to go and prepare for You to eat the Passover?"	26:17 Now on the first day of Unleavened Bread the [disciples] came to Jesus and asked, "Where do You want us to prepare for You to eat the Passover?"	14:12 On the first day of Unleavened Bread, when the Passover lamb was being sacrificed, His [disciples] said to Him, "Where do You want us to go and prepare for You to eat the Passover?"	22:7 Then came the first day of Unleavened Bread on which the Passover lamb had to be sacrificed. 22:9 They said to Him, "Where do You want us to prepare it?"	
2	Jesus sent two of His [apostles], Peter and John; and He said to them, "Go and prepare it for us <to> eat in the city.	26:18~ And He said, "Go into the city	14:13~ And He sent two of His [disciples] and said to them, "Go into the city,	22:8 And Jesus sent Peter and John, saying, "Go and prepare the Passover for us, so that we may eat it."	
3	"When you have entered the city, a certain man will meet you carrying a pitcher of water; follow him,	26:18~¹ to a certain man,	14:~13 and a man will meet you carrying a pitcher of water; follow him;	22:10~ And He said to them, "When you have entered the city, a man will meet you carrying a pitcher of water; follow him	
4	"and say to the owner of the house that he enters, 'The Teacher says to you, "My time is near. I am to keep the Passover at your house.	26:18~² and say to him, 'The Teacher says, "My time is near; I am to keep the Passover at your house	14:14~ and wherever he enters, say to the owner of the house, 'The Teacher says,	22:11 "And you shall say to the owner of the house, 22:~10 into the house that he enters. 22:11~ 'The Teacher says to you,	
5	"Where is the guest room in which I may eat the Passover with My disciples?" '	26:~18 with My disciples."'"	14:~14 "Where is My guest room in which I may eat the Passover with My disciples?"'	22:~11 "Where is the guest room in which I may eat the Passover with My disciples?"'	
6	"And he himself will show you a large upper room, furnished and ready; prepare it for us there."		14:15 "And he himself will show you a large upper room furnished and ready; prepare for us there."	22:12 "And he will show you a large, furnished upper room; prepare it there."	
7	[Peter and John] did as Jesus directed them, and they went [in]to the city and found everything just as He had told them; and they prepared the Passover.	26:19 [The disciples] did as Jesus had directed them; and they prepared the Passover.	14:16 [The disciples] went out and came to the city, and found it just as He had told them; and they prepared the Passover.	22:13 And they left and found everything just as He had told them; and they prepared the Passover.	
8	Now before the Passover Feast, Jesus, knowing that His hour had come [when] He would depart out of this world <and go> to The Father, having loved His own who were in the world, He loved them to the end.				13:1 Now before the Feast of the Passover, Jesus knowing that His hour had come [that] He would depart out of this world to the Father, having loved His own who were in the world, He loved them to the end.

7 - THE FINAL WEEK

Act 7: **Thursday - The Last Supper**

Scene 2: **The Last Supper Begins**

A house in Jerusalem, *Judea*   Thursday evening, April 2nd / 33 CE

The United Gospel Story of Jesus Christ

	Matthew	Mark	Luke
1 When it was evening, <and> the hour had come, Jesus came <and> reclined at the table with <His> twelve apostles.	26:20 ~~Now~~ when evening ~~came~~, Jesus ~~was~~ reclining at the table with [~~the~~] twelve ~~disciples~~.	14:17 When it was evening ~~He~~ came with [the] twelve.	22:14 When the hour had come, ~~He~~ reclined at the table, ~~and the~~ apostles ~~with Him~~.
2 He said to them, "I have earnestly desired to eat this Passover with you before I suffer, for I say to you, that I shall [not] eat it again until it is fulfilled			22:15 ~~And~~ He said to them, "I have earnestly desired to eat this Passover with you before I suffer; 22:16 for I say to you, I shall [~~never~~] again
3 And a dispute arose among them, as to which one of them was to be regarded [as the] greatest.			22:24 And ~~there~~ arose ~~also~~ a dispute among them as to which one of them was regarded [~~to be~~] greatest.
4 [Jesus] said to them, "The kings of the Gentiles lord it over them, and those who have authority over them are called 'Benefactors.'			22:25 ~~And~~ [He] said to them, "The kings of the Gentiles lord it over them; and those who have authority over them are called 'Benefactors.'
5 "But it is not this way with you, [for] the one who is the greatest among you must become like the youngest, and the leader like the servant.			22:26 "But it is not this way with you, [~~but~~] the one who is the greatest among you must become like the youngest, and the leader like the servant.
6 "For who is greater, the one who reclines at the table, or the one who serves? Is it not the one who reclines at the table?			22:27~ "For who is greater, the one who reclines at the table or the one who serves? Is it not the one who reclines at the table?
7 "But I am among you as the One who serves.			22:~27 But I am among you as the one who serves.
8 "You are those who have stood by Me in My trials, and just as My Father has granted Me a Kingdom, I grant that you may eat and drink at My table, in My Kingdom;			22:28 "You are those who have stood by Me in My trials; 22:29 and just as My Father has granted Me a kingdom, I grant ~~you~~ 22:30~ that you may eat and drink at My table in My kingdom,
9 "and you will sit on thrones, judging the twelve tribes of Israel."			22:~30 and you will sit on thrones judging the twelve tribes of Israel.

7 - THE FINAL WEEK

Act 7: Thursday - The Last Supper

Scene 3: Jesus Washes His Apostles' Feet

A house in Jerusalem, *Judea*   Thursday evening, April 2nd / 33 CE

	John
1 Jesus, knowing that The Father had given all things into His hands, and that He had come forth from God, and was going back to God, got up from supper, and He laid aside His garments, and girded Himself with a towel.	13:3 Jesus, knowing that the Father had given all things into His hands, and that He had come forth from God and was going back to God, 13:4 got up from supper, and laid aside His garments; and ~~taking~~ a towel, He girded Himself.
2 Then He poured water into the basin, and began to wash [His] [apostles'] feet, and to wipe them with the towel with which He was girded.	13:5 Then He poured water into the basin, and began to wash [~~the~~] [~~disciples~~'] feet and to wipe them with the towel with which He was girded.
3 [When] [Jesus] came to Simon, Peter said to Him, "Lord, do You wash my feet?"	13:6 [~~So~~] [~~He~~] came to Simon Peter. ~~He~~ said to Him, "Lord, do You wash my feet?
4 Jesus answered him, "What I do you do not realize now, but you will understand [later]."	13:7 Jesus answered ~~and said to~~ him, "What I do you do not realize now, but you will understand [~~hereafter~~]."
5 Peter said to Him, "Never shall You wash my feet!"	13:8~ Peter said to Him, "Never shall You wash my feet!"
6 Jesus answered, "If I do not wash you, you have no part with Me."	13:~8 Jesus answered ~~him~~, "If I do not wash you, you have no part with Me."
7 Peter said to Him, "Lord, then wash not only my feet, but also my hands, and my head."	13:9 ~~Simon~~ Peter said to Him, "Lord, then wash not only my feet, but also my hands and my head."
8 Jesus said to him, "He who has bathed is completely clean, [and] needs only to wash his feet.	13:10~ Jesus said to him, "He who has bathed needs only to wash his feet, [~~but~~] is completely clean;
9 "And you are already clean, because of the Word which I have spoken to you; but not all of you."	13:~10 and you are ~~clean~~, but not all of you." 15:3 "~~You are~~ already clean because of the word which I have spoken to you.
10 [Jesus] knew the one who was betraying Him, <and> for this reason He said, "Not all of you are clean."	13:11 ~~For~~ [He] knew the one who was betraying Him; for this reason He said, "Not all of you are clean."
11 When He had washed their feet, <Jesus> [took] His garments, and reclined at the table again.	13:12 ~~So~~ when He had washed their feet, ~~and~~ [taken] His garments and reclined at the table again,
12 <Then> He said to them, "Do you know what I have done to you?	13:~12 He said to them, "Do you know what I have done to you?
13 "You call Me Teacher, and Lord; and you are right, for so I am.	13:13 "You call Me Teacher and Lord; and you are right, for so I am.
14 "If I, the Lord and the Teacher, <have> washed your feet, then you [should] also wash one another's feet; for I gave you an example that you should do as I did to you.	13:14 "If I then, the Lord and the Teacher, washed your feet, you also [~~ought to~~] wash one another's feet. 13:15 "For I gave you an example that you ~~also~~ should do as I did to you.
15 "Truly, truly, I say to you, a slave is not greater than his master, <and> nor is one who is sent greater than the one who sent him.	13:16 "Truly, truly, I say to you, a slave is not greater than his master, nor is one who is sent greater than the one who sent him.
16 "If you know these things, you are blessed if you do them!	13:17 "If you know these things, you are blessed if you do them.
17 "I do not speak of all of you. I know the ones <whom> I have chosen; but it is that the Scripture may be fulfilled: 'He who eats My bread has lifted up his heel against Me.'[1]	13:18 "I do not speak of all of you. I know the ones I have chosen; but it is that the Scripture may be fulfilled, 'He who eats My bread has lifted up his heel against Me.'
18 "From now on, I am telling you before it comes to pass, so that when it does occur, you may believe that I am He.	13:19 "From now on I am telling you before it comes to pass, so that when it does occur, you may believe that I am He.
19 "Truly, truly, I say to you, he who receives whomever I send receives Me; and he who receives Me, receives [the One] who sent Me."	13:20 "Truly, truly, I say to you, he who receives whomever I send receives Me; and he who receives Me receives [~~Him~~] who sent Me."

1. Psalm 41:9

7 - THE FINAL WEEK

Act 7: Thursday - The Last Supper

Scene 4: One Of You Will Betray Me

A house in Jerusalem, *Judea* Thursday evening, April 2nd / 33 CE

The Four Gospels United in Harmony

Page 237

	Matthew	Mark	Luke	John
1 [After] Jesus had said this, as they were reclining at the table and eating, He became troubled in <His> spirit; and <He> testified, say[ing], "Truly, truly, I say to you, that *one of you will betray Me - one who is eating with Me.*" [1]	26:21 As they were eating, He [said], "Truly I say to you that one of you will betray Me."	14:18 As they were reclining at the table and eating, ~~Jesus~~ [said], "Truly I say to you that one of you will betray Me - one who is eating with Me."		13:21 [~~When~~] Jesus had said this, He became troubled in spirit, and testified ~~and~~ [said], "Truly, truly, I say to you, that one of you will betray Me."
2 They <all> began to be deeply grieved, and they each one by one began to say to say to Him, "Surely not I, Lord?"	26:22 Being deeply grieved, they each one began to say to Him, "Surely not I, Lord?"	14:19 They began to be grieved and one by one to say to Him "Surely not I?		
3 [Jesus] answered, and said to them, "It is one of the twelve.	26:23 ~~And~~ [He] answered,	14:20~ And ~~He~~ said to them, "It is one of the twelve,		
4 "Behold, *he who dips his hand with Mine in the bowl is the one who will betray Me.*[1]	26:~23 "He who ~~dipped~~ his hand with Me in the bowl is the one who will betray Me.	14:~20 one who dips with Me in the bowl.	22:21 "~~But~~ behold, ~~the~~ hand ~~of~~ the one betraying Me is with Mine ~~on~~ the ~~table~~."	
5 "For indeed, the Son of Man is going to go just as it has been written of Him -	26:24~ "The Son of Man is to go, just as it ~~is~~ written of Him;	14:21~ "For the Son of Man is to go just as it ~~is~~ written of Him;	22:22 "For indeed, the Son of Man is going as it has been ~~determined~~;	
6 "but woe to that man by whom He is betrayed! It would have been good for that man if he had not been born."	26:~24 but woe to that man by whom ~~the Son of Man~~ is betrayed! It would have been good for that man if he had not been born."	14:21 but woe to that man by whom ~~the Son of Man~~ is betrayed! It would have been good for that man if he had not been born."	22:~22 but woe to that man by whom He is betrayed!"	
7 The [apostles] began looking at one another, at a loss to know of [whom] He was speaking.			13:22 The [~~disciples~~] began looking at one another, at a loss to know of [which one] He was speaking.	
8 And they began to discuss among themselves which one of them it might be who was going to do this thing.			22:23 And they began to discuss among themselves which one of them it might be who was going to do this thing.	

1. Psalm 41:9

7 - THE FINAL WEEK	Scene 5: **Judas Is Revealed**	
Act 7: **Thursday - The Last Supper**	A house in Jerusalem, *Judea* Thursday evening, April 2nd / 33 CE	

	Matthew	John
1 Reclining there on Jesus' bosom was [the] [apostle] whom Jesus loved,[1] so Simon Peter gestured to him, and said, "Tell us of whom He is speaking."		13:23 There was reclining on Jesus' bosom [one of His] [disciples], whom Jesus loved. 13:24 So Simon Peter gestured to him, and said to him, "Tell us who it is of whom He is speaking."
2 He, leaning back on Jesus' bosom, said to Him, "Who is it, Lord?"		13:25 He, leaning back thus on Jesus' bosom, said to Him, "Lord, who is it?"
3 Jesus answered, "[It] is the one for whom I shall dip the morsel, and give it to him."		13:26~ Jesus then answered, "[That] is the one for whom I shall dip the morsel and give it to him."
4 So when He had dipped the morsel, He gave it to Judas, the son of Simon Iscariot.		13:~26 So when He had dipped the morsel, He took and gave it to Judas, the son of Simon Iscariot.
5 Judas said, "Surely it is not I, Rabbi?" Jesus [answered] him, "You have said it."	26:25 And Judas, who was betraying Him, said, "Surely it is not I, Rabbi?" Jesus [said to] him, "You have said it yourself."	
6 After the morsel, Satan entered into [Judas]. Therefore Jesus said to him, "What you do, do quickly."		13:27 After the morsel, Satan then entered into [him]. Therefore Jesus said to him, "What you do, do quickly."
7 No one reclining at the table knew [why] [Jesus] said this to him, [but] some were supposing that because Judas had the money box; [He] was saying to him, "Buy the things we need for the feast", or that he should give something to the poor.		13:28 Now no one of those reclining at the table knew [for what purpose] [He] had said this to him. 13:29 [For] some were supposing, because Judas had the money box, that [Jesus] was saying to him, "Buy the things we have need of for the feast"; or else, that he should give something to the poor.
8 So after receiving the morsel [Judas] immediately went out, and it was night.		13:30 So after receiving the morsel [he] went out immediately; and it was night.
9 [After] he had gone out, Jesus said, "Now is the Son of Man glorified, and God is glorified in Him! <And> God will glorify Him in Himself, and will glorify Him immediately."		13:31 [Therefore when] he had gone out, Jesus said, "Now is the Son of Man glorified, and God is glorified in Him; 13:32 if God is glorified in Him, God will also glorify Him in Himself, and will glorify Him immediately."

1. *John Zebedee - John 19:26; 20:2; 21:7, 20*

7 - THE FINAL WEEK

Act 7: Thursday - The Last Supper

Scene 6: The Blood of The New Covenant

A house in Jerusalem, *Judea*   Thursday evening, April 2nd / 33 CE

The Harmonious Gospel

	Matthew	Mark	Luke
1 While they were eating, Jesus took some bread; and after giv[ing] a blessing <of> thanks, He broke [the bread], and gave it to the [apostles].	26:26~ While they were eating, Jesus took some bread, and after a blessing, He broke [it] and gave it to the [disciples],	14:22~ While they were eating, He took some bread, and after a blessing He broke [it], and gave it to them,	22:19~ And when He had taken some bread and giv[en] thanks, He broke [it] and gave it to them,
2 And <He> said, "Take it, <and> eat. This is My body which is given for you. Do this in remembrance of Me."	26:~26 and said, "Take, eat; this is My body."	14:~22 and said, "Take it; this is My body."	22:~19 saying, "This is My body which is given for you; do this in remembrance of Me."
3 After they had eaten [Jesus] took the cup; and in the same way, [after] He had given thanks, He gave it to [the apostles], saying, "Take this, and share it among yourselves. Drink from it, all of you."	26:27 And when [He] had taken a cup and given thanks, He gave it to [them], saying, "Drink from it, all of you;	14:23~ And when [He] had taken a cup and given thanks, He gave it to [them],	22:20 And in the same way [He] took the cup after they had eaten, 22:17 And [when] He had taken a cup and given thanks, He said, "Take this and share it among yourselves;
4 <As> they all drank from it, [Jesus] said to them, "This cup is My blood of the new covenant, which is poured out for you <and> for many, for [the] forgiveness of sins.	26:28 for this is My blood of the covenant, which is poured out for many for forgiveness of sins.	14:~23 and they all drank from it. 14:24 And [He] said to them, "This is My blood of the covenant, which is poured out for many.	22:20 saying, "This cup which is poured out for you is the new covenant in My blood.
5 "Truly I say to you, I will not drink of this fruit of the vine again, until that day when the Kingdom of God comes, <and> I drink it new with you, in My Father's Kingdom."	26:29 "But I say to you, I will not drink of this fruit of the vine from now on until that day when I drink it new with you in My Father's kingdom."	14:25 "Truly I say to you, I will never again drink of the fruit of the vine until that day when I drink it new in the kingdom of God."	22:18 for I say to you, I will not drink of the fruit of the vine from now on until the kingdom of God comes."

Scene 7: My New Commandment: Love One Another

A house in Jerusalem, *Judea*   Thursday evening, April 2nd / 33 CE

	John
1 "A new commandment I give to you, that you love one another; even as I have loved you, that you also love one another.	13:34 "A new commandment I give to you, that you love one another, even as I have loved you, that you also love one another.
2 "By this all men will know that you are My disciples, if you have love for one another."	13:35 "By this all men will know that you are My disciples, if you have love for one another."

7 - THE FINAL WEEK

Act 7: Thursday - The Last Supper

Scene 8: Peter, You Will Deny Me Three Times

A house in Jerusalem, *Judea* Thursday evening, April 2nd / 33 CE

#	Matthew	Mark	Luke	John
1				13:33~ "Little children, I am with you a little while longer.
2				13:~33 You will seek Me; and as I said to the Jews, now I also say to you, 'Where I am going, you cannot come.'
3				13:36~ Simon Peter said to [Him], "Lord, where are You going?"
4				13:~36 Jesus answered, "Where I go, you cannot follow Me now; but you will follow later."
5				13:37~ Peter said to Him, "Lord, why can I not follow You right now?
6	"Little children, I am with you for only a little while longer." / "You will seek Me, and as I said to the Jews, I now say also to you; 'Where I am going, you cannot come.' " / Simon Peter said to [Jesus], "Lord, where are You going?" / Jesus answered, "Where I go, you cannot follow Me now, but you will follow later." / Peter said to Him, "Lord, why can I not follow You now?" / Jesus said to them, "You will all fall away because of Me this night, for it is written; 'I will *strike down the shepherd, and the of the flock sheep shall be scattered!*'[1]	26:31 Then Jesus said to them, "You will all fall away because of Me this night, for it is written, 'I will strike down the shepherd, and the sheep of the flock shall be scattered.'	14:27 And Jesus said to them, "You will all fall away because it is written, 'I will strike down the shepherd, and the sheep shall be scattered.'		
7	"But after I have been raised, I will go ahead of you to Galilee."	26:32 "But after I have been raised, I will go ahead of you to Galilee."	14:28 "But after I have been raised, I will go ahead of you to Galilee."		
8	Peter said to Him, "Even though all may fall away because of You, I will never fall away."	26:33 But Peter said to Him, "Even though all may fall away because of You, I will never fall away."	14:29 But Peter said to Him, "Even though all may fall away, yet I will not."		
9	<Jesus said to him,> "Simon, Simon, behold! Satan has demanded permission to sift you like wheat; but I have prayed for you, that your faith may not fail.			22:31 "Simon, Simon, behold, Satan has demanded permission to sift you like wheat; 22:32~ but I have prayed for you, that your faith may not fail;	
10	"And you, when you have turned again, strengthen your brothers."			22:~32 and you, when once you have turned again, strengthen your brothers."	
11	But [Peter] said, "Lord, I am ready to go with You both to prison and to death! I will lay down my life for You."			22:33 But [he] said to Him, "Lord, with You I am ready to go both to prison and to death!"	13:~37 I will lay down my life for You."
12	Jesus answered, and said to him, "Will you lay down your life for Me?	26:34~ Jesus said to him,	14:30~ And Jesus said to him,	22:34~ And He said,	13:38~ Jesus answered, "Will you lay down your life for Me?
13	"Truly, truly, I say to you Peter, that this very night, a rooster will not crow until you yourself have denied that you know Me, three times."	26:~34 "Truly I say to you that this very night, before a rooster crows you will deny Me three times."	14:~30 "Truly I say to you, that this very night, before a rooster crows twice you yourself will deny Me three times."	22:~34 "I say to you, Peter, the rooster will not crow today until you have denied three times that you know Me."	13:~38 Truly, truly, I say to you, a rooster will not crow until you deny Me three times."

1. Zechariah 13:7

continued >

7 - THE FINAL WEEK

Act 7: **Thursday - The Last Supper**

Scene 8: **Peter, You Will Deny Me Three Times**

continued

Synoptic = seeing together (as one)

	Matthew	Mark	Luke	John
14 But Peter kept insist[ing], "Even if I have to die with You, I will not deny You!"	26:35~ Peter ~~said to Him~~, "Even if I have to die with You, I will not deny You."	14:31~ But Peter kept ~~saying~~ [insistently], "Even if I have to die with You, I will not deny You!"		
15 And all the [apostles] were saying the same thing.	26:~35 All the [~~disciples~~] ~~said~~ the same thing ~~too~~.	14:~31 And ~~they~~ all were saying the same thing ~~also~~.		

Scene 9: **Two Swords Are Enough**

A house in Jerusalem, *Judea*   Thursday evening, April 2nd / 33 CE

	Luke
1 [Jesus] said to them, "When I sent you out without money belt [or] bag [or] sandals, you did not lack anything, did you?" They said, "No, nothing."	22:35 ~~And~~ [He] said to them, "When I sent you out without money belt [~~and~~] bag [~~and~~] sandals, you did not lack anything, did you?" They said, "No, nothing."
2 [Then] He said to them, "But now, whoever has a money belt is to take it along, likewise also a bag.	22:36~ [~~And~~] He said to them, "But now, whoever has a money belt is to take it along, likewise also a bag,
3 "And whoever has no sword is to sell his coat and buy one.	22:~36 and whoever has no sword is to sell his coat and buy one.
4 "For I tell you, that this which is written must be fulfilled in Me, *'And He was numbered with transgressors'*;[1.] for that which refers to Me has its fulfillment."	22:37 "For I tell you that this which is written must be fulfilled in Me, 'And He was numbered with transgressors'; for that which refers to Me has its fulfillment."
5 They said, "Lord, look, here are two swords." And He said to them, "It is enough."	22:38 They said, "Lord, look, here are two swords." And He said to them, "It is enough."

1. Isaiah 53:12

7 - THE FINAL WEEK Act 8: **The Holy Spirit and The Father**	Scene 1: **I Am The Way, and The Truth, and The Life** A house in Jerusalem, *Judea* Thursday evening, April 2nd / 33 CE

Page 242

The Four Gospels Harmoniously United

		John
1	"Do not let your heart be troubled. Believe in God, <and> believe also in Me.	14:1 "Do not let your heart be troubled; believe in God, believe also* in Me.
2	"In My Father's house are many places <to> dwell; if it were not so, I would have told you, [because] I go to prepare a place for you.	14:2 "In My Father's house are many dwelling places; if it were not so, I would have told you; [for] I go to prepare a place for you.
3	"<And> if I go and prepare a place for you, I will come again and receive you to Myself, <so> that where I am, there you may be also.	14:3 "If I go and prepare a place for you, I will come again and receive you to Myself, that where I am, there you may be also.
4	"And you know the way <to> where I am going."	14:4 "And you know the way where I am going."
5	Thomas said to Him, "Lord, we do not know where You are going. How do we know the way?"	14:5 Thomas said to Him, "Lord, we do not know where You are going, how do we know the way?"
6	Jesus said to him, "I am the way, and the truth, and the life; no one comes to The Father but through Me.	14:6 Jesus said to him, "I am the way, and the truth, and the life; no one comes to the Father but through Me.
7	"If you had known Me, you would have known My Father also. From now on you know Him, and have seen Him."	14:7 "If you had known Me, you would have known My Father also; from now on you know Him, and have seen Him."
8	Philip said, "Lord, show us The Father, and it is enough for us."	14:8 Philip said ~~to Him~~, "Lord, show us the Father, and it is enough for us."
9	Jesus said to him, "Have I been with you [this] long, and yet you have not come to know Me, Philip?	14:9~ Jesus said to him, "Have I been [~~so~~] long with you, and yet you have not come to know Me, Philip?
10	"He who has seen Me has seen The Father.	14:~9~ He who has seen Me has seen the Father;
11	"How can you say, 'Show us The Father'? Do you not believe that I am in The Father, and <that> The Father is in Me?	14:~9 how can you say, 'Show us the Father'? 14:10~ "Do you not believe that I am in the Father, and the Father is in Me?
12	"The words that I say to you, I do not speak on My own initiative, but The Father abiding in Me does His works.	14:~10 The words that I say to you I do not speak on My own initiative, but the Father abiding in Me does His works.
13	"Believe Me, that I am in The Father, and <that> The Father is in Me; otherwise believe because of the works themselves.	14:11 "Believe Me that I am in the Father and the Father is in Me; otherwise believe because of the works themselves.
14	"Truly, truly, I say to you, he who believes in Me, the works that I do, he will do also.	14:12~ "Truly, truly, I say to you, he who believes in Me, the works that I do, he will do also;
15	"And greater works than these he will do, because I go to The Father."	14:~12 and greater works than these he will do; because I go to the Father.

7 - THE FINAL WEEK
Act 8: The Holy Spirit and The Father
Scene 2: The Holy Spirit Helper
A house in Jerusalem, *Judea* Thursday evening, April 2nd / 33 CE

	John
1 "Whatever you ask in My Name, that I will do, so that the Father may be glorified in the Son.	14:13 "Whatever you ask in My name, that will I do, so that the Father may be glorified in the Son.
2 "If you ask anything <of> Me in My Name, I will do it.	14:14 "If you ask Me anything in My name, I will do it.
3 "If you love Me, you will keep My commandments,	14:15 "If you love Me, you will keep My commandments.
4 "<and> I will ask the Father, and He will give you another Helper, that He may be with you forever, that is the Spirit of Truth;	14:16 "I will ask the Father, and He will give you another Helper, that He may be with you forever; 14:17~ that is the Spirit of truth,
5 "whom the world cannot receive, because it does not see Him, or know Him; but you know Him, because He abides with you, and will be in you.	14:~17 whom the world cannot receive, because it does not see Him or know Him, but you know Him because He abides with you and will be in you.
6 "I will not leave you as orphans, I will come to you.	14:18 "I will not leave you as orphans; I will come to you.
7 "After a little while, the world will no longer see Me, but you will see Me; <and> because I live you will also live.	14:19 "After a little while the world will no longer see Me, but you will see Me; because I live, you will live also.
8 "In that day, you will know that I am in My Father, and <that> you <are> in Me, and I <am> in you.	14:20 "In that day you will know that I am in My Father, and you in Me, and I in you.
9 "[The one] who has My commandments, and keeps them, is the one who loves Me;	14:21~ "[He] who has My commandments and keeps them is the one who loves Me;
10 "and he who loves Me will be loved by My Father; and I will love him, and will disclose Myself to him."	14:~21 and he who loves Me will be loved by My Father, and I will love him and will disclose Myself to him."
11 Judas [Thaddaeus] said to Him, "Lord, what has happened that You are going to disclose Yourself to us, and not to the world?"	14:22 Judas [(not Iscariot)] said to Him, "Lord, what then has happened that You are going to disclose Yourself to us, and not to the world?"
12 Jesus answered, and said to him, "If anyone loves Me, he will keep My Word, and My Father will love him;	14:23~ Jesus answered and said to him, "If anyone loves Me, he will keep My word; and My Father will love him,
13 "and We will come to him, and make Our abode with him.	14:~23 and We will come to him and make Our abode with him.
14 "He who does not love Me does not keep My words; and the Word which you hear is not Mine, but The Father's who sent Me.	14:24 "He who does not love Me does not keep My words; and the word which you hear is not Mine, but the Father's who sent Me.
15 "These things I have spoken to you while <I am> abiding with you, but the Helper, the Holy Spirit whom The Father will send in My Name, He will teach you all things, and bring to your remembrance all that I <have> said to you."	14:25 "These things I have spoken to you while abiding with you. 14:26 "But the Helper, the Holy Spirit, whom the Father will send in My name, He will teach you all things, and bring to your remembrance all that I said to you.

The Gospel Story of Jesus

| | 7 - THE FINAL WEEK
Act 8: **The Holy Spirit
and The Father** | Scene 3: **I Go Away, and I Will Come To You**
A house in Jerusalem, *Judea*   Thursday evening, April 2nd / 33 CE | Page 244
Verse-By-Verse Edition |

		John
1	"Peace I leave with you! My peace I give to you, <but> not as the world gives, do I give to you.	14:27~ "Peace I leave with you; My peace I give to you, not as the world gives do I give to you.
2	"Do not let your heart be troubled, nor let it be fearful.	14:~27 Do not let your heart be troubled, nor let it be fearful.
3	"You <have> heard that I said to you, 'I go away, and I will come to you.'	14:28~ "You heard that I said to you, 'I go away, and I will come to you.'
4	"If you loved Me, you would have rejoiced because I go to The Father, for The Father is greater than I.	14:~28 If you loved Me, you would have rejoiced because I go to the Father, for the Father is greater than I.
5	"Now I have told you before it happens, so that when it happens, you [might] believe.	14:29 "Now I have told you before it happens, so that when it happens, you [~~may~~] believe.
6	"I will not speak much more with you <now>, [because] the ruler of the world is coming, and he has no <part> [of] Me.	14:30 "I will not speak much more with you, [~~for~~] the ruler of the world is coming, and he has no~~thing~~ [~~in~~] Me;
7	"But so that the world may know that I love The Father, I do exactly as The Father <has> commanded Me."	14:31~ but so that the world may know that I love the Father, I do exactly as the Father commanded Me.

Scene 4: **Abide In My Love, and Bear Fruit**
A house in Jerusalem, *Judea*   Thursday evening, April 2nd / 33 CE

		John
1	"I am the true vine, and My Father is the vinedresser.	15:1 "I am the true vine, and My Father is the vinedresser.
2	"Every branch in Me that does not bear fruit, He takes away;	15:2~ "Every branch in Me that does not bear fruit, He takes away;
3	"and every branch that bears fruit He prunes, so that it may bear more fruit.	15:~2 and every branch that bears fruit, He prunes ~~it~~ so that it may bear more fruit.
4	"Abide in Me, [as] I <abide> in you. As the branch cannot bear fruit of itself unless it abides in the vine, so neither can you <bear fruit> unless you abide in Me.	15:4 "Abide in Me, [and] I in you. As the branch cannot bear fruit of itself unless it abides in the vine, so neither can you unless you abide in Me.
5	"I am the vine, [and] you are the branches.	15:5~ "I am the vine, you are the branches;
6	"He who abides in Me, and I in him, bears much fruit; for apart from Me, you can do nothing.	15:~5 he who abides in Me and I in him, ~~he~~ bears much fruit, for apart from Me you can do nothing.
7	"If anyone does not abide in Me, he is thrown away as a branch and dries up, and <is> gather[ed] and cast into the fire, [where] they are burned.	15:6 "If anyone does not abide in Me, he is thrown away as a branch and dries up; and ~~they~~ gather ~~them~~, and cast ~~them~~ into the fire [and] they are burned.
8	"If you abide in Me, and My words abide in you, ask whatever you wish, and it will be done for you.	15:7 "If you abide in Me, and My words abide in you, ask whatever you wish, and it will be done for you.
9	"My Father is glorified by this, that you bear much fruit, and so prove to be My disciples.	15:8 "My Father is glorified by this, that you bear much fruit, and so prove to be My disciples.
10	"Just as The Father has loved Me, I have also loved you. Abide in My love!	15:9 "Just as the Father has loved Me, I have also loved you; abide in My love.
11	"If you keep My commandments you will abide in My love, just as I have kept My Father's commandments, and abide in His love.	15:10 "If you keep My commandments, you will abide in My love; just as I have kept My Father's commandments and abide in His love.
12	"These things I have spoken to you so that My joy may be in you, and that your joy may be made full!"	15:11 "These things I have spoken to you so that My joy may be in you, and that your joy may be made full.

7 - THE FINAL WEEK
Act 8: **The Holy Spirit and The Father**

Scene 5: **My Commandment Again: Love One Another**

A house in Jerusalem, *Judea* Thursday evening, April 2nd / 33 CE

		John
1	"This is My commandment; that you love one another, just as I have loved you!	*15:12* "This is My commandment, that you love one another, just as I have loved you.
2	"Greater love has no one than this, that one <would> lay down his life for his friends.	*15:13* "Greater love has no one than this, that one lay down his life for his friends.
3	"You are My friends, if you do what I command you.	*15:14* "You are My friends if you do what I command you.
4	"No longer do I call you slaves, for the slave does not know what his master is doing; but I have called you friends, for all <of the> things that I have heard from My Father, I have made <them> known to you.	*15:15* "No longer do I call you slaves, for the slave does not know what his master is doing; but I have called you friends, for all things that I have heard from My Father I have made known to you.
5	"You did not choose Me, but I chose you, and appointed you, <so> that you would go and bear fruit, and that your fruit would remain;	*15:16~* "You did not choose Me but I chose you, and appointed you that you would go and bear fruit, and that your fruit would remain,
6	"so that whatever you ask of The Father in My Name, He [will] give to you.	*15:~16* so that whatever you ask of the Father in My name He [~~may~~] give to you.
7	"This I command you; that you love one another."	*15:17* "This I command you, that you love one another.

Scene 6: **The World Hates Me and My Father**

A house in Jerusalem, *Judea* Thursday evening, April 2nd / 33 CE

		John
1	"If the world hates you, know that it has hated Me before it hated you.	*15:18* "If the world hates you, ~~you~~ know that it has hated Me before it hated you.
2	"If you were of the world, the world would love its own;	*15:19~* "If you were of the world, the world would love its own;
3	"but because you are not of the world, but I chose you out of the world, because of this the world hates you.	*15:~19* but because you are not of the world, but I chose you out of the world, because of this the world hates you.
4	"Remember the Word that I said to you; 'A slave is not greater than his master.'	*15:20~* "Remember the word that I said to you, 'A slave is not greater than his master.'
5	"If they <have> persecuted Me, <then> they will also persecute you;	*15:~20~* If they persecuted Me, they will also persecute you;
6	"<and> if they <have> kept My word, <then> they will also keep yours.	*15:~20* if they kept My word, they will keep yours also.
7	"All these things they will do to you for My name's sake, because they do not know the One who sent Me.	*15:21* "~~But~~ all these things they will do to you for My name's sake, because they do not know the One who sent Me.
8	"If I had not come and spoken to them, they would not have sin, but now they have no excuse for their sin.	*15:22* "If I had not come and spoken to them, they would not have sin, but now they have no excuse for their sin.
9	"[The one] who hates Me also hates My Father.	*15:23* "[~~He~~] who hates Me hates My Father also.
10	"If I had not done among them the works which no one else did, <then> they would not have sin; but now they have both seen <Me>, and hated Me, and My Father as well.	*15:24* "If I had not done among them the works which no one else did, they would not have sin; but now they have both seen and hated Me and My Father as well.
11	"But they have done this to fulfill the word that is written in their Law; 'They hated Me without a cause.'[1] "	*15:25* "But they have done this to fulfill the word that is written in their Law, 'They hated Me without a cause.'

1. Psalm 69:4; (35:19); (109:3)

7 - THE FINAL WEEK

Act 8: The Holy Spirit and The Father

Scene 7: More About The Holy Spirit of Truth

A house in Jerusalem, *Judea* — Thursday evening, April 2nd / 33 CE

	John
1 "When the Helper comes, whom I will send to you from The Father - that is the Spirit of Truth who proceeds from The Father - He will testify about Me.	15:26 "When the Helper comes, whom I will send to you from the Father, that is the Spirit of truth who proceeds from the Father, He will testify about Me,
2 "And you will also testify, because you have been with Me from the beginning.	15:27 and you will testify also, because you have been with Me from the beginning.
3 "These things I have spoken to you, so that you may be kept from stumbling,	16:1 "These things I have spoken to you so that you may be kept from stumbling.
4 "<because> they will make you outcasts from the synagogue, [and] an hour is coming [when] everyone who kills you [will] think that he is offering service to God.	16:2 "They will make you outcasts from the synagogue, [but] an hour is coming [for] everyone who kills you [to] think that he is offering service to God.
5 "These things they will do because they [do] not [know] The Father, or Me.	16:3 "These things they will do because they [have] not [known] the Father or Me.
6 "But I have spoken these things to you, so that when their [time] comes, you may remember that I told you of them.	16:4~ "But these things I have spoken to you, so that when their [hour] comes, you may remember that I told you of them.
7 "These things I did not say to you at the beginning, because I was with you, but now I am going to Him who sent Me;	16:~4 These things I did not say to you at the beginning, because I was with you. 16:5~ "But now I am going to Him who sent Me;
8 "and none of you asks Me, 'Where are You going?'	16:~5 and none of you asks Me, 'Where are You going?'
9 "[Now], because I have said these things to you, sorrow has filled your heart.	16:6 "[But] because I have said these things to you, sorrow has filled your heart.
10 "But I tell you the truth, it is to your advantage that I go away, for if I do not go away <then> the Helper will not come to you; [however], if I go <then> I will send Him to you.	16:7 "But I tell you the truth, it is to your advantage that I go away; for if I do not go away, the Helper will not come to you; [but] if I go, I will send Him to you.
11 "And when He comes, He will convict the world concerning sin, and righteousness, and judgment;	16:8 "And He, when He comes, will convict the world concerning sin and righteousness and judgment;
12 "concerning sin, because they do not believe in Me;	16:9 concerning sin, because they do not believe in Me;
13 "and concerning righteousness, because I go to The Father, and you <will> no longer see Me;	16:10 and concerning righteousness, because I go to the Father and you no longer see Me;
14 "and concerning judgment, because the ruler of this world has been judged.	16:11 and concerning judgment, because the ruler of this world has been judged.
15 "I have many more things to say to you, but you cannot bear them now; but when the Spirit of Truth comes, He will guide you into all <of the> truth,	16:12 "I have many more things to say to you, but you cannot bear them now. 16:13~ "But when He, the Spirit of truth, comes, He will guide you into all the truth;
16 "for He will not speak on His own initiative, but whatever He hears He will speak; and He will disclose to you what is to come.	16:~13 for He will not speak on His own initiative, but whatever He hears, He will speak; and He will disclose to you what is to come.
17 "He will glorify Me, for He will take [what is] Mine, and will disclose it to you.	16:14 "He will glorify Me, for He will take [of] Mine and will disclose it to you.
18 "All things that The Father has are Mine, therefore I said <that> He will take [what is] Mine, and disclose it to you."	16:15 "All things that the Father has are Mine; therefore I said that He takes [of] Mine and will disclose it to you.

7 - THE FINAL WEEK
Act 8: The Holy Spirit and The Father
Scene 8: I Am Going To The Father
A house in Jerusalem, *Judea*   Thursday evening, April 2nd / 33 CE

	John
1 "<After> a little while, you will no longer see Me; and again <after> a little while, [then] you will see Me."	16:16 "A little while, ~~and~~ you will no longer see Me; and again a little while, [~~and~~] you will see Me."
2 Some of His [apostles] said to one another, "What is this thing He is telling us, '<After> a little while and you will not see Me; and again <after> a little while, [then] you will see Me'; and, 'because I go to The Father'?	16:17 Some of His [~~disciples~~] ~~then~~ said to one another, "What is this thing He is telling us, 'A little while, and you will not see Me; and again a little while, [~~and~~] you will see Me'; and, 'because I go to the Father'?"
3 "What is this that He says, 'A little while'? We do not know what He is talking about."	16:18 ~~So they were saying~~, "What is this that He says, 'A little while'? We do not know what He is talking about."
4 Jesus knew that they wished to question Him, and He said to them, "Are you deliberating together about this, that I said, 'A little while, and you will not see Me; and again a little while, and you will see Me'?	16:19 Jesus knew that they wished to question Him, and He said to them, "Are you deliberating together about this, that I said, 'A little while, and you will not see Me, and again a little while, and you will see Me'?
5 "Truly, truly, I say to you, that you will weep and lament, but the world will rejoice; <and> you will grieve, but your grief will be turned into joy!	16:20 "Truly, truly, I say to you, that you will weep and lament, but the world will rejoice; you will grieve, but your grief will be turned into joy.
6 "Whenever a woman is in labor she has pain, because her hour has come;	16:21~ "Whenever a woman is in labor she has pain, because her hour has come;
7 "but when she gives birth to the child, she no longer remembers the anguish, because of the joy that a child has been born into the world.	16:~21 but when she gives birth to the child, she no longer remembers the anguish because of the joy that a child has been born into the world.
8 "Therefore, you <will> [also] have grief now, but I will see you again, and your heart will rejoice; and no one will take your joy away from you.	16:22 "Therefore you [~~too~~] have grief now; but I will see you again, and your heart will rejoice, and no one will take your joy away from you.
9 "In that day you will not question Me about anything.	16:23~ "In that day you will not question Me about anything.
10 "Truly, truly, I say to you, if you ask The Father for anything in My Name, He will give it to you.	16:~23 Truly, truly, I say to you, if you ask the Father for anything in My name, He will give it to you.
11 "Until now, you have [not] asked for [any]thing in My Name; ask and you will receive, so that your joy may be made full.	16:24 "Until now you have asked for [no]thing in My name; ask and you will receive, so that your joy may be made full.
12 "These things I have spoken to you in figurative language, <but> an hour is coming when I will no longer speak to you in figurative language, but <I> will tell you plainly of The Father.	16:25 "These things I have spoken to you in figurative language; an hour is coming when I will no longer speak to you in figurative language, but will tell you plainly of the Father.
13 "In that day you will ask in My Name, and I do not say to you that I will request of The Father on your behalf, for The Father Himself loves you, because you have loved Me, and have believed that I <have> [come] forth from The Father.	16:26 "In that day you will ask in My name, and I do not say to you that I will request of the Father on your behalf; for the Father Himself loves you, 16:27 because you have loved Me and have believed that I [came] forth from the Father.
14 "I came forth from The Father, and have come into the world, <and now> I am leaving the world, and going <back> to The Father."	16:28 "I came forth from the Father and have come into the world; I am leaving the world ~~again~~ and going to the Father."
15 His [apostles] said, "[Ah], now You are speaking plainly, and are not using a figure of speech.	16:29 His [~~disciples~~] said, "[~~Lo~~], now You are speaking plainly and are not using a figure of speech.
16 "Now we know that You know all things, and have no need for anyone to question You; by this we believe that You [have come] from God."	16:30 "Now we know that You know all things, and have no need for anyone to question You; by this we believe that You [came] from God."
17 Jesus answered them, "Do you now believe?	16:31 Jesus answered them, "Do you now believe?
18 "Behold, [the] hour [has come] for each of you to be scattered on his own, and to leave Me alone;	16:32~ "Behold, [an] hour [is coming], ~~and has already come~~, for you to be scattered, each [~~to~~] his own ~~home~~, and ~~to~~ leave Me alone;
19 "and yet I am not alone, because The Father is with Me.	16:~32 and yet I am not alone, because the Father is with Me.
20 "These things I have spoken to you so that in Me you may have peace.	16:33~ "These things I have spoken to you, so that in Me you may have peace.
21 "In the world you have tribulation, but take courage, I have overcome the world."	16:~33 In the world you have tribulation, but take courage; I have overcome the world."

7 – THE FINAL WEEK
Act 8: The Holy Spirit and The Father
Scene 9: Jesus Prays To The Father
A house in Jerusalem, *Judea* — Thursday evening, April 2nd / 33 CE

The Complete Gospel of Jesus Christ — Page 248

#		John
1	<After> Jesus spoke these things, He [raised] His eyes to heaven, and said, "Father, the hour has come! Glorify Your Son, <so> that the Son may glorify You;	17:1 Jesus spoke these things; and [~~lifting up~~] His eyes to heaven, He said, "Father, the hour has come; glorify Your Son, that the Son may glorify You,
2	"even as You gave Him authority over all flesh, that to all whom You have given Him, He may give eternal life!	17:2 even as You gave Him authority over all flesh, that to all whom You have given Him, He may give eternal life.
3	"This is eternal life, that they may know You, the only true God, and Jesus Christ, whom You have sent.	17:3 "This is eternal life, that they may know You, the only true God, and Jesus Christ whom You have sent.
4	"I glorified You on the earth, having accomplished the work which You have given Me to do.	17:4 "I glorified You on the earth, having accomplished the work which You have given Me to do.
5	"Now Father, glorify Me together with Yourself, with the glory which I had with You before the world was.	17:5 "Now, father, glorify Me together with Yourself, with the glory which I had with You before the world was.
6	"*I have manifested Your Name to the men whom You gave Me* [1] *out of the world; they were Yours, and You gave them to Me,* [2] *and they have kept Your Word.*	17:6 "I have manifested Your name to the men whom You gave Me out of the world; they were Yours and You gave them to Me, and they have kept Your word.
7	"Now they have come to know that everything You have given Me is from You, for I have given to them the words which You gave <to> Me;	17:7 "Now they have come to know that everything You have given Me is from You; 17:8~ for the words which You gave Me I have given to them;
8	"and they received them, and <have> truly understood that I came forth from You, and they believe that You sent Me.	17:~8 and they received them and truly understood that I came forth from You, and they believe~~d~~ that You sent Me.
9	"I ask on their behalf, I do not ask on behalf of the world, but of those whom You have given Me, for they are Yours.	17:9 "I ask on their behalf; I do not ask on behalf of the world, but of those whom You have given Me; for they are Yours;
10	"All things that are Mine are Yours, and Yours are Mine; and I have been glorified in them!	17:10 ~~and~~ all things that are Mine are Yours, and Yours are Mine; and I have been glorified in them.
11	"I am no longer in the world, and yet they themselves are in the world, and I come to You.	17:11~ "I am no longer in the world; and yet they themselves are in the world, and I come to You.
12	"Holy Father, keep them in Your Name - the Name which You have given <to> Me - that they may be one, even as We are.	17:~11 Holy Father, keep them in Your name, the name which You have given Me, that they may be one even as We are.
13	"While I was with them, I [kept] them in Your Name which You have given <to> Me;	17:12~ "While I was with them, I [~~was keeping~~] them in Your name which You have given Me;
14	"and I guarded them, and not one of them perished [except] the son of perdition, so that *the Scripture* [3] would be fulfilled.	17:~12 and I guarded them and not one of them perished [~~but~~] the son of perdition, so that the Scripture would be fulfilled.
15	"[And] now I come to You; and these things I speak in the world, so that they may have My joy made full [with]in themselves.	17:13 "[~~But~~] now I come to You; and these things I speak in the world so that they may have My joy made full in themselves.
16	"I have given them Your Word, and the world has hated them, because they are not of the world, even as I am not of the world.	17:14 "I have given them Your word; and the world has hated them, because they are not of the world, even as I am not of the world.
17	"I do not ask You to take them out of the world, but to keep them from the evil one.	17:15 "I do not ask You to take them out of the world, but to keep them from the evil one.
18	"They are not of the world, even as I am not of the world.	17:16 "They are not of the world, even as I am not of the world.
19	"Sanctify them in the truth; Your Word is truth!	17:17 "Sanctify them in the truth; Your word is truth.
20	"As You sent Me into the world, I have also sent them into the world.	17:18 "As You sent Me into the world, I also have sent them into the world.
21	"For their sakes I sanctify Myself, that they themselves may also be sanctified in truth.	17:19 "For their sakes I sanctify Myself, that they themselves also may be sanctified in truth.

1. *Psalm 22:22*   2. *Ezekiel 18:4*   3. *Psalm 41:9*

continued >

7 - THE FINAL WEEK
Act 8: The Holy Spirit and The Father

Scene 9: Jesus Prays To The Father
continued

Page 249
A Unified Four Gospel Harmony

	John
22 "I do not ask on behalf of these alone, but also for those who believe in Me through their word, that they may all be one;	17:20 "I do not ask on behalf of these alone, but for those also who believe in Me through their word; that they may all be one;
23 "even as You, Father, are in Me, and I <am> in You, that they may also be in Us, so that the world may believe that You sent Me.	17:21 even as You, father, are in Me and I in You, that they also may be in Us, so that the world may believe that You sent Me.
24 "The glory which You have given Me, I have given to them, that they may be one, just as We are one; I in them, and You in Me, that they may be perfected in unity;	17:22 "The glory which You have given Me I have given to them, that they may be one, just as We are one; 17:23~ I in them and You in Me, that they may be perfected in unity,
25 "so that the world may know that You sent Me, and loved them, even as You have loved Me.	17:~23 so that the world may know that You sent Me, and loved them, even as You have loved Me.
26 "Father, I also desire that [those] whom You have given Me be with Me where I am, so that they may see My glory which You have given Me; for You loved Me before the foundation of the world.	17:24 "Father, I desire that they also, whom You have given Me, be with Me where I am, so that they may see My glory which You have given Me, for You loved Me before the foundation of the world.
27 "O righteous Father! Although the world has not known You, yet I have known You; and these have known that You sent Me.	17:25 "O righteous Father, although the world has not known You, yet I have known You; and these have known that You sent Me;
28 "And I have made Your Name known to them, and will make it known, so that the love with which You <have> loved Me may be in them, and I in them."	17:26 and I have made Your name known to them, and will make it known, so that the love with which You loved Me may be in them, and I in them."
29 [After] Jesus had spoken these words, <He said,> "Get up, <and> let us go from here."	18:1~ [When] Jesus had spoken these words, 14:~31 Get up, let us go from here.

	Matthew	Mark	Luke	John
30 After singing a hymn, He went out and proceeded, as was His custom, to the Mount of Olives; and [His] [apostles] followed Him.	26:30 After singing a hymn, they went out to the Mount of Olives.	14:26 After singing a hymn, they went out to the Mount of Olives.	22:39 And He came out and proceeded as was His custom to the Mount of Olives; and [the] [disciples] also followed Him.	

CHAPTER 8
ARREST, TRIALS & CRUCIFIXION

The Arrest, Trials and Crucifixion of Jesus Christ.

Act 1 - Jesus Is Arrested at Gethsemane

		Page
Scene 1	The First Agonized Prayer of Jesus	252
2	Jesus Prays A Second Time	253
3	The Third Prayer of Jesus In The Garden	253
4	Judas Leads The Authorities To Jesus	254
5	Peter Defends Jesus With A Sword	255
6	Jesus Is Arrested	256

Act 2 - Jesus Is Accused By The High Priest

Scene 1	First, To The House of Annas	257
2	Then To The High Priest, Caiaphas	258
3	Peter's First Denial of Jesus	259
4	Peter's Second Denial	259
5	Jesus Is Charged With Blasphemy	260
6	Jesus Is Beaten	260
7	Peter Denies Jesus The Third Time	261

Act 3 - Jesus Is Questioned By The Sanhedrin

Scene 1	The Sanhedrin Council Condemns Jesus	262
2	The Jews Take Jesus To The Roman Governor	262

Act 4 - Jesus Is Questioned By The Romans

Scene 1	Pilate Hears The Accusation Against Jesus	263
2	Are You The King of The Jews?	264
3	Pilate Finds No Guilt In Jesus	265
4	Herod, Tetrarch of Galilee, Questions Jesus	266
5	We Romans Find No Guilt In This Man	266

Act 5 - Jesus Is Sentenced To Die

		Page
Scene 1	Shall I Release For You Jesus, or Barabbas?	267
2	The Jews Cry Out To Crucify Jesus	268
3	Pilate Sentences Jesus To Die	268
4	The Soldiers Mock and Scourge Jesus	269
5	Pilate Tries Again To Release Jesus	270
6	Jesus Is Handed Over To Be Crucified	271
7	Judas The Betrayer Hangs Himself	271

Act 6 - The Crucifixion of Jesus Christ

Scene 1	Simon of Cyrene Carries The Cross of Jesus	272
2	The Walk To Golgotha	272
3	Jesus Is Crucified	273
4	The Soldiers Divide His Clothing	274
5	Jesus Is Crucified Between Two Criminals	274
6	Pilate's Inscription of The Charge Against Jesus	275
7	Jesus Entrusts His Mother To John	275
8	Let This Christ Save Himself!	276
9	The Last Words of the Two Criminals	276

Act 7 - The Death of Jesus Christ

Scene 1	Darkness Falls Over The Land	277
2	Jesus Dies On The Cross	277
3	An Earthquake At The Death of Jesus	278
4	The Body of Jesus Is Taken Down	279

Act 8 - Jesus Is Laid In Joseph's Tomb

		Page
Scene 1	Joseph Asks Pilate For The Body of Jesus	280
2	The Body of Jesus Is Placed In Joseph's Tomb	281
3	Roman Soldiers Guard The Tomb	282

Act 9 - The Resurrection of Jesus Christ

Scene 1	An Earthquake at The Resurrection of Jesus	283
2	The Soldiers Are Paid To Lie	283

MAP OF JERUSALEM

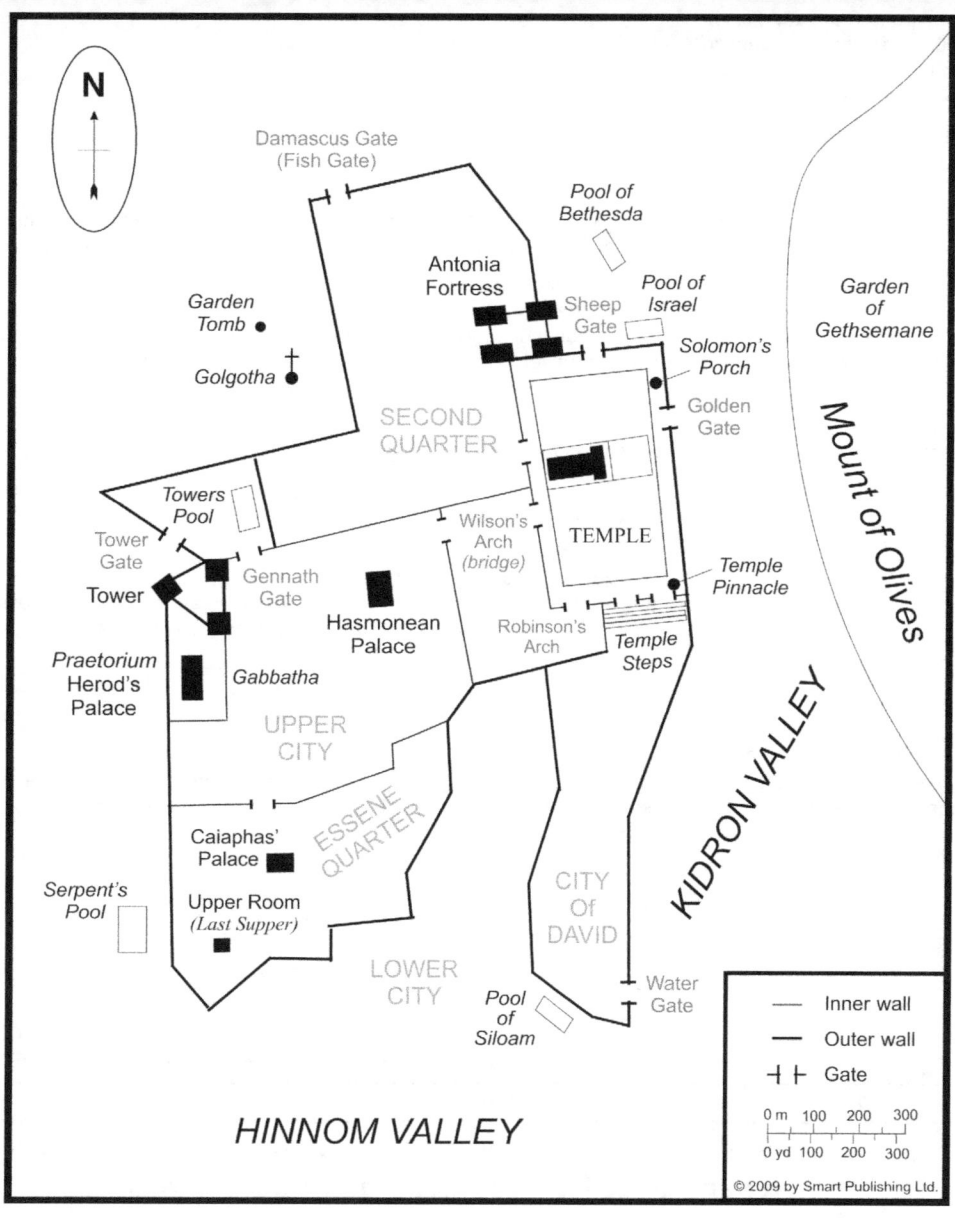

8 - TRIALS & CRUCIFIXION

Act 1: Jesus Is Arrested at Gethsemane

Scene 1: The First Agonized Prayer of Jesus

Garden of Gethsemane, Mount of Olives, Jerusalem, *Judea* — late Thursday evening, April 2nd / 33 CE

The Greatest Gospel

	Matthew	Mark	Luke	John
1 Jesus went forth with His [apostles] [through] the Kidron ravine, <and> came to a place called Gethsemane where there was a garden, in[to] which [they] entered.	26:36~ Then Jesus came with them to a place called Gethsemane,	14:32~ They came to a place named Gethsemane;		18:~1 He went forth with His [disciples] [over] the ravine of the Kidron, where there was a garden, in which [He] entered [with His disciples].
2 Now Judas <Iscariot>, who was betraying Him, also knew the [garden], for Jesus had often met there with His [apostles].				18:2 Now Judas also, who was betraying Him, knew the [place], for Jesus had often met there with His [disciples].
3 When [they] arrived at the place, [Jesus] said to them, "Sit here, while I go over there and pray. <And> pray that you may not enter into temptation."	26:~36 and said to His disciples, "Sit here while I go over there and pray."	14:~32 and [He] said to His disciples, "Sit here until I have prayed."	22:40 When [He] arrived at the place, [He] said to them, "Pray that you may not enter into temptation."	
4 [Jesus] took with Him Peter, and James and John, the two sons of Zebedee.	26:37~ And [He] took with Him Peter and the two sons of Zebedee,	14:33~ And [He] took with Him Peter and James and John,		
5 [Then] <He> began to be very distressed and troubled; and He said to them, "My soul is deeply grieved, to the point of death.	26:~37 [and] began to be grieved and distressed. 26:38~ Then He said to them, "My soul is deeply grieved, to the point of death;	14:~33 [and] began to be very distressed and troubled. 14:34~ And He said to them, "My soul is deeply grieved to the point of death;		
6 "Remain here, and keep watch with Me."	26:~38 remain here and keep watch with Me."	14:~34 remain here and keep watch."		
7 [Then] [Jesus] withdrew about a stone's throw beyond them, and fell down to the ground on His face.	26:39~ [And] [He] went a little beyond them and fell on His face	14:35~ [And] [He] went a little beyond them and fell to the ground	22:41~ [And] [He] withdrew from them about a stone's throw, and He knelt down	
8 And <He> began to pray, that if it were possible, the hour might pass Him by; saying, "Abba! My Father! All things are possible for You.	26:~39 and prayed, saying, "My Father,	14:~35 and began to pray that if it were possible, the hour might pass Him by. 14:36~ And He was saying, "Abba! Father! All things are possible for You;	22:~41 and began to pray, 22:42~ saying, "Father,	
9 "If You are willing, remove this cup, <and> let [it] pass from Me; *yet not as I will, but what You will be done."* [1.]	26:~39 if it is possible, let [this cup] pass from Me; yet not as I will, but as You will."	14:~36 remove this cup from Me; yet not what I will, but what You will."	22:~42 if You are willing, remove this cup from Me; yet not My will, but Yours be done."	
10 [Then] an angel from Heaven appeared to [Jesus], strengthening Him.			22:43 [Now] an angel from heaven appeared to [Him], strengthening Him.	
11 And being in agony, He was praying very fervently; and His sweat became like drops of blood, falling down upon the ground.			22:44 And being in agony He was praying very fervently; and His sweat became like drops of blood, falling down upon the ground.	

1. Isaiah 50:5

8 - TRIALS & CRUCIFIXION
Act 1: Jesus Is Arrested at Gethsemane

Scene 2: Jesus Prays A Second Time
Garden of Gethsemane, Mount of Olives, Jerusalem, *Judea*   late Thursday evening, April 2nd / 33 CE

	Matthew	Mark	Luke
1	When [Jesus] rose from prayer, He came to the [apostles], and found them sleeping from sorrow.	26:40~ And He came to the [disciples] and found them sleeping,	14:37~ And He came and found them sleeping,	22:45 When [He] rose from prayer, He came to the [disciples] and found them sleeping from sorrow,
2	<He> said to Peter, "Simon, are you asleep? Why are you sleeping? Could you men not keep watch with Me for one hour?	26:~40 and said to Peter, "So, you men could not keep watch with Me for one hour?	14:37~ and said to Peter, "Simon, are you asleep? Could you not keep watch for one hour?	22:46~ and said to them, "Why are you sleeping?
3	"Get up! Keep watching, and praying that you may not enter into temptation;	26:41 "Keep watching and praying that you may not enter into temptation;	14:38 "Keep watching and praying that you may not come into temptation;	22:~46 Get up and pray that you may not enter into temptation."
4	"the spirit is willing, but the flesh is weak."	26:~41 the spirit is willing, but the flesh is weak."	14:~38 the spirit is willing, but the flesh is weak."	
5	<Then> [Jesus] went away a second time, and <He> prayed again saying the same words; "My Father, if this cannot pass unless I drink it, Your will be done."	26:42 [He] went away a second time and prayed, again saying, "My Father, if this cannot pass away unless I drink it, Your will be done."	14:39 Again [He] went away and prayed saying the same words.	

Scene 3: The Third Prayer of Jesus In The Garden
Garden of Gethsemane, Mount of Olives, Jerusalem, *Judea*   late Thursday evening, April 2nd / 33 CE

	Matthew	Mark
1	Again [Jesus] came and found them sleeping, for their eyes were very heavy; and they did not know what to answer Him.	26:43 Again [He] came and found them sleeping, for their eyes were heavy.	14:40 And again [He] came and found them sleeping, for their eyes were very heavy; and they did not know what to answer Him.
2	And again He left them, and went away and prayed <for> a third time, saying the same thing once more.	26:44 And He left them again, and went away and prayed a third time, saying the same thing once more.	14:41~[1] the third time,
3	Then [Jesus] came to the <three> [apostles], and <He> said to them, "Are you still sleeping and resting? It is enough!	26:45~ Then [He] came to the [disciples] and said to them, "Are you still sleeping and resting?	14:41~ And [He] came 14:41~[2] and said to them, "Are you still sleeping and resting? It is enough;
4	"Behold, the hour has come, and the Son of Man is being betrayed into the hands of sinners.	26:~45 Behold, the hour is at hand and the Son of Man is being betrayed into the hands of sinners.	14:~41 the hour has come; behold, the Son of Man is being betrayed into the hands of sinners.
5	"Get up, <and> let us be going! Behold, the one who betrays Me is at hand!"	26:46 "Get up, let us be going; behold, the one who betrays Me is at hand!"	14:42 "Get up, let us be going; behold, the one who betrays Me is at hand!"

8 - TRIALS & CRUCIFIXION

Act 1: Jesus Is Arrested at Gethsemane

Scene 4: Judas Leads The Authorities To Jesus

Garden of Gethsemane, Mount of Olives, Jerusalem, *Judea*   around midnight, Thursday, April 2nd / 33 CE

A Harmonious Gospel Merger

	Matthew	Mark	Luke	John
1	Immediately, while [Jesus] was still speaking, behold, <the> one of the twelve called Judas came there, preceding a large crowd [of] the chief priests and the Pharisees, [with] the scribes and the elders of the people, <along with> the Roman cohort and officers.	26:47~ While [He] was still speaking, behold, Judas, one of the twelve, came ~~up accompanied by~~ a large crowd 26:~47 ~~who came~~ [from] the chief priests and the elders of the people.	14:43~ Immediately while [He] was still speaking, Judas, one of the twelve, came ~~up accompanied by~~ a crowd 14:~43 ~~who were~~ [from] the chief priests [and] the scribes and the elders.	22:47~ While [He] was still speaking, behold, a crowd came, ~~and the one~~ called Judas, one of the twelve, ~~was~~ preceding ~~them~~	18:3 Judas ~~then~~, ~~having received~~ the Roman cohort and officers came [from] the chief priests and the Pharisees, came there
2	<They were> [carrying] lanterns and torches, and swords and clubs.	26:~47~ [with] swords and clubs,	14:~43~ [with] swords and clubs,		18:~3 [with] lanterns and torches and ~~weapons~~.
3	Now Judas <Iscariot>, who was betraying [Jesus], had given them a signal, saying, "Whomever I kiss, He is the One. Seize Him, and lead Him away under guard."	26:48 Now [he] who was betraying [Him] gave them a sign, saying, "Whomever I kiss, He is the one; seize Him."	14:44 Now [he] who was betraying [Him] had given them a signal, saying, "Whomever I kiss, He is the one; seize Him and lead Him away under guard."		18:~5~ ~~And~~ Judas ~~also~~, who was betraying [Him],
4	[Upon arriving], Judas immediately approached Jesus, and said, "Hail, Rabbi!" and kissed Him.	26:49 Immediately Judas ~~went to~~ Jesus and said, "Hail, Rabbi!" and kissed Him.	14:45 [After coming], Judas immediately ~~went to Him, saying~~, "Rabbi!" and kissed Him.	22:~47 ~~and he~~ approached Jesus ~~to~~ kiss Him.	
5	Jesus said to him, "Judas, *are you betraying the Son of Man with a kiss*?" [1]			22:48 ~~But~~ Jesus said to him, "Judas, are you betraying the Son of Man with a kiss?"	
6	So Jesus, knowing all the things that were coming upon Him, said to them, "Whom do you seek?"				18:4 So Jesus, knowing all the things that were coming upon Him, ~~went forth and~~ said to them, "Whom do you seek?"
7	They answered Him, "Jesus the Nazarene." He said to them, "I am He."				18:5~ They answered Him, "Jesus the Nazarene." He said to them, "I am He."
8	When He said to them, "I am He," they drew back, and fell to the ground.				18:6 ~~So~~ when He said to them, "I am He," they drew back and fell to the ground.
9	[So] again [Jesus] asked them, "Whom do you seek?" <And again> they said, "Jesus the Nazarene."				18:7 [~~Therefore~~] [He] again asked them, "Whom do you seek?" ~~And~~ they said, "Jesus the Nazarene."
10	Jesus answered, "I told you that I am He; so if you seek Me, let these go <on> their way,"				18:8 Jesus answered, "I told you that I am He; so if you seek Me, let these go their way,"
11	to fulfill the Word which He spoke, *"Of those whom You have given <to> Me, I lost not one."* [2]				18:9 to fulfill the word which He spoke, "Of those whom You have given Me I lost not one."

1. Proverb 27:6   *2. 517.3 (John 6:39); 789.14 (John 17:12)*

8 - TRIALS & CRUCIFIXION
Act 1: Jesus Is Arrested at Gethsemane
Scene 5: Peter Defends Jesus With A Sword

Garden of Gethsemane, Mount of Olives, Jerusalem, *Judea* around midnight, Thursday, April 2nd / 33 CE

The Full Gospel Story of Jesus Christ

#	Matthew	Mark	Luke	John
1	<Judas the betrayer> was standing with [the crowd], and Jesus said to him, "Friend, do what you have come for."	*26:50~* And Jesus said to ~~him~~, "Friend, do what you have come for."			*18:~5* was standing with [~~them~~].
2	Then they came and laid hands on Jesus, and seized Him.	*26:~50* Then they came and laid hands on Jesus and seized Him.	*14:46* They laid hands on ~~Him~~ and seized Him.		
3	When those who were around [Jesus] saw what was happen[ing], they said, "Lord, shall we [defend] <You>?"			*22:49* When those who were around [Him] saw what was ~~going to~~ happen, they said, "Lord, shall we [~~strike with the sword~~]?"	
4	Then Simon Peter, having a sword, drew it and struck Malchus, the slave of the High Priest, and cut off his right ear.	*26:51* ~~And behold, one of those who were with Jesus reached and~~ drew ~~out his sword~~, and struck the slave of the high priest and cut off his ear.	*14:47* ~~But one of those who stood by~~ drew ~~his sword~~, and struck the slave of the high priest and cut off his ear.	*22:50* ~~And one of them~~ struck the slave of the high priest and cut off his right ear.	*18:10* Simon Peter then, having a sword, drew it and struck the high priest's slave, and cut off his right ear; ~~and the slave's name was~~ Malchus.
5	But Jesus said, "Stop! No more of this!"			*22:51~* But Jesus ~~answered and~~ said, "Stop! No more of this."	
6	And He touched [the slave's] ear, and healed him.			*22:~51* And He touched [~~his~~] ear and healed him.	
7	Then Jesus said to Peter, "Put your sword back in its sheath, for all those who take up the sword shall perish by the sword.	*26:52* Then Jesus said to ~~him~~, "Put your sword back ~~into~~ its ~~place~~; for all those who take up the sword shall perish by the sword.			*18:11~* ~~So~~ Jesus said to Peter, "Put ~~the~~ sword ~~into~~ ~~the~~ sheath;
8	"The cup which The Father has given <to> Me, shall I not drink it?				*18:~11* the cup which the Father has given Me, shall I not drink it?"
9	"Or do you not think that I can appeal to My Father, and He will at once put at My disposal more than twelve legions of angels?	*26:53* "Or do you think that I cannot appeal to My Father, and He will at once put at My disposal more than twelve legions of angels?			
10	"<But> how then will the Scriptures be fulfilled, which say that it must happen this way?"	*26:54* "How then will the Scriptures be fulfilled, which say that it must happen this way?"			

8 - TRIALS & CRUCIFIXION

Act 1: Jesus Is Arrested at Gethsemane

Scene 6: Jesus Is Arrested

Garden of Gethsemane, Mount of Olives, Jerusalem, *Judea* — around midnight Thursday, April 2nd / 33 CE

#		Matthew	Mark	Luke	John
1	Then Jesus said to the crowds <and the> chief priests, <with the> elders and <the> officers of the Temple who had come <out> against Him, "Have you come with swords and clubs to arrest Me, as you would against a robber?	26:55~ ~~At that time~~ Jesus said to ~~the~~ crowds, "Have you come ~~out~~ with swords and clubs to arrest Me as you would against a robber?	14:48 ~~And~~ Jesus said to ~~them~~, "Have you come ~~out~~ with swords and clubs to arrest Me, as you would against a robber?	22:52 Then Jesus said to the chief priests and officers of the temple ~~and~~ elders who had come against Him, "Have you come ~~out~~ with swords and clubs as you would against a robber?	
2	"Every day I used to sit with you in the Temple teaching, and you did not lay hands on Me.	26:~55 Every day I used to sit in the temple teaching and you did not ~~seize~~ Me.	14:49~ Every day I ~~was~~ with you in the temple teaching, and you did not ~~seize~~ Me;	22:53~ ~~While~~ I ~~was~~ with you ~~daily~~ in the temple, you did not lay hands on Me;	
3	"But all <of> this has taken place to fulfill the Scriptures of the prophets; this hour, and the power of darkness, are yours."	26:56 But all this has taken place to fulfill the Scriptures of the prophets."	14:~49 but this has taken place to fulfill the Scriptures."	22:~53 ~~but~~ this hour and the power of darkness are yours."	
4	So the Roman cohort and the commander, [with] the [attendants] of the Jews, arrested Jesus, and bound Him.				18:12 So the Roman cohort and the commander [~~and~~] the [~~officers~~] of the Jews, arrested Jesus and bound Him,
5	Then all the [apostles] left Him, and fled.	26:~56 Then all the [~~disciples~~] left Him and fled.	14:50 ~~And they~~ all left Him and fled.		
6	A young man was following Him, wearing nothing but a linen sheet over his naked body; and they seized him, but he pulled free of the linen sheet, and escaped naked.		14:51 A young man was following Him, wearing nothing but a linen sheet over his naked body; and they seized him. 14:52 But he pulled free of the linen sheet and escaped naked.		

8 - TRIALS & CRUCIFIXION

Act 2: Jesus Is Accused By The High Priest

Scene 1: First, To The House of Annas

House of Annas, Jerusalem, *Judea* — early Friday morning, April 3rd / 33 CE

The Complete Gospel of Jesus

#	Matthew	Mark	Luke	John
1	Having arrested [Jesus], those who seized [Him] led Him away, and brought Him to the house of *Annas*[1] first, for he was the father-in-law of *Caiaphas*,[2] who was <the> High Priest that year.	26:57~ Those who had seized [Jesus] led Him away	14:53~ They led Jesus away to	22:54~ Having arrested [Him], they led Him away and brought Him to the house of	18:13 and led Him to Annas first; for he was father-in-law of Caiaphas, who was high priest that year.
2	[When] [Annas] questioned Jesus about His disciples, and about His teaching, Jesus answered him, "I have spoken openly to the world.				18:19 [The high priest] [then] questioned Jesus about His disciples, and about His teaching. 18:20~ Jesus answered him, "I have spoken openly to the world;
3	"I always taught in synagogues and in the Temple, where all the Jews come together, and I spoke nothing in secret.				18:~20 I always taught in synagogues and in the temple, where all the Jews come together; and I spoke nothing in secret.
4	"Why do you question Me? Question those who have heard what I spoke. They know what I said."				18:21 "Why do you question Me? Question those who have heard what I spoke to them; they know what I said."
5	When Jesus had said this, one of the [attendants] standing nearby struck Him, <and> [said], "Is that the way You answer the High Priest?"				18:22 When He had said this, one of the [officers]* standing nearby struck Jesus, [saying], "Is that the way You answer the high priest?"
6	Jesus answered him, "If I have spoken wrongly, testify of the wrong; but if rightly, why do you strike Me?"				18:23 Jesus answered him, "If I have spoken wrongly, testify of the wrong; but if rightly, why do you strike Me?"
7	[Then] Annas sent Him bound to Caiaphas the High Priest, where all the chief priests [with] the elders and the scribes, were gathered together.	26:~57 to Caiaphas, the high priest, where the scribes and the elders were gathered together.	14:~53 the high priest; and all the chief priests and the elders and the scribes gathered together.	22:~54~ the high priest;	18:24 [So] Annas sent Him bound to Caiaphas the high priest.
8	Now Caiaphas was the one who had advised the Jews that it was expedient for one man to die on behalf of the people.				18:14 Now Caiaphas was the one who had advised the Jews that it was expedient for one man to die on behalf of the people.

1. Annas (23 BCE - c. 40 CE) - High Priest during 6-15 CE   2. Joseph Caiaphas (c. 14 BCE - 46 CE) - High Priest during 18-36 CE

8 - TRIALS & CRUCIFIXION

Act 2: Jesus Is Accused By The High Priest

Scene 2: Then To The High Priest, Caiaphas

Palace of Caiaphas, Jerusalem, *Judea* early Friday morning, April 3rd / 33 CE

A Four Gospel Harmony & Merger

#	Matthew	Mark	Luke	John
1	Simon Peter was following Jesus at a distance, and so was another [apostle].	26:58~ But Peter was following Him at a distance	14:54~ Peter had followed Him at a distance,	22:~54 but Peter was following at a distance.	18:15~ Simon Peter was following Jesus, and so was another [disciple].
2	[Since] that [apostle] was known to the High Priest, <he> entered with Jesus into the court of the High Priest, but Peter was standing outside at the door.				18:~15 [Now] that [disciple] was known to the high priest, and entered with Jesus into the court of the high priest, 18:16~ but Peter was standing at the door outside.
3	So the [apostle] who was known to the High Priest went and spoke to the doorkeeper, and <they> brought Peter into the courtyard.	26:~58~ as far as the courtyard of the high priest,	14:~54~1 right into the courtyard of the high priest;		18:~16 So the other [disciple], who was known to the high priest, went out and spoke to the doorkeeper, and brought Peter in.
4	[Peter] entered, and sat down with the [attendants] to see the outcome.	26:~58 and entered in, and sat down with the [officers]* to see the outcome.	14:54~2 and [he] was sitting with the [officers]*		
5	[Meanwhile], the chief priests and the whole *Council* [1.] kept trying to obtain testimony against Jesus, so that they might put Him to death;	26:59 [Now] the chief priests and the whole Council kept trying to obtain false testimony against Jesus, so that they might put Him to death.	14:55~ [Now] the chief priests and the whole Council kept trying to obtain testimony against Jesus to put Him to death.		
6	[but] they did not find any, even though many false witnesses came forward <who> [gave] testimony against Him, but their testimony was not consistent.	26:60~ They did not find any, even though many false witnesses came forward.	14:~55 [and] they were not finding any. 14:56 For many were [giving] false testimony against Him, but their testimony was not consistent.		
7	But later on, two <people> came forward <who> [gave] false testimony against Him,[2.] saying, "We heard this man state, 'I will destroy this Temple of God made with hands, and in three days I will build another, made without hands.'"	26:~60 But later on two came forward, 26:61 and said, "This man stated, 'I am able to destroy the temple of God and to rebuild it in three days.'"	14:57 Some stood up and began to [give] false testimony against Him, saying, 14:58 "We heard Him say, 'I will destroy this temple made with hands, and in three days I will build another made without hands.'"		
8	<So,> not even in this respect was their testimony consistent.		14:59 Not even in this respect was their testimony consistent.		
9	<Then> the High Priest stood up, and came forward, and <he> questioned Jesus, saying, "Do You not answer? What is it that these men are testifying against You?"	26:62 The high priest stood up and said to Him, "Do You not answer? What is it that these men are testifying against You?"	14:60 The high priest stood up and came forward and questioned Jesus, saying, "Do You not answer? What is it that these men are testifying against You?"		
10	But *Jesus kept silent, and <He> did not answer.*[3.]	26:63~ But Jesus kept silent.	14:61~ But He kept silent and did not answer.		

1. Hebrew word sanhedrin *means "sitting together" or "council"*

8 - TRIALS & CRUCIFIXION
Act 2: Jesus Is Accused By The High Priest

Scene 3: Peter's First Denial of Jesus
Palace of Caiaphas, Jerusalem, *Judea* early Friday morning, April 3rd / 33 CE

Quotations and references are italicized

	Matthew	Mark	Luke	John
1 Now after the [servants] and the [attendants] <who> were standing outside in the middle of the courtyard had kindled a charcoal fire, <they> sat down together, for it was cold and they were warming themselves.	26:69~ Now 26:69~2 outside in the courtyard,	14:~66~ below in the courtyard,	22:55~ After they had kindled a fire in the middle of the courtyard and had sat down together,	18:18~ Now the [slaves] and the [officers]* were standing there having made a charcoal fire, for it was cold and they were warming themselves;
2 Peter was <also> sitting among them and warming himself, [when] a servant-girl of the High Priest who kept the door came.	26:69~1 Peter was sitting 26:69~3 and a servant-girl came to him	14:~54 and warming himself at the fire. 14:66~ As Peter was 14:~66 one of the servant-girls of the high priest came,	22:~55 Peter was sitting among them. 22:56~ And a servant-girl,	18:~18 and Peter was also with them, standing and warming himself. 18:17~ [Then] the slave-girl who kept the door
3 Seeing Peter, as he sat warming himself in the firelight, she looked intently at him, and said to [him], "You too were with Jesus the Galilean. You are not also one of [His] disciples, are you?"	26:~69 and said, "You too were with Jesus the Galilean."	14:67 and seeing Peter warming himself, she looked at him and said, "You also were with Jesus the Nazarene."	22:~56 seeing him as he sat in the firelight and looking intently at him, said, "This man was with Him too."	18:~17~ said to [Peter], "You are not also one of [this man's] disciples, are you?"
4 But [Peter] denied it before them all, saying, "Woman, I am not. I neither know nor understand what you are talking about. I do not know Him."	26:70 But [he] denied it before them all, saying, "I do not know what you are talking about."	14:68~ But [he] denied it, saying, I neither know nor understand what you are talking about.	22:57 But [he] denied it, saying, "Woman, I do not know Him."	18:~17 He said, "I am not."
5 And [Peter] went out onto the porch.		14:~68 And [he] went out onto the porch.		

Scene 4: Peter's Second Denial
Palace of Caiaphas, Jerusalem, *Judea* early Friday morning, April 3rd / 33 CE

	Matthew	Mark	Luke	John
1 When [Peter] had gone out [through] the gateway <and onto the porch>, another servant-girl of the High Priest, being a relative of the one whose ear Peter <had> cut off, saw him, and said, "You are one of them too! Did I not see you in the garden with Him?"	26:71~ When [he] had gone out [to] the gateway, another servant-girl saw him	14:69~ The servant-girl saw him, and began once more to say 14:~69 "This is one of them!"	22:58~ A little later, another saw him and said, "You are one of them too!"	18:26 One of the slaves of the high priest, being a relative of the one whose ear Peter cut off, said, "Did I not see you in the garden with Him?"
2 <And she> said to the bystanders who were there, "This man was with Jesus of Nazareth!"	26:~71 and said to those who were there, "This man was with Jesus of Nazareth."	14:~69 to the bystanders,		
3 And again Peter denied it with an oath, and said, "I am not! I do not know the man."	26:72 And again he denied it with an oath, "I do not know the man."	14:70~ But again he denied it.	22:~58 But Peter said, "Man, I am not!"	18:~25 He denied it, and said, "I am not."

8 - TRIALS & CRUCIFIXION
Act 2: Jesus Is Accused By The High Priest

Scene 5: Jesus Is Charged With Blasphemy
Palace of Caiaphas, Jerusalem, Judea — early Friday morning, April 3rd / 33 CE

	Matthew	Mark
1 Again the High Priest question[ed] [Jesus], and said to Him, "I adjure You by the living God, that You tell us: Are You the Christ, the Son of God?"	26:~63 ~And~ the high priest said to Him, "I adjure You by the living God, that You tell us ~whether~ You are the Christ, the Son of God."	14:~61 Again the high priest ~was~ question[ing] [Him], and ~saying~ to Him, "Are You the Christ, the Son of ~the Blessed One~?"
2 Jesus said to him, "You have said it yourself; I am.	26:64 Jesus said to him, "You have said it yourself;	14:62~ ~And~ Jesus said, "I am;
3 "Nevertheless, I tell you <that> hereafter you shall see *the Son of Man sitting at the right hand of Power, and coming with the clouds of Heaven.*" [1]	26:~64 nevertheless I tell you, hereafter you ~will~ see the Son of Man sitting at the right hand of Power, and coming ~on~ the clouds of heaven.	14:~62 ~and~ you shall see the Son of Man sitting at the right hand of Power, and coming with the clouds of heaven."
4 Then the High Priest tore his robes, and said, "He has blasphemed!	26:~65 Then the high priest tore his robes and said, "He has blasphemed!	14:63~ ~Tearing~ his ~clothes~, the high priest said,
5 "What further need do we have of witnesses? Behold, you have now heard the blasphemy.	26:~65 What further need do we have of witnesses? Behold, you have now heard the blasphemy;	14:~63 "What further need do we have of witnesses? 14:64~ You have heard the blasphemy;
6 "What do you think? How does it seem to you?"	26:66~ what do you think?	14:~64~ how does it seem to you?"
7 And they all condemned [Jesus], <and> answered, "He deserves death."	26:~66 ~They~ answered, "He deserves death!"	14:~64 And they all condemned [Him] ~to be~ deserving ~of~ death.

1. Daniel 7:13

Scene 6: Jesus Is Beaten
Palace of Caiaphas, Jerusalem, Judea — early Friday morning, April 3rd / 33 CE

	Matthew	Mark	Luke
1 Then the men who were holding Jesus in custody were mocking Him, <and> some began to *spit in His face.*	26:67~ Then ~they~ [spat] in His face	14:~65~ Some began to spit ~at Him~,	22:63~ ~Now~ the men who were holding Jesus in custody were mocking Him
2 *And they blindfolded Him, and beat Him with their fists.* [1]	26:~67~ and beat Him with their fists;	14:~65~ and ~to~ blindfold Him, and ~to~ beat Him with their fists,	22:~63 and beating Him, 22:64~ and they blindfolded Him
3 [Then] the [attendants] slapped Him in the face, and said to Him, "Prophesy to us, You Christ! Who is the one who hit You?"	26:~67 [and] ~others~ slapped Him, 26:68 and said, "Prophesy to us, You Christ; who is the one who hit You?"	14:~65 and ~to say~ to Him, "Prophesy!" [And] the [~officers~]* ~received~ Him ~with~ slaps in the face.	22:~64 and ~were asking~ Him, ~saying~, "Prophesy, who is the one who hit You?"
4 And they were saying many other blasphem[ous] things against Him.			22:65 And they were saying many other things against Him, blasphem[ing].

1. Isaiah 50:6

8 - TRIALS & CRUCIFIXION

Act 2: Jesus Is Accused By The High Priest

Scene 7: Peter Denies Jesus The Third Time

Palace of Caiaphas, Jerusalem, *Judea* early Friday morning, April 3rd / 33 CE

Page 261

Seeing the Four Gospels as One

#	Matthew	Mark	Luke	John
1	After about an hour had passed, Simon Peter was standing and warming himself <in the courtyard>, so the bystanders said to him, "You are not also one of His disciples, are you?"	26:73~ A little later the bystanders	14:~70~ And after a little while the bystanders	22:59~ After about an hour had passed,	18:25~ Now Simon Peter was standing and warming himself. So they said to him, "You are not also one of His disciples, are you?"
2	Another man came up and began to insist, saying to Peter, "Surely you [were] with Him, for you too are a Galilean - even the way you talk gives you away!"	26:~73 came up and said to Peter, "Surely you too are one of them; for even the way you talk gives you away.	14:~70 were again saying to Peter, "Surely you are one of them, for you are a Galilean too.	22:~59 another man began to insist, saying, Certainly this man also [was] with Him, for he is a Galilean too.	
3	Then Peter began to curse and swear, <and he> denied it again, <and> said "I do not know this man <that> you are talking about!"	26:74~ Then he began to curse and swear, "I do not know the man!"	14:71 But he began to curse and swear, "I do not know this man you are talking about!"	22:60~ But Peter said, "Man, I do not know what you are talking about."	18:27~ Peter then denied it again,
4	And immediately, while he was still speaking, a rooster crowed.	26:~74 And immediately a rooster crowed.	14:72~ Immediately a rooster crowed a second time.	22:~60 Immediately, while he was still speaking, a rooster crowed.	18:~27 and immediately a rooster crowed.
5	<And> the Lord turned, and looked at Peter; and Peter remembered the word of the Lord - how Jesus had made the remark to him: "Before a rooster crows today, you will deny Me three times."	26:75~ And Peter remembered the word which Jesus had said, "Before a rooster crows, you will deny Me three times."	14:~72~ And Peter remembered how Jesus had made the remark to him "Before a rooster crows twice you will deny Me three times."	22:61 The Lord turned and looked at Peter. And Peter remembered the word of the Lord, how He had told him "Before a rooster crows today, you will deny Me three times."	
6	And [Peter] went out, and <he> began to weep bitterly.	26:~75 And [he] went out and wept bitterly.	14:~72 And [he] began to weep.	22:62 And [he] went out and wept bitterly.	

8 – TRIALS & CRUCIFIXION
Act 3: Jesus Is Questioned By The Sanhedrin

Scene 1: The Sanhedrin Council Condemns Jesus
Sanhedrin Council Chamber, The Temple, Jerusalem, *Judea*   early Friday morning, April 3rd / 33 CE

The Unified Four Gospel Harmony

	Matthew	Mark	Luke
1 Early in the morning, when it was day, all the chief priests and <the> scribes assembled with the whole *Council*[1.] of the elders of the people; <and> immediately <they> held a consultation.	27:1~ ~~Now~~ when morning ~~came~~, all the chief priests and the elders of the people	15:1~ Early in the morning the chief priests with the elders and scribes and the whole Council, immediately held a consultation;	22:66~ When it was day, ~~the~~ Council of elders of the people ~~both~~ chief priests and scribes, assembled,
2 [Then] they led [Jesus] [in]to their Council chamber, <and> [said], "If You are the Christ, tell us."			22:~66 [and] they led [Him] ~~away~~ [in]to their council chamber, [saying], 22:67~ "If You are the Christ, tell us."
3 He said to them, "If I tell you, you will not believe; and if I ask <you> a question, you will not answer.			22:~67 ~~But~~ He said to them, "If I tell you, you will not believe; 22:68 and if I ask a question, you will not answer.
4 "But from now on, the Son of Man will be seated at the right hand of the power of God."			22:69 "But from now on the Son of Man will be seated at the right hand of the power of God."
5 They all [asked], "Are You the Son of God, then?" And [Jesus] said to them, "Yes, I am."			22:70 ~~And~~ they all [said], "Are You the Son of God, then?" And [He] said to them, "Yes, I am."
6 Then they said, "What further need do we have of testimony? For we have heard it <for> ourselves, from His own mouth!"			22:71 Then they said, "What further need do we have of testimony? For we have heard it ourselves from His own mouth."
7 <And they> conferred together to put Jesus to death.	27:~1 conferred together ~~against~~ Jesus to put ~~Him~~ to death;		

1. Hebrew word sanhedrin *means "sitting together" or "council"*

Scene 2: The Jews Take Jesus To The Roman Governor
The Praetorium, Jerusalem, *Judea*   early Friday morning, April 3rd / 33 CE

	Matthew	Mark	Luke	John
1 Then the whole body of them got up, and they bound Jesus;	27:2~ and they bound ~~Him~~,	15:~1 and ~~binding~~ Jesus,	23:1~ Then the whole body of them got up	
2 and they led Him away from Caiaphas, and brought Him to the *Praetorium*,[1.] and delivered Him to *Pilate*,[2.] the <Roman> Governor.	27:~2 and led Him away and delivered Him to Pilate the governor.	15:~1 they led Him away and delivered Him to Pilate.	23:~1 and brought Him ~~before~~ Pilate.	18:28~ ~~Then~~ they led ~~Jesus~~ from Caiaphas ~~into~~ the Praetorium,
3 It was early, and they themselves did not enter to the Praetorium so that they would not be defiled, but might eat the Passover.				18:~28 ~~and~~ it was early; and they themselves did not enter into the Praetorium so that they would not be defiled, but might eat the Passover.

1. seat of Roman authority   2. Pontius Pilate - Roman Governor of Judea from 26 to 37 CE

8 - TRIALS & CRUCIFIXION	Scene 1: **Pilate Hears The Accusation Against Jesus**	
Act 4: **Jesus Is Questioned By The Romans**	The Praetorium, Jerusalem, *Judea* early Friday morning, April 3rd / 33 CE	

	Luke	John
1 Pilate, <the Roman Governor of Judea,> went out to [the Jews], and <he> said <to them>, "What accusation do you bring against this man?"		18:29 ~~Therefore~~ Pilate went out to [~~them~~] and said, "What accusation do you bring against this Man?"
2 They answered, and said to him, "If this man were not an evildoer, we would not have delivered Him to you."		18:30 They answered and said to him, "If this Man were not an evildoer, we would not have delivered Him to you."
3 Pilate said to them, "Take Him yourselves, and judge Him according to your law."		18:31~ ~~So~~ Pilate said to them, "Take Him yourselves, and judge Him according to your law."
4 The Jews said to him, "We are not permitted to put anyone to death"; to fulfill the word which Jesus spoke, signifying by what kind of death He was about to die.		18:~31 The Jews said to him, "We are not permitted to put anyone to death," 18:32 to fulfill the word of Jesus which He spoke, signifying by what kind ~~of~~ death He was about to die.
5 [Then] they began to accuse [Jesus], saying, "We found this man misleading our nation, and forbidding <us> to pay taxes to Caesar;	23:2~ [~~And~~] they began to accuse [~~Him~~], saying, "We found this man misleading our nation and forbidding to pay taxes to Caesar,	
6 "and saying that He Himself is [the Messiah], a King."	23:~2 and saying that He Himself is [~~Christ~~], a King."	
7 [When] Pilate <heard this, he> entered into the Praetorium again, and summoned Jesus.		18:33~ [~~Therefore~~] Pilate entered again into the Praetorium, and summoned Jesus

8 - TRIALS & CRUCIFIXION

Act 4: Jesus Is Questioned By The Romans

Scene 2: Are You The King of The Jews?

The Praetorium, Jerusalem, *Judea* early Friday morning, April 3rd / 33 CE

*Look for **The Red Letter Gospel***

#	Matthew	Mark	Luke	John
1	[When] Jesus stood before the Governor, Pilate asked Him, "Are You the King of the Jews?"	27:11~ [Now] Jesus stood before the governor, and the governor questioned Him, saying, "Are You the King of the Jews?"	15:2~ Pilate questioned Him, "Are You the King of the Jews?"	23:3~ So Pilate asked Him, saying, "Are You the King of the Jews?"	18:33 and said to Him, "Are You King of the Jews?"
2	Jesus answered <him>, "Are you [ask]ing this on your own initiative, or did others tell you about Me?"				18:34 Jesus answered, "Are you [say]ing this on your own initiative, or did others tell you about Me?"
3	Pilate answered, "I am not a Jew, am I?				18:35~ Pilate answered, "I am not a Jew, am I?
4	"Your own nation and the chief priests <have> delivered You to me. What have You done?"				18:~35 Your own nation and the chief priests delivered You to me; what have You done?"
5	Jesus answered, "My Kingdom is not of this world.				18:36~ Jesus answered, "My kingdom is not of this world.
6	"If My Kingdom were of this world then My servants would be fighting so that I would not be handed over to the Jews; but as it is, My Kingdom is not of this realm."				18:~36 If My kingdom were of this world, then My servants would be fighting so that I would not be handed over to the Jews; but as it is, My kingdom is not of this realm."
7	Therefore Pilate said to Him, "So You are a king?"				18:37~ Therefore Pilate said to Him, "So You are a king?"
8	Jesus answered him, "It is as you say; that I am a King.	27:~11 And Jesus said to him, "It is as you say."	15:~2 And He answered him, "It is as you say."	23:~3 And He answered him and said, "It is as you say."	18:37~1 Jesus answered, "You say correctly that I am a king.
9	"For this I have been born, and for this I have come into the world; to testify to the truth.				18:37~2 For this I have been born, and for this I have come into the world, to testify to the truth.
10	"Everyone who is of the truth hears My voice."				18:~37 Everyone who is of the truth hears My voice."
11	Pilate said to Him, "What is truth?"				18:38~ Pilate said to Him, "What is truth?"

8 - TRIALS & CRUCIFIXION

Act 4: Jesus Is Questioned By The Romans

Scene 3: Pilate Finds No Guilt In Jesus

The Praetorium, Jerusalem, *Judea*   early Friday morning, April 3rd / 33 CE

The Complete Four Gospel Harmony

Page 265

#	Matthew	Mark	Luke	John
1	[After] Pilate said this, he went out again to the Jews, and said to the chief priests and the crowds, "I find no guilt in this man."			23:4 [Then] Pilate said to the chief priests and the crowds, "I find no guilt in this man."	18:~38 And [when] he had said this, he went out again to the Jews and said to them, "I find no guilt in Him.
2	<Then> chief priests began to accuse [Jesus] harshly, and while He was being accused by the chief priests and <the> elders, *He did not answer.*[1.]	27:12 And while He was being accused by the chief priests and elders, He did not answer.	15:3 The chief priests began to accuse [Him] harshly.		
3	<So> Pilate questioned [Jesus] again, <and> said to Him, "Do You not hear how many things they testify [about] You, <and the> charges <that> they bring against You? Do You not answer?"	27:13 [Then] Pilate said to Him, "Do You not hear how many things they testify [against] You?"	15:4 [Then] Pilate questioned [Him] again, saying, "Do You not answer? See how many charges they bring against You!"		
4	But *Jesus made no further [reply], and He did not answer him with regard to even a single charge;*[1.] so the Governor was quite amazed.	27:14 And He did not answer him with regard to even a single charge, so the governor was quite amazed.	15:5 But Jesus made no further [answer]; so Pilate was amazed.		
5	But [the Jews] kept insisting, saying, "He stirs up the people, teaching all over Judea, starting from Galilee, even as far as this place!"			23:5 But [they] kept on insisting, saying, "He stirs up the people, teaching all over Judea, starting from Galilee even as far as this place."	
6	When Pilate heard [this], he asked whether [Jesus] was a Galilean; and when he learned that He belonged to *Herod's*[2.] jurisdiction, [Pilate] sent Him to Herod, who himself was also in Jerusalem at that time.			23:6 When Pilate heard [it], he asked whether [the man] was a Galilean. 23:7 And when he learned that He belonged to Herod's jurisdiction, [he] sent Him to Herod, who himself also was in Jerusalem at that time.	

1. Isaiah 53:7   2. Herod Antipater (Antipas) (20 BCE - 39 CE), Tetrarch of Galilee & Perea (4 BCE - 39 CE)

8 - TRIALS & CRUCIFIXION
Act 4: Jesus Is Questioned By The Romans

Scene 4: Herod, Tetrarch of Galilee, Questions Jesus
Hasmonean Palace, Jerusalem, *Judea* early Friday morning, April 3rd / 33 CE

The Gospel

	Luke
1 Now *Herod*,[1] <the Tetrarch of Galilee,> was very glad when he saw Jesus, for he had wanted to see Him for a long time, because he had been hearing about Him, and <he> was hoping to see some sign performed by Him.	23:8 Now Herod was very glad when he saw Jesus; for he had wanted to see Him for a long time, because he had been hearing about Him and was hoping to see some sign performed by Him.
2 [Herod] questioned [Jesus] at some length, [while] the chief priests and the scribes were standing there, <and> accusing Him vehemently; but [Jesus] <did not> answer him.[2]	23:9 A̶n̶d̶ [he] questioned [H̶i̶m̶] at some length; but [He] answer̶e̶d̶ him n̶o̶t̶h̶i̶n̶g̶. 23:10 [A̶n̶d̶] the chief priests and the scribes were standing there, accusing Him vehemently.
3 [Then] Herod with his soldiers, after treating [Jesus] with contempt and mocking Him, dressed Him in a gorgeous robe, and sent Him back to Pilate.	23:11 [A̶n̶d̶] Herod with his soldiers, after treating [H̶i̶m̶] with contempt and mocking Him, dressed Him in a gorgeous robe and sent Him back to Pilate.
4 Now Herod and Pilate became friends with one another that very day, for they had [previously] been enemies with each other.	23:12 Now Herod and Pilate became friends with one another that very day; for [b̶e̶f̶o̶r̶e̶] they had been enemies with each other.

1. *Herod Antipater (aka Antipas) (20 BCE - 39 CE) Tetrarch of Galilee & Perea (4 BCE - 39 CE)*   2. *Isaiah 53:7*

Scene 5: We Romans Find No Guilt In This Man
The Praetorium, Jerusalem, *Judea* Friday morning, April 3rd / 33 CE

	Luke
1 <Then> Pilate summoned the chief priests, and the rulers <of the Jews>, and the people; and <he> said to them <all>, "You brought this man to me as one who incites the people to rebellion.	23:13 Pilate summoned the chief priests and the rulers and the people, 23:14~ and said to them, "You brought this man to me as one who incites the people to rebellion,
2 "And behold, having examined Him before you, I have found no guilt in this man regarding the charges which you make against Him.	23:~14 and behold, having examined Him before you, I have found no guilt in this man regarding the charges which you make against Him.
3 "No, <and> nor has Herod, for he <has> sent Him back to us.	23:15~ "No, nor has Herod, for he sent Him back to us;
4 "And behold, <since> nothing deserving <of> death has been done by Him, I will punish Him, and release Him."	23:~15 and behold, nothing deserving death has been done by Him. 23:16 "T̶h̶e̶r̶e̶f̶o̶r̶e̶ I will punish Him and release Him."

8 - TRIALS & CRUCIFIXION

Act 5: Jesus Is Sentenced To Die

Scene 1: Shall I Release For You Jesus, or Barabbas?

The Praetorium, Jerusalem, *Judea*   Friday morning, April 3rd / 33 CE

The Unified Four Gospel Merger

#	Matthew	Mark	Luke	John
1	Now at the Passover Feast, the Governor was accustomed to release to the people any one prisoner whom they requested.	27:15 Now at the feast the governor was accustomed to release ~~for~~ the people any one prisoner whom they ~~wanted~~.	15:6 Now at the feast ~~he used~~ to release ~~for them~~ any one prisoner whom they requested.	23:17 {Now ~~he~~ was ~~obliged~~ to release to ~~them~~ at the feast one prisoner.}	18:39~ "But ~~you have a~~ custom ~~that I~~ release ~~some~~one ~~for you at the~~ Passover;
2	At that time they were holding a notorious prisoner named Barabbas, a robber who had been imprisoned with the insurrectionists who had committed murder in an insurrection in the city.	27:16 At that time they were holding a notorious prisoner, ~~called~~ Barabbas.	15:7 ~~The man~~ named Barabbas had been imprisoned with the insurrectionists who had committed murder in ~~the~~ insurrection.	23:19 (~~He was~~ ~~one~~ who had been ~~thrown into~~ prison ~~for~~ an insurrection ~~made~~ in the city, ~~and for~~ murder.)	18:~40 ~~Now~~ Barabbas ~~was~~ a robber.
3	So when the people <were> gathered together, the crowd began asking [Pilate] to do for them as [they] had been accustomed.	27:17~ So when the people gathered together,	15:8 The crowd ~~went up and~~ began asking [him] to do as ~~he~~ had been accustomed ~~to do~~ for them.		
4	Pilate answered them, saying, "Do you wish me to release for you the King of the Jews?"		15:9 Pilate answered them, saying, "Do you ~~want~~ me to release for you the King of the Jews?"		18:~39 do you wish ~~then that I~~ release for you the King of the Jews?"
5	But they cried out all together, saying, "Not this Man! Away with this man, and release for us Barabbas!"			23:18 But they cried out all together, saying, "Away with this man, and release for us Barabbas!	18:40~ ~~So~~ they cried out ~~again~~ saying, "Not this Man, ~~but~~ Barabbas.
6	[Now] [Pilate] was aware that the chief priests had handed [Jesus] over because of envy, <so> [he] [asked] them, "Whom do you want me to release for you? Barabbas, or Jesus who is called Christ?"	27:18 [~~For~~] [he] ~~knew~~ that because of envy ~~they~~ had handed [~~Him~~] over. 27:~17 [Pilate] [said] ~~to~~ them, "Whom do you want me to release for you? Barabbas, or Jesus who is called Christ?"	15:10 [~~For~~] [he] was aware that the chief priests had handed [~~Him~~] over because of envy.		
7	The chief priests and the elders stirred up <and> persuaded the crowds to ask [Pilate] to release Barabbas for them, and to put Jesus to death.	27:20 ~~But~~ the chief priests and the elders persuaded the crowds to ask for Barabbas and to put Jesus to death.	15:11 ~~But~~ the chief priests stirred up the crowd to ask [him] to release Barabbas for them ~~instead~~.		
8	[So] the Governor [asked] them <again>, "Which of the two do you want me to release for you?" And they said, "Barabbas!"	27:21 [~~But~~] the governor [said] ~~to~~ them, "Which of the two do you want me to release for you?" And they said, "Barabbas."			

8 - TRIALS & CRUCIFIXION

Act 5: **Jesus Is Sentenced To Die**

Scene 2: **The Jews Cry Out To Crucify Jesus**
The Praetorium, Jerusalem, *Judea*   Friday morning, April 3rd / 33 CE

FIVE COLUMN

	Matthew	Mark	Luke
1 [Then] Pilate said to them, "[And] what shall I do with Jesus, who is called Christ; whom you call the King of the Jews?"	27:22~ Pilate said to them, "[Then] what shall I do with Jesus who is called Christ?	15:12 ~~Answering again~~, Pilate said to them, "[Then] what shall I do with ~~Him~~ whom you call the King of the Jews?"	
2 They all shouted back, "Crucify Him!"	27:~22 They all ~~said~~, "Crucify Him!"	15:13 They shouted back, "Crucify Him!"	
3 While [Pilate] was sitting on the judgment seat, his wife sent him a message, saying, "Have nothing to do with that righteous Man, for last night I suffered greatly in a dream because of Him."	27:19 While [~~he~~] was sitting on the judgment seat, his wife sent him a message, saying, "Have nothing to do with that righteous Man; for last night I suffered greatly in a dream because of Him."		
4 Pilate, wanting to release Jesus, addressed [the crowd] again, but they kept on calling out, "Crucify! Crucify Him!"			23:20 Pilate, wanting to release Jesus, addressed [them] again, 23:21 but they kept on calling out, ~~saying~~, "Crucify, crucify Him!"
5 [So] Pilate said to them the third time, "Why, what evil has He done?	27:23~ [And] ~~he~~ said, "Why, what evil has He done?	15:14~ [But] Pilate said to them, "Why, what evil has He done?	23:22~ [And] [~~he~~] said to them the third time, "Why, what evil has ~~this man~~ done?
6 "I have found in Him no [reason] demanding [of] death, therefore I will punish Him, and release Him."			23:~22 I have found in Him no [~~guilt~~] demanding death; therefore I will punish Him and release Him."
7 But they were insistent, <and> with loud voices kept shouting [even] more, "Crucify Him!" And their voices began to prevail.	27:~23 But they kept shouting [~~all the~~] more, ~~saying~~ "Crucify Him!"	15:~14 But they shouted [~~all the~~] more, "Crucify Him!"	23:23 But they were insistent, with loud voices ~~asking that He be~~ crucified. And their voices began to prevail.

Scene 3: **Pilate Sentences Jesus To Die**
The Praetorium, Jerusalem, *Judea*   Friday morning, April 3rd / 33 CE

	Matthew	Mark	Luke
1 When Pilate saw that he was accomplishing nothing, but rather that a riot was starting, he took water and washed his hands in front of the crowd, saying, "I am innocent of this Man's blood; see to that yourselves."	27:24 When Pilate saw that he was accomplishing nothing, but rather that a riot was starting, he took water and washed his hands in front of the crowd, saying, "I am innocent of this Man's blood; see to that yourselves."		
2 And all the people said, "His blood shall be [up]on us, and [up]on our children!"	27:25 And all the people said, "His blood shall be on us and on our children!"		
3 Wishing to satisfy the crowd, Pilate [then] *pronounced sentence that their demand be granted;* [1.] and he released Barabbas for them, the man who had been thrown into prison for insurrection and murder,	27:26~ ~~Then~~ he released Barabbas for them;	15:15~ Wishing to satisfy the crowd, ~~Pilate~~ released Barabbas for them,	23:24 [And] Pilate pronounced sentence that their demand be granted. 23:25~ And he released the man ~~they were asking for~~ who had been thrown into prison for insurrection and murder,
4 [and] he delivered Jesus to their will.			23:~25 [~~but~~] he delivered Jesus to their will.

1. Isaiah 53:8

	8 - TRIALS & CRUCIFIXION Act 5: **Jesus Is Sentenced To Die**	Scene 4: **The Soldiers Mock and Scourge Jesus** The Praetorium, Jerusalem, *Judea* Friday morning, April 3rd / 33 CE		
		Matthew	**Mark**	**John**
1	Then *Pilate* <had> Jesus scourged; and after scourg[ing] [Him] [1] the soldiers of the Governor took Jesus into the Praetorium palace, and they gathered together the whole Roman cohort around Him.	27:~26 ~~but~~ after having [~~Jesus~~] scourg[~~ed~~], 27:27 ~~Then~~ soldiers of the governor took Jesus into the Praetorium ~~and~~ gathered the whole Roman cohort around Him.	15:~15~ and after having [~~Jesus~~] scourg[~~ed~~], 15:16 The soldiers took ~~Him~~ away into the palace (~~that is,~~ the Praetorium), and they ~~called~~ together the whole Roman cohort.	19:1 Pilate then ~~took~~ Jesus ~~and~~ scourged ~~Him~~.
2	[Then] the soldiers stripped [Jesus], and dressed Him in purple, and <they> put a scarlet <red> robe on Him.	27:28 ~~They~~ stripped [~~Him~~] and put a scarlet robe on Him.	15:17~ ~~They~~ dressed Him ~~up~~ in purple,	19:2~ [~~And~~] the soldiers 19:~2 put a ~~purple~~ robe on Him;
3	After twisting together a crown of thorns, they put it on His head, and a reed in His right hand.	27:29~ ~~And~~ after twisting together a crown of thorns, they put it on His head, and a reed in His right hand;	15:~17 ~~and~~ after twisting a crown of thorns, they put it on ~~Him~~;	19:~2~ twist~~ed~~ together a crown of thorns ~~and~~ put it on His head,
4	[Then] they began to come up and mock [Jesus], bowing down and kneeling before Him, and saying, "Hail, King of the Jews!"	27:~29 [~~and~~] they knel~~t~~ down before Him and mock~~ed~~ [~~Him~~], saying, "Hail, King of the Jews!"	15:18 [~~and~~] they began ~~to acclaim~~ [~~Him~~], "Hail, King of the Jews!" 15:~19 and bowing and kneeling before Him.	19:~3~ [~~and~~] they began to come up ~~to~~ [~~Him~~] and say, "Hail, King of the Jews!"
5	And they *slap[ped]* Him in the face, <and> spat on Him; [2] and <they> took the reed and began to beat Him on His head with <it>.	27:30 They spat on Him, and took the reed and began to beat Him on ~~the~~ head.	15:~19 They ~~kept~~ beat~~ing~~ His head with ~~a~~ reed, and sp~~itting~~ on Him,	19:~3 and ~~to give~~ Him slap[s] in the face.

1. Isaiah 53:5   2. Isaiah 50:6

8 - TRIALS & CRUCIFIXION

Act 5: Jesus Is Sentenced To Die

Scene 5: Pilate Tries Again To Release Jesus

The Praetorium, Jerusalem, *Judea* Friday morning, April 3rd / 33 CE

	John
1 [Then] Pilate came out, and said to [the crowd], "Behold, I am bringing Him out to you, so that you may know that I find no guilt in Him."	19:4 Pilate came out [again] and said to [them], "Behold, I am bringing Him out to you so that you may know that I find no guilt in Him."
2 [When] Jesus came out, wearing the crown of thorns and the [scarlet] robe, Pilate said to them, "Behold, the Man!"	19:5 Jesus [then] came out, wearing the crown of thorns and the [purple] robe. Pilate said to them, "Behold, the Man!"
3 When the chief priests and the [attendants] saw Him, they cried out saying, "Crucify! Crucify!"	19:6~ So when the chief priests and the [officers]* saw Him, they cried out saying, "Crucify, crucify!"
4 Pilate said to them, "Take Him yourselves and crucify Him, for I find no guilt in Him."	19:~6 Pilate said to them, "Take Him yourselves and crucify Him, for I find no guilt in Him."
5 The Jews answered him, "We have a law, and *by that law He ought to die, because He made Himself out to be the Son of God.*" [1]	19:7 The Jews answered him, "We have a law, and by that law He ought to die because He made Himself out to be the Son of God."
6 When Pilate heard this statement, he [became] more afraid; and he entered into the Praetorium again, and said to Jesus, "Where are You from?" But *Jesus gave him no answer.*[2]	19:8 Therefore when Pilate heard this statement, he [was] even more afraid; 19:9 and he entered into the Praetorium again and said to Jesus, "Where are You from?" But Jesus gave him no answer.
7 So Pilate said to Him, "Do You not speak to me? Do You not know that I have authority to release You, and I have authority to crucify You?"	19:10 So Pilate said to Him, "You do not speak to me? Do You not know that I have authority to release You, and I have authority to crucify You?"
8 Jesus answered, "You would have no authority over Me unless it had been given <to> you from above;	19:11~ Jesus answered, "You would have no authority over Me, unless it had been given you from above;
9 "for this reason, he who delivered Me to you has greater sin."	19:~11 for this reason he who delivered Me to you has the greater sin."
10 As a result of this, Pilate made efforts to release [Jesus], but the Jews cried out saying, "If you release this Man, you are no friend of Caesar! Everyone who makes himself out to be a king opposes Caesar."	19:12 As a result of this Pilate made efforts to release [Him], but the Jews cried out saying, "If you release this Man, you are no friend of Caesar; everyone who makes himself out to be a king opposes Caesar."
11 When Pilate heard these words, he brought Jesus out, and sat down on the judgment seat, at a place called The Pavement, [which is] *Gabbatha* in Hebrew.	19:13 Therefore when Pilate heard these words, he brought Jesus out, and sat down on the judgment seat at a place called The Pavement, [but] in Hebrew, Gabbatha.

1. Leviticus 24:16   2. Isaiah 53:7

8 - TRIALS & CRUCIFIXION	Scene 6: **Jesus Is Handed Over To Be Crucified**	
Act 5: **Jesus Is Sentenced To Die**	The Praetorium, Jerusalem, *Judea* Friday morning, April 3rd / 33 CE	

	Matthew	Mark	John
1 Now it was the day of preparation for the Passover, and [at] about *the sixth hour*[1] [Pilate] said to the Jews, "Behold, your King."			19:14 Now it was the day of preparation for the Passover; [it was] about the sixth hour. And [he] said to the Jews, "Behold, your King!"
2 So they cried out, "Away with Him! Away with Him! Crucify Him!"			19:15~ So they cried out, "Away with Him, away with Him, crucify Him!"
3 Pilate [asked] them, "Shall I crucify your King?"			19:~15~ Pilate [said to] them, "Shall I crucify your King?"
4 The chief priests answered, "We have no King but Caesar."			19:~15 The chief priests answered, "We have no king but Caesar."
5 So [Pilate] handed [Jesus] over to be crucified.	27:~26 [he] handed [Him] over to be crucified.	15:~15 [he] handed [Him] over to be crucified.	19:16 So [he] then handed [Him] over to them to be crucified.

1. *Jewish time - roughly 9 to 10 am*

Scene 7: **Judas The Betrayer Hangs Himself**
Jerusalem, *Judea* Friday morning, April 3rd / 33 CE

	Matthew
1 When Judas, who had betrayed [Jesus], saw that He had been condemned, he felt remorse;	27:3~ Then when Judas, who had betrayed [Him], saw that He had been condemned, he felt remorse
2 and <he> returned the thirty pieces of silver to the chief priests and <the> elders, saying, "I have sinned by betraying innocent blood."	27:~3 and returned the thirty pieces of silver to the chief priests and elders, 27:4~ saying, "I have sinned by betraying innocent blood."
3 But they said <to him>, "What is that to us? See to that yourself."	27:~4 But they said, "What is that to us? See to that yourself!"
4 [So] [Judas] threw the pieces of silver into the Temple sanctuary, and departed;	27:5~ [And] [he] threw the pieces of silver into the temple sanctuary and departed;
5 and he went away and hanged himself.	27:~5 and he went away and hanged himself.
6 The chief priests took the pieces of silver, and said, "It is not lawful to put them into the Temple treasury, since it is the price of blood."	27:6 The chief priests took the pieces of silver and said, "It is not lawful to put them into the temple treasury, since it is the price of blood."
7 [So] they conferred together; and with the money <they> bought the Potter's Field, as a burial place for strangers.	27:7 [And] they conferred together and with the money bought the Potter's Field as a burial place for strangers.
8 For this reason, that field has been called "The Field of Blood" to this day.	27:8 For this reason that field has been called the Field of Blood to this day.
9 Then that which was spoken through [Zechariah] the prophet was fulfilled: "And [I] took the thirty pieces of silver, the price of the one whose [value] had been set by the sons of Israel,[1]	27:9 Then that which was spoken through [Jeremiah] the prophet was fulfilled: "And [they] took the thirty pieces of silver, the price of the one whose [price] had been set by the sons of Israel;
10 "and [I] gave them for the Potter's Field, as the Lord directed me."[2]	27:10 and [they] gave them for the Potter's Field, as the Lord directed me."

1. *Zechariah 11:12*   2. *Zechariah 11:12-13 / Jeremiah 32:6-12*

8 - TRIALS & CRUCIFIXION
Act 6: The Crucifixion of Jesus Christ

Scene 1: Simon of Cyrene Carries The Cross of Jesus
Jerusalem, *Judea*   Friday morning, April 3rd / 33 CE

#		Matthew	Mark	Luke	John
1	After [the soldiers] had mocked [Jesus], they took the scarlet robe off <of> Him, and put His own garments back on.	27:31~ After [they] had mocked [Him], they took the scarlet robe off Him and put His own garments back on Him,	15:20~ After [they] had mocked [Him], they took the purple robe off Him and put His own garments on Him.		
2	[Then] they led Him away to crucify Him; and He went out, bearing His own cross.	27:~31 [and] led Him away to crucify Him.	15:~20 [And] they led Him out to crucify Him.	23:26~ [When] they led Him away,	19:17~ They took Jesus therefore, and He went out, bearing His own cross,
3	As they were coming out, to bear His cross, they seized <and> pressed into service a passer-by coming in from the country, a man of Cyrene named Simon, the father of Alexander and Rufus.	27:32 As they were coming out, they found a man of Cyrene named Simon, whom they pressed into service to bear His cross.	15:21 They pressed into service a passer-by coming from the country, Simon of Cyrene (the father of Alexander and Rufus), to bear His cross.	23:~26 they seized a man, Simon of Cyrene, coming in from the country,	
4	And <they> placed the cross on him to carry behind Jesus.			23:~26 and placed on him the cross to carry behind Jesus.	
5	Two others also, who were criminals, were being led away to be put to death with [Jesus].			23:32 Two others also, who were criminals, were being led away to be put to death with [Him].	

Scene 2: The Walk To Golgotha
Jerusalem, *Judea*   Friday morning, April 3rd / 33 CE

#		Luke
1	Following [Jesus] was a large crowd of people, and of women who were mourning and lamenting <for> Him.	23:27 And following [Him] was a large crowd of the people, and of women who were mourning and lamenting Him.
2	Turning to them, Jesus said, "Daughters of Jerusalem, [do not] weep for Me, but weep for yourselves, and for your children.	23:28 But Jesus turning to them said, "Daughters of Jerusalem, [stop] weeping for Me, but weep for yourselves and for your children.
3	"For behold, the days are coming when they will say, 'Blessed are the barren, and the wombs that never bore, and the breasts that never nursed!'	23:29 "For behold, the days are coming when they will say, 'Blessed are the barren, and the wombs that never bore, and the breasts that never nursed.'
4	*"Then they will begin to say to the mountains, 'Fall on us,' and to the hills, 'Cover us!'* [1]	23:30 "Then they will begin to say to the mountains, 'Fall on us,' and to the hills, 'Cover us.'
5	"[So,] if they do these things when the tree is green, what will happen when it is dry?"	23:31 "[For] if they do these things when the tree is green, what will happen when it is dry?"

1. *Hosea 10:8*

8 - TRIALS & CRUCIFIXION
Act 6: The Crucifixion of Jesus Christ
Scene 3: Jesus Is Crucified
Golgotha, Jerusalem, *Judea*   Friday morning, April 3rd / 33 CE

#	Matthew	Mark	Luke	John
1	Then they came to the place called *Golgotha*[1.] in Hebrew, which means, "The Place of a Skull".	27:33 ~And~ ~when~ they came to ~a~ place called Golgotha, which means Place of a Skull,	15:22 Then they ~brought~ ~Him~ to the place Golgotha, which ~is translated~, place of a Skull.	23:33~ ~When~ they came to the place called ~The~ Skull,	19:~17 to the place called ~the~ Place of a Skull, which ~is called~ in Hebrew, Golgotha.
2	The people stood by, looking on [while] the rulers were sneering at [Jesus], saying, "He saved others, let Him save Himself, if this is the Christ of God, His Chosen One."			23:35 ~And~ the people stood by, looking on. [~And even~] the rulers were sneering at [~Him~], saying, "He saved others; let Him save Himself if this is the Christ of God, His Chosen One."	
3	The soldiers also mocked Him, <and> coming up to [Jesus], they tried to *give Him sour wine to drink, mixed with myrrh* <and> *gall;*[2.] but after tasting it, He was unwilling to drink.	27:34 they gave Him wine to drink mixed with gall; ~and~ after tasting it, He was unwilling to drink.	15:23 They tried to give Him wine mixed with myrrh; but He ~did not take it~.	23:36 The soldiers also mocked Him, coming up to [~Him~], ~offering~ Him sour wine,	
4	[And] Jesus [said], "Father, forgive them; for they do not know what they are doing."			23:34~ [~But~] Jesus ~was~ [~saying~], "Father, forgive them; for they do not know what they are doing."	
5	And *they crucified Him*[3.] [at] *the third hour.*[4.]		15:24~ And they crucified Him, 15:25~ [~It was~] the third hour		

1. Latin: Calvary   2. Psalm 69:21   3. Psalm 22:16 / Zechariah 12:10; 13:6   4. Jewish time - approximately 9 to 10 am

8 - TRIALS & CRUCIFIXION
Act 6: The Crucifixion of Jesus Christ

Scene 4: The Soldiers Divide His Clothing
Golgotha, Jerusalem, *Judea* Friday morning, April 3rd / 33 CE

Using the NASB version of The Gospels

	Matthew	Mark	Luke	John
1 [After] they had *crucified Jesus,*[1] the soldiers divided His outer garments among themselves, and <they> made four parts, a part to every soldier, and also the tunic.	27:35~ And [when] they had crucified Him, they divided up His garments among themselves	15:~24~ and divided up His garments among themselves, 15:~25 [when] they crucified Him.	23:34~1 And they 23:~34 dividing up His garments among themselves.	19:23~ Then the soldiers, [when] they had crucified Jesus, took His outer garments and made four parts, a part to every soldier and also the tunic;
2 [Since] the tunic was woven in one piece <and> seamless, they said to one another, "Let us not tear it, but cast lots for it, to decide whose it shall be."	27:~35 by casting lots.	15:~24 casting lots for them to decide what each man should take.	23:34~2 cast lots,	19:~23 [now] the tunic was seamless, woven in one piece. 19:24~ So they said to one another, "Let us not tear it, but cast lots for it, to decide whose it shall be";
3 The soldiers did these things to fulfill the Scripture: *"They divided My outer garments among them[selves], and for My clothing they cast lots."*[2]				19:~25~ Therefore the soldiers did these things. 19:~24 this was to fulfill the Scripture: "They divided My outer garments among them, and for My clothing they cast lots."
4 [Then] [the soldiers] [sat] down, <and> began to keep watch over Him.	27:36 [And] [sitting] down, [they] began to keep watch over Him there.			
5 And <they were> saying, "If You are the King of the Jews, save Yourself!"			23:37 and saying, "If You are the King of the Jews, save Yourself!"	

1. Psalm 22:16 / Zechariah 12:10; 13:6   2. Psalm 22:18

Scene 5: Jesus Is Crucified Between Two Criminals
Golgotha, Jerusalem, *Judea* Friday morning, April 3rd / 33 CE

	Matthew	Mark	Luke	John
1 There at that time, they crucified two criminals with Him; one on His right, and the other on His left, [with] Jesus in between.	27:38 At that time two robbers were crucified with Him, one on the right and one on the left.	15:27 They crucified two robbers with Him, one on His right and one on His left.	23:~33 there they crucified Him and the criminals, one on the right and the other on the left.	19:18 There they crucified Him, and with Him two other men, one on either side [and] Jesus in between.
2 And the Scripture was fulfilled which says, *"He was numbered with transgressors."*[1]		15:28 {And the Scripture was fulfilled which says, "And He was numbered with transgressors."}		

1. Isaiah 53:12

8 - TRIALS & CRUCIFIXION
Act 6: The Crucifixion of Jesus Christ

Scene 6: Pilate's Inscription of The Charge Against Jesus
Golgotha, Jerusalem, *Judea*   Friday morning, April 3rd / 33 CE

Page 275

NASB = New American Standard Bible

#	Matthew	Mark	Luke	John
1	Pilate wrote an inscription of the charge against [Jesus], and they put it on the cross, up above His head.	27:37~ And above His head they put up the charge against [Him]	15:26~ The inscription of the charge against [Him]	23:38~ Now there was also an inscription above Him,	19:19~ Pilate also wrote an inscription and put it on the cross.
2	It was written in Hebrew, Latin, and Greek, and it read: "THIS IS JESUS THE NAZARENE, THE KING OF THE JEWS."	27:~37 which read, THIS IS JESUS THE KING OF THE JEWS.	15:~26 read, THE KING OF THE JEWS.	23:~38 THIS IS THE KING OF THE JEWS.	19:~19 It was written, "JESUS THE NAZARENE, THE KING OF THE JEWS." 19:~20 and it was written in Hebrew, Latin and in Greek.
3	Many of the Jews read this inscription, for the place where Jesus was crucified was near the city.				19:20~ Therefore many of the Jews read this inscription, for the place where Jesus was crucified was near the city;
4	The chief priests [said] to Pilate, "Do not write, 'The King of the Jews', but that He said, 'I am <the> King of the Jews.' "				19:21 So the chief priests of the Jews were [saying] to Pilate, "Do not write, 'The King of the Jews'; but that He said, 'I am King of the Jews.' "
5	Pilate answered, "I have written what I have written."				19:22 Pilate answered, "What I have written I have written."

Scene 7: Jesus Entrusts His Mother To John
Golgotha, Jerusalem, *Judea*   Friday morning, April 3rd / 33 CE

#		John
1	Standing by the cross of Jesus were His mother, and His mother's sister, <and> Mary the wife of [Cleopas], and Mary Magdalene.	19:~25 But standing by the cross of Jesus were His mother, and His mother's sister, Mary the wife of [Clopas], and Mary Magdalene.
2	When Jesus saw His mother, and the *disciple whom He loved* [1] standing nearby, He said to His mother, "Woman, behold, your son!"	19:26 When Jesus then saw His mother, and the disciple whom He loved standing nearby, He said to His mother, "Woman, behold, your son!"
3	Then He said to the [apostle], "Behold, your mother."	19:27~ Then He said to the [disciple], "Behold, your mother!"
4	<And> from that hour, [John] took her into his own household.	19:~27 From that hour [the disciple] took her into his own household.

1. John Zebedee - John 13:23; 20:2; 21:7, 20

8 - TRIALS & CRUCIFIXION
Act 6: **The Crucifixion of Jesus Christ**

Scene 8: **Let This Christ Save Himself!**

Golgotha, Jerusalem, *Judea*   Friday morning, April 3rd / 33 CE

A Unified Verse-By-Verse Gospel Harmony

#		Matthew	Mark
1	*Those passing by were hurling abuse at [Jesus], wagging their heads,*[1.] and saying, "Ha! You who are going to destroy the Temple and rebuild it in three days!	27:39 And those passing by were hurling abuse at [Him], wagging their heads 27:40~ and saying, "You who are going to destroy the temple and rebuild it in three days,	15:29 Those passing by were hurling abuse at [Him], wagging their heads and saying, "Ha! You who are going to destroy the temple and rebuild it in three days,
2	"If You are the Son of God, save Yourself, and come down from the cross!"	27:~40 save Yourself! If You are the Son of God, come down from the cross.	15:30 save Yourself, and come down from the cross!
3	In the same way, the chief priests also, along with the scribes and <the> elders, were mocking Him among themselves, and saying, "He saved others, <but> He cannot save Himself?	27:41 In the same way the chief priests also, along with the scribes and elders, were mocking Him and saying, 27:42~ "He saved others; He cannot save Himself.	15:31 In the same way the chief priests also, along with the scribes, were mocking Him among themselves and saying, "He saved others; He cannot save Himself.
4	"He is the King of Israel; let this Christ come down from the cross, so that we may see, and we will believe in Him!	27:~42 He is the King of Israel; let Him now come down from the cross, and we will believe in Him.	15:32~ Let this Christ, the King of Israel, now come down from the cross, so that we may see and believe!"
5	"*He trusts in God, <so> let God rescue Him now, if He delights in Him;*[2.] for He said, 'I am the Son of God.' "	27:43 "He trusts in God; let God rescue Him now, if He delights in Him; for He said, 'I am the Son of God.' "	

1. Psalm 22:6-7; 109:25   2. Psalm 72:8

Scene 9: **The Last Words of The Two Criminals**

Golgotha, Jerusalem, *Judea*   Friday morning, April 3rd / 33 CE

#		Matthew	Mark	Luke
1	One of the criminals who had been crucified with [Jesus] was also insulting Him with the same words, <and> saying, "Are You not the Christ? Save Yourself and us!"	27:44 The robbers who had been crucified with [Him] were also insulting Him with the same words.	15:~32 Those who were crucified with [Him] were also insulting Him.	23:39 One of the criminals who were hanged there was hurling abuse at Him, saying, "Are You not the Christ? Save Yourself and us!"
2	But the other <one> answered, and rebuking him said, "Do you not fear even God, since you are under the same sentence of condemnation?			23:40 But the other answered, and rebuking him said, "Do you not even fear God, since you are under the same sentence of condemnation?
3	"And we indeed are suffering justly, for we are receiving what we deserve for our deeds; but this man has done nothing wrong."			23:41 "And we indeed are suffering justly, for we are receiving what we deserve for our deeds; but this man has done nothing wrong."
4	And he [said], "Jesus, remember me when You come in[to] Your Kingdom!"			23:42 And he was [saying], "Jesus, remember me when You come in Your kingdom!"
5	And [Jesus] said to him, "Truly I say to you, <that> today you shall be with Me in Paradise."			23:43 And [He] said to him, "Truly I say to you, today you shall be with Me in Paradise."

8 - TRIALS & CRUCIFIXION

Act 7: The Death of Jesus Christ

Scene 1: Darkness Falls Over The Land

Golgotha, Jerusalem, *Judea* Friday afternoon, roughly noon to 3:00 pm, April 3rd / 33 CE

The Full Gospel United from Four

	Matthew	Mark	Luke
1 Now when *the sixth hour*[1.] came the sun was obscured, and darkness fell over the whole land until *the ninth hour*.[2.]	27:45 Now ~~from~~ the sixth hour darkness fell ~~upon all~~ the land until the ninth hour.	15:33 When the sixth hour came, darkness fell over the whole land until the ninth hour.	23:44 ~~It was~~ now ~~about~~ the sixth hour, and darkness fell over the whole land until the ninth hour, 23:45~ ~~because~~ the sun was obscured;
2 At about the ninth hour, Jesus cried out with a loud voice, <and> [said], *"Eloi, eloi, lama sabachthani?"*[3.] which is translated, *"My God, My God! Why have You forsaken Me?"*[3.]	27:46 About the ninth hour Jesus cried out with a loud voice, [saying], "Eli, eli, lama sabachthani? ~~that~~ is, "My God, My God, why have You forsaken Me?"	15:34 At the ninth hour Jesus cried out with a loud voice, "Eloi, eloi, lama sabachthani? which is translated, "My God, My God, why have You forsaken Me?"	
3 When some of the bystanders who were standing there heard [this], they began saying, "Behold, He is calling for Elijah."	27:47 ~~And~~ some of ~~those~~ who were standing there, when they heard [it], began saying, "~~This man~~ is calling for Elijah."	15:35 When some of the bystanders heard [it], they began saying, "Behold, He is calling for Elijah."	
4 [And] the rest of them said, "Let us see whether Elijah will come to take Him down, <and> save Him."	27:49 [~~But~~] the rest of them said, "Let us see whether Elijah will come to save Him."	15:~36 ~~saying~~, "Let us see whether Elijah will come to take Him down."	

1. *roughly noon to 1 pm, Jewish time*   2. *roughly 3 to 4 pm*   3. *Psalm 22:1*

Scene 2: Jesus Dies On The Cross

Golgotha, Jerusalem, *Judea* Friday afternoon, around 3:00 pm, April 3rd / 33 CE

	Matthew	Mark	Luke	John
1 After this, knowing that all things had [now] been accomplished, to fulfill *the Scripture*,[1.] Jesus said, "I am thirsty."				19:28 After this, Jesus, knowing that all things had [~~already~~] been accomplished, to fulfill the Scripture, said, "I am thirsty."
2 A jar full of sour wine was standing there, <and> immediately someone ran, and taking a sponge *he filled it with the sour wine, put it on a reed of hyssop, and brought it up to His mouth, and gave Him a drink*.[2.]	27:48 Immediately one ~~of them~~ ran, and taking a sponge, he filled it with sour wine ~~and~~ put it on a reed, and gave Him a drink.	15:36~ Someone ran ~~and~~ filled a sponge with sour wine, put it on a reed, and gave Him a drink,		19:29 A jar full of sour wine was standing there; ~~so they~~ put a sponge ~~full of~~ the sour wine ~~upon~~ a ~~branch~~ of hyssop and brought it up to His mouth.
3 [After] Jesus had received the sour wine, [He] cried out again with a loud voice, <and> said, "It is finished. Father, *into Your hands I commit My Spirit*."[3.]	27:50~ ~~And [Jesus]~~ cried out again with a loud voice	15:37~ ~~And [Jesus]~~ ~~uttered~~ a loud ~~cry~~	23:46~ ~~And [Jesus]~~, cr~~ying~~ out with a loud voice said, "Father, into Your hands I commit My spirit."	19:30~ ~~Therefore~~ [when] Jesus had received the sour wine, ~~He~~ said, "It is finished!"
4 Having said this, [Jesus] breathed His last, bowed His head, and yielded up His Spirit.	27:~50 and yielded up His spirit.	15:~37 ~~and~~ breathed His last.	23:~46 Having said this, [~~He~~] breathed His last.	19:~30 ~~And He~~ bowed His head and ~~gave~~ up His spirit.

1. *Psalm 22:15*   2. *Psalm 69:21*   3. *Psalm 31:5*

8 - TRIALS & CRUCIFIXION

Act 7: **The Death of Jesus Christ**

Scene 3: **An Earthquake At The Death of Jesus**

Jerusalem, *Judea*   Friday afternoon, around 3:00 pm, April 3rd / 33 CE

This Text is from the Word-For-Word Edition

	Matthew	Mark	Luke
1 And behold, the earth shook, and the rocks were split; and the veil of the Temple was torn in two, from top to bottom.	27:51 And behold, the veil of the temple was torn in two from top to bottom; ~~and~~ the earth shook and the rocks were split.	15:38 And the veil of the temple was torn in two from top to bottom.	23:~45 and the veil of the temple was torn in two.
2 When those who were keeping guard over Jesus saw the way <that> He breathed His last, <and> the earthquake and the things that were happening, <they> became very frightened, and began praising God.	27:~54~ ~~and~~ those who were ~~with him~~ keeping guard over Jesus, when ~~they~~ saw the earthquake and the things that were happening, became very frightened and	15:39~ When 15:39~2 saw the way He breathed His last	23:47~ ~~Now~~ when 23:47~2 saw ~~what had~~ happen~~ed~~, ~~he~~ began praising God,
3 [And] the centurion, who was standing right in front of [Jesus], said, "Truly this [righteous] man was the Son of God!"	27:~54 [~~Now~~] the centurion, 27:~54 said, "Truly this was the Son of God!"	15:39~1 the centurion, who was standing right in front of [Him], 15:~39 ~~he~~ said, "Truly this man was the Son of God!"	23:47~1 the centurion 23:~47 say~~ing~~, "~~Certainly~~ this man ~~was~~ [innocent *]."
4 [After] all the crowds who came together for this spectacle observed what had happened, they began to return <to their homes>, beating their breasts.			23:48 And all the crowds who came together for this spectacle, [when] they observed what had happened, began to return, beating their breasts.
5 All <of> His acquaintances and many <other> women were there, looking on from a distance [1]. <and> seeing these things.	27:55~ Many women were there looking on from a distance,	15:40~ There were ~~also some~~ women looking on from a distance,	23:49~ ~~And~~ all His acquaintances and ~~the~~ women 23:~49 were standing at a distance, seeing these things.
6 Among them was Mary Magdalene, and Mary the mother of Jesus, and Salome, the mother of the sons of Zebedee.	27:56 Among them was Mary Magdalene, and Mary the mother of [~~James and Joseph~~], and the mother of the sons of Zebedee.	15:~40 among whom ~~were~~ Mary Magdalene, and Mary the mother of [~~James the Less and Joses~~], and Salome.	
7 When [Jesus] was in Galilee they used to follow Him, while ministering to Him.	27:55~2 follow~~ed~~ ~~Jesus~~ 27:~55 while ministering to Him.	15:41~ When [He] was in Galilee, they used to follow Him ~~and~~ minister to Him;	
8 And there were many other women who had accompanied Him from Galilee to Jerusalem.	27:55~1 who had 27:55~3 from Galilee	15:~41 and there were many other women who ~~came up with~~ Him to Jerusalem.	23:~49~ who accompanied Him from Galilee

1. Psalm 38:11

8 - TRIALS & CRUCIFIXION	Scene 4: **The Body of Jesus Is Taken Down**	
Act 7: **The Death of Jesus Christ**	Golgotha, Jerusalem, *Judea* late Friday afternoon, April 3rd / 33 CE	
	Mark	**John**
1 Then, because it was *the day of preparation,*[1] that is, the day before the Sabbath, so that the bodies would not remain on the cross [during] the Sabbath, ([and] that was a *high Sabbath day*),[2] the Jews asked Pilate that their legs might be broken, and [their bodies] be taken away.	15:~42 that is, the day before the Sabbath,	19:31 Then the Jews, because it was the day of preparation, so that the bodies would not remain on the cross [on] the Sabbath ([for] that Sabbath was a high day), asked Pilate that their legs might be broken, and that [they] might be taken away.
2 So the soldiers came and broke the legs of the first [criminal], and of the other <one> who was crucified with Him;		19:32 So the soldiers came, and broke the legs of the first man and of the other who was crucified with Him;
3 but when <they> [came] to Jesus, they saw that He was already dead, <and so> they did not break His legs.		19:33 but [coming] to Jesus, when they saw that He was already dead, they did not break His legs.
4 One of the soldiers pierced His side with a spear, and immediately blood and water came out.		19:34 But one of the soldiers pierced His side with a spear, and immediately blood and water came out.
5 These things came to pass to fulfill the Scripture, *"Not a bone of Him shall be broken."*[3]		19:36 For these things came to pass to fulfill the Scripture, "Not a bone of Him shall be broken."
6 And another Scripture <which> says, *"They shall look [up]on [Me], whom they <have> pierced."*[4]		19:37 And again another Scripture says, "They shall look on [Him]* whom they pierced."

1. Friday, before sunset   2. the first day of the seven day Passover Feast   3. Psalm 34:20 / (Exodus 12:46) / (Numbers 9:12)   4. Zechariah 12:10; 13:6

8 - TRIALS & CRUCIFIXION
Act 8: Jesus Is Laid In Joseph's Tomb

Scene 1: Joseph Asks Pilate For The Body of Jesus
The Praetorium, Jerusalem, *Judea*   late Friday afternoon, April 3rd / 33 CE

#	Matthew	Mark	Luke	John
1	When it was <the> evening [of] the preparation day <for the Sabbath>, a rich man named Joseph, from Arimathea, came <to the Praetorium>.	27:57~ When it was evening, ~~there came~~ a rich man named Joseph, from Arimathea,	15:42~ When evening ~~had already come, because~~ [it was] the preparation day, 15:43~ Joseph ~~of~~ Arimathea came,	23:50~ ~~And~~ a man named Joseph, 23:~51~ ~~a man~~ from Arimathea, ~~a city of the Jews~~, 23:54~ [It was] the preparation day,	19:38~ ~~After these things~~ Joseph ~~of~~ Arimathea,
2	[He] was a prominent member of the <Jewish> *Council*[1] <of elders>; a good and righteous man, [who] had not consented to their plan and action.		15:43~1 a prominent member of the Council,	23:~50 [who] was a member of the Council, a good and righteous man 23:51~ ([he] had not consented to their plan and action),	
3	[He] himself was waiting for the Kingdom of God, <and> had become a disciple of Jesus, but a secret one for fear of the Jews.	27:~57 [~~who~~] himself had ~~also~~ become a disciple of Jesus.	15:43~2 [~~who~~] himself was waiting for the kingdom of God;	23:~51 ~~who~~ was waiting for the kingdom of God;	19:38~1 being a disciple of Jesus, but a secret one for fear of the Jews,
4	[Joseph] gathered up <his> courage, and <he> went in before Pilate, and <he> asked that he might take away the body of Jesus.	27:58~ [~~This man~~] went ~~to~~ Pilate and asked ~~for~~ the body of Jesus.	15:~43 ~~and~~ [he] gathered up courage and went in before Pilate, and asked ~~for~~ the body of Jesus.	23:52 [~~this man~~] went ~~to~~ Pilate and asked ~~for~~ the body of Jesus.	19:38~2 asked Pilate that he might take away the body of Jesus;
5	Pilate wondered if [Jesus] was dead by this time, and summoning [a] centurion, he questioned him as to whether He was already dead.		15:44 Pilate wondered if [~~He~~] was dead by this time, and summoning [~~the~~] centurion, he questioned him as to whether He was already dead.		
6	Ascertaining this from the centurion, Pilate granted permission <that> the body be given to Joseph.	27:~58 ~~Then~~ Pilate ~~ordered it to~~ be given to ~~him~~.	15:45 ~~And~~ ascertaining this from the centurion, ~~he~~ granted the body to Joseph.		19:38~3 ~~and~~ Pilate granted permission.

1. Hebrew word sanhedrin *means "sitting together" or "council"*

8 - TRIALS & CRUCIFIXION
Act 8: Jesus Is Laid In Joseph's Tomb
Scene 2: The Body of Jesus Is Placed In Joseph's Tomb

The Garden Tomb, Jerusalem, *Judea*   late Friday afternoon, April 3rd / 33 CE

#		Matthew	Mark	Luke	John
1	Joseph bought a clean linen cloth, and he came and took away the body <of Jesus>.	27:59~ And Joseph took the body 27:59~2 clean	15:46~ Joseph bought a linen cloth, took Him down,	23:53~ And he took it down	19:~38 So he came and took away His body.
2	Nicodemus, who had first come to [Jesus] by night, also came, bringing a mixture of myrrh and aloes, about [seventy-five] pounds [1] <in> weight.				19:39 Nicodemus, who had first come to [Him] by night, also came, bringing a mixture of myrrh and aloes, about [a hundred] pounds weight.
3	So they took the body of Jesus, and wrapped it in the linen cloth with the spices, as is the burial custom of the Jews.	27:59~1 and wrapped it in a 27:~59 linen cloth,	15:46~1 wrapped Him in the linen cloth	23:53~1 and wrapped it in a linen cloth,	19:40 So they took the body of Jesus and bound it in linen wrappings with the spices, as is the burial custom of the Jews.
4	Now in the place where [Jesus] was crucified there was a garden, and in the garden <was> [Joseph's] new *tomb which had been hewn out [of] the rock,* [2] in which no one had ever yet been laid.	27:~60~ in [his] own new tomb which he had hewn out [in] the rock;	15:46~3 in a tomb which had been hewn out [in] the rock;	23:~53 in a tomb cut [into] the rock, where no one had ever lain.	19:41 Now in the place where [He] was crucified there was a garden, and in the garden [a] new tomb in which no one had yet been laid.
5	Therefore, [since] the Sabbath was about to begin, [and] the tomb was nearby, they laid Jesus there.	27:60~ and laid it	15:46~2 and laid Him	23:53~2 and laid Him 23:~54 [and] the Sabbath was about to begin.	19:42 Therefore [because of] the Jewish day of preparation, [since] the tomb was nearby, they laid Jesus there.
6	[Then] [they] rolled a large stone against the entrance of the tomb, and went away.	27:~60 [and] [he] rolled a large stone against the entrance of the tomb and went away.	15:~46 [and] [he] rolled a stone against the entrance of the tomb.		
7	Now the women who had come out of Galilee with [Jesus] were sitting opposite the grave, looking <at> the tomb and to see how His body was laid.	27:~61 sitting opposite the grave.	15:~47 were looking on to see where He was laid.	23:55 Now the women who had come with [Him] out of Galilee followed, and saw the tomb and how His body was laid.	
8	Mary Magdalene was there, and Mary the mother of [Jesus].	27:61~ And Mary Magdalene was there, and the other Mary,	15:47~ Mary Magdalene and Mary the mother of [Joses]		
9	Then they returned, and prepared spices and perfumes;			23:56~ Then they returned and prepared spices and perfumes.	
10	and *on the Sabbath they rested, according to the commandment.* [3]			23:~56 And on the Sabbath they rested according to the commandment.	

1. 34 kg / Roman pound = approximately 11.5 oz.   2. Isaiah 53:9   3. Exodus 20:8-10 / 31:15 / Deuteronomy 5:12-14

8 - TRIALS & CRUCIFIXION	Scene 3: **Roman Soldiers Guard The Tomb**
Act 8: **Jesus Is Laid In Joseph's Tomb**	The Garden Tomb, Jerusalem, *Judea* Friday evening, April 3rd / 33 CE

	Matthew
1 On [that] day, after the [sun had set], the chief priests and the Pharisees gathered together with Pilate, and <they> said, "Sir, we remember that when He was alive, that deceiver said, 'After three days, I [will] rise again.'	27:62 ~~Now~~ on [~~the next~~] day, ~~the day~~ after the [~~preparation~~], the chief priests and the Pharisees gathered together with Pilate, 27:63 and said, "Sir, we remember that when He was ~~still~~ alive that deceiver said, 'After three days I [~~am to~~] rise again.'
2 "Therefore, give orders for the grave to be made secure until the third day, otherwise His disciples may come and steal Him away, and say to the people, 'He has risen from the dead,' and the last deception will be worse than the first."	27:64 "Therefore, give orders for the grave to be made secure until the third day, otherwise His disciples may come and steal Him away and say to the people, 'He has risen from the dead,' and the last deception will be worse than the first."
3 Pilate said to them, "You have a guard. Go, <and> make it as secure as you know how."	27:65 Pilate said to them, "You have a guard; go, make it as secure as you know how."
4 [So] they went and made the grave secure; and along with the guard, they set a seal on the stone.	27:66 [~~And~~] they went and made the grave secure, and along with the guard they set a seal on the stone.

8 - TRIALS & CRUCIFIXION
Act 9: The Resurrection of Jesus Christ

Scene 1: An Earthquake at The Resurrection of Jesus

The Garden Tomb, Jerusalem, Judea   early Sunday morning, April 5th / 33 CE

93% of Mark is paralleled in the other three

	Matthew
1 And behold, a severe earthquake occurred, for an angel of the Lord descended from heaven.	28:2~ And behold, a severe earthquake ~~had~~ occurred, for an angel of the Lord descended from heaven
2 <He> came and rolled away the stone, and sat upon it.	28:~2 and came and rolled away the stone and sat upon it.
3 *His appearance was like lightning*,[1] and *his clothing as white as snow*;[2]	28:3 ~~And~~ his appearance was like lightning, and his clothing as white as snow.
4 <and> the guards shook for fear of him, and became like dead men.	28:4 The guards shook for fear of him and became like dead men.
5 <And> the tombs were opened; and many bodies of the saints who had fallen asleep were raised, and coming out of the tombs after His resurrection, they entered the holy city, and appeared to many.	27:52 The tombs were opened, and many bodies of the saints who had fallen asleep were raised; 27:53 and coming out of the tombs after His resurrection they entered the holy city and appeared to many.

     1. *(Daniel 10:6)*   2. *(Daniel 7:9)*

Scene 2: The Soldiers Are Paid To Lie

Jerusalem, Judea   early Sunday morning, April 5th / 33 CE

	Matthew
1 Some of the guard[s] [went] into the city, and reported to the chief priests all that had happened.	28:11 Some of the guard [~~came~~] into the city and reported to the chief priests all that had happened.
2 When [the chief priests] had assembled with the elders, [they] consulted together.	28:12~ And when [~~they~~] had assembled with the elders [~~and~~] consulted together,
3 <Then> they gave a large sum of money to the soldiers, and said <to them>; "You are to say, 'His disciples came by night, and stole Him away while we were asleep.'	28:~12 they gave a large sum of money to the soldiers, 28:13 and said, "You are to say, 'His disciples came by night and stole Him away while we were asleep.'
4 "And if this should come to the Governor's ears, we will win him over, and keep you out of trouble."	28:14 "And if this should come to the governor's ears, we will win him over and keep you out of trouble."
5 [The guards] took the money, and did as they had been instructed; and this story was widely spread among the Jews, [as it] is to this day.	28:15 ~~And~~ [~~they~~] took the money and did as they had been instructed; and this story was widely spread among the Jews, [~~and~~] is to this day.

CHAPTER 9
APPEARANCES & ASCENSION OF JESUS

Events that occurred after The Resurrection of Jesus Christ.

	Page
Act 1 - Sunday Morning	
Scene 1 The Women Arrive At The Tomb	285
2 Two Angels Greet The Women At The Tomb	286
3 The Women Tell The Apostles	287
4 Peter and John Run To The Tomb	287
5 Jesus Appears To Mary Magdalene	288
Act 2 - Appearances To The Apostles	
Scene 1 Jesus Walks To Emmaus With Two Disciples	289
2 They Finally Recognize Jesus	290
3 Jesus Appears To The Ten Apostles	291
4 Jesus Proves That His Body Is Real	292
5 Jesus Bestows The Holy Spirit On The Apostles	292
6 Jesus Manifests Himself To Thomas	293
Act 3 - Reunion In Galilee	
Scene 1 Jesus Meets His Apostles At The Mountain	294
2 Appearance at The Sea of Galilee	294
3 A Catch of One Hundred and Fifty-Three Fish	295
4 Peter, Tend My Sheep	296
5 The Promise of The Father	297
Act 4 - The Great Commission	
Scene 1 Jesus Sends The Eleven To Preach The Gospel	298
2 These Signs Will Accompany You	298
Act 5 - The Ascension of Jesus Christ	
Scene 1 Jesus Christ Ascends To Heaven	299
2 They Went Out and Preached Everywhere	299
Act 6 - Epilogue	
Scene 1 Final Words	300

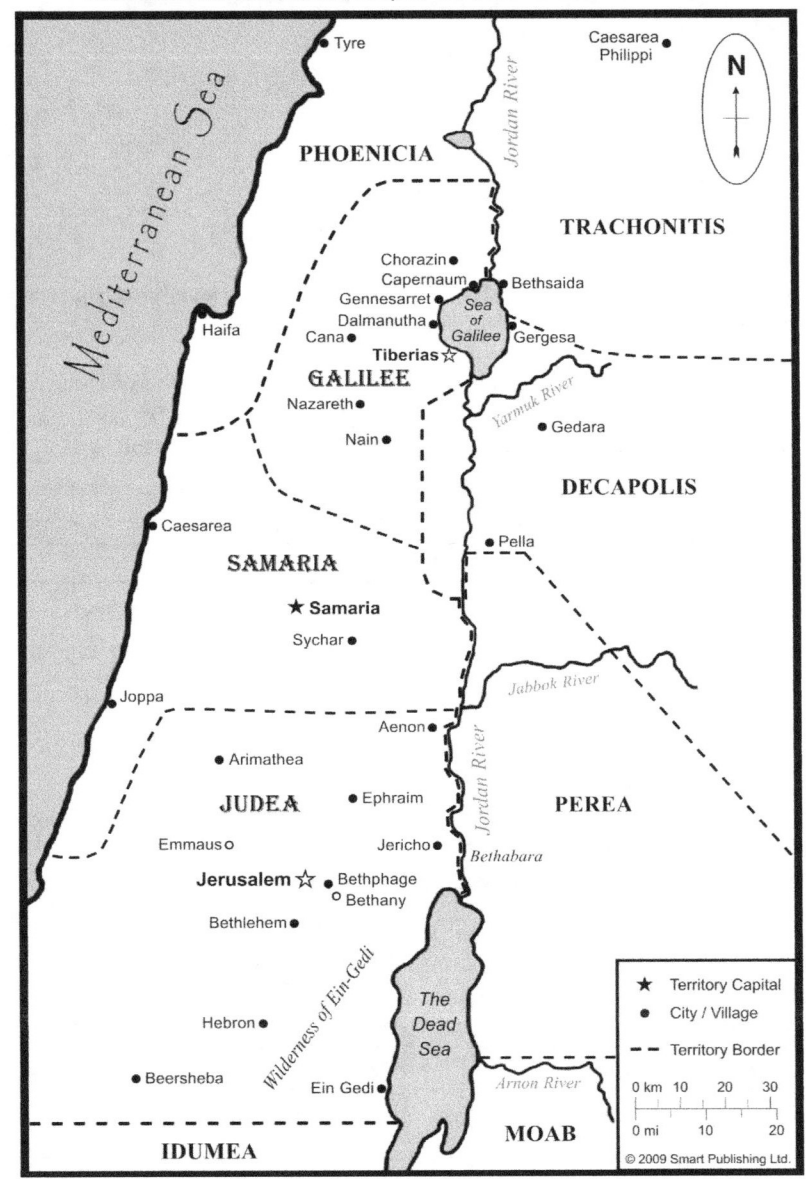

MAP OF ISRAEL

Locations mentioned in this Chapter are shown with a white center.

9 - APPEARANCES & ASCENSION

Act 1: Sunday Morning

Scene 1: The Women Arrive At The Tomb

The Garden Tomb, Jerusalem, Judea — early Sunday morning, April 5th / 33 CE

The Four Gospels Harmoniously United

	Matthew	Mark	Luke	John
1	When the Sabbath was over, as it began to dawn very early on the first day of the week, while it was still dark, Mary Magdalene, and Mary the mother of [Jesus], [with] Joanna and Salome, came to the tomb, bringing the spices which they had prepared, so that they might anoint <the body of> [Jesus].	28:1 ~~Now after~~ the Sabbath, as it began to dawn ~~toward~~ the first day of the week, Mary Magdalene and ~~the other~~ Mary came to ~~look at~~ the grave.	16:1 When the Sabbath was over, Mary Magdalene, and Mary the mother of [James], and Salome, ~~bought~~ spices, so that they might ~~come and~~ anoint [Him]. 16:2 Very early on the first day of the week, ~~they~~ came to the tomb ~~when the sun had risen~~.	24:1 ~~But~~ on the first day of the week, ~~at~~ early dawn ~~they~~ came to the tomb bringing the spices which they had prepared. 24:10~1 [and] Joanna	20:1~ ~~Now~~ on the first day of the week Mary Magdalene came early to the tomb, while it was still dark,
2	They were saying to one another, "Who will roll away the stone from the entrance of the tomb for us?"		16:3 They were saying to one another, "Who will roll away the stone for us from the entrance of the tomb?"		
3	And looking up, they saw that the stone had already been rolled away from the tomb, although it was extremely large.		16:4 Looking up, they saw that the stone had been rolled away, although it was extremely large.	24:2 And they ~~found~~ the stone rolled away from the tomb,	20:~1 and saw the stone already ~~taken~~ away from the tomb.

9 - APPEARANCES & ASCENSION

Act 1: Sunday Morning

Scene 2: Two Angels Greet The Women At The Tomb

The Garden Tomb, Jerusalem, Judea — early Sunday morning, April 5th / 33 CE

Verse-By-Verse Edition

#		Matthew	Mark	Luke
1	When they entered the tomb, they did not find the body of the Lord Jesus.		16:5~ Entering the tomb,	24:3 but when they entered, they did not find the body of the Lord Jesus.
2	While they were perplexed about this, behold, [a man] suddenly stood near them in dazzling clothing;			24:4 While they were perplexed about this, behold, [two men] suddenly stood near them in dazzling clothing;
3	<and> they saw [another] young man sitting at the right, wearing a white robe.		16:~5~ they saw [a] young man sitting at the right, wearing a white robe;	
4	The women were terrified, and <they> bowed their faces to the ground.		16:~5 and they were amazed.	24:5~ and as the women were terrified and bowed their faces to the ground,
5	The angel said to them, "Do not be afraid, for I know that you are looking for Jesus, the Nazarene who has been crucified.	28:5 The angel said to the women, "Do not be afraid; for I know that you are looking for Jesus who has been crucified.	16:6~ And he said to them, "Do not be amazed; you are looking for Jesus the Nazarene, who has been crucified.	24:~5~ the men said to them,
6	"Why do you seek the living among the dead?			24:~5 "Why do you seek the living One among the dead?
7	"He is not here, for He has risen, just as He said.	28:6~ He is not here, for He has risen, just as He said.	16:~6~ He has risen; He is not here;	24:6~ "He is not here, but He has risen.
8	"Remember how He spoke to you while He was still in Galilee, saying that the Son of Man must be delivered into the hands of sinful men, and be crucified, and <then> rise again <on> the third day?			24:~6 Remember how He spoke to you while He was still in Galilee, 24:7 saying that the Son of Man must be delivered into the hands of sinful men, and be crucified, and the third day rise again."
9	"Behold, see the place where they laid Him.	28:~6 Come, see the place where He was lying."	16:~6 behold, here is the place where they laid Him."	
10	"[Now] go quickly, and tell His [apostles] and Peter that He has risen from the dead.	28:7~ "Go quickly and tell His [disciples] that He has risen from the dead;	16:7~ "[But] go, tell His [disciples] and Peter,	
11	"And behold, He is going ahead of you to Galilee, <and> there you will see Him, just as He told you."	28:~7 and behold, He is going ahead of you to Galilee, there you will see Him; behold, I have told you."	16:~7 'He is going ahead of you to Galilee; there you will see Him, just as He told you.' "	
12	[The women] remembered His words, and they quickly fled from the tomb with fear, and great joy; and <they> ran to report it to [the] [apostles].	28:8~ And they left the tomb quickly with fear and great joy and ran to report it to [His] [disciples].	16:8~ They went out and fled from the tomb, 16:~8 for they were afraid.	24:8 And [they] remembered His words, 24:9~ and returned from the tomb
13	And they said nothing to anyone, for [fear] and astonishment gripped them.		16:~8~ for [trembling] and astonishment had gripped them; and they said nothing to anyone,	

9 - APPEARANCES & ASCENSION	Scene 3: **The Women Tell The Apostles**
Act 1: **Sunday Morning**	Jerusalem, *Judea* early Sunday morning, April 5ᵗʰ / 33 CE

The Harmonious Gospel

	Luke	John
1 Mary Magdalene, and Mary the mother of [Jesus], [and] the other women <who> were with them, <went and> reported all these things to the eleven apostles, and to all the rest.	24:~9 ~and~ reported all these things to the eleven and to all the rest. 24:10~ ~Now they were~ Mary Magdalene 24:~10 and Mary the mother of [James]; [~also~] the other women with them ~were telling these things to the~ apostles.	
2 But these words appeared to them as nonsense, and they would not believe them.	24:11 But these words appeared to them as nonsense, and they would not believe them.	
3 So [Mary] came to Simon Peter and <John>, the other *apostle whom Jesus loved*,¹· and <she> said to them, "They have taken the Lord out of the tomb, and we do not know where they have laid Him."		20:2 So [~she~] ~ran and~ came to Simon Peter and ~to~ the other disciple whom Jesus loved, and said to them, "They have taken ~away~ the Lord out of the tomb, and we do not know where they have laid Him."

1. John Zebedee - John 13:23; 19:26; 21:7, 20

Scene 4: **Peter and John Run To The Tomb**

The Garden Tomb, Jerusalem, *Judea* early Sunday morning, April 5ᵗʰ / 33 CE

	Luke	John
1 [Then] Simon Peter and [John] got up, and <they> ran to the tomb.	24:12~ [~But~] Peter got up and ran to the tomb;	20:3 [~So~] Peter and [~the other disciple~] ~went forth~, and ~they were going~ to the tomb. 20:6~ ~And so~ Simon
2 [They] were running together, [but] [John] ran faster than Peter, and came to the tomb first.		20:4 [~The two~] were running together; [~and~] [~the other disciple~] ran ~ahead~ faster than Peter and came to the tomb first;
3 Stooping and looking in, [John] saw only the linen wrappings lying there, but he did not go in.	24:~12~ stooping and looking in, [he] saw the linen wrappings only;	20:5 ~and~ stooping and looking in, [he] saw the linen wrappings lying there; but he did not go in.
4 Peter came following him, and <he> entered the tomb.		20:~6~ Peter ~also~ came, following him, and entered the tomb;
5 And he saw the linen wrappings lying there, [but] the facecloth which had been on [Jesus'] head <was> not lying with the linen wrappings, but <was> rolled up in a place by itself.		20:~6 and he saw the linen wrappings lying there, 20:7 [~and~] the face-cloth which had been on [His] head, not lying with the linen wrappings, but rolled up in a place by itself.
6 Then [John] also entered the tomb, and he saw, and <he> believed;		20:8 So [~the other disciple who had first come to~ the tomb] then also entered, and he saw and believed.
7 for they did not yet understand *the Scripture*,¹· that He must rise again from the dead.		20:9 For ~as~ yet they did not understand the Scripture, that He must rise again from the dead.
8 And [they] went away, marveling at what had happened.	24:~12 and [he] went away ~to his home~, marveling at what had happened.	20:10 So [~the disciples~] went away ~again to their own homes~.

1. Psalm 16:10

9 - APPEARANCES & ASCENSION

Act 1: Sunday Morning

Scene 5: Jesus Appears To Mary Magdalene

The Garden Tomb, Jerusalem, *Judea* Sunday morning, April 5th / 33 CE

Get the 552 page Word-For-Word Edition

#		Matthew	Mark	John
1	Now after [Jesus] had risen early on the first day of the week, He appeared first to Mary Magdalene, from whom He had cast out seven demons.		16:9 {Now after [He] had risen early on the first day of the week, He first appeared to Mary from whom He had cast out seven demons.	20:18⁻¹ Magdalene
2	[She] <had returned> to the tomb, and was standing outside, weeping.			20:11~ But [Mary] was standing outside the tomb weeping; and
3	As she wept, she stooped and looked into the tomb; and she saw <the> two angels in white, sitting one at the head, and one at the feet, <of> where the body of Jesus had been lying.			20:~11 so, as she wept, she stooped and looked into the tomb; 20:12 and she saw two angels in white sitting, one at the head and one at the feet, where the body of Jesus had been lying.
4	[One of them] said to her, "Woman, why are you weeping?"			20:13~ And [they] said to her, "Woman, why are you weeping?"
5	[Mary] [answered], "Because they have taken away my Lord, and I do not know where they have laid Him."			20:~13 [She] [said] to them, "Because they have taken away my Lord, and I do not know where they have laid Him."
6	When [Mary] said this, she turned around and saw Jesus standing there; [but] <she> did not know that it was Jesus.			20:14 When [she] had said this, she turned around and saw Jesus standing there, [and] did not know that it was Jesus.
7	Jesus said to her, "Woman, why are you weeping? Whom [do] you seek?"			20:15~ Jesus said to her, "Woman, why are you weeping? Whom [are] you seeking?"
8	Supposing Him to be the gardener, she said to Him, "Sir, if you have [removed] Him, tell me where you have laid Him, and I will take Him away."			20:~15 Supposing Him to be the gardener, she said to Him, "Sir, if you have [carried] Him away, tell me where you have laid Him, and I will take Him away."
9	And behold, Jesus greeted her, and said, "Mary!"	28:9~ And behold, Jesus met them and greeted [them].		20:16~ Jesus said to her, "Mary!"
10	She turned, and said to Him, "Rabboni!" which means "Teacher" in Hebrew; and [she] took hold of His feet and worshiped Him.	28:~9 And [they] came up and took hold of His feet and worshiped Him.		20:~16 She turned and said to Him in Hebrew, "Rabboni!" (which means, teacher).
11	Jesus said to her, "Stop clinging to Me, for I have not yet ascended to The Father;			20:17~ Jesus said to her, "Stop clinging to Me, for I have not yet ascended to the Father;
12	"but go to My brethren, and say to them, 'I ascend to My Father and your Father, [to] My God and your God.'"			20:~17 but go to My brethren and say to them, 'I ascend to My Father and your Father, [and] My God and your God.'"
13	Then Jesus said to [her], "Do not be afraid. Go and take word to My brethren to leave for Galilee, and there they will see Me."	28:10 Then Jesus said to [them], "Do not be afraid; go and take word to My brethren to leave for Galilee, and there they will see Me."		
14	Mary went and reported <this> to the [apostles], while they were mourning and weeping.		16:10 She went and reported to those who had been with Him, while they were mourning and weeping.	20:18~ Mary 20:18⁻² came announcing to the [disciples], "I have seen the Lord," .

continued >

9 - APPEARANCES & ASCENSION
Act 1: Sunday Morning
Scene 5: Jesus Appears To Mary Magdalene
continued

Matthew	Mark	John
15 <She said>, "I have seen the Lord!" and <she told them> [the] things that He had said to her. 16 <But> when they heard that [Jesus] was alive, and had been seen by her, they refused to believe it.	16:11 When they heard that [He] was alive and had been seen by her, they refused to believe it.}	20:~18 "I have seen the Lord," and that He had said [these] things to her.

---

9 - APPEARANCES & ASCENSION
Act 2: Appearances To The Apostles
Scene 1: Jesus Walks To Emmaus With Two Disciples
west of Jerusalem, *Judea*   Sunday afternoon, April 5th / 33 CE

	Mark	Luke
1 [Later] that day, [Jesus] appeared in a different form to two of them while they were walking [through] the country, on their way to a village named Emmaus, which was about *seven miles*[1] from Jerusalem.	16:12 {[After] that, [He] appeared in a different form to two of them while they were walking along on their way [to] the country.}	24:13 And behold, two of them were going that very day to a village named Emmaus, which was about seven miles from Jerusalem.
2 They were talking with each other about all the things [that] had taken place, and while they were talking, Jesus Himself approached, and began traveling with them;		24:14 And they were talking with each other about all these things [which] had taken place. 24:15 While they were talking and discussing, Jesus Himself approached and began traveling with them.
3 but their eyes were prevented from recognizing Him.		24:16 But their eyes were prevented from recognizing Him.
4 He [asked] them, "What are you <two> discussing, as you walk?" And they stood still, looking sad.		24:17 And He [said] to them, "What are these words that you are [exchanging] with one another as you are walking?" And they stood still, looking sad.
5 One of them, named Cleopas, answered and said to Him, "Are You the only one visiting Jerusalem [who is] unaware of the things which have happened here in these days?"		24:18 One of them, named Cleopas, answered and said to Him, "Are You the only one visiting Jerusalem [and] unaware of the things which have happened here in these days?
6 [Jesus] said to them, "What things?"		24:19~ And [He] said to them, "What things?"
7 They said, "The things about Jesus the Nazarene, who was a Prophet mighty in Word and deed, in the sight of God, and all the people;		24:~19 And they said to Him, "The things about Jesus the Nazarene, who was a prophet mighty in deed and word in the sight of God and all the people,
8 "and how the chief priests and our rulers delivered Him to the sentence of death, and crucified Him.		24:20 and how the chief priests and our rulers delivered Him to the sentence of death, and crucified Him.
9 "But we were hoping that it was He who was going to redeem Israel.		24:21~ But we were hoping that it was He who was going to redeem Israel.
10 "Indeed, besides all <of> this, it is the third day since these things <have> happened.		24:~21 Indeed, besides all this, it is the third day since these things happened.

1. *approximately 11 km*

continued >

9 - APPEARANCES & ASCENSION	Scene 1: **Jesus Walks To Emmaus With Two Disciples**	
Act 2: **Appearances To The Apostles**	*continued*	*A Harmonized Merger of the Four Gospels*

	Mark	**Luke**
11 "Also some women <from> among us amazed us. When they were at the tomb early in the morning, and did not find His body, they came saying that they had seen a vision of angels, who said that [Jesus] was alive!		24:22 "But also some women among us amazed us. When they were at the tomb early in the morning, 24:23 and did not find His body, they came, saying that they had also seen a vision of angels who said that [He] was alive.
12 "<Then> some of those who were with us went to the tomb, and <they> found it exactly as the women had said; but they did not see Him."		24:24 "Some of those who were with us went to the tomb and found it just exactly as the women also had said; but Him they did not see."
13 [Jesus] said to them, "O foolish men, and slow of heart to believe in all that the prophets have spoken.		24:25 And [He] said to them, "O foolish men and slow of heart to believe in all that the prophets have spoken!
14 "Was it not necessary for the Christ to suffer these things, and to enter into His glory?"		24:26 "Was it not necessary for the Christ to suffer these things and to enter into His glory?"
15 Then beginning with Moses, and all the prophets, [Jesus] explained to them the things concerning Himself in all <of> the Scriptures.		24:27 Then beginning with Moses and with all the prophets, [He] explained to them the things concerning Himself in all the Scriptures.
16 [As] they approached the village where they were going, [Jesus] acted as though He were going farther, [and so] they urged Him, saying, "Stay with us, for it is getting toward evening, and the day is now nearly over."		24:28 [And] they approached the village where they were going, and [He] acted as though He were going farther. 24:29~ [But] they urged Him, saying, "Stay with us, for it is getting toward evening, and the day is now nearly over."
17 So He went in [and] stay[ed] with them.		24:~29 So He went in [to] stay with them.

Scene 2: **They Finally Recognize Jesus**

Emmaus, *Judea*   late afternoon, Sunday, April 5th / 33 CE

	Mark	**Luke**
1 When [Jesus] had reclined at the table with them, He took the bread and blessed it; and breaking it, He began giving it to them.		24:30 When [He] had reclined at the table with them, He took the bread and blessed it, and breaking it, He began giving it to them.
2 Then their eyes were opened and they recognized Him; and He vanished from their sight.		24:31 Then their eyes were opened and they recognized Him; and He vanished from their sight.
3 They said to one another, "Were not our hearts burning within us while He was speaking to us on the road, [and] explaining the Scriptures to us?"		24:32 They said to one another, "Were not our hearts burning within us while He was speaking to us on the road, [while He was] explaining the Scriptures to us?"
4 And they got up that very hour, and returned to Jerusalem.	16:13~ {They went away}	24:33~ And they got up that very hour and returned to Jerusalem,

9 - APPEARANCES & ASCENSION Act 2: **Appearances To The Apostles**	Scene 3: **Jesus Appears To The Ten Apostles** Jerusalem, *Judea* Sunday evening, April 5th / 33 CE		Page 291 *The United Gospel Verse-By-Verse*

#	[Composite]	Mark	Luke	John
1	When it was evening that day, the first day of the week, the doors were shut where the [apostles] and those who were with them were, for fear of the Jews.	16:13⁻² {the others,	24:~33 and those who were with them,	20:19~ So when it was evening on that day, the first day of the week, and when the doors were shut where the [disciples] were, for fear of the Jews,
2	<The two men> found [them] gathered together as they were reclining at the table, and <they> reported to <them>, saying, "The Lord really has risen, and appeared to Simon."	16:13⁻¹ and reported it to 16:14⁻³ as they were reclining at the table;	24:~33~ and found gathered together [the eleven] 24:34 saying, "The Lord has really risen and has appeared to Simon."	
3	<And> they began to relate their experiences on the road, and how [they] recognized [Jesus] [by] the breaking of the bread.		24:35 They began to relate their experiences on the road and how [He] was recognized by [them] [in] the breaking of the bread.	
4	But [those who were gathered] did not believe them.	16:~13 but [they] did not believe them either.		
5	While they were telling these things, Jesus Himself came, and appeared to them.	16:14~ Afterward He appeared to the eleven themselves}	24:36~ While they were telling these things, He Himself	20:~19~ Jesus came and
6	<He> stood in their midst, and said to them, "Peace be with you!"		24:~36 stood in their midst and said to them, "Peace be to you."	20:~19 stood in their midst and said to them, "Peace be with you."
7	But they were frightened, and thought that they were seeing a spirit.		24:37 But they were startled and frightened and thought that they were seeing a spirit.	

9 - APPEARANCES & ASCENSION
Act 2: Appearances To The Apostles

Scene 4: Jesus Proves That His Body Is Real
Jerusalem, Judea Sunday evening, April 5th / 33 CE

#	Mark	Luke	John
1	[Jesus] said to them, "Why are you troubled, and why do doubts arise in your hearts?		24:38 And [He] said to them, "Why are you troubled, and why do doubts arise in your hearts?	
2	"See My hands, and My feet - that it is I Myself.		24:39~ "See My hands and My feet, that it is I Myself;	
3	"Touch Me, and see; for a spirit does not have flesh and bones, as you see that I have."		24:~39 touch Me and see, for a spirit does not have flesh and bones as you see that I have."	
4	And when [Jesus] had said this, He showed them both His hands, and His feet, and His side.		24:40 And when [He] had said this, He showed them His hands and His feet.	20:20~ And when [He] had said this, He showed them both His hands and His side.
5	The [apostles] rejoiced when they saw the Lord.			20:~20 The [disciples] then rejoiced when they saw the Lord.
6	While they still could not believe it, because of their joy and amazement, [Jesus] said to them, "Have you anything here to eat?"		24:41 While they still could not believe it because of their joy and amazement, [He] said to them, "Have you anything here to eat?"	
7	They gave Him a piece of broiled fish; and He took it, and ate it before them.		24:42 They gave Him a piece of a broiled fish; 24:43 and He took it and ate it before them.	
8	[Then] [Jesus] reproached them for their unbelief and hardness of heart, because they had not believed those who had seen Him after He had risen.	16:~14 {[and] [He] reproached them for their unbelief and hardness of heart, because they had not believed those who had seen Him after He had risen.}		

Scene 5: Jesus Bestows The Holy Spirit On The Apostles
Jerusalem, Judea Sunday evening, April 5th / 33 CE

#		John
1	[Then] Jesus said to them again, "Peace be with you! As the Father has sent Me, I also send you."	20:21 [So] Jesus said to them again, "Peace be with you; as the Father has sent Me, I also send you."
2	When He had said this, He breathed on them, and said to them, "Receive the Holy Spirit.	20:22 And when He had said this, He breathed on them and said to them, "Receive the Holy Spirit.
3	"If you forgive the sins of any, their sins have been forgiven; <and> if you retain the sins of any, they have been retained."	20:23 "If you forgive the sins of any, their sins have been forgiven them; if you retain the sins of any, they have been retained."
4	But Thomas, <the> one of the twelve called *Didymus*,[1.] was not with them when Jesus came, so <later> [they] [said] to him, "We have seen the Lord!"	20:24 But Thomas, one of the twelve, called Didymus, was not with them when Jesus came. 20:25~ So [the other disciples] were [saying] to him, "We have seen the Lord!"
5	But [Thomas] said to them, "Unless I see the imprint of the nails in His hands, and put my finger into the place of the nails, and put my hand into His side, I will not believe."	20:~25 But [he] said to them, "Unless I see in His hands the imprint of the nails, and put my finger into the place of the nails, and put my hand into His side, I will not believe."

1. Greek for twin or double

9 - APPEARANCES & ASCENSION
Act 2: Appearances To The Apostles

Scene 6: Jesus Manifests Himself To Thomas

Jerusalem, *Judea*   Monday, April 13th / 33 CE

	John
1 Eight days [later], His [apostles] were in-side again, and Thomas <was> with them.	20:26~ [After] eight days His [disciples] were again inside, and Thomas with them.
2 <Although> the doors [were] shut, Jesus came and stood in their midst, and said <to them>, "Peace be with you!"	20:~26 Jesus came, the doors [having been] shut, and stood in their midst and said, "Peace be with you."
3 Then He said to Thomas, "Reach here with your finger, and see My hands. And put your hand into My side; and do not [doubt], but believe."	20:27 Then He said to Thomas, "Reach here with your finger, and see My hands; and reach here your hand and put it into My side; and do not [be unbelieving], but believing."
4 Thomas said to Him, "My Lord, and my God!"	20:28 Thomas answered and said to Him, "My Lord and my God!"
5 Jesus said, "You have believed because you have seen Me, <but> blessed are [those] who did not see, and yet believe."	20:29 Jesus said to him, "Because you have seen Me, have you believed? Blessed are [they] who did not see, and yet believed."
6 This is the third time that Jesus was manifested to the [apostles], after He was raised from the dead.	21:14 This is now the third time that Jesus was manifested to the [disciples], after He was raised from the dead.

The Unified Gospel Story of Jesus Christ

9 - APPEARANCES & ASCENSION

Act 3: **Reunion In Galilee**

Scene 1: **Jesus Meets His Apostles At The Mountain**

Galilee   mid April / 33 CE

The Story of The Life of Jesus

	Matthew
1 The eleven [apostles] proceeded to the mountain which Jesus had designated [in] Galilee.	28:16 But the eleven [disciples] proceeded [to] Galilee, to the mountain which Jesus had designated.
2 When they saw [Jesus] they worshiped Him, but some were doubtful.	28:17 When they saw [Him], they worshiped Him; but some were doubtful.

Scene 2: **Appearance at The Sea of Galilee**

near Tiberius, Sea of Galilee, *Galilee*   late April / 33 CE

	John
1 After [this], Jesus manifested Himself again to the [apostles] at the Sea of [Galilee], and He manifested Himself in this way:	21:1 After [these things] Jesus manifested Himself again to the [disciples] at the Sea of [Tiberias], and He manifested Himself in this way.
2 Simon Peter, and Thomas, and *Nathanael,*[1.] and the sons of Zebedee, and two of His other [apostles], were together.	21:2 Simon Peter, and Thomas called Didymus, and Nathanael and the sons of Zebedee, and two others of His [discip]les were together.
3 Peter said to them, "I am going fishing," <and> they said, "We will come with you."	21:3~ Simon Peter said to them, "I am going fishing." They said to him, "We will also come with you."
4 <So> they went out in the boat, [but] that night they <did not> [catch] [anything].	21:~3 They went out and got into the boat; [and] that night they [caught] [nothing].
5 When the day was breaking, Jesus stood on the beach; yet [they] did not know that it was Jesus.	21:4 But when the day was now breaking, Jesus stood on the beach; yet [the disciples] did not know that it was Jesus.
6 [He] said to them, "Children, do you have any[thing] <to eat>?" They answered Him, "No."	21:5 So [Jesus] said to them, "Children, you do not have any [fish]*, do you?" They answered Him, "No."
7 [Jesus] said, "Cast the net on the right side of the boat, and you will find a catch."	21:6~ And [He] said to them, "Cast the net on the right-hand side of the boat and you will find a catch."
8 So they cast <the net>, and they were not able to haul it in because of the great number of fish.	21:~6 So they cast, and then they were not able to haul it in because of the great number of fish.

1. or Bartholomew - Scene 412.10 - Matthew 10:3 / Mark 3:18 / Luke 6:14

9 - APPEARANCES & ASCENSION

Act 3: Reunion In Galilee

Scene 3: A Catch of One Hundred and Fifty-Three Fish

near Tiberius, Sea of Galilee, *Galilee*   late April / 33 CE

90% of John is non-synoptic (unique)

	John
1 [John] said to Peter, "It is the Lord!"	21:7~ ~~Therefore~~ [~~that disciple whom Jesus loved~~] said to Peter, "It is the Lord."
2 When Peter heard that it was the Lord, he put on his garment (for he was [naked]), and threw himself into the sea.	21:~7 ~~So~~ when ~~Simon~~ Peter heard that it was the Lord, he put his ~~outer~~ garment on (for he was [~~stripped for work~~]), and threw himself into the sea.
3 The other [apostles] came in the little boat dragging the net full of fish, for they were not far from the land, but about [a] *hundred yards* [1.] away.	21:8 ~~But~~ the other [~~disciples~~] came in the little boat, for they were not far from the land, but about [~~one~~] hundred yards away, dragging the net full of fish.
4 When they got on[to] the land, they saw a charcoal fire already laid, [with] fish placed on it, and bread.	21:9 ~~So~~ when they got out on the land, they saw a charcoal fire already laid [~~and~~] fish placed on it, and bread.
5 Jesus said to them, "Bring some of the fish [that] you have caught."	21:10 Jesus said to them, "Bring some of the fish [~~which~~] you have ~~now~~ caught."
6 Peter drew the net to land, full of [one] hundred and fifty-three large fish; and although there were so many, the net was not torn.	21:11 ~~Simon~~ Peter ~~went up and~~ drew the net to land, full of large fish, [a] hundred and fifty-three; and although there were so many, the net was not torn.
7 Jesus said to them, "Come and have breakfast."	21:12~ Jesus said to them, "Come and have breakfast."
8 None of the [apostles] ventured to [ask] Him, "Who are You?" knowing that it was the Lord.	21:~12 None of the [~~disciples~~] ventured to [~~question~~] Him, "Who are You?" knowing that it was the Lord.
9 Jesus came and took the bread, and <He> gave it to them, [along with] the fish.	21:13 Jesus came and took the bread and gave it to them, and the fish likewise.

[1.] *about 91 meters*

9 - APPEARANCES & ASCENSION

Act 3: **Reunion In Galilee**

Scene 4: **Peter, Tend My Sheep**

near Tiberius, Sea of Galilee, *Galilee*   late April / 33 CE

The Four Gospels Unified Verse-By-Verse

	John
1 When they had finished breakfast, Jesus said to Peter, "Simon, son of John; do you love Me more than these?"	21:15~ ~~So~~ when they had finished breakfast, Jesus said to ~~Simon~~ Peter, "Simon, son of John, do you love Me more than these?"
2 [Peter] said to Him, "Yes, Lord; You know that I love You!"	21:~15~ [He] said to Him, "Yes, Lord; You know that I love You."
3 [Jesus] said to him, "Tend My lambs."	21:~15 [He] said to him, "Tend My lambs."
4 <Then> [Jesus] said to [Peter] a second time, "Simon, son of John, do you love Me?"	21:16~ [He] said to him ~~again~~ a second time, "Simon, son of John, do you love Me?"
5 <Again> [Peter] said to Him, "Yes, Lord; You know that I love You."	21:~16~ [He] said to Him, "Yes, Lord; You know that I love You."
6 He said to him, "Shepherd My sheep."	21:~16 He said to him, "Shepherd My sheep."
7 <Then> [Jesus] said to him [a] third time, "Simon, son of John, do you love Me?"	21:17~ [He] said to him [~~the~~] third time, "Simon, son of John, do you love Me?"
8 Peter was grieved because [Jesus] said to him the third time, "Do you love Me?" and he said to Him, "Lord, You know all things; You know that I love You!"	21:~17~ Peter was grieved because [He] said to him the third time, "Do you love Me?" And he said to Him, "Lord, You know all things; You know that I love You."
9 Jesus said to him, "Tend My sheep.	21:~17 Jesus said to him, "Tend My sheep.
10 "Truly, truly, I say to you, when you were younger, you used to gird yourself and walk wherever you wished; but when you grow old, you will stretch out your hands, and someone else will gird you, and bring you <to> where you do not wish to go."	21:18 "Truly, truly, I say to you, when you were younger, you used to gird yourself and walk wherever you wished; but when you grow old, you will stretch out your hands and someone else will gird you, and bring you where you do not wish to go."
11 Now [Jesus] said this <to> signify by what kind of death [Peter] would glorify God.	21:19~ Now this [He] said, signif~~ying~~ by what kind of death [he] would glorify God.
12 When [Jesus] had spoken this, He said to him, "Follow Me."	21:~19 ~~And~~ when [He] had spoken this, He said to him, "Follow Me!"
13 Turning around, Peter saw <John,> *the disciple whom Jesus loved,*[1] following them; the one who had leaned back on His bosom at the supper and said, "Lord, who is the one who betrays You?"	21:20 Peter, turning around, saw the disciple whom Jesus loved following them; the one who ~~also~~ had leaned back on His bosom at the supper and said, "Lord, who is the one who betrays You?"
14 So Peter, seeing him, said to Jesus, "Lord, and what about this man?"	21:21 So Peter seeing him said to Jesus, "Lord, and what about this man?"
15 Jesus said to [Peter], "If I want him to remain until I come, what is that to you? You follow Me."	21:22 Jesus said to [him], "If I want him to remain until I come, what is that to you? You follow Me!"
16 Therefore this saying went out among the brethren, that [John] would not die.	21:23~ Therefore this saying went out among the brethren that [~~that disciple~~] would not die;
17 Yet Jesus did not say that [John] would not die, but only, "If I want him to remain until I come, what is that to you?"	21:~23 yet Jesus did not say ~~to him~~ that [he] would not die, but only, "If I want him to remain until I come, what is that to you?"

1. *John Zebedee - John 13:23; 19:26; 20:2; 21:7*

9 - APPEARANCES & ASCENSION
Act 3: Reunion In Galilee

Scene 5: The Promise of The Father
near Tiberius, Sea of Galilee, *Galilee*   late April / 33 CE

	Luke
1 [Jesus] said to them, "These are My words which I spoke to you while I was still with you, that all <of the> things which are written about Me in the Law of Moses, and the Prophets, and the Psalms, must be fulfilled."	24:44 ~~Now~~ [He] said to them, "These are My words which I spoke to you while I was still with you, that all things which are written about Me in the Law of Moses and the Prophets and the Psalms must be fulfilled."
2 Then [Jesus] opened their minds to understand the Scriptures;	24:45 Then [~~He~~] opened their minds to understand the Scriptures,
3 and He said to them, "Thus it is written, that the Christ would suffer, and rise again from the dead <on> the third day;	24:46 and He said to them, "Thus it is written, that the Christ would suffer and rise again from the dead the third day,
4 "and that repentance for <the> forgiveness of sins would be proclaimed in His Name to all <of> the nations, beginning from Jerusalem.	24:47 and that repentance for forgiveness of sins would be proclaimed in His name to all the nations, beginning from Jerusalem.
5 "You are witnesses of these things.	24:48 "You are witnesses of these things.
6 "And behold, I am sending forth the promise of My Father upon you, but you are to stay in the city until you are clothed with power from on high!"	24:49 "And behold, I am sending forth the promise of My Father upon you; but you are to stay in the city until you are clothed with power from on high.

9 - APPEARANCES & ASCENSION

Act 4: **The Great Commission**

Scene 1: **Jesus Sends The Eleven To Preach The Gospel**

Jerusalem, *Judea* Friday, May 15th / 33 CE

Page 298

The Good News of Jesus Christ

	Matthew	Mark
1 <Later,> Jesus spoke to them, saying, "All authority has been given to Me in Heaven, and on earth.	28:18 ~~And~~ Jesus ~~came up and~~ spoke to them, saying, "All authority has been given to Me in heaven and on earth.	16:15~ {~~And He~~ said to them,
2 "Go therefore, into all the world, and preach the gospel to all creation;	28:19~ "Go therefore	16:~15 "Go into all the world and preach the gospel to all creation.
3 "and make disciples of all the nations, baptizing them in the Name of The Father, and <of> the Son, and <of> the Holy Spirit.	28:~19 and make disciples of all the nations, baptizing them in the name of the Father and the Son and the Holy Spirit,	
4 "Teach them to observe all that I <have> commanded you.	28:20~ teach~~ing~~ them to observe all that I commanded you;	
5 "He who has believed, and has been baptized, shall be saved;		16:16~ "He who has believed and has been baptized shall be saved;
6 "but he who has disbelieved shall be condemned."		16:~16 but he who has disbelieved shall be condemned.}

Scene 2: **These Signs Will Accompany You**

Jerusalem, *Judea* Friday, May 15th / 33 CE

	Matthew	Mark
1 "These signs will accompany those who have believed: in My Name they will cast out demons;		16:17~ {"These signs will accompany those who have believed: in My name they will cast out demons,
2 "they will speak with new tongues;		16:~17 they will speak with new tongues;
3 "they will pick up serpents,		16:18~ they will pick up serpents,
4 "and if they drink any deadly poison, it will not hurt them;		16:~18~ and if they drink any deadly poison, it will not hurt them;
5 "they will lay <their> hands on the sick, and they will recover.		16:~18 they will lay hands on the sick, and they will recover."}
6 "And [behold], I am with you [all] <the days>, [until] the end of the age."	28:~20 and [~~lo~~], I am with you [a~~lways~~]*, [~~to~~] the end of the age."	

9 - APPEARANCES & ASCENSION
Act 5: **The Ascension of Jesus Christ**

Scene 1: **Jesus Christ Ascends To Heaven**
Bethany, *Judea*   Friday, May 15th [1] / 33 CE

Page 299
The United Gospel Story

	Mark	Luke
1 [After] the Lord had spoken to [the apostles], He led them out as far as Bethany.	16:19~ {So [then, when] the Lord Jesus had spoken to [them],	24:50~ And He led them out as far as Bethany,
2 [Then] [Jesus] lifted up His hands, and blessed them.		24:~50 [and] [He] lifted up His hands and blessed them.
3 While He was blessing them, He [de]parted from them, and was [taken] up into Heaven, and *sat down at the right hand of God.*[1]	16:~19 He was [received] up into heaven and sat down at the right hand of God.}	24:51 While He was blessing them, He parted from them and was [carried] up into heaven.
4 After worshiping Him, [the apostles] returned to Jerusalem with great joy, and <they> were continually in the Temple, praising God.		24:52 And [they], after worshiping Him, returned to Jerusalem with great joy, 24:53 and were continually in the temple praising God.

1. *Psalm 110:1 / Acts 1:3*

Scene 2: **They Went Out and Preached Everywhere**

	Mark
1 [Then] Jesus sent out through [the apostles], from east to west, the sacred and imperishable proclamation of eternal salvation.	16:~20 {And they promptly reported all these instructions to Peter and his companions. And [after that], Jesus Himself sent out through [them] from east to west the sacred and imperishable proclamation of eternal salvation.
2 And they went out and preached everywhere, while the Lord worked with them, and confirmed the Word by the signs that followed.	16:20~ And they went out and preached everywhere, while the Lord worked with them, and confirmed the word by the signs that followed.}

9 - APPEARANCES & ASCENSION

Act 6: Epilogue

Scene 1: Final Words

FIVE COLUMN

	John	John
1 *No one has seen God at any time;* [1]	1:18~ No one has seen God at any time;	
2 the only begotten God who is in the bosom of The Father, He has explained Him.	1:~18 the only begotten God who is in the bosom of the Father, He has explained Him.	
3 He came to His own, and those who were His own did not receive Him.	1:11 He came to His own, and those who were His own did not receive Him.	
4 But as many as received Him, to them He gave the right to become children of God, even to those who believe in His Name;	1:12 But as many as received Him, to them He gave the right to become children of God, even to those who believe in His name,	
5 who were born not of blood, nor of the will of the flesh, nor of the will of man, but of God.	1:13 who were born, not of blood nor of the will of the flesh nor of the will of man, but of God.	
6 For <although> the Law was given through Moses,[2] grace and truth [came] through Jesus Christ.	1:17 For the Law was given through Moses; grace and truth [were realized]* through Jesus Christ.	
7 Of His fullness, we have all received, [which is] grace upon grace.	1:16 For of His fullness we have all received, [and] grace upon grace.	
8 [One] [3] who has seen is testifying, and <he> wrote these things;	21:24~ This is [the disciple] who is testifying to these things and wrote these things,	19:35~ And [he] who has seen has testified,
9 and we know that his testimony is true, and <that> he is telling the truth, so that you may also believe.	21:~24 and we know that his testimony is true.	19:~35 and his testimony is true; and he knows that he is telling the truth, so that you also may believe.
10 And there are also many other things which Jesus did, <and> many other signs <which> [He] performed in the presence of the disciples which are not written in this book,	20:30 [Therefore] many other signs [Jesus] also performed in the presence of the disciples, which are not written in this book; 21:25~ And there are also many other things which Jesus did,	
11 which if they were written in detail, I suppose that even the world itself [could] not contain the books that would be written;	21:~25 which if they were written in detail, I suppose that even the world itself [would] not contain the books that would be written.	
12 but these have been written so that you may believe that Jesus is the *Christ*,[4] the Son of God;	20:31~ but these have been written so that you may believe that Jesus is the Christ, the Son of God;	
13 and that <by> believing, you may have life in His Name.	20:~31 and that believing you may have life in His name.	

1. *Exodus 33:20*   2. *Exodus 20:1-17 / Deuteronomy 5:1-22; 33:4*   3. *John Zebedee - John 13:23; 19:26; 20:2; 21:7*   4. **Hebrew:** Meshiach = *Greek:* Christos = *English:* Christ

~ End ~

Seven Articles

That detail why

Five Column: The Synoptic Gospel

was created.

Written by: Daniel John

© 2014 Smart Publishing Ltd.

# Article 1
WHY MERGE THE GOSPELS?

One might ask;

> "Why merge the four Gospels? It is important to preserve each of the four individual accounts of the life and teachings of Jesus Christ because each of them contains unique sayings, events and stories that are not found within the others."

Yes, that is true, and the world will always have the four Gospels as they now appear in all of the versions of the New Testament of the *Holy Bible* that have ever been printed. However, because there is overlap and duplication among so much similarity, the many benefits that are derived from reading a single, concise account have long been recognized, and the first attempt to produce a merger of the content of the four Gospel texts into a single storyline was likely the work titled *Diatessaron* (meaning "out of/from/through" "four"), which was created by a Syrian student of Justin Martyr named Tatian, in about 160 CE.

Due to the differences in the specific details that each Gospel account records, no single instance of a parallel saying or event could by itself be considered complete or accurate if it lacked a detail that is mentioned in the text of one or more of the other Gospel accounts. For this reason, the only way to know the full detail of all of the things that Jesus Christ said, and did, and taught, is to read all four of the Gospel accounts. As to why these particular four Gospel accounts have been preserved together, in lieu of any and all others, see *Note 5.1 - Why Are There Four Gospels?* on page *xx*.

At 83,680 words, using the *New American Standard Bible* (NASB) - each English translation will vary - reading all four of the Gospel accounts back-to-back is time consuming, and the differences in the chronological sequencing of their story-lines and details can be confusing. To eliminate the confusion caused by the large amount of overlap and repetition it is logical and desirable to merge and harmonize the words of the four Gospel accounts into a single, complete storyline - one that contains the full detail of every saying and event from each of the four Gospels. Why read four overlapping yet different versions of the same event, when you really want to see everything that happened all together, and in a logical order?

As the intent of *FIVE COLUMN: The Synoptic Gospel* is to focus the full picture of the life and teachings of Jesus Christ, all four of the New Testament Gospels were used to produce a complete and unified account that is almost 22% shorter in length than reading the four Gospel accounts back-to-back, making this Gospel story both faster to read, and much easier to understand.

Article 2
HAVE THE GOSPELS BEEN MERGED BEFORE?

One might ask;

> "How many *synoptic* mergers have been created that combine, harmonize and unify the words of the four New Testament Gospel accounts?"

The four familiar Gospel accounts have long been read together, both as a **harmony** with the texts of several Gospels in columns side-by-side, and also as a **merger** or synopsis, where the individual words of the parallel and overlapping verses are combined or unified in some way. Although there may have been even earlier works that combine and unify the words of the Gospels, *Diatessaron* was compiled by Tatian using the four familiar Gospels around 160 CE, which is about 130 years after the death and resurrection of Jesus Christ.

Tatian created his merger *Diatessaron* by adding material from the Gospels of *Matthew*, *Mark* and *Luke*, to *The Gospel of John*. In those many places where the texts from two or more of the four Gospels closely parallel each other, Tatian chose one set of verses (usually the longest, most detailed version of the saying or event) from one Gospel over the other(s).

Despite its editorial shortcomings, being a more complete narrative than reading even any two of the Gospel accounts separately, *Diatessaron* was widely read throughout the early Christian Church, from Rome in the west to Constantinople in the east, where it was used exclusively as The Gospel by the Eastern and Coptic Churches for more than 200 years.

In 405 CE, the Roman Catholic Church produced the *Vulgate (Common)* version of the New Testament in Latin. The *Vulgate* opened with the same four Gospel records of the life of Jesus that Tatian had used, except once again as four separate accounts.

Since at least Tatian's *Diatessaron,* many harmonies and several mergers of the words of the three closely related "synoptic" Gospels have been created, and also a few works that include the text of *The Gospel of John*. Learning from past examples, and using a precise system of notation, this book goes beyond all previous mergers and harmonies by splitting the parallel verses into sets of individual words, which were then carefully aligned on a word-for-word, and thought-for-thought, basis.

In the end, with each and every word from each of the four Gospel accounts of the New Testament included or accounted for, *FIVE COLUMN: The Synoptic Gospel* is the most complete and accurate word-for-word merged harmonization of the texts of the four Gospel accounts of the New Testament that has ever been produced.

Article 3
WHY INCLUDE THE GOSPEL OF JOHN?

One might ask;

> "Why is *The Gospel of John* included in *The Synoptic Gospel*?"
> or, "Why include *John* in any harmonization or merger of the New Testament Gospels?"

One might ask this because *John's Gospel* has not traditionally been held to be truly "synoptic" with the other three accounts of *Matthew*, *Mark* and *Luke*. The major reason for this is that less than 10% of *The Gospel of John* overlaps, repeats, or parallels the sayings, teachings and events that are chronicled within the other three accounts. Among the three "synoptic" accounts, some 65% of *The Gospel of Matthew* is paralleled within *Mark* and *Luke*, and 80% of *Luke* is repeated in *Mark* and *Matthew*, and fully 93% of *Mark's* material is shared by the other two.

Another distinction of *John's* narrative is its theology, which confirms Jesus not only as the *Messiah* (Christ) and Son of God, but also uniquely as the Divine "Word" (Greek: *logos*) of God. A further distinction that some have noted is that *John's Gospel* does not appear to contain any "true" parables, which are sayings and stories that use the symbolic language of allegory to represent hidden spiritual truths and deeper symbolic meanings.

So, if *The Gospel of John* is so different from the other three, why include it in a harmony or a textual merger with them? Part of the answer is that because only 10% of *John's Gospel* overlaps and parallels the other three, *John* therefore contributes the most unique material to the combined Gospel story of the life of Jesus. This being the case, to exclude it would produce a short and very incomplete account of the life and teachings of Jesus Christ. If a Gospel must be excluded, it would be more logical to exclude *The Gospel of Mark*, which overlapping almost 93% of its content with the other three only contributes about 7% as new stories and material to the combined Gospel story.

As for the authenticity of the Gospel that bears the name of *John*, though it was likely the last of the four accounts to be written, it has always since its completion been accepted by the early Church as a reliable record of the "good news" message of the life and teachings of Jesus Christ.

Some seventy or so years after *The Gospel of John* was completed, in about the year 160 CE, a Syrian student of Justin Martyr named Tatian created a merger of the four Gospel texts which he called *Diatessaron*, meaning "out of/from/through" "four". To create this work Tatian used 96% of *The Gospel of John* as a backbone, to which he then added additional material from the Gospels of *Matthew*, *Mark* and *Luke* that was not mentioned within *John*.

Being more complete than reading even any two of the Gospel accounts, *Diatessaron* was used throughout the early Church and exclusively by the eastern Coptic Churches for more than two hundred years, until the Latin *Vulgate* New Testament was completed by Jerome on appointment from the Roman Catholic Church in 405 CE. Perhaps because Tatian was eventually branded by the Church as a heretic, the *Vulgate Bible* did not use the *Diatessaron*, but included the same four Gospel accounts that Tatian had used.

In the *Vulgate Bible, The Gospel of John* was placed in sequence after the other three, as most New Testaments still arrange the Gospels to this day. However, being the fourth of four Gospels does not mean a position of lesser importance, but it was placed as the fourth because it was known to have been written last, and because in many ways it differs from the closer synchronicity of the other three. Interestingly, some versions of *The Bible* have put *John* as the first Gospel and book of their New Testament canons.

As for the writer of this record of the life of Jesus, it has traditionally been held that the author is John Zebedee, who, along with his elder brother James, were, according to some traditions, possibly related to Jesus as cousins through His mother Mary, and their mother Salome. James and John were among the twelve men that Jesus called to serve as His *apostles*, which means something like "one who is sent [forth]" as with a message. Jesus named James and his younger brother John "Boanerges", which means "sons of thunder."[1.]

Of the twelve apostles, John may have been the closest to Jesus, and "*the one that Jesus loved*,"[2.] who, along with his brother James, and also Peter, were the only witnesses on several significant occasions during the ministry of Jesus, such as when He was transfigured on the mountain with Moses and Elijah, and when He resurrected to life a little girl who had died, and also during His final prayers in the Garden of Gethsemane, on the night that He was arrested.

It can be debated about whether or not the writer or dictator of *The Gospel of John* is actually this John Zebedee, the beloved apostle of Jesus, but there is too much unique material and important details in his account that would only have been known by an actual witness to the events. And where *John's* account does parallel and overlap stories and content from the other three Gospels, it may do so specifically to add details that were lacking within the others.

1. Mark 3:17   2. John 13:23; 19:26; 20:2; 21:7, 20

Article 3 - continued

While some believe that John was a simple fisherman who probably could not read or write, he could still have dictated his version of the sayings of Jesus, and the events from His life, to a scribe, or to whomever it was who wrote the original Greek words of the account that bears his name. It is likely however, that John the apostle could read and write, and even in Greek, or that he had learned to do so by the end of his life, as John "the Evangelizer" was a leader of the early Church, and especially after James the Just, the brother of Jesus and head of the Jerusalem Church, had been put to death around 62 CE, followed shortly after by Peter in 64 CE.

This same John likely authored at least the first two of the three letters that bear his name (*1st*, *2nd* and *3rd John*), and some people believe that he may have also written the *Book of Revelation (Greek: Apocalypse)*.

As a leader of the early Christian Church, John the Apostle himself had disciples, and he taught the young *Polycarp*, who became the bishop of Smyrna (*c. 69 - 155 CE*); who went on to disciple the bishop *Irenaeus* of Gaul (*c. 130 - 202 CE*); who tutored the early third century Roman theologian *Hippolytus* (*c. 170 - 235 CE*).

As a leader of the mother Church in Jerusalem, John would have seen and had access to all of the Gospel accounts that would have existed after 80 CE, the period around when *John's Gospel* appears to have been written. By that time, some fifty years after the death of Jesus Christ, there were at least a dozen accounts in circulation of the sayings, teachings, and stories of His life and ministry; and many more such "gospels" would continue to be written for the next one hundred years or so. Interestingly, some of these later accounts would be influenced by the style and/or the theology of *John's Gospel*, and also by the writings and teachings of those whom John had taught, and by those who had been taught by them.

That more than 90% of *The Gospel of John* is unique, unparalleled material not shared with the other three New Testament Gospels may be due to the fact that John decided to not repeat stories about the life of Jesus for which he perhaps felt he could not add much new or significant information. Being a later account of the life of Jesus, it appears that perhaps John chose to tell his unique stories precisely because they were not already mentioned within any of the other Gospel accounts that existed at that time, and because there were few other people still alive who had witnessed those momentous events. The content of *John's Gospel* includes, with the exception of the last Passover, all of the other Feasts and Festivals that the Gospels mention that Jesus attended in Jerusalem, along with most of the events that occurred in Judea during His ministry, and particularly during the final year of his life.

As less than 10% of *John's* account parallels the content of the other three Gospels, it appears that perhaps as John neared the end of his long life he chose to retell certain stories that were already mentioned in order to specifically add important details and information which the other accounts, for whatever reason, did not include.

As a leader in the early Jerusalem Church, it appears that John may have also chosen to compose his account to address certain issues of importance to the Church at that time, such as questions about the station of Jesus Christ in relation to God, and the purpose of His mission as the Word of God, and the promised Messiah of the Jewish peoples.

As to whether the author of *John's Gospel* could be someone other than John Zebedee, the apostle chosen by Jesus who led the early Church in Jerusalem, it is unlikely that someone could write a "strange" or different Gospel, and then put the name of "John" the great apostle on it, and have the early Church accept it as such.

For all of these reasons, as a final thought on the importance of *John's Gospel*, even for inclusion in the FIVE COLUMN Four Gospel Harmony and *The Synoptic Gospel* word-for-word Merger, no one would say that *John's* account is the least of the four Gospels, and many people would say that if they could have only one Gospel account, then they would likely choose *The Gospel of John*.

In conclusion, *John's* account has always been accepted as a fine, true Gospel record of the life and teachings of Jesus Christ, and it has been included in the Four Gospel Harmony of FIVE COLUMN and the word-for-word *fifth column* Merger of *The Synoptic Gospel* because more than 90% of *John* is unique, unparalleled material that is not shared with the other three New Testament Gospel accounts. As such, in the end, to not include *The Gospel of John* in any merged harmonization of the Gospel accounts would produce a very short and incomplete picture of the teaching life and healing ministry of Jesus Christ.

Article 4

PARALLEL WORDING DIFFERENCES

Within the four Gospels of the New Testament, many teachings and stories of Jesus Christ are mentioned in two or three of the accounts, while some sayings and events from His life are mentioned in all four. Within the many sets of parallel and overlapping verses there are almost always differences in the specific words and word-forms that each account records.

One common type of wording difference is the use of synonyms to convey the same basic meaning of thought, such as when "Rabbi" is used in one Gospel, and "Teacher", or "Master", or even "Lord", in another; or "young donkey" in one account, and "colt" or "foal" in the other(s).

A second type of difference occurs within the parallel verses when the Gospels all use the same root word, but with different endings (*suffixes*), as when they describe the action as taking place in different tenses - such as the present and the past, or even the future. Examples of this include "walk" "walking" and "walked", and "say" "saying" and "said". Different suffixes on the same root word also occur when something is mentioned as being single in one Gospel, and as plural in another.

Whatever the wording differences between the texts of the synoptic verses, in those many places of duplicated repetition, only one word or word-form could be retained and copied into the unified *fifth column* text of FIVE COLUMN aka *The Synoptic Gospel*, and this requires that a choice be made as to which word, words, or word-forms would be used, and which would not be retained and copied into the *fifth column*. Word retention choices were generally made so that each line of text within the *fifth column* flowed logically and smoothly to the next line; and where the choice concerned the action tense of a word or sentence, the preference was to leave the action in the present tense.

For more information on the choices that were made to harmonize the wording differences among the parallel sections of the four Gospels, see *Note 1 - How This Book Was Compiled*, which begins on page *xi*.

It is noted that for every word choice that was made to produce the unified text of *The Synoptic Gospel* another person might see it another way, and make a different choice. As such, FIVE COLUMN, *The Synoptic Gospel*, and the works that are based upon its text, are open to review and comment. If you have constructive feedback or a suggestion that would improve this work, please see the last page of this book. All feedback and suggestions for the improvement of this work are greatly appreciated, especially those that enhance future editions.

Article 5

ORDERING THE GOSPEL STORYLINE

In order to chronologically arrange all of the sayings and events from the four Gospel accounts of the New Testament it is necessary to establish a timeline for the earthly life and ministry of Jesus Christ. Establishing a timeline is problematic because the events recorded within the four Gospel accounts are not all presented in the same chronological order, and this is most clearly seen in the many sections of overlapping and parallel verses.

As they begin, the four Gospels describe events in more or less the same chronological sequence, but they soon diverge throughout the middle sections of their stories, before coming together again to recount the events of the final week of Jesus in Jerusalem, including the last supper that He ate with His apostles, and His arrest, trials, crucifixion and death. Part of the reason for the differing sequences of events among the four Gospels is that *Matthew* and *Luke* ordered some of the stories of their narratives according to something other than the more straightforward chronological timeline that is used in *Mark*, and especially in *John*.

This means that no matter which of the four Gospel accounts is used as a backbone to anchor a timeline for the life of Jesus, the sequence of verses from the other three Gospels will need to be broken and reordered many times in order to include all of the teachings and events within the same timeline.

Over the centuries, beginning with the use of *The Gospel of John* by Tatian in his *Diatessaron* (*c. 160 CE*), each Gospel has been used as the backbone against which to anchor a timeline for all of the events of the other accounts. While problems and conflicts will result no matter which Gospel you start with, and which Gospel's verses you add to that, some combinations result in fewer primary and secondary breaks within the overall sequence that is produced when all of the sayings and stories from the four Gospels are combined.

After trials with all combinations, the arrangement that appears to produce the fewest number of conflicts and breaks within the overall sequence of the storyline, and is therefore used in this book, is to align the verses of *Mark* to *The Gospel of John*. To this the verses of *Matthew's* Gospel were added, and then the content of *Luke* was merged with that. Under this arrangement, *Luke's* Gospel, being the last considered, is the most divided, and has the most verses out of their original sequence.

As the Scriptural sequence of events from each Gospel account conflicts with each of the others in a few or many places, the correct chronological sequence for every event and verse cannot always be accurately determined. When a choice had to be made, the sayings and events were ordered so that the overall combined storyline flowed as smoothly and logically as possible, from the beginning of the story to the end. For more information on the timeline of the life and ministry of Jesus Christ that is used in *FIVE COLUMN*, and this reprint of its *fifth column* text, see *Note 3.2* on page *xviii*.

Article 6
RE-VERSING THE GOSPEL

Early in the 13th century, the Arch-Bishop of Canterbury, Stephen Langton, divided the words of the longer books of *The Bible* into the arrangement of chapters that is still in use today.

Some three hundred years later, in 1551, a French Catholic who became a Protestant, named Robert Estienne, divided the chapters of Langton into sets of verses, which made it even easier to reference everything. While the verse divisions that Estienne added are very useful, the assignment of those verses was inconsistent, and resulted in some very lengthy groupings of words composed of multiple sentences, which often contained several ideas, and too much information.

This example of a single, long verse from *The Gospel of John* consists in English of three full sentences, and contains as many as ten interrelated pieces of information:

> *"You are of your father the Devil, and you want to do the desires of your father. He was a murderer from the beginning, and does not stand in the truth because there is no truth in him. Whenever he speaks a lie, he speaks from his own nature, for he is a liar and the father of lies."*
> ~ Jesus Christ (*John 8:44*)

At 59 words and 283 characters it is a lot of text, and perhaps contains too many details for one single verse. While some see this as Estienne overlooking a division in the flickering light of a dying candle at the end of long day, the New Testament is full of verses longer than this, with the 76 words of *Revelation 20:4* consisting of around 380 characters.

Another inconsistency in the assignment of verses can be seen in the parallel sections of the Gospels, where two or more of the accounts mention the same saying, or are describing the same event. In many sets of parallel verses a grouping of words from one of the Gospels was divided into two verses, while the parallel text from another Gospel(s) was left as a single, long verse. Although Estienne was a printer by trade, these types of inconsistencies might not have occurred if he had consulted a harmony of the Gospels, where he could have seen the four texts in parallel columns side-by-side; or, if he had remembered how he had previously divided that same section of words the first time that he saw it in the other Gospel(s).

As with the original four Gospels, for ease of reference, the sequence of words within the *fifth column* of FIVE COLUMN: *The Synoptic Gospel* is divided into concise Verses that generally contain a single major or important thought, idea, or action, or two, if they are closely related in meaning. In general, the Verses of this book are on average slightly shorter than those of the four original Gospels.

To be able to quickly reference any Verse in this book, the entire combined narrative is laid out like a play, with *Chapters*, *Acts* and *Scenes*. Each *Scene* of action is identified with a three digit *scene reference number*, which chronologically indicates when in time the Scene may have happened, in relation to all of the other Scenes of action in the combined Gospel story.

Each *Verse* within each Scene is designated by a one or two digit *verse reference number*, which follows the three digit *scene reference number*. For more information on the reference system that designates the Verses of FIVE COLUMN and *The Synoptic Gospel*, see *Note 2* which begins on page *xiv*.

As an example of the difference between the old verse system used within the four Gospels and the Verses of this book, consider where in *John 13:38*, Jesus says to Peter, *"... a rooster will not crow until you deny Me three times."* While a reference of *John 13:38* is useful, it does not tell you much about when Jesus may have spoken these words, except that as there are 21 chapters in *John's Gospel*, then perhaps this event in the 13th chapter likely happened more than half way through *John's* narrative of the life of Jesus.

Further, a reference of *John, Chapter thirteen, Verse thirty-eight*, does not tell you that these words are part of a larger set of parallel verses, with *Matthew 26:34*, *Mark 14:30*, and *Luke 22:34*, and that the full text and reference for these words of Jesus is actually these four verses taken together.

By contrast, *The Synoptic Gospel* lists these words of Jesus as Verse 778.13 (or TSG 778.13), where the first number designates the *Chapter* (7 - The Final Week), the second number is the *Act* (7 - Thursday - The Last Supper), the third number is the *Scene* (8 - Peter, You Will Deny Me Three Times), and following a period is the *Verse reference* - Verse 13 - the text of which reads as:

> *"Truly, truly, I say to you Peter, that this very night, a rooster will not crow until you yourself have denied that you know Me three times."*
> ~ 778.13

Although the reference system used in FIVE COLUMN: *The Synoptic Gospel* is a four part notation (*Chapter*, *Act*, *Scene* and *Verse*) the result is a shorter reference than the current three parts of *Book*, *Chapter* and *Verse*. This concise four part notation makes all of the sayings and events from the life and ministry of Jesus Christ easy to reference and quick to locate, with the reference itself indicating when in time the Scene occurred in relation to the rest of the combined Gospel story.

Article 7
THE FUTURE OF THE FOUR GOSPELS

In that the meaning of the words from the four individual Gospel accounts are all found within a single text, *FIVE COLUMN* and *The Synoptic Gospel* are complete, and our knowledge of the things that Jesus Christ said and did cannot be significantly increased from the manuscripts of the four New Testament Gospels that currently exist, including the Nestle-Aland *Novum Testamentum Graece* which forms the basis of this work, as is used in the *New American Standard Bible* (NASB) version of the four New Testament Gospels.

The first New Testament to include *The Synoptic Gospel* account of the life and teachings of Jesus Christ will likely be in a *New American Standard Bible* edition of *The Bible*. In time, the precisely merged Gospel story of this book, or something similar to it, may eventually replace the four Gospels in the New Testaments of the majority of *Bibles* throughout the world, even as the *Diatessaron* was once the only Gospel account used within the early Eastern and Coptic Churches for hundreds of years.

Perhaps given enough time, some future generation will be unaware that the Gospel story of the life of Jesus Christ that is found in the New Testament was based on four related but separate accounts, that had once existed together as a merger for three hundred years, and then side-by-side for the next 1,600 years. If this seems unlikely, consider that most people today have not heard of *Diatessaron*, nor are many people aware that within the early Church perhaps as many as thirty different "gospel" collections of the stories, sayings and teachings of Jesus Christ once also existed, in addition to *Matthew*, *Mark*, *Luke* and *John*.

As all people are to hear the Gospel message of Jesus Christ, *FIVE COLUMN* and *The Synoptic Gospel* are powerful tools to help spread that Good News. And as for the four individual Gospel accounts themselves, they will always continue to exist in the countless New Testaments of all of the *Bibles* that have been printed, in all of the languages of the world.

As to the future of this work, improvements will continue to be made to the *FIVE COLUMN* Four Gospel Harmony, and to the *fifth column Synoptic Gospel* word-for-word Merger, by those who are interested. For more information on improving future editions of this work, please see the last page of this book.

Appendix 1

The Synoptic Gospel Scene Contents

APPENDIX 1 - THE SYNOPTIC GOSPEL SCENE CONTENTS

The 360 Scenes of **FIVE COLUMN** and *The Synoptic Gospel* including the Date, Location and the original Gospel Verses.

CHAPTER 0 - PROLOGUE	Verses	Location	Date	Page
Act 1 - Foreword				
Scene 1 Prologue	L 1:1-4	-	-	2
2 The Word of God	J 1:1-5, 9-10, 14	-	-	2
Act 2 - The Genealogy of Jesus				
Scene 1 The Genealogy of The Messiah	M 1:1-17	-	-	3
2 The Genealogy of The Son of God	L 3:~23-38	-	-	5

* M = **M**atthew
K = Mar**K**
L = **L**uke
J = **J**ohn

CHAPTER 1 - THE BIRTH OF JESUS	Verses	Location	Date	Page
Act 1 - The Prophecy About John				
Scene 1 The Birth of John Is Foretold To Zacharias	K 1:1 / L 1:5-23	The Temple, Jerusalem, Judea	mid June / 7 BCE	6
2 Elizabeth Becomes Pregnant With John	L 1:24-25	Judean hill country, Judea	summer / 7 BCE	7
Act 2 - The Annunciation To Mary				
Scene 1 Gabriel Tells Mary That She Will Birth A Son	L 1:26-38	Nazareth, Galilee	late December / 7 BCE	8
2 Mary Visits Elizabeth	L 1:39-56	Judean hill country, Judea	late December / 7 BCE	9
Act 3 - The Birth of John				
Scene 1 The Birth and Naming of John	L 1:57-64	Judean hill country, Judea	late March / 6 BCE	10
2 The Prophecy of Zacharias About John	L 1:65-80	Judean hill country, Judea	late March / 6 BCE	11
Act 4 - The Birth of Jesus				
Scene 1 An Angel Solves Joseph's Dilemma	M 1:18-25~	Nazareth, Galilee	spring / 6 BCE	12
2 Joseph and Mary Journey To Bethlehem	L 2:1-5	Bethlehem, Judea	late September / 6 BCE	12
3 The Birth of Jesus	L 2:6-7	Bethlehem, Judea	late September / 6 BCE	13
4 Angelic Announcement To The Shepherds	L 2:8-20	Bethlehem, Judea	late September / 6 BCE	13
5 The Naming of Jesus	M 1:~25 / L 2:21	Bethlehem, Judea	early October / 6 BCE	14
Act 5 - Jesus Is Presented In The Temple				
Scene 1 Righteous Simeon Prophesies About Jesus	L 2:22-35	The Temple, Jerusalem, Judea	early November / 6 BCE	14
2 Anna The Prophetess	L 2:36-38	The Temple, Jerusalem, Judea	early November / 6 BCE	15
3 Return To Nazareth	L 2:39-40	Nazareth, Galilee	early November / 6 BCE	15

The Story of The Life of Jesus

CHAPTER 1 - THE BIRTH OF JESUS - continued	Verses	Location	Date	Page
Act 6 - To Egypt and Back				
Scene 1 King Herod and The Magi From The East	M 2:1-12	Jerusalem, Judea	late autumn / 6 BCE	16
2 Joseph Is Warned To Flee to Egypt	M 2:13-15~	Nazareth, Galilee > Egypt	late autumn / 6 BCE	17
3 Herod Orders The Death of The Male Babies	M 2:16-18	Jerusalem, Judea	winter / 5 BCE	17
4 Joseph, Mary and Jesus Return From Egypt	M 2:~15, 19-23	Egypt > Nazareth, Galilee	spring / 4 BCE	18
Act 7 - Young Jesus In The Temple				
Scene 1 I Had To Be In My Father's House	L 2:41-52	The Temple, Jerusalem, Judea	Passover, March / 7 BCE	19

CHAPTER 2 - THE MESSIAH IS ANOINTED	Verses	Location	Date	Page
Act 1 - John Becomes The Baptist				
Scene 1 John Begins His Ministry of Baptism	M 3:1-6 / K 1:2-6 / L 3:1-6 / J 1:6-8	Jordan River, Judea	spring / 29 CE	21
2 John Warns The Pharisees	M 3:7-10 / L 3:7-9	Jordan River, Judea	spring / 29 CE	22
3 The Teachings of John The Baptist	L 3:10-14	Jordan River, Judea	spring / 29 CE	23
4 John Preaches About The Coming Messiah	M 3:11-12 / K 1:7-8 / L 3:15-18	Jordan River, near Bethabara, Perea	summer / 29 CE	23
5 John Denies That He Is The Christ or Elijah	J 1:19-28	Jordan River, near Bethabara, Perea	summer / 29 CE	24
Act 2 - The Baptism of Jesus				
Scene 1 John Is At First Unwilling To Baptize Jesus	M 3:13-15 / K 1:9~ / J 1:29-31	Jordan River, near Bethabara, Perea	late summer / 29 CE	25
2 Jesus Is Baptized By John In The Jordan River	M 3:16-17 / K 1:~9-11 / L 3:21-22	Jordan River, near Bethabara, Perea	late summer / 29 CE	26
3 John Testifies that Jesus Is The Son of God	J 1:15, 32-34	Jordan River, near Bethabara, Perea	late summer / 29 CE	26
Act 3 - The Messiah Is Tempted				
Scene 1 Jesus Fasts In The Wilderness For Forty Days	M 4:1-2 / K 1:12-13~ / L 4:1-2	Judean wilderness, Judea	late summer / 29 CE	27
2 Satan Tries to Tempt Jesus	M 4:3-11 / K 1:~13 / L 4:3-13	Judean wilderness, Judea	early autumn / 29 CE	28

CHAPTER 3 - THE FIRST YEAR of His Ministry	Verses	Location	Date	Page
Act 1 - Jesus Begins His Ministry				
Scene 1 Jesus Meets Andrew and Simon	L 3:23~ / J 1:35-42	Jordan River, Judea	early autumn / 29 CE	30
2 Jesus Meets Philip and Nathanael	J 1:43-51	Judea	early autumn / 29 CE	31
3 Jesus Turns Water Into Wine At A Wedding	J 2:1-12	Cana, Galilee	autumn / 29 CE	32
Act 2 - The First Passover				
Scene 1 Jesus Expels The Merchants From The Temple	J 2:13-25	The Temple, Jerusalem, Judea	Passover - April / 30 CE	33
2 A Pharisee Named Nicodemus	J 3:1-21	Jerusalem, Judea	Passover - April / 30 CE	34
3 The Disciples of Jesus Begin Baptizing	J 3:22-30, 4:1-2	Jordan River, Aenon, Judea	late spring / 30 CE	35
4 Believe In The Son and Have Eternal Life	J 3:31-36	Jordan River, Aenon, Judea	late spring / 30 CE	35

APPENDIX 1 - THE SYNOPTIC GOSPEL SCENE CONTENTS

CHAPTER 3 - THE FIRST YEAR - continued	Verses	Location	Date	Page
Act 3 - A Journey Through Samaria				
Scene 1 King Herod Imprisons John The Baptist	M 4:12; 14:3-5 / K 1:14~; 6:17-20 / L 3:19-20 / J 4:3-4	Judea	late spring / 30 CE	36
2 The Woman At Jacob's Well	J 4:5-12	Sychar, Samaria	late spring / 30 CE	37
3 I Am The Living Water	J 4:13-30	Sychar, Samaria	late spring / 30 CE	38
4 Many Samaritans Believe In Jesus	J 4:31-44	Sychar, Samaria	late spring / 30 CE	39
Act 4 - Jesus Settles In Capernaum				
Scene 1 Through Nazareth and Cana	M 4:13~ / L 4:14 / J 4:45-46~	Nazareth & Cana, Galilee	late spring / 30 CE	40
2 Healing The Son of A Royal Official	J 4:~46-54	Capernaum, Galilee	late spring / 30 CE	40
3 Jesus Resides In Capernaum	M 4:~13-17 / K 1:~14-15 / L 4:15	Capernaum, Galilee	late spring / 30 CE	41
4 Jesus Calls Peter and Andrew, and Others	M 4:18-20 / K 1:16-18 / L 5:1-9, ~10	Sea of Galilee, near Capernaum, Galilee	late spring / 30 CE	42
5 Jesus Calls James and John	M 4:21-22 / K 1:19-20 / L 5:10~, 11	Sea of Galilee, near Capernaum, Galilee	late spring / 30 CE	43
Act 5 - Jesus Heals Many				
Scene 1 Healing A Demoniac on The Sabbath	K 1:21-28 / L 4:31-38~	Capernaum, Galilee	a Sabbath, summer / 30 CE	44
2 Jesus Heals Simon Peter's Mother-in-Law	M 8:14-15 / K 1:29-31 / L 4:~38-39	Capernaum, Galilee	a Sabbath, summer / 30 CE	45
3 Many Come To Be Healed	M 8:16-17 / K 1:32-34 / L 4:40-41	Capernaum, Galilee	Saturday evening, summer / 30 CE	45
4 Preaching and Healing Throughout Galilee	M 4:23-25 / K 1:35-39 / L 4:42-44	Galilee	a Sunday, summer / 30 CE	46
5 Cleansing A Leper	M 8:2-4 / K 1:40-45 / L 5:12-16	Galilee	summer / 30 CE	47
6 Resurrecting The Son of A Widow	L 7:11-18	Nain, Galilee	summer / 30 CE	48
Act 6 - John Enquires About Jesus				
Scene 1 John Asks Jesus, "Are You The Expected One?"	M 11:2-6 / L 7:19-23	Capernaum, Galilee	summer / 30 CE	49
2 John Is Elijah Who Was To Come	M 11:7-15 / L 7:24-30	Capernaum, Galilee	summer / 30 CE	50
3 To What Shall I Compare This Generation?	M 11:16-19 / L 7:31-35	Capernaum, Galilee	summer / 30 CE	51
Act 7 - Jesus Attends A Feast				
Scene 1 Jesus Heals A Man at The Bethesda Pool	J 5:1-14	Bethesda Pool, Jerusalem, Judea	a Sabbath, summer / 30 CE	52
2 The Father and The Son	J 5:15-23	Jerusalem, Judea	a Sabbath, summer / 30 CE	53
3 Those Who Believe My Words Will Live	J 5:24-30	Jerusalem, Judea	a Sabbath, summer / 30 CE	54
4 My Testimony About Myself	J 5:31-47	Jerusalem, Judea	a Sabbath, summer / 30 CE	55
5 The Parable of The Good Samaritan	L 10:25-37	Jerusalem, Judea	a Sabbath, summer / 30 CE	56
6 Jesus Visits Martha and Mary	L 10:38-42	Bethany, Judea	summer / 30 CE	57

One Complete Gospel United from Four

CHAPTER 3 - THE FIRST YEAR - *continued*	Verses	Location	Date	Page
Act 8 - Events In Capernaum				
Scene 1 The Man Paralyzed In A Bed	M 9:2 / K 2:1-5 / L 5:17-20	Capernaum, Galilee	summer / 30 CE	58
2 Jesus Is Accused of Blasphemy	M 9:3-8 / K 2:6-13 / L 5:21-26	Capernaum, Galilee	summer / 30 CE	59
3 Jesus Calls Matthew Levi	M 9:9 / K 2:14 / L 5:27-28	Capernaum, Galilee	summer / 30 CE	60
4 Matthew Gives A Reception For Jesus	M 9:10-13 / K 2:15-17 / L 5:29-32	Capernaum, Galilee	summer / 30 CE	60
5 Why Do You Not Fast?	M 9:14-15 / K 2:18-20 / L 5:33-35	Capernaum, Galilee	summer / 30 CE	61
6 New Cloth and Wineskins	M 9:16-17 / K 2:21-22 / L 5:36-39	Capernaum, Galilee	summer / 30 CE	61
7 Picking Grain On The Sabbath	M 12:1-8 / K 2:23-28 / L 6:1-5	Galilee	a Sabbath, late summer / 30 CE	62
8 Healing A Withered Hand On The Sabbath	M 12:9-15~ / K 3:1-7~, 9 / L 6:6-11	Galilee	a Sabbath, late summer / 30 CE	63
9 Lord, Teach Us To Pray	L 11:1-4	Galilee	late summer / 30 CE	64
Act 9 - The Death of John The Baptist				
Scene 1 The Demand of Herodias	M 14:6-9 / K 6:21-26	Jerusalem, Judea	late summer / 30 CE	65
2 King Herod Has John Beheaded	M 14:10-13~ / K 6:27-29 / J 6:1	Jerusalem, Judea	late summer / 30 CE	65

CHAPTER 4 - THE SECOND YEAR of Ministry	Verses	Location	Date	Page
Act 1 - Jesus Chooses Twelve Apostles				
Scene 1 Miracles of Healing	M 12:~15-21 / K 3:~8, 10-12 / L 6:18~, 19	Capernaum, Galilee	spring / 31 CE	68
2 Jesus Appoints Twelve Apostles	M 5:1; 10:2-4 / K 3:13-19 / L 6:12-16 / J 11:~16~	Mount Eremos, near Capernaum, Galilee	spring / 31 CE	69
Act 2 - The Sermon On The Mount				
Scene 1 The Beatitudes	M 5:2-12 / K 3:~7-8~ / L 6:17, ~18, 20-26	Mount Eremos, near Capernaum, Galilee	spring / 31 CE	75
2 You Are The Salt of The Earth	M 5:13 / K 4:23; 9:50 / L 14:34-35	Mount Eremos, near Capernaum, Galilee	spring / 31 CE	76
3 You Are The Light of The World	M 5:14-16 / K 4:21-22 / L 8:16-17; 11:33	Mount Eremos, near Capernaum, Galilee	spring / 31 CE	76
4 The Eye Is The Lamp of The Body	M 6:22-23 / L 11:34-36	Mount Eremos, near Capernaum, Galilee	spring / 31 CE	77
5 I Have Come To Fulfill The Law	M 5:17-20	Mount Eremos, near Capernaum, Galilee	spring / 31 CE	77
6 Forgive Your Brother	M 5:21-24	Mount Eremos, near Capernaum, Galilee	spring / 31 CE	78
7 Settle With Your Opponent	M 5:25-26 / L 12:57-59	Mount Eremos, near Capernaum, Galilee	spring / 31 CE	78
8 On Adultery and Divorce	M 5:27-32	Mount Eremos, near Capernaum, Galilee	spring / 31 CE	79
9 Make No Oath By Heaven or Earth	M 5:33-37	Mount Eremos, near Capernaum, Galilee	spring / 31 CE	80

APPENDIX 1 - THE SYNOPTIC GOSPEL SCENE CONTENTS

CHAPTER 4 - THE SECOND YEAR - continued	Verses	Location	Date	Page
Act 3 - The Sermon on True Wealth				
Scene 1 Give To Everyone Who Asks of You	M 5:38-42 / L 6:29-30, 34, 38	Mount Eremos, near Capernaum, Galilee	spring / 31 CE	75
2 Love Your Enemy	M 5:43-48 / L 6:27-28, 32-33, 35-36	Mount Eremos, near Capernaum, Galilee	spring / 31 CE	76
3 When You Give To The Poor	M 6:1-4	Mount Eremos, near Capernaum, Galilee	spring / 31 CE	76
4 When You Pray	M 6:5-8	Mount Eremos, near Capernaum, Galilee	spring / 31 CE	77
5 The Lord's Prayer	M 6:9-15 / K 11:25-26	Mount Eremos, near Capernaum, Galilee	spring / 31 CE	77
6 When You Fast	M 6:16-18	Mount Eremos, near Capernaum, Galilee	spring / 31 CE	78
7 Life Is Not About Possessions	L 12:13-21	Mount Eremos, near Capernaum, Galilee	spring / 31 CE	78
8 Store Up Treasure In Heaven	M 6:19-21 / L 12:33-34	Mount Eremos, near Capernaum, Galilee	spring / 31 CE	79
9 Do Not Worry About Food or Clothing	M 6:25-34 / L 12:22-32	Mount Eremos, near Capernaum, Galilee	spring / 31 CE	80
Act 4 - The Sermon on Spiritual Fruit				
Scene 1 On Judging Another Person	M 7:1-5 / L 6:37, 39, 41-42	Mount Eremos, near Capernaum, Galilee	spring / 31 CE	81
2 Ask, and It Will Be Given To You	M 7:7-14 / L 6:31; 11:5-13	Mount Eremos, near Capernaum, Galilee	spring / 31 CE	82
3 The Fruit of False Prophets	M 7:6, 15-20 / L 6:43-44	Mount Eremos, near Capernaum, Galilee	spring / 31 CE	83
4 Build On The Solid Foundation of The Word	M 7:21-27 / L 6:46-49	Mount Eremos, near Capernaum, Galilee	spring / 31 CE	84
5 Jesus Finishes His Sermon	M 7:28 - 8:1 / L 7:1	Mount Eremos, near Capernaum, Galilee	spring / 31 CE	84
Act 5 - Events In Galilee				
Scene 1 Healing A Centurion's Servant	M 8:5-13 / L 7:2-10	Capernaum, Galilee	spring / 31 CE	85
2 Perfumed Feet In The Home of A Pharisee	L 7:36-50	Capernaum, Galilee	summer / 31 CE	86
3 Preaching The Kingdom of God	L 8:1-3	Galilee	summer / 31 CE	87
4 Jesus Denounces The Unrepentant Cities	M 11:20-24 / L 10:12-15	Galilee	summer / 31 CE	87
5 Come to Me - My Burden Is Light	M 11:25-30 / L 10:21-22	Galilee	summer / 31 CE	88
Act 6 - On Good and Evil Spirits				
Scene 1 You Heal By Beelzebul	M 12:22-24 / K 3:20-22 / L 11:14-16	Capernaum, Galilee	summer / 31 CE	89
2 How Can Satan Cast Out Satan?	M 12:25-29 / K 3:23-27 / L 11:17-22	Capernaum, Galilee	summer / 31 CE	90
3 The Unforgivable Sin	M 12:30-32 / K 3:28-30 / L 11:23; 12:10	Capernaum, Galilee	summer / 31 CE	91
4 On Good and Evil	M 12:33-37 / L 6:45	Capernaum, Galilee	summer / 31 CE	91
5 A Wicked Generation Seeks A Sign	M 12:38-42 / L 11:29-32	Capernaum, Galilee	summer / 31 CE	98
6 On Unclean Spirits	M 12:43-45 / L 11:24-28	Capernaum, Galilee	summer / 31 CE	98
7 Woe To You Pharisees!	L 11:37-44	Capernaum, Galilee	summer / 31 CE	93
8 Woe To You Lawyers As Well!	L 11:45-46, 52 - 12:1	Capernaum, Galilee	summer / 31 CE	93
9 Who Are My Mother and My Brothers?	M 12:46-50 / K 3:31-35 / L 8:19-21	Capernaum, Galilee	summer / 31 CE	94

All The Words of Jesus Christ in Red

CHAPTER 4 - THE SECOND YEAR - continued	Verses	Location	Date	Page
Act 7 - Parables About The Kingdom				
Scene 1 The Parable of The Sower a)	M 13:1-9 / K 4:1-9 / L 8:4-8	Sea of Galilee, Capernaum, Galilee	summer / 31 CE	95
2 Why Do You Speak To Them In Parables?	M 13:10-11, 13-17 / K 4:10-13 / L 8:9-10; 10:23-24	Capernaum, Galilee	summer / 31 CE	96
3 The Parable of The Sower b) Explained	M 13:12, 18-23 / K 4:14-20, 24-25 / L 8:11-15, 18	Capernaum, Galilee	summer / 31 CE	97
4 The Parable of The Tares a)	M 13:24-30 / K 4:26-29	Capernaum, Galilee	summer / 31 CE	98
5 The Kingdom of Heaven Is Like A Mustard Seed	M 13:31-32 / K 4:30-32 / L 13:18-19	Capernaum, Galilee	summer / 31 CE	99
6 More Parables About The Kingdom of Heaven	M 13:33-36~, 44-52 / K 4:33-34 / L 13:20-21	Capernaum, Galilee	summer / 31 CE	100
7 The Parable of The Tares b) Explained	M 13:~36-43, 53	Capernaum, Galilee	summer / 31 CE	101
Act 8 - Mighty Miracles				
Scene 1 Jesus Calms The Stormy Sea	M 8:18, 23-27 / K 4:35-41 / L 8:22-25	Sea of Galilee, Galilee	summer / 31 CE	102
2 A Demon-Possessed Man Named Legion	M 8:28-29 / K 5:1-10 / L 8:26-31	Gergesa, Decapolis	summer / 31 CE	103
3 Jesus Sends The Demons Into The Swine	M 8:30-34 / K 5:11-20 / L 8:32-39	Gergesa, Decapolis	summer / 31 CE	104
4 Jairus Implores Jesus To Heal His Daughter a)	M 9:1, 18-19 / K 5:21-23, ~42~ / L 8:40-42~	Capernaum, Galilee	summer / 31 CE	105
5 A Woman Is Healed of Her Hemorrhage	M 9:20-22 / K 5:24-34 / L 8:~42-48	Capernaum, Galilee	summer / 31 CE	106
6 Jesus Heals The Daughter of Jairus b)	M 9:23-26 / K 5:35-42~, ~42-43 / L 8:49-56	Capernaum, Galilee	summer / 31 CE	107
7 Two Blind Men and A Mute Demon	M 9:27-34	Capernaum, Galilee	summer / 31 CE	108
8 Reading In His Hometown On The Sabbath	M 13:54~ / K 6:1-2~ / L 4:16-21	Nazareth, Galilee	A Sabbath, late summer / 31 CE	109
9 The Nazarenes Take Offense At Jesus	M 13:~54-58 / K 6:~2-6~ / L 4:22-30	Nazareth, Galilee	A Sabbath, late summer / 31 CE	110
Act 9 - Jesus Sends The Apostles				
Scene 1 Jesus Sends His Twelve Apostles To Preach	M 9:35 - 10:1 / K 6:~6-7 / L 9:1-2	Capernaum, Galilee	late summer / 31 CE	111
2 Jesus Instructs The Apostles	M 10:5-10 / K 6:8-9 / L 9:3	Capernaum, Galilee	late summer / 31 CE	112
3 Peace, To Those Who Receive You	M 10:11-15 / K 6:10-11 / L 9:4-5	Capernaum, Galilee	late summer / 31 CE	112
4 I Send You Out As Sheep Among Wolves	M 10:16-20 / L 12:11-12	Capernaum, Galilee	late summer / 31 CE	113
5 You Will Be Persecuted, But Do Not Fear	M 10:21-31 / L 6:40; 12:2-7	Capernaum, Galilee	late summer / 31 CE	114
6 Whoever Confesses The Son of Man	M 10:32-33 / L 12:8-9	Capernaum, Galilee	late summer / 31 CE	115
7 I Have Not Come To Bring Peace	M 10:34-36 / L 12:49-53	Capernaum, Galilee	late summer / 31 CE	115
8 He Who Is Worthy of Me	M 10:37 - 11:1	Capernaum, Galilee	late summer / 31 CE	116
9 The Apostles Go Out and Preach The Gospel	K 6:12-13 / L 9:6	Galilee	late summer / 31 CE	116

APPENDIX 1 - THE SYNOPTIC GOSPEL SCENE CONTENTS

CHAPTER 5 - THE THIRD YEAR of His Ministry	Verses	Location	Date	Page
Act 1 - The Bread of Life				
Scene 1 The Apostles Return	M 14:~13-14 / K 6:30-34 / L 9:10-11 / J 6:2-3	Galilee	early spring / 32 CE	118
2 Jesus Feeds A Crowd of Five Thousand	M 14:15-21 / K 6:35-44 / L 9:12-17 / J 6:4-14	near Tiberias Galilee	April / 32 CE	119
3 Jesus Walks On The Sea of Galilee	M 14:22-27 / K 6:45-50 / J 6:15-20	Sea of Galilee, Galilee	spring / 32 CE	121
4 Peter Joins Jesus On The Sea	M 14:28-33 / K 6:51-52 / J 6:21	Sea of Galilee, Galilee	spring / 32 CE	122
5 Healing In Gennesaret	M 14:34-36 / K 6:53-56	Gennesaret, Galilee	spring / 32 CE	122
6 I Am The Bread of Life	J 6:22-36	Capernaum, Galilee	spring / 32 CE	123
7 The Will of The Father	J 6:37-50	Capernaum, Galilee	spring / 32 CE	124
8 Eat My Flesh, and Drink My Blood	J 6:51-59	Capernaum, Galilee	spring / 32 CE	125
9 Some Disciples Stumble At This	J 6:60-71	Capernaum, Galilee	spring / 32 CE	126
Act 2 - In Galilee, and Beyond				
Scene 1 Eating With Unwashed Hands	M 15:1-14 / K 7:1-16	Capernaum, Galilee	summer / 32 CE	127
2 The Things From The Heart Defile The Man	M 15:15-20 / K 7:17-23	Capernaum, Galilee	summer / 32 CE	128
3 The Wisdom of A Canaanite Woman	M 15:21-28 / K 7:24-30	District of Tyre near Sidon, Phoenicia	summer / 32 CE	129
4 Jesus Restores The Hearing of A Deaf Man	M 15:29-31 / K 7:31-37	Decapolis	summer / 32 CE	130
5 Jesus Feeds Four Thousand People	M 15:32-38 / K 8:1-9	Decapolis	summer / 32 CE	131
6 The Pharisees and Sadducees Seek A Sign	M 15:39 - 16:4~ / K 8:10-12 / L 12:54-56	Dalmanutha, Galilee	summer / 32 CE	132
7 Beware Of The Leaven of The Pharisees	M 16:~4-12 / K 8:13-21	Sea of Galilee, Galilee	summer / 32 CE	133
8 Healing A Blind Man at Bethsaida	K 8:22-26	Bethsaida, Trachonitis	summer / 32 CE	134
9 Healing A Crippled Woman on The Sabbath	L 13:10-17	Bethsaida, Trachonitis	a Sabbath, summer / 32 CE	134
Act 3 - A Trip To Trachonitis				
Scene 1 Who Do The People Say That I Am?	M 16:13-20 / K 8:27-30 / L 9:18-21	Caesarea Philippi, Trachonitis	summer / 32 CE	135
2 Jesus Rebukes Peter	M 16:21-23 / K 8:31-33 / L 9:22	Caesarea Philippi, Trachonitis	summer / 32 CE	136
3 If Anyone Wishes To Follow Me	M 16:24-28 / K 8:34 - 9:1 / L 9:23-27	Caesarea Philippi, Trachonitis	summer / 32 CE	137
4 Jesus Is Transfigured With Moses and Elijah	M 17:1-9 / K 9:2-10 / L 9:28-36~	Mount Hermon, Trachonitis	summer / 32 CE	138
5 Why Must Elijah Come First?	M 17:10-13 / K 9:11-13 / L 9:~36	Mount Hermon, Trachonitis	summer / 32 CE	139
6 Jesus Cures A Demon-Possessed Boy	M 17:14-18 / K 9:14-27 / L 9:37-43~	near Mount Hermon, Trachonitis	summer / 32 CE	140
7 Why Could We Not Drive Out The Demon?	M 17:19-21 / K 9:28-29 / L 17:5-6	Trachonitis	summer / 32 CE	141
8 Follow Me	M 8:19-22 / K 9:30 / L 9:57-62	Galilee	summer / 32 CE	142

A Unified Four Gospel Harmony + Merger A-15

	CHAPTER 5 - THE THIRD YEAR - *continued*	VERSES	Location	Date	Page
	Act 4 - Return To Capernaum				
Scene 1	Jesus Foreshadows His Death and Resurrection	M 17:22-23 / K 9:31-32 / L 9:~43-45	Galilee	summer / 32 CE	143
2	Paying The Poll-Tax	M 17:24-27 / K 9:33~	Capernaum, Galilee	summer / 32 CE	143
3	The Greatest In The Kingdom of Heaven	M 18:1-5 / K 9:~33-37 / L 9:46-48	Capernaum, Galilee	summer / 32 CE	144
4	Do Not Cause The Children To Stumble	M 18:6, 10, 14 / K 9:42 / L 17:2	Capernaum, Galilee	summer / 32 CE	145
5	On Stumbling Blocks and Hell Fire	M 18:7-9 / K 9:43-49 / L 17:1	Capernaum, Galilee	summer / 32 CE	145
6	If Your Brother Sins	M 18:15-20 / L 17:3-4	Capernaum, Galilee	summer / 32 CE	146
7	On Forgiveness and The Unforgiving Slave	M 18:21-35	Capernaum, Galilee	summer / 32 CE	147
8	He Who Is Not Against Us Is For Us	K 9:38-41 / L 9:49-50	Capernaum, Galilee	summer / 32 CE	148
	Act 5 - Jesus Sends Seventy Disciples				
Scene 1	The Trials of Discipleship	L 14:25-33	Capernaum, Galilee	summer / 32 CE	149
2	Jesus Sends Seventy Disciples To Preach	L 10:1-11, 16	Capernaum, Galilee	summer / 32 CE	149
3	King Herod Is Perplexed About Jesus	M 14:1-2 / K 6:14-16 / L 9:7-9	Jerusalem, Judea	summer / 32 CE	150
	Act 6 - On Dining Etiquette				
Scene 1	A Sabbath Meal With Pharisees	L 14:1-6	Capernaum, Galilee	a Sabbath, summer / 32 CE	150
2	Do Not Take The Place of Honor	L 14:7-11	Capernaum, Galilee	a Sabbath, summer / 32 CE	151
3	Invite The Poor, and Be Blessed	L 14:12-15	Capernaum, Galilee	a Sabbath, summer / 32 CE	151
4	The Seventy Disciples Return	L 10:17-20	Capernaum, Galilee	summer / 32 CE	151
	Act 7 - A Collection of Parables				
Scene 1	The Joy Over One Sinner Who Repents	M 18:11-13 / L 15:1-10	Capernaum, Galilee	summer / 32 CE	152
2	The Prodigal Son	L 15:11-24	Capernaum, Galilee	summer / 32 CE	153
3	Rejoice! Your Lost Brother Has Been Found	L 15:25-32	Capernaum, Galilee	summer / 32 CE	154
4	The Shrewd Manager	L 16:1-9	Capernaum, Galilee	summer / 32 CE	155
5	He Who Is Faithful With Little Things	M 6:24 / L 16:10-17	Capernaum, Galilee	summer / 32 CE	156
6	Lazarus and The Rich Man	L 16:19-31	Capernaum, Galilee	summer / 32 CE	157
7	Pray, and Don't Lose Heart	L 18:1-8	Capernaum, Galilee	summer / 32 CE	158
8	The Pharisee and The Tax Collector	L 18:9-14	Capernaum, Galilee	summer / 32 CE	158

APPENDIX 1 - THE SYNOPTIC GOSPEL SCENE CONTENTS

CHAPTER 6 - THE FINAL YEAR of His Ministry	Verses	Location	Date	Page
Act 1 - The Feast of Tabernacles (Booths)				
Scene 1 His Brothers Did Not Believe In Him	J 7:1-9	Galilee	October / 32 CE	161
2 Why Do You Seek To Kill Me?	J 7:10-24	The Temple, Jerusalem, Judea	Feast of Tabernacles, October / 32 CE	162
3 Where I Am Going You Cannot Come	J 7:25-36	The Temple, Jerusalem, Judea	Feast of Tabernacles, October / 32 CE	163
4 Come To Me, and Drink	J 7:37-44	The Temple, Jerusalem, Judea	Feast of Tabernacles, October / 32 CE	164
5 The Pharisees Are Divided	J 7:45 - 8:1	The Temple, Jerusalem, Judea	Feast of Tabernacles, October / 32 CE	164
Act 2 - Discussions In The Temple				
Scene 1 Jesus Forgives An Adulteress	J 8:2-11	The Temple, Jerusalem, Judea	October / 32 CE	165
2 My Testimony and Judgment Is True	J 8:12-20	The Temple Treasury, Jerusalem, Judea	October / 32 CE	166
3 You Are From Below, I Am From Above	J 8:21-30	The Temple Treasury, Jerusalem, Judea	October / 32 CE	167
4 Abraham Is Our Father	J 8:31-42	The Temple, Jerusalem, Judea	October / 32 CE	168
5 Your Father Is The Devil	J 8:43-47	The Temple, Jerusalem, Judea	October / 32 CE	169
6 You Have A Demon!	J 8:48-59	The Temple, Jerusalem, Judea	October / 32 CE	170
Act 3 - Healing A Man Born Blind				
Scene 1 Jesus Cures A Man Who Was Born Blind	J 9:1-12	Jerusalem, Judea	a Sabbath, October / 32 CE	171
2 The Pharisees Question The Man and His Parents	J 9:13-23	Jerusalem, Judea	a Sabbath, October / 32 CE	172
3 They Question The Man A Second Time	J 9:24-34	Jerusalem, Judea	a Sabbath, October / 32 CE	173
4 Do You Believe In The Son of Man?	J 9:35-41	Jerusalem, Judea	a Sabbath, October / 32 CE	173
Act 4 - The Good Shepherd				
Scene 1 I Am The Door of The Sheep	J 10:1-10	Jerusalem, Judea	a Sabbath, October / 32 CE	174
2 I Am The Good Shepherd	J 10:11-16	Jerusalem, Judea	a Sabbath, October / 32 CE	174
3 I Lay Down My Life To Take It Again	J 10:17-21	Jerusalem, Judea	a Sabbath, October / 32 CE	175
4 Repent And Bear Fruit, or Perish	L 13:1-9	Jerusalem, Judea	a Sabbath, October / 32 CE	175
Act 5 - The Feast of Dedication				
Scene 1 Depart From Me, All You Evildoers!	L 13:22-33 / J 10:22	Galilee	December / 32 CE	176
2 I And The Father Are One	J 10:23-30	The Temple, Jerusalem, Judea	Feast of Dedication, December / 32 CE	177
3 The Jews Try To Stone Jesus For Blasphemy	J 10:31-42	The Temple, Jerusalem, Judea	Feast of Dedication, December / 32 CE	177
Act 6 - The Resurrection of Lazarus				
Scene 1 Jesus Hears That Lazarus Has Died	J 11:1-16~, ~16	Galilee	winter / 33 CE	178
2 I Am The Resurrection and The Life	J 11:18-29, 31	Bethany, Judea	winter / 33 CE	179
3 Mary Goes To Meet Jesus	J 11:30, 32-37	Bethany, Judea	winter / 33 CE	179
4 Jesus Calls Lazarus Forth From The Tomb	J 11:17, 38-46	Bethany, Judea	winter / 33 CE	180
5 The Pharisees Plot To Kill Jesus	J 11:47-54	Jerusalem, Judea	winter / 33 CE	181

The Unified Four Gospel Harrmony

CHAPTER 6 - THE FINAL YEAR - *continued*	Verses	Location	Date	Page
Act 7 - Further Teachings				
Scene 1 Teachings On Divorce	M 19:1-8 / K 10:1-9	Judea	early spring / 33 CE	182
2 Teachings On Adultery	M 19:9-11 / K 10:10-12 / L 16:18	Judea	early spring / 33 CE	183
3 A Word About Eunuchs	M 19:12	Judea	early spring / 33 CE	183
4 Let The Children Come To Me	M 19:13-15 / K 10:13-16 / L 18:15-17	Judea	early spring / 33 CE	184
5 What Must I Do To Obtain Eternal Life?	M 19:16-22 / K 10:17-22 / L 18:18-23	Judea	early spring / 33 CE	185
6 It Is Hard For The Wealthy To Enter The Kingdom	M 19:23-26 / K 10:23-27 / L 18:24-27	Judea	early spring / 33 CE	186
7 What Will There Be For Us?	M 19:27-30 / K 10:28-31 / L 18:28-30	Judea	early spring / 33 CE	187
8 The Generous Landowner	M 20:1-16	Judea	early spring / 33 CE	188
9 The Unworthy Slaves	L 17:7-10	Judea	early spring / 33 CE	188
Act 8 - The Road To Jerusalem				
Scene 1 Shall We Command Fire From Heaven?	L 9:51-56	Samaria	late March / 33 CE	189
2 The Ten Lepers of Samaria	L 17:11-19	Samaria	late March / 33 CE	189
3 What Will Happen To The Son of Man	M 20:17-19 / K 10:32-34 / L 18:31-34	Samaria	late March / 33 CE	190
4 To Sit On My Right and On My Left	M 20:20-24 / K 10:35-41	Samaria	late March / 33 CE	191
5 The Greatest Is The One Who Serves	M 20:25-28 / K 10:42-45	Samaria	late March / 33 CE	191
6 Jesus Restores The Sight of Bartimaeus	M 20:29-34 / K 10:46-52 / L 18:35-43	Jericho, Judea	late March / 33 CE	192
7 The Salvation of Zaccheus	L 19:1-10	Jericho, Judea	late March / 33 CE	193
8 The Parable of The Good and Faithful Servants	M 25:14-30 / L 19:11-28	Judea	late March / 33 CE	194
Act 9 - Anointed For Burial				
Scene 1 Mary Anoints Jesus With Perfume	M 26:6-7 / K 14:3 / J 11:55 - 12:3	Bethany, Judea	Saturday evening, March 28th / 33 CE	196
2 The Disciples Question The Waste	M 26:8-13 / K 14:4-9 / J 12:4-11	Bethany, Judea	Saturday evening, March 28th / 33 CE	197

APPENDIX 1 - THE SYNOPTIC GOSPEL SCENE CONTENTS

CHAPTER 7 - THE FINAL WEEK	Verses	Location	Date	Page
Act 1 - Sunday - Arrival In Jerusalem				
Scene 1 The Lord Has Need of Your Donkey	M 21:1-3, 6 / K 11:1-3 / L 19:29-31 / J 12:12~	Bethphage, Judea	Sunday, March 29th / 33 CE	200
2 Jesus Rides on The Colt	M 21:4-5, 7 / K 11:4-7 / L 19:32-35 / J 12:14-15	Bethphage, Judea	Sunday, March 29th / 33 CE	201
3 The Approach To Jerusalem	M 21:8 / K 11:8 / L 19:36 / J 12:~12-13~	Bethphage, Judea	Sunday, March 29th / 33 CE	201
4 Hosanna, To The Son of David!	M 21:9 / K 11:9-10 / L 19:37-40 / J 12:~13, 16-19	Bethphage, Judea	Sunday, March 29th / 33 CE	202
5 Jesus Weeps For Jerusalem	L 19:41-44	Bethphage, Judea	Sunday, March 29th / 33 CE	203
6 Jesus Enters Jerusalem	M 21:10-11 / K 11:11~, 15~	Jerusalem, Judea	Sunday, March 29th / 33 CE	203
7 Jesus Cleanses The Temple, The Final Time	M 21:12-13 / K 11:~11~, ~15-18 / L 19:45-46	The Temple, Jerusalem, Judea	Sunday, March 29th / 33 CE	204
8 Healing In The Temple	M 21:14-17 / K 11:~11	The Temple, Jerusalem, Judea	Sunday, March 29th / 33 CE	204
Act 2 - Monday				
Scene 1 Jesus Curses A Fig Tree	M 21:18-22 / K 11:12-14, 20-24	east of Jerusalem, Judea	Monday, March 30th / 33 CE	205
2 Who Gave You This Authority?	M 21:23-27 / K 11:27-33 / L 20:1-8	The Temple, Jerusalem, Judea	Monday, March 30th / 33 CE	206
3 Who Did the Will of His Father?	M 21:28-32	The Temple, Jerusalem, Judea	Monday, March 30th / 33 CE	207
4 The Parable of The Evil Vine-Growers	M 21:33-46 / K 12:1-12~ / L 20:9-19	The Temple, Jerusalem, Judea	Monday, March 30th / 33 CE	208
5 To Serve Me, You Must Follow Me	J 12:20-26	The Temple, Jerusalem, Judea	Monday, March 30th / 33 CE	209
6 A Voice From Heaven	J 12:27-33	The Temple, Jerusalem, Judea	Monday, March 30th / 33 CE	210
7 Believe In The Light	J 12:34-43	The Temple, Jerusalem, Judea	Monday, March 30th / 33 CE	210
8 Believe In Me, and The One Who Sent Me	L 19:47-48 / J 12:44-50	The Temple, Jerusalem, Judea	Monday, March 30th / 33 CE	211
Act 3 - Tuesday				
Scene 1 Be Prepared For The Wedding Feast	M 22:1-14 / L 14:16-24; 17:20-21	The Temple, Jerusalem, Judea	Tuesday, March 31st / 33 CE	212
2 The Pharisees Plot To Trap Jesus	M 22:15-16~ / K 12:~12-13 / L 20:20	Jerusalem, Judea	Tuesday, March 31st / 33 CE	213
3 Is It Lawful To Pay Taxes To Caesar?	M 22:~16-22 / K 12:14-17 / L 20:21-26	The Temple, Jerusalem, Judea	Tuesday, March 31st / 33 CE	213
4 In the Next Life, Whose Wife Will She Be?	M 22:23-33 / K 12:18-27 / L 20:27-40	The Temple, Jerusalem, Judea	Tuesday, March 31st / 33 CE	214
5 The Greatest Commandment	M 22:34-40 / K 11:19; 12:28-34 / L 21:37	The Temple, Jerusalem, Judea	Tuesday, March 31st / 33 CE	215
Act 4 - Wednesday - Woe To The Pharisees				
Scene 1 How Is The Christ The Son of David?	M 22:41-46 / K 12:35-37 / L 20:41-44; 21:38	The Temple, Jerusalem, Judea	Wednesday, April 1st / 33 CE	216
2 Beware of The Scribes and The Pharisees	M 23:1-13 / K 12:38-39 / L 20:45-46	The Temple, Jerusalem, Judea	Wednesday, April 1st / 33 CE	217
3 The Hypocrisy Of The Scribes and The Pharisees	M 23:14-24 / K 12:40 / L 20:47	The Temple, Jerusalem, Judea	Wednesday, April 1st / 33 CE	218
4 First, Clean The Inside of The Cup	M 23:25-28	The Temple, Jerusalem, Judea	Wednesday, April 1st / 33 CE	219
5 You Shed The Blood of The Prophets	M 23:29-36 / L 11:47-51	The Temple, Jerusalem, Judea	Wednesday, April 1st / 33 CE	219
6 A Second Lament For Jerusalem	M 23:37-39 / L 13:34-35	The Temple, Jerusalem, Judea	Wednesday, April 1st / 33 CE	220
7 The Greatest Contributor To The Treasury	K 12:41-44 / L 21:1-4	The Temple, Jerusalem, Judea	Wednesday, April 1st / 33 CE	220

CHAPTER 7 - THE FINAL WEEK - continued	Verses	Location	Date	Page
Act 5 - Wednesday - The End of The Age				
Scene 1 The Temple Will Be Destroyed	M 24:1-2 / K 13:1-2 / L 21:5-6	The Temple, Jerusalem, Judea	Wednesday, April 1st / 33 CE	221
2 The Signs of The End of The Age	M 24:3-8 / K 13:3-8 / L 21:7-11	Mount of Olives, Jerusalem, Judea	Wednesday, April 1st / 33 CE	222
3 Your Testimony When They Persecute You	M 24:9~ / K 13:9, 11 / L 21:12-15	Mount of Olives, Jerusalem, Judea	Wednesday, April 1st / 33 CE	223
4 You Will Be Hated Because of My Name	M 24:~9-14 / K 13:10, 12-13 / L 21:16-19	Mount of Olives, Jerusalem, Judea	Wednesday, April 1st / 33 CE	223
5 Do Not Turn Back!	M 24:15-22 / K 13:14-20 / L 17:31-33; 21:20-24	Mount of Olives, Jerusalem, Judea	Wednesday, April 1st / 33 CE	224
6 False Christs Will Arise	M 24:23-27 / K 13:21-23 / L 17:22-24	Mount of Olives, Jerusalem, Judea	Wednesday, April 1st / 33 CE	225
7 Signs In The Sun, Moon and Stars	M 24:29-31 / K 13:24-27 / L 21:25-28	Mount of Olives, Jerusalem, Judea	Wednesday, April 1st / 33 CE	226
Act 6 - Wednesday - The Return				
Scene 1 The Parable of The Fig Tree	M 24:32-39 / K 13:28-32 / L 17:25-30; 21:29-33	Mount of Olives, Jerusalem, Judea	Wednesday, April 1st / 33 CE	227
2 One Will Be Taken, and The Other Will Be Left	M 24:28, 40-42 / K 13:33 / L 17:34-37	Mount of Olives, Jerusalem, Judea	Wednesday, April 1st / 33 CE	228
3 Be On the Alert!	M 24:43-44 / K 13:34-37 / L 12:39-40; 21:34-36	Mount of Olives, Jerusalem, Judea	Wednesday, April 1st / 33 CE	229
4 Be Dressed In Readiness	M 24:45-51 / L 12:35-38, 41-48	Mount of Olives, Jerusalem, Judea	Wednesday, April 1st / 33 CE	230
5 The Lamps of The Ten Virgins	M 25:1-13	Mount of Olives, Jerusalem, Judea	Wednesday, April 1st / 33 CE	231
6 Separating The Sheep From The Goats	M 25:31 - 26:2 / K 14:1~ / L 22:1	Mount of Olives, Jerusalem, Judea	Wednesday, April 1st / 33 CE	232
7 Judas Plots With The Jews To Betray Jesus	M 26:3-5, 14-16 / K 14:~1-2, 10-11 / L 22:2-6 / J 13:2	Jerusalem, Judea	Wednesday, April 1st / 33 CE	233
Act 7 - Thursday - The Last Supper				
Scene 1 Preparing The Venue	M 26:17-19 / K 14:12-16 / L 22:7-13 / J 13:1	Jerusalem, Judea	Thursday, April 2nd / 33 CE	234
2 The Last Supper Begins	M 26:20 / K 14:17 / L 22:14-16, 24-30	A house in Jerusalem, Judea	Thursday evening, April 2nd / 33 CE	235
3 Jesus Washes His Apostles' Feet	J 13:3-20; 15:3	A house in Jerusalem, Judea	Thursday evening, April 2nd / 33 CE	236
4 One Of You Will Betray Me	M 26:21-24 / K 14:18-21 / L 22:21-23 / J 13:21-22	A house in Jerusalem, Judea	Thursday evening, April 2nd / 33 CE	237
5 Judas Is Revealed	M 26:25 / J 13:23-32	A house in Jerusalem, Judea	Thursday evening, April 2nd / 33 CE	238
6 The Blood of The New Covenant	M 26:26-29 / K 14:22-25 / L 22:17-20	A house in Jerusalem, Judea	Thursday evening, April 2nd / 33 CE	239
7 My New Commandment: Love One Another	J 13:34-35	A house in Jerusalem, Judea	Thursday evening, April 2nd / 33 CE	239
8 Peter, You Will Deny Me Three Times	M 26:31-35 / K 14:27-31 / L 22:31-34 / J 13:33, 36-38	A house in Jerusalem, Judea	Thursday evening, April 2nd / 33 CE	240
9 Two Swords Are Enough	L 22:35-38	A house in Jerusalem, Judea	Thursday evening, April 2nd / 33 CE	241

APPENDIX 1 - THE SYNOPTIC GOSPEL SCENE CONTENTS

CHAPTER 7 - THE FINAL WEEK - continued

Act 8 - The Holy Spirit and The Father

	Verses	Location	Date	Page
Scene 1 I Am The Way, and The Truth, and The Life	J 14:1-12	A house in Jerusalem, Judea	Thursday evening, April 2nd / 33 CE	242
2 The Holy Spirit Helper	J 14:13-26	A house in Jerusalem, Judea	Thursday evening, April 2nd / 33 CE	243
3 I Go Away, and I Will Come To You	J 14:27-31~	A house in Jerusalem, Judea	Thursday evening, April 2nd / 33 CE	244
4 Abide In My Love, and Bear Fruit	J 15:1-2, 4-11	A house in Jerusalem, Judea	Thursday evening, April 2nd / 33 CE	244
5 My Commandment Again: Love One Another	J 15:12-17	A house in Jerusalem, Judea	late Thursday evening, April 2nd / 33 CE	245
6 The World Hates Me and My Father	J 5:18-25	A house in Jerusalem, Judea	late Thursday evening, April 2nd / 33 CE	245
7 More About The Holy Spirit of Truth	J 15:26 - 16:15	A house in Jerusalem, Judea	late Thursday evening, April 2nd / 33 CE	246
8 I Am Going To The Father	J 16:16-33	A house in Jerusalem, Judea	late Thursday evening, April 2nd / 33 CE	247
9 Jesus Prays To The Father	M 26:30 / K 14:26 / L 22:39 / J 14:~31; 17:1 - 18:1~	A house in Jerusalem, Judea	late Thursday evening, April 2nd / 33 CE	248

CHAPTER 8 - TRIALS AND CRUCIFIXION

Act 1 - Jesus Is Arrested at Gethsemane

	Verses	Location	Date	Page
Scene 1 The First Agonized Prayer of Jesus	M 26:36-39 / K 14:32-36 / L 22:40-44 / J 18:~1-2	Garden of Gethsemane, Mount of Olives, Jerusalem	midnight - Friday morning, April 3rd / 33 CE	252
2 Jesus Prays A Second Time	M 26:40-42 / K 14:37-39 / L 22:45-46	Garden of Gethsemane, Mount of Olives, Jerusalem	early Friday morning, April 3rd / 33 CE	253
3 The Third Prayer of Jesus In The Garden	M 26:43-46 / K 14:40-42	Garden of Gethsemane, Mount of Olives, Jerusalem	early Friday morning, April 3rd / 33 CE	253
4 Judas Leads The Authorities To Jesus	M 26:47-49 / K 14:43-45 / L 22:47-48 / J 18:3-5~, 6-9	Garden of Gethsemane, Mount of Olives, Jerusalem	early Friday morning, April 3rd / 33 CE	254
5 Peter Defends Jesus With A Sword	M 26:50-54 / K 14:46-47 / L 22:49-51 / J 18:~5, 10-11	Garden of Gethsemane, Mount of Olives, Jerusalem	early Friday morning, April 3rd / 33 CE	255
6 Jesus Is Arrested	M 26:55-56 / K 14:48-52 / L 22:52-53 / J 18:12	Garden of Gethsemane, Mount of Olives, Jerusalem	early Friday morning, April 3rd / 33 CE	256

Act 2 - Jesus Is Accused by The High Priest

	Verses	Location	Date	Page
Scene 1 First, To The House of Annas	M 26:57 / K 14:53 / L 22:54~ / J 18:13-14, 19-24	House of Annas, Jerusalem, Judea	early Friday morning, April 3rd / 33 CE	257
2 Then To The High Priest, Caiaphas	M 26:58-63~ / K 14:~54, 55-61~ / L 22:~54 / J 18:15-16	Palace of Caiaphas, Jerusalem, Judea	early Friday morning, April 3rd / 33 CE	258
3 Peter's First Denial of Jesus	M 26:69-70 / K 14:~54, 66-68 / L 22:55-57 / J 18:17-18	Palace of Caiaphas, Jerusalem, Judea	early Friday morning, April 3rd / 33 CE	259
4 Peter's Second Denial	M 26:71-72 / K 14:69-70~ / L 22:58 / J 18:~25-26	Palace of Caiaphas, Jerusalem, Judea	early Friday morning, April 3rd / 33 CE	259
5 Jesus Is Charged With Blasphemy	M 26:~63-66 / K 14:~61-64	Palace of Caiaphas, Jerusalem, Judea	early Friday morning, April 3rd / 33 CE	260
6 Jesus Is Beaten	M 26:67-68 / K 14:65 / L 22:63-65	Palace of Caiaphas, Jerusalem, Judea	early Friday morning, April 3rd / 33 CE	260
7 Peter Denies Jesus The Third Time	M 26:73-75 / K 14:~70-72 / L 22:59-62 / J 18:25~, 27	Palace of Caiaphas, Jerusalem, Judea	early Friday morning, April 3rd / 33 CE	261

Act 3 - Jesus Is Questioned by The Sanhedrin

	Verses	Location	Date	Page
Scene 1 The Sanhedrin Council Condemns Jesus	M 27:1 / K 15:1~ / L 22:66-71	Sanhedrin Council Chamber, The Temple, Jerusalem	early Friday morning, April 3rd / 33 CE	262
2 The Jews Take Jesus To The Roman Governor	M 27:2 / K 15:~1 / L 23:1 / J 18:28	The Praetorium, Jerusalem, Judea	early Friday morning, April 3rd / 33 CE	262

CHAPTER 8 - TRIALS & CRUCIFIXION -continued

	Verses	Location	Date	Page
Act 4 - Jesus Is Questioned by The Romans				
Scene 1 Pilate Hears The Accusation Against Jesus	L 23:2 / J 18:29-33~	The Praetorium, Jerusalem, Judea	early Friday morning, April 3rd / 33 CE	263
2 Are You The King of The Jews?	M 27:11 / K 15:2 / L 23:3 / J 18:~33-38~	The Praetorium, Jerusalem, Judea	early Friday morning, April 3rd / 33 CE	264
3 Pilate Finds No Guilt In Jesus	M 27:12-14 / K 15:3-5 / L 23:4-7 / J 18:~38	The Praetorium, Jerusalem, Judea	early Friday morning, April 3rd / 33 CE	265
4 Herod, Tetrarch of Galilee, Questions Jesus	L 23:8-12	Hasmonean Palace, Jerusalem, Judea	early Friday morning, April 3rd / 33 CE	266
5 We Romans Find No Guilt In This Man	L 23:13-16	The Praetorium, Jerusalem, Judea	Friday morning, April 3rd / 33 CE	266
Act 5 - Jesus Is Sentenced To Die				
Scene 1 Shall I Release For You Jesus, or Barabbas?	M 27:15-18, 20-21 / K 15:6-11 / L 23:17-19 / J 18:39-40	The Praetorium, Jerusalem, Judea	Friday morning, April 3rd / 33 CE	267
2 The Jews Cry Out To Crucify Jesus	M 27:19, 22-23 / K 15:12-14 / L 23:20-23	The Praetorium, Jerusalem, Judea	Friday morning, April 3rd / 33 CE	268
3 Pilate Sentences Jesus To Die	M 27:24-26~ / K 15:15~ / L 23:24-25	The Praetorium, Jerusalem, Judea	Friday morning, April 3rd / 33 CE	268
4 The Soldiers Mock and Scourge Jesus	M 27:~26~, 27-30 / K 15:~15~, 16-19 / J 19:1-3	The Praetorium, Jerusalem, Judea	Friday morning, April 3rd / 33 CE	269
5 Pilate Tries Again To Release Jesus	J 19:4-13	The Praetorium, Jerusalem, Judea	Friday morning, April 3rd / 33 CE	270
6 Jesus Is Handed Over To Be Crucified	M 17:~26 / K 15:~15 / J 19:14-16	The Praetorium, Jerusalem, Judea	Friday morning, April 3rd / 33 CE	271
7 Judas The Betrayer Hangs Himself	M 27:3-10	Jerusalem, Judea	Friday morning, April 3rd / 33 CE	271
Act 6 - The Crucifixion of Jesus Christ				
Scene 1 Simon of Cyrene Carries The Cross of Jesus	M 27:31-32 / K 15:20-21 / L 23:26, 32 / J 19:17~	Jerusalem, Judea	Friday morning, April 3rd / 33 CE	272
2 The Walk To Golgotha	L 23:27-31	Jerusalem, Judea	Friday morning, April 3rd / 33 CE	272
3 Jesus Is Crucified	M 27:33-34 / K 15:22-24~, 25~ / L 23:33~, 34~, 35-36 / J 19:~17	Golgotha, Jerusalem, Judea	Friday morning, April 3rd / 33 CE	273
4 The Soldiers Divide His Clothing	M 27:35-36 / K 15:~24, ~25 / L 23:~34, 37 / J 19:23-25~	Golgotha, Jerusalem, Judea	Friday morning, April 3rd / 33 CE	274
5 Jesus Is Crucified Between Two Criminals	M 27:38 / K 15:27-28 / L 23:~33 / J 19:18	Golgotha, Jerusalem, Judea	Friday morning, April 3rd / 33 CE	274
6 Pilate's Inscription of The Charge Against Jesus	M 27:37 / K 15:26 / L 23:38 / J 19:19-22	Golgotha, Jerusalem, Judea	Friday morning, April 3rd / 33 CE	275
7 Jesus Entrusts His Mother To John	J 19:~25-27	Golgotha, Jerusalem, Judea	Friday morning, April 3rd / 33 CE	275
8 Let This Christ Save Himself!	M 27:39-43 / K 15:29-32~	Golgotha, Jerusalem, Judea	Friday morning, April 3rd / 33 CE	276
9 The Last Words of The Two Criminals	M 27:44 / K 15:~32 / L 23:39-43	Golgotha, Jerusalem, Judea	Friday morning, April 3rd / 33 CE	276
Act 7 - The Death of Jesus Christ				
Scene 1 Darkness Falls Over The Land	M 27:45-47, 49 / K 15:33-35, ~36 / L 23:44-45~	Golgotha, Jerusalem, Judea	noon to 3:00 pm, Friday afternoon, April 3rd	277
2 Jesus Dies On The Cross	M 27:48, 50 / K 15:36~, 37 / L 23:46 / J 19:28-30	Golgotha, Jerusalem, Judea	3:00 pm, Friday afternoon, April 3rd / 33 CE	277
3 An Earthquake At The Death of Jesus	M 27:51, 54-56 / K 15:38-41 / L 23:~45, 47-49	Jerusalem, Judea	3:00 pm, Friday afternoon, April 3rd / 33 CE	278
4 The Body of Jesus Is Taken Down	K 15:~42 / J 19:31-34, 36-37	Golgotha, Jerusalem, Judea	late Friday afternoon, April 3rd / 33 CE	279
Act 8 - Jesus Is Laid In Joseph's Tomb				
Scene 1 Joseph Asks Pilate For The Body of Jesus	M 27:57-58 / K 15:42~, 43-45 / L 23:50-52, 54 / J 19:38~	The Praetorium, Jerusalem, Judea	late Friday afternoon, April 3rd / 33 CE	280
2 The Body of Jesus Is Placed In Joseph's Tomb	M 27:59-61 / K 15:46-47 / L 23:53, 55-56 / J 19:~38-42	The Garden Tomb, Jerusalem, Judea	late Friday afternoon, April 3rd / 33 CE	281
3 Roman Soldiers Guard The Tomb	M 27:62-66	The Garden Tomb, Jerusalem, Judea	Friday evening, April 3rd / 33 CE	282

APPENDIX 1 - THE SYNOPTIC GOSPEL SCENE CONTENTS

CHAPTER 8 - TRIALS & CRUCIFIXION -continued	Verses	Location	Date	Page
Act 9 - The Resurrection of Jesus Christ				
Scene 1 An Earthquake At The Resurrection of Jesus	M 27:52-53; 28:2-4	The Garden Tomb, Jerusalem, Judea	early Sunday morning, April 5th / 33 CE	283
2 The Soldiers Are Paid To Lie	M 28:11-15	Jerusalem, Judea	early Sunday morning, April 5th / 33 CE	283

CHAPTER 9 - APPEARANCES and ASCENSION	Verses	Location	Date	
Act 1 - Sunday Morning				
Scene 1 The Women Arrive At The Tomb	M 28:1 / K 16:1-4 / L 24:1-2, ~10~ / J 20:1	The Garden Tomb, Jerusalem, Judea	early Sunday morning, April 5th / 33 CE	285
2 Two Angels Greet The Women At The Tomb	M 28:5-8 / K 16:5-8 / L 24:3-9~	The Garden Tomb, Jerusalem, Judea	early Sunday morning, April 5th / 33 CE	286
3 The Women Tell The Apostles	L 24:~9-11 / J 20:2	Jerusalem, Judea	early Sunday morning, April 5th / 33 CE	287
4 Peter and John Run To The Tomb	L 24:12 / J 20:3-10	The Garden Tomb, Jerusalem, Judea	early Sunday morning, April 5th / 33 CE	287
5 Jesus Appears To Mary Magdalene	M 28:9-10 / K 16:9-11 / J 20:11-18	The Garden Tomb, Jerusalem, Judea	Sunday morning, April 5th / 33 CE	288
Act 2 - Appearances To The Apostles				
Scene 1 Jesus Walks To Emmaus With Two Disciples	K 16:12 / L 24:13-29	west of Jerusalem, Judea	Sunday afternoon, April 5th / 33 CE	289
2 They Finally Recognize Jesus	K 16:13~ / L 24:30-33~	Emmaus, Judea	Sunday, late afternoon, April 5th / 33 CE	290
3 Jesus Appears To The Ten Apostles	K 16:~13-14 / L 24:~33-37 / J 20:19	Jerusalem, Judea	Sunday evening, April 5th / 33 CE	291
4 Jesus Proves That His Body Is Real	L 24:38-43 / J 20:20	Jerusalem, Judea	Sunday evening, April 5th / 33 CE	292
5 Jesus Bestows The Holy Spirit On The Apostles	J 20:21-25	Jerusalem, Judea	Sunday evening, April 5th / 33 CE	292
6 Jesus Manifests Himself To Thomas	J 20:26-29	Jerusalem, Judea	Monday, April 13th / 33 CE	293
Act 3 - Reunion In Galilee				
Scene 1 Jesus Meets His Apostles At The Mountain	M 28:16-17	Galilee	April /33 CE	294
2 Appearance At The Sea of Galilee	J 21:1-6	near Tiberius, Sea of Galilee, Galilee	late April / 33 CE	294
3 A Catch of One Hundred and Fifty-Three Fish	J 21:7-14	near Tiberius, Sea of Galilee, Galilee	late April / 33 CE	295
4 Peter, Tend My Sheep	J 21:15-23	near Tiberius, Sea of Galilee, Galilee	late April / 33 CE	296
5 The Promise of The Father	L 24:44-49	near Tiberius, Sea of Galilee, Galilee	late April / 33 CE	297
Act 4 - The Great Commission				
Scene 1 Jesus Sends The Eleven To Preach The Gospel	M 28:18-20~ / K 16:15-16	Jerusalem, Judea	Friday, May 15th / 33 CE	298
2 These Signs Will Accompany You	M 28:~20 / K 16:17-18	Jerusalem, Judea	Friday, May 15th / 33 CE	298
Act 5 - The Ascension of Jesus Christ				
Scene 1 Jesus Christ Ascends To Heaven	K 16:19 / L 24:50-53	Bethany, Judea	Friday, May 15th / 33 CE	299
2 They Went Out and Preached Everywhere	K 16:20	-	-	299
Act 6 - Epilogue				
Scene 1 Final Words	J 1:11-13, 16-18; 19:35; 20:30-31; 21:24-25	-	-	300

~ End ~

Appendix 2

Gospel Verse Cross-Reference

APPENDIX 2 - GOSPEL VERSE CROSS-REFERENCE

Bold Verses are part of a parallel set with another Gospel(s)   TSG = The Synoptic Gospel Verse Reference

1	TSG	3	TSG	4	TSG	5	TSG	6	TSG	7	TSG	8	TSG	9	TSG	10	TSG
1:1	021.1	2:10	161.10	**4:4**	232.2	**5:13**	422.1-3	5:47	432.4	**6:33**	439.11	**8:4**	355.4-5	**9:4**	382.3	9:38	491.4
1:2	021.2-4	2:11	161.11-12	**4:5**	232.3	5:14	423.1-2	5:48	432.12	6:34	439.13	**8:5**	451.1,3	**9:5**	382.4	**10:1**	491.5
1:3	021.5-7	2:12	161.13	**4:6**	232.4-5	**5:15**	423.3-4	6:1	433.1	**7:1**	441.1	8:6	451.2	**9:6**	382.5	**10:2**	412.5-8
1:4	021.8-10	2:13	162.1	**4:7**	232.6	5:16	423.5	6:2	433.2	7:2	441.2	8:7	451.4	**9:7**	382.6	**10:3**	412.9-14
1:5	021.11-13	2:14	162.2	**4:8**	232.7	5:17	425.1	6:3	433.3	**7:3**	441.3	8:8	451.5	**9:8**	382.7	**10:4**	412.15-16
1:6	021.14-15	2:15	162.3 / 164.2	**4:9**	232.8-9	5:18	425.2	6:4	433.3-4	**7:4**	441.4	8:9	451.6	**9:9**	383.1-2	10:5	492.1
1:7	021.16-18	2:16	163.1	**4:10**	232.10	5:19	425.3-4	6:5	434.1	**7:5**	441.5	**8:10**	451.7	**9:10**	384.1-2	10:6	492.1
1:8	021.19-21	2:17	163.2	**4:11**	232.11-12	5:20	425.5	6:6	434.2	7:6	443.1	8:11	451.8	**9:11**	384.3	10:7	492.2
1:9	021.22-24	2:18	163.2	**4:12**	331.6	5:21	426.1-2	6:7	434.3	7:7	442.4	8:12	451.9	**9:12**	384.4	10:8	492.3-4
1:10	021:25-27	2:19	164.1	4:13	341.3 / 343.1	5:22	426.3-5	6:8	434.3-4	7:8	442.5	8:13	451.10-11	**9:13**	384.5-6	**10:9**	492.6
1:11	021.28	2:20	164.1	4:14	343.2	5:23	426.6	6:9	435.1	7:9	442.7	**8:14**	352.2	**9:14**	385.1-2	**10:10**	492.6
1:12	021.29-30	2:21	164.3	4:15	343.2	5:24	426.6-7	6:10	435.2	7:10	442.6	8:15	352.4-5	**9:15**	385.3-4	**10:11**	493.1
1:13	021.31-33	2:22	164.4-5	4:16	343.3	**5:25**	427.2-3	6:11	435.3	7:11	442.8	**8:16**	353.1-2	**9:16**	386.1	10:12	493.2
1:14	021.34-36	2:23	164.5-6	**4:17**	343.4	5:26	427.4	6:12	435.4	7:12	442.9	8:17	353.3	**9:17**	386.2-3	10:13	493.3
1:15	021.37-39	**3:1**	211.1,4,7	**4:18**	344.1	5:27	428.1	6:13	435.5-6	7:13	442.10	**8:18**	481.1	**9:18**	484.3-4	**10:14**	493.4
1:16	021.40	3:2	211.7	**4:19**	344.10	5:28	428.2	**6:14**	435.7	7:14	442.11	**8:19**	538.1-2	9:19	484.5	10:15	493.5
1:17	021.41-43	**3:3**	211.8-9	**4:20**	344.11	5:29	428.3	**6:15**	435.8	7:15	443.2	**8:20**	538.3	**9:20**	485.2,4	10:16	494.1
1:18	141.1	**3:4**	211.11	**4:21**	345.1-2	5:30	428.4	6:16	436.1	**7:16**	443.3-4	**8:21**	538.4	**9:21**	485.4	10:17	494.2
1:19	141.2	**3:5**	211.12	**4:22**	345.3	5:31	428.5	6:17	436.2	7:17	443.5	**8:22**	538.5	**9:22**	485.5,9,12	10:18	494.3
1:20	141.3	**3:6**	211.13	**4:23**	354.4-5	5:32	428.6-7	6:18	436.2-3	**7:18**	443.6	**8:23**	481.2	**9:23**	486.4	**10:19**	494.4
1:21	141.4	**3:7**	212.1	4:24	354.6	5:33	429.1	6:19	438.1	7:19	443.8	**8:24**	481.4-6	**9:24**	486.5-6	10:20	494.5
1:22	141.5	**3:8**	212.2	4:25	354.7	5:34	429.2	**6:20**	438.2-3	7:20	443.7	**8:25**	481.6	**9:25**	486.7-9	10:21	495.1
1:23	141.5	**3:9**	212.3	**5:1**	412.1,3	5:35	429.2-3	**6:21**	438.4	7:21	444.1	**8:26**	481.7-9	9:26	486.11	10:22	495.2
1:24	141.6	**3:10**	212.4	**5:2**	421.3	5:36	429.4	**6:22**	424.1	7:22	444.2	**8:27**	481.11	9:27	487.1	10:23	495.3
1:25	141.7 / 145.1	**3:11**	214.1-3	5:3	421.5	5:37	429.5	**6:23**	424.2-3	7:23	444.3-4	**8:28**	482.1-3,6	9:28	487.2	**10:24**	495.4
2:1	161.1	**3:12**	214.4-5	5:4	421.6	5:38	431.1	6:24	575.4-5	**7:24**	444.5	8:29	482.7-8	9:29	487.3	10:25	495.5-6
2:2	161.1	**3:13**	221.1	5:5	421.7	**5:39**	431.1-2	6:25	439.1	**7:25**	444.6	8:30	483.1	9:30	487.3-4	**10:26**	495.7
2:3	161.2	3:14	221.5	**5:6**	421.8	5:40	431.3	6:26	439.2-3	**7:26**	444.7	8:31	483.1-2	9:31	487.4	**10:27**	495.8
2:4	161.3	**3:15**	221.6-7	5:7	421.10	5:41	431.4	6:27	439.4	**7:27**	444.8	8:32	483.3-4	9:32	487.5	**10:28**	495.9-10
2:5	161.4	**3:16**	222.2-3	5:8	421.11	**5:42**	431.5	6:28	439.6-7	7:28	445.1	8:33	483.5	9:33	487.6	**10:29**	495.11
2:6	161.5	**3:17**	222.4	5:9	421.12	5:43	432.1	6:29	439.7	7:29	445.1	8:34	483.6,9	9:34	487.7	**10:30**	495.12
2:7	161.6	**4:1**	231.1-2	5:10	421.13	**5:44**	432.2	6:30	439.8			8:1	445.2	9:35	491.1-2	**10:31**	495.12
2:8	161.7-8	**4:2**	231.3	**5:11**	421.14	5:45	432.7-8	6:31	439.9			8:2	355.1	9:2	381.3,6	**10:32**	496.1
2:9	161.9	**4:3**	232.1	**5:12**	421.15	5:46	432.10	6:32	439.10			8:3	355.2-3	9:3	382.1-2	**10:33**	496.2

MATTHEW 10 — MATTHEW 19

11	TSG	12	TSG	13	TSG	13	TSG	14	TSG	15	TSG	16	TSG	17	TSG	19	TSG
10:34	497.3	11:28	455.6	12:33	464.1	13:19	473.2	13:55	489.2-3	14:33	514.7	15:33	525.4	17:2	534.2-3	18:11	571.9
10:35	497.4,6	11:29	455.7	12:34	464.2-3	13:20	473.3	13:56	489.4-5	14:34	515.1	15:34	525.5,8	17:3	534.4	18:12	571.2
10:36	497.7	11:30	455.7	12:35	464.3	13:21	473.3-4	13:57	489.5-6	14:35	515.2-3	15:35	525.6	17:4	534.7	18:13	571.3
10:37	498.1	12:1	387.1	12:36	464.4	13:22	473.5	13:58	489.15	14:36	515.4	15:36	525.6-7	17:5	534.9-10	18:14	544.3
10:38	498.2	12:2	387.2	12:37	464.4	13:23	473.6	14:1	553.1	15:1	521.1,6	15:37	525.9	17:6	534.11	18:15	546.1-2
10:39	498.3	12:3	387.3	12:38	465.1	13:24	474.4	14:2	553.2	15:2	521.6-7	15:38	525.10	17:7	534.12	18:16	546.4
10:40	498.4	12:4	387.4-5	12:39	465.2	13:25	474.5	14:3	331.1-2	15:3	521.8	15:39	526.1	17:8	534.13	18:17	546.5-6
10:41	498.5-6	12:5	387.6	12:40	465.3	13:26	474.6	14:4	331.2	15:4	521.10	16:1	526.2	17:9	534.14	18:18	546.7
10:42	498.7	12:6	387.7	12:41	465.4-5	13:27	474.7	14:5	331.3-4	15:5	521.11	16:2	526.3-4	17:10	535.1	18:19	546.8
11:1	498.8	12:7	387.8	12:42	465.6-7	13:28	474.8-9	14:6	391.1-2	15:6	521.11-12	16:3	526.5-6	17:11	535.2	18:20	546.9
11:2	361.1	12:8	387.10	12:43	466.1	13:29	474.10	14:7	391.2-3	15:7	521.13	16:4	526.7-8 / 527.1	17:12	535.4-5	18:21	547.1
11:3	361.2	12:9	388.1	12:44	466.2	13:30	474.11	14:8	391.5	15:8	521.13	16:5	527.1-2	17:13	535.6	18:22	547.2
11:4	361.4	12:10	388.1-3	12:45	466.3-4	13:31	475.1-2	14:9	391.6	15:9	521.13	16:6	527.3	17:14	536.3-4	18:23	547.3
11:5	361.4	12:11	388.6	12:46	469.1-2	13:32	475.3	14:10	392.1	15:10	521.14	16:7	527.4	17:15	536.4-5	18:24	547.4
11:6	361.5	12:12	388.7-8	12:47	469.3	13:33	476.1-2	14:11	392.2	15:11	521.15	16:8	527.5	17:16	536.7	18:25	547.5
11:7	362.1-2	12:13	388.9-10	12:48	469.4	13:34	476.10	14:12	392.3	15:12	521.17	16:9	527.6,8	17:17	536.8-9	18:26	547.6
11:8	362.3-4	12:14	388.12	12:49	469.5	13:35	476.12	14:13	392.4 / 511.4-5	15:13	521.18	16:10	527.9	17:18	536.15-16	18:27	547.7
11:9	362.5	12:15	388.13-14 / 411.2	12:50	469.7	13:36	476.13 / 477.1	14:14	511.6-8	15:14	521.19-20	16:11	527.10	17:19	537.1	18:28	547.8
11:10	362.6					13:1	471.1	13:37	477.2	14:15	512.1	15:15	522.1	16:12	527.11	17:20	537.2,4	18:29	547.9
11:11	362.7-8	12:16	411.3	13:2	471.2-3	13:38	477.2-4	14:16	512.2	15:16	522.2	16:13	531.1-2	17:21	537.5	18:30	547.10
11:12	362.9	12:17	411.4	13:3	471.3-4	13:39	477.4-5	14:17	512.8	15:17	522.3	16:14	531.3	17:22	541.1	18:31	547.11
11:13	362.10	12:18	411.4-5	13:4	471.5	13:40	477.6	14:18	512.9	15:18	522.4	16:15	531.4	17:23	541.1-2,4	18:32	547.12
11:14	362.11	12:19	411.6	13:5	471.6	13:41	477.7	14:19	512.10-13	15:19	522.5	16:16	531.5	17:24	542.1	18:33	547.13
11:15	362.12	12:20	411.7	13:6	471.7	13:42	477.7	14:20	512.14-16	15:20	522.6-7	16:17	531.6	17:25	542.1-2	18:34	547.14
11:16	363.1-2	12:21	411.8	13:7	471.8	13:43	477.8-9	14:21	512.17	15:21	523.1	16:18	531.7	17:26	542.3	18:35	547.15
11:17	363.2	12:22	461.3	13:8	471.9	13:44	476.3	14:22	513.1-2	15:22	523.3-4	16:19	531.8	17:27	542.4-5	19:1	671.1
11:18	363.3	12:23	461.4	13:9	471.10	13:45	476.4	14:23	513.3-4	15:23	523.5-6	16:20	531.9	18:1	543.3	19:2	671.1-2
11:19	363.4-5	12:24	461.5-6	13:10	472.1	13:46	476.4	14:24	513.4-5	15:24	523.7	16:21	532.1	18:2	543.5	19:3	671.3
11:20	454.1	12:25	462.1-4	13:11	472.2	13:47	476.5	14:25	513.6	15:25	523.8	16:22	532.2	18:3	543.6	19:4	671.4,7
11:21	454.2	12:26	462.5	13:12	473.9-10	13:48	476.5-6	14:26	513.8	15:26	523.9	16:23	532.3-4	18:4	543.7	19:5	671.8
11:22	454.3	12:27	462.6	13:13	472.3	13:49	476.7	14:27	513.9	15:27	523.10	16:24	533.1	18:5	543.8	19:6	671.8-9
11:23	454.4	12:28	462.7	13:14	472.4	13:50	476.7	14:28	514.1	15:28	523.11-12	16:25	533.2	18:6	544.2	19:7	671.5
11:24	454.5	12:29	462.10	13:15	472.5-6	13:51	476.8	14:29	514.1-2	15:29	524.1-2	16:26	533.3-4	18:7	545.1	19:8	671.6
11:25	455.1	12:30	463.1	13:16	472.7	13:52	476.9	14:30	514.3	15:30	524.2	16:27	533.6	18:8	545.2-4	19:9	672.2
11:26	455.2	12:31	463.2-3	13:17	472.8	13:53	477.10	14:31	514.4	15:31	524.8,10	16:28	533.7	18:9	545.5	19:10	672.5
11:27	455.3-5	12:32	463.4-5	13:18	473.1	13:54	488.1-2 / 489.1	14:32	514.5	15:32	525.2-3	17:1	534.1	18:10	544.1	19:11	672.6

20	TSG	21	TSG	21	TSG	22	TSG	23	TSG	24	TSG	24	TSG	25	TSG	26	TSG
19:12	673.1-3	20:16	678.14	21:16	718.2-3	22:4	731.5	22:38	735.6	23:26	744.2	24:21	755.10	25:4	765.2	25:38	766.7
19:13	674.1-2	20:17	683.1-3	21:17	718.4	22:5	731.4,6,8	22:39	735.7	23:27	744.3	24:22	755.11	25:5	765.3	25:39	766.8
19:14	674.3	20:18	683.3-4	21:18	721.1-2	22:6	731.9	22:40	735.8	23:28	744.4	24:23	756.2	25:6	765.4	25:40	766.9
19:15	674.6	20:19	683.5-6	21:19	721.2-5	22:7	731.10	22:41	741.2	23:29	745.1	24:24	756.3	25:7	765.5	25:41	766.10
19:16	675.1	20:20	684.1	21:20	721.7	22:8	731.11	22:42	741.2-3	23:30	745.2	24:25	756.4	25:8	765.5	25:42	766.11
19:17	675.2-3	20:21	684.2-3	21:21	721.8-10	22:9	731.11	22:43	741.4-5	23:31	745.3	24:26	756.5	25:9	765.6	25:43	766.12
19:18	675.4-8	20:22	684.4-5	21:22	721.11	22:10	731.14	22:44	741.5	23:32	745.7	24:27	756.6	25:10	765.7	25:44	766.13
19:19	675.10-11	20:23	684.6-7	21:23	722.1-3	22:11	731.15	22:45	741.6	23:33	745.8	24:28	762.5	25:11	765.8	25:45	766.14
19:20	675.12	20:24	684.8	21:24	722.4	22:12	731.15	22:46	741.7	23:34	745.4-5	24:29	757.1-3	25:12	765.8	25:46	766.16
19:21	675.13-14	20:25	685.1	21:25	722.5-6	22:13	731.16	23:1	742.1	23:35	745.5-6	24:30	757.5-6	25:13	765.9	26:1	766.14
19:22	675.15	20:26	685.2	21:26	722.7	22:14	731.17	23:2	742.1	23:36	745.7	24:31	757.7	25:14	688.2-3	26:2	766.14
19:23	676.1	20:27	685.2	21:27	722.8-9	22:15	732.1	23:3	742.1-2	23:37	746.1-2	24:32	761.1	25:15	688.4-5	26:3	767.1
19:24	676.3	20:28	685.3	21:28	723.1	22:16	732.2 / 733.1	23:4	742.3	23:38	746.3	24:33	761.2	25:16	688.7	26:4	767.1
19:25	676.4	20:29	686.1	21:29	723.2	22:17	733.2	23:5	742.4	23:39	746.4	24:34	761.3	25:17	688.8	26:5	767.2
19:26	676.5	20:30	686.1-3	21:30	723.3	22:18	733.3	23:6	742.5	24:1	751.1	24:35	761.4	25:18	688.9	26:6	691.5
19:27	677.1	20:31	686.4	21:31	723.4-5	22:19	733.3-4	23:7	742.5	24:2	751.3	24:36	761.5	25:19	688.10-11	26:7	691.7
19:28	677.2	20:32	686.5,8	21:32	723.6-7	22:20	733.4	23:8	742.6	24:3	752.1-2	24:37	761.7	25:20	688.12	26:8	692.1
19:29	677.3,5	20:33	686.8	21:33	724.1-2	22:21	733.4-5	23:9	742.7	24:4	752.3	24:38	761.7	25:21	688.13	26:9	692.1-2
19:30	677.6	20:34	686.9-10	21:34	724.3	22:22	733.6-7	23:10	742.8	24:5	752.3	24:39	761.8,11	25:22	688.14	26:10	692.4
20:1	678.1	21:1	711.1-2	21:35	724.4,6-7	22:23	734.1	23:11	742.9	24:6	752.4	24:40	762.2	25:23	688.15	26:11	692.5
20:2	678.2	21:2	711.2-3	21:36	724.8	22:24	734.1	23:12	742.9	24:7	752.5-6	24:41	762.3	25:24	688.16	26:12	692.6
20:3	678.3	21:3	711.4	21:37	724.10	22:25	734.2	23:13	74210	24:8	752.8	24:42	762.6	25:25	688.16-17	26:13	692.7
20:4	678.3	21:4	712.5	21:38	724.11	22:26	734.3	23:14	743.1	24:9	753.2 / 754.4	24:43	763.3	25:26	688.18-19	26:14	767.3-4
20:5	678.4	21:5	712.5	21:39	724.12	22:27	734.4	23:15	743.2	24:10	754.2	24:44	763.5	25:27	688.19	26:15	767.5-6
20:6	678.5	21:6	711.5	21:40	724.13	22:28	734.5	23:16	743.3	24:11	754.1	24:45	764.7	25:28	688.20	26:16	767.7
20:7	678.6	21:7	712.4	21:41	724.14-15	22:29	734.6	23:17	743.4	24:12	754.1	24:46	764.8	25:29	688.22-23	26:17	771.1
20:8	678.7	21:8	713.2	21:42	724.16-17	22:30	734.7-8	23:18	743.5	24:13	754.6	24:47	764.8	25:30	688.24	26:18	771.2-5
20:9	678.8	21:9	714.2-3, 5	21:43	724.18	22:31	734.9	23:19	743.6	24:14	754.7	24:48	764.9	25:31	766.1	26:19	771.7
20:10	678.9	21:10	716.1	21:44	724.19	22:32	734.9-10	23:20	743.7	24:15	755.2	24:49	764.9	25:32	766.2	26:20	772.1
20:11	678.10	21:11	716.2	21:45	724.20	22:33	734.11	23:21	743.8	24:16	755.2	24:50	764.10	25:33	766.3	26:21	774.1
20:12	678.10	21:12	717.1-2	21:46	724.21	22:34	735.1	23:22	743.9	24:17	755.4	24:51	764.10	25:34	766.4	26:22	774.2
20:13	678.11	21:13	717.3	22:1	731.2	22:35	735.2	23:23	743.10	24:18	755.5	25:1	765.1	25:35	766.5	26:23	774.3
20:14	678.11-12	21:14	718.1	22:2	731.2	22:36	735.3	23:24	743.11	24:19	755.6	25:2	765.2	25:36	766.5	26:24	774.4
20:15	678.13	21:15	718.2	22:3	731.3-4	22:37	735.4-5	23:25	744.1	24:20	755.9	25:3	765.2	25:37	766.6	26:25	775.5

MATTHEW 26 — The Synoptic Gospel — MARK 1 — MARK 5

26	TSG	27	TSG	28	TSG	28	TSG	1	TSG	2	TSG	3	TSG	4	TSG	5	TSG
26:26	776.1	*27:14*	843.4	*27:49*	871.4	*28:19*	941.1-2	*1:1*	111.1	*1:37*	354.2	*2:28*	387.10	*4:1*	471.1-3	*4:37*	481.5-6
26:27	776.2	*27:15*	851.1	*27:50*	872.3-4	28:20	941.3 / 942.6	*1:2*	211.8-9	*1:38*	354.3	*3:1*	388.1	*4:2*	471.3-4	*4:38*	481.4,6
26:28	776.3	*27:16*	851.2	*27:51*	873.1			*1:3*	211.9	*1:39*	354.4-5	*3:2*	388.2	*4:3*	471.4	*4:39*	481.8-9
26:29	776.4	*27:17*	851.3,6	*27:52*	891.3	**Bold Verses** are part		*1:4*	211.4,7	*1:40*	355.1	*3:3*	388.4	*4:4*	471.5	*4:40*	481.7,10
26:30	789.30	*27:18*	851.6	*27:53*	891.3	of a parallel set with		*1:5*	211.12-13	*1:41*	355.2	*3:4*	388.5	*4:5*	471.6	*4:41*	481.11
26:31	778.6	*27:19*	852.3	*27:54*	873.3-4	another Gospel(s)		*1:6*	211.11	*1:42*	355.3	*3:5*	388.9-10	*4:6*	471.7	*5:1*	482.1
26:32	778.7	*27:20*	851.7	*27:55*	873.5,7-8			*1:7*	214.1-2	*1:43*	355.4	*3:6*	388.12	*4:7*	471.8	*5:2*	482.2-3
26:33	778.8	*27:21*	851.8	*27:56*	873.6			*1:8*	214.1-3	*1:44*	355.4-5	*3:7*	388.13 / 421.2	*4:8*	471.9	*5:3*	482.4-5
26:34	778.12-13	*27:22*	852.1-2	*27:57*	881.1,3	TSG =		*1:9*	221.1 / 222.1	*1:45*	355.6-8	*3:8*	411.1 / 421.2	*4:9*	471.10	*5:4*	482.5
26:35	778.14-15	*27:23*	852.5-7	*27:58*	881.4,6	The Synoptic Gospel		*1:10*	222.2-3	*2:1*	381.1	3:9	388.14	*4:10*	472.1	*5:5*	482.6
26:36	811.1,3	*27:24*	853.1	*27:59*	882.1	Verse Reference		*1:11*	222.4	*2:2*	381.1-2	*3:10*	411.2	*4:11*	472.2-3	*5:6*	482.7
26:37	811.4-5	*27:25*	853.2	*27:60*	882.4-6			*1:12*	231.1	*2:3*	381.3	*3:11*	411.3	*4:12*	472.3,6	*5:7*	482.7-8
26:38	811.5	*27:26*	853.3 / 854.1	*27:61*	882.7-8			*1:13*	231.2 / 232.12	*2:4*	381.4-5	*3:12*	411.3	*4:13*	473.9	*5:8*	482.9
26:39	811.6-8		/ 856.5	*27:62*	883.1			*1:14*	331.6 / 343.4	*2:5*	381.6	*3:13*	412.1-3	*4:14*	473.1	*5:9*	482.10-11
26:67	826.1-3	*27:27*	854.1	*27:63*	883.1			*1:15*	343.4	*2:6*	382.1	*3:14*	412.3-4	*4:15*	473.2	*5:10*	482.12
26:68	826.3	*27:28*	854.2	*27:64*	883.2			*1:16*	344.1	*2:7*	382.1-2	*3:15*	412.4	*4:16*	473.3	*5:11*	483.1
26:69	823.1-3	*27:29*	854.3-4	*27:65*	883.3			*1:17*	344.10	*2:8*	382.3	*3:16*	412.5	*4:17*	473.3-4	*5:12*	483.1-2
26:70	823.4	*27:30*	854.5	*27:66*	883.4			*1:18*	344.11	*2:9*	382.4	*3:17*	412.7-8	*4:18*	473.5	*5:13*	483.3-4
26:71	824.1-2	*27:31*	861.1-2	*28:1*	911.1			*1:19*	345.1-2	*2:10*	382.5	*3:18*	412.6,9-15	*4:19*	473.5	*5:14*	483.5-6
26:72	824.3	*27:32*	861.3	28:2	891.1			*1:20*	345.3	*2:11*	382.5	*3:19*	412.16	*4:20*	473.6	*5:15*	483.7
26:73	827.1-2	*27:33*	863.1	28:3	891.2			*1:21*	351.1	*2:12*	382.6-8	*3:20*	461.1	*4:21*	423.1,3-4	*5:16*	483.8
26:74	827.3-4	*27:34*	863.3	28:4	891.2			*1:22*	351.2	*2:13*	382.9	*3:21*	461.2	*4:22*	423.6	*5:17*	483.9
26:75	827.5-6	*27:35*	864.1-2	28:5	912.4			*1:23*	351.3-4	*2:14*	383.1-2	*3:22*	461.5-6	*4:23*	422.5	*5:18*	483.10
27:1	831.1,7	*27:36*	864.4	28:6	912.5,7			*1:24*	351.4-6	*2:15*	384.1-2	*3:23*	462.1-2	*4:24*	473.7	*5:19*	483.10-11
27:2	832.1	*27:37*	866.1-2	28:7	912.8-9			*1:25*	351.7	*2:16*	384.3	*3:24*	462.3	*4:25*	473.9-10	*5:20*	483.12
27:3	857.1-2	*27:38*	865.1	28:8	912.10			*1:26*	351.8	*2:17*	384.4,6	*3:25*	462.4	*4:26*	474.1	*5:21*	484.1-2
27:4	857.2-3	*27:39*	868.1	28:9	915.9-10			*1:27*	351.9-10	*2:18*	385.1-2	*3:26*	462.5	*4:27*	474.1	*5:22*	484.3-4
27:5	857.4	*27:40*	868.1	28:10	915.13			*1:28*	351.11	*2:19*	385.3-4	*3:27*	462.10	*4:28*	474.2	*5:23*	484.4
27:6	857.5	*27:41*	868.2	28:11	892.1			*1:29*	352.1	*2:20*	385.4	*3:28*	463.2	*4:29*	474.3	*5:24*	485.1
27:7	857.6	*27:42*	868.2-3	28:12	892.2-3			*1:30*	352.2-3	*2:21*	386.1	*3:29*	463.3	*4:30*	475.1	*5:25*	485.2
27:8	857.7	*27:43*	868.4	28:13	892.3			*1:31*	352.4-5	*2:22*	386.2-3	3:30	463.6	*4:31*	475.2-3	5:26	485.3
27:9	857.8	*27:44*	869.1	28:14	892.4			*1:32*	353.1	*2:23*	387.1	*3:31*	469.1-2	*4:32*	475.3	*5:27*	485.4
27:10	857.9	*27:45*	871.1	28:15	892.5			*1:33*	353.1	*2:24*	387.2	*3:32*	469.3	*4:33*	476.10	*5:28*	485.4
27:11	842.1,7	*27:46*	871.2	28:16	931.1			*1:34*	353.1-2,5	*2:25*	387.3	*3:33*	469.4	*4:34*	476.10-11	*5:29*	485.5
27:12	843.2	*27:47*	871.3	28:17	931.2			*1:35*	354.1	*2:26*	387.4-5	*3:34*	469.5	*4:35*	481.1	5:30	485.6
27:13	843.3	*27:48*	872.2	28:18	941.1			*1:36*	354.2	*2:27*	387.9	*3:35*	469.7	*4:36*	481.2-3	*5:31*	485.7

APPENDIX 2 - GOSPEL VERSE CROSS-REFERENCE

5	TSG	6	TSG	7	TSG	8	TSG	9	TSG	9	TSG	10	TSG	11	TSG	12	TSG
5:32	485.9	6:24	391.4	7:4	521.4-5	8:3	525.3	8:23	528.2-3	9:21	536.11-12	10:7	671.8	10:43	685.2	11:26	435.8
5:33	485.10	6:25	391.5	7:5	521.6-7	8:4	525.4	8:24	528.4	9:22	536.5,12	10:8	671.8	10:44	685.2	11:27	722.1-2
5:34	485.12-13	6:26	391.6	7:6	521.13	8:5	525.5	8:25	528.5	9:23	536.13	10:9	671.9	10:45	685.3	11:28	722.3
5:35	486.1	6:27	392.1-2	7:7	521.13	8:6	525.6-7	8:26	528.6	9:24	536.14	10:10	672.1	10:46	686.1	11:29	722.4
5:36	486.2	6:28	392.2	7:8	521.8	7:32	524.3	8:27	531.1-2	9:25	536.15	10:11	672.2	10:47	686.2-3	11:30	722.5
5:37	486.3	6:29	392.3	7:9	521.9	7:33	524.4-5	8:28	531.3	9:26	536.16	10:12	672.3	10:48	686.4	11:31	722.6
5:38	486.4	6:30	511.1	7:10	521.10	7:34	524.5	8:29	531.4-5	9:27	536.17	10:13	674.1-2	10:49	686.5-6	11:32	722.7
5:39	486.5	6:31	511.2	7:11	521.11	7:35	524.6	8:30	531.9	9:28	537.1	10:14	674.3	10:50	686.7	11:33	722.8-9
5:40	486.6-7	6:32	511.3	7:12	521.11	7:36	524.7	8:31	532.1	9:29	537.5	10:15	674.4	10:51	686.8	12:1	724.1-2
5:41	486.8	6:33	511.4-5	7:13	521.12	7:37	524.9	8:32	532.2	9:30	538.1	10:16	674.5-6	10:52	686.9-10	12:2	724.3
5:42	484.3 / 486.9-10	6:34	511.6-7	7:14	521.14	8:1	525.1-2	8:33	532.3	9:31	541.1-2	10:17	675.1	11:1	711.1-2	12:3	724.4
		6:35	512.1	7:15	521.14-15	8:2	525.2	8:34	533.1	9:32	541.3	10:18	675.2	11:2	711.2-3	12:4	724.5
5:43	486.10	6:36	512.1	7:16	521.16	8:3	525.3	8:35	533.2	9:33	542.1 / 543.1	10:19	675.5-9	11:3	711.4	12:5	724.7-8
6:1	488.1	6:37	512.2,6	7:17	522.1	8:4	525.4	8:36	533.3	9:34	543.2	10:20	675.12	11:4	712.1	12:6	724.10
6:2	488.2 / 489.1	6:38	512.7-8	7:18	522.2-3	8:5	525.5	8:37	533.4	9:35	543.4	10:21	675.13-14	11:5	712.2	12:7	724.11
6:3	489.2-5	6:39	512.10-11	7:19	522.3	8:6	525.6-7	8:38	533.5	9:36	543.5-6	10:22	675.15	11:6	712.3	12:8	724.12
6:4	489.6	6:40	512.11	7:20	522.3-4	8:7	525.8	9:1	533.7	9:37	543.8-9	10:23	676.1	11:7	712.4	12:9	724.13-14
6:5	489.15	6:41	512.12-14	7:21	522.5	8:8	525.9	9:2	534.1-2	9:38	548.1	10:24	676.2	11:8	713.2	12:10	724.16-17
6:6	489.16 / 491.1	6:42	512.14	7:22	522.5	8:9	525.10	9:3	534.3	9:39	548.2	10:25	676.3	11:9	714.2-3	12:11	724.17
6:7	491.5-6	6:43	512.16	7:23	522.6	8:10	526.1	9:4	534.4	9:40	548.3	10:26	676.4	11:10	714.4-5	12:12	724.20-21 / 732.1
6:8	492.1,5-6	6:44	512.17	7:24	523.1-2	8:11	526.2	9:5	534.7	9:41	548.4	10:27	676.5	11:11	716.1 / 717.1		
6:9	492.6	6:45	513.1-2	7:25	523.3-4	8:12	526.3,7-8	9:6	534.8	9:42	544.2	10:28	677.1		/ 718.4	12:13	732.2
6:10	493.1	6:46	513.3	7:26	523.3,5	8:13	527.1	9:7	534.9-10	9:43	545.2	10:29	677.2-3	11:12	721.1-2	12:14	733.1-2
6:11	493.4	6:47	513.4	7:27	523.9	8:14	527.2	9:8	534.13	9:44	545.3	10:30	677.3-5	11:13	721.2-3	12:15	733.3
6:12	499.1	6:48	513.5-7	7:28	523.10	8:15	527.3	9:9	534.14	9:45	545.4	10:31	677.6	11:14	721.4	12:16	733.4
6:13	499.2	6:49	513.8	7:29	523.11	8:16	527.4	9:10	534.15	9:46	545.4	10:32	683.1-2	11:15	716.1 / 717.1-2	12:17	733.5-6
6:14	553.1-2	6:50	513.8-9	7:30	523.13	8:17	527.5-6	9:11	535.1	9:47	545.5	10:33	683.3-5	11:16	717.2	12:18	734.1
6:15	553.3	6:51	514.5-6	7:31	524.1	8:18	527.7-8	9:12	535.2-3	9:48	545.6	10:34	683.5-6	11:17	717.3	12:19	734.1
6:16	553.4	6:52	514.6	7:32	524.3	8:19	527.8	9:13	535.4	9:49	545.7	10:35	684.1-2	11:18	717.4	12:20	734.2
6:17	331.1-2	6:53	515.1	7:33	524.4-5	8:20	527.9	9:14	536.1	9:50	422.1-2,4	10:36	684.3	11:19	735.13	12:21	734.3
6:18	331.2	6:54	515.2	7:34	524.5	8:21	527.10	9:15	536.2	10:1	671.1-2	10:37	684.4	11:20	721.1,5	12:22	734.3-4
6:19	331.3	6:55	515.2-3	7:35	524.6	8:22	528.1	9:16	536.3	10:2	671.3	10:38	684.5	11:21	721.6	12:23	734.5
6:20	331.3-5	6:56	515.4	7:36	524.7	8:23	528.2-3	9:17	536.4-5	10:3	671.4	10:39	684.6-7	11:22	721.8	12:24	734.6
6:21	391.1	7:1	521.1	7:37	524.9	8:24	528.4	9:18	536.6-7	10:4	671.5	10:40	684.8	11:23	721.9-10	12:25	734.7-8
6:22	391.2	7:2	521.2	8:1	525.1-2	8:25	528.5	9:19	536.8-9	10:5	671.6	10:41	684.9	11:24	721.11	12:26	734.9
6:23	391.3	7:3	521.3	8:2	525.2	8:26	528.6	9:20	536.10	10:6	671.6-7	10:42	685.1	11:25	435.7	12:27	734.10

Five Column

MARK 12 — LUKE 2 — A-29

12	TSG	13	TSG	14	TSG	15	TSG	15	TSG	16	TSG	1	TSG	1	TSG	2	TSG
12:28	735.2-3	13:20	755.12	14:19	774.2	14:54	822.1,3-4 / 823.2	15:16	854.1	16:5	912.1,3	1:1	011.1	1:37	121.11	1:73	132.4
12:29	735.4	13:21	756.2	14:20	774.3			15:17	854.2-3	16:6	912.4-5,7	1:2	011.1	1:38	121.12-13	1:74	132.5
12:30	735.5	13:22	756.3	14:21	774.4	14:55	822.5-6	15:18	854.4	16:7	912.8-9	1:3	011.2	1:39	122.1	1:75	132.5
12:31	735.7-8	13:23	756.4	14:22	776.1	14:56	822.6	15:19	854.4-5	16:8	912.10-11	1:4	011.2	1:40	122.1	1:76	132.6
12:32	735.9	13:24	757.1-2	14:23	776.2-3	14:57	822.7	15:20	861.1-2	16:9	915.1	1:5	111.2	1:41	122.2	1:77	132.7
12:33	735.10	13:25	757.3	14:24	776.3	14:58	822.7	15:21	861.3	16:10	915.12	1:6	111.3	1:42	122.3	1:78	132.7
12:34	735.11-12	13:26	757.5	14:25	776.4	14:59	822.8	15:22	863.1	16:11	915.14	1:7	111.4	1:43	122.4	1:79	132.8
12:35	741.2,4	13:27	757.6	14:26	789.30	14:60	822.9	15:23	863.3	16:12	921.1	1:8	111.5	1:44	122.4	1:80	132.11
12:36	741.5	13:28	761.1	14:27	778.6	14:61	822.10 / 825.1	15:24	863.5 / 864.1-2	16:13	922.4 / 923.1-3	1:9	111.5	1:45	122.5	2:1	142.1
12:37	741.6-7	13:29	761.2	14:28	778.7	14:62	825.2-3	15:25	863.5 / 864.1	16:14	923.2,5 / 924.8	1:10	111.6	1:46	122.6	2:2	142.2
12:38	742.1,5	13:30	761.3	14:29	778.8	14:63	825.4-5	15:26	866.1-2	16:15	941.1	1:11	111.6	1:47	122.6	2:3	142.2
12:39	742.5	13:31	761.4	14:30	778.12-13	14:64	825.5-6	15:27	865.1	16:16	941.4	1:12	111.7	1:48	122.6-7	2:4	142.3
12:40	743.1	13:32	761.5	14:31	778.14-15	14:65	826.1-3	15:28	865.2	16:17	942.1-2	1:13	111.8	1:49	122.7	2:5	142.3-4
12:41	747.1-2	13:33	762.6	14:32	811.1,3	14:66	823.1-2 /	15:29	868.1	16:18	942.3-5	1:14	111.9	1:50	122.8	2:6	143.1
12:42	747.2	13:34	763.2	14:33	811.4-5	14:67	823.3	15:30	868.1	16:19	951.1,3	1:15	111.9-10	1:51	122.9	2:7	143.1-2
12:43	747.3	13:35	763.4	14:34	811.5	14:68	823.4-5	15:31	868.2	16:20	952.1-2	1:16	111.10	1:52	122.10	2:8	144.1
12:44	747.3	13:36	763.4	14:35	811.6-7	14:69	824.1-2	15:32	868.3 / 869.1			1:17	111.11	1:53	122.11	2:9	144.2-3
13:1	751.1-2	13:37	763.7	14:36	811.7-8	14:70	824.3 / 827.1-2	15:33	871.1	**Bold Verses** are part of a parallel set with another Gospel(s)		1:18	111.12	1:54	122.12	2:10	144.3
13:2	751.3	14:1	766.14 / 767.1	14:37	812.1-2	14:71	827.3	15:34	871.2			1:19	111.13	1:55	122.12	2:11	144.4
13:3	752.1	14:2	767.2	14:38	812.3	14:72	827.4-6	15:35	871.3			1:20	111.14	1:56	122.13	2:12	144.5
13:4	752.1-2	14:3	691.5-7	14:39	812.4	15:1	831.1 / 832.1	15:36	871.4 / 872.2			1:21	111.15	1:57	131.1	2:13	144.6
13:5	752.3	14:4	692.1	14:40	813.1	15:2	842.1,7	15:37	872.3-4			1:22	111.16	1:58	131.2	2:14	144.6-7
13:6	752.3	14:5	692.1-2	14:41	813.2-4	15:3	843.2	15:38	873.1	TSG = The Synoptic Gospel Verse Reference		1:23	111.17	1:59	131.3	2:15	144.8
13:7	752.4	14:6	692.4	14:42	813.5	15:4	843.3	15:39	873.3-4			1:24	112.1-2	1:60	131.3	2:16	144.9
13:8	752.5-8	14:7	692.5	14:43	814.1-2	15:5	843.4	15:40	873.5-6			1:25	112.2	1:61	131.4	2:17	144.10
13:9	753.1-3	14:8	692.6	14:44	814.3	15:6	851.1	15:41	873.7-8			1:26	121.1	1:62	131.5	2:18	144.11
13:10	754.7	14:9	692.7	14:45	814.4	15:7	851.2	15:42	874.1 / 881.1			1:27	121.2	1:63	131.6	2:19	144.11
13:11	753.4	14:10	767.3-4	14:46	815.2	15:8	851.3	15:43	881.1-4			1:28	121.3	1:64	131.7	2:20	144.12
13:12	754.3-4	14:11	767.6-7	14:47	815.4	15:9	851.4	15:44	881.5			1:29	121.4	1:65	132.9	2:21	145.1
13:13	754.5-6	14:12	771.1	14:48	816.1	15:10	851.6	15:45	881.6			1:30	121.5	1:66	132.10	2:22	151.1
13:14	755.2	14:13	771.2-3	14:49	816.2-3	15:11	851.7	15:46	882.1,4-6			1:31	121.6	1:67	132.1	2:23	151.2
13:15	755.4	14:14	771.4-5	14:50	816.5	15:12	852.1	15:47	882.7-8			1:32	121.7-8	1:68	132.1	2:24	151.3
13:16	755.5	14:15	771.6	14:51	816.6	15:13	852.2	16:1	911.1			1:33	121.8	1:69	132.2	2:25	151.4
13:17	755.7	14:16	771.7	14:52	816.6	15:14	852.5,7	16:2	911.1			1:34	121.9	1:70	132.2	2:26	151.5
13:18	755.10	14:17	772.1	14:53	821.1,6	15:15	853.3 / 854.1 / 856.5	16:3	911.2			1:35	121.10	1:71	132.3	2:27	151.6
13:19	755.11	14:18	774.1					16:4	911.3			1:36	121.11	1:72	132.3-4	2:28	151.6

APPENDIX 2 - GOSPEL VERSE CROSS-REFERENCE

LUKE 2 — LUKE 9

2	TSG	3	TSG	4	TSG	5	TSG	6	TSG	7	TSG	7	TSG	8	TSG	9	TSG
2:29	151.7	3:13	213.4	4:11	232.5	5:2	344.2	5:38	386.3	6:35	432.6-8	7:22	361.4	8:8	471.9-10	8:44	485.4-5
2:30	151.7	3:14	213.5-6	4:12	232.6	5:3	344.3	5:39	386.4	6:36	432.9	7:23	361.5	8:9	472.1	8:45	485.6-7
2:31	151.7	3:15	214.1	4:13	232.11	5:4	344.4	6:1	387.1	6:37	441.1	7:24	362.1-2	8:10	472.2-3	8:46	485.8
2:32	151.7	3:16	214.1-3	4:14	341.1-2	5:5	344.5	6:2	387.2	6:38	431.8-9	7:25	362.3-4	8:11	473.1	8:47	485.10-11
2:33	151.10	3:17	214.4-5	4:15	343.5	5:6	344.6	6:3	387.3	6:39	441.6	7:26	362.5	8:12	473.2	8:48	485.12
2:34	151.8	3:18	214.6	4:16	488.1-3	5:7	344.7	6:4	387.4-5	6:40	495.4	7:27	362.6	8:13	473.3-4	8:49	486.1
2:35	151.8-9	3:19	331.1-2	4:17	488.3-4	5:8	344.8	6:5	387.9-10	6:41	441.3	7:28	362.7-8	8:14	473.5	8:50	486.2
2:36	152.1-2	3:20	331.1	4:18	488.4-5	5:9	344.9	6:6	388.1	6:42	441.4-5	7:29	362.12	8:15	473.6	8:51	486.3-4,7
2:37	152.2-3	3:21	222.1-2	4:19	488.5	5:10	344.10 / 345.1	6:7	388.2	6:43	443.6	7:30	362.13	8:16	423.3-4	8:52	486.4-5
2:38	152.4	3:22	222.3-4	4:20	488.6	5:11	345.3	6:8	388.4	6:44	443.3-4	7:31	363.1	8:17	423.6	8:53	486.6
2:39	153.1	3:23	022.1-2 / 311.1	4:21	488.7	5:12	355.1	6:9	388.5	6:45	464.3	7:32	363.2	8:18	473.7,9-10	8:54	486.8
2:40	153.2	3:24	022.3-7	4:22	489.2	5:13	355.2-3	6:10	388.9-10	6:46	444.3	7:33	363.3	8:19	469.1	8:55	486.9-10
2:41	171.1	3:25	022.8-12	4:23	489.8-9	5:14	355.4-5	6:11	388.11	6:47	444.5	7:34	363.4	8:20	469.3	8:56	486.10
2:42	171.1	3:26	022.13-17	4:24	489.7	5:15	355.6-7	6:12	412.1	6:48	444.5-6	7:35	363.5	8:21	469.4-6	9:1	491.5
2:43	171.2-3	3:27	022.18-22	4:25	489.10	5:16	355.8	6:13	412.2-3	6:49	444.7-8	7:36	452.1	8:22	481.1-3	9:2	491.6
2:44	171.3-4	3:28	022.23-27	4:26	489.11	5:17	381.1-3	6:14	412.5-10	7:1	445.1-2	7:37	452.2	8:23	481.4-6	9:3	492.1,5-6
2:45	171.4	3:29	022.28-32	4:27	489.12	5:18	381.3	6:15	412.11-13,15	7:2	451.1	7:38	452.3	8:24	481.6,8-9	9:4	493.1
2:46	171.5	3:30	022.33-37	4:28	489.13	5:19	381.4-5	6:16	412.14,16	7:3	451.1-2	7:39	452.4	8:25	481.10-11	9:5	493.4
2:47	171.6	3:31	022.38-42	4:29	489.14	5:20	381.6	6:17	421.1-2	7:4	451.3	7:40	452.5	8:26	482.1	9:6	499.1-2
2:48	171.7	3:32	022.43-47	4:30	489.14	5:21	382.1-2	6:18	411.2 / 421.2	7:5	451.3	7:41	452.6	8:27	482.2-4	9:7	553.1-2
2:49	171.8	3:33	022.48-53	4:31	351.1	5:22	382.3	6:19	411.2	7:6	451.4-5	7:42	452.7	8:28	482.7-8	9:8	553.3
2:50	171.9	3:34	022.54-58	4:32	351.2	5:23	382.4	6:20	421.3	7:7	451.5	7:43	452.8-9	8:29	482.4-5,9	9:9	553.4-5
2:51	171.10	3:35	022.59-63	4:33	351.3-4	5:24	382.5	6:21	421.8-9	7:8	451.6	7:44	452.10-11	8:30	482.10-11	9:10	511.1,3
2:52	171.11	3:36	022.64-68	4:34	351.4-6	5:25	382.6	6:22	421.14	7:9	451.7	7:45	452.12	8:31	482.12	9:11	511.4,7-8
3:1	211.1-2	3:37	022.69-73	4:35	351.7-8	5:26	382.7-8	6:23	421.15	7:10	451.12	7:46	452.13	8:32	483.1,3	9:12	512.1
3:2	211.3-4	3:38	022.74-77	4:36	351.9-10	5:27	383.1	6:24	421.16	7:11	356.1	7:47	452.14-15	8:33	483.4	9:13	512.2,6,8
3:3	211.7	4:1	231.1-2	4:37	351.11	5:28	383.2	6:25	421.17-18	7:12	356.2	7:48	452.16	8:34	483.5	9:14	512.10,17
3:4	211.9	4:2	231.2-3	4:38	351.11 / 352.1-3	5:29	384.1-2	6:26	421.19	7:13	356.3	7:49	452.17	8:35	483.6-7	9:15	512.11
3:5	211.10	4:3	232.1			5:30	384.3	6:27	432.2	7:14	356.4-5	7:50	452.18	8:36	483.8	9:16	512.12-13
3:6	211.10	4:4	232.2	4:39	352.4-5	5:31	384.4	6:28	432.3	7:15	356.5-6	8:1	453.1-2	8:37	483.9-10	9:17	512.14,16
3:7	212.1	4:5	232.7	4:40	353.1-2	5:32	384.6	6:29	431.2-3	7:16	356.6-7	8:2	453.2	8:38	483.10-11	9:18	531.2
3:8	212.2-3	4:6	232.8	4:41	353.4-5	5:33	385.1-2	6:30	431.5-6	7:17	356.8	8:3	453.2-3	8:39	483.11-12	9:19	531.3
3:9	212.4	4:7	232.9	4:42	354.1-3	5:34	385.3	6:31	442.9	7:18	356.9	8:4	471.2-3	8:40	484.2	9:20	531.4-5
3:10	213.1	4:8	232.10	4:43	354.3	5:35	385.4	6:32	432.10-11	7:19	361.1	8:5	471.4-5	8:41	484.3-4	9:21	531.9
3:11	213.2	4:9	232.3-4	4:44	354.4	5:36	386.1	6:33	432.5	7:20	361.2	8:6	471.6-7	8:42	484.3 / 485.1	9:22	532.1
3:12	213.3	4:10	232.4	5:1	344.2	5:37	386.2	6:34	431.7	7:21	361.3	8:7	471.8	8:43	485.2	9:23	533.1

THE GREATEST GOSPEL

LUKE 9 — LUKE 16

9	TSG	10	TSG	11	TSG	11	TSG	12	TSG	13	TSG	14	TSG	15	TSG	16	TSG
9:24	533.2	9:59	538.4	10:33	375.10	11:27	466.5	12:9	496.2	12:45	764.9	13:22	651.1	14:23	731.13	15:24	572.13-14
9:25	533.3	9:60	538.5	10:34	375.10-11	11:28	466.6	12:10	463.4-5	12:46	764.10	13:23	651.2-3	14:24	731.13	15:25	573.1
9:26	533.5	9:61	538.6	10:35	375.12	11:29	465.2	12:11	494.4	12:47	764.11	13:24	651.3	14:25	551.1	15:26	573.1
9:27	533.7	9:62	538.7	10:36	375.13	11:30	465.3	12:12	494.4	12:48	764.12-13	13:25	651.4	14:26	551.1	15:27	573.2
9:28	534.1	10:1	552.1	10:37	375.14-15	11:31	465.6-7	12:13	437.1	12:49	497.1	13:26	651.5	14:27	551.2	15:28	573.3
9:29	534.2-3	10:2	552.2	10:38	376.1	11:32	465.4-5	12:14	437.2	12:50	497.2	13:27	651.6	14:28	551.3	15:29	573.4
9:30	534.4	10:3	552.3	10:39	376.2	11:33	423.3-4	12:15	437.3	12:51	497.3	13:28	651.7	14:29	551.4	15:30	573.5
9:31	534.5	10:4	552.4	10:40	376.3	11:34	424.1-2	12:16	437.4	12:52	497.5	13:29	651.8	14:30	551.4	15:31	573.6
9:32	534.6	10:5	552.5	10:41	376.4	11:35	424.4	12:17	437.4	12:53	497.4,6	13:30	651.9	14:31	551.5	15:32	573.7
9:33	534.7-8	10:6	552.6	10:42	376.4-5	11:36	424.5	12:18	437.5	12:54	526.3-4	13:31	651.10	14:32	551.6	16:1	574.1
9:34	534.9	10:7	552.7-8	11:1	389.1	11:37	467.1	12:19	437.6	12:55	526.5	13:32	651.11	14:33	551.7	16:2	574.2
9:35	534.10	10:8	552.8	11:2	389.2	11:38	467.2	12:20	437.7	12:56	526.6	13:33	651.12	14:34	422.1-2	16:3	574.3
9:36	534.11,13 / 535.7	10:9	552.9	11:3	389.3	11:39	467.3	12:21	437.8	12:57	527.1	13:34	746.1-2	14:35	422.3,5	16:4	574.4
		10:10	552.10	11:4	389.4-5	11:40	467.4	12:22	439.1	12:58	527.2-3	13:35	746.3-4	15:1	571.1	16:5	574.5-6
9:37	536.1-2	10:11	552.10-11	11:5	442.1	11:41	467.5	12:23	439.1	12:59	527.4	14:1	561.1	15:2	571.1	16:6	574.6-7
9:38	536.4	10:12	454.5	11:6	442.1	11:42	467.6	12:24	439.2-3	13:1	644.1	14:2	561.2	15:3	571.2	16:7	574.8-9
9:39	536.5-6	10:13	454.2	11:7	442.2	11:43	467.7	12:25	439.4	13:2	644.2	14:3	561.2	15:4	571.2	16:8	574.10-11
9:40	536.7	10:14	454.3	11:8	442.3	11:44	467.8	12:26	439.5	13:3	644.3	14:4	561.2-3	15:5	571.3	16:9	574.12
9:41	536.8-9	10:15	454.4	11:9	442.4	11:45	468.1	12:27	439.6-7	13:4	644.4	14:5	561.4	15:6	571.4	16:10	575.1
9:42	536.10,15-17	10:16	552.12-13	11:10	442.5	11:46	468.2	12:28	439.8	13:5	644.5	14:6	561.5	15:7	571.5	16:11	575.2
9:43	536.18 / 541.1	10:17	564.1	11:11	442.6	11:47	745.1	12:29	439.9	13:6	644.6	14:7	562.1-2	15:8	571.6	16:12	575.3
9:44	541.1	10:18	564.2	11:12	442.7	11:48	745.3	12:30	439.10	13:7	644.7	14:8	562.2	15:9	571.7	16:13	575.4-5
9:45	541.3-4	10:19	564.3	11:13	442.8	11:49	745.4-5	12:31	439.11	13:8	644.8	14:9	562.2	15:10	571.8	16:14	575.6
9:46	543.2	10:20	564.4	11:14	461.3-4	11:50	745.5	12:32	439.12	13:9	644.8	14:10	562.3	15:11	572.1	16:15	575.7-8
9:47	543.4-5	10:21	455.1-2	11:15	461.5-6	11:51	745.6-7	12:33	438.2-3	13:10	529.1	14:11	562.4	15:12	572.1	16:16	575.9
9:48	543.6,8-9	10:22	455.3-4	11:16	461.7	11:52	468.3-4	12:34	438.4	13:11	529.1	14:12	563.1	15:13	572.2	16:17	575.10
9:49	548.1	10:23	472.2,7	11:17	462.1-4	11:53	468.5	12:35	764.1	13:12	529.2	14:13	563.2	15:14	572.3	16:18	672.2,4
9:50	548.2-3	10:24	472.8	11:18	462.5-6	11:54	468.5	12:36	764.2	13:13	529.3	14:14	563.2	15:15	572.4	16:19	576.1
9:51	681.1	10:25	375.1	11:19	462.6	12:1	468.6	12:37	764.3-4	13:14	529.4	14:15	563.3	15:16	572.5	16:20	576.2
9:52	681.1-2	10:26	375.2	11:20	462.7	12:2	495.7	12:38	764.5	13:15	529.5	14:16	731.2	15:17	572.6	16:21	576.2
9:53	681.2	10:27	375.3-4	11:21	462.8	12:3	495.8	12:39	763.3	13:16	529.6	14:17	731.3	15:18	572.7	16:22	576.3
9:54	681.3	10:28	375.5	11:22	462.9	12:4	495.9	12:40	763.5	13:17	529.7	14:18	731.6	15:19	572.8	16:23	576.4-5
9:55	681.4	10:29	375.6	11:23	463.1	12:5	495.10	12:41	764.6	13:18	475.1	14:19	731.7	15:20	572.9-10	16:24	576.5
9:56	681.4-5	10:30	375.7	11:24	466.1-2	12:6	495.11	12:42	764.7	13:19	475.2-3	14:20	731.8	15:21	572.11	16:25	576.6
9:57	538.2	10:31	375.8	11:25	466.2	12:7	495.12	12:43	764.8	13:20	476.1	14:21	731.10-11	15:22	572.12	16:26	576.7
9:58	538.3	10:32	375.9	11:26	466.3	12:8	496.1	12:44	764.8	13:21	476.2	14:22	731.12	15:23	572.13	16:27	576.8

17	TSG	18	TSG	19	TSG	19	TSG	20	TSG	21	TSG	22	TSG	22	TSG	23	TSG
16:28	576.8	17:33	755.5	18:32	683.5	19:25	688.21	20:13	724.9-10	21:2	747.2	21:38	741.1	22:36	779.2-3	23:1	832.1
16:29	576.9	17:34	762.1	18:33	683.5-6	19:26	688.22-23	20:14	724.11	21:3	747.3	22:1	766.14	22:37	779.4	23:2	841.5-6
16:30	576.10	17:35	762.3	18:34	683.7	19:27	688.25	20:15	724.12-13	21:4	747.3	22:2	767.1-2	22:38	779.5	23:3	842.1,7
16:31	576.11	17:36	762.2	18:35	686.1	19:28	688.26	20:16	724.14-15	21:5	751.1,3	22:3	767.3	22:39	789.30	23:4	843.1
17:1	545.1	17:37	762.4-5	18:36	686.2	19:29	711.1	20:17	724.16-17	21:6	751.3	22:4	767.4	22:40	811.3	23:5	843.5
17:2	544.2	18:1	577.1	18:37	686.2	19:30	711.2-3	20:18	724.19	21:7	752.1-2	22:5	767.6	22:41	811.6-7	23:6	843.6
17:3	546.1-2	18:2	577.1	18:38	686.3	19:31	711.4	20:19	724.20-21	21:8	752.3	22:6	767.7	22:42	811.7-8	23:7	843.6
17:4	546.3	18:3	577.2	18:39	686.4	19:32	712.1	20:20	732.1-2	21:9	752.4	22:7	771.1	22:43	811.9	23:8	844.1
17:5	537.3	18:4	577.3	18:40	686.5,8	19:33	712.2	20:21	733.1	21:10	752.4-5	22:8	771.2	22:44	811.10	23:9	844.2
17:6	537.4	18:5	577.3	18:41	686.8	19:34	712.3	20:22	733.2	21:11	752.6-7	22:9	771.1	22:45	812.1	23:10	844.2
17:7	679.1	18:6	577.4	18:42	686.9	19:35	712.4	20:23	733.3	21:12	753.1-3	22:10	771.3-4	22:46	812.2-3	23:11	844.3
17:8	679.2	18:7	577.4	18:43	686.10-11	19:36	713.2	20:24	733.3-4	21:13	753.3	22:11	771.4-5	22:47	814.1,4	23:12	844.4
17:9	679.3	18:8	577.5-6	19:1	687.1	19:37	714.1	20:25	733.5	21:14	753.5	22:12	771.6	22:48	814.5	23:13	845.1
17:10	679.4	18:9	578.1	19:2	687.1	19:38	714.2-3, 5	20:26	733.6-7	21:15	753.5	22:13	771.7	22:49	815.3	23:14	845.1-2
17:11	682.1	18:10	578.2	19:3	687.1	19:39	714.6	20:27	734.1	21:16	754.2-4	22:14	772.1	22:50	815.4	23:15	845.3-4
17:12	682.2	18:11	578.3	19:4	687.2	19:40	714.7	20:28	734.1	21:17	754.5	22:15	772.2	22:51	815.5	23:16	845.4
17:13	682.2	18:12	578.4	19:5	687.3	19:41	715.1	20:29	734.2	21:18	754.5	22:16	772.2	22:52	816.1	23:17	851.1
17:14	682.3-4	18:13	578.5	19:6	687.4	19:42	715.1	20:30	734.3	21:19	754.6	22:17	776.2	22:53	816.2-3	23:18	851.5
17:15	682.5	18:14	578.6	19:7	687.5	19:43	715.2	20:31	734.3	21:20	755.1	22:18	776.4	22:54	821.1,6 / 822.1	23:19	851.2
17:16	682.6	18:15	674.1-2	19:8	687.6-7	19:44	715.3-4	20:32	734.4	21:21	755.2	22:19	776.1	22:55	823.1-2	23:20	852.4
17:17	682.7	18:16	674.3	19:9	687.8	19:45	717.1	20:33	734.5	21:22	755.3	22:20	776.2-3	22:56	823.2-3	23:21	852.4
17:18	682.8	18:17	674.4	19:10	687.10	19:46	717.3	20:34	734.6-7	21:23	755.6	22:21	774.3	22:57	823.4	23:22	852.5-6
17:19	682.9	18:18	675.1	19:11	688.1	19:47	728.8	20:35	734.7	21:24	755.7-8	22:22	774.4	22:58	824.1,3	23:23	852.7
17:20	731.1	18:19	675.2	19:12	688.2	19:48	728.9	20:36	734.8	21:25	757.1,4	22:23	774.6	22:59	827.1-2	23:24	853.3
17:21	731.1	18:20	675.5-9	19:13	688.3-5	20:1	722.1-2	20:37	734.9	21:26	757.3-4	22:24	772.3	22:60	827.3-4	23:25	853.3
17:22	756.1	18:21	675.12	19:14	688.6	20:2	722.3	20:38	734.10	21:27	757.5	22:25	772.4	22:61	827.5	23:26	861.2-4
17:23	756.2	18:22	675.13-14	19:15	688.10-11	20:3	722.4	20:39	734.12	21:28	757.7	22:26	772.5	22:62	827.6	23:27	862.1
17:24	756.6	18:23	675.15	19:16	688.12	20:4	722.5	20:40	734.12	21:29	761.1	22:27	772.6-7	22:63	826.1-2	23:28	862.2
17:25	761.6	18:24	676.1	19:17	688.13	20:5	722.6	20:41	741.4	21:30	761.1	22:28	772.8	22:64	826.2-3	23:29	862.3
17:26	761.7	18:25	676.3	19:18	688.14	20:6	722.7	20:42	741.5	21:31	761.2	22:29	772.8	22:65	826.4	23:30	862.4
17:27	761.7-8	18:26	676.4	19:19	688.15	20:7	722.8	20:43	741.5	21:32	761.3	22:30	772.8-9	22:66	831.1-2	23:31	862.5
17:28	761.9	18:27	676.5	19:20	688.16-17	20:8	722.9	20:44	741.6	21:33	761.4	22:31	778.9	22:67	831.2-3	23:32	861.5
17:29	761.10	18:28	677.1	19:21	688.16	20:9	724.1-2	20:45	742.1	21:34	763.1	22:32	778.9-10	22:68	831.3	23:33	863.1 / 865.1
17:30	761.11	18:29	677.2-3	19:22	688.18-19	20:10	724.3-4	20:46	742.5	21:35	763.1	22:33	778.11	22:69	831.4	23:34	863.4 / 864.1-2
17:31	755.4-5	18:30	677.3-5	19:23	688.19	20:11	724.5	20:47	743.1	21:36	763.6	22:34	778.12-13	22:70	831.5	23:35	863.2
17:32	755.5	18:31	683.2-3	19:24	688.20	20:12	724.6	21:1	747.1-2	21:37	735.13	22:35	779.1	22:71	831.6	23:36	863.3

LUKE 24 — JOHN 1 — JOHN 6

Bold Verses are part of a parallel set with another Gospel(s)

24	TSG	24	TSG	1	TSG	2	TSG	3	TSG	4	TSG	5	TSG	5	TSG	6	TSG
23:37	864.5	24:18	921.4	1:1	012.1	1:38	311.4-5	2:24	321.13	3:36	324.8-9	4:37	334.7	5:20	372.7-8	**6:10**	512.10-11,17
23:38	866.1-2	24:19	921.5-6	1:2	012.2	1:39	311.6-7	2:25	321.14	4:1	323.3	4:38	334.8	5:21	372.9	**6:11**	512.12-14
23:39	869.1	24:20	921.7	1:3	012.3	1:40	311.8	3:1	322.1	4:2	323.1	4:39	334.9	5:22	372.10	6:12	512.15
23:40	869.2	24:21	921.8-9	1:4	012.4	1:41	311.9	3:2	322.2	**4:3**	331.6	4:40	334.10	5:23	372.10-11	**6:13**	512.16
23:41	869.3	24:22	921.10	1:5	012.7	1:42	311.9-10	3:3	322.3	4:4	331.6	4:41	334.11	5:24	373.1	6:14	512.18
23:42	869.4	24:23	921.10	1:6	211.5	1:43	312.1	3:4	322.4	4:5	332.1	4:42	334.12	5:25	373.2	**6:15**	513.1,3
23:43	869.5	24:24	921.11	1:7	211.5	1:44	312.2	3:5	322.5	4:6	332.2-3	4:43	334.13	5:26	373.3	**6:16**	513.1,3
23:44	871.1	24:25	921.12	1:8	211.6	1:45	312.3	3:6	322.6	4:7	332.3-4	4:44	334.13	5:27	373.4	**6:17**	513.1-2,4
23:45	871.1 / 873.1	24:26	921.13	1:9	012.6	1:46	312.4-5	3:7	322.7	4:8	332.4	**4:45**	341.1	5:28	373.5	**6:18**	513.5
23:46	872.3-4	24:27	921.14	1:10	012.8	1:47	312.6	3:8	322.8	4:9	332.5	4:46	341.2 / 342.1	5:29	373.5-7	**6:19**	513.6,8
23:47	873.3-4	24:28	921.15	1:11	961.3	1:48	312.7-8	3:9	322.9	4:10	332.6	4:47	342.2	5:30	373.8	**6:20**	513.9
23:48	873.2	24:29	921.15-16	1:12	961.4	1:49	312.9	3:10	322.10	4:11	332.7	4:48	342.3	5:31	374.1	6:21	514.5-6
23:49	873.5,8	24:30	922.1	1:13	961.5	1:50	312.10-11	3:11	322.11	4:12	332.8	4:49	342.4	5:32	374.2	6:22	516.1
23:50	881.1-3	24:31	922.2,4	1:14	012.5,9	1:51	312.11	3:12	322.12	4:13	333.1	4:50	342.5-6	5:33	374.3	6:23	516.2
23:51	881.1-3	24:32	922.5	1:15	223.4	2:1	313.1-2	3:13	322.13	4:14	333.1-2	4:51	342.7	5:34	374.4	6:24	516.3
23:52	881.4	24:33	922.4 / 923.1	1:16	961.7	2:2	313.2	3:14	322.14	4:15	333.3	4:52	342.8	5:35	374.5	6:25	516.4
23:53	882.1,4-5	24:34	923.2	1:17	961.6	2:3	313.3	3:15	322.14	4:16	333.4	4:53	342.9	5:36	374.6-7	6:26	516.5
23:54	881.1	24:35	923.3	1:18	961.1-2	2:4	313.4	3:16	322.15	4:17	333.5-6	4:54	342.10	5:37	374.8-9	6:27	516.6-7
23:55	882.7	**24:36**	923.4-5	1:19	215.1	2:5	313.5	3:17	322.16	4:18	333.6	5:1	371.1	5:38	374.10	6:28	516.8
23:56	882.9	24:37	923.6	1:20	215.2	2:6	313.6	3:18	322.17-18	4:19	333.7	5:2	371.2	5:39	374.11	6:29	516.9
24:1	911.1	24:38	924.1	1:21	215.3-4	2:7	313.7	3:19	322.19	4:20	333.8	5:3	371.3-4	5:40	374.12	6:30	516.10
24:2	911.3	24:39	924.2-3	1:22	215.5	2:8	313.8	3:20	322.20	4:21	333.9	5:4	371.4	5:41	374.13	6:31	516.11
24:3	912.1	**24:40**	924.4	1:23	215.6	2:9	313.9	3:21	322.21	4:22	333.10	5:5	371.5	5:42	374.14	6:32	516.12
24:4	912.2	24:41	924.6	1:24	215.7	2:10	313.9-10	3:22	323.1	4:23	333.11	5:6	371.6	5:43	374.15-16	6:33	516.13
24:5	912.3-5	24:42	924.7	1:25	215.7	2:11	313.11	3:23	323.2	4:24	333.12	5:7	371.7	5:44	374.17	6:34	516.14
24:6	912.5-6	24:43	924.7	1:26	215.8	2:12	313.12	3:24	323.2	4:25	333.13	5:8	371.8	5:45	374.18	6:35	516.15
24:7	912.6	24:44	935.1	1:27	215.8	2:13	321.1	3:25	323.4	4:26	333.14	5:9	371.9-10	5:46	374.19	6:36	516.16
24:8	912.10	24:45	935.2	1:28	215.9	2:14	321.2	3:26	323.4	4:27	333.15	5:10	371.10	5:47	374.20	6:37	517.1
24:9	912.10 / 913.1	24:46	935.3	1:29	221.2	2:15	321.3-4	3:27	323.5	4:28	333.16	5:11	371.11	6:1	392.4	6:38	517.2
24:10	911.1 / 913.1	24:47	935.4	1:30	221.3	2:16	321.5	3:28	323.6	4:29	333.16	5:12	371.12	6:2	511.4	6:39	517.3
24:11	913.2	24:48	935.5	1:31	221.4	2:17	321.6	3:29	323.7-8	4:30	333.17	5:13	371.12	6:3	511.1	6:40	517.4-5
24:12	914.1,3,8	24:49	935.6	1:32	223.1	2:18	321.7	3:30	323.9	4:31	334.1	5:14	371.13	6:4	512.3	6:41	517.6
24:13	921.1	24:50	951.1-2	1:33	223.1	2:19	321.8	3:31	324.1-3	4:32	334.1	5:15	372.1	6:5	512.3	6:42	517.7
24:14	921.2	**24:51**	951.3	1:34	223.3	2:20	321.9	3:32	324.4	4:33	334.2	5:16	372.2	6:6	512.4	6:43	517.8
24:15	921.2	24:52	951.4	1:35	311.2	2:21	321.10	3:33	324.5	4:34	334.3	5:17	372.3	6:7	512.5	6:44	517.8
24:16	921.2	24:53	951.4	1:36	311.2	2:22	321.11	3:34	324.6	4:35	334.4-5	5:18	372.4	**6:8**	512.8	6:45	517.9-10
24:17	921.3			1:37	311.3	2:23	321.12	3:35	324.7	4:36	334.6	5:19	372.5-6	**6:9**	512.8	6:46	517.11

APPENDIX 2 - GOSPEL VERSE CROSS-REFERENCE

JOHN 6 — JOHN 12   A-34

6	TSG	7	TSG	8	TSG	8	TSG	9	TSG	10	TSG	11	TSG	11	TSG	12	TSG
6:47	517.12	7:12	612.3	7:48	615.3	8:31	624.1	9:8	631.8	10:3	641.3	10:39	653.8	11:32	663.2	12:11	692.9
6:48	517.13	7:13	612.4	7:49	615.4	8:32	624.1	9:9	631.9	10:4	641.4	10:40	653.9	11:33	663.3	12:12	711.1 / 713.1
6:49	517.14	7:14	612.5	7:50	615.5	8:33	624.2	9:10	631.10	10:5	641.5	10:41	653.10	11:34	663.4	12:13	713.1-2 /
6:50	517.15	7:15	612.6	7:51	615.5	8:34	624.3	9:11	631.11-12	10:6	641.6	10:42	653.10	11:35	663.5		714.2-3
6:51	518.1-2	7:16	612.7	7:52	615.6	8:35	624.4	9:12	631.13	10:7	641.7	11:1	661.1-2	11:36	663.5	12:14	712.4-5
6:52	518.3	7:17	612.8	7:53	615.7	8:36	624.5	9:13	632.1	10:8	641.8	11:2	661.1-2 / 692.7	11:37	663.6	12:15	712.5
6:53	518.4	7:18	612.9-10	8:1	615.7	8:37	624.6	9:14	632.1	10:9	641.9	11:3	661.3	11:38	664.1-2	12:16	714.8
6:54	518.5	7:19	612.11-12	8:2	621.1	8:38	624.7	9:15	632.2	10:10	641.10	11:4	661.4	11:39	664.2-3	12:17	714.9
6:55	518.6	7:20	612.13	8:3	621.2	8:39	624.8-9	9:16	632.3-4	10:11	642.1	11:5	661.5	11:40	664.4	12:18	714.10
6:56	518.7	7:21	612.14	8:4	621.2	8:40	624.10	9:17	632.5	10:12	642.2	11:6	661.5	11:41	664.4-5	12:19	714.11
6:57	518.8	7:22	612.15	8:5	621.3	8:41	624.10-11	9:18	632.6	10:13	642.3	11:7	661.6	11:42	664.6	12:20	725.1
6:58	518.9	7:23	612.16	8:6	621.4-5	8:42	624.12	9:19	632.6	10:14	642.4	11:8	661.7	11:43	664.7	12:21	725.1 / 412.9
6:59	518.10	7:24	612.17	8:7	621.6	8:43	625.1	9:20	632.7	10:15	642.4-5	11:9	661.8	11:44	664.8-9	12:22	725.2
6:60	519.1	7:25	613.1	8:8	621.7	8:44	625.2-4	9:21	632.7-8	10:16	642.6-7	11:10	661.9	11:45	664.10	12:23	725.3
6:61	519.2	7:26	613.2	8:9	621.8	8:45	625.5	9:22	632.9	10:17	643.1	11:11	661.10	11:46	664.11	12:24	725.4
6:62	519.2	7:27	613.4	8:10	621.9	8:46	625.6-7	9:23	632.10	10:18	643.2-3	11:12	661.11	11:47	665.1	12:25	725.5
6:63	519.3-4	7:28	613.4-5	8:11	621.9-10	8:47	625.8-9	9:24	633.1	10:19	643.4	11:13	661.12	11:48	665.2	12:26	725.6-7
6:64	519.5	7:29	613.6	8:12	622.1	8:48	626.1	9:25	633.2	10:20	643.4	11:14	661.13	11:49	665.3	12:27	726.1
6:65	519.6	7:30	613.7	8:13	622.2	8:49	626.2	9:26	633.3	10:21	643.5	11:15	661.13	11:50	665.3	12:28	726.2-3
6:66	519.7	7:31	613.8	8:14	622.3-4	8:50	626.3	9:27	633.4	10:22	651.1	11:16	412.12 /	11:51	665.4	12:29	726.4
6:67	519.8	7:32	613.9	8:15	622.5	8:51	626.4	9:28	633.5	10:23	652.1		661.14	11:52	665.5	12:30	726.5
6:68	519.9	7:33	613.10	8:16	622.6	8:52	626.5	9:29	633.6	10:24	652.2	11:17	664.1	11:53	665.6	12:31	726.6
6:69	519.10	7:34	613.11	8:17	622.7	8:53	626.6	9:30	633.7	10:25	652.3-4	11:18	662.2	11:54	665.7	12:32	726.7
6:70	519.11	7:35	613.12-13	8:18	622.8	8:54	626.7	9:31	633.8	10:26	652.4	11:19	662.1	11:55	691.1	12:33	726.8
6:71	519.12	7:36	613.14	8:19	622.9-10	8:55	626.8-9	9:32	633.9	10:27	652.5	11:20	662.1	11:56	691.2	12:34	727.1-2
7:1	611.1	7:37	614.1	8:20	622.11	8:56	626.10	9:33	633.10	10:28	652.6	11:21	662.3	11:57	691.3	12:35	727.3-4
7:2	611.2	7:38	614.2	8:21	623.1-2	8:57	626.11	9:34	633.11	10:29	652.7	11:22	662.4	12:1	691.4	12:36	727.5-6
7:3	611.2	7:39	614.3	8:22	623.3	8:58	626.12	9:35	634.1	10:30	652.8	11:23	662.5	12:2	691.5-6	12:37	727.7
7:4	611.2-3	7:40	614.4	8:23	623.4	8:59	626.13	9:36	634.2	10:31	653.1	11:24	662.6	12:3	691.7-8	12:38	727.8
7:5	611.4	7:41	614.4-5	8:24	623.5	9:1	631.1	9:37	634.3	10:32	653.2	11:25	662.7	12:4	692.2	12:39	727.9
7:6	611.5	7:42	614.5	8:25	623.6-7	9:2	631.1	9:38	634.4	10:33	653.3	11:26	662.7	12:5	692.2	12:40	727.9
7:7	611.6	7:43	614.6	8:26	623.8	9:3	631.2	9:39	634.5	10:34	653.4	11:27	662.8	12:6	692.3	12:41	727.10
7:8	611.7	7:44	614.6	8:27	623.9	9:4	631.3	9:40	634.6	10:35	653.5	11:28	662.9	12:7	692.4,6	12:42	727.11
7:9	611.8	7:45	615.1	8:28	623.9-10	9:5	631.4	9:41	634.7	10:36	653.5	11:29	662.10	12:8	692.5	12:43	727.11
7:10	612.1	7:46	615.2	8:29	623.11	9:6	631.5	10:1	641.1	10:37	653.6	11:30	663.1	12:9	692.8	12:44	728.1
7:11	612.2	7:47	615.3	8:30	623.12	9:7	631.6-7	10:2	641.2	10:38	653.7	11:31	662.11	12:10	692.9	12:45	728.2

JOHN 13 — FIVE COLUMN — JOHN 21

13	TSG	14	TSG	15	TSG	16	TSG	17	TSG	18	TSG	19	TSG	20	TSG	21	TSG
12:46	728.3	13:32	775.9	14:30	783.6	16:8	787.10	17:11	789.11-12	18:21	821.3	19:17	861.2 / 863.1	20:10	914.8	21:15	934.1-3
12:47	728.4	13:33	778.1-2	14:31	783.7 / 789.29	16:9	787.11	17:12	789.13-14	18:22	821.4	19:18	865.1	20:11	915.2-3	21:16	934.4-6
12:48	728.5	13:34	777.1	15:1	784.1	16:10	787.12	17:13	789.15	18:23	821.5	19:19	866.1-2	20:12	915.3	21:17	934.7-9
12:49	728.6	13:35	777.2	15:2	784.2	16:11	787.13	17:14	789.16	18:24	821.6	19:20	866.2-3	20:13	915.4-5	21:18	934.10
12:50	728.7	13:36	778.3-4	15:3	773.8	16:12	787.14	17:15	789.17	18:25	824.3 / 827.1	19:21	866.4	20:14	915.6	21:19	934.11-12
13:1	771.8	13:37	778.5,11	15:4	784.3	16:13	787.14-15	17:16	789.18	18:26	824.1	19:22	866.5	20:15	915.7-8	21:20	934.13
13:2	767.3-4	13:38	778.12-13	15:5	784.4-5	16:14	787.16	17:17	789.19	18:27	827.3-4	19:23	864.1-2	20:16	915.9	21:21	934.14
13:3	773.1	14:1	781.1	15:6	784.6	16:15	787.17	17:18	789.20	18:28	832.1-2	19:24	864.2-3	20:17	915.10-11	21:22	934.15
13:4	773.1	14:2	781.2-3	15:7	784.7	16:16	788.1	17:19	789.21	18:29	841.1	19:25	864.3 / 867.1	20:18	915.1,12-13	21:23	934.16-17
13:5	773.2	14:3	781.3	15:8	784.8	16:17	788.2	17:20	789.22	18:30	841.2	19:26	867.2	20:19	923.1,4-5	21:24	961.8
13:6	773.3	14:4	781.4	15:9	784.9	16:18	788.3	17:21	789.23	18:31	841.3-4	19:27	867.3-4	20:20	924.4-5	21:25	961.10-11
13:7	773.4	14:5	781.5	15:10	784.10	16:19	788.4	17:22	789.24	18:32	841.4	19:28	872.1	20:21	925.1		
13:8	773.5	14:6	781.6	15:11	784.11	16:20	788.5	17:23	789.24-25	18:33	841.7 / 815.1	19:29	872.2	20:22	925.2		
13:9	773.6	14:7	781.7	15:12	785.1	16:21	788.6-7	17:24	789.26	18:34	842.2	19:30	872.3-4	20:23	925.3		
13:10	773.7-8	14:8	781.8	15:13	785.2	16:22	788.8	17:25	789.27	18:35	842.3	19:31	874.1	20:24	925.4		~ End ~
13:11	773.9	14:9	781.9-10	15:14	785.3	16:23	788.9-10	17:26	789.28	18:36	842.4-5	19:32	874.2	20:25	925.4-5		
13:12	773.10-11	14:10	781.11-12	15:15	785.4	16:24	788.11	18:1	789.29 / 811.1	18:37	842.6-8	19:33	874.3	20:26	926.1-2		
13:13	773.12	14:11	781.13	15:16	785..5-6	16:25	788.12	18:2	811.2	18:38	842.9 / 843.1	19:34	874.4	20:27	926.3		
13:14	773.13	14:12	781.14-15	15:17	785.7	16:26	788.13	18:3	814.1-2	18:39	851.1,4	19:35	961.8	20:28	926.4		
13:15	773.13	14:13	782.1 / 789.29	15:18	786.1	16:27	788.13	18:4	814.6	18:40	851.2,5	19:36	874.5	20:29	926.5		
13:16	773.14	14:14	782.2	15:19	786.2	16:28	788.14	18:5	814.3,7 / 815.1	19:1	854.1	19:37	874.6	20:30	961.9		
13:17	773.15	14:15	782.3	15:20	786.3-4	16:29	788.15	18:6	814.8	19:2	854.2-3	19:38	881.1,3-4,6 /	20:31	961.11		
13:18	773.16	14:16	782.4	15:21	786.5	16:30	788.16	18:7	814.9	19:3	854.4-5		882.1	21:1	932.1		
13:19	773.17	14:17	782.4-5	15:22	786.6	16:31	788.17	18:8	814.10	19:4	855.1	19:39	882.2	21:2	932.2 / 412.10		
13:20	773.18	14:18	782.6	15:23	786.7	16:32	788.18-19	18:9	814.11	19:5	855.2	19:40	882.3	21:3	932.3-4		
13:21	774.1	14:19	782.7	15:24	786.8	16:33	788.20-21	18:10	815.4	19:6	855.3-4	19:41	882.4	21:4	932.5		
13:22	774.5	14:20	782.8	15:25	786.9	17:1	789.1	18:11	815.6-7	19:7	855.5	19:42	882.5	21:5	932.6		
13:23	775.1	14:21	782.9-10	15:26	787.1	17:2	789.2	18:12	816.4	19:8	855.6	20:1	911.1,3	21:6	932.7-8		
13:24	775.1	14:22	782.11	15:27	787.2	17:3	789.3	18:13	821.1	19:9	855.6	20:2	913.3	21:7	933.1-2		
13:25	775.2	14:23	782.12-13	16:1	787.3	17:4	789.4	18:14	821.7	19:10	855.7	20:3	914.1	21:8	933.3		
13:26	775.3-4	14:24	782.14	16:2	787.4	17:5	789.5	18:15	822.1-2	19:11	855.8-9	20:4	914.2	21:9	933.4		
13:27	775.6	14:25	782.15	16:3	787.5	17:6	789.6	18:16	822.2-3	19:12	855.10	20:5	914.3	21:10	933.5		
13:28	775.7	14:26	782.15	16:4	787.6-7	17:7	789.7	18:17	823.2-4	19:13	855.11	20:6	914.4-5	21:11	933.6		
13:29	775.7	14:27	783.1-2	16:5	787.7	17:8	789.7-8	18:18	823.1-2	19:14	856.1	20:7	914.5	21:12	933.7-8		
13:30	775.8	14:28	783.3-4	16:6	787.8	17:9	789.9	18:19	821.2	19:15	856.2-4	20:8	914.6	21:13	933.9		
13:31	775.9	14:29	783.5	16:7	787.9	17:10	789.10	18:20	821.2	19:16	856.5	20:9	914.7	21:14	926.6		

IMPROVING FIVE COLUMN: *The Synoptic Gospel*

This edition of the **FIVE COLUMN** Four Gospel Harmony, and *The Synoptic Gospel* *fifth column* word-for-word Merger of their texts, is as complete and accurate as possible at the time of its publication, and **FIVE COLUMN** and the works that are based upon its text, is open to comment, review and criticism. As the many eyes and minds of the group are better than a few, it is hoped that interested people would share their input to help further enhance and refine future editions of this work. Everyone is encouraged to submit their comments, corrections, suggestions and personal Testimonials, using the form at: *synopticgospel.com/feedback* or email: *feedback@synopticgospel.com*

All input to help improve this unified Synoptic Gospel is greatly appreciated, and may enhance future editions of this work. Thank You!

Reviews: To formally review this work in media visit: *synopticgospel.com/reviews*

Websites: fivecolumn.com   synopticgospel.com   thegreatestgospel.com   theredlettergospel.com   solascriptura.ca

Youtube: youtube.com/SynopticGospel   facebook.com/SynopticGospel

---

If you purchased this book from Amazon, please help encourage people to read this Gospel message, by leaving a positive and honest review at:

Amazon: amazon./dp/1988271797   Goodreads: goodreads.com/book/show/156508969   *Thank You!*

Other formats of this publication, **FIVE COLUMN**: *Verse-By-Verse* Edition
PDF: ISBN 978-1-998271-92-7   Hard Cover: ISBN 978-1-998271-93-4

Editions of **FIVE COLUMN**: *Word-For-Word Edition* (554 Pages)
PDF: ISBN 978-0-993914-06-5   Paperback: ISBN 978-0-993914-01-9   Hard Cover: ISBN 978-0-993914-07-2

The unified *Fifth Column* text of this book is reprinted as **The Synoptic Gospel**: *The Story of The Life of Jesus*
ePub: ISBN 978-1-988271-49-1   Kindle: ISBN 978-0-993914-03-4
Standard Edition - PDF: ISBN 978-1-988271-27-9   Paperback: ISBN 978-1-988271-30-9   Hard Cover: ISBN 978-1-988271-28-6
Complete Edition - PDF: ISBN 978-1-988271-41-5   Paperback: ISBN 978-1-988271-44-6   Hard Cover: ISBN 978-1-988271-83-5
Audiobook - Download (.m4b): ISBN 978-1-988271-00-2   DVD (.m4b): ISBN 978-0-9939140-9-6

Editions of **The Red Letter Gospel**: *All the Words of Jesus Christ in Red*
ePub: ISBN 978-1-988271-10-1   PDF: ISBN 978-1-988271-06-4   Kindle: ISBN 978-1-988271-07-1
Standard Edition - Paperback: ISBN 978-1-988271-37-8   Hard Cover: ISBN 978-1-988271-33-0
Complete Edition - Paperback: ISBN 978-1-988271-47-7   Hard Cover: ISBN 978-1-988271-84-3

are available at: *synopticgospel.com/purchase*

SMART PUBLISHING

Audiobook available! (*iTunes .m4b*)
The Synoptic Gospel: *The Story of The Life of Jesus*
Hear the entire Gospel Story in under seven hours!   Narrated by: Daniel John
Available for instant **Download** at: *synopticgospel.com/audiobook*

Notes: